eGrade Plus

for *Managerial Accounting: Tools for Business Decision-Making,* Canadian Edition

Check with your instructor to find out if you have access to eGrade Plus!

Study More Effectively with a Multimedia Text

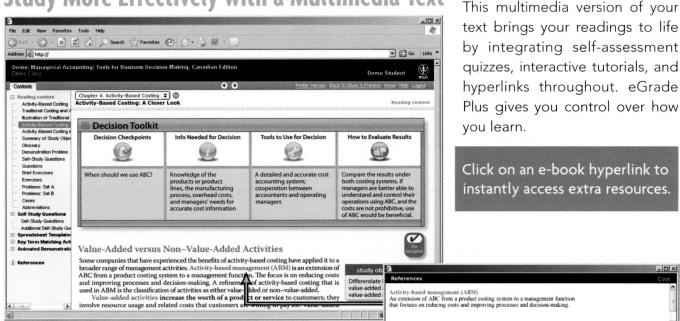

This multimedia version of your text brings your readings to life by integrating self-assessment quizzes, interactive tutorials, and hyperlinks throughout. eGrade Plus gives you control over how you learn.

Click on an e-book hyperlink to instantly access extra resources.

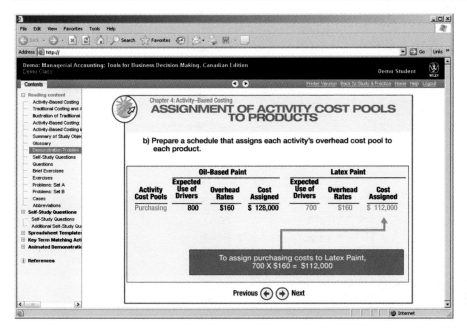

Preparing for a test has never been easier! eGrade Plus brings all of your course materials together and takes the stress out of organizing your study aids. A streamlined study routine saves you time and lets you focus on learning.

Grasp key concepts by exploring the various interactive tools in Study & Practice.

John Wiley & Sons Canada, Ltd.

Complete and Submit Assignments Online Efficiently

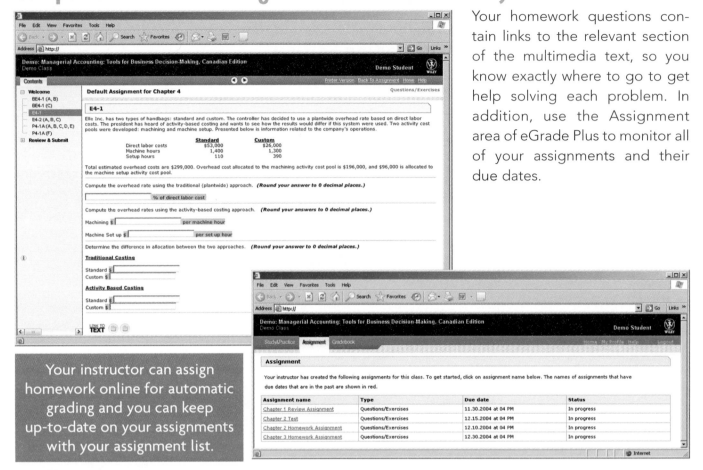

Your homework questions contain links to the relevant section of the multimedia text, so you know exactly where to go to get help solving each problem. In addition, use the Assignment area of eGrade Plus to monitor all of your assignments and their due dates.

Your instructor can assign homework online for automatic grading and you can keep up-to-date on your assignments with your assignment list.

Keep Track of Your Progress

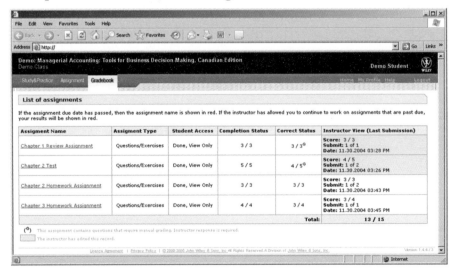

Your personal Gradebook lets you review your answers and results from past assignments as well as any feedback your instructor may have for you.

Keep track of your progress and review your completed questions at any time.

MANAGERIAL ACCOUNTING
Tools for Business Decision-Making

JERRY J. WEYGANDT PhD, CPA

Arthur Andersen Alumni Professor of Accounting
University of Wisconsin
Madison, Wisconsin

DONALD E. KIESO PhD, CPA

KPMG Peat Marwick Emeritus Professor of Accounting
Northern Illinois University
DeKalb, Illinois

PAUL D. KIMMEL PhD, CPA

Associate Professor of Accounting
University of Wisconsin—Milwaukee
Milwaukee, Wisconsin

IBRAHIM M. ALY PhD

Concordia University
Montreal, Quebec

Canadian Edition

John Wiley & Sons Canada, Ltd.

Library and Archives Canada Cataloguing in Publication

Managerial Accounting: Tools for Business Decision-Making

Canadian ed.
Includes index.
ISBN-13 978-0-470-83546-3
ISBN-10 0-470-83546-X

1. Managerial accounting--Textbooks. I. Weygandt, Jerry J.

HF5657.4.M357 2005   658.15'11   C2005-900799-0

Production Credits

Publisher: *John Horne*
Editorial Manager: *Karen Staudinger*
Publishing Services Director: *Karen Bryan*
Developmental Editor: *Zoë Craig*
Senior Marketing Manager: *Isabelle Moreau*
New Media Editor: *Elsa Passera*
Associate Editor: *Gail Brown*
Editorial Assistant: *Lindsay Humphreys*
Cover Design: *Interrobang Graphic Design, Inc.*
Design and Typesetting: *Appleby Color Lab*
Printing and Binding: *Tri-Graphic Printing Limited*

Printed and bound in Canada
10 9 8 7 6 5 4 3 2 1

WILEY

John Wiley & Sons Canada, Ltd.
6045 Freemont Blvd.
Mississauga, Ontario L5R 4J3

Visit our website at: www.wiley.ca

US Edition

Jerry J. Weygandt, PhD, CPA, is Arthur Andersen Alumni Professor of Accounting at the University of Wisconsin-Madison. He holds a PhD in accounting from the University of Illinois. Articles by Professor Weygandt have appeared in the *Accounting Review, Journal of Accounting Research, Accounting Horizons, Journal of Accountancy,* and other academic and professional journals. These articles have examined such financial reporting issues as accounting for price-level adjustments, pensions, convertible securities, stock option contracts, and interim reports. Professor Weygandt is author of other accounting and financial reporting books and is a member of the American Accounting Association, the American Institute of Certified Public Accountants, and the Wisconsin Society of Certified Public Accountants. He has served on numerous committees of the American Accounting Association and as a member of the editorial board of the *Accounting Review*; he also has served as President and Secretary-Treasurer of the American Accounting Association. In addition, he has been actively involved with the American Institute of Certified Public Accountants and has been a member of the Accounting Standards Executive Committee (AcSEC) of that organization. He has served on the FASB task force that examined the reporting issues related to accounting for income taxes and is presently a trustee of the Financial Accounting Foundation. Professor Weygandt has received the Chancellor's Award for Excellence in Teaching and the Beta Gamma Sigma Dean's Teaching Award. He is on the board of directors of M & I Bank of Southern Wisconsin and the Dean Foundation. He is the recipient of the Wisconsin Institute of CPA's Outstanding Educator's Award and the Lifetime Achievement Award. In 2001 he received the American Accounting Association's Outstanding Accounting Educator Award.

Donald E. Kieso, PhD, CPA, received his bachelor's degree from Aurora University and his doctorate in accounting from the University of Illinois. He has served as chairman of the Department of Accountancy and is currently the KPMG Peat Marwick Emeritus Professor of Accounting at Northern Illinois University. He has public accounting experience with Price Waterhouse & Co. (San Francisco and Chicago) and Arthur Andersen & Co. (Chicago) and research experience with the Research Division of the American Institute of Certified Public Accountants (New York). He has done postdoctorate work as a Visiting Scholar at the University of California at Berkeley and is a recipient of NIU's Teaching Excellence Award and four Golden Apple Teaching Awards. Professor Kieso is the author of other accounting and business books and is a member of the American Accounting Association, the American Institute of Certified Public Accountants, and the Illinois CPA Society. He has served as a member of the Board of Directors of the Illinois CPA Society, the AACSB's Accounting Accreditation Committees, the State of Illinois Comptroller's Commission, as Secretary-Treasurer of the Federation of Schools of Accountancy, and as Secretary-Treasurer of the American Accounting Association. Professor Kieso is currently serving on the Board of Trustees and Executive Committee of Aurora University, as a member of the Board of Directors of Castle BancGroup Inc., and as Treasurer and Director of Valley West Community Hospital. He served as a charter member of the national Accounting Education Change Commission. He is the recipient of the Outstanding Accounting Educator Award from the Illinois CPA Society, the FSA's Joseph A. Silvoso Award of Merit, the NIU Foundation's Humanitarian Award for Service to Higher Education, the Distinguished Service Award from the Illinois CPA Society, and the Community Citizen of the Year Award from Rotary International.

Paul D. Kimmel, PhD, CPA, received his bachelor's degree from the University of Minnesota and his doctorate in accounting from the University of Wisconsin. He is an Associate Professor at the University of Wisconsin-Milwaukee, and has public accounting experience with Deloitte & Touche (Minneapolis). He was the recipient of the UWM School of Business Advisory Council Teaching Award, the Reggie Taite Excellence in Teaching Award, and a three-time winner of the Outstanding Teaching Assistant Award at the University of Wisconsin. He is also a recipient of the Elijah Watts Sells Award for Honorary Distinction for his results on the CPA exam. He is a member of the American Accounting Association and has published articles in Accounting Review, Accounting Horizons, Advances in Management Accounting, Managerial Finance, Issues in Accounting Education, Journal of Accounting Education, as well as other journals. His research interests include accounting for financial instruments and innovation in accounting education. He has published papers and given numerous talks on incorporating critical thinking into accounting education, and helped prepare a catalog of critical thinking resources for the Federated Schools of Accountancy.

Canadian Edition

Ibrahim M. Aly, PhD, is an associate professor in the Department of Accountancy at the John Molson School of Business, Concordia University, where he has been on faculty since 1989. Professor Aly holds a PhD and MBA (with distinction) in accounting from the University of North Texas, as well as an MS and BComm in accounting with distinction from Cairo University, Egypt. Professor Aly has taught at a variety of universities in Egypt, Saudi Arabia, the USA and Canada and he has developed and coordinated many accounting courses at both the undergraduate and graduate levels. He participated in the Symposium on Models of Accounting Education, sponsored by the Accounting Education Change Commission of the American Accounting Association. Throughout his many years of teaching, Professor Aly's method of instruction has consistently been met with high praise from his students. He won the College of Business Teaching Innovation Award for two consecutive years.

Professor Aly has published in reputable refereed journals in the fields of managerial accounting, financial accounting, behavioural accounting and accounting education, in addition, he has previously published a book on management accounting entitled *Readings in Management Accounting: New Rules for New Games in Manufacturing and Service Organizations,* Kendall/Hunt Publishing Company. He has presented his work at over thirty scholarly national and international conferences, and been chosen as the Department of Accountancy Research Professor. He has organized the Department's Luncheon Presentations Series, and the PhD Visiting Speaker Series, both of which provide an indispensable academic service to graduate students and professors.

The Canadian edition of *Managerial Accounting: Tools for Business Decision-Making* builds on the successes of the previous two US editions as well as the current US third edition. This edition has been further strengthened for use in the Canadian academic market. For those familiar with the US edition, much of the text will be recognizable to you. Changes were made only where it would make the text more cognizant of the Canadian environment and more relevant to Canadian students. To this end, the Canadian edition has been changed in a few important ways:

- The text incorporates the economic, legal, and cultural environment distinctive to Canada.
- The companies in the feature stories have been revised to reflect the Canadian business environment. Canadian business experiences have been used wherever possible.
- The end-of-chapter materials have been expanded.

Our goals are straightforward: We want this book to present the fundamental concepts of managerial accounting in an easy-to-understand fashion. We want to present only those concepts that students need to know. And we want students to leave the course feeling confident that they will be able to apply the basic decision skills that they learned in this course when they enter the workforce. As a result, as you read through the list of features of this edition and review the text, the common theme you will notice is that the focus is to simplify and clarify the presentation of basic concepts and to strengthen the students' decision-making skills. We are very excited about this edition of the text. Our efforts were driven by the following key beliefs:

"No more, no less—exactly what you need."

Our instructional objective is to provide students with an understanding of those concepts that are fundamental to the use of managerial accounting. Most students will forget procedural details within a short period of time. On the other hand, concepts, if well taught, should be remembered for a lifetime. Concepts are especially important in a world where the details are constantly changing.

"Don't just sit there—do something."

Students learn best when they are actively engaged. The overriding pedagogical objective of this book is to provide students with continual opportunities for active learning. One of the best tools for active learning is strategically placed questions. Our discussions are framed by questions, often beginning with rhetorical questions and ending with review questions. Even our selection of analytical devices, called *Decision Tools*, is referenced using key questions to emphasize the purpose of each. In addition, technology offers many opportunities to enhance the learning environment. Through the use of *eGrade Plus*, as well as our website at http://www.wiley.com/canada/managerial/, we offer many opportunities for active learning.

"I'll believe it when I see it."

Students will be most willing to commit time and energy to a topic when they believe that it is relevant to their future careers. There is no better way to demonstrate relevance than to ground discussion in the real world. By using high-profile companies like WestJet, Petro-Canada and Inco Limited to frame our discussion of accounting issues, we demonstrate the relevance of accounting while teaching students about companies with which they are familiar. In addition, because the economy has shifted toward service industries, many of the companies used as examples are service-based. This shift is emphasized by our *Business Insight—Service Company Perspective* feature, as well as references to service companies. There are also numerous problems and cases focused on service companies.

"You'll need to make a decision."

All business people must make decisions, and managerial accounting concerns itself with developing tools to help managers make effective decisions. Decision making involves critical evaluation and analysis of the information at hand, and this takes practice. We have therefore integrated important analytical tools throughout the book. After each new decision tool is presented, we summarize the key features of that tool in a *Decision Toolkit*. At the end of each chapter, the Using the Decision Toolkit activity provides a comprehensive demonstration of an analysis of a real-world problem using the decision tools presented in the chapter. The case material requires the student to employ these decision tools. Our goal is to provide students with a set of decision-making tools they can take with them long after the course is over.

Key Features of Each Chapter

Chapter 1, Managerial Accounting

- Compares and contrasts managerial accounting with financial accounting.
- Identifies three broad functions of management.
- Defines three classes of manufacturing costs, organizational structure, and business ethics issues.
- Distinguishes between product costs and period costs.
- Presents the costs of goods manufactured section of the income statement.
- Presents an overview of trends in managerial accounting including shift toward service industries, value chain management, enterprise resource planning, just-in-time inventory, activity-based costing, theory of constraints, and the balanced scorecard.

Chapter 2, Job-Order Cost Accounting

- Provides an overview of cost accounting systems.
- Illustrates the flow of costs in a job order cost system.
- Presents the use of job cost sheets.
- Demonstrates the use of predetermined overhead rate.
- Illustrates the basic entries for job order cost system.
- Provides a simple presentation of overapplied and underapplied overhead.

Chapter 3, Process Cost Accounting

- Explains the difference between job order and process costing systems.
- Illustrates the flow of costs and end-of-period accounting procedures for process costing.
- Demonstrates calculation of physical units of production, equivalent units of production, and unit costs.
- Shows how to assign costs to units of output and prepare a production cost report.

Chapter 4, Activity-Based Costing

- Explains the need for activity-based costing (ABC).
- Contrasts ABC to traditional costing systems.
- Identifies numerous activities, activity cost pools, and cost drivers.
- Discusses the implications of value-added and non-value added activities.
- Illustrates the use of ABC in service industries.
- Reviews the benefits and limitations of ABC.
- Discusses the implications of activity levels.

Chapter 5, Decision-Making: Cost-Volume-Profit

- Distinguishes between variable and fixed costs, and explains relevant range and mixed costs.
- Identifies components and assumptions of CVP analysis.
- Discusses concept of contribution margin and illustrates CVP income statement.
- Illustrates calculation of break-even point.
- Discusses margin of safety and target net income.
- Illustrates CVP income statement.

- Appendix explains sales mix and its effect on break-even analysis.
- Promotes understanding of how operating leverage affects profitability.

Chapter 6, Incremental Analysis

- Presents the concept of incremental analysis through a simple example.
- Explains the concepts of relevant cost, opportunity cost, and sunk cost.
- Applies incremental analysis in the following decision settings:
  - Accept an order at a special price
  - Make or buy
  - Sell or process further, including discussion of joint costs
  - Keep or replace equipment
  - Eliminate an unprofitable segment
  - Allocate limited resources across multiple products.

Chapter 7, Variable Costing: A Decision-Making Perspective

- Explains the difference between absorption costing and variable costing.
- Discusses the effect that changes in production level and sales level have on net income measured under absorption costing versus variable costing.
- Discusses the relative merits of absorption costing versus variable costing for management decision making.

Chapter 8, Pricing

- Demonstrates how to calculate target cost when a product's price is determined by the market.
- Illustrates how to compute target selling price using cost-plus pricing.
- Demonstrates how to use time and materials pricing when services are provided.
- Discusses the objective of transfer pricing.
- Illustrates how to determine a transfer price using the cost-based, market-based, and negotiated approaches.
- Explains the issues involved when goods are transferred between countries with different tax rates.

Chapter 9, Budgetary Planning

- Discusses the benefits of budgeting.
- Illustrates the process of assembling information for a master budget.
- Prepares a budgeted income statement, balance sheet, and cash budget.
- Discusses the use of budgets in merchandising, service, and not-for-profit enterprises.

Chapter 10, Budgetary Control and Responsibility Accounting

- Explains how budgets are used to control costs and operations.
- Contrasts static budgets and flexible budgets.
- Uses a case study to illustrate usefulness of flexible budgets.

- Illustrates responsibility reporting systems.
- Defines cost centres, profit centres, and investment centres.
- Illustrates the calculation and use of return on investment and (in a chapter appendix) residual income.

Chapter 11, Standard Costs and Balance Scorecard

- Differentiates between a standard and a budget.
- Discusses the advantages of standard costs and methods of computing.
- Illustrates computation of direct materials variance, direct labor variance, and manufacturing overhead variance.
- Demonstrates analysis through comparison of actual costs with standard costs.
- Discusses the basic features and usefulness of the balanced scorecard.
- The appendix illustrates the journal entries for a standard cost system.

Chapter 12, Capital Budgeting

- Discusses nature of capital budgeting decisions.
- Describes and illustrates four methods of evaluating capital expenditures:
  - Cash payback technique
  - Net present value method
  - Internal rate of return method
  - Annual rate of return technique
- Discusses the profitability index, post audits, and the implications of intangible benefits when making capital budgeting decisions.

Outstanding Problem Material

A major goal in developing this Canadian edition was to offer a comprehensive problem set that would surpass the needs of Canadian instructors. To that end, this book has more problem material—and a greater variety of problem material—than any other text available in Canada. This provides instructors with unprecedented flexibility in using the problem material in class for demonstration purposes, for student practice, or as homework assignments.

The assignment material also includes numerous problems, exercises, and cases adapted from **CGA** and **CMA** professional examinations, providing students with the opportunity to become exposed to professional exam-type

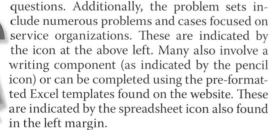

questions. Additionally, the problem sets include numerous problems and cases focused on service organizations. These are indicated by the icon at the above left. Many also involve a writing component (as indicated by the pencil icon) or can be completed using the pre-formatted Excel templates found on the website. These are indicated by the spreadsheet icon also found in the left margin.

The decision tools presented in a chapter are used throughout the homework material, questions, exercises, and problems. The assignment material includes the following:

- **Self-Study Questions** comprise a practice test to enable students to check their understanding of important concepts. These questions are keyed to the Study Objectives, so students can go back and review sections of the chapter in which they find they need further work. Answers appear on the last page of the chapter. A *web icon* tells students that they can answer the Self-Study Questions in an interactive format on the text's website. They can also take an additional Self-Test on the website to further help them master the material.

- **Questions** provide a full review of chapter content and help students prepare for class discussions and testing situations.

- **Brief Exercises** build students' confidence and test their basic skills. Each exercise focuses on a single *Study Objective*.

- Each of the **Exercises** focuses on one or more of the *Study Objectives*. These tend to take a little longer to complete and present more of a challenge to students than Brief Exercises. The Exercises help instructors and students make a manageable transition to more challenging problems. Certain exercises, marked with a 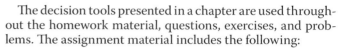, help students practice business writing skills.

- **Problems** stress the application of the concepts presented in the chapter. Two sets of problems—A and B—have corresponding problems keyed to the same *Study Objectives*, thus giving instructors greater flexibility in assigning homework. Certain problems, marked with the icon, help build business writing skills.

- Each Brief Exercise, Exercise, and Problem has a **description of the concept** covered and is keyed to the *Study Objectives*.

- **Spreadsheet Exercises and Problems**, identified by an icon, can be solved using Excel templates found on the website.

- A rich variety of **Cases** help students build decision-making skills by analyzing real-world scenarios. They are designed to broaden the learning experience by providing more real-world decision making, analysis, and critical-thinking activities. Many of the cases include group activities designed to promote teamwork, or focus on building communication, managerial, or research skills. Additionally, many cases also focus on ethical issues.

Technology for Teaching and Learning

Managerial Accounting, Canadian Edition offers instructors and students a unique and comprehensive set of technology tools to aid in instruction and learning. These have been carefully developed and integrated with the text and serve to expand the educational experience.

eGrade Plus

 *Managerial Accounting,* Canadian Edition is available with Wiley's *eGrade Plus* course management system. It offers an on-line suite of teaching tools, assignments, interactive assessments, and a complete "e-version" of the book. It also includes an integrated set of on-line instructor's tools to help in class preparation, the creation of assignments, the automated assigning and grading of homework or quizzes, tracking of students' progress, and administration of courses. *eGrade Plus* provides instructors with the most comprehensive and flexible resources available on the market. Ask your Wiley sales representative for a demonstration of this powerful new tool or visit www.wiley.com/canada/managerial for an on-line demonstration of the powerful teaching functionality now available.

Spreadsheets

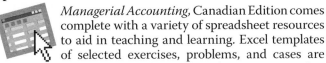 *Managerial Accounting,* Canadian Edition comes complete with a variety of spreadsheet resources to aid in teaching and learning. Excel templates of selected exercises, problems, and cases are available for download on the text's website at www.wiley.com/canada/managerial. These formatted spreadsheets aid students in preparing and solving assignments. A special icon indicates which assignment material is available in Excel format. Additionally, students can purchase the Excel Working Papers which provide a set of templates of the text's complete exercises, problems, and cases.

The *Managerial Accounting* Website at:
http://www.wiley.com/canada/managerial

 A resource and learning tool, the website serves as a launching pad to numerous activities, resources, and related sites. On the website you will find *Animated Demonstration Problems, Self Tests, Rapid Review Sheets* and *web links*. In addition, there are links to companies discussed in the text and items available for downloading such as *PowerPoint presentations*.

Resources for Instructors

For the instructor, we have designed an extensive support package to help you maximize your teaching effectiveness, including print and technology tools. We offer useful supplements for instructors with various levels of experience and different instructional circumstances.

INSTRUCTOR'S RESOURCE CD

Responding to the changing needs of instructors and to developments in distance learning and electronic classrooms, the Instructor's Resource CD provides all the instructor support material in an electronic format that is easy to navigate and use. This CD contains supplements for use in the classroom, for printing out material, for uploading to your own website, or for downloading and modifying. The CD gives you the flexibility to access and prepare instructional material based on your individual needs. The CD contains the following:

Solutions Manual

The Solutions Manual contains detailed solutions to all exercises and problems in the textbook and suggested answers to the questions and cases. Print is large and bold for easy readability. Each chapter includes an *assignment classification table* (identifies end-of-chapter items by study objectives), an *assignment characteristics table* (describes each problem and identifies difficulty level and estimated completion time), and a *Bloom's taxonomy table* (classifies end-of-chapter items by Bloom's taxonomy of learning objective and study objective).

Instructor's Manual

The Instructor's Manual is a comprehensive resource guide designed to assist professors in preparing lectures and assignments, and it includes sample syllabi for preparing for the course. The print is set in a size large enough for easy reading or for use as transparency masters.

Included for each chapter are an *assignment classification table*; an *assignment characteristics table*; a *list of study objectives* in extra-large, boldface print for transparencies; a *chapter review* of the significant topics and points contained in the chapter; *enhanced lecture outlines* with teaching tips and references to text material; *suggestions for integrating supplements* into the classroom; a *20-minute quiz* in the form of 10 true/false and 5 multiple-choice questions (with solutions); and illustrations, including diagrams, graphs, questions, and exercises, for use as classroom handouts, overhead transparencies, in-class quizzes, or demonstrations (solutions are provided).

Test Bank

The Test Bank is a comprehensive testing package that allows instructors to tailor examinations according to study objectives and learning skills, and it includes over 800 examination questions and exercises accompanied by solutions. The Test Bank includes the helpful *Summary of Questions by Objectives* and *Summary of Objectives by*

Questions, tools effective in linking test items to study objectives. Each chapter also includes a chart indicating the placement of questions in Bloom's taxonomy. An estimated completion time for each question and exercise is also provided.

The Test Bank provides an achievement test and solutions bank for every two chapters in the textbook. Three comprehensive tests and a final exam are also provided. The tests consist of problems and exercises as well as multiple-choice, matching, and true/false questions. These materials are also available in Word files.

Computerized Test Bank

The Computerized Test Bank offers a number of valuable options that allow instructors to create multiple versions of the same test by scrambling questions; generate a large number of test questions randomly or manually; and modify and customize test questions by changing existing problems or adding your own.

Checklist of Key Figures

The Checklist of Key Figures is a listing of key amounts for textbook problems, allowing students to verify the accuracy of their answers as they work through the assignments.

PowerPoint Presentation Material

This PowerPoint lecture aid contains a combination of key concepts, images, and problems from the textbook for use in the classroom. Designed according to the organization of the material in the textbook, this series of electronic transparencies can be used to reinforce managerial accounting principles visually and graphically.

Resources for Students

Excel Working Papers

The Excel Working Papers CD compiles all the accounting forms you will need to successfully complete your study work for *Managerial Accounting*, Canadian Edition. The templates on this CD include custom forms for all relevant end-of-chapter exercises, problems, and cases. The Excel Working Papers provide you with the option of printing forms and completing them manually, or entering data electronically and then printing out a completed form. By entering data electronically, you can then paste homework to a new file and e-mail the worksheet to your instructor.

Student Study Guide

The *Student Study Guide* is a comprehensive review of accounting and a powerful tool for students to use in the classroom. Tied to study objectives, it guides students through chapter content and provides resources for use during lectures. This is an excellent resource when preparing for exams.

Each chapter of the *Student Study Guide* includes a chapter review consisting of 20–30 key points; a demonstration problem linked to study objectives in the textbook; and additional opportunities for students to practice their knowledge and skills through true/false, multiple-choice, and matching questions related to key terms and exercises linked to study objectives. Solutions to the exercises explain the hows and whys so that students get immediate feedback.

ACKNOWLEDGMENTS

I would like to express my appreciation to the many people who have contributed to the development of this textbook. First, the following professors have thoroughly reviewed the manuscript at several stages in the development of the text. I gratefully acknowledge their valuable contribution, constructive criticism, and many suggestions, which have significantly improved the content and pedagogy of the final product.

Reviewers for *Managerial Accounting*, Canadian Edition

Tashia Batstone, *Memorial University of Newfoundland*

Hilary Becker, *Carleton University*

Margo Burtch, *Seneca College of Applied Arts and Technology*

Anthony Moung-yin Chan, *Ryerson University*

Gail Lynn Cook, *Brock University*

K. Suzanne Coombs, *Kwantlen University College*

Chris Duff, *Royal Roads University*

Gerry Dupont, *Carleton University*

Thomas R. Friedrich, *British Columbia Institute of Technology*

Masuma Jaffer, *Seneca College of Applied Arts and Technology*

Johnny Jermias, *Simon Fraser University*

Cynthia Lone, *Red River Community College*

Winston Marcellin, *George Brown College*

Sayed Ahmed Naqi, *Lakehead University*

Joe Nemi, *Humber College Institute of Technology and Advanced Learning*

Audra Ong, *University of Windsor*

Jeffrey Pittman, *Memorial University of Newfoundland*

Giuseppina Salvaggio, *Dawson College*

Nancy Tait, *Fleming College*

Ancillary Authors, Contributors, and Proofers

Alison Arnot–Feature Story writer

David Schwinghamer–copyeditor

Zofia Laubitz–proofreader

Gail Lynn Cook, *Brock University*–Test Bank author

Ilene Gilborn, *Mount Royal College*–Solutions Manual author

Sayed Ahmed Naqi, *Lakehead University*–PowerPoint author

Jeffrey Pittman, *Memorial University of Newfoundland*–Instructor's Manual author

I would like to extend my sincere appreciation to the US authors of this textbook for their willingness to share their work with me. They have advanced the discussion of management accounting from that established in traditional textbooks, which focused on "number-crunchers," to a more modern view of accountants as critical participants in the business decision-making process. The features of this book will help accounting students discover a reasonable balance between learning managerial accounting techniques and gaining essential application skills and how to apply them when they enter the workforce.

I express my gratitude to the many fine people at John Wiley and Sons Canada who have professionally guided this text through the development and publication process. In particular, I acknowledge the publisher, John Horne, for his interest in and support of this first Canadian edition of the textbook. In addition, I extend my appreciation to Wiley Canada's editorial staff, who were terrific in guiding me through this challenging process, especially Zoë Craig, Developmental Editor. I also extend my appreciation to all other members of the publishing team at John Wiley & Sons Canada who worked together to complete this project successfully. Thank you all for your patience and assistance.

Finally, special thanks and gratitude are extended to my family for their support and encouragement.

Suggestions and comments from users—instructors and students alike—will be appreciated.

Ibrahim Aly
Montreal, Quebec
January 2005

How to Use the Study Aids in this Book

CHAPTER 4

Activity-Based Costing

Storage Solutions

RONA Inc. was having difficulty accounting for the costs of its warehousing and distribution. So the Boucherville, Quebec–based distributor and retailer of hardware, home improvement, and gardening supplies introduced an activity-based costing system to keep better track of its route-to-market costs.

"The costs are reallocated to the product based on the characteristics of each product and the activities required to complete an order," says RONA's controller for distribution, Martin Beauregard, CMA. The value of the product inside a carton has little bearing on the cost to ship it; it depends on the process required. For example, electric saws are stored at 40 cases per pallet, which takes up one cubic metre of space. With its new system, RONA can determine that it costs, say, $40 per cubic metre per year—or $1 per case—to store this product.

But with 40,000 SKUs, 28 separate processes in its warehouses, more than 3,000 vendors, and 535 stores, cally was not accomplished easily. several sectors, with the activities fo example, storage in the yard is chea products require more labour and ta breaking down this information and able to determine the actual cost req

"In the past, we allocated the co explains. "We knew our average co X percent, so we were using that pe quire more manipulation than othe were not accurate measures.

With value-chain analytics soft push the products through different is the most cost-effective. Usually through their warehouse, but it may to retail outlets. The software will RONA to instruct suppliers on the b "Now, people in merchandising have propriate allocation with suppliers,"

RONA Inc.: www.rona.ca

The Feature Story helps you picture how the chapter topic relates to the real world of accounting and business.

The Navigator is a learning system designed to guide you through each chapter and help you succeed in learning the material. It consists of (1) a checklist at the beginning of the chapter, that outlines text features and study skills you will need, and (2) a series of check boxes that prompt you to use the learning aids in the chapter and set priorities as you study. the navigator

THE NAVIGATOR

- [ ] Scan *Study Objectives*
- [ ] Read *Feature Story*
- [ ] Read *Chapter Preview*
- [ ] Read text and answer *Before You Go On* p. 150, p. 156, p. 159
- [ ] Work *Using the Decision Toolkit*
- [ ] Review *Summary of Study Objectives*
- [ ] Review *Using the Decision Toolkit—A Summary*
- [ ] Work *Demonstration Problem*
- [ ] Answer *Self-Study Questions*
- [ ] Complete assignments

Study Objectives at the beginning of each chapter provide you with a framework for learning the specific concepts and procedures covered in the chapter. Each study objective reappears in the margin at the point where the concept is discussed. Finally, you can review off the study objectives in the **Summary** at the end of the chapter text.

STUDY OBJECTIVES

After studying this chapter, you should be able to:

1. Recognize the difference between traditional costing and activity-based costing.
2. Identify the steps in the development of an activity-based costing system.
3. Know how companies identify the activity cost pools used in activity-based costing.
4. Know how companies identify and use the activity cost drivers in activity-based costing.
5. Understand the benefits and limitations of activity-based costing.
6. Differentiate between value-added and non–value-added activities.
7. Understand the value of using activity levels in activity-based costing.
8. Apply activity-based costing to service industries.

the navigator

PREVIEW OF CHAPTER 4

As indicated in our feature story about RONA, the traditional costing systems described in earlier chapters are not the best answer for every company. Because RONA suspected that the traditional system was hiding significant differences in its real cost structure, it looked for a new method of assigning costs. Similar searches by other companies for ways to improve operations and gather more accurate data for decision-making have resulted in the development of powerful new management tools, including **activity-based costing (ABC)**, which this chapter explains and illustrates.

The chapter is organized as follows:

ACTIVITY-BASED COSTING

Traditional Costing and Activity-Based Costing	Illustration of Traditional Costing versus Activity-Based Costing	Activity-Based Costing: A Closer Look	Activity-Based Costing in Service Industries
▶ Traditional costing systems ▶ Need for a new approach ▶ Activity-based costing	▶ Unit costs under traditional costing ▶ Unit costs under ABC ▶ Comparing unit costs	▶ Benefits of ABC ▶ Limitations of ABC ▶ When to use ABC ▶ Value-added versus non–value-added activities ▶ Classification of activity levels	▶ Traditional costing example ▶ Activity-based costing example

the navigator

The **Preview** links the Feature Story with the major topics of the chapter and describes the purpose of the chapter. It then shows a graphic outline of major topics and subtopics that will be discussed. This narrative and visual preview gives you a mental framework upon which to arrange the information you are learning.

Traditional Costing and Activity-Based Costing

Traditional Costing Systems

study objective 1

Recognize the difference between traditional costing and activity-based costing.

It is probably impossible to determine the exact cost of a product or service. However, for decision-makers to make better management decisions, they must have the most accurate cost estimates possible. A product's cost can be estimated most accurately when this cost can be traced directly to the product produced or the service provided. Direct material and direct labour costs are the easiest to determine, because these can be traced directly to the product by examining material requisition forms and payroll time sheets. Overhead costs, on the other hand, are an indirect or common cost that generally cannot be easily or directly traced to individual products or services. Instead, we use estimates to assign overhead costs to products and services.

Often the most difficult part of calculating accurate unit costs is determining the proper amount of **overhead cost** to assign to each product, service, or job. In our coverage of job order costing in Chapter 2 and of process costing in Chapter 3, we used a single or plantwide overhead rate throughout the year for the entire factory operation. That rate was called the **predetermined overhead rate**. For job order costing, we assumed that **direct labour cost** was the relevant activity base for assigning all overhead [...] we assumed that **machine hours** was the relevant ac[...] the process or department.

The use of direct labour as the activity base mad[...] systems were first developed. At that time, direct lab[...] manufacturing cost. Therefore, it was widely accepte[...] tween direct labour and overhead costs. As a result, [...] basis for allocating overhead.

Even in today's increasingly automated environ[...] appropriate basis for assigning overhead costs to p[...] labour when (a) direct labour is a significant part of [...] a high correlation between direct labour and chang[...] simplified (one-stage) traditional costing system tha[...] costs is shown in Illustration 4-1.

Study Objectives reappear in the margins at the point where the related topic is discussed. End-of-chapter assignments are keyed to Study Objectives.

Colour illustrations visually reinforce important concepts and therefore often contain material that may appear on exams. **Infographics**, a special type of illustration, pictorially link concepts to the real world and provide visual reminders of key concepts.

---

146 Chapter 4 ▶ Activity-Based Costing

Illustration 4-2 ▶
Activities and related cost drivers

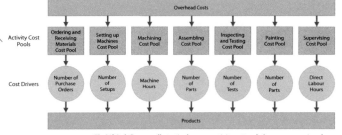

In the first step (as shown at the top of the illustration), the company's overhead costs are allocated to activity cost pools. In this simplified example, four activity cost pools have been identified: purchasing, storing, machining, and supervising. After the costs are allocated to the activity cost pools, the company uses cost drivers to measure the costs to be assigned to the individual products (either axles or steering wheels) based on each product's use of each activity. For example, if axles require more activity by the purchasing department, as measured by the number of required purchase orders, then more of the overhead cost from the purchasing pool will be allocated to the axles.

Not all products or services share equally in these activities. When a product's manufacturing operation is more complex, it is likely to have more activities and cost drivers. If there is little or no correlation between changes in the cost driver and the consumption of the overhead cost, inaccurate **product costs** will result. The design of a more complex activity-based costing system with seven activity cost pools is shown in Illustration 4-3 for Lift Jack Company. Lift Jack Company manufactures two automotive jacks—an automobile scissors jack and a truck hydraulic jack.

Alternative Terminology
Product costs are also called *inventory costs*.

Illustration 4-3 ▼
ABC system design—Lift Jack Company

Overhead Costs

Activity Cost Pools						
Ordering and Receiving Materials Cost Pool	Setting up Machines Cost Pool	Machining Cost Pool	Assembling Cost Pool	Inspecting and Testing Cost Pool	Painting Cost Pool	Supervising Cost Pool

Cost Drivers						
Number of Purchase Orders	Number of Setups	Machine Hours	Number of Parts	Number of Tests	Number of Parts	Direct Labour Hours

Products

The Lift Jack Company illustration has seven activity cost pools. In some companies, a large number of activities can be related to a cost pool. For example, at Clark-Hurth (a division of Clark Equipment Company), a manufacturer of axles and transmissions, over 170 activities were

To answer these questions, management needs reliable and relevant cost information. We now explain and illustrate the various cost categories that management uses.

Manufacturing Costs

Manufacturing consists of activities and processes that convert raw materials into finished goods. In contrast, merchandising sells goods in the same form in which they are purchased. Manufacturing costs are typically classified as shown in Illustration 1-3.

Manufacturing Costs

Direct Materials   Direct Labour   Manufacturing Overhead

Illustration 1-3 ◄
Classifications of manufacturing costs

Ilustrations like this one convey information in pictures to help you visualize and apply the ideas as you study.

Direct Materials

To obtain the materials that will be converted into the finished product, the manufacturer purchases raw materials. **Raw materials** are the basic materials and parts used in the manufacturing process. For example, auto manufacturers such as General Motors of Canada Ltd., Honda Canada Ltd., and Ford Motor Co. of Canada, Ltd. use steel, plastics, and tires as raw materials in making cars.

Raw materials that can be physically and directly associated with the finished product during the manufacturing process are called **direct materials**. Examples include flour in the baking of bread, syrup in the bottling of soft drinks, and steel in the making of automobiles. In the feature story, direct materials for Alcoa Canada include alumina, bauxite ore, and carbon.

But some raw materials cannot be easily associated with the finished product. These are called indirect materials. **Indirect materials** have one of two characteristics: either they do not physically become part of the finished product, such as lubricants and polishing compounds, or they cannot be traced because their physical association with the finished product is too small in terms of cost, such as cotter pins and lock washers. Indirect materials are accounted for as part of the **manufacturing overhead**.

Helpful Hints clarify concepts being discussed.

Helpful Hint A manufacturer uses masking tape to protect certain sections of its product while other sections are painted. The tape is removed and thrown away when the paint is dry. Is the tape a direct or indirect material? Answer: indirect.

Direct Labour

The work of factory employees that can be physically and directly associated with converting raw materials into finished goods is called **direct labour**. Bottlers at Cott Corp. and bakers at McCain Foods Ltd., are employees whose activities are usually classified as direct labour. Indirect labour refers to the work of factory employees that has no physical association with the finished product, or for which it is impractical to trace costs to the goods produced. Examples include wages of maintenance people, timekeepers, and supervisors. Like indirect materials, indirect labour is classified as **manufacturing overhead**.

BUSINESS INSIGHT ► Management Perspective

More and more Canadian automakers are focusing on engine design and selling the finished product, leaving the manufacture of seats, frames, electronics, and other parts, as well as their associated costs, in the hands of other companies. This outsourcing has resulted in auto parts maker Magna International Inc. rivalling General Motors of Canada Ltd. as the sector's largest employer. Industry experts say the 1965 auto pact between Canada and the United States allowed for the growth of auto parts companies. For its part, Magna has invested in new manufacturing technologies to help automakers reduce the weight of their vehicles, as well as the costs.

Source: "Magna Poised to Become Largest Auto Sector Employer," Ottawa Business Journal, April 6, 2004.

Helpful Hints in the margins are like having an instructor with you as you read. They further clarify concepts being discussed.

Key terms and concepts are printed in blue where they are first explained in the text. They are listed and defined again in the end-of-chapter **Glossary**.

y Control and Responsibility Accounting

r responsibility accounting, any individual who has control and is accountable for d set of activities can be recognized as a responsibility centre. Thus, responsibility ng may extend from the lowest level of control to the top layers of management. ponsibility has been established, the effectiveness of an individual's performance is ured and reported for the specified activity. It is then reported upward throughout nization.

onsibility accounting is especially valuable in a decentralized company. Decen-n means that the control of operations is given to many managers throughout the tion. The term segment is sometimes used to identify an area of responsibility in zed operations. Under responsibility accounting, segment reports are prepared pe-, such as monthly, quarterly, and annually, to evaluate a manager's performance. onsibility accounting is an essential part of any effective system of budgetary con-reporting of costs and revenues under responsibility accounting differs from bud-two ways:

1. ..... istinction is made between controllable and noncontrollable items.
2. Performance reports either emphasize or include only the items that can be controlled by the individual manager.

Responsibility accounting is used in both profit and not-for-profit entities. The former try to maximize net income. The latter want to minimize the cost of providing services.

BUSINESS INSIGHT ► Service Company Perspective

In 2001, SR Telecom Inc., a Montreal-based manufacturer of broadband fixed wireless networks seemed doomed to the fate of many high-tech companies at that time. It was spending too much and carrying a huge debt load. However, the company soon turned its fortunes around by streamlining its operations and using the market turmoil to cheaply acquire assets that broadened its product portfolio. The company was basically a one-product operation providing wireless connections to carry data to rural and remote regions, mainly in developing nations, where the installation of copper or fibre cable was too costly. But, with the growth of the Internet, demand for broadband access increased and wireless technologies had advanced, providing SR Telecom with new opportunities.

In order to grow, though, the company needed to improve its operations. Its production cycle was too slow, and it was making too much equipment before orders even came in. The company was stockpiling large inventories, while its accounts receivable were too high. As the inventories were gradually worked off, contracts with suppliers of components and raw materials were renegotiated to get just-in-time delivery. Production began only on orders that could be shipped out once they were finished. This reduced working inventory on the production floor at any one time to $1.5 million, from approximately $10 million, and cut the company's 10-week production cycle down to three weeks. These significant improvements were the result of employee teams that renewed their efforts to control costs at every level.

Source: Andrew Wahl, "Out of the Wilderness," Canadian Business, May 26, 2003.

Business Insight examples give you more glimpses into how real companies make decisions using accounting information. These high-interest boxes are classified by four different points of view: management perspectives, international perspectives, service company perspectives, and e-business insights.

One of the special types of **Business Insight** boxes, **Service Company Perspectives** highlight accounting practices in this growing segment of our economy.

Controllable versus Noncontrollable Revenues and Costs

In all costs and revenues can be controlled at some level of responsibility in a company. This truth emphasizes the adage used by the CEO of any organization that "the buck stops here." Under responsibility accounting, the critical issue is whether or not the cost or revenue can be controlled at the level of responsibility that it is associated with.

A cost is considered to be **controllable** at a particular level of managerial responsibility if the manager has the power to incur it in a specific period of time. From this criterion, the following can be concluded:

1. All costs are controllable by top management because of its broad range of authority.
2. Fewer costs are controllable as one moves down to each lower level of managerial responsibility because the manager's authority decreases at each level.

In general, costs that are incurred directly by a level of responsibility can be controlled at that level. In contrast, costs that are incurred indirectly and allocated to a responsibility level are considered to be **noncontrollable** at that level.

Illustration 5-16 ◀
Comparative CVP income statements

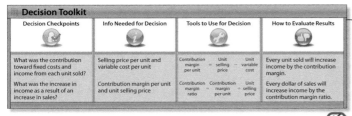

| | No Change | | With Change | |
	Total	Per Unit	Total	Per Unit
Sales	$500,000	$ 500	$600,000	$ 500
Variable costs	300,000	300	360,000	300
Contribution margin	200,000	$200	240,000	$200
Fixed costs	200,000		200,000	
Net income	$ 0		$ 40,000	

VARGO VIDEO COMPANY
CVP Income Statements
Month Ended June 30, 2005

Study these CVP income statements carefully. The concepts used in these statements will be used often in this and later chapters.

Decision Toolkit

Decision Checkpoints	Info Needed for Decision	Tools to Use for Decision	How to Evaluate Results
What was the contribution toward fixed costs and income from each unit sold?	Selling price per unit and variable cost per unit	Contribution margin per unit = Unit selling price − Unit variable cost	Every unit sold will increase income by the contribution margin.
What was the increase in income as a result of an increase in sales?	Contribution margin per unit and unit selling price	Contribution margin ratio = Contribution margin per unit ÷ Unit selling price	Every dollar of sales will increase income by the contribution margin ratio.

Each chapter presents **decision tools** that help decision makers analyze and solve business problems. At the end of the text discussion, a **Decision Toolkit** summarizes the key features of a decision tool and reviews why and how you would use it.

Break-Even Analysis

A key relationship in CVP analysis is the level of activity at which total revenues equal total costs (both fixed and variable). This level of activity is called the **break-even point**. At this volume of sales, the company will realize no income and will suffer no loss. The process of finding the break-even point is called **break-even analysis**. Knowledge of the break-even point is useful to management when it decides whether to introduce new product lines, change sales prices on established products, or enter new market areas.

The break-even point can be:

1. Calculated with a mathematical equation
2. Calculated by using contribution margin
3. Derived from a cost-volume-profit (CVP) graph

The break-even point can be expressed **in either sales units or sales dollars.**

study objective 6
Identify the three ways to determine the break-even point.

Mathematical Equation

A common equation that is used for CVP analysis is shown in Illustration 5-17.

| Sales | = | Variable Costs | + | Fixed Costs | + | Net Inc |

Identifying the break-even point is a special case of CVP analysis. Because ne[...] is zero at the break-even point, **break-even occurs when total sales equal varia[...] plus fixed costs.**

BEFORE YOU GO ON . . .

▶Review It

1. What are the effects of a change in activity on (a) a variable cost and (b) a fixed cost?
2. What is the relevant range, and how do costs behave within this range?
3. What steps are used in applying the high-low method to mixed costs?

▶Do It

Helena Company reports the following total costs at two levels of production:

	10,000 units	20,000 units
Direct materials	$20,000	$40,000
Maintenance	8,000	10,000
Amortization	4,000	4,000

Classify each cost as either variable, fixed, or mixed.

Action Plan

- Recall that a variable cost varies in total directly and proportionately with each change.
- Recall that a fixed cost remains the same in total with each change.
- Recall that a mixed cost changes in total but not proportionately with each change.

Solution

Direct materials is a variable cost. Maintenance is a mixed cost. Amortization is a fixed cost.

Related exercise material: BE5–1, BE5–2, BE5–3, E5–1, E5–2, and E5–3.

Cost-Volume-Profit Analysis

Cost-volume-profit (CVP) analysis is the study of the effects that changes in costs and volume have on a company's profits. CVP analysis is important in profit planning. It is also a critical factor in such management decisions as setting selling prices, determining product mix, and maximizing the use of production facilities.

study objective 4
List the five components of cost-volume-profit analysis.

Basic Components

CVP analysis considers the interrelationships among the components shown in Illustration 5-9.

Illustration 5-9 ▶
Components of CVP analysis

| Volume or level of activity | Unit selling prices | Variable cost per unit | Total cost per unit | Sales mix |

The following assumptions underlie each CVP analysis:

1. The behaviour of both costs and revenues is linear throughout the relevant range of the activity index.
2. All costs can be classified with reasonable accuracy as either variable or fixed.
3. Changes in activity are the only factors that affect costs.
4. All units that are produced are sold.
5. When more than one type of product is sold, the sales mix will remain constant. That is, the percentage that each product represents of total sales will stay the same. The sales mix complicates CVP analysis because different products will have different cost relationships. In this chapter, we assume a single product is being sold. Sales mix issues are addressed in Appendix 5A.

When these five assumptions are not valid, the results of CVP analysis may be inaccurate.

Before You Go On sections follow each key topic. *Review It* questions prompt you to stop and review the key points you have just studied. If you cannot answer these questions, you should go back and read the section again.

Brief *Do It* exercises ask you to put to work your newly acquired knowledge. They outline an *Action Plan* necessary to complete the exercise, and the *Solution* helps you see how the exercise should be solved. The *Do It* exercises are keyed to similar homework exercises.

CASTLE AND FIELD, CAs
Plano Moulding Company Audit

Illustration 4-18 ◄
Comparison of traditional costing with ABC in a service company

	Traditional Costing		ABC	
Revenue		$260,000		$260,000
Expenses				
Direct professional labour	$ 70,000		$ 70,000	
Applied overhead	140,000		165,100	
Total expenses		210,000		235,100
Operating income		$ 50,000		$ 24,900
Profit margin		19.2%		9.6%

The comparison shows that the assignment of overhead costs under traditional costing is distorted. The total cost assigned to performing the audit of Plano Moulding Company is greater under activity-based costing by $25,100, or 18 percent, and the profit margin is only half as much. Traditional costing gives the false impression of an operating profit of $50,000. This is more than double the operating income of $24,900 using ABC.

BEFORE YOU GO ON . . .

► Review It

1. What is the main barrier to effectively using ABC in a service-company environment?
2. What is the main advantage to be gained by using ABC in a service-company environment?

Using the Decision Toolkit

Preece Company manufactures a line of high-end exercise equipment of commercial quality. Assume that the chief accountant has proposed changing from a traditional costing system to an activity-based costing system. The financial vice-president is not convinced, so she requests that the next large order for equipment be costed under both systems for purposes of comparison and analysis. An order from Slim-Way Salons, Inc., for 150 low-impact treadmills is received and is identified as the order to be used for dual costing. The following cost data relate to the Slim-Way order:

Data Relevant to Both Costing Systems:

Direct materials	$55,500
Direct labour hours	820
Direct labour rate per hour	$18.00

Data Relevant to the Traditional Costing System:

Predetermined overhead rate is 300% of direct labour cost.

Data Relevant to the Activity-Based Costing System:

Activity Cost Pools	Cost Drivers	Activity-Based Overhead Rate	Expecte of Cost per Tre
Engineering design	Engineering hours	$30 per hour	3
Machine setup	Setups	$200 per setup	
Machining	Machine hours	$25 per hour	7
Assembly	Number of subassemblies	$8 per subassembly	1,4
Packaging and shipping	Packaging/shipping hours	$15 per hour	1
Building occupancy	Machine hours	$6 per hour	7

> A **Using the Decision Toolkit** exercise follows the final set of **Review It** questions in the chapter. It asks you to use business information and the decision tools presented in the chapter. You should think through the questions related to the decision before you study the printed **Solution**.

Instructions

Calculate the total cost of the Slim-Way Salons, Inc., order under (a) the traditional costing system and (b) the activity-based costing system. (c) As a result of this comparison, which costing system is Preece likely to adopt? Why?

Solution

(a) Traditional costing system:

Direct materials	$ 55,500
Direct labour (820 × $18)	14,760
Overhead assigned ($14,760 × 300%)	44,280
Total costs assigned to Slim-Way order	$114,540
Number of low-impact treadmills	150
Cost per unit	$763.60

(b) Activity-based costing system:

Direct materials		$ 55,500
Direct labour (820 × $18)		14,760
Overhead activity costs:		
Engineering design (330 hours @ $30)	$ 9,900	
Machine setup (22 setups @ $200)	4,400	
Machining (732 machine hours @ $25)	18,300	
Assembly (1,450 subassemblies @ $8)	11,600	
Packaging and shipping (152 hours @ $15)	2,280	
Building occupancy (732 hours @ $6)	4,392	50,872
Total costs assigned to Slim-Way order		$121,132
Number of low-impact treadmills		150
Cost per unit		$807.55

(c) Preece Company will likely adopt ABC because of the difference in the cost per unit (which ABC found to be higher). More importantly, ABC provides greater insight into the sources and causes of the cost per unit. Managers have a better understanding of which activities to control in order to reduce costs. ABC will provide better product costing and greater profitability for the company.

Summary of Study Objectives

1. *Recognize the difference between traditional costing and activity-based costing.* A traditional costing system allocates overhead to products based on a predetermined plantwide or department-wide volume of unit-based output rates, such as direct labour or machine hours. An ABC system allocates overhead to identified activity cost pools, and costs are then assigned to products using related cost drivers that measure the activities (resources) consumed.

2. *Identify the steps in the development of an activity-based costing system.* The development of an activity-based costing system involves four steps: (1) Identify and classify the major activities that pertain to the manufacture of specific products, and allocate manufacturing overhead costs to the appropriate cost pools. (2) Identify the cost driver that has a strong correlation to the costs accumulated in each activity cost pool.

(3) Calculate the activity-based overhead rate per cost driver. (4) Use the cost drivers to assign overhead costs for each activity cost pool to products or services.

3. *Know how companies identify the activity cost pools used in activity-based costing.* To identify activity cost pools, a company must perform an analysis of each operation or process, documenting and timing every task, action, or transaction.

4. *Know how companies identify and use the activity cost drivers in activity-based costing.* Cost drivers that are identified for activity cost pools must (a) accurately measure the actual consumption of the activity by the various products, and (b) have data on them that is easily available.

5. *Understand the benefits and limitations of activity-based costing.* What makes ABC a more accurate

Summary of Study Objectives

1. **Distinguish between variable and fixed costs.** Variable costs are costs that vary in total directly and proportionately with changes in the activity index. Fixed costs are costs that remain the same in total regardless of changes in the activity index.

2. **Explain significance of the relevant range.** The relevant range is the range of activity in which a company expects to operate during a year. It is important in CVP analysis because the behaviour of costs is linear throughout the relevant range.

3. **Explain the concept of mixed costs.** Mixed costs increase in total but not proportionately with changes in the activity level. For CVP analysis, mixed costs must be classified into their fixed and variable elements. One method that management may use is the high-low method.

4. **List the five components of cost-volume-profit analysis.** The five components of CVP analysis are (a) volume or level of activity, (b) unit selling prices, (c) variable cost per unit, (d) total fixed costs, and (e) sales mix.

5. **Explain what the contribution margin is and how it can be expressed.** Contribution margin is the amount of revenue remaining after deducting variable costs. It is identified in a CVP income statement, which classifies costs as variable or fixed. It can be expressed as a per unit amount or as a ratio.

6. **Identify the three ways to determine the break-even point.** The break-even point can be (a) calculated with a mathematical equation, (b) calculated by using a contribution margin technique, and (c) derived from a CVP graph.

7. **State the formulas for determining the sales required to earn the target net income.** One formula is: required sales = variable costs + fixed costs + target net income. Another formula is: fixed costs + target net income ÷ contribution margin ratio = required sales.

8. **State the formulas for determining the sales required to earn the target net income after tax.** One formula is: required sales = variable costs + fixed costs + target net income before tax. Another formula is: (fixed costs + target net income before tax) ÷ contribution margin ratio = required sales.

9. **Define margin of safety, and state the formulas for calculating it.** Margin of safety is the difference between actual or expected sales and sales at the break-even point. The formulas for margin of safety are: actual (expected) sales − break-even sales = margin of safety in dollars; margin of safety in dollars ÷ actual (expected) sales = margin of safety ratio.

10. **Understand how operating leverage affects profitability.** Operating leverage is how much a company's net income reacts to a change in sales. Operating leverage is determined by a company's relative use of fixed versus variable costs. Companies with high fixed costs relative to variable costs have a high operating leverage. A company with a high operating leverage will experience a sharp increase (decrease) in net income with an increase (decrease) in sales. The degree of operating leverage can be measured by dividing the contribution margin by net income.

11. **Explain the term "sales mix" and its effect on break-even sales (Appendix 5A).** The sales mix is the relative proportion in which each product is sold when a company sells more than one product. For a multi-product company, break-even sales in units is determined by using the weighted-average unit contribution margin of all the products. If the company sells many different products, calculating the break-even point using unit information is not practical. Instead, in a company with many products, break-even sales in dollars is calculated using the weighted-average contribution margin ratio.

The **Summary of Study Objectives** reviews the main points related to the Study Objectives. It provides you with another opportunity to review what you have learned as well as to see how the key topics within the chapter fit together.

---

4. **Identify the relevant costs in a make-or-buy decision.** In a make-or-buy decision, the relevant costs are (a) the variable manufacturing costs that will be saved, (b) the purchase price, and (c) opportunity costs.

5. **Identify the relevant costs in deciding whether to sell or process materials further.** The decision rule for whether to sell or process materials further is as follows: Process further as long as the incremental revenue from processing is more than the incremental processing costs.

6. **Identify the relevant costs in deciding whether to keep or replace equipment.** The relevant costs to be considered in determining whether equipment should be kept or replaced are the effects on variable costs and

the cost of the new equipment. Also, any disposal value of the existing asset must be considered.

7. **Identify the relevant costs in deciding whether to eliminate an unprofitable segment.** In deciding whether to eliminate an unprofitable segment, the relevant information is the contribution margin, if any, produced by the segment and the disposition of the segment's fixed expenses.

8. **Determine the sales mix when a company has limited resources.** When a company has limited resources, it is necessary to find the contribution margin per unit of the limited resource. This amount is then multiplied by the units of limited resource to determine which product maximizes net income.

At the end of each chapter, the **Decision Toolkit—A Summary** reviews the contexts and techniques useful for decision making that were covered in the chapter.

Decision Toolkit—A Summary

Decision Checkpoints	Info Needed for Decision	Tools to Use for Decision	How to Evaluate Results
Which alternative should the company choose?	All relevant costs and opportunity costs	Compare the relevant cost of each alternative.	Choose the alternative that maximizes net income.
How many units of products A and B should we produce with a limited resource?	Contribution margin per unit, limited resource required per unit	$\dfrac{\text{Contribution margin per unit of limited resource}} = \dfrac{\text{Contribution margin per unit}}{\text{Limited resource per unit}}$	Any additional capacity of the limited resource should be applied toward the product with the higher contribution margin per unit of the limited resource.

The **Glossary** defines all the **key terms** and concepts introduced in the chapter. Page references help you find any terms you need to study further. A **web icon** tells you that there is a Key Term Matching Activity on the website that can help you master the material.

Key Term Matching Activity

Glossary

Incremental analysis The process of identifying the financial data that change under alternative courses of action. (p. 247)

Joint costs For joint products, all costs incurred before the point at which the two products are separately identifiable. This point is known as the split-off point. (p. 251)

Joint products Multiple end products produced from a single raw material and a common process. (p. 251)

Opportunity cost The potential benefit that may be obtained from following an alternative course of action. (p. 247)

Relevant costs Those costs and revenues that differ across alternatives. (p. 247)

Sunk cost A cost that cannot be changed by any present or future decision. (p. 247)

Theory of constraints A specific approach that is used to identify and manage constraints in order to achieve the company's goals. (p. 256)

260   Chapter 6   ▶   Incremental Analysis

Demonstration Problem

Animated
Demonstration
Problem

Canada Bearings Corporation manufactures and sells three different types of high-quality sealed ball bearings. The bearings vary in their quality specifications—mainly in terms of their smoothness and roundness. They are referred to as Fine, Extra-Fine, and Super-Fine bearings. Machine time is limited. More machine time is required to manufacture the Extra-Fine and Super-Fine bearings. Additional information follows:

	Product		
	Fine	Extra-Fine	Super-Fine
Selling price	$6.00	$10.00	$16.00
Variable costs and expenses	4.00	6.50	11.00
Contribution margin	$2.00	$ 3.50	$ 5.00
Machine hours required	0.02	0.04	0.08
Total fixed costs: $234,000			

Instructions

Answer each of the following questions.

(a) Ignoring the machine-time constraint, what strategy would be best?
(b) What is the contribution margin per unit of the limited resource for each type of bearing?
(c) If additional machine time could be obtained, how should the additional capacity be used?

Action Plan
• To determine how best to use a limited resource, calculate the contribution margin per unit of the limited resource for each product type.

Solution to Demonstration Problem

(a) The Super-Fine bearings have the highest contribution margin per unit. Thus, ignoring any manufacturing constraints, it would appear that the company should shift toward production of more Super-Fine units.

(b) The contribution margin per unit of the limited resource is calculated as follows:

	Fine	Extra-Fine	Super-Fine
Contribution margin per unit ÷	$2	$3.5	$5
Limited resource consumed per unit	÷ 0.02	÷ 0.04	÷ 0.08
	$100.00	$87.50	$62.50

5. The Fine bearings have the highest contribution margin per limited resource, even though they have the lowest contribution margin per unit. Because of this resource constraint, any additional capacity should be used to make Fine bearings.

the navigator

Self-Study Questions

Additional Self-Study Questions

Answers are at the end of the chapter.

(SO 1) 1. Three of the steps in management's decision-making process are to (1) review the results of the decision, (2) determine and evaluate possible courses of action, and (3) make the decision. The steps are prepared in the following order:
(a) 1, 2, 3.   (c) 2, 1, 3.
(b) 3, 2, 1.   (d) 2, 3, 1.

(SO 2) 2. Incremental analysis is the process of identifying the financial data that:
(a) do not change under alternative courses of action.
(b) change under alternative courses of action.
(c) are mixed under alternative courses of action.
(d) No correct answer is given.

3. It costs a company $14 of variable costs and $6 of   (SO 2)
fixed costs to ...
A foreign bu...
$18 each. If...
duced with...
(a) decrease...
(b) increase...

4. It costs a co...
of fixed cost...
$30. A fore...
units at $18...
and produce...
net income...
(a) increase...
(b) increase...

Self-Study Questions provide a practice test, keyed to Study Objectives, that gives you an opportunity to check your knowledge of important topics. Answers appear on the last page of the chapter. **Web icons** tell you that you can answer these **Self-Study Questions** interactively on the website. Also, there is an additional **Self-Test** on the website that can further help you master the material.

Questions allow you to explain your understanding of concepts and relationships covered in the chapter. Use them to help prepare for class discussion and tests.

A **Demonstration Problem** is the final step before you begin homework. These sample problems provide you with an **Action Plan** in the margin that lists the strategies needed to approach and solve the problem. The Solution demonstrates both the form and content of complete answers.

A **web icon** tells you that there is an animated version of the **Demonstration Problem** that you can walk through on the text companion website.

---

164   Chapter 4   ▶   Activity-Based Costing

Self-Study Questions

Additional Self-Study Questions

Answers are at the end of the chapter.

(SO 1) 1. Activity-based costing (ABC):
(a) can be used only in a process cost system.
(b) focuses on units of production.
(c) focuses on activities that are performed to produce a product.
(d) uses only a single basis of allocation.

(SO 1) 2. Activity-based costing:
(a) is the initial phase of converting to a just-in-time operating environment.
(b) can be used only in a job-order costing system.
(c) is a two-stage overhead cost allocation system that identifies activity cost pools and cost drivers.
(d) uses direct labour as its main cost driver.

(SO 3) 3. Any activity that causes resources to be consumed is called a:
(a) just-in-time activity.
(b) facility-level activity.
(c) cost driver.
(d) non–value-added activity.

(SO 4) 4. The overhead rate for machine setups is $100 per setup. Products A and B have 80 and 60 setups, respectively. The overhead assigned to each product is:
(a) product A $8,000, product B $8,000.
(b) product A $8,000, product B $6,000.
(c) product A $6,000, product B $6,000.
(d) product A $6,000, product B $8,000.

5. Donna Crawford Co. has identified an activity   (SO 4)
cost pool and has allocated estimated overhead of $1,920,000 to it. It has determined the expected use of cost drivers for that activity to be 160,000 inspections. Widgets require 40,000 inspections; gadgets, 30,000 inspections; and targets, 90,000 inspections. The overhead assigned to each product is:
(a) widgets $40,000, gadgets $30,000, targets $90,000.
(b) widgets $480,000, gadgets $360,000, targets $108,000.
(c) widgets $360,000, gadgets $480,000, targets $1,080,000.
(d) widgets $480,000, gadgets $360,000, targets $1,080,000.

6. An activity that adds costs to the product but   (SO 6)
does not increase its market value is a:
(a) value-added activity.
(b) cost driver.
(c) cost-benefit activity.
(d) non–value-added activity.

7. The following activity is value-added: (SO 6)
(a) storage of raw materials.
(b) moving parts from machine to machine.
(c) shaping a piece of metal on a lathe.
(d) All of the above

8. A relevant facility-level cost driver for heating   (SO 7)
costs is:
(a) machine hours.   (c) floor space.
(b) direct material.   (d) direct labour cost.

the navigator

Questions

1. Under what conditions is direct labour a valid basis for allocating overhead?

2. What has happened in recent industrial history to reduce the usefulness of direct labour as the main basis for allocating overhead to products?

3. In an automated manufacturing environment, what basis of overhead allocation is often more relevant than direct labour hours?

4. What is generally true about overhead allocation to high-volume products versus low-volume products under a traditional costing system?

5. (a) What are the principal differences between activity-based costing (ABC) and traditional product costing?
(b) What assumptions must be met for ABC costing to be useful?

6. What is the formula for calculating activity-based overhead rates?

7. What are the steps in developing an activity-based costing system?

8. Explain the preparation and use of an activity flow-chart in an ABC system.

9. What is an activity cost pool?

10. What is a cost driver?

11. What makes a cost driver accurate and appropriate?

12. What is the formula for assigning activity cost pools to products?

13. What are the benefits of activity-based costing?

14. What are the limitations of activity-based costing?

15. Under what conditions is ABC generally the better overhead costing system?

16. What refinement has been made to increase the efficiency and effectiveness of ABC for use in managing costs?

17. What is the benefit of classifying activities as value-added and non–value-added?

18. In what ways is the application of ABC to service industries the same as its application to manufacturing companies?

19. How is the classification of levels of activity relevant to ABC?

Brief Exercises help you focus on one Study Objective at a time and thus help you build confidence in your basic skills and knowledge. (Keyed to Study Objectives.)

Brief Exercises

BE4–1 Infortrac Inc. sells a high-speed retrieval system for mining information. It provides the following information for the year:

	Budgeted	Actual
Overhead cost	$1,000,000	$950,000
Machine hours	50,000	45,000
Direct labour hours	100,000	90,000

Identify differences between costing systems.
(SO 1)

Overhead is applied based on direct labour hours. (a) Calculate the predetermined overhead rate. (b) Determine the amount of overhead applied for the year. (c) Explain how an activity-based costing system might differ in terms of calculating a predetermined overhead rate.

Some Exercises and Problems focus on accounting situations faced by Service Companies. The **service company icon** highlights these homework materials.

BE4–2 Sassafras Inc. has conducted an analysis of overhead costs for one of its product lines using a traditional cost system (volume-based) and an activity-based costing system. Here are its results:

	Traditional Costing	ABC
Sales revenues	$600,000	$600,000
Overhead costs:		
Product RX3	$34,000	$50,000
Product Y12	36,000	20,000
	$70,000	$70,000

Identify differences between costing systems.
(SO 1)

Explain how a difference in the overhead costs between the two systems may have occurred.

BE4–3 Altex Co. identifies the following activities that pertain to manufacturing overhead: materials handling, machine setups, factory machine maintenance, factory supervision, and quality control. For each activity, identify an appropriate cost driver.

Identify cost drivers.
(SO 4)

BE4–4 Ayala Company manufactures four products in a single production facility. The company uses activity-based costing. The following activities have been identified through the company's activity analysis: (a) inventory control, (b) machine setups, (c) employee training, (d) quality inspections, (e) material ordering, (f) drilling operations, and (g) building maintenance.

For each activity, name a cost driver that might be used to assign overhead costs to products.

Identify cost drivers.
(SO 4)

BE4–5 Gomez Company identifies three activities in its manufacturing process: machine setups, machining, and inspections. The estimated annual overhead cost for each activity is $180,000, $325,000, and $87,500, respectively. The cost driver for each activity and the expected annual usage are as follows: number of setups 2,500, machine hours 25,000, number of inspections 1,750. Calculate the overhead rate for each activity.

Calculate activity-based overhead rates.
(SO 4)

BE4–6 Coats Galore, Inc. uses activity-based costing as the basis for information about prices for its six lines of seasonal coats. Calculate the activity-based overhead rates using the following budgeted data for each of the activity cost pools:

Activity Cost Pools	Estimated Overhead	Expected Use of Cost Drivers per Activity
Designing	$ 450,000	12,000 designer hours
Sizing and cutting	4,000,000	160,000 machine hours
Stitching and trimming	1,440,000	80,000 labour hours
Wrapping and packing	336,000	32,000 finished units

Exercises, which are more difficult than Brief Exercises, help you continue to build confidence in your ability to use the material learned in the chapter. (Keyed to Study Objectives.)

Spreadsheet Exercises and Problems, identified by an icon, are selected problems that can be solved using the Excel templates on the text companion website.

Exercises

E4–1 Elle Inc. makes two types of handbags: standard and custom. The controller has decided to use a plantwide overhead rate based on direct labour costs. The president has heard of activity-based costing and wants to see how the results would differ if this system were used. Two activity cost pools were developed: machining and setup. Presented below is information related to the company's operations:

	Standard	Custom
Direct labour costs	$50,000	$100,000
Machine hours	1,000	1,000
Setup hours	100	400

Assign overhead using traditional costing and ABC.
(SO 1, 4)

Total estimated overhead costs are $300,000. The overhead cost allocated to the machining activity cost pool is $200,000, and $100,000 is allocated to the machine setup activity cost pool.

Instructions

(a) Calculate the overhead rate using the traditional (plantwide) approach.
(b) Calculate the overhead rates using the activity-based costing approach.
(c) Determine the difference in allocation between the two approaches.

E4–2 Perdon Inc. has conducted the following analysis related to its product lines, using a traditional cost system (volume-based) and an activity-based costing system. Both the traditional and the activity-based costing systems include direct materials and direct labour costs.

		Total Costs	
Product	Sales Revenue	Traditional	ABC
Product 540X	$200,000	$55,000	$50,000
Product 137Y	160,000	50,000	35,000
Product 249S	80,000	15,000	35,000

Explain difference between traditional and activity-based costing.
(SO 1)

Instructions

(a) For each product line, calculate the operating income using the traditional costing system.
(b) For each product line, calculate the operating income using the activity-based costing system.
(c) Using the following formula, calculate the percentage difference in operating income for each of Perdon's product lines: Operating Income (ABC) less Operating Income (traditional cost) divided by Operating Income (traditional cost). Round the percentage to two decimals.
(d) Explain why the costs for Product 540X are approximately the same using either the traditional or activity-based costing system.

E4–3 International Fabrics has budgeted overhead costs of $900,000. It has allocated overhead on a plantwide basis to its two products (wool and cotton) using direct labour hours which are estimated to be 450,000 for the current year. The company has decided to experiment with activity-based costing and has created two activity cost pools and related activity cost drivers. These two cost pools are as follows: cutting (cost driver is machine hours) and design (cost driver is number of setups). Overhead allocated to the cutting cost pool is $300,000 and $600,000 is allocated to the design cost pool. Additional information related to these pools is as follows:

	Wool	Cotton	Total
Machine hours	100,000	100,000	200,000
Number of setups	1,000	500	1,500

Assign overhead using traditional costing and ABC.
(SO 1, 4)

Instructions

(a) Determine the amount of overhead allocated to the wool product line and the cotton product line using activity-based costing.
(b) What is the difference between the allocation of overhead to the wool and cotton product lines using activity-based costing versus the traditional approach, assuming direct labour hours were incurred evenly between the cutting and design activities?

230   Chapter 5   ▶   Decision-Making: Cost-Volume-Profit

Instructions

(a) Calculate the break-even point in units for the company.
(b) Determine the number of units to be sold at the break-even point for each product line.
(c) Verify that the mix of sales units determined in (b) will generate a zero net income.

Determine break-even point in dollars for two divisions.
(SO 11)

*E5–17 Mega Electronix sells television sets and DVD players. The business is divided into two divisions along product lines. A variable cost income statement for a recent quarter's activity is presented below:

	TV Division	DVD Division	Total
Sales	$600,000	$400,000	$1,000,000
Variable costs	450,000	240,000	690,000
Contribution margin	$150,000	$160,000	310,000
Fixed costs			124,000
Net income			$ 186,000

Instructions

(a) Determine the percentage of sales and contribution margin for each division.
(b) Calculate the company's weighted-average contribution margin ratio.
(c) Calculate the company's break-even point in dollars.
(d) Determine the sales level in dollars for each division at the break-even point.

Problems: Set A

Determine variable and fixed costs, calculate break-even point, prepare CVP graph, and determine net income.
(SO 1, 3, 5, 6)

P5–18A The Peace Barber Shop employs four barbers. One barber, who also serves as the manager, is paid a salary of $1,800 per month. The other barbers are paid $1,500 per month. In addition, each barber is paid a commission of $4 per haircut. Other monthly costs are as follows: store rent $800 plus 60 cents per haircut; amortization on equipment $500; barber supplies 40 cents per haircut; utilities $300; and advertising $200. The price of a haircut is $11.

Instructions

(a) Determine the variable cost per haircut and the total monthly fixed costs.
(b) Calculate the break-even point in units and dollars.
(c) Prepare a CVP graph, assuming a maximum of 1,500 haircuts in a month. Use increments of 300 haircuts on the horizontal axis and $3,300 increments on the vertical axis.
(d) Determine the net income, assuming 1,500 haircuts are given in a month.

Determine contribution margin ratio, break-even point in dollars, and margin of safety.
(SO 5, 6, 7, 9)

P5–19A Montreal Seating Co., a manufacturer of chairs, had the following data for 2005:

Sales	2,400 units
Sales price	$40 per unit
Variable costs	$14 per unit
Fixed costs	$19,500

Instructions

(a) What is the contribution margin ratio?
(b) What is the break-even point in dollars?
(c) What is the margin of safety in units and dollars?
(d) If the company wishes to increase its total dollar by how much will it need to increase its sales if

Prepare CVP income statement; calculate break-even point, contribution margin ratio, margin of safety ratio, and sales for target net income.
(SO 5, 6, 7, 9)

P5–20A Boisclair Company bottles and distributes sold for $1.00 per 500-ml bottle to retailers, who cha ment estimates the following revenues and costs:

Net sales	$2,500,000	Selli
Direct materials	360,000	Selli
Direct labour	650,000	Adm
Manufacturing overhead—variable	370,000	Adm
Manufacturing overhead—fixed	260,000	

Each **Problem** helps you pull together and apply several concepts from the chapter. Two sets of **Problems—A** and **B**—are keyed to the same Study Objectives and provide additional opportunities to apply concepts learned in the chapter. (Keyed to multiple Study Objectives.)

Certain exercises and problems, marked with a pencil icon ✎➤, help you practice **business writing skills**, which are much in demand among employers.

---

272   Chapter 6   ▶   Incremental Analysis

(d) The company has the option of making and buying at the same time. What would be your answer to (c) if this alternative was considered? Show calculations to support your answer.
(e) What qualitative factors should Kamloops Outdoors Corporation consider in determining whether it should make or buy the lip balm tubes?

(CMA Canada-adapted)

Problems: Set B

Prepare incremental analysis for special order and identify non-financial factors in decision.
(SO 3)

P6–24B Oakbrook Company is currently producing 18,000 units per month, which is 80% of its production capacity. Variable manufacturing costs are currently $13.20 per unit, and fixed manufacturing costs are $72,000 per month. Oakbrook pays a 9% sales commission to its salespeople, has $30,000 in fixed administrative expenses per month, and is averaging $432,000 in sales per month.

A special order received from a foreign company would enable Oakbrook Company to operate at 100% capacity. The foreign company offered to pay 80% of Oakbrook's current selling price per unit. If the order is accepted, Oakbrook will have to spend an extra $2.00 per unit to package the product for overseas shipping. Also, Oakbrook would need to lease a new stamping machine to imprint the foreign company's logo on the product, at a monthly cost of $5,000. The special order would require a sales commission of $4,000.

Instructions

(a) Calculate the number of units involved in the special order and the foreign company's offered price per unit.
(b) What is the manufacturing cost of producing one unit of Oakbrook's product for regular customers?
(c) Prepare an incremental analysis of the special order. Should management accept the order?
(d) What is the lowest price that Oakbrook could accept for the special order to earn net income of $1.20 per unit?
(e) ✎➤ What non-financial factors should management consider in making its decision?

Calculate contribution margin and prepare incremental analysis for maximizing operating income and replacing equipment.
(SO 6)

P6–25B Sharp Aerospace has a five-year contract to supply North Plane with four specific spare parts for its fleet of airplanes. The following table provides information on selling prices, costs, and the number of units of each part that the company needs to produce annually according to the contract with North Plane:

	A10	A20	A30	A40
Sales	$1,500,000	$875,000	$450,000	$2,400,000
Variables costs	1,235,000	425,000	187,000	1,875,000
Contribution margin	$ 265,000	$450,000	$263,000	$ 525,000
Production in units	1,000	250	750	600
Machine hours/unit	2	4	1.5	3

Fixed overhead costs amount to $820,000 and are allocated based on the number of units produced. The company has a maximum annual capacity of 6,000 machine hours.

Instructions

(a) If Sharp Aerospace could manufacture only one of the four parts, which spare part should it produce, based on the contribution margin? Explain why.
(b) Polaris Airline wants to buy 200 units of part A10 at 110% of the price currently paid by North Plane. Assume that for any of the four parts, Sharp Aerospace has to supply North Plane with at least 90% of the number of units specified in the contract. Should Sharp Aerospace accept the order for 200 units of part A10?
(c) A new technology is available that costs $2.5 million and would increase Sharp Aerospace's annual capacity by 25%. Should the company purchase the new technology? Assume that the technology has an estimated life of four years and that Sharp Aerospace can sell, at the same prices paid by North Plane, all the units it can produce of any of the four parts. Show all your calculations.

(CGA-adapted)

moderate price range. Debbie MacNeil, the manager of Bricktown, has determined that during the last two years the sales mix and contribution margin of its offerings are as follows:

	Percent of Total Sales	Contribution Margin Ratio
Appetizers	10%	50%
Main entrees	55%	30%
Desserts	10%	60%
Beverages	25%	75%

Debbie is considering a variety of options to try to improve the profitability of the restaurant. Her goal is to generate a target net income of $155,000. The company has fixed costs of $400,000 per year.

Instructions

(a) Calculate the total restaurant sales and the sales of each product line that would be necessary in order to achieve the desired target net income.

(b) Debbie believes the restaurant could greatly improve its profitability by reducing the complexity and selling price of its entrees to increase the number of clients that it serves, and by then more heavily marketing its appetizers and beverages. She is proposing to reduce the contribution margin on the main entrees to 15% by dropping the average selling price. She envisions an expansion of the restaurant that would increase fixed costs by 50%. At the same time, she is proposing to change the sales mix to the following:

	Percent of Total Sales	Contribution Margin Ratio
Appetizers	15%	50%
Main entrees	30%	15%
Desserts	15%	60%
Beverages	40%	75%

Calculate the total restaurant sales, and the sales of each product line that would be necessary to achieve the desired target net income.

(c) Suppose that Debbie drops the selling price on entrees, and increases fixed costs as proposed in part (b), but customers are not swayed by her marketing efforts, and the product mix remains what it was in part (a). Calculate the total restaurant sales and the sales of each product line that would be necessary to achieve the desired target net income. Comment on the potential risks and benefits of this strategy.

under alternative sales strategies and evaluate.
(SO 5, 6, 9, 11)

Cases

> The **Cases** help you build decision-making skills by analyzing accounting information in a less structured situation. These cases require evaluation of a manager's decision, or they lead to a decision among alternative courses of action. The case section includes situations that involve research, group work, communication, and ethics.

C5–43 Clay Company has decided to introduce a new product. The new product can be manufactured by either a capital-intensive method or a labour-intensive method. The manufacturing method will not affect the quality of the product. The estimated manufacturing costs under the two methods are as follows:

	Capital-Intensive	Labour-Intensive
Direct materials	$5 per unit	$5.50 per unit
Direct labour	$6 per unit	$7.20 per unit
Variable overhead	$3 per unit	$4.80 per unit
Fixed manufacturing costs	$2,440,000	$1,390,000

Clay's market research department has recommended an introductory unit sales price of $30. The incremental selling expenses are estimated to be $500,000 annually pl[...] each unit sold, regardless of the manufacturing method.

> The **web icon** in the cases section indicates that there are additional cases on the text companion website.

Additional Cases

> The **group icon** indicates a case that can be worked on in groups.

would cost $90,000, with a useful life of six years and no salvage value. The company uses straight-line amortization on all plant assets.

Instruction

(a) What was Labrador's break-even point in units last year?

(b) How many units of product would Labrador have had to sell in the past year to earn $247,500 in net income after taxes?

(c) If it holds the sales price constant and makes the suggested changes, how many units of product must the company sell in the coming year to break even?

(d) If it holds the sales price constant and makes the suggested changes, how many units of product will Labrador have to sell to make the same net income before taxes as last year?

(e) If Labrador wishes to maintain the same contribution margin ratio, what selling price per unit of product must it charge next year to cover the increased materials costs?

(CMA Canada-adapted)

C5–48 Ronnie Drake is an accountant for Benson Company. Early this year, Ronnie made a highly favourable projection of sales and profits over the next three years for Benson's hot-selling computer PLEX. As a result of the projections Ronnie presented to senior management, management decided to expand production in this area. This decision led to dislocations of some plant personnel, who were reassigned to one of the company's newer plants in another province. However, no one was fired, and in fact the company expanded its workforce slightly.

Unfortunately, Ronnie rechecked his calculations on the projections a few months later and found that he had made an error that would have reduced his projections substantially. Luckily, sales of PLEX have exceeded projections so far, and management is satisfied with its decision. Ronnie, however, is not sure what to do. Should he confess his honest mistake and jeopardize his possible promotion? He suspects that no one will catch the error because sales of PLEX have exceeded his projections, and it appears that profits will materialize close to his projections.

Instructions

(a) Who are the stakeholders in this situation?

(b) Identify the ethical issues involved in this situation.

(c) What are the possible alternative actions for Ronnie? What would you do in Ronnie's position?

> Through the **Ethics Cases** you will reflect on typical ethical dilemmas, analyze the issues involved, and decide on an appropriate course of action.

Answers to Self-Study Questions

1. d   2. c   3. a   4. a   5. c   6. d   7. a   8. b   9. d   10. d

> **Answers to Self-Study Questions** provide feedback on your understanding of concepts.

> After you complete your homework assignment, it's a good idea to go back to **The Navigator** checklist at the start of the chapter to see if you have used all of the chapter's study aids.

 Remember to go back to the Navigator Box at the beginning of the chapter to check off your completed work.

This questionnaire aims to find out something about your preferences for the way you work with information. You will have a preferred learning style and one part of that learning style is your preference for the intake and the output of ideas and information.

Circle the letter of the answer that best explains your preference. Circle more than one if a single answer does not match your perception. Leave blank any question that does not apply.

1. You are about to give directions to a person who is standing with you. She is staying in a hotel in town and wants to visit your house later. She has a rental car. Would you
   (a) draw a map on paper?
   (b) tell her the directions?
   (c) write down the directions (without a map)?
   (d) pick her up at the hotel in your car?

2. You are not sure whether a word should be spelled "dependent" or "dependant." Do you
   (c) see the word in your mind and choose by the way it looks?
   (a) sound it out in your mind?
   (b) look it up in the dictionary?
   (d) write both versions down on paper and choose one?

3. You have just received a copy of your itinerary for a world trip. This is of interest to a friend. Would you
   (b) call her immediately and tell her about it?
   (c) send her a copy of the printed itinerary?
   (a) show her on a map of the world?
   (d) share what you plan to do at each place you visit?

4. You are going to cook something as a special treat for your family. Do you
   (d) cook something familiar without the need for instructions?
   (a) thumb through the cookbook looking for ideas from the pictures?
   (c) refer to a specific cookbook where there is a good recipe?

5. A group of tourists has been assigned to you to find out about wildlife reserves or parks. Would you
   (d) drive them to a wildlife reserve or park?
   (a) show them slides and photographs?
   (c) give them pamphlets or a book on wildlife reserves or parks?
   (b) give them a talk on wildlife reserves or parks?

6. You are about to purchase a new CD player. Other than price, what would most influence your decision?
   (b) The salesperson telling you what you want to know.
   (c) Reading the details about it.
   (d) Playing with the controls and listening to it.
   (a) Its fashionable and upscale appearance.

7. Recall a time in your life when you learned how to do something like playing a new board game. Try to avoid choosing a very physical skill, e.g., riding a bike. How did you learn best? By
   (a) visual clues—pictures, diagrams, charts?
   (c) written instructions?
   (b) listening to somebody explaining it?
   (d) doing it or trying it?

8. You have an eye problem. Would you prefer that the doctor
   (b) tell you what is wrong?
   (a) show you a diagram of what is wrong?
   (d) use a model to show what is wrong?

9. You are about to learn to use a new program on a computer. Would you
   (d) sit down at the keyboard and begin to experiment with the program's features?
   (c) read the manual that comes with the program?
   (b) call a friend and ask questions about it?

10. You are staying in a hotel and have a rental car. You would like to visit friends whose address/location you do not know. Would you like them to
    (a) draw you a map on paper?
    (b) tell you the directions?
    (c) write down the directions (without a map)?
    (d) pick you up at the hotel in their car?

11. Apart from price, what would most influence your decision to buy a particular book?
    (d) You have used a copy before.
    (b) A friend talking about it.
    (c) Quickly reading parts of it.
    (a) The appealing way it looks.

12. A new movie has arrived in town. What would most influence your decision to go (or not go)?
    (b) You heard a radio review about it.
    (c) You read a review about it.
    (a) You saw a preview of it.

13. Do you prefer a lecturer or teacher who likes to use
    (c) a textbook, handouts, readings?
    (a) flow diagrams, charts, graphs?
    (d) field trips, labs, practical sessions?
    (b) discussion, guest speakers?

	(a)	(b)	(c)	(9)
Count your choices:	☐	☐	☐	☐
	V	A	R	K

Now match the letter or letters you have recorded most to the same letter or letters in the Learning Styles Chart on the text companion website. You may have more than one learning style preference—many people do.

Next to each letter in the chart are suggestions that will refer you to different learning aids throughout this text.

www.wiley.com/canada/managerial

CONTENTS

CHAPTER 1

Managerial Accounting

Costs Are Key

Chances are that the foil wrapped around your food, the tire rims on your car, or the screens keeping insects out of your home were made from aluminum created by Alcoa, the world's leading aluminum producer. The multinational corporation based in Pittsburgh, Pennsylvania, has three smelters in Quebec—in Baie-Comeau, Deschambault, and Bécancour. These smelters produce one million metric tonnes of aluminum each year, or 20 percent of the company's worldwide capacity.

Alain Boucher, vice-president, finance, for Alcoa Canada, explains that these smelters produce aluminum in various alloys that are used for a variety of purposes. "These products have different shapes, lengths, heights, and also different metallic components depending on customer specifications," he says.

Aluminum production has four cost components, Mr. Boucher continues. Raw material costs cover alumina, a powder refined from bauxite ore, and carbon, needed to conduct energy and one of the chemical components used to produce aluminum. Other raw materials may also be used, depending on the product. The second cost is for the energy itself. "About a third of the cost is energy," Mr. Boucher stresses. Quebec has been attractive to aluminum producers mainly because of its traditionally low energy costs, though this may change as North American energy costs rise. The third cost component is labour, which can range from manual tasks to technical engineering knowledge. The final cost factor is maintenance. Smelters have huge equipment and many large vehicles, all of which need to be maintained. Plus there are general overhead and administration costs.

Alcoa's key performance indicators include financial, health and safety, and environmental measures. "A big component of our process is to make sure we produce good aluminum at a low cost, but also in a safe environment and with a process that is environmentally friendly," Mr. Boucher says. Among the measures Alcoa management keeps track of is "current efficiency," which is the amount of aluminum that should be produced based on the amount of energy used. The company also tracks the number of person-hours required for the amount of metal produced. And then there are environmentally driven measures, such as plant emissions.

Managing costs is key to running a profitable aluminum smelter, Mr. Boucher says. "Aluminum is a commodity," he says. "The price is established on the world market... The best way to generate profit in this business is to manage your costs properly."

the navigator

The **Navigator** is a learning system that prompts you to use the learning aids in the chapter and helps you set priorities as you study.

THE NAVIGATOR

- [ ] Scan *Study Objectives*
- [ ] Read *Feature Story*
- [ ] Read *Chapter Preview*
- [ ] Read text and answer *Before You Go On* p. 10, p. 13, p. 17, p. 22
- [ ] Work *Using the Decision Toolkit*
- [ ] Review *Summary of Study Objectives*
- [ ] Review *Using the Decision Toolkit—A Summary*
- [ ] Work *Demonstration Problem*
- [ ] Answer *Self-Study Questions*
- [ ] Complete assignments

STUDY OBJECTIVES

Study Objectives give you a framework for learning the specific concepts covered in the chapter.

After studying this chapter, you should be able to:

1. Explain the distinguishing features of managerial accounting.
2. Identify the three broad functions of management.
3. Define the three classes of manufacturing costs.
4. Distinguish between product and period costs.
5. Explain the difference between a merchandising income statement and a manufacturing income statement.
6. Indicate how the cost of goods manufactured is determined.
7. Explain the difference between a merchandising balance sheet and a manufacturing balance sheet.
8. Identify changes in managerial accounting.

the navigator

This book focuses on issues in the feature story about Alcoa Canada. These include determining and controlling the costs of materials, labour, and overhead and the relationship between costs and profits. In a previous financial accounting course, you learned about the form and content of **financial statements for external users** of financial information, such as shareholders and creditors. These financial statements are the main product of financial accounting. Managerial accounting focuses primarily on the preparation of **reports for internal users** of financial information, such as the managers and officers of a company. Managers are evaluated on the results of their decisions. In today's rapidly changing global environment, managers must often make decisions that determine their company's fate— and their own. Managerial accounting provides tools that help management make decisions and evaluate the effectiveness of those decisions.

The chapter is organized as follows:

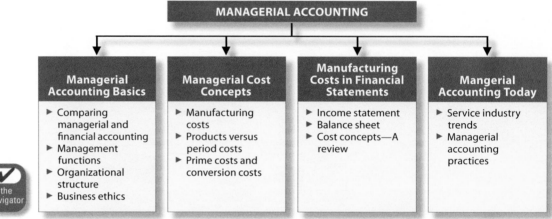

Managerial Accounting Basics

Managerial accounting, also called management accounting, is a field of accounting that provides economic and financial information for managers and other internal users. The activities that are part of managerial accounting (and the chapters that discuss them in this textbook) are as follows:

1. Explaining manufacturing and non-manufacturing costs and how they are reported in the financial statements (Chapter 1).
2. Calculating the cost of providing a service or manufacturing a product (Chapters 2, 3, and 4).
3. Determining the behaviour of costs and expenses as activity levels change, and analyzing cost-volume-profit relationships within a company (Chapter 5).
4. Accumulating and presenting relevant data for management decision-making (Chapter 6).
5. Evaluating the impact on decision-making of alternative approaches for costing inventory (Chapter 7).
6. Determining prices for external and internal transactions (Chapter 8).
7. Assisting management in profit planning and formalizing these plans in budgets (Chapter 9).
8. Providing a basis for controlling costs and expenses by comparing actual results with planned objectives and standard costs (Chapters 10 and 11).
9. Accumulating and presenting data for capital expenditure decisions (Chapter 12).

Managerial accounting applies to all types of businesses—service, merchandising, and manufacturing. It also applies to all forms of business organizations—proprietorships, partnerships, and corporations. Managerial accounting is needed in not-for-profit entities as well as in profit-oriented enterprises.

In the past, managerial accountants were mostly involved in **cost accounting**—collecting and reporting costs to management. Recently, this role has changed significantly. First, the methods used to determine product costs are constantly being refined and improved.

This change has been particularly important as the manufacturing environment has become more automated. Second, today's managerial accountants are now responsible for strategic cost management—that is, they help management evaluate how well the company is using its resources. One implication is that the managerial accountant is now responsible for collecting various types of non-financial information.

In addition, when they are making critical management decisions, many companies now use cross-functional teams. For example, when designing a new product line or planning a new production facility, companies will frequently create cross-functional teams with personnel from production, operations, marketing, engineering, quality control, and management accounting. The role of the managerial accountant within these teams is that of information expert: he or she collects, synthesizes, analyzes, and interprets information for the other members of the team.

As a result of these changes, there are many opportunities for managerial accountants to advance within a company. Top corporate financial executives often have a background that includes managerial accounting experience. Whatever your position within a company—marketing, sales, or production—knowledge of managerial accounting greatly improves your opportunities for advancement.

Comparing Managerial and Financial Accounting

There are both similarities and differences between managerial and financial accounting. First, both fields deal with the economic events of a business. Thus, their interests overlap. For example, determining the unit cost of manufacturing a product is part of managerial accounting. Reporting the total cost of goods manufactured and sold is part of financial accounting. In addition, both managerial and financial accounting require that a company's economic events be quantified and communicated to interested parties.

The principal differences between financial accounting and managerial accounting are summarized in Illustration 1-1. The varied needs for economic data among interested parties are the reason for many of the differences.

study objective 1
Explain the distinguishing features of managerial accounting.

Financial Accounting		Managerial Accounting
• External users: shareholders, creditors, and regulators	Primary Users of Reports	• Internal users: officers and managers
• Financial statements	Types and Frequency of Reports	• Internal reports
• Quarterly and annually		• As frequently as needed
• General-purpose	Purpose of Reports	• Special-purpose for specific decisions
• Pertains to business as a whole	Content of Reports	• Pertains to subunits of the business
• Highly aggregated (condensed)		• Very detailed
• Limited to double-entry accounting and cost data		• Extends beyond double-entry accounting to any relevant data
• In accordance with generally accepted accounting principles		• Standard is relevance to decisions
• Audit by CA	Verification Process	• No independent audits

Illustration 1-1 ◀

Differences between financial and managerial accounting

Management Functions

study objective 2

Identify the three broad functions of management.

Management's activities and responsibilities can be classified into three broad functions:

1. Planning
2. Directing
3. Controlling

In performing these functions, managers make decisions that have a significant impact on the organization.

Planning requires management to look ahead and to establish objectives. These objectives are often diverse: maximizing short-term profits and market share, maintaining a commitment to environmental protection, and contributing to social programs. A key objective of management is to add **value** to the business under its control. Value is usually measured by the trading price of the company's shares and by the potential selling price of the company.

Directing involves coordinating a company's various activities and human resources to produce a smoothly running operation. This involves implementing planned objectives and providing necessary incentives to motivate employees. For example, manufacturers such as General Motors of Canada Ltd., Magna International Inc., and Maple Leaf Foods Inc. must coordinate their purchasing, manufacturing, warehousing, and selling. Service corporations such as Air Canada, BCT.TELUS Communications Inc., and Nortel Networks Corp. must coordinate their scheduling, sales, service, and acquisitions of equipment and supplies. Directing also involves selecting executives, appointing managers and supervisors, and hiring and training employees.

The third management function, **controlling**, is the process of keeping the company's activities on track. In controlling operations, managers determine whether planned goals are being achieved. When there are deviations from target objectives, managers must decide what changes are needed to get back on track.

How do managers achieve control? A smart manager in a small operation can make personal observations, ask good questions, and know how to evaluate the answers. But using this approach in a large organization would result in chaos. Imagine the president of BCE Inc. trying to determine whether planned objectives are being met without some record of what has happened and what is expected to occur. Thus, a formal system of evaluation is typically used in large businesses. These systems rely on budgets, responsibility centres, and performance evaluation reports.

Business Insight examples illustrate interesting situations in real companies and show how decisions are made based on accounting information. Examples labelled as **e-Business Insights** describe how e-business technology is being used in accounting applications.

BUSINESS INSIGHT ▶ Management Perspective

Automation and computerization have changed not only the way managers and employees interact; they have also changed the communication processes between customer and supplier.

In the early 1980s, the apparel industry was a paperwork nightmare with mountains of mail flowing among vendors, suppliers, merchants, and factories. Canadian women's apparel manufacturer Nygård International turned to computer-driven enterprise systems to fix the problem. Its Automatic Reorder to Sales (ARTS2) system links all Nygård stores and major retail accounts. Whenever items are sold, the retail outlets' cash register transactions trigger reorder forms. These reorders are sent electronically to the ARTS2 plant in Winnipeg, allowing it to coordinate material supply and production schedules quickly and efficiently. Orders that previously took three weeks are now filled within a few hours. Plus, with ARTS2, garments are made only when needed, thus reducing inventory costs.

The system is also linked to major suppliers, who are notified as orders are placed, which coordinates the flow of component parts like zippers and buttons. Currently, 85% of the company's customers and suppliers are linked, but Nygård plans to eventually restrict its supplier base to those suppliers who are also automated.

Decision-making is not a separate management function. Rather, it is what results from judgement in planning, directing, and controlling.

Organizational Structure

To help management functions go smoothly, most companies prepare **organization charts** that show the interrelationships of activities and the delegation of authority and responsibility within the company. A typical organization chart showing the delegation of responsibility is shown in Illustration 1-2.

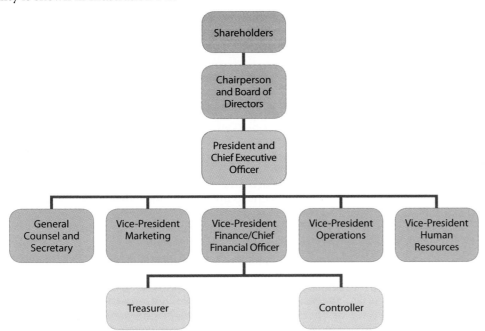

Illustration 1-2 ◄

Corporation organization chart

Shareholders own the corporation, but they manage it indirectly through a **board of directors** they elect. Even not-for-profit organizations have boards of directors. The board formulates the operating policies for the company. The board also selects officers, such as a president and one or more vice-presidents, to execute policy and to perform daily management functions.

The **chief executive officer (CEO)** has overall responsibility for managing the business. Obviously, even in a small business, in order to accomplish organizational objectives, the company relies on the delegation of responsibilities. As the organization chart shows, the CEO delegates responsibility to other officers. Each member of the organization has a clearly defined role to play.

Responsibilities within the company are frequently classified as either line or staff positions. Employees with **line positions** are directly involved in the company's main revenue-generating operating activities. Examples of line positions would be the vice-president of operations, vice-president of marketing, plant managers, supervisors, and production personnel. Employees with **staff positions** are involved in activities that support the efforts of the line employees. In a manufacturing firm, employees in the finance, legal, and purchasing departments and in human resources have staff positions. While the activities of staff employees are vital to the company, these employees are really only there to serve the line employees involved in the company's main operations.

The **chief financial officer (CFO)** is responsible for all of the accounting and finance issues the company faces. The CFO is supported by the **controller** and the **treasurer**. The controller's responsibilities include (1) maintaining the accounting records, (2) maintaining an adequate system of internal control, and (3) preparing financial statements, tax returns, and internal reports. The treasurer has custody of the corporation's funds and is responsible for maintaining the company's cash position.

Also serving the CFO are the **internal audit staff**. Their responsibilities include reviewing the reliability and integrity of financial information provided by the controller and treasurer. They also ensure that internal control systems are functioning properly to safeguard corporate assets. In addition, they investigate compliance with policies and regulations, and in many companies they determine whether resources are being used in the most economical and efficient way.

The vice-president of operations oversees employees with line positions. For example, the company might have multiple plant managers, and each one would report to the vice-president of operations. Each plant would also have department managers, such as fabricating, painting, and shipping managers, with each of them reporting to the plant manager.

All employees in an organization are expected to act ethically in their business activities. Given the importance of ethical behaviour to corporations and their owners (shareholders), an increasing number of organizations provide codes of business ethics for their employees.

Business Ethics

Recent business scandals have resulted in massive investment losses and large employee layoffs. A 2003 survey of fraud by international accounting firm KPMG reported a 13-percent increase in instances of corporate fraud compared to five years earlier. It noted that while employee fraud (such things as expense-account abuse, payroll fraud, and theft of assets) represented 60 percent of all instances of fraud, financial reporting fraud (the intentional misstatement of financial reports) was the most costly to companies.

Managerial accounting affects employee behaviour. The systems designed by managerial accountants are used to control and evaluate the actions of managers. Unfortunately, these various systems and controls sometimes create unintended incentives for managers to take unethical actions. For example, budgets are prepared by companies as part of the planning process. Because the budget is used also as an evaluation tool, some managers try to "game" the budgeting process by underestimating their division's predicted performance so that it will be easier to meet their performance targets. Or, if the budget is set at unattainable levels, managers sometimes take unethical actions to meet the targets and thus earn bonuses or keep their jobs. For example, in 2004, Nortel Network Corporation fired CEO Frank Dunn and two other senior executives in connection with an internal probe of the company's financial practices. Later that year, Nortel fired seven more financial managers as it continued to sort out the accounting scandal that led to the dismissal of its president. The financial shenanigans drew the attention of federal prosecutors from the U.S. Attorney's office in Dallas, and from the Royal Canadian Mounted Police. Securities regulators in both countries are also looking into Nortel's accounting irregularities. Nortel said it expected to restate its results for 2001, 2002, and 2003. Among other things, the company said it actually lost money in the first half of 2003, whereas it had previously reported a net profit of $40 million. Nortel said it would try to recover about $10 million in bonuses that were paid to the fired executives in 2003.[1]

These unethical actions also take place in the U.S. For example, in recent years airlines manufacturer Boeing has been plagued by a series of scandals, including charges of overbilling, corporate espionage, and illegal conflicts of interest. Some long-time employees of Boeing blame the decline in ethics on a change in the corporate culture that took place after Boeing merged with McDonnell Douglas. They suggest that evaluation systems that were implemented after the merger to monitor results and evaluate employee performance made employees believe they needed to succeed no matter what.

The fraudulent activities of managers at Enron, Worldcom, Nortel and others resulted in huge financial losses and thousands of lost jobs. The U.S. Congress responded with the *Sarbanes-Oxley Act* of 2002, which has numerous implications for managers and accountants. One result of Sarbanes-Oxley was to clarify top management's responsibility for a company's financial statements. CEOs and CFOs must now certify that the financial statements give a fair presentation of the company's operating results and its financial condition. In addition, top management must certify that the company maintains an adequate system of internal controls to safeguard the company's assets and ensure accurate financial reports. Also, more attention is now paid to the composition of the company's board of directors. In particular, the audit committee of the board of directors must be comprised entirely of independent members (that is, non-employees) and it must have at least one member who is considered a financial expert. Finally, to increase the likelihood of compliance with these and other new rules, the penalties for misconduct were substantially increased.

As discussed in the December 2003 issue of *CA Magazine*, "In Canada, after the Bre-X Minerals Ltd., Cinar, Livent Inc. and other scandals, steps were also taken to remedy market and financial manipulations. the Canadian Securities Administrators, federal and provincial

---

[1] Jeffry Bartash, CBS.MarketWatch.com, May 14, 2004; Ian Austen, *New York Times*, August 20, 2004

securities regulators, the Office of the Superintendent of Financial Institutions (OSFI) and the accounting profession set up the Canadian Public Accountability Board (CPAB), which is charged with overseeing the independence and transparency of the Canadian accounting system. According to the OSFI, 'The mission of the CPAB is to contribute to public confidence in the integrity of financial reporting of Canadian public companies by promoting high quality, independent auditing.'

The Ontario Securities Commission (OSC), in conjunction with the Canadian Securities Administrators, hopes to be as effective as US regulatory bodies in restoring investor confidence by introducing on January 1, 2004, regulations governing the composition and duties of audit committees, as well as their members' behaviour. The proposed regulations will also be adopted by all provincial and territorial securities regulators, except for British Columbia. 'The rules are as robust as parallel rules required by the US Sarbanes-Oxley legislation, but address unique Canadian concerns,' said OSC chair David Brown in a release announcing the proposed rules."[2]

To provide guidance for managerial accountants, the Institute of Management Accountants (IMA) has developed a code of ethical standards entitled *Standards of Ethical Conduct for Practitioners of Management Accounting and Financial Management*. The code states that management accountants should not commit acts in violation of these standards. Nor should they condone such acts by others within their organizations. In Canada, all three professional accounting organizations—The Society of Management Accountants of Canada (SMAC), The Canadian Institute of Chartered Accountants (CICA), and The Certified General Accountants' Association of Canada (CGAAC)—play an important role in promoting high standards of ethics in the accounting profession. These standards of ethics can be used as guidelines in dealing with the public and the association's members. The **Code of Professional Ethics** provides the following codes of conduct regarding **competence, confidentiality, integrity, and objectivity**:

Competence

Management accountants have a responsibility to:
- maintain professional competence
- perform professional duties in accordance with relevant laws, regulations, and technical standards
- prepare complete and clear reports and recommendations

Confidentiality

Management accountants have a responsibility to:
- refrain from disclosing confidential information
- inform subordinates as to how to handle confidential information
- refrain from using confidential information for unethical or illegal advantage

Integrity

Management accountants have a responsibility to:
- avoid conflicts of interest
- refrain from activity that would prejudice their ability to carry out their duties ethically
- refuse gifts, favours, or hospitality that would influence their actions
- refrain from subverting attainment of the organization's legitimate and ethical objectives
- recognize and communicate professional limitations that would preclude responsible judgement
- communicate unfavourable as well as favourable information
- refrain from engaging in or supporting any activity that would discredit the accounting profession

Objectivity

Management accountants have a responsibility to:
- communicate information fairly and objectively
- disclose fully all relevant information that could reasonably be expected to influence a user's understanding of the reports, comments, and recommendations presented

---

[2] Gilles des Roberts, "On the hot seat", *CA Magazine*, December 2003

Accounting Organizations and Professional Accounting Careers in Canada

In Canada, three different professional accounting designations are available to qualify a candidate who would like to pursue a career in accounting. The Society of Management Accountants of Canada (SMAC) offers the CMA (Certified Management Accountant) designation. Certified management accountants are strategic financial management professionals who have gained the knowledge and skills necessary to provide leadership, innovation, and an integrating perspective to organizational decision-making in the global marketplace. To earn the CMA designation, prospective members must complete a university degree, pass an entrance examination, and complete a two-year strategic leadership program while gaining practical work experience in a management accounting environment. Each provincial and territorial office of CMA Canada provides additional information on applying for membership, course exemptions, writing the Entrance Examination, program costs, and practical experience requirements. The SMAC issues Management Accounting guidelines on fundamental areas of practice and research studies. It publishes the *CMA Magazine* and sponsors a research program that supports management accounting research. For more information on the SMAC, visit its website at *www.cma-canada.org*.

The Canadian Institute of Chartered Accountants (CICA) offers the CA (Chartered Accountant) designation. The CA education program focuses on external financial reports and the auditing of those reports. The education requirements for the CA designation require all students to complete a university degree, meet specific course requirements, and pass a comprehensive professional accreditation examination. Students must also train in an approved public accounting office for a period determined by the provincial and territorial institutes. The CICA publishes *CAmagazine* and sponsors a research program that supports financial accounting research. For more information on the CA designation, visit the CICA website at *www.cica.ca*.

The Certified General Accountants' Association of Canada (CGAAC) administers a set of courses with a national examination for those pursuing the designation of CGA (Certified General Accountant). The education requirements for the CGA designation require all students to complete a university degree, meet specific course requirements, and pass a comprehensive professional accreditation examination. Students must also complete a practical work experience requirement in industry, government, or a public accounting firm. The education requirement stresses having a broad base in accounting and financial management. The CGAAC publishes *CGA Magazine* and sponsors a research program that supports accounting research. For more information on the CGAAC, visit its website at *www.cga-online.org*.

BEFORE YOU GO ON . . .

▶ Review It

1. Compare financial accounting and managerial accounting, identifying the principal differences.
2. Identify and discuss the three broad functions of management.
3. What are line positions? What are staff positions? Give examples.

Related exercise materials: BE1–6, BE1–7, E1–3, and E1–4.

Managerial Cost Concepts

study objective 3

Define the three classes of manufacturing costs.

To perform the three management functions effectively, management needs information. One very important type of information concerns costs. For example, questions such as the following should be asked:

1. What costs are involved in making a product or providing a service?
2. If production volume is decreased, will costs decrease?
3. What impact will automation have on total costs?
4. How can costs be controlled best?

To answer these questions, management needs reliable and relevant cost information. We now explain and illustrate the various cost categories that management uses.

Manufacturing Costs

Manufacturing consists of activities and processes that convert raw materials into finished goods. In contrast, merchandising sells goods in the same form in which they are purchased. Manufacturing costs are typically classified as shown in Illustration 1-3.

Manufacturing Costs

Direct Materials   Direct Labour   Manufacturing Overhead

Illustration 1-3 ◀

Classifications of manufacturing costs

Ilustrations like this one convey information in pictures to help you visualize and apply the ideas as you study.

Direct Materials

To obtain the materials that will be converted into the finished product, the manufacturer purchases raw materials. **Raw materials** are the basic materials and parts used in the manufacturing process. For example, auto manufacturers such as General Motors of Canada Ltd., Honda Canada Ltd., and Ford Motor Co. of Canada, Ltd. use steel, plastics, and tires as raw materials in making cars.

Raw materials that can be physically and directly associated with the finished product during the manufacturing process are called **direct materials**. Examples include flour in the baking of bread, syrup in the bottling of soft drinks, and steel in the making of automobiles. In the feature story, direct materials for Alcoa Canada include alumina, bauxite ore, and carbon.

But some raw materials cannot be easily associated with the finished product. These are called indirect materials. **Indirect materials** have one of two characteristics: either they do not physically become part of the finished product, such as lubricants and polishing compounds, or they cannot be traced because their physical association with the finished product is too small in terms of cost, such as cotter pins and lock washers. Indirect materials are accounted for as part of the **manufacturing overhead**.

Helpful Hints clarify concepts being discussed.

Helpful Hint A manufacturer uses masking tape to protect certain sections of its product while other sections are painted. The tape is removed and thrown away when the paint is dry. Is the tape a direct or indirect material? Answer: indirect.

Direct Labour

The work of factory employees that can be physically and directly associated with converting raw materials into finished goods is called **direct labour**. Bottlers at Cott Corp. and bakers at McCain Foods Ltd., are employees whose activities are usually classified as direct labour. **Indirect labour** refers to the work of factory employees that has no physical association with the finished product, or for which it is impractical to trace costs to the goods produced. Examples include wages of maintenance people, timekeepers, and supervisors. Like indirect materials, indirect labour is classified as **manufacturing overhead**.

BUSINESS INSIGHT ▶ Management Perspective

More and more Canadian automakers are focusing on engine design and selling the finished product, leaving the manufacture of seats, frames, electronics, and other parts, as well as their associated costs, in the hands of other companies. This outsourcing has resulted in auto parts maker Magna International Inc. rivalling General Motors of Canada Ltd. as the sector's largest employer. Industry experts say the 1965 auto pact between Canada and the United States allowed for the growth of auto parts companies. For its part, Magna has invested in new manufacturing technologies to help automakers reduce the weight of their vehicles, as well as the costs.

Source: "Magna Poised to Become Largest Auto Sector Employer," *Ottawa Business Journal*, April 6, 2004.

Manufacturing Overhead

Manufacturing overhead consists of costs that are indirectly associated with the manufacture of the finished product. These costs may also be manufacturing costs that cannot be classified as direct materials or direct labour. Manufacturing overhead includes indirect materials, indirect labour, amortization on factory buildings and machines, and insurance, taxes, and maintenance on factory facilities.

One study found the following proportions of the three different product costs as a percentage of the total product cost: direct materials 54 percent, direct labour 13 percent, and manufacturing overhead 33 percent. Note that the direct labour component is the smallest. This component of product cost is dropping substantially because of automation. In some companies, direct labour has become as little as five percent of the total cost.

Allocating materials and labour costs to specific products is fairly straightforward. Good record keeping can tell a company how much plastic is used in making each type of gear, or how many hours of factory labour are used to assemble a part. But allocating overhead costs to specific products presents problems. How much of the purchasing agent's salary is attributable to the hundreds of different products made in the same plant? What about the grease that keeps the machines humming, or the computers that make sure paycheques come out on time? Boiled down to its simplest form, the question becomes, which products cause the incurrence of which costs. In subsequent chapters, we show various methods of allocating overhead to products.

Alternative Terminology
Terms such as *factory overhead*, *indirect manufacturing costs*, and *burden* are sometimes used instead of manufacturing overhead.

Alternative Terminology notes present synonymous terms that are used in practice.

Product versus Period Costs

study objective 4

Distinguish between product and period costs.

Each of the manufacturing cost components (direct materials, direct labour, and manufacturing overhead) are product costs. As the term suggests, **product costs** are costs that are a necessary and integral part of producing the finished product. Product costs are recorded as inventory when they are incurred. Under the matching principle, these costs do not become expenses until the finished goods inventory is sold. The expense is the cost of goods sold.

Period costs are costs that are matched with the revenue of a specific time period rather than included as part of the cost of a saleable product. These are non-manufacturing costs. Period costs include selling and administrative expenses. They are deducted from revenues in the period in which they are incurred, in order to determine net income.

The above relationships and cost terms are summarized in Illustration 1-4. Our main concern in this chapter is with product costs.

Alternative Terminology
Product costs are also called *inventoriable costs*.

Illustration 1-4 ▶

Product versus period costs

Helpful Hint An unethical manager may choose to inflate the company's earnings by improperly including period costs (such as selling and administrative expenses not related to production) in the ending inventory balances.

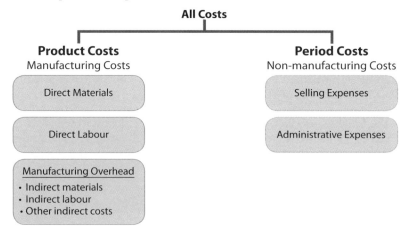

Prime Costs and Conversion Costs

Prime costs and conversion costs are two other terms that are used in manufacturing accounting systems. **Prime costs** are the sum of all direct materials costs and direct labour costs. These are all direct manufacturing costs. **Conversion costs** are the sum of all direct labour costs and manufacturing overhead costs, which together are the costs of converting raw materials into a final product.

BEFORE YOU GO ON . . .

►Review It

1. What are the major cost classifications in manufacturing a product?
2. What are product and period costs, and what is their relationship to the manufacturing process?

►Do It

A bicycle company has these costs: tires, the salaries of employees who put tires on the wheels, factory building amortization, wheel nuts, spokes, the salary of the factory manager, handlebars, and the salaries of factory maintenance employees. Classify each cost as direct materials, direct labour, or overhead.

Action Plan

- Classify as direct materials any raw materials that can be physically and directly associated with the finished product.
- Classify as direct labour the work of factory employees that can be physically and directly associated with the finished product.
- Classify as manufacturing overhead any costs that are indirectly associated with the finished product.

Solution

Tires, spokes, and handlebars are direct materials. The salaries of employees who put tires on the wheels are direct labour. All of the other costs are manufacturing overhead.

Related exercise material: BE1–4, BE1–5, BE1–7, E1–1, and E1–2.

Manufacturing Costs in Financial Statements

The financial statements of a manufacturer are very similar to those of a merchandiser. The main differences are in the cost of goods sold section in the income statement and the current assets section in the balance sheet.

Income Statement

Under a periodic inventory system, the income statements of a merchandiser and a manufacturer differ in the cost of goods sold section. For a merchandiser, the cost of goods sold is calculated by adding the beginning merchandise inventory to the **cost of goods purchased** and subtracting the ending merchandise inventory. For a manufacturer, the cost of goods sold is calculated by adding the beginning finished goods inventory to the **cost of goods manufactured** and subtracting the ending finished goods inventory, as shown in Illustration 1-5.

study objective 5

Explain the difference between a merchandising income statement and a manufacturing incoming statement.

Illustration 1-5 ◄

Cost of goods sold components

Helpful Hint A periodic inventory system is assumed here.

Merchandiser

| Beginning Merchandise Inventory | + | Cost of Goods Purchased | − | Ending Merchandise Inventory | = | Cost of Goods Sold |

Manufacturer

| Beginning Finished Goods Inventory | + | Cost of Goods Manufactured | − | Ending Finished Goods Inventory | = |

The cost of goods sold sections for merchandising and manufacturing companies in Illustration 1-6 show the different presentations. The other sections of an income statement are similar for merchandisers and manufacturers.

MERCHANDISING COMPANY Income Statement (partial) Year Ended December 31, 2005			MANUFACTURING COMPANY Income Statement (partial) Year Ended December 31, 2005		
Cost of goods sold			Cost of goods sold		
Merchandise inventory, January 1	$ 70,000		Finished goods inventory, January 1	$ 90,000	
Cost of goods purchased	650,000		Cost of goods manufactured (see Illustration 1-8)	370,000	
Cost of goods available for sale	720,000		Cost of goods available for sale	460,000	
Merchandise inventory, December 31	400,000		Finished goods inventory, December 31	80,000	
Cost of goods sold	$320,000		Cost of goods sold	$380,000	

Illustration 1-6 ▲

Cost of goods sold sections of merchandising and manufacturing income statements

Several accounts are involved in determining the cost of goods manufactured. To eliminate excessive detail, income statements typically show only the total cost of goods manufactured. The details are presented in a cost of goods manufactured schedule. The form and content of this schedule are shown in Illustration 1-8 (page 15).

Determining the Cost of Goods Manufactured

Helpful Hint Does the amount of "total manufacturing costs for the current year" include the amount of "beginning work in process inventory?" Answer: No.

An example may help show how the cost of goods manufactured is determined. Assume that ATI Technologies Inc. has graphics cards in various stages of production on January 1. In total, these partially completed units are called **beginning work in process inventory**. The costs assigned to beginning work in process inventory are based on the **manufacturing costs incurred in the prior period**.

The manufacturing costs incurred in the current year are used first to complete the work in process on January 1. They then are used to start the production of other graphics cards. The sum of the direct materials costs, direct labour costs, and manufacturing overhead incurred in the current year is the **total manufacturing cost** for the current period.

We now have two cost amounts: (1) the cost of the beginning work in process and (2) the total manufacturing cost for the current period. The sum of these costs is the **total cost of work in process** for the year.

At the end of the year, some graphics cards may again be only partially completed. The costs of these units become the cost of the **ending work in process inventory**. To find the **cost of goods manufactured**, we subtract this cost from the total cost of work in process. Illustration 1-7 shows how to determine cost of goods manufactured.

Illustration 1-7 ▶

Cost of goods manufactured formula

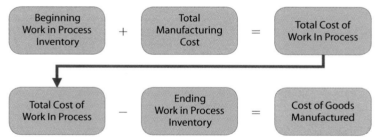

Cost of Goods Manufactured Schedule

An internal report shows each of the cost elements in Illustration 1-7. This report is called the **cost of goods manufactured schedule**. The schedule for Olsen Manufacturing Company (using assumed data) is shown in Illustration 1-8. Note that the schedule presents detailed data for direct materials and for manufacturing overhead.

Review Illustration 1-7 and then examine the cost of goods manufactured schedule in Illustration 1-8. You should be able to distinguish between the total manufacturing cost and the cost of goods manufactured. The difference is the effect of the change in work in process during the period.

OLSEN MANUFACTURING COMPANY
Cost of Goods Manufactured Schedule
Year Ended December 31, 2005

Work in process, January 1			$ 18,400
Direct materials			
Raw materials inventory, January 1	$ 16,700		
Raw materials purchases	152,500		
Total raw materials available for use	169,200		
Less: Raw materials inventory, December 31	22,800		
Direct materials used		$146,400	
Direct labour		175,600	
Manufacturing overhead			
Indirect labour	14,300		
Factory repairs	12,600		
Factory utilities	10,100		
Factory amortization	9,440		
Factory insurance	8,360		
Total manufacturing overhead		54,800	
Total manufacturing cost			376,800
Total cost of work in process			395,200
Less: Work in process, December 31			25,200
Cost of goods manufactured			$370,000

Illustration 1-8 ◄

Cost of goods manufactured schedule.

Numbers or categories in the financial statements are often highlighted in **red type** to draw your attention to key information.

Each chapter presents useful information about how decision-makers analyze and solve business problems. **Decision Toolkits** summarize the key features of a decision tool and review why and how to use it.

Decision Toolkit

Decision Checkpoints	Info Needed for Decision	Tools to Use for Decision	How to Evaluate Results
Is the company maintaining control over the costs of production?	Cost of material, labour, and overhead	Cost of goods manufactured schedule	Compare the cost of goods manufactured to the revenue expected from product sales.

Balance Sheet

The balance sheet for a merchandising company shows just one category of inventory. In contrast, the balance sheet for a manufacturer may have three inventory accounts. They are shown in Illustration 1-9.

Raw Materials Inventory

Shows the cost of raw materials on hand.

Work in Process Inventory

Shows the cost applicable to units that have been started into production but are only partially completed.

Finished Goods Inventory

Shows the cost of completed goods on hand.

Illustration 1-9 ◄

Inventory accounts for a manufacturer

Finished goods inventory is to a manufacturer what merchandise inventory is to a merchandiser. It represents the goods that are available for sale.

The current assets sections presented in Illustration 1-10 contrast the presentations of inventories for merchandising and manufacturing companies. Manufacturing inventories

study objective 7

Explain the difference between a merchandising balance sheet and a manufacturing balance sheet.

are generally listed in the order of their liquidity—the order in which they are expected to be realized in cash. Thus, finished goods inventory is listed first. The remainder of the balance sheet is similar for the two types of companies.

MERCHANDISING COMPANY Balance Sheet December 31, 2005			MANUFACTURING COMPANY Balance Sheet December 31, 2005		
Current assets			Current assets		
Cash		$100,000	Cash		$180,000
Receivables (net)		210,000	Receivables (net)		210,000
Merchandise inventory		400,000	Inventories		
Prepaid expenses		22,000	Finished goods	$80,000	
Total current assets		$732,000	Work in process	25,200	
			Raw materials	22,800	128,000
			Prepaid expenses		18,000
			Total current assets		$536,000

Illustration 1-10 ▲

Current assets sections of merchandising and manufacturing balance sheets

Each step in the accounting cycle for a merchandiser applies to a manufacturer. For example, before preparing financial statements, adjusting entries are required. The adjusting entries for a manufacturer are essentially the same as those of a merchandiser. The closing entries are also similar for manufacturers and merchandisers.

Decision Toolkit

Decision Checkpoints	Info Needed for Decision	Tools to Use for Decision	How to Evaluate Results
What is the composition of a manufacturing company's inventory?	Amount of raw materials, work in process, and finished goods inventories	Balance sheet	Determine whether there is sufficient finished goods inventory, raw materials, and work in process to meet expected demand.

Cost Concepts—A Review

You have learned a number of cost concepts in this chapter. Because many of these concepts are new, we now provide an extended example for review.

Assume that Northridge Company manufactures and sells pre-hung metal doors. Recently, it has also decided to start selling pre-hung wood doors. An old warehouse that the company owns will be used to manufacture the new product. Northridge identifies the following costs as being associated with manufacturing and selling the pre-hung wood doors:

1. The material cost (wood) for each door is $10.
2. Labour costs required to construct a wood door are $8 per door.
3. Amortization on the factory equipment used to make the wood doors is $25,000 per year.
4. Property taxes on the factory building used to make the wood doors are $6,000 per year.
5. Advertising costs for the pre-hung wood doors total $2,500 per month or $30,000 per year.
6. Sales commissions for pre-hung wood doors that are sold are $4 per door.
7. Salaries for employees who maintain the factory facilities are $28,000.
8. The salary of the plant manager in charge of pre-hung wood doors is $70,000.
9. The cost of shipping pre-hung wood doors is $12 per door sold.

These manufacturing and selling costs can be assigned to the various categories shown in Illustration 1-11.

Remember that the total manufacturing cost is the sum of the **product costs**—direct materials, direct labour, and manufacturing overhead. If Northridge Company produces 10,000 pre-hung wood doors the first year, the total manufacturing cost would be $309,000, as shown in Illustration 1-12.

Knowing the total manufacturing cost, Northridge can calculate the manufacturing cost per unit: assuming 10,000 units, the cost to produce one pre-hung wood door is $30.90 ($309,000 ÷ 10,000 units).

The cost concepts discussed in this chapter will be used extensively in subsequent chapters. Study Illustration 1-11 carefully. If you do not understand any of these classifications, go back and reread the appropriate section in this chapter.

| | Product Costs | | | |
Cost Item	Direct Materials	Direct Labour	Manufacturing Overhead	Period Costs
1. Material cost ($10/door)	X			
2. Labour cost ($8/door)		X		
3. Amortization on new equipment ($25,000/year)			X	
4. Property taxes on factory building ($6,000/year)			X	
5. Advertising cost ($30,000/year)				X
6. Sales commissions ($4/door)				X
7. Maintenance salaries—factory facilities ($28,000/year)			X	
8. Salary of plant manager ($70,000)			X	
9. Cost of shipping pre-hung doors ($12/door)				X

Illustration 1-11 ◄

Assigment of costs to cost categories

Cost Number and Item	Manufacturing Cost
1. Material cost ($10 × 10,000)	$100,000
2. Labour cost ($8 × 10,000)	80,000
3. Amortization on factory equipment	25,000
4. Property taxes on factory building	6,000
5. Maintenance salaries—factory facilities	28,000
6. Salary of plant manager	70,000
Total manufacturing cost	$309,000

Illustration 1-12 ◄

Calculation of total manufacturing cost

BEFORE YOU GO ON . . .

►Review It

1. How does the content of an income statement for a merchandiser differ from that for a manufacturer?
2. How is work in process inventory reported in the cost of goods manufactured schedule?
3. How does the content of the balance sheet for a merchandiser differ from that for a manufacturer?

the navigator

Managerial Accounting Today

study objective 8

Identify changes in managerial accounting.

To compete successfully in today's deregulated global environment, many Canadian and American manufacturing and service industries have begun implementing strategic management programs. These are designed to improve quality, reduce costs, and regain the competitive position the companies once held in the world marketplace. This approach focuses on the long-term goals and objectives of the organization as well as a full analysis of the environment in which the business is operating. The analysis covers all the internal operations and resources of the organization, as well as the external aspects of its environment. It includes competitors, suppliers, customers, and legal and regulatory changes, as well as the economy as a whole.

This new approach requires changes to traditional management accounting, which has been widely criticized for being too narrow, highly quantitative, and aimed toward the needs of financial reporting, and for contributing little to the overall policy and direction of the organization. In this regard, one author says, management accounting needs to be released from the factory floor so that it can meet market challenges directly.[1] The result is a new variety of management accounting that expands the information provided to decision-makers. The following section explains the expanding role of management accounting in the twenty-first century.

Service Industry Trends

During the most recent decade, the Canadian and U.S. economies in general shifted toward an emphasis on providing services, rather than goods. Today over 50 percent of Canadian and U.S. workers are employed by service companies, and that percentage is expected to increase in coming years. Much of this chapter focused on manufacturers. But most of the techniques that you will learn in this course are equally applicable to service entities.

Managers of service companies look to managerial accounting to answer many questions. Illustration 1-13 presents examples of such questions. In some instances, the managerial accountant may need to develop new systems for measuring the cost of serving individual customers. In others, he or she may need new operating controls to improve the quality and efficiency of specific services. Many of the examples we present in subsequent chapters will relate to service companies.

Illustration 1-13 ▶

Service industries and companies and the managerial accounting questions they face

Industry/Company	Questions Faced by Service-Company Managers
Transportation (WestJet Airlines)	• whether to buy new or used planes • whether or not to service a new route
Package delivery services (Purolator, Fedex)	• what fee structure to use • what mode of transportation to use
Telecommunications (BCE Inc.)	• what fee structure to use • whether to service a new community • how many households it will take to break even • whether to invest in a new satellite or lay new cable
Professional services (lawyers, accountants, physicians)	• how much to charge for particular services • how much office overhead to allocate to particular jobs • how efficient and productive individual staff members are
Financial institutions (Bank of Montreal, TD Waterhouse)	• which services to charge for, and which to provide for free • whether to build a new branch office or to install a new ATM • whether fees should vary depending on the size of the customers' accounts
Health care (TLC The Laser Center Inc.)	• whether to invest in new equipment • how much to charge for various services • how to measure the quality of the services provided

---

[1] M. Bromwich, "The Case for Strategic Management Accounting: The Role of Accounting Information for Strategy in Competitive Markets," *Accounting, Organizations and Society*, 1990, pp. 27-46.

Managerial Accounting Practices

As discussed earlier, the practice of managerial accounting has changed significantly in recent years to better meet the needs of managers. The following sections explain some newly developed managerial accounting practices.

The Value Chain

The **value chain** refers to all activities associated with providing a product or service. For a manufacturer, these include research and development, product design, the acquisition of raw materials, production, sales and marketing, delivery, customer relations, and subsequent service. Illustration 1-14 shows the value chain for a manufacturer. In recent years, companies have made huge advances in analyzing all stages of the value chain in an effort to improve productivity and eliminate waste. Japanese automobile manufacturer Toyota pioneered many of the change efforts.

Illustration 1-14 ▼

A manufacturer's value chain

Research & development and Product design   Acquisition of raw materials   Production   Sales & marketing   Delivery   Customer relations and subsequent service

In the 1980s, many companies purchased giant machines to replace humans in the manufacturing process. These machines were designed to produce large batches of products. In recent years, these manufacturing processes have been recognized as being very wasteful. They require vast amounts of inventory storage capacity and much movement of materials. Consequently, many companies have re-engineered their manufacturing processes. As one example, the manufacturing company Pratt and Whitney has replaced many of its large machines with smaller, more flexible ones, and has begun reorganizing its plants for a more efficient flow of goods. With these changes, Pratt and Whitney was able to reduce the time that its turbine engine blades spend in the grinding section from 10 days to two hours. It also cut the total amount of time spent making a blade from 22 days to seven days. The improvements that have resulted from analyses of the value chain have made companies far more responsive to customer needs, and profitability has also improved.

Technological Change

Many companies now use **enterprise resource planning (ERP)** software systems to manage their value chains. ERP systems provide a comprehensive, centralized, and integrated source of information that is used to manage all major business processes, from purchasing to manufacturing to recording human resources. In large companies, an ERP system might replace as many as 200 individual software packages. For example, an ERP system can eliminate the need for individual software packages for personnel, inventory management, receivables, and payroll. Because the value chain goes beyond the walls of the company, ERP systems also collect information from and provide it to the company's major suppliers, customers, and business partners. The largest ERP provider, the German corporation SAP, has more than 22,000 customers worldwide.

Technology is also affecting the value chain through business-to-business (B2B) e-commerce on the Internet. The Internet has dramatically changed the way corporations do business with one another. Interorganizational information systems connected over the Internet enable customers and suppliers to share information nearly instantaneously. In addition, the Internet has changed the marketplace, often having the effect of cutting out intermediaries (the "middle-men"). The automobile, airline, hotel, and electronics industries have made commitments to purchase some or all of their supplies and raw materials in the huge B2B electronic marketplaces. For example, Hilton Hotels recently committed itself to purchasing as much as $1.5 billion of bedsheets, pest control services, and other items from an on-line supplier, PurchasePro.com.

Just-in-Time Inventory Methods

Many companies have significantly lowered their inventory levels and costs by using **just-in-time (JIT) inventory** methods. Under a just-in-time method, goods are manufactured or purchased just in time for use. As noted in the feature story, Alcoa Canada is famous for having developed a system for making products in response to individual customer requests, with each product custom-made to meet each customer's particular specifications. Another example is Dell Corporation, which takes less than 48 hours to assemble a computer to customer specifications and put it on a truck. By integrating its information systems with those of its suppliers, Dell reduced its inventories to nearly zero. This is a huge advantage in an industry where products become obsolete nearly overnight. JIT is discussed further in Chapter 4.

Quality

JIT inventory systems also require an increased emphasis on product quality. If products are produced only as they are needed, it is very costly for the company to have to stop production because of defects or machine breakdowns. Many companies have installed **total quality management (TQM)** systems to reduce defects in finished products. The goal is to achieve zero defects. These systems require timely data on defective products, rework costs, and the cost of honouring warranty contracts. Often this information is used to help redesign the product in a way that makes it less likely to have a defect. Or it may be used to re-engineer the production process to reduce setup time and decrease the potential for error. TQM systems also provide information on non-financial measures, such as customer satisfaction, the number of service calls, and the time needed to generate reports. Attention to these measures, which employees can control, leads to increased profitability.

recorded against the original order. Vesey's uses a just-in-time system to fill orders: it buys seeds in large quantities, but packages them in increments, as needed. In addition to tracking inventory, the system produces sales reports by week or by category. This helps management with estimates on future sales and inventory requirements, which is crucial in Vesey's business. With a live product that needs to be sold and planted within a certain amount of time, Vesey's can't have any surplus.

Focus on Activities

As discussed earlier, overhead costs have become an increasingly large component of product and service costs. By definition, overhead costs cannot be directly traced to individual products. But to determine each product's cost, overhead must be **allocated** to the various products. In order to obtain more accurate product costs, many companies now allocate overhead using **activity-based costing (ABC)**. Under ABC, overhead is allocated based on each product's use of activities. For example, the company can keep track of the cost of setting up machines for each batch of a production process. Then a particular product can be allocated part of the total setup cost based on the number of setups that product required.

Activity-based costing is beneficial because it results in more accurate product costing and in more careful scrutiny of all activities in the **supply chain**. For example, if a product's cost is high because it requires a high number of setups, management will be motivated to determine how to produce the product using as few machine setups as possible. ABC is now widely used by both manufacturing and service companies. Chapter 4 discusses ABC further.

Theory of Constraints

All companies have certain aspects of their business that create "bottlenecks"—constraints that limit the company's potential profitability. An important aspect of managing the value chain is identifying these constraints. The **theory of constraints** refers to the practice of (1) identifying constraints that impede a company's ability to provide a good or service, and (2) addressing the constraint to maximize profitability. Automobile manufacturer General Motors of Canada Ltd. is using the theory of constraints in all of its North American plants. The company has found that it is most profitable when it focuses on fixing bottlenecks, rather than worrying about whether all aspects of the company are functioning at full capacity. This has greatly improved the company's ability to effectively use overtime labour while meeting customer demand. Chapter 6 discusses applications of the theory of constraints.

Balanced Scorecard

As various innovations in business practices have been implemented, managers have sometimes focused too enthusiastically on the latest innovation, and paid less attention to other areas of the business. For example, in focusing on improving quality, companies sometimes lose sight of cost/benefit considerations. Similarly, in focusing on reducing inventory levels through just-in-time, companies sometimes lose sales due to inventory shortages. The **balanced scorecard** is a performance-measurement approach that uses both financial and non-financial measures to evaluate all aspects of a company's operations in an *integrated* way. The performance measures are linked by cause and effect to ensure that they all connect to the company's overall objectives.

For example, the company may want to increase its return on assets, a common financial performance measure (calculated as net income divided by average total assets). It will then identify a series of linked goals that, if each one is accomplished, will ultimately result in an increase in return on assets. For example, in order to increase return on assets, sales must increase. In order to increase sales, customer satisfaction must be increased. In order to increase customer satisfaction, product defects must be reduced. In order to reduce product defects, employee training must be increased. Note the linkage, which starts with employee training and ends with return on assets. Each objective will have associated performance measures.

Use of the balanced scorecard is widespread among some well-known and respected companies. For example, Hilton Hotels Corporation uses the balanced scorecard to evaluate the performance of employees at all of its hotel chains. Wal-Mart employs the balanced scorecard, and actually extends its use to evaluations of its suppliers. For example, Wal-Mart recently awarded Welch's the "Dry Grocery Division Supplier of the Year Award" for its balanced scorecard results. The balanced scorecard is discussed further in Chapter 11.

BEFORE YOU GO ON . . .

▶Review It

1. Describe, in sequence, the main components of a manufacturer's value chain.
2. What is an enterprise resource planning (ERP) system? What are its primary benefits?
3. Why is product quality important for companies that implement a just-in-time inventory system?
4. Explain what is meant by "balanced" in the balanced scorecard approach.

Using the Decision Toolkit
exercises, which follow the final set of Review It questions in the chapter, ask you to use business information and the decision tools presented in the chapter. We encourage you to think through the questions related to the decision before you study the **Solution**.

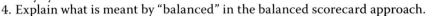

Using the Decision Toolkit

Giant Manufacturing Co. Ltd. specializes in manufacturing many different models of bicycles. Assume that a new model, the Jaguar, has been well accepted. As a result, the company has established a separate manufacturing facility to produce these bicycles. The company produces 1,000 bicycles per month. Giant's monthly manufacturing cost and other expense data related to these bicycles are as follows:

1. Rent on manufacturing equipment (lease cost) $2,000/month
2. Insurance on manufacturing building $750/month
3. Raw materials (frames, tires, etc.) $80/bicycle
4. Utility costs for manufacturing facility $1,000/month
5. Supplies for general office $800/month
6. Wages for assembly line workers in manufacturing facility $30/bicycle
7. Amortization on office equipment $650/month
8. Miscellaneous materials (lubricants, solders, etc.) $1.20/bicycle
9. Property taxes on manufacturing building $2,400/year
10. Manufacturing supervisor's salary $3,000/month
11. Advertising for bicycles $30,000/year
12. Sales commissions $10/bicycle
13. Amortization on manufacturing building $1,500/month

Instructions

(a) Prepare an answer sheet with the following column headings:

	Product Costs			
Cost Item	Direct Materials	Direct Labour	Manufacturing Overhead	Period Costs

Enter each cost item on your answer sheet, placing an "X" under the appropriate headings.

(b) Calculate the total manufacturing cost for the month.

Solution

(a)

Cost Item	Direct Materials	Direct Labour	Manufacturing Overhead	Period Costs
			Product Costs	
1. Rent on equipment ($2,000/month)			X	
2. Insurance on manufacturing building ($750/month)			X	
3. Raw materials ($80/bicycle)	X			
4. Manufacturing utilities ($1,000/month)			X	
5. Office supplies ($800/month)				X
6. Wages for workers ($30/bicycle)		X		
7. Amortization on office equipment ($650/month)				X
8. Miscellaneous materials ($1.20/bicycle)			X	
9. Property taxes on building ($2,400/year)			X	
10. Manufacturing supervisor's salary ($3,000/month)			X	
11. Advertising costs ($30,000/year)				X
12. Sales commissions ($10/bicycle)				X
13. Amortization on manufacturing building ($1,500/month)			X	

(b)

Cost Item	Manufacturing Cost
Rent on equipment	$ 2,000
Insurance	750
Raw materials ($80 × 1,000)	80,000
Manufacturing utilities	1,000
Labour ($30 × 1,000)	30,000
Miscellaneous materials ($1.20 × 1,000)	1,200
Property taxes ($2,400 ÷ 12)	200
Manufacturing supervisor's salary	3,000
Amortization on building	1,500
Total manufacturing cost	$119,650

the navigator

Summary of Study Objectives

The **Summary of Study Objectives** repeats the main points related to the Study Objectives. It gives you an opportunity to review what you have learned.

1. **Explain the distinguishing features of managerial accounting.** The distinguishing features of managerial accounting are:

- the primary users of reports—internal users, who are officers, department heads, managers, and supervisors in the company
- the type and frequency of reports—internal reports that are issued as frequently as needed
- the purpose of reports—to provide special-purpose information for a particular user for a specific decision
- the content of reports—pertains to subunits of the business and may be very detailed; may extend beyond double-entry accounting system; reporting standard is relevance to the decision being made
- the verification of reports—no independent audits

2. **Identify the three broad functions of management.** The three functions are planning, directing and motivating, and controlling. Planning requires management to look ahead and to establish objectives. Directing and motivating involve coordinating the diverse activities and human resources of a company to produce a smoothly running operation. Controlling is the process of keeping the activities on track.

3. **Define the three classes of manufacturing costs.** Manufacturing costs are typically classified as either (1) direct materials, (2) direct labour, or (3) manufacturing overhead. Raw materials that can be physically and directly associated with the finished product during the manufacturing process are called direct materials. The work of factory employees that can be physically and directly associated with converting raw materials into

finished goods is considered direct labour. Manufacturing overhead consists of costs that are indirectly associated with the manufacture of the finished product.

4. ***Distinguish between product and period costs.*** Product costs are costs that are a necessary and integral part of producing the finished product. Product costs are also called inventoriable costs. Under the matching principle, these costs do not become expenses until the inventory to which they attach is sold. Period costs are costs that are identified with a specific time period rather than with a saleable product. These costs relate to non-manufacturing costs and therefore are not inventoriable costs. Prime costs and conversion costs are two other terms that are used in manufacturing accounting systems. Prime costs are the sum of all direct materials costs and direct labour costs. These are all direct manufacturing costs. Conversion costs are the sum of all direct manufacturing labour costs and the manufacturing overhead costs, which are the costs of converting raw materials into a final product in a manufacturing firm.

5. ***Explain the difference between a merchandising income statement and a manufacturing income statement.*** The difference between merchandising and manufacturing income statements is in the cost of goods sold section. A manufacturing cost of goods sold section shows the beginning and ending finished goods inventories and the cost of goods manufactured.

6. ***Indicate how the cost of goods manufactured is determined.*** The cost of the beginning work in process is added to the total manufacturing costs for the current year to arrive at the total cost of work in process for the year. The ending work in process is then subtracted from the total cost of work in process to arrive at the cost of goods manufactured.

7. ***Explain the difference between a merchandising balance sheet and a manufacturing balance sheet.*** The difference between merchandising and manufacturing balance sheets is in the current assets section. In the current assets section of a manufacturing company's balance sheet, three inventory accounts are presented: finished goods inventory, work in process inventory, and raw materials inventory.

8. ***Identify changes in managerial accounting.*** Managerial accounting has experienced many changes in recent years. Among these are a shift toward meeting the needs of service companies and improving practices to better meet the needs of managers. Improved practices include a focus on managing the value chain through techniques such as just-in-time inventory, and technological applications such as enterprise resource planning (ERP). In addition, techniques have been developed to improve decision-making, such as the theory of constraints and activity-based costing (ABC). Finally, the balanced scorecard is now used by many companies in order to have a more comprehensive view of the company's operations.

Decision Toolkit—A Summary

The **Decision Toolkit—A Summary** reviews the contexts and techniques useful for decision-making that were covered in the chapter

Decision Checkpoints	Info Needed for Decision	Tools to Use for Decision	How to Evaluate Results
Is the company maintaining control over the costs of production?	Cost of material, labour, and overhead	Cost of goods manufactured schedule	Compare the cost of goods manufactured to the revenue expected from product sales.
What is the composition of a manufacturing company's inventory?	Amount of raw materials, work in process, and finished goods inventories	Balance sheet	Determine whether there is sufficient finished goods inventory, raw materials, and work in process to meet expected demand.

the navigator

Glossary

www.wiley.com/canada/managerial

Key Term Matching Activity

Activity-based costing (ABC) A method of allocating overhead based on each product's use of activities. (p. 21)

Balanced scorecard A performance-measurement approach that uses both financial and non-financial measures that are tied to company objectives to evaluate a company's operations in an integrated way. (p. 21)

Board of directors The group of officials elected by the shareholders of a corporation to formulate operating policies, select officers, and otherwise manage the company. (p. 7)

Chief executive officer (CEO) The corporate officer who has overall responsibility for managing the business and delegates that responsibility to other corporate officers. (p. 7)

Chief financial officer (CFO) The corporate officer who is responsible for all of the accounting and finance issues of the company. (p. 7)

Controller The financial officer who is responsible for a company's accounting records, system of internal control, and preparation of financial statements, tax returns, and internal reports. (p. 7)

Conversion costs The sum of direct manufacturing labour costs and manufacturing overhead costs. (p. 12)

Cost of goods manufactured Total cost of work in process less the cost of the ending work in process inventory. (p. 14)

Direct labour The work of factory employees that can be physically and directly associated with converting raw materials into finished goods. (p. 11)

Direct materials Raw materials that can be physically and directly associated with manufacturing the finished product. (p. 11)

Enterprise resource planning (ERP) system Software that provides a comprehensive, centralized, integrated source of information that is used to manage all major business processes. (p. 19)

Indirect labour Work of factory employees that has no physical association with the finished product, or for which it is impractical to trace the costs to the goods produced. (p. 11)

Indirect materials Raw materials that do not physically become part of the finished product or cannot be traced because their physical association with the finished product is too small. (p. 11)

Just-in-time (JIT) inventory An inventory system in which goods are manufactured or purchased just in time for use. (p. 20)

Line positions Jobs that are directly involved in a company's main revenue-generating operating activities. (p. 7)

Managerial accounting A field of accounting that provides economic and financial information for managers and other internal users. (p. 4)

Manufacturing overhead Manufacturing costs that are indirectly associated with the manufacture of the finished product. (p. 11)

Period costs Costs that are matched with the revenue of a specific time period and charged to expenses as incurred. (p. 12)

Prime costs The sum of direct materials costs and direct labour costs. (p. 12)

Product costs Costs that are a necessary and integral part of producing the finished product. (p. 12)

Staff positions Jobs that support the efforts of line employees. (p. 7)

Supply chain All activities from the receipt of an order to the delivery of a product or service. (p. 21)

Theory of constraints The practice of identifying constraints that impede a company's ability to provide a good or service, and dealing with the constraints to maximize profitability. (p. 21)

Total cost of work in process Cost of the beginning work in process plus the total manufacturing costs for the current period. (p. 14)

Total manufacturing cost The sum of direct materials, direct labour, and manufacturing overhead incurred in the current period. (p. 14)

Total quality management (TQM) Systems implemented to reduce defects in finished products with the goal of achieving zero defects. (p. 20)

Treasurer The financial officer who is responsible for custody of a company's funds and for maintaining its cash position. (p. 7)

Value chain All activities associated with providing a product or service. (p. 19)

> **Demonstration Problems** are a final review before you begin homework. **Action Plans** that appear in the margins give you tips about how to approach the problem, and the **Solution** provided demonstrates both the form and content of complete answers.

Demonstration Problem

Superior Manufacturing Company has the following cost and expense data for the year ending December 31, 2005:

Raw materials, January 1	$ 30,000	Insurance, factory	$ 14,000
Raw materials, December 31	20,000	Property taxes—factory building	6,000
Raw materials purchased	205,000	Sales (net)	1,500,000
Indirect materials	15,000	Delivery expenses	100,000
Work in process, January 1	80,000	Sales commissions	150,000
Work in process, December 31	50,000	Indirect labour	90,000
Finished goods, January 1	110,000	Factory machinery rent	40,000
Finished goods, December 31	120,000	Factory utilities	65,000
Direct labour	350,000	Amortization—factory building	24,000
Factory manager's salary	35,000	Administrative expenses	300,000

> The **Excel icon** indicates there is an Excel spreadsheet template for this problem on the text companion website.
>
> The **Web icon** indicates there is an animated version of the demonstration problem on the text companion website.

Instructions

(a) Prepare a cost of goods manufactured schedule for Superior Company for 2005.

(b) Prepare an income statement for Superior Company for 2005.

(c) Assume that Superior Company's ledgers show the following balances in its current asset accounts: Cash $17,000, Accounts Receivable (net) $120,000, Prepaid Expenses $13,000, and Short-Term Investments $26,000. Prepare the current assets section of the balance sheet for Superior Company as at December 31, 2005.

Action Plan

- Start with beginning work in process as the first item in the cost of goods manufactured schedule.

- Sum the direct materials used, direct labour, and total manufacturing overhead to determine the total current manufacturing cost.

- Sum the beginning work in process and total current manufacturing cost to determine the total cost of work in process.

- The cost of goods manufactured is the total cost of work in process less the ending work in process.

- In the cost of goods sold section of the income statement, show the beginning and ending finished goods inventory and cost of goods manufactured.

- In the balance sheet, list manufacturing inventories in the order of their expected realization in cash, with finished goods first.

Solution to Demonstration Problem

(a)

SUPERIOR MANUFACTURING COMPANY
Cost of Goods Manufactured Schedule
Year Ended December 31, 2005

Work in process, January 1			$ 80,000
Direct materials			
Raw materials inventory, January 1	$ 30,000		
Raw materials purchased	205,000		
Total raw materials available for use	235,000		
Less: Raw materials inventory, December 31	20,000		
Direct materials used		$215,000	
Direct labour		350,000	
Manufacturing overhead			
Indirect labour	90,000		
Factory utilities	65,000		
Factory machinery rent	40,000		
Factory manager's salary	35,000		
Amortization on building	24,000		
Indirect materials	15,000		
Factory insurance	14,000		
Property taxes	6,000		
Total manufacturing overhead		289,000	
Total manufacturing cost			854,000
Total cost of work in process			934,000
Less: Work in process, December 31			50,000
Cost of goods manufactured			$884,000

(b)

SUPERIOR MANUFACTURING COMPANY Income Statement Year Ended December 31, 2005		
Sales (net)		$1,500,000
Cost of goods sold		
Finished goods inventory, January 1	$110,000	
Cost of goods manufactured	884,000	
Cost of goods available for sale	994,000	
Less: Finished goods inventory, December 31	120,000	
Cost of goods sold		874,000
Gross profit		626,000
Operating expenses		
Administrative expenses	300,000	
Sales commissions	150,000	
Delivery expenses	100,000	
Total operating expenses		550,000
Net income		$ 76,000

(c)

SUPERIOR MANUFACTURING COMPANY Balance Sheet (partial) As at December 31, 2005		
Current assets		
Cash		$ 17,000
Short-term investments		26,000
Accounts receivable (net)		120,000
Inventories		
Finished goods	$120,000	
Work in process	50,000	
Raw materials	20,000	190,000
Prepaid expense		13,000
Total current assets		$366,000

the navigator

Self-Study Questions

www.wiley.com/canada/managerial

Additional Self-Study Questions

Answers are at the end of the chapter.

(SO 1) 1. Managerial accounting:
(a) is governed by generally accepted accounting principles.
(b) emphasizes special-purpose information.
(c) pertains to the entity as a whole and is highly aggregated.
(d) is limited to cost data.

(SO 2) 2. Which of the following is not one of the categories in *Standards of Ethical Conduct for Practitioners of Management Accounting and Financial Management*?

(a) Confidentiality   (c) Integrity
(b) Competence   (d) Independence

3. The management of an organization performs (SO 2) several broad functions. They are:
(a) planning, directing and motivating, and selling.
(b) planning, directing and motivating, and controlling.
(c) planning, manufacturing, and controlling.
(d) directing and motivating, manufacturing, and controlling.

(SO 3) 4. Direct materials are a:

	Product Cost	Manufacturing Overhead	Period Cost
(a)	Yes	Yes	No
(b)	Yes	No	No
(c)	Yes	Yes	Yes
(d)	No	No	No

(SO 4) 5. Indirect labour is a:
(a) non-manufacturing cost.
(b) raw materials cost.
(c) product cost.
(d) period cost.

(SO 3) 6. Which of the following costs would be included in the manufacturing overhead of a computer manufacturer?
(a) The cost of the $\frac{3}{12}$-inch disk drives
(b) The wages earned by computer assemblers
(c) The cost of the memory chips
(d) Amortization on testing equipment

(SO 3) 7. Which of the following is *not* an element of manufacturing overhead?
(a) Sales manager's salary
(b) Plant manager's salary
(c) Factory repairman's wages
(d) Product inspector's salary

(SO 5) 8. For the year, Redder Company has cost of goods manufactured of $600,000, beginning finished goods inventory of $200,000, and ending finished goods inventory of $250,000. The cost of goods sold is:
(a) $450,000.   (c) $550,000.
(b) $500,000.   (d) $600,000.

(SO 6) 9. A cost of goods manufactured schedule shows beginning and ending inventories for:
(a) raw materials and work in process only.
(b) work in process only.
(c) raw materials only.
(d) raw materials, work in process, and finished goods.

(SO 7) 10. In a manufacturer's balance sheet, three inventories may be reported: (1) raw materials, (2) work in process, and (3) finished goods. In what sequence do these inventories generally appear on a balance sheet?
(a) 1, 2, 3   (c) 3, 1, 2
(b) 2, 3, 1   (d) 3, 2, 1

Questions

1. (a) "Managerial accounting is a field of accounting that provides economic information for all interested parties." Do you agree? Explain.
   (b) Tina Thomas believes that managerial accounting serves only manufacturing firms. Is Tina correct? Explain.

2. Distinguish between managerial and financial accounting regarding the (a) primary users of reports, (b) types and frequency of reports, and (c) purpose of reports.

3. How do the content of reports and the verification of reports differ between managerial and financial accounting?

4. (a) Identify the four categories of ethical standards for management accountants.
   (b) Is the responsibility of the management accountant limited to only his or her own acts? Explain.

5. Kent Krause is studying for the next accounting mid-term examination. Summarize for Kent what he should know about management functions.

6. "Decision-making is management's most important function." Do you agree? Why or why not?

7. Explain the primary difference between line positions and staff positions, and give examples of each.

8. What changes were enacted under the *Sarbanes-Oxley Act* to address unethical accounting practices?

9. Alan Bruski is studying for his next accounting examination. Explain to Alan what he should know about the differences between the income statements for a manufacturing company and for a merchandising company.

10. Sandy Cesska is unsure about the difference between the balance sheets of a merchandising company and a manufacturing company. Explain the difference to Sandy.

11. What do SMAC, CICA, and CGAAC stand for?

12. How are manufacturing costs classified?

13. Tony Siebers claims that the distinction between direct and indirect materials is based entirely on physical association with the product. Is Tony correct? Why or why not?

14. Trenton Hipp is confused about the differences between a product cost and a period cost. Explain the differences to Trenton.

15. Explain the following cost terms: direct raw materials costs, direct manufacturing labour costs, direct manufacturing costs, indirect manufacturing costs, prime costs, and conversion costs.

16. Identify the differences in the cost of goods sold section of an income statement for a merchandising company and one for a manufacturing company.

17. Determining the cost of goods manufactured involves the following factors: (A) beginning work in process inventory, (B) total manufacturing costs,

and (C) ending work in process inventory. Identify the meaning of X in the following formulas:
(a) A + B = X
(b) A + B − C = X

18. Gruber Manufacturing has beginning raw materials inventory $12,000, ending raw materials inventory $15,000, and raw materials purchases $180,000. What is the cost of direct materials used?

19. Jelk Manufacturing Inc. has beginning work in process $26,000, direct materials used $240,000, direct labour $200,000, total manufacturing overhead $150,000, and ending work in process $32,000. What is the total manufacturing cost?

20. Using the data in question 19, what are (a) the total cost of work in process and (b) the cost of goods manufactured?

21. In what order should manufacturing inventories be listed in a balance sheet?

22. What is an enterprise resource planning (ERP) system? What are its primary benefits?

23. Explain what is meant by "balanced" in the balanced-scorecard approach.

24. What is activity-based costing, and what are its potential benefits?

25. What is the value chain? Describe, in sequence, the main components of a manufacturer's value chain.

26. Why is product quality important for companies that implement a just-in-time inventory system?

Brief Exercises

BE1–1 Complete the following comparison table between managerial and financial accounting:

	Financial Accounting	Managerial Accounting
Primary users		
Type of reports		
Frequency of reports		
Purpose of reports		
Content of reports		
Verification		

Distinguish between managerial and financial accounting.
(SO 1)

BE1–2 The Institute of Management Accountants has promulgated ethical standards for managerial accountants. Identify the four specific standards.

Identify ethical standards.
(SO 2)

BE1–3 Three functions of an organization's management follow:

1. Planning
2. Directing
3. Controlling

Identify which of the following statements best describes each of the above functions:

(a) _____ Requires management to look ahead and to establish objectives. A key objective of management is to add value to the business.
(b) _____ Involves coordinating the diverse activities and human resources of a company to produce a smoothly running operation. This function relates to the implementation of planned objectives.
(c) _____ Is the process of keeping the activities on track. Management must determine whether goals are being met and what changes are necessary when there are deviations.

Identify the three management functions.
(SO 2)

BE1–4 Determine whether each of the following costs should be classified as direct materials (DM), direct labour (DL), or manufacturing overhead (MO):

(a) _____ Frames and tires used in manufacturing bicycles
(b) _____ Wages paid to production workers
(c) _____ Insurance on factory equipment and machinery
(d) _____ Amortization on factory equipment

Classify manufacturing costs.
(SO 3)

BE1–5 Indicate whether each of the following costs of an automobile manufacturer would be classified as direct materials, direct labour, or manufacturing overhead:

(a) _____ Windshield
(b) _____ Engines
(c) _____ Wages of assembly line workers
(d) _____ Amortization of factory machinery

(e) _____ Factory machinery lubricants
(f) _____ Tires
(g) _____ Steering wheel
(h) _____ Salaries of painting supervisors

Classify manufacturing costs.
(SO 6)

Identify product and period costs.
(SO 4)

BE1–6 Identify whether each of the following costs should be classified as product costs or period costs:

(a) ____ Manufacturing overhead
(b) ____ Selling expenses
(c) ____ Administrative expenses
(d) ____ Advertising expenses
(e) ____ Direct labour
(f) ____ Direct materials

Classify manufacturing costs.
(SO 3, 4)

BE1–7 Presented below are Apex Company's monthly manufacturing cost data for its personal computer products:

(a) Utilities for manufacturing equipment, $116,000
(b) Raw material (CPU, chips, etc.), $85,000
(c) Amortization on manufacturing building, $880,000
(d) Wages for production workers, $191,000

Enter each cost item in the following table, placing an "X" under the appropriate heading.

| | Product Costs | | |
	Direct Materials	Direct Labour	Factory Overhead
(a)			
(b)			
(c)			
(d)			

Calculate total manufacturing costs and total cost of work in process.
(SO 6)

BE1–8 Sielert Manufacturing Company has the following data: direct labour $249,000, direct materials used $180,000, total manufacturing overhead $208,000, and beginning work in process $25,000. Calculate (a) the total manufacturing cost and (b) the total cost of work in process.

Prepare current assets section.
(SO 7)

BE1–9 In alphabetical order below are current asset items for Osgood Company's balance sheet at December 31, 2005. Prepare the current assets section (including a complete heading).

Accounts receivable	$200,000	Prepaid expenses	$38,000
Cash	62,000	Raw materials	68,000
Finished goods	71,000	Work in process	87,000

Determine missing amounts in calculating total manufacturing cost.
(SO 6)

BE1–10 Presented below are incomplete 2005 manufacturing cost data for Vang Corporation. Determine the missing amounts.

	Direct Materials Used	Direct Labour Used	Factory Overhead	Total Manufacturing Cost
(a)	$35,000	$61,000	$ 50,000	?
(b)	?	75,000	140,000	$296,000
(c)	55,000	?	111,000	300,000

Determine missing amounts in calculating cost of goods manufactured.
(SO 6)

BE1–11 Use the data from BE1–10 above and the data below. Determine the missing amounts.

	Total Manufacturing Cost	Work in Process (January 1)	Work in Process (December 31)	Cost of Goods Manufactured
(a)	?	$120,000	$82,000	?
(b)	$296,000	?	98,000	$321,000
(c)	300,000	463,000	?	715,000

Exercises

Identify positions within organizational structure.
(SO 2)

E1–1 The following is a list of terms related to a company's organizational structure:

1. ____ Board of directors
2. ____ Chief financial officer
3. ____ Treasurer
4. ____ Controller
5. ____ Line position
6. ____ Chief executive officer
7. ____ Staff position

Instructions

Match each of the above terms with the appropriate statement below.

(a) Employee who has overall responsibility for managing the business
(b) Employees who are directly involved in the company's primary revenue-generating activities
(c) Employee with overall responsibility for all accounting and finance issues
(d) Group of people elected by the shareholders that selects and oversees company officers and formulates operating policies
(e) Employee who provides support services to those employees who are directly involved in the company's primary revenue-generating activities
(f) Employee who maintains accounting records and the system of internal controls, and prepares financial statements, tax returns, and internal reports
(g) Employee who has custody of the company's funds and maintains the company's cash position

E1–2   Burrand Corporation, a manufacturer of furniture, usually incurs the following costs and expenses in its factory:

Classify costs into three classes of manufacturing costs.
(SO 3)

1. _____ Salaries for assembly line inspectors
2. _____ Insurance on factory machines
3. _____ Property taxes on the factory building
4. _____ Factory repairs
5. _____ Upholstery used in manufacturing furniture
6. _____ Wages paid to assembly line workers
7. _____ Factory machinery amortization
8. _____ Glue, nails, paint, and other small parts used in production
9. _____ Factory supervisors' salaries
10. _____ Wood used in manufacturing furniture

Instructions

Classify the above items into the following categories: (a) direct materials, (b) direct labour, and (c) manufacturing overhead.

E1–3   Caroline Company reports the following costs and expenses in May:

Determine the total amount of various types of costs.
(SO 3, 4)

Factory utilities	$ 8,500	Direct labour	$69,100
Amortization—factory equipment	12,650	Sales salaries	49,400
Amortization—delivery trucks	3,800	Property taxes on factory building	2,500
Indirect factory labour	48,900	Repairs to office equipment	1,300
Indirect materials	95,800	Factory repairs	2,000
Direct materials used	137,600	Advertising	18,000
Factory manager's salary	8,000	Office supplies used	2,640

Instructions

Determine the total amount of (a) manufacturing overhead, (b) product costs, and (c) period costs.

E1–4   Sota Company is a manufacturer of personal computers. Various costs and expenses associated with its operations are as follows:

Classify various costs into different cost categories.
(SO 3, 4)

1. _____ Property taxes on the factory building
2. _____ Production superintendents' salaries
3. _____ Memory boards and chips used in assembling computers
4. _____ Amortization on the factory equipment
5. _____ Salaries for assembly line quality control inspectors
6. _____ Sales commissions paid for sales of personal computers
7. _____ Electrical components used in assembling computers
8. _____ Wages of workers assembling personal computers
9. _____ Soldering materials used on factory assembly lines
10. _____ Salaries for the night security guards for the factory building

The company intends to classify these costs and expenses into the following categories: (a) direct materials, (b) direct labour, (c) manufacturing overhead, and (d) period costs.

Instructions

List items 1 to 10. For each item, indicate the cost category to which it belongs.

Determine missing amounts in cost of goods manufactured schedule.
(SO 6)

E1-5 The cost of goods manufactured schedule shows each of the cost elements. Complete the following schedule for Madlock Manufacturing Company:

MADLOCK MANUFACTURING COMPANY
Cost of Goods Manufactured Schedule
Year Ended December 31, 2005

Work in process, January 1			$210,000
Direct materials			
Raw materials inventory, January 1	$?		
Add: Raw materials purchases	158,000		
Less: Raw materials inventory, December 31	7,500		
Direct materials used		$190,000	
Direct labour		?	
Manufacturing overhead			
Indirect labour	18,000		
Factory amortization	36,000		
Factory utilities	68,000		
Total overhead		122,000	
Total manufacturing cost			?
Total cost of work in process			?
Less: Work in process, December 31			81,000
Cost of goods manufactured			$530,000

Determine the missing amount of different cost items.
(SO 6)

E1-6 Manufacturing cost data for Darlinda Company are presented below:

	Case A	Case B	Case C
Direct materials used	(a)	$ 68,400	$130,000
Direct labour	$ 57,000	86,000	(g)
Manufacturing overhead	46,500	81,600	102,000
Total manufacturing cost	180,650	(d)	253,700
Work in process, January 1, 2005	(b)	16,500	(h)
Total cost of work in process	221,500	(e)	327,000
Work in process, December 31, 2005	(c)	11,000	70,000
Cost of goods manufactured	185,275	(f)	(i)

Instructions

Indicate the missing amounts for letters (a) to (i).

Determine the missing amount of different cost items, and prepare a condensed cost of goods manufactured schedule.
(SO 6)

E1-7 Incomplete manufacturing cost data for Motta Company for 2005 are presented below:

	Direct Materials Used	Direct Labour Used	Manufacturing Overhead	Total Manufacturing Cost	Work in Process (Jan. 1)	Work in Process (Dec. 31)	Cost of Goods Manufactured
1.	$117,000	$140,000	$ 77,000	(a)	$33,000	(b)	$360,000
2.	(c)	200,000	132,000	$440,000	(d)	$40,000	470,000
3.	80,000	100,000	(e)	255,000	60,000	80,000	(f)
4.	70,000	(g)	75,000	288,000	45,000	(h)	270,000

Instructions

(a) Indicate the missing amount for each letter.
(b) Prepare a condensed cost of goods manufactured schedule for situation 1 for the year ended December 31, 2005.

Prepare a cost of goods manufactured schedule and a partial income statement.
(SO 5, 6)

E1-8 Berger Corporation has the following cost records for June 2005:

Indirect factory labour	$ 4,500	Factory utilities	$ 400
Direct materials used	20,000	Depreciation—factory equipment	1,400
Work in process, June 1, 2005	3,000	Direct labour	25,000
Work in process, June 30, 2005	3,800	Maintenance—factory equipment	1,800
Finished goods, June 1, 2005	5,000	Indirect materials	2,200
Finished goods, June 30, 2005	7,500	Factory manager's salary	3,000

Instructions

(a) Prepare a cost of goods manufactured schedule for June 2005.
(b) Prepare an income statement through gross profit for June 2005, assuming net sales are $97,100.

E1–9 Marla Manufacturing Company produces blankets. From its accounting records, it prepares the following schedule and financial statements on a yearly basis:

(a) Cost of goods manufactured schedule
(b) Income statement
(c) Balance sheet

The following items are found in its ledger and accompanying data:

1. ____ Direct labour
2. ____ Raw materials inventory, January 1
3. ____ Work in process inventory, December 31
4. ____ Finished goods inventory, January 1
5. ____ Indirect labour
6. ____ Amortization—factory machinery
7. ____ Work in process, January 1
8. ____ Finished goods inventory, December 31
9. ____ Factory maintenance salaries
10. ____ Cost of goods manufactured
11. ____ Amortization—delivery equipment
12. ____ Cost of goods available for sale
13. ____ Direct materials used
14. ____ Heat and electricity for factory
15. ____ Repairs to roof of factory building
16. ____ Cost of raw materials purchases

Instructions

For each item, indicate by using the appropriate letter or letters, the schedule and/or financial statement(s) in which the item will appear.

> Indicate in which schedule or financial statement(s) different cost items will appear.
> (SO 5, 6, 7)

E1–10 An analysis of the accounts of Yellowknife Manufacturing reveals the following manufacturing cost data for the month ended June 30, 2005:

Inventories	Beginning	Ending
Raw materials	$9,000	$13,100
Work in process	5,000	8,000
Finished goods	9,000	6,000

Costs incurred:

Raw materials purchases	$64,000	Manufacturing overhead	$19,900
Direct labour	57,000		

Specific overhead costs:

Indirect labour	$5,500	Machinery repairs	$1,800
Factory insurance	4,000	Factory utilities	3,100
Machinery amortization	4,000	Miscellaneous factory costs	1,500

Assume that all raw materials used were direct materials.

> Prepare cost of goods manufactured schedule, and present ending inventories on balance sheet.
> (SO 6, 7)

Instructions

(a) Prepare the cost of goods manufactured schedule for the month ended June 30, 2005.
(b) Show the presentation of the ending inventories on the June 30, 2005, balance sheet.

E1–11 Kam Motor Company manufactures automobiles. During September 2005 the company purchased 5,000 headlights at a cost of $9 per light. Kam withdrew 4,650 lights from the warehouse during the month. Fifty of these lights were used to replace the headlights in autos used by travelling sales staff. The remaining 4,600 lights were put in autos manufactured during the month.

Of the autos put into production during September 2005, 90% were completed and transferred to the company's storage lot. Of the cars completed during the month, 75% were sold by September 30.

> Determine cost to appear in accounts, and indicate financial statements accounts would appear in.
> (SO 4, 5, 6, 7)

Instructions

(a) Determine the cost of headlights that would appear in each of the following accounts at September 30, 2005: Raw Materials, Work in Process, Finished Goods, Cost of Goods Sold, and Selling Expenses.

(b) ◁▭▭▭▷ Write a short memo to the chief accountant, indicating whether and where each of the accounts in (a) would appear on the income statement or on the balance sheet at September 30, 2005.

Identify various managerial accounting processes.
(SO 8)

E1–12   The following is a list of terms related to managerial accounting practices:

1. Theory of constraints	4. Balanced scorecard
2. Activity-based costing	5. Value chain
3. Just-in-time inventory	6. Enterprise resource planning

Instructions

(a) _____ a system that provides a comprehensive, centralized, integrated source of information used to manage all major business processes

(b) _____ the group of activities associated with providing a product or service

(c) _____ an approach used to reduce the cost associated with handling and holding inventory by reducing the amount of inventory on hand

(d) _____ a method used to allocate overhead to products based on each product's use of the activities that cause the incurrence of the overhead cost

(e) _____ an approach used to identify those factors that limit a company's productive capacity and to deal with those limitations in order to maximize profitability

(f) _____ a performance-measurement technique that attempts to consider and evaluate all aspects of performance using financial and non-financial measures in an integrated fashion

Problems: Set A

Calculate prime cost, conversion cost, and cost of goods manufactured.
(SO 3, 4, 6)

P1–13A   The following incomplete data are for Atlantic Pride Manufacturing:

	January 1, 2005	December 31, 2005
Direct materials	$40,000	$60,000
Work in process	80,000	50,000
Finished goods	56,000	70,000

Additional information for 2005:

Direct materials	$200,000
Direct manufacturing labour payroll	160,000
Direct manufacturing labour rate per hour	10
Factory overhead rate per direct manufacturing labour hour	8

Instructions

Calculate the following manufacturing costs for 2005: (a) prime cost, (b) conversion cost, and (c) cost of goods manufactured.

Income statement schedules for cost of goods sold, and cost of goods manufactured.
(SO 3, 4, 5, 6)

P1–14A   The following incomplete income statement information is available for Sawchule Ltd. for Year 2005:

Sales	$560,000
Beginning inventory of finished goods	270,000
Cost of goods manufactured	260,000
Net income	50,000
Nonmanufacturing costs	170,000

The beginning inventory of work in process was $110,000 and there was no ending inventory of work in process.

Instructions

(a) What was the gross profit in 2005?
(b) What was the cost of goods sold in 2005?
(c) What was the cost of the ending inventory of finished goods in 2005?
(d) What was the total manufacturing cost in 2005?

P1−15A Thin-Tech Corp. recorded the following manufacturing costs for 2005:

Inventories	January 1, 2005	December 31, 2005
Direct materials	$36,000	$30,000
Work in process	18,000	12,000
Finished goods	4,000	72,000

Calculate prime cost, conversion cost, and cost of goods manufactured.
(SO 3, 4, 6)

Additional information for the month of March 2005:

Direct materials purchased	$84,000
Direct labour cost incurred	60,000
Direct labour rate per hour	7.50
Factory overhead rate per direct labour hour	10

Instructions

(a) What was the prime cost for 2005?
(b) What was the conversion cost for 2005?
(c) What was the cost of goods manufactured for 2005?

P1−16A Jeff Horne, a CMA, wants to know the total cost of preparing a corporate tax return for his client Ontario Limited. His labour cost is $150 per hour. He estimates overhead costs will be $180 to prepare the return, it will require 45 hours to prepare, and total direct material costs will be $500.

Calculate direct cost, indirect cost, prime cost, conversion cost, and total job cost.
(SO 3, 4, 6)

Instructions

(a) What would the total direct cost be?   (d) What would the total conversion cost be?
(b) What would the total indirect cost be?   (e) What would the total job cost be?
(c) What would the total prime cost be?

P1−17A Lair Company specializes in manufacturing motorcycle helmets. The company has enough orders to keep the factory production at 1,000 motorcycle helmets per month. Lair's monthly manufacturing cost and other expense data are as follows:

Classify manufacturing costs into different categories and calculate unit cost.
(SO 3, 4)

Maintenance costs on factory building	$ 300
Factory manager's salary	4,000
Advertising for helmets	10,000
Sales commissions	3,000
Amortization on factory building	700
Rent on factory equipment	6,000
Insurance on factory building	3,000
Raw materials (frames, tires, etc.)	20,000
Utility costs for factory	800
Supplies for general office	200
Wages for assembly line workers	44,000
Amortization on office equipment	500
Miscellaneous materials (lubricants, solders, etc.)	2,000

Instructions

(a) Prepare an answer sheet with the following column headings. Enter each cost item on your answer sheet, placing the dollar amount under the appropriate heading. Total the dollar amounts in each column.

	Product Costs			
Cost Item	Direct Materials	Direct Labour	Manufacturing Overhead	Period Costs

(b) Calculate the cost to produce one motorcycle helmet.

Classify manufacturing costs into different categories and calculate unit cost.
(SO 3, 4)

P1–18A   Tomlin Company, a manufacturer of tennis racquets, started production in November 2005. For the previous five years, Tomlin had been a retailer of sports equipment. After a thorough survey of tennis racquet markets, Tomlin decided to turn its retail store into a tennis racquet factory.

The raw materials cost for a tennis raquet is $23 per racquet. Workers on the production line are paid $13 per hour on average. A racquet usually takes two hours to complete. In addition, the rent on the equipment used to produce racquets amounts to $1,300 per month. Indirect materials cost $3 per raquet. A supervisor was hired to oversee production and is paid $3,500 per month.

Janitorial costs are $1,400 monthly. Advertising costs for the racquets will be $6,000 per month. The factory building amortization expense is $8,400 per year. Property taxes on the factory building will be $4,320 per year.

Instructions

(a) Prepare an answer sheet with the following column headings. Assuming that Tomlin manufactures, on average, 2,000 tennis raquets per month, enter each cost item on your answer sheet, placing the dollar amount per month under the appropriate heading. Total the dollar amounts in each column.

	Product Costs			
Cost Item	Direct Materials	Direct Labour	Manufacturing Overhead	Period Costs

(b) Calculate the cost to produce one racquet.

Indicate missing amounts of different cost items, and prepare condensed cost of goods manufactured schedule, income statement, and partial balance sheet.
(SO 5, 6, 7)

P1–19A   Incomplete manufacturing costs, expenses, and selling data for two different cases are as follows:

	Case 1	Case 2
Direct materials used	$ 8,300	(g)
Direct labour	3,000	$ 4,000
Manufacturing overhead	6,000	5,000
Total manufacturing cost	(a)	20,000
Beginning work in process inventory	1,000	(h)
Ending work in process inventory	(b)	2,000
Sales	22,500	(i)
Sales discounts	1,500	1,200
Cost of goods manufactured	15,800	21,000
Beginning finished goods inventory	(c)	4,000
Goods available for sale	17,300	(j)
Cost of goods sold	(d)	(k)
Ending finished goods inventory	1,200	2,500
Gross profit	(e)	6,000
Operating expenses	2,700	(l)
Net income	(f)	3,200

Instructions

(a) Indicate the missing amount for each letter.
(b) Prepare a condensed cost of goods manufactured schedule for Case 1.
(c) Prepare an income statement and the current assets section of the balance sheet for Case 1. Assume that in Case 1 the other items in the current assets section are as follows: cash $3,000, receivables (net) $10,000, raw materials $700, and prepaid expenses $200.

Prepare cost of goods manufactured schedule, partial income statement, and partial balance sheet.
(SO 5, 6, 7)

P1–20A   The following data were taken from the records of Cruz Manufacturing Company for the year ended December 31, 2005:

Raw materials		Accounts receivable	$ 27,000
inventory, January 1	$ 47,000	Factory insurance	7,400
Raw materials		Factory machinery	
inventory, December 31	44,200	amortization	7,700
Finished goods		Factory utilities	12,900
inventory, January 1	85,000	Office utilities	8,600
Finished goods		Sales	475,000
inventory, December 31	77,800	Sales discounts	2,500
Work in process		Plant manager's salary	30,000
inventory, January 1	9,500	Factory property taxes	6,100
Work in process		Factory repairs	800
inventory, December 31	8,000	Raw materials purchases	67,500
Direct labour	145,100	Cash	28,000
Indirect labour	18,100		

Instructions

(a) Prepare a cost of goods manufactured schedule. (Assume all raw materials used were direct materials.)

(b) Prepare an income statement through gross profit.

(c) Prepare the current assets section of the balance sheet at December 31.

P1–21A Agler Company is a manufacturer of toys. Its controller, Joyce Rotzen, resigned in August 2005. An inexperienced assistant accountant has prepared the following income statement for the month of August 2005:

Prepare cost of goods manufactured schedule and correct income statement. (SO 5, 6)

AGLER COMPANY
Income Statement
Month Ended August 31, 2005

Sales (net)		$675,000
Less: Operating expenses		
Raw materials purchased	$200,000	
Direct labour cost	160,000	
Advertising expense	75,000	
Selling and administrative salaries	70,000	
Rent on factory facilities	60,000	
Amortization on sales equipment	50,000	
Amortization on factory equipment	35,000	
Indirect labour cost	20,000	
Utilities expense	10,000	
Insurance expense	5,000	685,000
Net loss		$ (10,000)

Before August 2005, the company was profitable every month. The company's president is concerned about the accuracy of the income statement. As her friend, you have been asked to review the income statement and make necessary corrections. After examining other manufacturing cost data, you have acquired additional information as follows:

1. Inventory balances at the beginning and end of August:

	August 1	August 31
Raw materials	$19,500	$30,000
Work in process	25,000	21,000
Finished goods	40,000	64,000

2. Only 60% of the utilities expense and 70% of the insurance expense apply to factory operations; the remaining amounts should be charged to selling and administrative activities.

Instructions

(a) Prepare a cost of goods manufactured schedule for August 2005.

(b) Prepare a correct income statement for August 2005.

Calculate selected costs for income statement and schedules of cost of goods manufactured and sold. (SO 3, 4, 5, 6)

P1–22A The following data are given for X Firm (in millions of dollars).

Beginning and ending inventories	0
Sales	$390
Direct materials used	80
Direct labour cost	180
Factory overhead	?
Selling and administrative expenses	?
Gross profit	70
Net income (no income taxes)	22

Instructions

Calculate the following amounts:

(a) cost of goods sold
(b) total factory overhead cost
(c) selling and administrative expenses
(d) total product costs
(e) total period costs
(f) prime cost
(g) conversion cost
(h) cost of goods manufactured

Determine missing amounts, prepare cost of goods manufactured and calculate inventory values. (SO 3, 4, 5, 6)

P1–23A On January 31, 2005, the manufacturing facility of a medium-sized company was severely damaged by an accidental fire. As a result, the company's direct materials, work in process, and finished goods inventories were destroyed. The company did have access to certain incomplete accounting records, which revealed the following:

1. Beginning inventories, January 1, 2005:

Direct materials	$32,000	Finished goods	$30,000
Work in process	68,000		

2. Key ratios for the month of January 2005:

Gross profit = 20% of sales
Prime costs = 70% of manufacturing costs
Factory overhead = 40% of conversion costs
Ending work in process is always 10% of the monthly manufacturing costs.

3. All costs are incurred evenly in the manufacturing process.
4. Actual operations data for the month of January 2005:

Sales	$900,000	Direct labour incurred	$360,000
Direct materials purchases	320,000		

Instructions

(a) From the above data, reconstruct a cost of goods manufactured schedule.
(b) Calculate the total cost of inventory lost, and identify each category where possible (i.e., direct materials, work in process, and finished goods), at January 30, 2005.

(CMA Canada-adapted)

Problems: Set B

Classify manufacturing costs into different categories and calculate unit cost. (SO 3, 4)

P1–24B Bjerg Company specializes in manufacturing a unique model of bicycle helmet. The model is well accepted by consumers, and the company has enough orders to keep the factory production at 10,000 helmets per month (80% of its full capacity). Bjerg's monthly manufacturing cost and other expense data are as follows:

Rent on factory equipment	$ 7,000	Miscellaneous materials	
Insurance on factory building	1,500	(lubricants, solders, etc.)	$ 1,100
Raw materials		Factory manager's salary	5,700
(plastics, polystyrene, etc.)	75,000	Property taxes on factory building	400
Utility costs for factory	900	Advertising for helmets	14,000
Supplies for general office	300	Sales commissions	7,000
Wages for assembly line workers	43,000	Amortization on factory building	1,500
Amortization on office equipment	800		

Instructions

(a) Prepare an answer sheet with the following column headings. Enter each cost item on your answer sheet, placing the dollar amount under the appropriate heading. Total the dollar amounts in each column.

	Product Costs			
Cost Item	Direct Materials	Direct Labour	Manufacturing Overhead	Period Costs

(b) Calculate the cost to produce one helmet.

P1–25B Copa Company, a manufacturer of stereo systems, started its production in October 2005. For the preceding three years, Copa had been a retailer of stereo systems. After a thorough survey of stereo system markets, Copa decided to turn its retail store into a stereo equipment factory.

Classify manufacturing costs into different categories and calculate unit cost. (SO 3, 4)

Raw materials cost for a stereo system total $74 per unit. Workers on the production lines are paid $12 per hour on average. A stereo system usually takes five hours to complete. In addition, rent on the equipment used to assemble stereo systems amounts to $4,900 per month. Indirect materials cost $5 per system. A supervisor was hired to oversee production; her monthly salary is $3,000.

Janitorial costs are $1,300 monthly. Advertising costs for the stereo systems are $8,500 per month. The factory building amortization expense is $7,200 per year. Property taxes on the factory building are $9,000 per year.

Instructions

(a) Prepare an answer sheet with the following column headings. Assuming that Copa manufactures, on average, 1,300 stereo systems per month, enter each cost item on your answer sheet, placing the dollar amount per month under the appropriate heading. Total the dollar amounts in each column.

	Product Costs			
Cost Item	Direct Materials	Direct Labour	Manufacturing Overhead	Period Costs

(b) Calculate the cost to produce one stereo system.

P1–26B Incomplete manufacturing costs, expenses, and selling data for two different cases are as follows.

Indicate missing amounts of different cost items, and prepare condensed cost of goods manufactured schedule, income statement, and partial balance sheet. (SO 5, 6, 7)

	Case 1	Case 2
Direct materials used	$ 7,600	(g)
Direct labour	5,000	$ 8,000
Manufacturing overhead	8,000	4,000
Total manufacturing cost	(a)	18,000
Beginning work in process inventory	1,000	(h)
Ending work in process inventory	(b)	3,000
Sales	24,500	(i)
Sales discounts	2,500	1,400
Cost of goods manufactured	17,000	22,000
Beginning finished goods inventory	(c)	3,300
Goods available for sale	18,000	(j)
Cost of goods sold	(d)	(k)
Ending finished goods inventory	3,400	2,500
Gross profit	(e)	7,000
Operating expenses	2,500	(l)
Net income	(f)	5,000

Instructions

(a) Indicate the missing amount for each letter.

(b) Prepare a condensed cost of goods manufactured schedule for Case 1.

(c) Prepare an income statement and the current assets section of the balance sheet for Case 1. Assume that in Case 1 the other items in the current assets section are as follows: cash $4,000, receivables (net) $15,000, raw materials $600, and prepaid expenses $400.

Prepare cost of goods manufactured schedule, partial income statement, and partial balance sheet.
(SO 5, 6, 7)

P1–27B The following data were taken from the records of Stellar Manufacturing Company for the fiscal year ended June 30, 2005:

Raw materials		Accounts teceivable	$ 27,000
inventory, July 1, 2004	$ 48,000	Factory insurance	4,600
Raw materials		Factory machinery	
inventory, June 30, 2005	39,600	amortization	16,000
Finished goods		Factory utilities	27,600
inventory, July 1, 2004	96,000	Office utilities	8,650
Finished goods		Sales	554,000
inventory, June 30, 2005	95,900	Sales discounts	4,200
Work in process		Plant manager's salary	29,000
inventory, July 1, 2004	19,800	Factory property taxes	9,600
Work in process		Factory repairs	1,400
inventory, June 30, 2005	18,600	Raw materials purchases	96,400
Direct labour	149,250	Cash	32,000
Indirect labour	24,460		

Instructions

(a) Prepare a cost of goods manufactured schedule. (Assume all raw materials used were direct materials.)

(b) Prepare an income statement through gross profit.

(c) Prepare the current assets section of the balance sheet at June 30, 2005.

Prepare cost of goods manufactured schedule and correct income statement.
(SO 5, 6)

P1–28B Tombert Company is a manufacturer of computers. Its controller resigned in October 2005. An inexperienced assistant accountant has prepared the following income statement for the month of October 2005:

TOMBERT COMPANY
Income Statement
Month Ended October 31, 2005

Sales (net)		$780,000
Less: Operating expenses		
Raw materials purchased	$264,000	
Direct labour cost	190,000	
Advertising expense	90,000	
Selling and administrative salaries	75,000	
Rent on factory facilities	60,000	
Amortization on sales equipment	45,000	
Amortization on factory equipment	31,000	
Indirect labour cost	28,000	
Utilities expense	12,000	
Insurance expense	8,000	803,000
Net loss		$ (23,000)

Before October 2005, the company was profitable every month. The company's president is concerned about the accuracy of the income statement. As his friend, you have been asked to review the income statement and make necessary corrections. After examining other manufacturing cost data, you have acquired additional information as follows:

1. Inventory balances at the beginning and end of October:

	October 1	October 31
Raw materials	$18,000	$34,000
Work in process	16,000	14,000
Finished goods	30,000	48,000

2. Only 70% of the utilities expense and 60% of the insurance expense apply to factory operations. The remaining amounts should be charged to selling and administrative activities.

Instructions

(a) Prepare a cost of goods manufactured schedule for October 2005.

(b) Prepare a correct income statement for October 2005.

P1–29B Nova Chemicals Corp. incurred the following manufacturing costs for the year 2005:

Calculate raw materials purchased, cost of goods manufactured, and cost of goods sold.
(SO 3, 4, 5, 6)

Raw materials used in production	$ 28,000	Selling and administration	
Total manufacturing cost added	160,000	expenses	$43,000
Factory overhead	66,000		

Inventories:

Raw materials, January 1	$ 9,600	Work in process, December 31	$13,000
Raw materials, December 31	10,400	Finished goods, January 1	9,600
Work in process, January 1	14,600	Finished goods, December 31	9,200

Instructions

(a) For 2005, what was the cost of raw materials purchased?
(b) For 2005, what was the cost of goods manufactured?
(c) For 2005, what was the cost of goods sold?

P1–30B The following information is for Montreal Gloves Inc. for the year 2005:

Calculate cost of goods manufactured and cost of goods sold.
(SO 3, 4, 5, 6)

Manufacturing costs	$3,000,000
Number of gloves manufactured	300,000 pairs
Beginning inventory	0 pairs

Sales in 2005 were 298,500 pairs of gloves for $18 per pair.

Instructions

(a) What is the cost of goods sold for 2005?
(b) What is the amount of the gross profit for 2005?
(c) What is the cost of finished goods ending inventory for 2005?

P1–31B Laframboise Inc. manufactures toys. It expects to sell 80,000 units in 2005. At the start of 2005, the company had enough beginning inventory of raw materials to produce 96,000 units. The beginning inventory of finished units totalled 8,000, and the target ending inventory was 10,000 units. The selling price per unit is $6 and the company keeps no work in process inventory. The direct materials cost for each unit is $2 and direct labour is $1. Factory overhead is $0.40 per unit.

Calculate cost of goods manufactured and cost of goods sold.
(SO 3, 4, 5, 6)

Instructions

(a) What will the total costs incurred for direct materials be for 2005?
(b) What will the total costs incurred for direct manufacturing labour be for 2005?
(c) What will the total costs incurred for manufacturing overhead be for 2005?
(d) What will the cost of goods sold be for 2005?

P1–32B Last night, the sprinkler system at Plant A was accidentally set off. The ensuing deluge destroyed most of the cost records in Plant A for the month just completed (May). The plant manager has come to you in a panic—he has to complete his report for head office by the end of today. He wants you to give him the numbers he needs for his report. He can provide you with some fragments of information he has been able to salvage:

Determine missing amounts, and calculate selected costs for schedules of cots of goods manufactured and sold.
(SO 3, 4, 6)

Raw materials:	beginning	$ 25,000
	ending	55,000
Work in process:	beginning	15,000
Finished goods:	sold in May	400,000
	ending	50,000
Manufacturing overhead:	beginning	0
Accrued wages payable:	beginning	10,000
	ending	20,000

Other information:

1. Total direct materials requisitions for the month were $180,000.
2. A total of 10,000 direct labour hours were worked during the month at an average wage of $15/hour.
3. Overhead is applied to production at $10/direct labour hour.
4. On May 31, there was one job (#XL235) left in work in process. It included $4,000 of direct materials and had received 20 direct labour hours to date (it was started on May 30).

Instructions

Calculate the following:

(a) the material purchases during May
(b) the cost of work in process inventory at the end of May
(c) the amount paid to the labour force in May
(d) the cost of goods sold in May
(e) the cost of goods transferred from work in process inventory to finished goods inventory in May
(f) the cost of finished goods inventory at the beginning of May

(CGA-adapted)

Additional Cases

Cases

C1–33　A fire on the premises of Bydo Inc. destroyed most of its records. Below is an incomplete set of data for operations in 2005:

Sales	?
Raw materials, beginning inventory	$13,000
Purchases	13,000
Raw materials, ending inventory	?
Direct materials	20,000
Direct labour	25,000
Factory overhead	8,000
Manufacturing costs added during the year	?
Work in process, beginning inventory	8,000
Work in process, ending inventory	7,000
Cost of goods manufactured	?
Finished goods, beginning inventory	6,000
Finished goods, ending inventory	?
Cost of goods sold	55,000
Gross profit	9,000
Operating expenses	?
Operating income (loss)	(4,000)

Instructions

Prepare an income statement for 2005. Include separate schedules for cost of goods sold and cost of goods manufactured.

(CGA-adapted)

C1–34　On January 31, a snowstorm damaged the office of a small business and some of the accounting information stored in the computer's memory was lost. The following information pertaining to January activities was retrieved from other sources:

Direct materials purchased	$18,000
Work in process—beginning inventory	2,000
Direct materials—beginning inventory	6,000
Direct materials—ending inventory	10,000
Finished goods—beginning inventory	12,000
Finished goods—ending inventory	2,500
Sales	60,000
Manufacturing overhead and direct labour incurred	22,000
Gross profit percentage based on net sales	40%

Instructions

(a) What was the cost of direct materials used in January?
(b) Assume that $20,000 of direct materials was used in January. What amount of work in process inventory was transferred out to finished goods during January?

(c) Assume that $20,000 of direct materials was used in January and that the cost of goods available for sale in January amounted to $40,000. What did the ending work in process inventory amount to?

C1–35 In January 2005, Sayers Manufacturing incurred the following costs in manufacturing Detecto, its only product:

Direct materials purchased	$900,000	Utility expenses	$92,500
Direct labour incurred	710,000	Amortization (equipment)	2,800
Benefits	75,000	Supplies (factory)	10,000
Overtime premium	50,000	Factory rent	31,300
Supervisory salaries	125,000		

An analysis of the accounting records showed the following balances in the inventory accounts at the beginning and end of January:

	January 1	January 31
Direct materials	$ 80,000	$ 90,000
Work in process	110,000	74,600
Finished goods	95,000	108,000

Sayers treats overtime premiums and benefits as indirect costs.

Instructions

(a) Determine the cost of goods manufactured for January 2005.
(b) What was the cost of goods sold for January 2005?

(CMA Canada-adapted)

C1–36 XYZ Company reports the following data for the month of June:

	June 1	June 30
Direct materials	$ 50	$ 80
Work in process	140	180
Finished goods	240	250

The following information is available for June:

1. Direct materials purchases were $140.
2. Direct costs of production were $220.
3. Variable costs of production were $280.
4. Indirect costs of production were $180.
5. Selling and administrative costs were $210.

Instructions

(a) What were the total costs of production?
(b) What was the cost of materials used?
(c) What was the cost of direct labour?
(d) What was the cost of variable overhead?
(e) What was fixed manufacturing overhead?
(f) What was the cost of goods manufactured?
(g) What was the cost of goods sold?
(h) What were the conversion costs?
(i) What were the prime costs?
(j) What were the period costs?

C1–37 Match Manufacturing Company specializes in producing fashion outfits. On July 31, 2005, a tornado touched down at its factory and general office. The inventories in the warehouse and the factory were completely destroyed, as was the general office nearby. Next morning, through a careful search of the disaster site, however, Ross Clarkson, the company's controller, and Catherine Harper, the cost accountant, were able to recover a small amount of manufacturing cost data for the current month.

"What a horrible experience," sighed Ross. "And the worst part is that we may not have enough records to use in filing an insurance claim."

"It was terrible," replied Catherine. "However, I managed to recover some of the manufacturing cost data that I was working on yesterday afternoon. The data indicate that our direct labour cost in July totalled $240,000 and that we had purchased $345,000 of raw materials.

Also, I recall that the amount of raw materials used for July was $350,000. But I'm not sure this information will help. The rest of our records were blown away."

"Well, not exactly," said Ross. "I was working on the year-to-date income statement when the tornado warning was announced. My recollection is that our sales in July were $1.26 million and our gross profit ratio has been 40% of sales. Also, I can remember that our cost of goods available for sale was $770,000 for July."

"Maybe we can work something out from this information!" exclaimed Catherine. "My experience tells me that our manufacturing overhead is usually 60% of direct labour."

"Hey, look what I just found," cried Catherine. "It's a copy of this June's balance sheet, and it shows that our inventories as at June 30 were finished goods $38,000, work in process $25,000, and raw materials $19,000."

"Super!" yelled Ross. "Let's go work something out."

In order to file an insurance claim, Match Manufacturing must determine the amount of its inventories as at July 31, 2005, the date of the tornado touchdown.

Instructions

With the class divided into groups, determine the amount of cost in the Raw Materials, Work in Process, and Finished Goods inventory accounts as at the date of the tornado.

C1–38   Wayne Terrago, controller for Robbin Industries, was reviewing production cost reports for the year. One amount in these reports continued to bother him—advertising. During the year, the company had instituted an expensive advertising campaign to sell some of its slower-moving products. It was still too early to tell whether the advertising campaign was successful.

There had been much internal debate about how to report the advertising cost. The vice-president of finance argued that advertising costs should be reported as a cost of production, just like direct materials and direct labour. He therefore recommended that this cost be identified as manufacturing overhead and reported as part of inventory costs until sold. Others disagreed. Terrago believed that this cost should be reported as an expense of the current period, based on the conservatism principle. Others argued that it should be reported as prepaid advertising and reported as a current asset.

The president finally had to decide the issue. He argued that these costs should be reported as inventory. His arguments were practical ones. He noted that the company was experiencing financial difficulty and expensing this amount in the current period might jeopardize a planned bond offering. Also, by reporting the advertising costs as inventory rather than as prepaid advertising, less attention would be directed to them by the financial community.

Instructions

(a) Who are the stakeholders in this situation?
(b) What are the ethical issues involved in this situation?
(c) What would you do if you were Wayne Terrago?

Answers to Self-Study Questions

1. b   2. d   3. b   4. b   5. c   6. d   7. a   8. c   9. a   10. d

Remember to go back to the Navigator Box at the beginning of the chapter to check off your completed work.

CHAPTER 2

Job-Order Cost Accounting

Print on Demand

Ottawa-based Dollco Printing prints a variety of magazines, catalogues, manuals, and promotional materials, ranging from association journals to advertising flyers. "Each job is customized to the specific client," says Jovalyn Humphreys, CMA, Dollco's accounting manager. Even for recurring jobs like magazines, client specifications can change from one issue to the next.

More than 7,000 of these projects run through Dollco's presses each year. And each job varies in the amount and type of service to be provided—from prepress, printing, binding, and finishing, to mailing and distribution. Tracking costs in such an environment can be a challenge.

"Up front, you know what the specifications are," Ms. Humphreys says. These specifications include the publication size, type of paper, and amount of colour required. "Depending on those specifications, you know how the work has to be laid out, what press you're going to use, what's going to be required in terms of bindery work, and if there's any mailing work."

Each job is assigned a code and costs are fully integrated, Ms. Humphreys explains. Labour and direct materials are tracked through the shop floor. When working on a project, employees enter the job code into the machines and punch it into their time clock. Employee and machine time is then charged to that job. General overhead and administration costs have been factored into the labour rates.

Outside purchases are handled in a similar way. When Dollco buys material for a specific job, the purchasing department will code it accordingly, linking it to that job. If material is taken out of inventory, the employee is responsible for charging it to the job.

Many of Dollco's projects are won through a bidding process. Potential customers will provide their specifications, and, using its integrated system that includes accounting, sales, production, and materials, Dollco generates an estimate based on those criteria. However, Ms. Humphreys says, "If you know it's going to be a longer-term project, you might decide to lower your margins for that job."

the navigator

Dollco Printing: www.dollco.com

THE NAVIGATOR

- [ ] Scan *Study Objectives*

- [ ] Read *Feature Story*

- [ ] Read *Chapter Preview*

- [ ] Read text and answer *Before You Go On* p. 50, p. 59, p. 64

- [ ] Work *Using the Decision Toolkit*

- [ ] Review *Summary of Study Objectives*

- [ ] Review *Using the Decision Toolkit—A Summary*

- [ ] Work *Demonstration Problem*

- [ ] Answer *Self-Study Questions*

- [ ] Complete assignments

STUDY OBJECTIVES

After studying this chapter, you should be able to:

1. Explain the characteristics and purposes of cost accounting.
2. Describe the flow of costs in a job-order cost accounting system.
3. Explain the nature and importance of a job cost sheet.
4. Indicate how the predetermined overhead rate is determined and used.
5. Prepare entries for jobs completed and sold.
6. Distinguish between underapplied and overapplied manufacturing overhead.

the navigator

The feature story about Ottawa-based Dollco Printing described the job-order costing system used in printing a variety of jobs. It demonstrated that accurate costing is critical to the company's success. For example, in order to submit accurate bids on new jobs and to know whether it profited from past jobs, the company needs a good costing system. This chapter shows how these printing costs would be assigned to specific jobs, such as the printing of an individual magazine. We begin the discussion in this chapter with an overview of the flow of costs in a job-order cost accounting system. We then use a case study to explain and illustrate the documents, entries, and accounts in this type of cost accounting system.

This chapter is organized as follows.

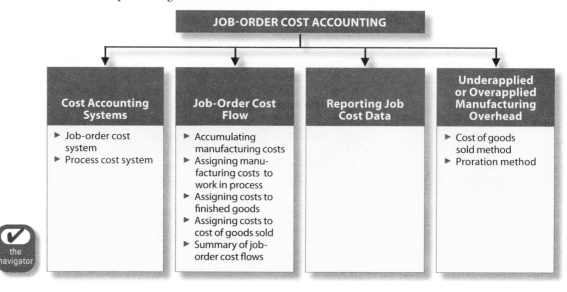

JOB-ORDER COST ACCOUNTING

Cost Accounting Systems	Job-Order Cost Flow	Reporting Job Cost Data	Underapplied or Overapplied Manufacturing Overhead
▶ Job-order cost system ▶ Process cost system	▶ Accumulating manufacturing costs ▶ Assigning manufacturing costs to work in process ▶ Assigning costs to finished goods ▶ Assigning costs to cost of goods sold ▶ Summary of job-order cost flows		▶ Cost of goods sold method ▶ Proration method

Cost Accounting Systems

study objective 1

Explain the characteristics and purposes of cost accounting.

Cost accounting involves the measuring, recording, and reporting of product costs. From the data that are collected, both the total cost and the unit cost of each product are determined. For a company to be successful, its cost accounting system has to provide accurate information about its product costs. As you will see in later chapters, this information is used to determine which products to produce, what prices to charge, and what amounts to produce. Accurate product cost information is also vital for evaluations of employee performance.

A **cost accounting system** uses specific accounts for the various manufacturing costs. These accounts are fully integrated into the general ledger of a company. **An important feature of a cost accounting system is the use of a perpetual inventory system.** Such a system **provides immediate, up-to-date information on the cost of a product.** There are two basic types of cost accounting systems: (1) a job-order cost system and (2) a process cost system. Although cost accounting systems differ greatly from company to company, most of them are based on one of these two traditional product costing systems.

Job-Order Cost System

Under a **job-order cost system**, costs are assigned to each **job** or to each **batch** of goods. Examples of a job would be the manufacture of a mainframe computer by IBM Canada and the production of a movie by The Canadian Broadcasting Corporation. An example of a batch would be the printing of 225 wedding invitations by a local print shop, such as Dollco Printing, or the printing of a weekly issue of *Fortune* magazine by a high-tech printer such as Quebecor Inc. Jobs or batches may be completed to fill a specific customer order or to replenish inventory.

An important feature of job-order costing is that each job (or batch) has its own distinguishing characteristics. For example, each house is custom-built, each consulting engagement is unique, and each printing job is different. **The objective is to calculate the cost per job.** At each point in the manufacture of a product or the provision of a service, the job and its associated costs can be identified. A job-order cost system measures costs for each completed job, rather than for set time periods. The recording of costs in a job-order cost system is shown in Illustration 2-1.

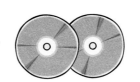

Dollco Printing
Job-Order Cost System
Two Jobs: Wedding Invitations and Menus

Black ink $ 225 envelopes $ Typesetting $ Coloured ink $

Typesetting $ Smith & Jones   Yellow stock $

225 invitations $ Vellum stock, pure white $ Lamination $ 50 copies $

Job # 9501   **Job # 9502**

Each job has distinguishing characteristics and related costs.

Illustration 2-1 ◀

Job-order cost system

Process Cost System

A **process cost system** is used when a large volume of similar products are manufactured. Production is continuous to ensure that adequate inventories of the finished product(s) are available. A process cost system is used in the manufacture of cereal by Kellogg Canada, the refining of petroleum by Petro-Canada, and the production of automobiles by General Motors of Canada Ltd. Process costing accumulates product-related costs **for a period of time** (such as a week or a month) instead of assigning costs to specific products or job orders. In process costing, the costs are assigned to departments or processes for a set (predetermined) period of time. The recording of costs in a process cost system is shown in Illustration 2-2.

Process Cost System
Compact Disc Production

1. Oil is pumped   2. Benzene is removed   3. The benzene is made into pellets...   4. ...from which compact discs are produced

Similar products are produced over a specified time period.

Illustration 2-2 ◀

Process cost system

The process cost system will be discussed further in Chapter 3. The main features of the job-order and process cost systems are summarized in illustration 2-3.

Job-Order Costing	Process Costing
1. Distinct products with low volumes: Home building, ship building, film production, aircraft manufacture, custom machining, furniture manufacture, printing, consulting	1. Homogeneous products with high volumes: Chemicals, gasoline, microchips, soft drinks, processed food, electricity
2. Cost added up by job or batch	2. Costs added by process or department
3. Unit cost calculated by dividing total job costs by units produced	3. Unit cost calculated by dividing total process costs during the period by units produced during that period

Illustration 2-3 ◀

Main features of job-order and process cost systems

A company may use both types of cost systems. For example, General Motors of Canada Ltd. would use process cost accounting for its standard model cars, such as Saturns and Corvettes, and job-order cost accounting for a custom-made limousine for Canada's prime minister. The goal of both systems is to provide unit cost information for product pricing, cost control, inventory valuation, and financial statement presentation. End-of-period inventory values are calculated by using unit cost data.

BUSINESS INSIGHT ▶ Management Perspective

Many companies suffer from poor cost accounting. As a result, they sometimes make products that they should not be selling at all and buy others that they could more profitably make themselves. Also, inaccurate cost data can lead companies to misallocate capital and it can frustrate plant managers' efforts to improve efficiency.

For example, consider the case of a diversified company in the business of rebuilding diesel locomotives. The managers thought they were making money, but a consulting firm found that costs had been seriously underestimated. The company bailed out of the business, and not a moment too soon. Says the consultant who advised the company, "The more contracts it won, the more money it lost." A company cannot stay in business very long that way!

BEFORE YOU GO ON . . .

▶ Review It

1. What is cost accounting?
2. What does a cost accounting system consist of?
3. How does a job-order cost system differ from a process cost system?

Job-Order Cost Flow

study objective 2

Describe the flow of costs in a job-order cost accounting system.

The flow of costs (direct materials, direct labour, and manufacturing overhead) in job-order cost accounting parallels the physical flow of the materials as they are converted into finished goods. As shown in Illustration 2-4, manufacturing costs are assigned to the Work in Process Inventory account. When a job is completed, the cost of the job is transferred to the Finished Goods Inventory account. Later, when the goods are sold, their cost is transferred to Cost of Goods Sold.

Illustration 2-4 provides a basic overview of the flow of costs in a manufacturing setting. A more detailed presentation of the flow of costs is shown in Illustration 2-5. It indicates that there are two major steps in the flow of costs: (1) *accumulating* the manufacturing costs incurred and (2) *assigning* the accumulated costs to the work done. As shown, manufacturing costs incurred are accumulated in entries 1 to 3 by debits to Raw Materials Inventory, Factory Labour, and Manufacturing Overhead. When these costs are incurred, no attempt is made to associate them with specific jobs. The remaining entries (entries 4 to 8) assign the manufacturing costs incurred. In the remainder of this chapter, pages 51–64, we will use a case study to explain how a job-order system operates.

Illustration 2-4 ▼

Flow of costs in job-order cost accounting

Manufacturing Costs	Work in Process Inventory	Finished Goods Inventory	Cost of Goods Sold
Raw Materials	Assigned to	Completed	Sold
Factory Labour			
Manufacturing Overhead			

Job-Order Cost Accounting

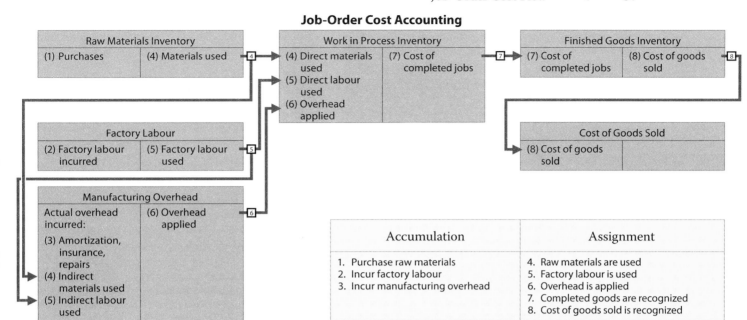

Illustration 2-5 ▲

Job-order cost accounting system

Accumulating Manufacturing Costs

In a job-order cost system, manufacturing costs are recorded in the period when they are incurred. To illustrate, we will use the January transactions of Wallace Manufacturing Company, which makes machine tools and dies. (Dies are devices used for cutting out, stamping, or forming metals and plastics.)

Raw Materials Costs

The costs of raw materials that are purchased are debited to Raw Materials Inventory when the materials are received. This account is debited for the invoice cost and freight costs that are chargeable to the purchaser. It is credited for purchase discounts that are taken and purchase returns and allowances. **At this point there is no attempt to associate the cost of materials with specific jobs or orders.** The procedures for ordering, receiving, recording, and paying for raw materials are similar to the purchasing procedures of a merchandising company.

To illustrate, assume that Wallace Manufacturing purchases 2,000 handles (Stock No. AA2746) at $5 per unit ($10,000) and 800 modules (Stock No. AA2850) at $40 per unit ($32,000) for a total cost of $42,000 ($10,000 + $32,000). The entry to record this purchase on January 4 is:

	(1)		
Jan. 4	Raw Materials Inventory	42,000	
	Accounts Payable		42,000
	To record the purchase of raw materials on account.		

Raw Materials Inventory is a general ledger account. It is also referred to as a **control account** because it summarizes the detailed data regarding specific inventory accounts in the subsidiary ledger. The subsidiary ledger consists of individual records for each item of raw materials. The records may take the form of accounts (or cards) that are manually or mechanically prepared. Or the records may be kept as computer data files. The records are referred to as **materials inventory records** (or **stores ledger cards**). The card for Stock No. AA2746 following the purchase is shown in Illustration 2-6.

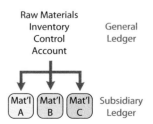

Illustration 2-6 ▶

Materials inventory card

	Receipts			Issues			Balance		
Date	Units	Cost	Total	Units	Cost	Total	Units	Cost	Total
Jan. 4	2,000	$5	$10,000				2,000	$5	$10,000

Item: Handles   Part No: AA2746

Postings are made daily to the subsidiary ledger. After all postings have been completed, the sum of the balances in the raw materials subsidiary ledger should equal the balance in the Raw Materials Inventory control account.

Factory Labour Costs

The procedures for accumulating factory labour costs are similar to those for calculating the payroll for a merchandising company. Time clocks and time cards are used to determine the total hours worked; gross and net earnings for each employee are listed in a payroll register; and individual employee earnings records are maintained. To help ensure that its data are accurate, a company should follow the principles of internal control.

In a manufacturing company, the cost of factory labour consists of (1) the gross earnings of factory workers, (2) employer payroll taxes on these earnings, and (3) fringe benefits incurred by the employer (such as sick pay, pensions, and vacation pay). **Labour costs are debited to Factory Labour when they are incurred.**

To illustrate, assume that Wallace Manufacturing incurs $32,000 of factory labour costs. Of that amount, $27,000 is for wages payable and $5,000 is for payroll taxes payable in January. The entry is:

	(2)		
Jan. 31	Factory Labour	32,000	
	Factory Wages Payable		27,000
	Employer Payroll Taxes Payable		5,000
	To record factory labour costs.		

Factory labour is then assigned to work in process and manufacturing overhead, as explained later in the chapter.

Manufacturing Overhead Costs

A company may have many types of overhead costs. These costs may be recognized **daily**, as is done for machinery repairs and the use of indirect materials and indirect labour. Or overhead costs may be recorded **periodically** through adjusting entries. Property taxes, amortization, and insurance are recorded periodically, for example. A **summary entry** summarizes the totals from multiple transactions. Wallace Manufacturing Company's summary entry for manufacturing overhead is as follows (using assumed data):

	(3)		
Jan. 31	Manufacturing Overhead	13,800	
	Utilities Payable		4,800
	Prepaid Insurance		2,000
	Accounts Payable (for repairs)		2,600
	Accumulated Amortization		3,000
	Property Taxes Payable		1,400
	To record overhead costs.		

Manufacturing Overhead is a control account. The subsidiary ledger consists of individual accounts for each type of cost, such as Factory Utilities, Factory Insurance, and Factory Repairs.

Assigning Manufacturing Costs to Work in Process

study objective 3

Explain the nature and importance of a job cost sheet.

As shown in Illustration 2-5, assigning manufacturing costs to work in process results in the following entries: (1) **debits** are made to Work in Process Inventory, and (2) **credits** are made to Raw Materials Inventory, Factory Labour, and Manufacturing Overhead. The journal entries to assign costs to work in process are usually made and posted **monthly**.

An essential accounting record in assigning costs to jobs is the **job cost sheet**, shown in Illustration 2-7. A **job cost sheet** is a form that is used to record the costs that are chargeable to a specific job and to determine the total and unit costs of the completed job.

Illustration 2-7 ◀

Job cost sheet

		Wallace Manufacturing Company	
		Job Cost Sheet	

Job No. _____   Quantity _____
Item _____   Date Requested _____
For _____   Date Completed _____

Date	Direct Materials	Direct Labour	Manufacturing Overhead

Cost of completed job
Direct materials $ _____
Direct labour _____
Manufacturing overhead _____
Total cost $ _____
Unit cost (total dollars ÷ quantity) $ _____

Helpful Hint In today's electronic environment, job cost sheets are maintained as computer files.

Postings to job cost sheets are made daily, directly from supporting documents.

A separate job cost sheet is kept for each job. The job cost sheets make up the subsidiary ledger for the Work in Process Inventory account. **Each entry to Work in Process Inventory must be accompanied by a corresponding posting to one or more job cost sheets.**

BUSINESS INSIGHT ▶ @-Business Insight

Montreal-based Ice.com is a rare Web success story. The on-line jewellery retailer set up shop in 2000, after a money-losing venture in California forced the owners to refocus. In its reincarnation, Ice.com was able to keep costs down, while providing an easy-to-use site where customers could buy affordable jewellery. Within a year, it was turning a profit; sales for 2003 were at least US$20 million. Part of the success involves Ice.com's product. The profit margins in on-line jewellery retail are better than for other products since it's easy and inexpensive to ship merchandise that is high in value but small in size. Plus, the owner's mother runs Ice.com's biggest supplier, Delmar International, which is conveniently located in the same building in downtown Montreal. With merchandise supplied by Delmar, Ice.com doesn't incur the cost of stocking inventory. The on-line jeweller can then pass these savings on to its customers, with prices up to 70% lower than department stores.

Source: Zena Olijnyk, "Dot-Com Wonder Boys," *Canadian Business*, April 14, 2003.

Raw Materials Costs

Raw materials costs are assigned when the materials are issued by the storeroom. To have effective internal control over issues of materials, the storeroom worker should receive a written authorization before any materials are released to production. Authorizations for issuing raw materials are made on a prenumbered **materials requisition slip**. This form is signed by an authorized employee, such as a department supervisor. The materials issued may be used directly on a job, or they may be considered indirect materials. As shown in Illustration 2-8, the requisition should indicate the quantity and type of materials withdrawn and the account to be charged. Direct materials are charged to Work in Process Inventory, and indirect materials to Manufacturing Overhead.

Helpful Hint Approvals are an important part of a materials requisition slip because they help determine which individuals are accountable for the inventory.

Illustration 2-8 ▶

Materials requisition slip

Helpful Hint The internal control principle of documentation includes prenumbering to improve accountability.

Wallace Manufacturing Company
Materials Requisition Slip

Deliver to: _____Assembly Department_____   Req. No.: _____R247_____
Charge to: ___Work in Process–Job No. 101___   Date: ___Jan. 6, 2004___

Quantity	Description	Stock No.	Cost per Unit	Total
200	Handles	AA2746	$5.00	$1,000

Requested by: _____Bruce Howart_____   Received by: ___Herb Crowley___
Approved by: _____Kap Shin_____   Costed by: ___Heather Remmecs___

The requisition is prepared in duplicate. A copy is retained in the storeroom as evidence of the materials released. The original is sent to accounting, where the cost per unit and total cost of the materials used are determined. Any of the inventory costing methods (FIFO, LIFO, or average cost) may be used in costing the requisitions. After the requisition slips have been costed, they are posted daily to the materials inventory records. Also, **requisitions for direct materials are posted daily to the individual job cost sheets**.

Periodically, the requisitions are sorted, totalled, and journalized. For example, if $24,000 of direct materials and $6,000 of indirect materials are used by Wallace Manufacturing in January, the entry is:

---

(4)

Jan. 31	Work in Process Inventory	24,000	
	Manufacturing Overhead	6,000	
	Raw Materials Inventory		30,000
	To assign materials to jobs and overhead.		

The requisition slips show total direct materials costs of $12,000 for Job No. 101; $7,000 for Job No. 102; and $5,000 for Job No. 103. The posting of requisition slip R247 for materials and other assumed postings to the job cost sheets are shown in Illustration 2-9. After all postings have been completed, the sum of the direct materials columns of the job cost sheets should equal the direct materials debited to Work in Process Inventory.

Illustration 2-9 ▶

Job cost sheets—direct materials

Helpful Hint Postings to control accounts are made monthly, and postings to job cost sheets are made daily.

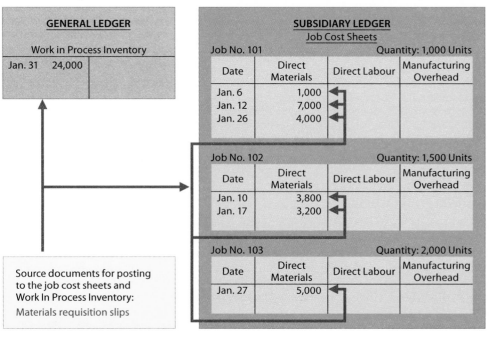

The materials inventory record for Part No. AA2746 is shown in Illustration 2-10. It shows the posting of requisition slip R247 for 200 handles and an assumed requisition slip for 760 handles costing $3,800 on January 10 for Job No. 102.

Item: Handles							Part No: AA2746		
	Receipt			Issues			Balance		
Date	Units	Cost	Total	Units	Cost	Total	Units	Cost	Total
Jan 4	2,000	$5	$10,000				2,000	$5	$10,000
Jan 6				200	$5	$1,000	1,800	5	9,000
Jan 10				760	5	3,800	1,040	5	5,200

Illustration 2-10 ◄

Materials inventory card following issues

Factory Labour Costs

Factory labour costs are assigned to jobs on the basis of time tickets that are prepared when the work is performed. The **time ticket** indicates the employee, the hours worked, the account and job to be charged, and the total labour cost. In many companies, these data are accumulated through the use of bar coding and scanning devices. When they start and end work, employees scan bar codes on their identification badges and bar codes that are associated with each job they work on. When direct labour is involved, the job number must be indicated, as shown in Illustration 2-11. All time tickets should be approved by the employee's supervisor.

Helpful Hint In some companies, different-coloured time tickets are used for direct and indirect labour.

Illustration 2-11 ◄

Time ticket

Wallace Manufacturing Company					
Time Ticket					
			Date: January 6, 2005		
Employee: John Nash			Employee No.: 124		
Charge to: Work in Process			Job No.: 101		
	Time			Hourly Rate	Total cost
Start	Stop	Total Hours			
0800	1200	4		10.00	40.00
Approved by: _Bob Kadler_			Costed by: _M. Chen_		

The time tickets are later sent to the payroll department. There, the total time reported for an employee for a pay period is reconciled with the total hours worked, as shown on the employee's time card. Then the employee's hourly wage rate is applied, and the total labour cost is calculated. Finally, the time tickets are sorted, totalled, and journalized. The account Work in Process Inventory is debited for direct labour, and Manufacturing Overhead is debited for indirect labour. For example, if the $32,000 total factory labour cost consists of $28,000 of direct labour and $4,000 of indirect labour, the entry is as follows:

	(5)		
Work in Process Inventory		28,000	
Manufacturing Overhead		4,000	
Factory Labour			32,000
To assign labour to jobs and overhead.			

As a result of this entry, Factory Labour is left with a zero balance, and gross earnings are assigned to the appropriate manufacturing accounts.

Let's assume that the labour costs that are chargeable to Wallace Manufacturing's three jobs are $15,000, $9,000, and $4,000. The Work in Process Inventory and job cost sheets after posting are shown in Illustration 2-12. As in the case of direct materials, the postings to the direct labour columns of the job cost sheets should equal the posting of direct labour to Work in Process Inventory.

Illustration 2-12 ▶

Job cost sheets—direct labour

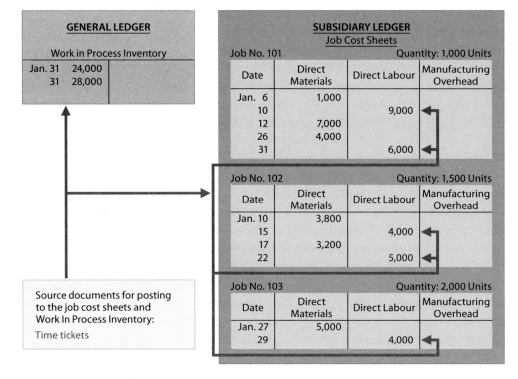

Helpful Hint Prove the $28,000 by totalling the charges by jobs:

101	$15,000
102	9,000
103	4,000
	$28,000

Manufacturing Overhead Costs

We have seen that the actual costs of direct materials and direct labour can be charged to specific jobs based on the actual costs incurred. In contrast to this, manufacturing overhead involves production operations **as a whole**. As a result, overhead costs cannot be assigned to specific jobs on the basis of the actual costs incurred. Instead, manufacturing overhead is assigned to work in process and to specific jobs **on an estimated basis by using a predetermined overhead rate**.

BUSINESS INSIGHT ▶ Management Perspective

A job-cost computer program provides summaries of material and labour costs by job. The program accumulates the costs for each job, sends data to accounts receivable for billings, assigns overhead costs, and provides up-to-date management reports. The reports generated by such systems are basically the same as those shown for Wallace Manufacturing. The major difference between manual and computerized systems is the time involved in converting data into information and in getting feedback (reports) to management.

Predetermined Overhead Rate

study objective 4

Indicate how the predetermined overhead rate is determined and used.

The **predetermined overhead rate** is based on the relationship between the estimated annual overhead costs and the expected annual operating activity. This relationship is expressed through a common **activity base**. The activity may be stated in terms of direct labour costs, direct labour hours, machine hours, or any other measure that will provide a fair basis for applying overhead costs to jobs. The predetermined overhead rate is established at the beginning of the year. Small companies will often have a single, company-wide predetermined overhead rate. Large companies, however, often have rates that vary from department to department. Illustration 2-13 shows the formula for calculating the predetermined overhead rate:

Illustration 2-13 ▶

Formula for predetermined overhead rate

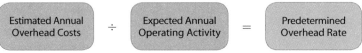

We stated earlier that overhead involves a company's production operations as a whole. In order to know what "the whole" is, the logical thing to do would be to wait until the end of the year's operations, when all factory overhead costs for the period would be available. This way, the costs for jobs could be allocated based on the actual factory overhead rate(s) times the actual quantity of the activity base(s) that each job used. This method of costing is called the **actual costing system**. In this method, the direct and indirect costs are assigned to a cost object by using the actual costs incurred during the accounting period. Practically, however, this method is unworkable. Managers cannot wait that long for information about the costs of specific jobs that were completed during the year. They need to be able to price products accurately on a more timely basis. This problem is solved by using a predetermined overhead rate, which makes it possible to determine the costs of a job immediately. Illustration 2-14 shows how manufacturing overhead is assigned to work in process.

Helpful Hint In contrast to overhead, the actual costs for direct materials and direct labour are used to assign costs to Work in Process.

Illustration 2-14 ◄

Using predetermined overhead rates

Wallace Manufacturing uses direct labour cost as the activity base. Assuming that annual overhead costs are expected to be $280,000 and that $350,000 of direct labour costs are anticipated for the year, the overhead rate is 80 percent, calculated as follows:

$$\$280,000 \div \$350,000 = 80\%$$

This means that for every dollar of direct labour that a job requires, 80 cents of manufacturing overhead will be assigned to the job. The use of a predetermined overhead rate enables the company to determine the approximate total cost of each job **when the job is completed**. The use of a predetermined overhead rate is referred to as the normal costing system.

The **normal costing system** is a costing system that traces direct costs (direct material and direct labour) to a cost object by using the actual cost data used during the accounting period; it allocates indirect costs (factory overhead) based on the predetermined rate(s) times the actual quantity of the activity base(s) used. The major differences between the actual job-order and normal job-order costing systems are summarized in Illustration 2-15.

Illustration 2-15 ◄

Actual costing system compared to normal costing system

Costs	Actual Costing System	Normal Costing System
Direct cost		
Direct material	• actual direct raw material cost rate times the actual quantity of direct material used.	• actual direct raw material cost rate times the actual quantity of direct material used
Direct labour	• actual direct labour cost rate times the actual hours used	• actual direct labour cost rate times the actual hours used
Indirect cost		
Factory overhead	• actual factory overhead rate(s) times the actual quantity used of the activity base(s)	• predetermined factory overhead rate(s) times the actual quantity used of the activity base(s)
Time and accuracy	• more accurate, but untimely information	• less accurate, but more timely information

Historically, direct labour costs or direct labour hours have often been used as the activity base. The reason was the relatively high correlation between direct labour and manufacturing overhead. In recent years, **there has been a trend toward using machine hours as the activity**

base, due to the increased reliance on automation in manufacturing operations. Or, as mentioned in Chapter 1, many companies have instead implemented activity-based costing in order to more accurately allocate overhead costs based on the activities that give rise to these costs.

For Wallace Manufacturing, the total amount of manufacturing overhead is assigned to work in process. It is then **applied to specific jobs when the direct labour costs are assigned.** The overhead applied for January is $22,400 ($28,000 × 80%), recorded as follows:

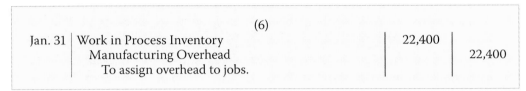

		(6)		
Jan. 31	Work in Process Inventory		22,400	
	Manufacturing Overhead			22,400
	To assign overhead to jobs.			

The overhead applied to each job will be 80 percent of the direct labour cost of the job for the month. After posting, the Work in Process Inventory account and the job cost sheets will appear as shown in Illustration 2-16. Note that the debit of $22,400 to Work in Process Inventory equals the sum of the overhead applied to jobs: $12,000 (Job No. 101) + $7,200 (Job No. 102) + $3,200 (Job No. 103).

Illustration 2-16 ▶

Job cost sheets—manufacturing overhead applied

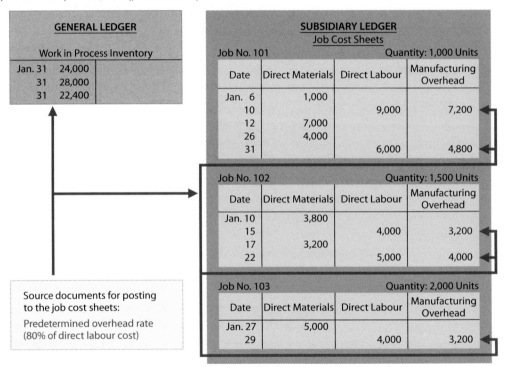

At the end of each month, **the balance in Work in Process Inventory should equal the sum of the costs shown on the job cost sheets of unfinished jobs.** Assuming that all jobs are unfinished, Illustration 2-17 shows proof of the agreement of the control and subsidiary accounts for Wallace Manufacturing.

Illustration 2-17 ▶

Proof of job cost sheets to Work in Process Inventory.

Work in Process Inventory			Job Cost Sheets	
Jan. 31	24,000		No. 101	$39,000
31	28,000		102	23,200
31	22,400		103	12,200
	74,400	◀		74,400

Decision Toolkit

Decision Checkpoints	Info Needed for Decision	Tools to Use for Decision	How to Evaluate Results
What is the cost of a job?	Cost of material, labour, and overhead assigned to a specific job	Job cost sheet	Compare the costs to those of previous periods and to those of competitors to ensure that costs are reasonable. Compare costs to the expected selling price or service fees that are charged to determine the overall profitability.

BEFORE YOU GO ON . . .

► Review It

1. What source documents are used in assigning manufacturing costs to Work in Process Inventory?
2. What is a job cost sheet, and what is its main purpose?
3. What is the formula for calculating a predetermined overhead rate?

► Do It

Danielle Company is working on two job orders. The job cost sheets show the following:

   Direct materials—Job No. 120, $6,000; Job No. 121, $3,600
   Direct labour—Job No. 120, $4,000; Job No. 121, $2,000
   Manufacturing overhead—Job No. 120, $5,000; Job No. 121, $2,500

Prepare the three summary entries to record the assignment of costs to Work in Process from the data on the job cost sheets.

Action Plan

• Recognize that Work in Process Inventory is the control account for all unfinished job cost sheets.
• Debit Work in Process Inventory for the materials, labour, and overhead charged to the job cost sheets.
• Credit the accounts that were debited when the manufacturing costs were accumulated.

Solution

The three summary entries are:

Work in Process Inventory ($6,000 + $3,600)	9,600	
Raw Materials Inventory		9,600
To assign materials to jobs.		
Work in Process Inventory ($4,000 + $2,000)	6,000	
Factory Labour		6,000
To assign labour to jobs.		
Work in Process Inventory ($5,000 + $2,500)	7,500	
Manufacturing Overhead		7,500
To assign overhead to jobs.		

Related exercise material: BE2–3, BE2–4, BE2–7, E2–2, E2–3, E2–7, and E2–8.

Assigning Costs to Finished Goods

When a job is completed, the costs are summarized and the lower section of the job cost sheet is completed. For example, if we assume that Wallace Manufacturing's Job No. 101 is completed on January 31, the job cost sheet will be as in Illustration 2-18.

Illustration 2-18 ▶

Completed job cost sheet

Wallace Manufacturing Company
Job Cost Sheet

Job No: 101   Quantity: 1,000
  Item: Magnetic Sensors   Date Requested: February 5
  For: Tanner Company   Date Completed: January 31

Date	Direct Materials	Direct Labour	Manufacturing Overhead
Jan. 6	$ 1,000		
10		$ 9,000	$ 7,200
12	7,000		
26	4,000		
31		6,000	4,800
	$12,000	$15,000	$12,000

Cost of completed job
  Direct materials $ 12,000
  Direct labour   15,000
  Manufacturing overhead   12,000
  Total cost $ 39,000
  Unit cost ($39,000 ÷ 1,000) $ 39.00

When a job is finished, an entry is made to transfer its total cost to Finished Goods Inventory. The entry for Wallace Manufacturing is:

(7)

Jan. 31	Finished Goods Inventory	39,000	
	Work in Process Inventory		39,000
	To record completion of Job No. 101.		

Finished Goods Inventory is a control account. It controls individual finished goods records in a finished goods subsidiary ledger. Postings to the receipts columns are made directly from completed job cost sheets. The finished goods inventory record for Job No. 101 is shown in Illustration 2-19.

Illustration 2-19 ▶

Finished goods record

Item: Magnetic sensors   Job No: 101

	Receipts			Issues			Balance		
Date	Units	Cost	Total	Units	Cost	Total	Units	Cost	Total
Jan. 31	1,000	$39	$39,000				1,000	$39	$39,000
31				1,000	$39	$39,000			

Assigning Costs to Cost of Goods Sold

The cost of goods sold is recognized when each sale occurs. To illustrate the entries when a completed job is sold, assume that on January 31 Wallace Manufacturing sells for $50,000 on account Job No. 101, which cost $39,000. The entries to record the sale and recognize the cost of goods sold are as follows:

	(8)			
Jan. 31	Accounts receivable		50,000	
	Sales			50,000
	To record sale of Job No. 101.			
31	Cost of Goods Sold		39,000	
	Finished Goods Inventory			39,000
	To record cost of Job No. 101.			

The units sold, the cost per unit, and the total cost of goods sold for each job that has been sold are recorded in the issues section of the finished goods record, as shown in Illustration 2-19 above.

Summary of Job-Order Cost Flows

A completed flowchart for a job-order cost accounting system is shown in Illustration 2-20. All postings are keyed to entries 1 to 8 in Wallace Manufacturing's accounts presented in the cost flow graphic in Illustration 2-5. Illustration 2-21 provides a summary of the flow of documents in a job-order cost system.

Illustration 2-20 ▼

Flow of costs in a job-order cost system

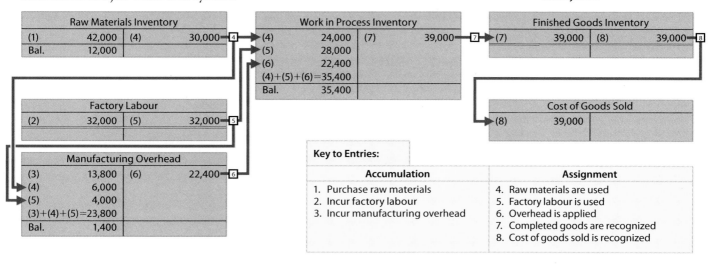

Illustration 2-21 ◀

Flow of documents in a job-order cost system

Flow of Documents

Materials Requisition Slips → Job Cost Sheet
Labour Time Tickets → Job Cost Sheet
Predetermined Overhead Rates → Job Cost Sheet

The job cost sheet summarizes the cost of jobs completed and not completed at the end of the accounting period. Jobs completed are transferred to finished goods to await sale.

Reporting Job Cost Data

At the end of a period, financial statements are prepared that present summarized data for all the jobs manufactured and sold. The cost of goods manufactured schedule in job-order costing is the same as in Chapter 1, with one exception: **The schedule shows manufacturing**

Helpful Hint Monthly financial statements are usually prepared for management use only.

overhead applied, rather than actual overhead costs. This amount is added to direct materials and direct labour to determine the total manufacturing cost. The schedule is prepared directly from the Work in Process Inventory account. Illustration 2-22 shows a condensed schedule for Wallace Manufacturing Company for January.

Illustration 2-22 ▶

Cost of goods manufactured schedule

WALLACE MANUFACTURING COMPANY Cost of Goods Manufactured Schedule Month Ended January 31, 2005		
Work in process, January 1		$ 0
Direct materials used	$24,000	
Direct labour	28,000	
Manufacturing overhead applied	22,400	
Total manfacturing cost		74,400
Total cost of work in process		74,400
Less: Work in process, January 31		35,400
Cost of goods manufactured		$39,000

Note that the cost of goods manufactured ($39,000) agrees with the amount transferred from Work in Process Inventory to Finished Goods Inventory in journal entry no. 7 in Illustration 2-20.

The income statement and balance sheet are the same as those illustrated in Chapter 1. For example, the partial income statement for Wallace Manufacturing for the month of January is shown in Illustration 2-23.

Illustration 2-23 ▶

Partial income statement

WALLACE MANUFACTURING COMPANY Income Statement (partial) Month Ended January 31, 2005		
Sales		$50,000
Cost of goods sold		
Finished goods inventory, January 1	$ 0	
Cost of goods manufactured (See Illustration 2-22)	39,000	
Cost of goods available for sale	39,000	
Less: Finished goods inventory, January 31	0	
Cost of goods sold		39,000
Gross profit		$11,000

Underapplied or Overapplied Manufacturing Overhead

When Manufacturing Overhead has a **debit balance**, overhead is said to be underapplied. **Underapplied overhead** means that the overhead assigned to Work in Process is less than the overhead incurred. Conversely, when Manufacturing Overhead has a **credit balance**, overhead is overapplied. **Overapplied overhead** means that the overhead assigned to Work in Process is greater than the overhead incurred. These concepts are shown in Illustration 2-24.

Illustration 2-24 ▶

Underapplied and overapplied overhead

Manufacturing Overhead	
Actual (costs incurred)	Applied (costs assigned)

If actual is **greater** than applied, manufacturing overhead is underapplied.
If actual is **less** than applied, manufacturing overhead is overapplied.

Cost of Goods Sold Method

At the end of the year, all manufacturing overhead transactions are complete. Accordingly, any balance in Manufacturing Overhead is eliminated by an adjusting entry. Generally the end-of-period underapplied or overapplied overhead costs are treated in one of two methods. The more common method is to make an adjustment to Cost of Goods Sold. Here, the underapplied or overapplied overhead costs are closed into **Cost of Goods Sold**. Thus, **underapplied overhead is debited to Cost of Goods Sold. Overapplied overhead is credited to Cost of Goods Sold.** To illustrate, assume that Wallace Manufacturing has a $2,500 credit balance in Manufacturing Overhead at December 31. The adjusting entry for the overapplied overhead is:

Dec. 31	Manufacturing Overhead	2,500	
	Cost of Goods Sold		2,500
	To transfer overapplied overhead to cost of goods sold.		

After this entry is posted, Manufacturing Overhead will have a zero balance. In preparing an income statement for the year, the amount reported for cost of goods sold will be the account balance **after the adjustment** for either under- or overapplied overhead.

BUSINESS INSIGHT ▶ Management Perspective

Nonmanufacturing companies have overhead; however, some will charge more to cover this overhead than others. A look at the mutual fund industry shows how service fees can vary; for example, Canadian mutual fund companies charge up to double what Americans pay in service fees. And a study by Toronto-based independent research company FundMonitor.com revealed that investors paying premium fees for their mutual funds, believing that they would in turn have better management and higher returns, can end up losing money. The study of 3,600 mutual funds sold in Canada measured whether there was a correlation between what investors paid in fees and fund performance. It found that most funds weren't returning more for the extra investment; some funds actually showed a negative correlation, most likely because management fees had eaten up any extra returns the fund might have earned. Investors were, in fact, paying more to do worse. However, for funds that focus on the global science or technology sectors or those buying emerging markets, higher prices actually did deliver better returns. Still, service fees take a bigger bite than some investors realize. Pennsylvania-based Vanguard Group Inc. estimates that a $10,000 investment in a fund with a 2% management fee that brings in 12% annually would total about $1 million after 40 years — that is, before fees. After the service fees have cut into the compound interest, the investor gets half as much, or $500,000.

Source: Kevin Libin, "Big Bucks, Big Whammy," *Canadian Business*, August 19, 2002.

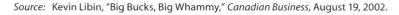

Proration Method

The second method is called the **proration** method. It can be argued that, when underapplied or overapplied overhead is material in amount at the end of the year, the amount should be allocated among Work in Process Inventory, Finished Goods Inventory, and Cost of Goods Sold. In this method, therefore, the under- or overapplied overhead is prorated among these three accounts. This is done by first determining the ratio of each account's balance to the total of the three account balances together, and then applying this ratio to the under- or overapplied overhead amount. The result of this method is that the total of these ending account balances equals the actual costs incurred. To illustrate, assume that Wallace Manufacturing has $10,000 of underapplied overhead in Manufacturing Overhead at December 31 and the following account balances at year end:

Work in Process Inventory	$ 10,000
Finished Goods Inventory	20,000
Cost of Goods Sold	70,000
Total costs	$100,000

If we considered the $10,000 of underapplied overhead in Manufacturing Overhead at December 31 is material, the adjusting journal entry to close the underapplied overhead would be:

Dec. 31	Manufacturing Overhead		10,000
	Work in Process Inventory ($10,000 ÷ $100,000) × $10,000	1,000	
	Finished Goods Inventory ($20,000 ÷ $100,000) × $10,000	2,000	
	Cost of Goods Sold ($70,000 ÷ $100,000) × $10,000	7,000	
	To close manufacturing overhead.		

However, most firms do not believe this type of allocation is worth the cost and effort. The under- or overapplied overhead is usually adjusted to Cost of Goods Sold because most of the jobs will be completed and sold during the year.

Decision Toolkit

Decision Checkpoints	Info Needed for Decision	Tools to Use for Decision	How to Evaluate Results
Has the company over- or underapplied overhead for the period?	Actual overhead costs and overhead applied	Manufacturing Overhead account	If the account balance is a credit, the overhead applied exceeded the actual overhead cost. If the account balance is a debit, the overhead applied was less than the actual overhead cost.

BEFORE YOU GO ON . . .

▶ Review It

1. When are entries made to record the completion and sale of a job?
2. What costs are included in the total manufacturing cost in the cost of goods manufactured schedule?
3. How is under- or overapplied manufacturing overhead reported in monthly financial statements?

Using the Decision Toolkit

Doctor Garage Inc. is a large manufacturer and marketer of unique, custom-made residential garage doors, as well as a major supplier of industrial and commercial doors, grilles, and counter shutters for the new construction, repair, and remodel markets. Doctor Garage Inc. has developed plans for continued expansion of a network of service operations that sell, install, and service manufactured fireplaces, garage doors, and related products.

Doctor Garage Inc. uses a job cost system and applies overhead to production on the basis of direct labour cost. In calculating a predetermined overhead rate for the year 2005, the company estimated manufacturing overhead to be $24 million and direct labour costs to be $20 million. In addition, the following information is available:

Actual costs incurred during 2005	
Direct materials used	$30,000,000
Direct labour cost incurred	21,000,000

Manufacturing costs incurred during 2005	
Insurance—factory	$ 500,000
Indirect labour	7,500,000
Maintenance	1,000,000
Rent on building	11,000,000
Amortization on equipment	2,000,000

Instructions

Answer each of the following questions.

(a) Why is Doctor Garage Inc. using a job-order costing system?

(b) On what basis does Doctor Garage Inc. allocate its manufacturing overhead? Calculate the predetermined overhead rate for the current year.

(c) Calculate the amount of the under- or overapplied overhead for 2005.

(d) Doctor Garage Inc. had beginning and ending balances in its work in process and finished goods accounts as follows:

	January 1, 2005	December 31, 2005
Work in process	$ 5,000,000	$ 4,000,000
Finished goods	13,000,000	11,000,000

Determine the (1) cost of goods manufactured and (2) cost of goods sold for Doctor Garage Inc. during 2005. Assume that any under- or overapplied overhead should be included in the cost of goods sold.

(e) During 2005, Job G408 was started and completed. Its cost sheet showed a total cost of $100,000, and the company prices its product at 50% above its cost. What is the price to the customer if the company follows this pricing strategy?

Solution

(a) The company is using a job-order system because each job (or batch) must have its own distinguishing characteristics. For example, each type of garage door would be different, and therefore a different cost per garage door should be assigned.

(b) The company allocates its overhead on the basis of direct labour cost. The predetermined overhead rate is 120%, calculated as follows:

$$\$24,000,000 \div \$20,000,000 = 120\%$$

(c)	Actual manufacturing overhead	$22,000,000	
	Applied overhead cost ($21,000,000 × 120%)	25,200,000	
	Overapplied overhead	$ 3,200,000	
(d)	1. Work in process, January 1, 2005		$ 5,000,000
	Direct materials used	$30,000,000	
	Direct labour	21,000,000	
	Manufacturing overhead applied	25,200,000	
	Total manufacturing cost		76,200,000
	Total cost of work in process		81,200,000
	Less: Work in process, December 31, 2005		4,000,000
	Cost of goods manufactured		$77,200,000
	2. Finished goods inventory, January 1, 2005	$13,000,000	
	Cost of goods manufactured (see above)	77,200,000	
	Cost of goods available for sale	90,200,000	
	Finished goods inventory, December 31, 2005	11,000,000	
	Cost of goods sold (unadjusted)	79,200,000	
	Less: Overapplied overhead	3,200,000	
	Cost of goods sold	$76,000,000	

(e)	G408 cost	$ 100,000
	Markup percentage	× 50%
	Profit	$ 50,000
	Price to customer: $150,000 ($100,000 + 50,000)	

Summary of Study Objectives

1. **Explain the characteristics and purposes of cost accounting.** Cost accounting involves the procedures for measuring, recording, and reporting product costs. From the data accumulated, the total cost and the unit cost of each product are determined. The two basic types of cost accounting systems are job-order cost and process cost.

2. **Describe the flow of costs in a job-order cost accounting system.** In job-order cost accounting, manufacturing costs are first accumulated in three accounts: Raw Materials Inventory, Factory Labour, and Manufacturing Overhead. The accumulated costs are then assigned to Work in Process Inventory and eventually to Finished Goods Inventory and Cost of Goods Sold.

3. **Explain the nature and importance of a job cost sheet.** A job cost sheet is a form used to record the costs that are chargeable to a specific job and to determine the total and unit costs of the completed job. Job cost sheets make up the subsidiary ledger for the Work in Process Inventory control account.

4. **Indicate how the predetermined overhead rate is determined and used.** The predetermined overhead rate is based on the relationship between estimated annual overhead costs and expected annual operating activity. This is expressed in terms of a common activity base, such as direct labour cost. The rate is used in assigning overhead costs to work in process and to specific jobs.

5. **Prepare entries for jobs completed and sold.** When jobs are completed, the cost is debited to Finished Goods Inventory and credited to Work in Process Inventory. When a job is sold, the entries are as follows: (a) Debit Cash or Accounts Receivable and credit Sales for the selling price. And (b) debit Cost of Goods Sold and credit Finished Goods Inventory for the cost of the goods.

6. **Distinguish between underapplied and overapplied manufacturing overhead.** Underapplied manufacturing overhead means that the overhead assigned to work in process is less than the overhead incurred. Overapplied overhead means that the overhead assigned to work in process is greater than the overhead incurred.

Decision Toolkit—A Summary

Decision Checkpoints	Info Needed for Decision	Tools to Use for Decision	How to Evaluate Results
What is the cost of a job?	Cost of material, labour, and overhead assigned to a specific job	Job cost sheet	Compare the costs to those of previous periods and to those of competitors to ensure that costs are reasonable. Compare costs to the expected selling price or to service fees that are charged to determine the overall profitability.
Has the company over- or underapplied overhead for the period?	Actual overhead costs and overhead applied	Manufacturing Overhead account	If the account balance is a credit, the overhead applied exceeded the actual overhead cost. If the account balance is a debit, the overhead applied was less than the actual overhead cost.

Glossary

Key Term Matching Activity

Actual costing system A cost accounting system in which costs are assigned to a cost object by using data on actual costs incurred during the accounting period. (p. 57)

Cost accounting An area of accounting that involves measuring, recording, and reporting product costs. (p. 48)

Cost accounting system Manufacturing cost accounts that are fully integrated into the general ledger of a company. (p. 48)

Job cost sheet A form used to record the costs that are chargeable to a job and to determine the total and unit costs of the completed job. (p. 53)

Job-order cost system A cost accounting system in which costs are assigned to each job or batch. (p. 48)

Materials requisition slip A document authorizing the issue of raw materials from the storeroom to production. (p. 53)

Normal costing system A cost accounting system that traces direct costs to a cost object by using the actual cost data incurred during the accounting period and that allocates indirect costs based on the predetermined rate(s) times the actual quantity of the cost-allocation base(s). (p. 57)

Overapplied overhead A situation in which overhead assigned to work in process is greater than the overhead incurred. (p. 62)

Predetermined overhead rate A rate based on the relationship between the estimated annual overhead costs and the expected annual operating activity, expressed in terms of a common activity base. (p. 56)

Process cost system A system of accounting that is used when a large volume of similar products are manufactured. (p. 49)

Proration The process of assigning overapplied or underapplied overhead costs to the inventory accounts Work in Process and Finished Goods, and to Cost of Goods Sold. (p. 63)

Summary entry A journal entry that summarizes the totals from multiple transactions. (p. 52)

Time ticket A document that indicates the employee, the hours worked, the account and job to be charged, and the total labour cost. (p. 55)

Underapplied overhead A situation in which the overhead assigned to work in process is less than the overhead incurred. (p. 62)

Demonstration Problem

During February, Cardella Manufacturing works on two jobs: A16 and B17. Summary data for these jobs are as follows:

Manufacturing Costs Incurred

Raw materials purchased on account: $54,000
Factory labour: $76,000, plus $4,000 of employer payroll taxes
Manufacturing overhead exclusive of indirect materials and indirect labour: $59,800

Animated
Demonstration
Problem

Assignment of Costs

Direct materials: Job No. A16, $27,000; Job No. B17, $21,000
Indirect materials: $3,000
Direct labour: Job No. A16, $52,000; Job No. B17, $26,000
Indirect labour: $2,000
Manufacturing overhead rate: 80% of direct labour costs

Job A16 was completed and sold on account for $150,000. Job B17 was only partially completed.

Instructions

(a) Journalize the February transactions in the sequence used in the chapter.
(b) What was the amount of under- or overapplied manufacturing overhead?
(c) Assuming the under- or overapplied overhead for the year is not allocated to inventory accounts, prepare the adjusting entry to assign the amount to Cost of Goods Sold.

Action Plan

- In accumulating costs, debit three accounts: Raw Materials Inventory, Factory Labour, and Manufacturing Overhead.
- When Work in Process Inventory is debited, credit one of the three accounts listed above.
- Debit Finished Goods Inventory for the cost of completed jobs. Debit Cost of Goods Sold for the cost of jobs sold.
- Overhead is underapplied when Manufacturing Overhead has a debit balance.

Solution to Demonstration Problem

(a)

			(1)		
Feb. 28		Raw Materials Inventory		54,000	
		Accounts Payable			54,000
		Purchase of raw materials on account.			

			(2)		
	28	Factory Labour		80,000	
		Factory Wages Payable			76,000
		Employer Payroll Taxes Payable			4,000
		To record factory labour costs.			

			(3)		
	28	Manufacturing Overhead		59,800	
		Accounts Payable, Accumulated Amortization, and Prepaid Insurance			59,800
		To record overhead costs.			

			(4)		
	28	Work in Process Inventory		48,000	
		Manufacturing Overhead		3,000	
		Raw Materials Inventory			51,000
		To assign raw materials to production.			

			(5)		
	28	Work in Process Inventory		78,000	
		Manufacturing Overhead		2,000	
		Factory Labour			80,000
		To assign factory labour to production.			

			(6)		
	28	Work in Process Inventory		62,400	
		Manufacturing Overhead (80% × $78,000)			62,400
		To assign overhead to jobs.			

			(7)		
Feb. 28		Finished Goods Inventory		120,600	
		Work in Process Inventory			120,600
		To record completion of Job A16: direct materials $27,000, direct labour $52,000, and manufacturing overhead $41,600.			

			(8)		
	28	Accounts Receivable		150,000	
		Sales			150,000
		To record sale of Job A16.			
	28	Cost of Goods Sold		120,600	
		Finished Goods Inventory			120,600
		To record cost of sale for Job A16.			

(b) Manufacturing Overhead has a debit balance of $2,400 as shown below:

Manufacturing Overhead			
(3)	59,800	(6)	62,400
(4)	3,000		
(5)	2,000		
Bal.	2,400		

Thus, manufacturing overhead is underapplied for the month.

(c) The adjusting entry for the underapplied overhead is:

Cost of Goods Sold	2,400	
Manufacturing Overhead		2,400
To close underapplied overhead to cost of goods sold.		

After this entry is posted, Manufacturing Overhead will have a zero balance. In preparing an income statement for the year, the amount reported for cost of goods sold will be the account balance after the adjustment for underapplied overhead.

Self-Study Questions

Additional Self-Study Questions

www.wiley.com/canada/managerial/

Answers are at the end of the chapter.

(SO 1)   1. Cost accounting involves the measuring, recording, and reporting of:
    (a) product costs.
    (b) future costs.
    (c) manufacturing processes.
    (d) managerial accounting decisions.

(SO 2)   2. In accumulating raw materials costs, the cost of raw materials purchased in a perpetual system is debited to:
    (a) Raw Materials Purchases.
    (b) Raw Materials Inventory.
    (c) Purchases.
    (d) Work in Process.

(SO 2)   3. When incurred, factory labour costs are debited to:
    (a) Work in Process.
    (b) Factory Wages Expense.
    (c) Factory Labour.
    (d) Factory Wages Payable.

(SO 3)   4. The source documents for assigning costs to job cost sheets are:
    (a) invoices, time tickets, and the predetermined overhead rate.
    (b) materials requisition slips, time tickets, and the actual overhead costs.
    (c) materials requisition slips, the payroll register, and the predetermined overhead rate.
    (d) materials requisition slips, time tickets, and the predetermined overhead rate.

(SO 3)   5. In recording the issue of raw materials in a job-order cost system, it would be incorrect to:
    (a) debit Work in Process Inventory.
    (b) debit Finished Goods Inventory.
    (c) debit Manufacturing Overhead.
    (d) credit Raw Materials Inventory.

6. The entry when direct factory labour is assigned (SO 3)
to jobs is a debit to:
    (a) Work in Process Inventory and a credit to Factory Labour.
    (b) Manufacturing Overhead and a credit to Factory Labour.
    (c) Factory Labour and a credit to Manufacturing Overhead.
    (d) Factory Labour and a credit to Work in Process Inventory.

7. The formula for calculating the predetermined (SO 4)
manufacturing overhead rate is estimated annual overhead costs divided by an expected annual operating activity. The operating activity is:
    (a) direct labour cost.   (c) machine hours.
    (b) direct labour hours. (d) any of the above.

8. In Crawford Company, the predetermined over- (SO 4)
head rate is 80% of the direct labour cost. During the month, $210,000 of factory labour costs are incurred, of which $180,000 is direct labour and $30,000 is indirect labour. The actual overhead incurred was $200,000. The amount of overhead debited to Work in Process Inventory should be:
    (a) $120,000.   (c) $168,000.
    (b) $144,000.   (d) $160,000.

9. In Mynex Company, Job No. 26 is completed at (SO 5)
a cost of $4,500 and later sold for $7,000 cash. A correct entry is:
    (a) Debit Finished Goods Inventory $7,000 and credit Work in Process Inventory $7,000.
    (b) Debit Cost of Goods Sold $7,000 and credit Finished Goods Inventory $7,000.
    (c) Debit Finished Goods Inventory $4,500 and credit Work in Process Inventory $4,500.
    (d) Debit Accounts Receivable $7,000 and credit Sales $7,000.

Questions

1. Tim Turner is studying for an accounting midterm examination. What should Tim know about how management may use job cost data?

2. (a) Kent Krause is not sure about the differences between cost accounting and a cost accounting system. Explain the differences to Kent. (b) Name an important feature of a cost accounting system.

3. (a) Distinguish between the two types of cost accounting systems. (b) Can a company use both types of cost accounting systems?

4. What type of industry is likely to use a job-order cost system? Give some examples.

5. What type of industry is likely to use a process cost system? Give some examples.

6. Your roommate asks for your help in understanding the major steps in the flow of costs in a job-order cost system. Identify the steps for your roommate.

7. There are three inventory control accounts in a job order system. Identify the control accounts and their subsidiary ledgers.

8. What source documents are used in accumulating direct labour costs?

9. "Entries to manufacturing overhead are normally only made daily." Do you agree? Explain.

10. Alan Bruski is confused about the source documents that are used in assigning materials and labour costs. Identify the documents and give the entry for each document.

11. What is the purpose of a job cost sheet?

12. Indicate the source documents that are used in charging costs to specific jobs.

13. Differentiate between a "materials inventory record" and a "materials requisition slip," as used in a job-order cost system.

14. Joe Gruber believes actual manufacturing overhead should be charged to jobs. Do you agree? Why or why not?

15. What relationships are involved in calculating a predetermined overhead rate?

16. How can the agreement of Work in Process Inventory and job-cost sheets be verified?

17. Jane Jelk believes that the cost of goods manufactured schedule in job-order cost accounting is the same as in manufacturing accounting. Is Jane correct? Explain.

18. Alex Cesska is confused about under- and overapplied manufacturing overhead. Define the terms for Alex, and indicate the balance in the manufacturing overhead account that is applicable to each term.

19. "Under- or overapplied overhead is reported in the income statement when monthly financial statements are prepared." Do you agree? If not, indicate the proper presentation.

20. "At the end of the year, under- or overapplied overhead is closed to Income Summary." Is this correct? If not, indicate the usual treatment of this account.

Brief Exercises

Prepare flowchart of job-order cost accounting system, and identify transactions.
(SO 2)

BE2–1 Sandy Tool & Die begins operations on January 1. Because all work is done to customer specifications, the company decides to use a job-order cost accounting system. Prepare a flowchart of a typical job-order system with arrows showing the flow of costs. Identify the eight transactions.

Prepare entries in accumulating manufacturing costs.
(SO 2)

BE2–2 During the first month of operations, Sandy Tool & Die accumulated the following manufacturing costs: raw materials, $3,000 on account; factory labour, $5,000, of which $4,500 relates to factory wages payable and $500 relates to payroll taxes payable; and utilities payable, $2,000. Prepare separate journal entries for each type of manufacturing cost.

Prepare entry for assignment of raw materials costs.
(SO 2)

BE2–3 In January, Sandy Tool & Die requisitions raw materials for production as follows: Job No. 1, $900; Job No. 2, $1,200; Job No. 3, $500; and general factory use, $600. Prepare a summary journal entry to record the raw materials used.

Prepare entry for assignment of factory labour costs.
(SO 2)

BE2–4 Factory labour data for Sandy Tool & Die is given in BE2–2. During January, time tickets show that the factory labour of $5,000 was used as follows: Job No. 1, $1,200; Job No. 2, $1,600; Job No. 3, $1,700; and general factory use, $500. Prepare a summary journal entry to record factory labour used.

BE2–5   Data pertaining to job cost sheets for Sandy Tool & Die are given in BE2–3 and BE2–4. Prepare the job cost sheets for each of the three jobs. (*Note*: You may omit the column for manufacturing overhead.)

Prepare job cost sheets.
(SO 3)

BE2–6   Burrand Company estimates that annual manufacturing overhead costs will be $600,000. Estimated annual operating activity bases are as follows: direct labour cost $500,000; direct labour hours 50,000; and machine hours 100,000. Calculate the predetermined overhead rate for each activity base.

Calculate predetermined overhead rates.
(SO 4)

BE2–7   During the first quarter, Sota Company incurs the following direct labour costs: January $40,000; February $30,000; and March $50,000. For each month, prepare the entry to assign the overhead to production, using a predetermined rate of 120% of the direct labour cost.

Assign manufacturing overhead to production.
(SO 4)

BE2–8   In March, Caroline Company completes Job Nos. 10 and 11. Job No. 10 cost $25,000 and Job No. 11 cost $32,000. On March 31, Job No. 10 is sold to the customer for $35,000 in cash. Journalize the entries for the completion of the two jobs and the sale of Job No. 10.

Prepare entries for completion and sale of completed jobs.
(SO 5)

BE2–9   At December 31, balances in Manufacturing Overhead are as follows: Apex Company—debit $1,200; Lopez Company—credit $900. Prepare the adjusting entry for each company at December 31, assuming the adjustment is made to Cost of Goods Sold.

Prepare adjusting entries for under- and overapplied overhead.
(SO 6)

Exercises

E2–1   The gross earnings of the factory workers for Darlinda Company during the month of January are $80,000. The employer's payroll taxes for the factory payroll are $8,000. The fringe benefits to be paid by the employer on this payroll are $4,000. Of the total accumulated cost of factory labour, 85% is related to direct labour and 15% is for indirect labour.

Prepare entries for factory labour.
(SO 2)

Instructions

(a) Prepare the entry to record the factory labour costs for the month of January.
(b) Prepare the entry to assign factory labour to production.

E2–2   Dooley Manufacturing uses a job-order cost accounting system. On May 1, the company has a balance in Work in Process Inventory of $3,200 and two jobs in process: Job No. 429 for $2,000; and Job No. 430 for $1,200. During May, a summary of source documents reveals the following:

Prepare journal entries for manufacturing costs.
(SO 2, 3, 4, 5)

Job Number	Materials Requisition Slips		Labour Time Tickets	
429	$2,500		$2,400	
430	3,500		3,000	
431	4,400	$10,400	7,600	$13,000
General use		800		1,200
		$11,200		$14,200

Dooley Manufacturing applies manufacturing overhead to jobs at an overhead rate of 90% of the direct labour cost. Job No. 429 is completed during the month.

Instructions

(a) Prepare summary journal entries to record the (1) requisition slips, (2) time tickets, (3) assignment of manufacturing overhead to jobs, and (4) completion of Job No. 429.
(b) Post the entries to Work in Process Inventory, and prove the agreement of the control account with the job cost sheets.

Analyze job cost sheet and prepare entries for manufacturing costs.
(SO 2, 3, 4, 5)

E2–3 A job order cost sheet for Bjerg Company is shown below:

Job No. 92			For 2,000 Units
Date	Direct Materials	Direct Labour	Manufacturing Overhead
Beg. bal. Jan. 1	5,000	6,000	4,200
8	6,000		
12		8,000	6,400
25	2,000		
27		4,000	3,200
	13,000	18,000	13,800

Cost of completed job:	
Direct materials	$13,000
Direct labour	18,000
Manufacturing overhead	13,800
Total cost	$44,800
Unit cost ($44,800 ÷ 2,000)	$ 22.40

Instructions

(a) Use the data to answer the following questions:
   1. What was the balance in Work in Process Inventory on January 1 if this was the only unfinished job?
   2. If manufacturing overhead is applied on the basis of the direct labour cost, what overhead rate was used in each year?

(b) ▭▭▶ Prepare the summary entries at January 31 to record the current year's transactions for Job No. 92.

Analyze manufacturing costs and determine missing amounts.
(SO 2, 5)

E2–4 Manufacturing cost data for Copa Company, which uses a job-order cost system, are presented below:

	Case A	Case B	Case C
Direct materials	$ (a)	$ 83,000	$ 63,150
Direct labour used	50,000	100,000	(h)
Manufacturing overhead applied	42,500	(d)	(i)
Total manufacturing cost	165,650	(e)	250,000
Work in Process, January 1, 2005	(b)	15,500	18,000
Total cost of work in process	201,500	(f)	(j)
Work in Process, December 31, 2005	(c)	11,800	(k)
Cost of goods manufactured	192,300	(g)	262,000

Instructions

Indicate the missing amount for each letter. Assume that in all cases manufacturing overhead is applied on the basis of the direct labour cost and the rate is the same.

Calculate manufacturing overhead rate and under- or overapplied overhead.
(SO 4, 6)

E2–5 Rodriguez Company applies manufacturing overhead to jobs based on machine hours used. Overhead costs are expected to total $300,000 for the year, and machine usage is estimated at 125,000 hours.

   In January, $28,000 of overhead costs are incurred and 12,000 machine hours are used. For the remainder of the year, $294,000 of overhead costs are incurred and 118,000 machine hours are used.

Instructions

(a) Calculate the manufacturing overhead rate for the year.
(b) What is the amount of under- or overapplied overhead at January 31? How should this amount be reported in the financial statements prepared on January 31?
(c) What is the amount of under- or overapplied overhead at December 31?
(d) Assuming the under- or overapplied overhead for the year is not allocated to inventory accounts, prepare the adjusting entry to assign the amount to Cost of Goods Sold.

E2–6 A job cost sheet for Battle Company follows:

Job Cost Sheet

Job No.: 469   Quantity: 2,000
Item: White Lion Cages   Date Requested: July 2
For: Tesla Company   Date Completed: July 31

Date	Direct Materials	Direct Labour	Manufacturing Overhead
July 10	825		
12	900		
15		440	528
22		380	456
24	1,600		
27	1,500		
31		540	648

Cost of completed job:
  Direct materials   _____
  Direct labour   _____
  Manufacturing overhead   _____
Total cost   _____
Unit cost   _____

Instructions

(a) Answer the following questions.
   1. What are the source documents for direct materials, direct labour, and manufacturing overhead costs assigned to this job?
   2. What is the predetermined manufacturing overhead rate?
   3. What are the total cost and the unit cost of the completed job?
(b) ▭▭▭▷ Prepare the entry to record the completion of the job.

E2–7 Laird Corporation had the following transactions:

  1. Purchased raw materials on account, $46,300.
  2. Raw materials of $36,000 were requisitioned to the factory. An analysis of the materials requisition slips indicated that $8,800 was classified as indirect materials.
  3. Factory labour costs incurred were $53,900, of which $49,000 was for factory wages payable and $4,900 was for employer payroll taxes payable.
  4. Time tickets indicated that $50,000 was direct labour and $3,900 was indirect labour.
  5. Overhead costs incurred on account were $80,500.
  6. Manufacturing overhead was applied at the rate of 150% of the direct labour cost.
  7. Goods costing $88,000 were completed and transferred to finished goods.
  8. Finished goods that cost $75,000 to manufacture were sold on account for $103,000.

Instructions

Journalize the transactions. (Omit explanations.)

E2–8 Tombert Printing Corp. uses a job-order cost system. The following data summarize the operations related to the first quarter's production:

  1. Materials purchased on account, $192,000; factory wages incurred, $87,300
  2. Materials requisitioned and factory labour used by job:

Job Number	Materials	Factory Labour
A20	$ 32,240	$18,000
A21	42,920	22,000
A22	36,100	15,000
A23	39,270	25,000
General factory use	4,470	7,300
	$155,000	$87,300

  3. Manufacturing overhead costs incurred on account, $39,500
  4. Amortization on machinery and equipment, $14,550

5. Manufacturing overhead rate: 70% of direct labour cost
6. Jobs completed during the quarter: A20, A21, and A23

Instructions

Prepare entries to record the operations summarized above. (Prepare a schedule showing the individual cost elements and total cost for each job in item 6.)

Prepare cost of goods manufactured schedule and partial financial statements.
(SO 2, 5)

E2–9   At May 31, 2005, the accounts of Yellow Knife Manufacturing Company show the following:

1. May 1 inventories—finished goods $12,600; work in process $14,700; and raw materials $8,200
2. May 31 inventories—finished goods $11,500; work in process $17,900; and raw materials $7,100
3. Debit postings to Work in Process: direct materials $62,400; direct labour $32,000; and manufacturing overhead applied $48,000
4. Total sales: $200,000

Instructions

(a) Prepare a condensed cost of goods manufactured schedule.
(b) Prepare an income statement for May through gross profit.
(c) Indicate the balance sheet presentation of the manufacturing inventories at May 31, 2005.

Calculate work in process and finished goods from job cost sheets.
(SO 2, 3, 5)

E2–10   Tomlin Company begins operations on April 1. Information from job cost sheets shows the following:

	Manufacturing Costs Assigned			
Job Number	April	May	June	Month Completed
10	$5,200	$4,400		May
11	6,100	3,900	$3,000	June
12	1,200			April
13		4,700	4,500	June
14		3,900	3,600	Not complete

Job No. 12 was completed in April. Job No. 10 was completed in May. Job Nos. 11 and 13 were completed in June. Each job was sold for 50% above its cost in the month following completion.

Instructions

(a) What is the balance in Work in Process Inventory at the end of each month?
(b) What is the balance in Finished Goods Inventory at the end of each month?
(c) What is the gross profit for May, June, and July?

Problems: Set A

Calculate predetermined overhead rate and job cost.
(SO 2, 3, 4)

P2–11A   Mitchell Corp. has the following estimated costs for 2005:

Direct materials	$ 60,000
Direct labour	2,000,000
Rent on factory building	150,000
Sales salaries	250,000
Amortization on factory equipment	80,000
Indirect labour	120,000
Production supervisor's salary	150,000
Machine hours	20,000

Mitchell Corp. estimates that 20,000 direct labour hours will be worked during the year. Manufacturing overhead is applied on the basis of machine-hours.

Instructions

(a) What will the overhead rate per machine hour be?
(b) What will the direct labour rate per hour be?

(c) What should the total cost be of a job that will take 200 machine hours, $15,000 of direct materials, and $5,000 of direct labour cost, using a *normal* cost system?

P2–12A Elite Manufacturing uses a job-order cost system and applies overhead to production on the basis of direct labour hours. On January 1, 2005, Job No. 25 was the only job in process. The costs incurred prior to January 1 on this job were as follows: direct materials $10,000; direct labour $6,000; and manufacturing overhead $9,000. Job No. 23 was completed at a cost of $45,000 and was part of finished goods inventory. There was a $5,000 balance in the Raw Materials Inventory account.

Prepare entries in job-order cost system and job cost sheets.
(SO 2, 3, 4, 5, 6)

During the month of January, the company began production on Jobs No. 26 and 27, and completed Job Nos. 25 and 26. Job Nos. 23 and 25 were sold on account during the month for $67,000 and $74,000, respectively. The following additional events occurred during the month.

1. Purchased additional raw materials for $45,000 on account.
2. Incurred factory labour costs of $35,500. Of this amount, $6,500 related to employer payroll taxes.
3. Incurred manufacturing overhead costs as follows: indirect materials $10,000; indirect labour $7,500; amortization expense $12,000; and various other manufacturing overhead costs on account for $6,000.
4. Assigned direct materials and direct labour to jobs as follows:

Job No.	Direct Materials	Direct Labour
25	$ 5,000	$ 3,000
26	20,000	12,000
27	15,000	9,000

5. The company uses direct labour hours as the activity base to assign overhead. Direct labour hours incurred on each job were as follows: Job No. 25, 200; Job No. 26, 800; and Job No. 27, 600.

Instructions

(a) Calculate the predetermined overhead rate for 2005, assuming Elite Manufacturing estimates total manufacturing overhead costs of $400,000, direct labour costs of $300,000, and direct labour hours of 20,000 for the year.
(b) Open job cost sheets for Job Nos. 25, 26, and 27. Enter the January 1 balances on the job cost sheet for Job No. 25.
(c) Prepare the journal entries to record the purchase of raw materials, the factory labour costs incurred, and the manufacturing overhead costs incurred during the month of January.
(d) Prepare the journal entries to record the assignment of direct materials, direct labour, and manufacturing overhead costs to production. In assigning manufacturing overhead costs, use the overhead rate calculated in (a). Post all costs to the job cost sheets as necessary.
(e) Total the job cost sheets for any job(s) completed during the month. Prepare the journal entry (or entries) to record the completion of any job(s) during the month.
(f) Prepare the journal entry (or entries) to record the sale of any job(s) during the month.
(g) What is the balance in the Work in Process Inventory account at the end of the month? What does this balance consist of?
(h) What is the amount of over- or underapplied overhead?

P2–13A For the year ended December 31, 2005, the job cost sheets of Sprague Company contained the following data:

Prepare entries in job-order cost system and partial income statement.
(SO 2, 3, 4, 5, 6)

Job Number	Explanation	Direct Materials	Direct Labour	Manufacturing Overhead	Total Cost
7650	Balance, January 1	$18,000	$20,000	$25,000	$ 63,000
	Current year's costs	27,000	30,000	37,500	94,500
7651	Balance, January 1	12,000	18,000	22,500	52,500
	Current year's costs	28,000	40,000	50,000	118,000
7652	Current year's costs	40,000	64,000	80,000	184,000

Other data:

1. Raw Materials Inventory totalled $20,000 on January 1. During the year, $100,000 of raw materials were purchased on account.

2. Finished goods on January 1 consisted of Job No. 7648 for $98,000 and Job No. 7649 for $62,000.
3. Job No. 7650 and Job No. 7651 were completed during the year.
4. Job Nos. 7648, 7649, and 7650 were sold on account for $490,000.
5. Manufacturing overhead incurred on account totalled $120,000.
6. Other manufacturing overhead consisted of indirect materials $12,000; indirect labour $18,000; and amortization on factory machinery $19,500.

Instructions

(a) Prove the agreement of Work in Process Inventory with job cost sheets for the unfinished work. (*Hint*: Use a single T account for Work in Process Inventory.) Calculate each of the following, then post each to the T account: (1) beginning balance, (2) direct materials, (3) direct labour, (4) manufacturing overhead, and (5) completed jobs.
(b) Prepare the adjusting entry for manufacturing overhead, assuming the balance is allocated entirely to Cost of Goods Sold.
(c) Determine the gross profit to be reported for 2005.

Prepare entries in job-order cost system and cost of goods manufactured schedule.
(SO 2, 3, 4, 5)

P2–14A   Steve Taylor is a contractor specializing in custom-built whirlpool baths. On May 1, 2005, his ledger contains the following data:

Raw Materials Inventory	$30,000
Work in Process Inventory	12,600
Manufacturing Overhead	2,500 (dr.)

The Manufacturing Overhead account has debit totals of $12,500 and credit totals of $10,000. Subsidiary data for Work in Process Inventory on May 1 follow:

	Job Cost Sheets		
Job by Customer	Direct Materials	Direct Labour	Manufacturing Overhead
Farley	$2,500	$2,000	$1,600
Hendricks	2,000	1,200	960
Minor	900	800	640
	$5,400	$4,000	$3,200

During May, the following costs were incurred: (a) raw materials purchased on account $5,000, (b) labour paid $8,000, (c) manufacturing overhead paid $1,400. A summary of materials requisition slips and time tickets for May reveals the following:

Job by Customer	Materials Requisition Slips	Time Tickets
Farley	$ 500	$ 400
Hendricks	600	1,000
Minor	2,300	1,300
Bennett	2,400	3,300
	5,800	6,000
General use	1,500	2,000
	$7,300	$8,000

Overhead was charged to jobs on the basis of $0.80 per dollar of direct labour cost. The whirlpool baths for customers Farley, Hendricks, and Minor were completed during May. Each bath was sold for $12,500 cash.

Instructions

(a) Prepare journal entries for the May transactions: (1) for the purchase of raw materials, factory labour costs incurred, and manufacturing overhead costs incurred; (2) for the assignment of direct materials, labour, and overhead to production; and (3) for the completion of jobs and the sale of goods.
(b) Post the entries to Work in Process Inventory.
(c) Reconcile the balance in Work in Process Inventory with the costs of unfinished jobs.
(d) Prepare a cost of goods manufactured schedule for May.

P2–15A Aquatic Manufacturing uses a job-order cost system in each of its three manufacturing departments. Manufacturing overhead is applied to jobs on the basis of direct labour cost in Department A, direct labour hours in Department B, and machine hours in Department C.

In establishing the predetermined overhead rates for 2005, the following estimates were made for the year:

Calculate predetermined overhead rates, apply overhead, and indicate statement presentation of under- or overapplied overhead. (SO 2, 4, 6)

	Department		
	A	B	C
Manufacturing overhead	$930,000	$800,000	$750,000
Direct labour cost	$600,000	$100,000	$600,000
Direct labour hours	50,000	40,000	40,000
Machine hours	100,000	120,000	150,000

During January, the job cost sheets showed the following costs and production data:

	Department		
	A	B	C
Direct materials used	$92,000	$86,000	$64,000
Direct labour cost	$48,000	$35,000	$50,400
Manufacturing overhead incurred	$76,000	$74,000	$61,500
Direct labour hours	4,000	3,500	4,200
Machine hours	8,000	10,500	12,600

Instructions

(a) Calculate the predetermined overhead rate for each department.
(b) Calculate the total manufacturing costs assigned to jobs in January in each department.
(c) Calculate the under- or overapplied overhead for each department at January 31.
(d) Indicate the statement presentation of the under- or overapplied overhead at January 31.

P2–16A Freedo Company's fiscal year ends on June 30. The following accounts are found in its job-order cost accounting system for the first month of the new fiscal year:

Analyze manufacturing accounts and determine missing amounts. (SO 2, 3, 4, 5, 6)

Raw Materials Inventory

July 1	Beginning balance	19,000	July 31	Requisitions	(a)
31	Purchases	90,400			
July 31	Ending balance	(b)			

Work in Process Inventory

July 1	Beginning balance	(c)	July 31	Jobs completed	(f)
31	Direct materials	80,000			
31	Direct labour	(d)			
31	Overhead	(e)			
July 31	Ending balance	(g)			

Finished Goods Inventory

July 1	Beginning balance	(h)	July 31	Cost of goods sold	(j)
31	Completed jobs	(i)			
July 31	Ending balance	(k)			

Factory Labour

July 31	Factory wages	(l)	July 31	Wages assigned	(m)

Manufacturing Overhead

July 31	Indirect materials	8,900	July 31	Overhead applied	117,000
31	Indirect labour	16,000			
31	Other overhead	(n)			

Other data:

1. On July 1, two jobs were in process: Job No. 4085 and Job No. 4086, with costs of $19,000 and $8,200, respectively.

2. During July, Job Nos. 4087, 4088, and 4089 were started. On July 31, only Job No. 4089 was unfinished. This job had charges for direct materials of $2,000 and direct labour of $1,000, plus manufacturing overhead. Manufacturing overhead was applied at the rate of 130% of the direct labour cost.
3. On July 1, Job No. 4084, costing $135,000, was in the finished goods warehouse. On July 31, Job No. 4088, costing $143,000, was in finished goods.
4. Overhead was underapplied by $3,000 in July.

Instructions

List the letters (a) through (n) and indicate the amount for each letter. Show all calculations.

Calculate job costs, inventories and prepare income statement in service organization.
(SO 2, 3, 4, 5, 6)

P2–17A Price-Gordon Architectural Consultants Ltd. uses a modified job-order costing system to keep track of project costs. During October 2005, the firm worked on four projects. The following table provides a summary of the cost of materials used and the number of consulting hours worked on each of the four projects in October:

Project Number	Cost of Materials	Consulting Hours Worked
80	$120	138
84	85	145
85	100	160
86	150	187

The records for September showed that 20 hours had been worked and $68 worth of materials had been used on Project 80. Projects 80 and 86 were completed in October, and bills were sent to the clients.

Consultants at Price-Gordon billed clients at $100 per consulting hour. The actual labour cost to the firm (based on salary cost) was $40 per hour. Overhead is charged to projects based on the consultants' time spent on the project. Total overhead for the current fiscal year, based on expected activity of 10,000 consulting hours, was estimated to be $267,000. This total overhead cost included a fixed portion of $84,000, which covered rent, amortization, and so on. Actual overhead for October was $21,455. Price-Gordon closes overapplied and underapplied overhead to Cost of Goods Sold at month end.

Instructions

(a) Determine the product costs for Project 80.
(b) Determine the balance in Work in Process as at October 31.
(c) Prepare the income statement for October 2005, including the appropriate amount of overapplied or underapplied overhead. Other expenses for October were $2,340.94.

(CMA Canada-adapted)

Prepare entries and close out under-or over-applied overhead.
(SO 4, 5, 6)

P2–18A Laramie Ltd. uses a normal job-order cost system. At the beginning of the month of June, two orders were in process, as follows:

	Order 8A	Order 10A
Raw materials	$1,000	$900
Direct labour	1,200	200
Manufacturing overhead absorbed	1,800	300

There was no inventory of finished goods on June 1. During the month of June, orders 11A and 12A, were put into process.

Raw materials requirements amounted to $13,000, direct labour expenses for the month were $20,000, and actual manufacturing overhead recorded during the month amounted to $28,000.

The only order in process at the end of June was order 12A, and the costs incurred for this order were $1,150 of raw materials and $1,000 of direct labour. In addition, order 11B, which was 100% complete, was still on hand as of June 30. Total costs allocated to this order were $3,300. The firm's overhead allocation rate in June was the same as the rate used in May and is based on labour cost.

Instructions

Prepare journal entries, with supporting calculations, to record the cost of goods manufactured, the cost of goods sold, and the closing of the over- or underapplied manufacturing overhead to Cost of Goods Sold.

(CMA Canada-adapted)

P2–19A Handy Widget Co. does a wide variety of metalwork on a custom basis. During the month of June 2005, six jobs were worked on. A summary of the job cost sheets on these jobs is given below:

Job No.	Direct Materials	Direct Labour	Factory Overhead Applied	Total Cost of Job
43	$ 410	$ 360	$ 288	$1,058
44	850	790	632	2,272
45	110	85	68	263
46	1,500	1,140	912	3,552
47	950	850	680	2,480
48ª	270	115	92	477
	$4,090	$3,340	$2,672	$10,102

ª Ending work in process

Handy Widget has used the same overhead rate on all jobs. Job No. 43 was the only job in process at the beginning of the month. At that time, it had incurred direct labour costs of $150 and total costs of $570.

Instructions

(a) What is the predetermined overhead rate being used by the Handy Widget Co.?
(b) Assume that during June the factory overhead was overapplied by $600. What was the actual factory overhead cost incurred during the month?
(c) What was the total amount of direct materials placed into production during June?
(d) How much direct labour cost was incurred during June?
(e) What was the cost of goods manufactured for June?
(f) The beginning finished goods inventory was $2,550. What was the cost of goods sold for the month if the ending finished goods inventory was $3,550?

(CGA-adapted)

Problems: Set B

P2–20B Consulting firm CMA Financial employs 30 full-time staff. The estimated compensation per employee is $75,000 for 2,000 hours. All direct labour costs are charged to clients. Any other costs are included in a single indirect cost pool, and are allocated based on labour hours. Actual indirect costs were $780,000. Estimated indirect costs for the coming year are $750,000. The firm expects to have 60 clients in the coming year.

Instructions

(a) What will the overhead rate per direct labour hour be?
(b) What will the direct labour rate per hour be?
(c) What should the total cost be of a job that will take 270 direct labour hours, using a normal cost system?

P2–21B Medina Manufacturing uses a job-order cost system and applies overhead to production based on direct labour costs. On January 1, 2005, Job No. 50 was the only job in process. The costs incurred prior to January 1 on this job were as follows: direct materials $20,000; direct labour $12,000; and manufacturing overhead $16,000. As at January 1, Job No. 49 had been completed at a cost of $90,000 and was part of finished goods inventory. There was a $15,000 balance in the Raw Materials Inventory account.

During the month of January, Medina Manufacturing began production on Job Nos. 51 and 52, and completed Job Nos. 50 and 51. Job Nos. 49 and 50 were also sold on account during the month for $122,000 and $158,000, respectively. The following additional events occurred during the month:

1. Purchased additional raw materials of $90,000 on account.
2. Incurred factory labour costs of $65,000. Of this amount, $13,000 was for employer payroll taxes.

3. Incurred manufacturing overhead costs as follows: indirect materials $14,000; indirect labour $15,000; amortization expense $19,000; and various other manufacturing overhead costs on account $20,000.

4. Assigned direct materials and direct labour to the jobs as follows:

Job No.	Direct Materials	Direct Labour
50	$10,000	$ 5,000
51	39,000	25,000
52	30,000	20,000

Instructions

(a) Calculate the predetermined overhead rate for 2005, assuming Medina Manufacturing estimates total manufacturing overhead costs of $980,000, direct labour costs of $700,000, and direct labour hours of 20,000 for the year.

(b) Open job cost sheets for Job Nos. 50, 51, and 52. Enter the January 1 balances on the job cost sheet for Job No. 50.

(c) Prepare the journal entries to record the purchase of raw materials, the factory labour costs incurred, and the manufacturing overhead costs incurred during the month of January.

(d) Prepare the journal entries to record the assignment of direct materials, direct labour, and manufacturing overhead costs to production. In assigning manufacturing overhead costs, use the overhead rate calculated in (a). Post all costs to the job cost sheets as necessary.

(e) Total the job cost sheets for any job(s) completed during the month. Prepare the journal entry (or entries) to record the completion of any job(s) during the month.

(f) Prepare the journal entry (or entries) to record the sale of any job(s) during the month.

(g) What is the balance in the Finished Goods Inventory account at the end of the month? What does this balance consist of?

Prepare entries in job-order cost system and partial income statement.
(SO 2, 3, 4, 5, 6)

P2–22B   For the year ended December 31, 2005, the job cost sheets of Amend Company contained the following data:

Job Number	Explanation	Direct Materials	Direct Labour	Manufacturing Overhead	Total Cost
7640	Balance, January 1	$25,000	$24,000	$28,800	$ 77,800
	Current year's costs	30,000	36,000	43,200	109,200
7641	Balance, January 1	11,000	18,000	21,600	50,600
	Current year's costs	40,000	48,000	57,600	145,600
7642	Current year's costs	48,000	50,000	60,000	158,000

Other data:

1. Raw materials inventory totalled $15,000 on January 1. During the year, $140,000 of raw materials were purchased on account.

2. Finished goods on January 1 consisted of Job No. 7638 for $87,000 and Job No. 7639 for $92,000.

3. Job No. 7640 and Job No. 7641 were completed during the year.

4. Job Nos. 7638, 7639, and 7641 were sold on account for $530,000.

5. Manufacturing overhead incurred on account totalled $115,000.

6. Other manufacturing overhead consisted of indirect materials $14,000, indirect labour $20,000, and amortization on factory machinery $8,000.

Instructions

(a) Prove the agreement of Work in Process Inventory with the job cost sheets for unfinished work. (*Hint*: Use a single T account for Work in Process Inventory.) Calculate each of the following, then post each to the T account: (1) beginning balance, (2) direct materials, (3) direct labour, (4) manufacturing overhead, and (5) completed jobs.

(b) Prepare the adjusting entry for manufacturing overhead, assuming the balance is allocated entirely to Cost of Goods Sold.

(c) Determine the gross profit to be reported for 2005.

P2–23B Zion Inc. is a construction company specializing in custom patios. The patios are constructed of concrete, brick, fibreglass, and lumber, depending on the customer's preference. On June 1, 2005, the general ledger for Zion Inc. contains the following data:

Prepare entries in job-order cost system and cost of goods manufactured schedule.
(SO 2, 3, 4, 5)

Raw Materials Inventory	$4,200	Manufacturing Overhead Applied	$32,640
Work in Process Inventory	$5,540	Manufacturing Overhead Incurred	$31,650

Subsidiary data for Work in Process Inventory on June 1 are as follows:

Job Cost Sheets

Cost Elements	Powell	Aurora	Hayden
		Custom Job	
Direct materials	$ 600	$ 800	$ 900
Direct labour	320	540	580
Manufacturing overhead	400	675	725
	$1,320	$2,015	$2,205

During June, raw materials purchased on account were $3,900, and all wages were paid. Additional overhead costs were amortization on equipment for $700 and miscellaneous costs of $400 incurred on account.

A summary of materials requisition slips and time tickets for June shows the following:

Job by Customer	Materials Requisition Slips	Time Tickets
Powell	$ 800	$ 450
Elgin	2,000	800
Aurora	500	360
Hayden	1,300	800
Chan	300	390
	4,900	2,800
General use	1,500	1,200
	$6,400	$4,000

Overhead was charged to jobs at the same rate of $1.25 per dollar of direct labour cost. The patios for customers Powell, Aurora, and Hayden were completed during June and sold for a total of $18,900. Each customer paid in full.

Instructions

(a) Journalize the June transactions: (1) for the purchase of raw materials, factory labour costs incurred, and manufacturing overhead costs incurred; (2) for the assignment of direct materials, labour, and overhead to production; and (3) for the completion of jobs and sale of goods.
(b) Post the entries to Work in Process Inventory.
(c) Reconcile the balance in Work in Process Inventory with the costs of unfinished jobs.
(d) Prepare a cost of goods manufactured schedule for June.

P2–24B Stein Manufacturing Company uses a job-order cost system in each of its three manufacturing departments. Manufacturing overhead is applied to jobs on the basis of direct labour cost in Department D, direct labour hours in Department E, and machine hours in Department K.

Calculate predetermined overhead rate, apply overhead, and indicate statement presentation of under- or overapplied overhead.
(SO 4, 6)

In establishing the predetermined overhead rates for 2006, the following estimates were made for the year:

	Department		
	D	E	K
Manufacturing overhead	$1,200,000	$1,500,000	$900,000
Direct labour cost	$1,500,000	$1,250,000	$450,000
Direct labour hours	100,000	125,000	40,000
Machine hours	400,000	500,000	120,000

During January, the job cost sheets showed the following costs and production data:

	Department		
	D	E	K
Direct materials used	$140,000	$126,000	$78,000
Direct labour cost	$120,000	$110,000	$37,500
Manufacturing overhead incurred	$98,000	$129,000	$74,000
Direct labour hours	8,000	11,000	3,500
Machine hours	34,000	45,000	10,400

Instructions

(a) Calculate the predetermined overhead rate for each department.
(b) Calculate the total manufacturing costs assigned to jobs in January in each department.
(c) Calculate the under- or overapplied overhead for each department at January 31.
(d) Indicate the statement presentation of the under- or overapplied overhead at January 31.
(e) If the amount in (d) was the same at December 31, how would it be reported in the year-end financial statements?

Analyze manufacturing accounts and determine missing amounts.
(SO 2, 3, 4, 5, 6)

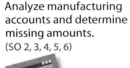

P2–25B   Vargas Corporation's fiscal year ends on November 30. The following accounts are found in its job-order cost accounting system for the first month of the new fiscal year:

Raw Materials Inventory

Dec. 1	Beginning balance	(a)	Dec. 31	Requisitions	16,850
31	Purchases	19,225			
Dec. 31	Ending balance	7,975			

Work in Process Inventory

Dec. 1	Beginning balance	(b)	Dec. 31	Jobs completed	(e)
31	Direct materials	(c)			
31	Direct labour	8,800			
31	Overhead	(d)			
Dec. 31	Ending balance	(f)			

Finished Goods Inventory

Dec. 1	Beginning balance	(g)	Dec. 31	Cost of goods sold	(i)
31	Completed jobs	(h)			
Dec. 31	Ending balance	(j)			

Factory Labour

Dec. 31	Factory wages	12,025	Dec. 31	Wages assigned	(k)

Manufacturing Overhead

Dec. 31	Indirect materials	1,900	Dec. 31	Overhead applied	(m)
31	Indirect labour	(l)			
31	Other overhead	1,245			

Other data:

1. On December 1, two jobs were in process: Job No. 154 and Job No. 155. These jobs had combined direct materials costs of $9,750 and direct labour costs of $15,000. Overhead was applied at a rate that was 75% of the direct labour cost.
2. During December, Job Nos. 156, 157, and 158 were started. On December 31, Job No. 158 was unfinished. This job had charges for direct materials of $3,800 and direct labour of $4,800, plus manufacturing overhead. All jobs except Job No. 158 were completed in December.
3. On December 1, Job No. 153 was in the finished goods warehouse. It had a total cost of $5,000. On December 31, Job No. 157 was the only job finished that was not sold. It had a cost of $4,000.
4. Manufacturing overhead was $230 overapplied in December.

Instructions

List the letters (a) through (m) and indicate the amount for each letter. Show all calculations.

P2–26B   Nicole Limited is a company that produces machinery to customer orders, using a normal job cost system. Manufacturing overhead is applied to production using a predetermined rate. This overhead rate is set at the beginning of each fiscal year by forecasting the year's overhead and relating it to direct labour costs. The budget for 2004 follows:

Calculate predetermined overhead rate and proration of overhead.
(SO 4, 5, 6)

Direct labour	$1,200,000
Manufacturing overhead	720,000

As at the end of the year, two jobs were incomplete. These were 1768B, with total direct labour charges of $11,000, and 1819C, with total direct labour charges of $39,000. On these jobs, machine hours were 287 hours for 1768B and 647 hours for 1819C. Direct materials issued for 1768B amounted to $22,000 and for 1819C they amounted to $42,000.

Total charges to the Manufacturing Overhead Control account for the year were $897,000, and direct labour charges made to all jobs amounted to $1,583,600, representing 247,216 direct labour hours.

There were no beginning inventories. In addition to the ending work in process just described, the ending finished goods inventory account showed a balance of $72,000.

Sales for the year amounted to $2,700,680, cost of goods sold totalled $648,000, and selling, general, and administrative expenses were $1,857,870.

The amounts for inventories and the cost of goods sold were not adjusted for any over- or underapplication of manufacturing overhead to production. It is the company's practice to allocate any over- or underapplied overhead to inventories and the cost of goods sold.

Instructions

(a) Calculate the under- or overapplied manufacturing overhead for 2004.
(b) Prorate the amount calculated in (1) based on the ending balances (before prorating) of Work in Process, Finished Goods, and Cost of Goods Sold.
(c) Prepare an income statement for the company for the year. The income tax rate is 40%.
(CMA Canada-adapted)

P2–27B   On November 30, 2004, there was a fire in the factory of Able Manufacturing Limited, where you work as the controller. The work in process inventory was completely destroyed, but both the materials and finished goods inventory were undamaged.

Analyze job-order cost system and calculate work-in-process.
(SO 2, 3, 4, 6)

Able uses normal job-order costing and its fiscal year end is December 31. Selected information for the period ending October 31, 2004, and November 30, 2004, follows:

	October 31, 2004	November 30, 2004
Stores (including both direct and indirect materials)	$ 79,250	$ 73,250
Work-in-process inventory	58,875	?
Finished goods inventory	60,000	63,000
Cost of goods sold (year to date)	576,000	656,000
Accounts payable (relates to materials purchased only)	17,960	53,540
Manufacturing overhead incurred (year to date)	129,500	163,300
Manufacturing overhead applied	128,700	?

Other information for November 2004:

Cash payments to suppliers	$40,000
Payroll (including $15,375 indirect)	83,500
Indirect materials used	4,848
Overapplied overhead (during November only)	1,750

Instructions

Calculate the normal cost of the work in process inventory lost during the fire.
(CGA-adapted)

P2–28B   Information for Merit Manufacturing Ltd. at May 1, 2005, is given below:

Prepare t-accounts in comprehensive manufacturing job cost system and compare process costing.
(SO 2, 3, 4, 5)

Inventories:	
Raw materials (all direct)	$2,500
Work in process	1,040
Finished goods	1,890

Transactions in May 2005:

1. Purchased $22,400 of direct materials on account.

2. Transferred $18,800 of direct materials into production.
3. Production wages totalled $6,500, of which direct labour accounted for $5,000.
4. The salary in May for the production supervisor was $3,000.
5. The total utility cost was $520, of which $410 was variable and $110 was fixed.
6. Transferred $1,300 of indirect material from factory supplies into production.
7. Amortization on factory assets for May was $22,500.
8. Amortization of prepaid insurance on factory assets was $1,600.

Other information:

1. The company transfers actual overhead costs during each month to the work in process inventory account. It uses separate accounts to record the incurrence of fixed and variable overhead.
2. During May, goods with a value of $52,450 were completed and transferred to finished goods.
3. During May, finished goods with a value of $51,315 were sold on account for $74,670.

Instructions

(a) Using T accounts, show the flow of costs into and out of the factory overhead, inventory, and cost of goods sold accounts for the month of May. Also calculate the value of each of the inventories of materials, work in process, and finished goods at the end of May 2005. Be sure to use separate accounts as necessary.
(b) Name an industry or product for which job-order costing would be appropriate and one for which process costing would be appropriate. Identify four differences between the production processes for job-order and process costing.

(CGA-adapted)

Additional Cases

Cases

C2–29   Wang Products Company uses a job-order cost system. For a few months, there has been an ongoing battle between the sales department and the production department concerning a special-order product, TC-1. TC-1 is a seasonal product that is manufactured in batches of 1,000 units. TC-1 is sold at cost plus a markup of 40% of cost.

The sales department is unhappy because fluctuating unit production costs significantly affect selling prices. Sales personnel complain that this has caused excessive customer complaints and the loss of many orders for TC-1.

The production department maintains that each job order must be fully costed based on the costs incurred during the period in which the goods are produced. Production personnel maintain that the only real solution to the problem is for the sales department to increase sales in the slow periods.

Sandra Devona, president of the company, asks you as the company accountant to collect quarterly data for the past year on TC-1. From the cost accounting system, you accumulate the following production quantity and cost data:

Costs	Quarter			
	1	2	3	4
Direct materials	$100,000	$220,000	$ 80,000	$200,000
Direct labour	60,000	132,000	48,000	120,000
Manufacturing overhead	105,000	153,000	97,000	125,000
Total	$265,000	$505,000	$225,000	$445,000
Production in batches	5	11	4	10
Unit cost (per batch)	$ 53,000	$ 45,909	$ 56,250	$ 44,500

Instructions

(a) What manufacturing cost element is responsible for the fluctuating unit costs? Why?
(b) What is your recommended solution to the problem of the fluctuating unit cost?
(c) Restate the quarterly data based on your recommended solution.

C2–30   Avid Assemblers uses normal job-order costing to assign costs to products. The company assembles and packages 20 different products according to customer specifications. Products are worked on in batches of 30 to 50 units. Each batch is given a job number.

On October 1, the company had the following balances:

Raw materials	$ 7,800
Work in process	45,726
Finished goods	23,520

Work in process consisted of the following jobs:

	Job 22	Job 24	Job 25
Direct materials	$4,200	$3,190	$2,800
Direct labour	8,500	7,210	6,500
Applied overhead	5,100	4,326	3,900
Total	$17,800	$14,726	$13,200
Number of units	30	50	35

Finished goods consisted of Job 23, with the following costs:

Direct materials	$7,200
Direct labour	10,200
Applied overhead	6,120
Total	$23,520
Number of units	50

Shown below are the direct cost data related to jobs started in October:

	Job 26	Job 27	Job 28	Total
Direct materials	$4,180	$3,600	$1,200	$ 8,980
Direct labour	9,200	8,340	2,910	20,450
Number of units	40	50	40	

Other information:

1. Direct materials and direct labour added to beginning work in process in October were as follows:

	Job 22	Job 24	Job 25	Total
Direct materials	$ 950	$ 410	$1,200	$ 2,560
Direct labour	2,000	3,500	4,500	10,000

2. Overhead is applied at a predetermined rate based on the direct labour cost.
3. Actual expenses for October were as follows:

Supervisory salaries	$4,000
Factory rent	2,000
Amortization (machines)	3,000
Indirect labour	5,000
Supplies (factory)	1,100
Selling expenses	8,500
Property tax and insurance	1,250
CPP, EI, and other benefits*	3,200

* 80 percent of employer contributions and benefits relate to factory personnel.

4. Purchases of direct materials (raw materials) during October amounted to $8,500. Indirect materials (supplies) are handled in a separate account.
5. Only Job Nos. 27 and 28 are still in process at closing on October 31. Finished goods consisted only of Job No. 25 at month end.
6. Avid writes off any over- and underapplied overhead to Cost of Goods Sold in the month in which it is incurred.

Instructions

(a) What is the predetermined overhead rate used by Avid to apply overhead to jobs?
(b) What is the unit cost of Job No. 24 in October?
(c) What are the October 31 balances for the following inventory accounts?
   1. Raw Materials
   2. Work in Process
   3. Finished Goods
(d) What is the cost of goods manufactured in October? (You do not have to prepare a statement.)
(e) Determine the over- or underapplied overhead for October and prepare the journal entry to dispose of this amount.

(CMA Canada-adapted)

C2–31   The following data were taken from the records of Cougar Enterprises, a Canadian manufacturer that uses a normal job-order costing system:

Work in Process, December 1

Job Number	70	75	80
Direct materials	$1,800	$2,400	$1,500
Direct labour	1,200	2,400	600
Applied overhead	600	1,350	450
Total	$3,600	$6,150	$2,550

During December, jobs numbered 70 through 90 were worked on, and the following costs were incurred:

Job Number	70	75	80	85	90	Total
Direct materials	$600	$ 900	$1,200	$1,350	$1,500	$5,550
Direct labour	$750	$1,500	$3,000	$2,250	$6,000	$13,500
Direct labour hours	50	100	200	150	400	900

Additional information:

1. Total overhead costs are applied to jobs on the basis of direct labour hours worked. At the beginning of the year, the company estimated that total overhead costs for the year would be $150,000, and the total labour hours worked would be 12,500.
2. The balance in the Departmental Overhead Control account on December 1 was $160,010. Actual direct labour hours for the previous 11 months (January through November) were 11,250.
3. There were no jobs in finished goods on December 1.
4. Expenses for December were as follows (not yet recorded in the books of account):

Direct materials purchased	$ 7,500
Salaries	
Production clerk	1,500
Supervisor	2,200
Amortization (plant and equipment)	2,490
Factory supplies	1,500
Sales staff salaries	9,200
Utilities (factory)	1,800
Administrative expenses	9,500
	$35,690

5. The company writes off all over- or under-applied overhead to Cost of Goods Sold at the end of the year.
6. Jobs numbered 70, 80, 85, and 90 were completed during December. Only job 90 remained in finished goods on December 31.
7. The company charges its customers 250 percent of total manufacturing cost.
8. Cost of goods sold to December 1 was $358,750.

Instructions

(a) Using the information given, calculate the following amounts:
   1. the predetermined overhead rate used to apply overhead to products.
   2. the cost of ending work in process inventory.

3. the cost of goods manufactured in December.

4. the unadjusted gross margin for December.

(b) Prepare the summary journal entries to the control accounts required to record all the transactions for December that relate to production. (*Note*: You should not make entries for individual jobs)

(c) Calculate the over- or underapplied overhead for the year. What effect would this amount have on net income?

(CMA Canada-adapted)

C2–32 Baehr Company is a manufacturer with a fiscal year that runs from July 1 to June 30. The company uses a normal job-order accounting system for its production costs.

A predetermined overhead rate based on direct labour hours is used to apply overhead to individual jobs. Three budgets of overhead costs were prepared for the 2005 fiscal year as follows:

Direct labour hours	100,000	120,000	140,000
Variable overhead costs	$325,000	$390,000	$455,000
Fixed overhead costs	216,000	216,000	216,000
Total overhead	$541,000	$606,000	$671,000

Although the annual ideal capacity is 150,000 direct labour hours, company officials have determined 120,000 direct labour hours to be the normal capacity for the year.

The following information is for November 2005 when Jobs X-50 and X-51 were completed:

Inventories, November 1	
Raw materials and supplies	$ 10,500
Work in process (Job X-50)	54,000
Finished goods	112,500
Purchases of raw materials and supplies	
Raw materials	$135,000
Supplies	15,000
Materials and supplies requisitioned for production	
Job X-50	$ 45,000
Job X-51	37,500
Job X-52	25,500
Supplies	12,000
	$120,000
Factory direct labour hours	
Job X-50	3,500 DLH
Job X-51	3,000 DLH
Job X-52	2,000 DLH
Labour costs	
Direct labour wages	$ 51,000
Indirect labour wages (4,000 hours)	15,000
Supervisory salaries	6,000
	$ 72,000
Building occupancy costs (heat, light, amortization)	
Factory facilities	$ 6,500
Sales offices	1,500
Administration offices	1,000
	$ 9,000
Factory equipment costs	
Power	$ 4,000
Repairs and maintenance	1,500
Amortization	1,500
Other	1,000
	$ 8,000

Instructions

(a) What is the predetermined rate to be used to apply overhead to individual jobs during the fiscal year?
(b) Prepare a schedule showing the costs assigned to each of Jobs X-50, X-51, and X-52.
(c) What is the cost of goods manufactured for November?
(d) What is the cost assigned to work in process on November 30?
(e) Determine whether overhead for November is overapplied or underapplied, and by what amount.

(CMA Canada-adapted)

C2–33   Triple C Ltd. is in the business of manufacturing cabinets, computer stands, and countertops. Most of its jobs are contracts for home builders. The following information is available for the month of July:

	Costs Incurred to July 1		Added in July		
Job Number	Direct Materials	Direct Labour	Direct Materials	Direct Labour	Status at July 31
101	$9,000	$2,000	$ 0	$1,000	Completed but not sold
103	2,500	1,500	?	?	Not completed
111	600	100	500	3,000	Completed but not sold
115			800	200	Not completed

Activity in accounts:

Opening Account	Balance July 1	Purchased in July	Issued/Used in July	Ending Balance July 31
Direct Materials	$3,000	$6,000	$4,900	$?
Direct Labour			8,000	

On July 1, finished goods inventory consisted of one job, 105, with a total cost of $18,000. This job was sold during July.
(*Note*: Manufacturing overhead is applied at 120% of the direct labour cost.)

Instructions

Calculate the costs of completed jobs 101 and 111, and the account balances in Direct Materials Inventory, Work in Process Inventory, and Finished Goods Inventory, as at July 31.

(CGA-adapted)

C2–34   ESU Printing provides printing services to many different corporate clients. Although ESU bids on most jobs, some jobs, particularly new ones, are negotiated on a "cost-plus" basis. Cost-plus means that the buyer is willing to pay the actual cost plus a return (profit) on these costs to ESU.

Clara Biggio, controller for ESU, has recently returned from a meeting where ESU's president stated that he wanted her to find a way to charge most of the company's costs to projects that are on a cost-plus basis. The president noted that the company needed more profits to meet its stated goals this period. By charging more costs to the cost-plus projects and therefore less costs to the jobs that were bid, the company should be able to increase its profits for the current year.

Clara knew why the president wanted to take this action. Rumours were that he was looking for a new position and if the company reported strong profits, the president's opportunities would be better. Clara also recognized that she could probably increase the cost of certain jobs by changing the basis that is used to allocate the manufacturing overhead.

Instructions

(a) Who are the stakeholders in this situation?
(b) What are the ethical issues in this situation?
(c) What would you do if you were Clara Biggio?

Answers to Self-Study Questions

1. a   2. b   3. c   4. d   5. b   6. a   7. d   8. b   9. c

Remember to go back to the Navigator Box at the beginning of the chapter to check off your completed work.

CHAPTER 3

Process Cost Accounting

Sweets Worth Waiting For

In Canada, the Ganong name means chocolate, the high-quality boxed chocolate and candies received as gifts on Valentine's Day and other special occasions. Now in its fifth generation, the Ganong family has been making its delectable treats in St. Stephen, New Brunswick, since 1873. Ganong Bros. Limited currently has offices in Moncton, Toronto, and Vancouver, and exports to the United States and the United Kingdom.

Making candy, for example jellybeans, is a process—a movement of the product from one department to another, in this case, from the kitchen, to the pan room, to polishing, and then packaging, says CMA Cathy Hastey, controller at Ganong's.

In the kitchen, the raw materials for jellybean centres are mixed in a kettle and cooked in 238-kilogram batches, with no colour or flavour. The mixture is then deposited in a mould and sent into a "hot room," where it sits for 24 hours, Ms. Hastey explains.

The pan room then receives the jellybean centres and divides them into pans, where sugar, colour, and flavour are added. After sitting for another day, the jellybeans enter the polishing stage, where they receive their final coating, which then needs another day to dry.

The finished jellybeans go to packaging, where different flavours are mixed together and packed to specific weight requirements.

"When the process is started, everything is a raw material. When it comes out of the centre stage, it has a product number for a centre," Ms. Hastey explains. "Whatever costs are associated with making the centre come forward as material in the panning stage. In the panning stage, the materials are charged to work in process and then come back out of work in process as a jellybean. That jellybean carries all material, labour, and overhead costs for all stages." This allows Ms. Hastey to track the production costs for each product.

This process is not just for jellybeans, 60,000 kilograms of which Ganong Bros. Limited produces every week. The same process applies to the hundreds of different chocolates, gumdrops, and fruit snacks the company produces. A box of chocolates with a variety of centres would require this days-long process for each piece. That's definitely something worth savouring.

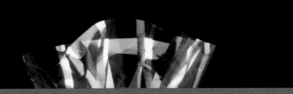

Ganong Bros. Limited: www.ganong.com

THE NAVIGATOR

- [ ] Scan *Study Objectives*

- [ ] Read *Feature Story*

- [ ] Read *Chapter Preview*

- [ ] Read text and answer *Before You Go On* p. 97, p. 106, p. 107

- [ ] Work *Using the Decision Toolkit*

- [ ] Review *Summary of Study Objectives*

- [ ] Review *Decision Toolkit—A Summary*

- [ ] Work *Demonstration Problem*

- [ ] Answer *Self-Study Questions*

- [ ] Complete assignments

STUDY OBJECTIVES

After studying this chapter, you should be able to:

1. Understand who uses process cost systems.
2. Explain the similarities and differences between job-order cost and process cost systems.
3. Explain the flow of costs in a process cost system.
4. Make the journal entries to assign manufacturing costs in a process cost system.
5. Calculate equivalent units using the weighted-average method.
6. Explain the four necessary steps to prepare a production cost report.
7. Prepare a production cost report.
8. Prepare a production cost report for a sequential department setting.
9. Calculate equivalent units using the FIFO method (Appendix 3A).

the navigator

The cost accounting system used by companies such as Ganong Bros. Limited is called a process cost accounting system. In contrast to job-order cost accounting, which focuses on the individual job, process cost accounting focuses on the processes involved in mass-producing products that are identical or very similar in nature. The purpose of this chapter is to explain and illustrate process cost accounting.

The chapter is organized as follows:

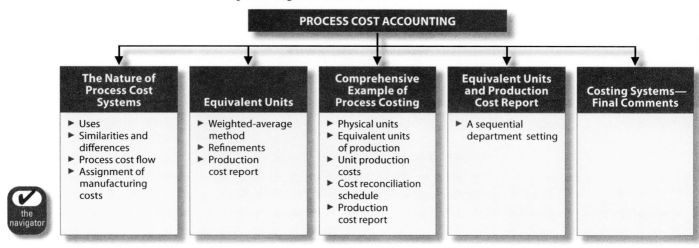

PROCESS COST ACCOUNTING

The Nature of Process Cost Systems	Equivalent Units	Comprehensive Example of Process Costing	Equivalent Units and Production Cost Report	Costing Systems—Final Comments
► Uses ► Similarities and differences ► Process cost flow ► Assignment of manufacturing costs	► Weighted-average method ► Refinements ► Production cost report	► Physical units ► Equivalent units of production ► Unit production costs ► Cost reconciliation schedule ► Production cost report	► A sequential department setting	

The Nature of Process Cost Systems

Uses of Process Cost Systems

study objective 1

Understand who uses process cost systems.

Process cost systems are used to apply costs to similar products that are mass-produced in a continuous way. Ganong Bros. Limited uses a process cost system: Production of the jellybeans, once it begins, continues until the jellybeans are fully made, and the processing is the same for the entire run—with precisely the same amount of materials, labour, and overhead. Each finished pan of jellybeans is like all the others.

A company such as Stelco uses process costing in the manufacturing of steel. Kellogg and General Mills use process costing for cereal production, Petro-Canada uses process costing for its oil refining, and Quebec-based Sico Inc. uses process costing for its paint products. At a bottling company like Cott Corp., the manufacturing process begins with the blending of the beverages. Next the beverage is dispensed into bottles that are moved into position by automated machinery. The bottles are then capped, packaged, and forwarded to the finished goods warehouse. This process is shown in Illustration 3-1.

Illustration 3-1 ►

Manufacturing processes

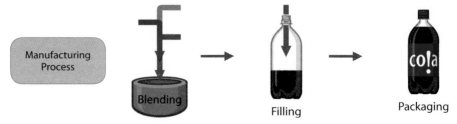

For Cott Corp., as well as the other companies just mentioned, once production begins, it continues until the finished product emerges, and each unit of finished product is like every other unit.

In comparison, costs in a job-order cost system are assigned to a *specific job*. Examples are the construction of a customized home, the making of a motion picture, or the manufacturing of a specialized machine. Illustration 3-2 provides examples of companies that mostly use either a process cost system or a job-order cost system.

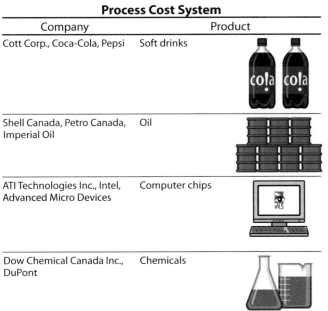

Process Cost System			Job-Order Cost System		
Company	Product		Company	Product	
Cott Corp., Coca-Cola, Pepsi	Soft drinks		Cossette Communications, J. Walter Thompson, Quebecor Inc.	Advertising & printing	
Shell Canada, Petro Canada, Imperial Oil	Oil		CBC, Walt Disney, Warner Brothers	Television and motion pictures	
ATI Technologies Inc., Intel, Advanced Micro Devices	Computer chips		CGI Group Inc.	Service	
Dow Chemical Canada Inc., DuPont	Chemicals		TLC the Laser Centre Inc., MDS, Extendicare	Patient health care	

Illustration 3-2 ▲

Process cost and job-order cost companies and products

Similarities and Differences between Job-Order Cost and Process Cost Systems

In a job-order cost system, costs are assigned to each job. In a process cost system, costs are tracked through a series of connected manufacturing processes or departments, rather than by individual jobs. Thus, process cost systems are used when a large volume of uniform or relatively homogeneous products is produced. The basic flow of costs in these two systems is shown in Illustration 3-3.

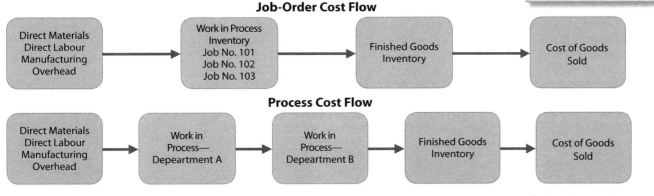

Job-Order Cost Flow

Direct Materials Direct Labour Manufacturing Overhead → Work in Process Inventory Job No. 101 Job No. 102 Job No. 103 → Finished Goods Inventory → Cost of Goods Sold

Process Cost Flow

Direct Materials Direct Labour Manufacturing Overhead → Work in Process— Depeartment A → Work in Process— Depeartment B → Finished Goods Inventory → Cost of Goods Sold

The basic similarities and differences between these two systems are highlighted in the following analysis.

Illustration 3-3 ▲

Job-order cost and process cost flow systems

> **study objective 2**
>
> Explain the similarities and differences between job-order cost and process cost systems.

Similarities

Job-order cost and process cost systems are similar in three ways:

1. **The manufacturing cost elements.** Both costing systems track three manufacturing cost elements—direct materials, direct labour, and manufacturing overhead.
2. **The accumulation of the costs of materials, labour, and overhead.** In both costing systems, raw materials are debited to Raw Materials Inventory; factory labour is debited to Factory Labour; and manufacturing overhead costs are debited to Manufacturing Overhead.

3. **The flow of costs.** As noted above, all manufacturing costs are accumulated by debits to Raw Materials Inventory, Factory Labour, and Manufacturing Overhead. These costs are then assigned to the same accounts in both costing systems—Work in Process, Finished Goods Inventory, and Cost of Goods Sold. **The methods of assigning costs, however, differ significantly.** These differences are explained and illustrated later in the chapter.

Differences

The differences between a job-order cost and a process cost system are as follows:

1. **The number of work in process accounts used.** In a job-order cost system, only one work in process account is used. In a process cost system, several work in process accounts are used.
2. **Documents used to track costs.** In a job-order cost system, costs are charged to individual jobs and summarized in a job cost sheet. In a process cost system, costs are summarized in a production cost report for each department.
3. **The point at which costs are totalled.** In a job-order cost system, the total cost is determined when the job is completed. In a process cost system, the total cost is determined at the end of a period of time.
4. **Unit cost calculations.** In a job-order cost system, the unit cost is the total cost per job divided by the units produced. In a process cost system, the unit cost is total manufacturing cost for the period divided by the units produced during the period.

The major differences between a job-order cost and a process cost system are summarized in Illustration 3-4.

Illustration 3-4 ▶

Job-order versus process cost systems

Features	Job-Order Cost System	Process Cost System
Work in process accounts	• one for each job	• one for each process
Documents used	• job cost sheets	• production cost reports
Determination of total manufacturing costs	• each job	• each period
Unit cost calculations	• cost of each job ÷ units produced for the job	• total manufacturing costs ÷ units produced during the period

Process Cost Flow

study objective 3

Explain the flow of costs in a process cost system.

Illustration 3-5 shows the flow of costs in the process cost system for Tyler Company. Tyler Company manufactures automatic can openers that are sold to retail outlets. Manufacturing consists of two processes: machining and assembly. In the machining department, the raw materials are shaped, honed, and drilled. In the assembly department, the parts are assembled and packaged.

Illustration 3-5 ▶

Flow of costs in a process cost system

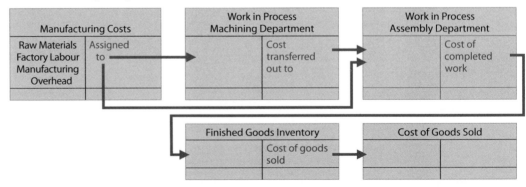

As the flow of costs indicates, materials, labour, and manufacturing overhead can be added in both the machining and assembly departments. When the machining department finishes its work, the partially completed units are transferred to the assembly department. In the assembly department, the goods are finished and are then transferred to the finished goods inventory. Upon sale, the goods are removed from the finished goods inventory. Within each department, a similar set of activities is performed on each unit that is processed.

Assignment of Manufacturing Costs—Journal Entries

study objective 4

Make the journal entries to assign manufacturing costs in a process cost system.

As indicated earlier, the accumulation of the costs of materials, labour, and manufacturing overhead is the same in a process cost system as in a job-order cost system. All raw materials are debited to Raw Materials Inventory when the materials are purchased. All factory labour is debited to Factory Labour when the labour costs are incurred. And overhead costs are debited to Manufacturing Overhead as they are incurred. However, the assignment of the three manufacturing cost elements to Work in Process in a process cost system is different from in a job-order cost system. We will now look at how these manufacturing cost elements are assigned in a process cost system.

Materials Costs

All raw materials that are issued for production are materials costs for the production department. Materials requisition slips may be used in a process cost system, but **fewer requisitions are generally used than in a job-order cost system, because the materials are used for processes rather than for specific jobs**. Requisitions are issued less often in a process cost system because the requisitions are for larger quantities of material.

Materials are usually added to production at the beginning of the first process. However, in subsequent processes, other materials may be added at various points. For example, in the manufacture of Ganong chocolate bars, the chocolate and other ingredients are added at the beginning of the first process, and the wrappers and cartons are added at the end of the packaging process. At Tyler Company, materials are entered at the beginning of each process. The entry to record the materials used is:

Work in Process—Machining	XXXX	
Work in Process—Assembly	XXXX	
Raw Materials Inventory		XXXX
To record materials used.		

At ice cream maker Dairyland, materials are added in three departments: milk and flavouring in the mixing department; extras, such as cherries and walnuts, in the prepping department; and cardboard containers in the pinting (packaging) department.

Factory Labour Costs

In a process cost system, as in a job-order cost system, time tickets can be used to determine the cost of labour that should be assigned to production departments. Since labour costs are assigned to a process rather than a job, the labour cost that is chargeable to a process can be obtained from the payroll register or a department's payroll summaries.

Labour costs for Tyler Company's machining department will include the wages of employees who shape, hone, and drill the raw materials. The entry to assign these costs for Tyler is:

Work in Process—Machining	XXXX	
Work in Process—Assembly	XXXX	
Factory Labour		XXXX
To assign factory labour to production.		

Manufacturing Overhead Costs

The goal when overhead is assigned in a process cost system is to allocate the overhead costs to the production departments on basis that is objective and fair. That basis is the activity that "drives" or causes the costs. A major driver of overhead costs in continuous manufacturing operations is **machine time used**, not direct labour. Thus, **machine hours are widely**

used to allocate manufacturing overhead costs. The entry to allocate overhead to the two processes Tyler uses is as follows:

Work in Process—Machining	XXXX	
Work in Process—Assembly	XXXX	
Manufacturing Overhead		XXXX
To assign overhead to production.		

BUSINESS INSIGHT ▶ Management Perspective

Mines are big business and much of the mining process, such as drilling, has been automated for years. But one of the most dangerous jobs—loading explosives into production holes—has remained a hands-on process. That is, until now. The technology to automate this perilous task now exists, thanks to the emulsion-loading automation project (ELAP), a private-public collaboration led by Ottawa-based DYI Technologies Inc. Now, miners can deposit explosive emulsive foam into production holes from a remote location, either underground or even from an office on the surface. The tele-remote operation is autonomous; it can find the holes itself, judge the correct length, load, and detonate. It can even call for help if needed. Not only does the ELAP technology—which is marketed by Australian company Orica Mining Services as Automation of Charging—provide a safer working environment for miners, it also improves productivity and saves money. Mining companies will no longer have to pay for the "dead" time (often up to three hours) it takes workers to enter and leave the mine. Although the technology will be expensive, costing about $1.5 million, it will save lives and labour costs.

Source: Andrew Young, ELAP project manager, DYI Technologies; Andy Holloway, "The Mine Machine," *Canadian Business*, Nov. 25, 2002; Orica press release, Sept. 4, 2003.

Transfer to Next Department

At the end of the month, an entry is needed to record the cost of the goods transferred out of the department. For Tyler, the transfer is from the machining department to the assembly department, and the following entry is made:

Work in Process—Assembly	XXXX	
Work in Process—Machining		XXXX
To record transfer of units to the assembly department.		

Transfer to Finished Goods

The units completed in the assembly department are transferred to the finished goods warehouse. The entry for this transfer is as follows:

Finished Goods Inventory	XXXX	
Work in Process—Assembly		XXXX
To record transfer of units to finished goods.		

Transfer to Cost of Goods Sold

Finally, when finished goods are sold, the entry to record the cost of goods sold is as follows:

Cost of Goods Sold	XXXX	
Finished Goods Inventory		XXXX
To record cost of units sold.		

BEFORE YOU GO ON . . .

►Review It

1. What type of manufacturing companies might use a process cost accounting system?
2. What are the main similarities and differences between a job-order cost system and a process cost system?

►Do It

Ruth company manufactures ZEBO through two processes: blending and bottling. In June, raw materials used were $18,000 for blending and $4,000 for bottling; factory labour costs were $12,000 for blending and $5,000 for bottling; manufacturing overhead costs were $6,000 for blending and $2,500 for bottling. Units completed at a cost of $19,000 in the blending department were transferred to the bottling department. Units completed at a cost of $11,000 in the bottling department were transferred to the finished goods inventory. Journalize the assignment of these costs to the two processes and the transfers of the units.

Action Plan

- In process cost accounting, keep separate work in process accounts for each process.
- When the costs are assigned to production, debit the separate work in process accounts.
- Transfer the cost of completed units to the next process or to Finished Goods Inventory.

Solution

The entries are:

Work in Process—Blending	18,000	
Work in Process—Bottling	4,000	
Raw Materials Inventory		22,000
To record materials used.		
Work in Process—Blending	12,000	
Work in Process—Bottling	5,000	
Factory Labour		17,000
To assign factory labour to production.		
Work in Process—Blending	6,000	
Work in Process—Bottling	2,500	
Manufacturing Overhead		8,500
To assign overhead to production.		
Work in Process—Bottling	19,000	
Work in Process—Blending		19,000
To record transfer of units to the bottling department.		
Finished Goods Inventory	11,000	
Work in Process—Bottling		11,000
To record transfer of units to finished goods.		

Related exercise material: BE3–1, BE3–2, BE3–3, E3–1, and E3–2.

the navigator

Equivalent Units

Suppose you were asked to calculate the cost of instruction at your college for each full-time equivalent student. You are provided with the following information:

study objective 5

Calculate equivalent units using the weighted-average method.

Costs:	
Total cost of instruction	$9,000,000
Student population:	
Full-time students	900
Part-time students	1,000

Part-time students take 60 percent of the classes of a full-time student during the year. To calculate the number of full-time equivalent students per year, you would make the following calculation:

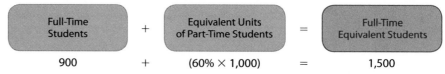

Full-Time Students	+	Equivalent Units of Part-Time Students	=	Full-Time Equivalent Students
900	+	(60% × 1,000)	=	1,500

The cost of instruction per full-time equivalent student is therefore the total cost of instruction ($9,000,000) divided by the number of full-time equivalent students (1,500), which is $6,000 ($9,000,000 ÷ 1,500).

In a process cost system, the same idea—called equivalent units of production—is used. **Equivalent units of production** measure the work done during the period, expressed in fully completed units. This concept is used to determine the cost per unit of completed product.

Weighted-Average Method

The formula to calculate equivalent units of production is shown in Illustration 3-6.

Illustration 3-6 ▶

Equivalent units of production formula

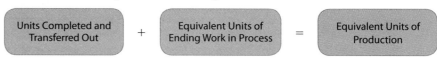

Units Completed and Transferred Out	+	Equivalent Units of Ending Work in Process	=	Equivalent Units of Production

To better understand this concept of equivalent units, consider the following two examples:

Example 1: The blending department's entire output during the period consists of ending work in process of 4,000 units which are 60 percent complete as to materials, labour, and overhead. The equivalent units of production for the blending department are therefore 2,400 units (4,000 × 60%).

Example 2: The packaging department's output during the period consists of 10,000 units completed and transferred out, and 5,000 units in ending work in process which are 70 percent completed. The equivalent units of production are therefore 13,500 [10,000 + (5,000 × 70%)].

This method of calculating equivalent units is referred to as the **weighted-average method**. It considers the degree of completion (weighting) of the units completed and transferred out and the ending work in process. An alternative method, called the FIFO method, is discussed in the appendix to this chapter.

Refinements on the Weighted-Average Method

Williams Waffle Company has produced frozen waffles since 1970. Three departments are used to produce these waffles: mixing, baking, and freezing/packaging. In the mixing department, dry ingredients, including flour, salt, and baking powder, are mixed with liquid ingredients, including eggs and vegetable oil, to make waffle batter. Information for the mixing department at the end of June is provided in Illustration 3-7.

Illustration 3-7 ▶

Information for mixing department

Mixing Department			
		Percentage Complete	
	Physical Units	Materials	Conversion Costs
Work in process, June 1	100,000	100%	70%
Started into production	800,000		
Total units	900,000		
Units transferred out	700,000		
Work in process, June 30	200,000	100%	60%
Total units	900,000		

Illustration 3-7 indicates that the beginning work in process is 100 percent complete as to materials cost and 70 percent complete as to conversion costs. **Conversion cost refers to the sum of labour costs and overhead costs**. In other words, both the dry and liquid ingredients (materials) are added at the beginning of the process to make waffles. The conversion costs (labour and overhead) for the mixing of these ingredients were incurred uniformly and are 70 percent complete. The ending work in process is 100 percent complete as to materials cost and 60 percent complete as to conversion costs.

We then use the mixing department information to determine the equivalent units. **In calculating equivalent units, the beginning work in process is not part of the equivalent units of production formula**. The units transferred out to the baking department are fully complete as to both materials and conversion costs. The ending work in process is fully complete as to materials, but only 60 percent complete as to conversion costs. **Two equivalent unit calculations are therefore necessary:** one for materials and the other for conversion costs. Illustration 3-8 shows these calculations.

Helpful Hint Question: When are separate unit cost calculations needed for materials and conversion costs? Answer: Whenever the two types of costs do not occur in the process at the same time.

	Equivalent Units	
	Materials	Conversion Costs
Units transferred out	700,000	700,000
Work in process, June 30		
200,000 × 100%	200,000	
200,000 × 60%		120,000
Total equivalent units	900,000	820,000

Illustration 3-8 ◄

Calculation of equivalent units—mixing department

The earlier formula that we used to calculate equivalent units of production can be refined to show the calculations for materials and for conversion costs, as Illustration 3-9 shows.

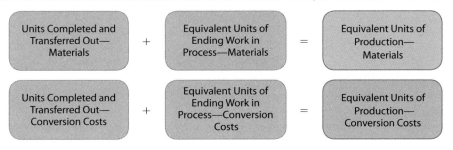

Illustration 3-9 ◄

Refined equivalent units of production formula

Production Cost Report

As mentioned earlier, a production cost report is prepared for each department in a process cost system. A **production cost report** is the key document management uses to understand the activities in a department; it shows the production quantity and cost data for that department. For example, in producing waffles, Williams Waffle Company would have three production cost reports: Mixing, Baking, and Freezing/Packaging. Illustration 3-10 shows the flow of costs to make a waffle and the related production cost reports for each department.

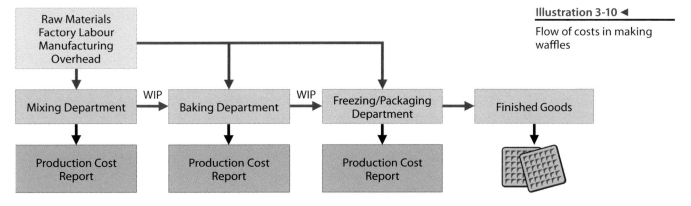

Illustration 3-10 ◄

Flow of costs in making waffles

study objective 6

Explain the four necessary
steps to prepare a
production cost report.

To be ready to complete a production cost report, the company must perform four steps:

1. Calculate the physical unit flow.
2. Calculate the equivalent units of production.
3. Calculate the unit production costs.
4. Prepare a cost reconciliation schedule.

Together, these four steps make up the process costing system. The next section explores these steps in an extended example.

Comprehensive Example of Process Costing Using Weighted-Average Method

Assumed data for the mixing department at Williams Waffle Company for the month of June are shown in Illustration 3-11. We will use this information to complete a production cost report for this department.

Illustration 3-11 ▶

Unit and cost data—mixing department

Mixing Department	
Units	
Work in process, June 1	100,000
Direct materials: 100% complete	
Conversion costs: 70% complete	
Units started into production during June	800,000
Units completed and transferred out to baking department	700,000
Work in process, June 30	200,000
Direct materials: 100% complete	
Conversion costs: 60% complete	
Costs	
Work in process, June 1	
Direct materials: 100% complete	$50,000
Conversion costs: 70% complete	35,000
Cost of work in process, June 1	$85,000
Costs incurred during production in June	
Direct materials	$400,000
Conversion costs	170,000
Costs incurred in June	$570,000

Calculate the Physical Unit Flow (Step 1)

Physical units are the actual units to be accounted for during a period, regardless of any work performed. To keep track of these units, it is necessary to add the units started (or transferred) into production during the period to the units in process at the beginning of the period. This amount is referred to as the **total units to be accounted for**.

The total units are then accounted for by the output of the period. The output consists of units transferred out during the period and any units in process at the end of the period. This amount is referred to as the **total units accounted for**. Illustration 3-12 shows the flow of physical units for Williams Waffle Company for the month of June for the mixing department.

Illustration 3-12 ◄

Physical unit flow—mixing department

Mixing Department	
	Physical Units
Units to be accounted for	
Work in process, June 1	100,000
Started (transferred) into production	800,000
Total units	900,000
Units accounted for	
Completed and transferred out	700,000
Work in process, June 30	200,000
Total units	900,000

The records indicate that 900,000 units must be accounted for in the mixing department. Of this sum, 700,000 units were transferred to the baking department and 200,000 units were still in process.

Calculate Equivalent Units of Production (Step 2)

Once the physical flow of the units is determined, it is necessary to measure the mixing department's productivity in equivalent units of production. In the mixing department, materials are added at the beginning of the process, and conversion costs are incurred evenly during the process. Thus, two calculations of equivalent units are required: one for materials, and one for conversion costs. Illustration 3-13 shows the equivalent unit calculation.

Helpful Hint Materials are not always added at the beginning of the process. For example, materials are sometimes added uniformly during the process.

Illustration 3-13 ◄

Calculation of equivalent units—mixing department

	Equivalent Units	
	Materials	Conversion Costs
Units transferred out	700,000	700,000
Work in process, June 30		
200,000 × 100%	200,000	
200,000 × 60%		120,000
Total equivalent units	900,000	820,000

Remember that the beginning work in process is ignored in this calculation.

Calculate Unit Production Costs (Step 3)

Now that we know the equivalent units of production, we can calculate the unit production costs. **Unit production costs** are costs expressed in terms of equivalent units of production. When equivalent units of production are different for materials and for conversion costs, three unit costs are calculated: (1) materials cost, (2) conversion cost, and (3) the total manufacturing cost.

The calculation of the total materials cost for waffles is shown in Illustration 3-14.

Illustration 3-14 ◄

Materials cost calculation

Work in process, June 1	
Direct materials cost	$ 50,000
Costs added to production during June	
Direct materials cost	400,000
Total materials cost	$450,000

Illstration 3-15 shows the calculation of the unit materials cost.

Illustration 3-15 ▶

Unit materials cost calculation

Total Materials Cost	÷	Equivalent Units of Materials	=	Unit Materials Cost
$450,000	÷	900,000	=	$0.50

The calculation of the total conversion cost is shown in Illustration 3-16.

Illustration 3-16 ▶

Total conversion cost calculation

Work in process, June 1	
Conversion cost	$ 35,000
Costs added to production during June	
Conversion costs	170,000
Total conversion cost	$205,000

Illustration 3-17 shows the calculation of the unit conversion cost.

Illustration 3-17 ▶

Unit conversion cost calculation

Total Conversion Cost	÷	Equivalent Units of Conversion Costs	=	Unit Conversion Cost
$205,000	÷	820,000	=	$0.25

The total manufacturing cost per unit is therefore calculated as in Illustration 3-18, which follows.

Illustration 3-18 ▶

Total manufacturing cost per unit

Unit Materials Cost	+	Unit Conversion Cost	=	Total Manufacturing Cost per Unit
$0.50	+	$0.25	=	$0.75

Prepare a Cost Reconciliation Schedule (Step 4)

We are now ready to determine the cost of goods transferred out of the mixing department to the baking department and the costs in ending work in process. The total cost that was charged to the mixing department in June is shown in Illustration 3-19.

Illustration 3-19 ▶

Costs charged to mixing department

Costs to be accounted for	
Work in process, June 1	$ 85,000
Started into production	570,000
Total cost	$655,000

The total costs charged to the mixing department in June are therefore $655,000.

Illustration 3-20 shows a cost reconciliation schedule, which is then prepared to assign these costs to (1) the units transferred out to the baking department and (2) the ending work in process.

Illustration 3-20 ▶

Cost reconciliation schedule—mixing department

Mixing Department Cost Reconciliation Schedule		
Costs accounted for		
Transferred out (700,000 × $0.75)		$525,000
Work in process, June 30		
Materials (200,000 × $0.50)	$100,000	
Conversion cost (120,000 × $0.25)	30,000	130,000
Total cost		$655,000

The total manufacturing cost per unit, $0.75, is used in costing the units that were completed and transferred to the baking department. In contrast, the unit cost of materials and the unit cost of conversion are needed in costing the units that are still in process. The **cost reconciliation schedule** shows that the **total costs accounted for** (Illustration 3-20) equal the **total costs to be accounted for** (see Illustration 3-19).

Preparing the Production Cost Report

study objective 7

Prepare a production cost report.

At this point, we are ready to prepare the production cost report for the mixing department. As indicated earlier, this report is an internal document for management that shows the production quantity and cost data for a production department.

There are four steps in preparing a production cost report: (1) Prepare a physical unit schedule. (2) Calculate the equivalent units. (3) Calculate the unit costs. (4) Prepare a cost reconciliation schedule. The production cost report for the mixing department is shown in Illustration 3-21. The four steps are identified in the report.

Illustration 3-21 ◄

Production cost report

Mixing Department
Production Cost Report
Month Ended June 30, 2005

	Physical Units	Equivalent Units Materials	Equivalent Units Conversion Costs	
Quantities	Step 1	Step 2		
Units to be accounted for				
Work in process, June 1	100,000			
Started into production	800,000			
Total units	900,000			
Units accounted for				
Transferred out	700,000	700,000	700,000	
Work in process, June 30	200,000	200,000	120,000	(200,000 × 60%)
Total units	900,000	900,000	820,000	

		Materials	Conversion Costs	Total
Costs				
Unit costs — Step 3				
Costs in June	(a)	$450,000	$205,000	$655,000
Equivalent units	(b)	900,000	820,000	
Unit costs [(a) ÷ (b)]		$0.50	$0.25	$0.75
Costs to be accounted for				
Work in process, June 1				$ 85,000
Started into production				570,000
Total costs				$655,000

Cost Reconciliation Schedule — Step 4		
Costs accounted for		
Transferred out (700,000 × $0.75)		$525,000
Work in process, June 30		
Materials (200,000 × $0.50)	$100,000	
Conversion costs (120,000 × $0.25)	30,000	130,000
Total costs		$655,000

Helpful Hint What are the two self-checks in the report? Answer: (1) Total physical units accounted for must equal the total units to be accounted for. (2) Total costs accounted for must equal the total costs to be accounted for.

Helpful Hint Because production cost reports are used as the basis for evaluating department productivity and efficiency, the units, costs, and computations reported therein should be independently accumulated and analyzed to prevent misstatements by department managers.

Production cost reports give a basis for evaluating the productivity of a department. In addition, the cost data can be used to judge whether unit costs and total costs are reasonable. By comparing the quantity and cost data to goals, top management can also judge whether current performance is meeting planned objectives.

Calculate Equivalent Units for a Sequential Process Setting

Most manufacturing firms have sequential processing facilities. In this setting, goods are transferred from one department to another in a sequence. For example, the production of waffles at Williams Waffle Company occurs in three departments: Mixing, Baking, and Freezing/Packaging.

Manufacturing costs always follow the physical flow of goods. The costs of completed units from the mixing department are treated as input material costs in the baking department. Such a sequential process requires the use of an additional cost component called "transferred in." This cost component has a percentage of completion factor of 100%. The **transferred-in cost** component is treated the same as any other cost component in the calculations of the equivalent units of production and the cost per equivalent unit of production.

The next department may also add additional raw material to the units that have been transferred in or it may add labour and overhead costs. Any costs added in by the next department require their own cost component for calculating the equivalent units of production and cost per equivalent unit. In this setting, the final cost of the product is added up cumulatively as the product moves through the production sequence.

Assumed data for the freezing/packaging department at Williams Waffle for the month of June are shown in illustration 3-22. The freezing/packaging department uses the weighted-average process costing method.

Illustration 3-22 ▶

Unit and cost data—freezing/packaging department

Freezing/Packaging Department	
Units	
Work in process, June 1	200,000
Transferred in, 100% complete	
Direct materials, 0% complete	
Conversion, 90% complete	
Units transferred in from baking department during June	700,000
Units completed during June and transferred	
out to finished goods inventory	800,000
Work in process, June 31	100,000
Transferred in, 100% complete	
Direct material, 0% complete	
Conversion, 75% complete	
Costs	
Work in process, June 1	
Transferred in, 100% complete	$170,000
Direct material, 0% complete	0
Conversion, 90% complete	36,000
Cost of work in process, June 1	$206,000
Costs incurred during production in June	
Transferred in from baking department	$595,000
Direct materials	120,000
Conversion costs	139,000
Total costs during June	$854,000

A completed production cost report for the freezing/packaging department is shown in illustration 3-23. Calculations to support the amounts reported follow the report.

Illustration 3-23 ◀

Production cost report

Freezing/Packaging Department
Production Cost Report
Month Ended June 30, 2005

Quantities	Physical Units	Transferred In	Direct Materials	Conversion Costs	
	Step 1	Step 2			
Units to be accounted for					
Work in process	200,000				
Units transferred in	700,000				
Total units	900,000				
Units accounted for					
Transferred out		800,000	800,000	800,000	
Work in process, June 30		100,000	0	75,000	(100,000 × 75%)
Total units		900,000	800,000	875,000	

Costs Step 3						Total
Unit costs						
Costs in June	(a)	$765,000	$120,000	$175,000		$1,060,000
Equivalent units	(b)	900,000	800,000	875,000		
Unit costs [(a) ÷ (b)]		$0.85	$0.15	$0.20		$1.20

Costs to be accounted for	
Work in process, June 1	$ 206,000
Started into production	854,000
Total costs	$1,060,000

Cost Reconciliation Schedule: Step 4		
Costs accounted for		
Transferred out (800,000 × $1.20)		$ 960,000
Work in process, June 30		
Transferred in (100,000 × $0.85)	$85,000	
Direct materials (0 × $0.15)	0	
Conversion costs (75,000 × $0.20)	15,000	100,000
Total cost		$1,060,000

Additional calculations to support the production cost report data:

Transferred in	$170,000 + $595,000 =	$ 765,000
Direct materials	$0 + $120,000 =	$ 120,000
Conversion costs	$36,000 + $139,000 =	$ 175,000
Total cost		$1,060,000

⊞ Decision Toolkit

Decision Checkpoints	Info Needed for Decision	Tools to Use for Decision	How to Evaluate Results
What is the cost of a product?	Cost of materials, labour, and overhead assigned to processes used to make the product	Production cost report	Compare costs to previous periods and to competitors to ensure that costs are reasonable. Compare costs to the expected selling price to determine overall profitability.

the navigator

BEFORE YOU GO ON . . .

▶ Review It

1. How do physical units differ from equivalent units of production?
2. What are the formulas for calculating unit costs of production?
3. How are costs assigned to units transferred out and units in process?
4. What are the four steps in preparing a production cost report?

▶ Do It

In March, Rodayo Manufacturing had the following unit production costs: materials $6 and conversion costs $9. On March 1, it had no work in process. During March, 12,000 units were transferred out. At March 31, 800 units that were 25 percent complete as to conversion costs and 100 percent complete as to materials were in ending work in process. Assign the costs to the units transferred out and the units in process.

Action Plan

- Assign the total manufacturing cost of $15 per unit to the 12,000 units transferred out.
- Assign the materials cost and conversion costs based on equivalent units of production to the units in process.

Solution

The assignment of costs is as follows:

Costs accounted for		
Transferred out (12,000 × $15)		$180,000
Work in process, March 31		
Materials (800 × $6)	$4,800	
Conversion costs (200[1] × $9)	1,800	6,600
Total costs		$186,600

[1] 800 × 25%

Related exercise material: BE3–4, BE3–5, BE3–6, BE3–7, BE3–8, BE3–10, E3–3, E3–4, E3–6, E3–8, E3–11, and E3–12.

Costing Systems—Final Comments

Companies often use a combination of a process cost and a job-order cost system, called operations costing. **Operations costing** is similar to process costing as standardized methods are used to manufacture the product. At the same time, the product may have some customized, individual features that require the use of a job-order cost system.

Consider, for example, the automobile manufacturer Ford Motor Company of Canada Ltd. Each vehicle at a particular plant goes through the same assembly line, but different materials (such as seat coverings, paint, and tinted glass) may be used for different vehicles. Similarly, Kellogg's Pop-Tarts Toaster Pastries go through numerous processes—mixing, filling, baking, frosting, and packaging. The pastry dough, though, comes in three flavours— plain, chocolate, and graham—and fillings include Smucker's real fruit, chocolate fudge, vanilla creme, brown sugar cinnamon, and S'mores.

A cost-benefit trade-off occurs as a company decides which costing system to use. A job-order system, for example, provides detailed information about the cost of the product. Because each job has its own distinguishing characteristics, an accurate cost per job can be provided. This information is useful in controlling costs and pricing products. However, the cost of implementing a job-order cost system is often high because of the accounting costs involved.

On the other hand, for a company like Celestica Inc., which makes computer chips, is there a benefit in knowing whether the cost of the one hundredth chip produced is different from the that of one thousandth chip produced? Probably not. An average cost of the product will be good enough for control and pricing purposes. In summary, when it decides to use one of these systems, or a combination system, a company must weigh the costs of implementing the system against the benefits of having the additional information.

Service companies are often thought of as having specific, non-routine tasks, such as providing consulting services or working on a major lawsuit. These tasks would normally require job-order costing rather than process costing. However, some service companies have repetitive, routine functions, such as retail checkout. Montreal-based Optimal Robotics Corp. has developed a device to automate this function and save stores money. The U-Scan is an automated self-checkout system that allows shoppers to scan, bag, and pay for their purchases with little or no assistance. While they have been slow to embrace the technology, Canadian retailers are beginning to install the devices. Both Loblaws and Dominion have jumped on board. Although retailers complain about the high installation costs, Optimal Robotics says the machines pay for themselves within a year. The company claims the self-checkouts can save retailers up to 120 cashier-hours a week per location. At $8 per hour, that's $46,000. Process costing will help retailers account for these expenses and potential savings.

Sources: Toronto Star, Jan. 20, 2003; Optimal Robotics Corp. news release, Feb. 1, 2002; Razel Robin, "Bye-Bye Bag Boy," Canadian Business, July 9, 2001.

BEFORE YOU GO ON . . .

► Review It

1. In what circumstances would a manufacturer use operations costing instead of process costing?
2. Describe the cost-benefit trade-off in deciding what costing system to use.

Decision Toolkit

Decision Checkpoints	Info Needed for Decision	Tools to Use for Decision	How to Evaluate Results
What costing method should be used?	Type of product produced	Cost of accounting system; benefits of additional information	The benefits of providing the additional information should exceed the costs of the accounting system that is needed to develop the information.

APPENDIX 3A ► FIFO METHOD

In Chapter 3, we demonstrated the weighted-average method of calculating equivalent units. Some companies use a different method to calculate equivalent units, called the **first-in, first-out (FIFO) method.** This appendix shows how the FIFO method is used.

Equivalent Units under FIFO

study objective 9

Calculate equivalent units using the FIFO method.

Under the FIFO method, the calculation of equivalent units is done on a first-in, first-out basis. Some companies prefer the FIFO method because the FIFO cost assumption usually matches the actual physical flow of the goods. Under the FIFO method, it is assumed therefore that the beginning work in process is completed before new work is started.

Using the FIFO method, equivalent units are the sum of the following work:

1. Work done to finish the units of beginning work in process inventory
2. Work done to complete the units started into production during the period (referred to as the **units started and completed**)
3. Work done to start, but only partially complete, the units in ending work in process inventory

Normally, in a process costing system, some units will always be in process at both the beginning and the end of the period.

Illustration

Illustration 3A-1 shows the physical flow of units for the assembly department of Shutters Inc. In addition, the illustration indicates the degree of completion of the work in process in regard to conversion costs.

Illustration 3A-1 ▶

Physical unit flow— assembly department

Assembly Department	
	Physical Units
Units to be accounted for	
Work in process, June 1 (40% complete)	500
Started (transferred) into production	8,000
Total units	8,500
Units accounted for	
Completed and transferred out	8,100
Work in process, June 30 (75% complete)	400
Total units	8,500

In this case, the units completed and transferred out (8,100) plus the units in ending work in process (400) equals the total units to be accounted for (8,500). We then calculate the equivalent units using FIFO as follows:

1. The 500 units of beginning work in process were 40 percent complete. Thus, 300 equivalent units (60% × 500 units) were required to complete the beginning inventory.
2. The units started and completed during the current month are the units transferred out minus the units in beginning work in process. For the assembly department, the number of units started and completed is 7,600 (8,100 − 500).
3. The 400 units of ending work in process were 75 percent complete. Thus, the number of equivalent units is 300 (400 × 75%).

Thus, the number of equivalent units for the assembly department is 8,200, as shown in Illustration 3A-2.

Illustration 3A-2 ▶

Calculation of equivalent units—FIFO method

Assembly Department			
Production Data	Physical Units	Work Added this Period	Equivalent Units
Work in process, June 1	500	60%	300
Started and completed	7,600	100%	7,600
Work in process, June 30	400	75%	300
Total	8,500		8,200

Comprehensive Example

To provide a complete illustration of the FIFO method, we will use the data for the mixing Department at Williams Waffle Company for the month of June, as shown in Illustration 3A-3.

Mixing Department	
Units	
Work in process, June 1	100,000
Direct materials: 100% complete	
Conversion costs: 70% complete	
Units started into production during June	800,000
Units completed and transferred out to Baking Department	700,000
Work in process, June 30	200,000
Direct materials: 100% complete	
Conversion costs: 60% complete	
Costs	
Work in process, June 1	
Direct materials: 100% complete	$50,000
Conversion costs: 70% complete	35,000
Cost of work in process, June 1	$85,000
Costs incurred during production in June	
Direct materials	$400,000
Conversion costs	170,000
Costs incurred in June	$570,000

Illustration 3A-3 ◄

Unit and cost data—mixing department

Calculate the Physical Unit Flow (Step 1)

Illustration 3A-4 shows the physical flow of units for the month of June for the mixing department of Williams Waffle Company.

Mixing Department	
	Physical Units
Units to be accounted for	
Work in process, June 1	100,000
Started (transferred) into production	800,000
Total units	900,000
Units accounted for	
Completed and transferred out	700,000
Work in process, June 30	200,000
Total units	900,000

Illustration 3A-4 ◄

Physical unit flow—mixing department

Under the FIFO method, the physical units schedule is often expanded to explain the transferred-out section. As a result, in this section the beginning work in process and the units started and completed are reported. These two items further explain the completed and transferred out section, as shown in Illustration 3A-5.

Mixing Department	
	Physical Units
Units to be accounted for	
Work in process, June 1	100,000
Started (transferred) into production	800,000
Total units	900,000
Units accounted for	
Completed and transferred out	
Work in process, June 1	100,000
Started and completed	600,000
	700,000
Work in process, June 30	200,000
Total units	900,000

The records indicate that 900,000 units must be accounted for in the mixing department. Of this sum, 700,000 units were transferred to the baking department and 200,000 units were still in process.

Calculate Equivalent Units of Production (Step 2)

As with the method presented in the chapter, once the physical flow of the units is determined, it is necessary to determine the equivalent units of production. In the mixing department, materials are added at the beginning of the process, and conversion costs are incurred evenly during the process. Thus, two calculations of equivalent units are required: one for materials and one for conversion costs.

Equivalent Units for Materials

Since materials are entered at the beginning of the process, no additional materials costs are required to complete the beginning work in process. In addition, 100 percent of the materials costs have been incurred on the ending work in process. Thus, the calculation of equivalent units for materials is as shown in Illustration 3A-6.

Mixing Department—Materials			
Production Data	Physical Units	Materials Added this Period	Equivalent Units
Work in process, June 1	100,000	0%	0
Started and finished	600,000	100%	600,000
Work in process, June 30	200,000	100%	200,000
Total	900,000		800,000

Equivalent Units for Conversion Costs

The 100,000 units of beginning work in process were 70 percent complete in terms of conversion costs. Thus, 30,000 equivalent units (30% × 100,000 units) of conversion costs were required to complete the beginning inventory. In addition, the 200,000 units of ending work in process were 60 percent complete in terms of conversion costs. Thus, the equivalent units for conversion costs is 750,000, calculated as in Illustration 3A-7.

Mixing Department—Conversion Costs			
Production Data	Physical Units	Materials Added this Period	Equivalent Units
Work in process, June 1	100,000	30%	30,000
Started and finished	600,000	100%	600,000
Work in process, June 30	200,000	60%	120,000
Total	900,000		750,000

Calculate Unit Production Costs (Step 3)

Now that we know the equivalent units of production, we can calculate the unit production costs. Unit production costs are costs expressed in terms of equivalent units of production. When equivalent units of production are different for materials and conversion costs, three unit costs are calculated: (1) materials costs, (2) conversion costs, and (3) the total manufacturing cost.

Under the FIFO method, the unit costs of production are based entirely on the production costs incurred during the month. Thus, the costs in beginning work in process are not relevant, because they were incurred on work done in the previous month. As Illustration 3A-3 indicated, the costs incurred during production in June were:

Direct materials	$400,000
Conversion costs	170,000
Total costs	$570,000

The calculation of the unit materials cost, unit conversion cost, and total unit cost for waffles is as follows in Illustration 3A-8.

Total Materials Cost	÷	Equivalent Units of Materials	=	Unit Materials Cost
$400,000	÷	800,000	=	$0.50

Total Conversion Costs	÷	Equivalent Units of Conversion Costs	=	Unit Conversion Cost
$170,000	÷	750,000	=	$0.227 (rounded)

Unit Materials Cost	+	Unit Conversion Cost	=	Total Manufacturing Cost per Unit
$0.50	+	$0.227	=	$0.727

As shown, the unit costs are $0.50 for materials, $0.227 for conversion costs, and $0.727 for the total manufacturing cost.

Prepare a Cost Reconciliation Schedule (Step 4)

We are now ready to determine the cost of goods transferred out of the mixing department into the baking department, and the costs in ending work in process. The total costs that were charged to the mixing department in June are shown in Illustration 3A-9.

Costs to be accounted for	
Work in process, June 1	$ 85,000
Started into production	570,000
Total costs	$655,000

The total costs charged to the mixing department in June are $655,000. A cost reconciliation is then prepared to assign these costs to (1) the units transferred out to the baking department and (2) the ending work in process. Under the FIFO method, the first goods to be completed during the period are the units in beginning work in process. Thus, the cost of the beginning work in process is always assigned to the goods transferred to finished goods (or the next department). The FIFO method also means that ending work in process will only be assigned production costs that are incurred in the current period. Illustration 3A-10 shows a cost reconciliation schedule for the mixing department.

Illustration 3A-10

Cost reconciliation schedule—mixing department

Mixing Department—Materials Cost Reconciliation Schedule		
Costs accounted for		
Transferred out		
Work in process, June 1		$ 85,000
Costs to complete beginning work in process		
Conversion costs (30,000 × $0.227)		6,810
Total costs		91,810
Units started and completed (600,000 × $0.727)		435,950 ª
Total costs transferred out		527,760
Work in process, June 30		
Materials (200,000 × $0.50)	$100,000	
Conversion costs (120,000 × $0.227)	27,240	127,240
Total cost		$655,000
ª Any rounding errors should be adjusted in the "Units started and completed" section.		

As you can see, the total costs accounted for ($655,000) equal the total costs to be accounted for ($655,000).

Preparing the Production Cost Report

At this point, we are ready to prepare the production cost report for the mixing department. This report is an internal document for management that shows the production quantity and cost data for a production department.

There are four steps in preparing a production cost report: (1) Prepare a physical unit schedule. (2) Calculate the equivalent units. (3) Calculate the unit costs. (4) Prepare a cost reconciliation schedule. The production cost report for the mixing department is shown in Illustration 3A-11, with the four steps identified in the report.

Mixing Department
Production Cost Report
Month Ended June 30, 2006

| | Physical Units | Equivalent Units | | Total |
		Materials	Conversion Costs	
		Step 2		
Quantities	**Step 1**			
Units to be accounted for				
Work in process, June 1	100,000			
Started in production	800,000			
Total units	900,000			
Units accounted for				
Completed and transferred out				
Work in process, June 1	100,000	0	30,000	
Started and completed	600,000	600,000	600,000	
Work in process, June 30	200,000	200,000	120,000	
Total units	900,000	800,000	750,000	
Costs **Step 3**				
Unit costs				
Costs in June (excluding beginning work in process) (a)		$400,000	$170,000	$570,000
Equivalent units (b)		800,000	750,000	
Unit costs [(a) ÷ (b)]		$0.50	$0.227	$0.727
Costs to be accounted for				
Work in process, June 1				$ 85,000
Started into production				570,000
Total costs				$655,000
Cost Reconciliation Schedule **Step 4**				
Costs accounted for				
Transferred out				
Work in process, June 1				$ 85,000
Cost to complete beginning work in process				
Conversion costs (30,000 × $0.227)				6,810
Total costs				91,810
Units started and completed (600,000 × $0.727)				435,950
Total costs transferred out				527,760
Work in process, June 30				
Materials (200,000 × $0.50)			$100,000	
Conversion costs (120,000 × $0.227)			27,240	127,240
Total cost				$655,000

Helpful Hint What are the two self-checks in the report? Answer: (1) Total physical units accounted for must equal the total units to be accounted for. (2) Total costs accounted for must equal the total costs to be accounted for.

As indicated earlier, production cost reports give a basis for evaluating the productivity of a department. In addition, the cost data can be used to judge whether unit costs and total costs are reasonable. By comparing the quantity and cost data to goals, top management can also judge whether current performance is meeting planned objectives.

FIFO and Weighted Average

The weighted-average method of calculating equivalent units has **one major advantage:** It is simple to understand and apply. In cases where prices do not fluctuate significantly from period to period, the weighted-average method will be very similar to the FIFO method. In addition, companies that have been using just-in-time procedures effectively for inventory control will have minimal inventory balances, and therefore differences between the weighted-average and the FIFO methods will not be significant.

Conceptually, the FIFO method is better than the weighted-average method because **current performance is measured** using only costs incurred in the current period. Managers are therefore not held responsible for costs from prior periods that they may have had no control over. In addition, the FIFO method **provides current cost information**, which can be used to establish **more accurate pricing strategies** for goods that are manufactured and sold in the current period.

▦ Using the Decision Toolkit

Essence Company manufactures a high-end aftershave lotion called Eternity, in 10-ounce, shaped glass bottles. Because the market for aftershave lotion is highly competitive, the company is very concerned about keeping its costs under control. Eternity is manufactured through three processes: mixing, filling, and corking. Materials are added at the beginning of the process, and labour and overhead are incurred uniformly throughout each process. The company uses a weighted-average method to cost its product.

A partially completed production cost report for the month of May for the mixing department follows:

ESSENCE COMPANY
Mixing Department
Production Cost Report
Month Ended May 31, 2005

	Physical Units	Equivalent Units	
		Materials	Conversion Costs
	Step 1	Step 2	
Quantities			
Units to be accounted for			
Work in process, May 1	1,000		
Started into production	2,000		
Total units	3,000		
Units accounted for			
Transferred out	2,200	?	?
Work in process, May 31	800	?	?
Total units	3,000	?	?

		Materials	Conversion Costs	Total
Costs				
Unit costs Step 3				
Costs in May	(a)	?	?	?
Equivalent units	(b)	?	?	
Unit costs [(a) ÷ (b)]		?	?	?
Costs to be accounted for				
Work in process, May 1				$ 56,300
Started into production				119,320
Total costs				$175,620
Cost Reconciliation Schedule Step 4				
Costs accounted for				
Transferred out				?
Work in process, May 31				
Materials			?	
Conversion costs			?	?
Total cost				?

Additional information:

1. Work in process, May 1: 1,000 units

Materials cost (100% complete)	$49,100	
Conversion costs (70% complete)	7,200	$ 56,300
Materials cost for May: 2,000 units		$100,000
Conversion costs for May		$ 19,320

2. Work in process, May 31, 800 units, 100% complete as to materials and 50% complete as to conversion costs

Instructions

(a) Prepare a production cost report for the mixing department for May.
(b) Prepare the journal entry to record the transfer of goods from the mixing department to the filling department.
(c) Explain why Essence Company is using a process cost system to account for its costs.

Solution

(a) A completed production cost report for the mixing department is shown below. Calculations to support the amounts reported are shown after the report.

ESSENCE COMPANY
Mixing Department
Production Cost Report
Month Ended May 31, 2005

		Equivalent Units	
	Physical Units	Materials	Conversion Costs
	Step 1	Step 2	
Quantities			
Units to be accounted for			
Work in process, May 1	1,000		
Started into production	2,000		
Total units	3,000		
Units accounted for			
Transferred out	2,200	2,200	2,200
Work in process, May 31	800	800	400 (800 × 50%)
Total units	3,000	3,000	2,600

Costs		Materials	Conversion Costs	Total
Unit costs Step 3				
Costs in May	(a)	$149,100	$26,520	$175,620
Equivalent units	(b)	3,000	2,600	
Unit costs [(a) ÷ (b)]		$49.70	$10.20	$59.90

Costs to be accounted for	
Work in process, May 1	$ 56,300
Started into production	119,320
Total costs	$175,620

Cost Reconciliation Schedule Step 4

Costs accounted for		
Transferred out (2,200 × $59.90)		$131,780
Work in process, May 31		
Materials (800 × $49.70)	$39,760	
Conversion costs (400 × $10.20)	4,080	43,840
Total Costs		$175,620

Additional calculations to support production cost report data:

Materials cost—$49,100 + $100,000
Conversion costs—$7,200 + $19,320

(b)
Work in Process—Filling	131,780	
Work in Process—Mixing		131,780

(c) Process cost systems are used to apply costs to similar products that are mass-produced in a continuous way. Essence Company uses a process cost system: production of the aftershave lotion, once it begins, continues until the aftershave lotion emerges. The processing is the same for the entire run—with precisely the same amount of materials, labour, and overhead. Every bottle of Eternity aftershave lotion is identical.

Summary of Study Objectives

1. *Understand who uses process cost systems.* Process cost systems are used by companies that mass-produce similar products in a continuous way. Once production begins, it continues until the finished product emerges. Each unit of finished product identical to every other unit.

2. *Explain the similarities and differences between job-order cost and process cost systems.* Job-order cost systems are similar to process cost systems in three ways: (1) Both systems track the same cost elements—direct materials, direct labour, and manufacturing overhead. (2) Costs are accumulated in the same accounts—Raw Materials Inventory, Factory Labour, and Manufacturing Overhead. (3) Accumulated costs are assigned to the same accounts—Work in Process, Finished Goods Inventory, and Cost of Goods Sold. However, the method of assigning costs differs significantly.

There are four main differences between the two cost systems: (1) A process cost system uses separate accounts for each production department or manufacturing process, rather than the single work in process account used in a job-order cost system. (2) In a process cost system, costs are summarized in a production cost report for each department; in a job-order cost system, costs are charged to individual jobs and summarized in a job cost sheet. (3) Costs are totalled at the end of a time period in a process cost system and at the completion of a job in a job-order cost system. (4) In a process cost system, the unit cost is calculated as follows: Total manufacturing costs for the period divided by the units produced during the period. In a job-order cost system, the calculation of the unit cost is as follows: Total cost per job divided by the units produced.

3. *Explain the flow of costs in a process cost system.* Manufacturing costs for raw materials, labour, and overhead are assigned to work in process accounts for various departments or manufacturing processes, and the costs of units completed in a department are transferred from one department to another as those units move through the manufacturing process. The costs of completed work are transferred to Finished Goods Inventory. When inventory is sold, costs are transferred to Cost of Goods Sold.

4. *Make the journal entries to assign manufacturing costs in a process cost system.* Entries to assign the costs of raw materials, labour, and overhead consist of a credit to Raw Materials Inventory, Factory Labour, and Manufacturing Overhead, and a debit to Work in Process for each of the departments that are doing the processing.

Entries to record the cost of goods transferred to another department are a credit to Work in Process for the department whose work is finished and a debit for the department that the goods are transferred to.

The entry to record the units completed and transferred to the warehouse is a credit for the department whose work is finished and a debit to Finished Goods Inventory.

Finally, the entry to record the sale of goods is a credit to Finished Goods Inventory and a debit to Cost of Goods Sold.

5. *Calculate equivalent units using the weighted-average method.* Equivalent units of production measure the work done during a period, expressed in fully completed units. This concept is used to determine the cost per unit of completed product. Equivalent units are the sum of units completed and transferred out plus equivalent units of ending work in process.

6. *Explain the four necessary steps to prepare a production cost report.* The four steps to complete a production cost report are as follows: (1) Calculate the physical unit flow—that is, the total units to be accounted for. (2) Calculate the equivalent units of production. (3) Calculate the unit production costs, expressed in equivalent units of production. (4) Prepare a cost reconciliation schedule, which shows that the total costs accounted for equal the total costs to be accounted for.

7. *Prepare a production cost report.* The production cost report contains both quantity and cost data for a production department. There are four sections in the report: (1) the number of physical units, (2) the equivalent units determination, (3) the unit costs, and (4) the cost reconciliation schedule.

8. *Prepare a production cost report for a sequential department setting.* In this setting, goods are transferred from one department to another. Such a

sequential process requires the use of an additional cost component called "transferred in." This cost component has a percentage of completion factor of 100%. The transferred-in cost component is treated the same way as any other cost component in the calculations of the equivalent units of production and the cost per equivalent unit of production.

9. *Calculate equivalent units using the FIFO method.* Equivalent units under the FIFO method are the sum of the work performed to (1) finish the units of beginning work in process inventory, if any; (2) complete the units started into production during the period; and (3) start, but only partially complete, the units in ending work in process inventory.

Decision Toolkit—A Summary

Decision Checkpoints	Info Needed for Decision	Tools to Use for Decision	How to Evaluate Results
What is the cost of a product?	Costs of materials, labour, and overhead assigned to processes used to make the product	Production cost report	Compare costs to previous periods and to competitors to ensure that costs are reasonable. Compare costs to the expected selling price to determine overall profitability.
What costing method should be used?	Type of product produced	Cost of accounting system; benefits of additional information	The benefits of providing the additional information should exceed the costs of the accounting system that is needed to develop the information.

Glossary

www.wiley.com/canada/managerial

Key Term Matching Activity

Conversion costs   The sum of labour costs and overhead costs. (p. 99)

Cost reconciliation schedule   A schedule that shows that the total costs accounted for equal the total costs to be accounted for. (p. 103)

Equivalent units of production   A measure of the work done during the period, expressed in fully completed units. (p. 98)

FIFO (First-in, First-out) method   A process costing method in which the cost assigned to the beginning work in process inventory is separated from current-period production costs. The cost per equivalent unit is related to the current period only. (p. 107)

Operations costing   A combination of a process cost and a job-order cost system, in which products are manufactured mainly by standardized methods, with some customization. (p. 106)

Physical units   Actual units to be accounted for during a period, regardless of any work performed. (p. 100)

Process cost system   An accounting system that is used to apply costs to similar products that are mass-produced in a continuous way. (p. 92)

Production cost report   An internal report for management that shows both the production quantity and cost data for a production department. (p. 99)

Total units (costs) accounted for   The sum of the units (costs) transferred out during the period plus the units (costs) in process at the end of the period. (pp. 100, 103)

Total units (costs) to be accounted for   The sum of the units (costs) started (or transferred) into production during the period plus the units (costs) in process at the beginning of the period. (pp. 100, 103)

Transferred-in cost   It is used in a sequential (or multiple-department) process setting. A cost component that has a percentage of completion factor of 100% and is treated the same as any other cost component in the calculations of the equivalent units of production and the cost per equivalent unit of production. (p. 104)

Unit production costs   Costs expressed in terms of equivalent units of production. (p. 101)

Weighted-average method   A method used to calculate equivalent units of production and which considers the degree of completion (weighting) of the units completed and transferred out and the ending work in process. (p. 98)

Demonstration Problem

www.wiley.com/canada/managerial

Animated Demonstration Problem

Karlene Industries produces plastic ice cube trays in two processes: heating and stamping. All materials are added at the beginning in the heating department. Karlene uses the weighted-average method to calculate equivalent units.

On November 1, 2005, 1,000 trays that were 70% complete were in process in the heating department. During November, 12,000 trays were started into production. On November 30, 2,000 trays that were 60% complete were in process.

The following cost information for the heating department is also available:

Work in process, November 1:		Costs incurred in November:	
Materials	$ 640	Material	$3,000
Conversion costs	360	Labour	2,300
Cost of work in process, Nov. 1	$1,000	Overhead	4,050

Instructions

(a) Prepare a production cost report for the heating department for the month of November, using the weighted-average method.

(b) Journalize the transfer of costs to the stamping department.

Action Plan

• Calculate the physical unit flow— that is, the total units to be accounted for.

• Calculate the equivalent units of production.

• Calculate the unit production costs, expressed in terms of equivalent units of production.

• Prepare a cost reconciliation schedule, which shows that the total costs accounted for equal the total costs to be accounted for.

Solution to Demonstration Problem

(a)

KARLENE INDUSTRIES
Heating Department
Production Cost Report
Month Ended November 30, 2005

	Physical Units	Equivalent Units		
		Materials	Conversion Costs	Total
	Step 1	Step 2		
Quantities				
Units to be accounted for				
Work in process, November 1	1,000			
Started in production	12,000			
Total units	13,000			
Units accounted for				
Transferred out	11,000	11,000	11,000	
Work in process, November 30	2,000	2,000	1,200	
Total units	13,000	13,000	12,200	
Costs Step 3				
Unit costs				
Costs in November (a)		$3,640	$6,710	$10,350
Equivalent units (b)		13,000	12,200	
Unit costs [(a) ÷ (b)]		$0.28	$0.55	$0.83
Costs to be accounted for				
Work in process, November 1				$ 1,000
Started into production				9,350
Total costs				$10,350
Cost Reconciliation Schedule Step 4				
Costs accounted for				
Transferred out (11,000 × $0.83)				$ 9,130
Work in process, November 30				
Materials (2,000 × $0.28)			$560	
Conversion costs (1,200 × $0.55)			660	1,220
Total cost				$10,350

(b)

Work in Process—Stamping	9,130	
Work in Process—Heating		9,130
To record transfer of units to the stamping department.		

✔ the navigator

Note: All questions, exercises, and problems below with an asterisk (*) relate to material in Appendix 3A.

Self-Study Questions

www.wiley.com/canada/managerial

Additional Self-Study Questions

Answers are at the end of the chapter.

(SO 1) 1. Which of the following items is *not* a characteristic of a process cost system?
(a) Once production begins, it continues until the finished product emerges.
(b) The products produced are heterogeneous in nature.
(c) The focus is on continually producing homogeneous products.
(d) When the finished product emerges, all units have precisely the same amount of materials, labour, and overhead.

(SO 2) 2. Indicate which of the following statements is *not* correct.
(a) Both a job-order and a process cost system track the same three manufacturing cost elements—direct materials, direct labour, and manufacturing overhead.
(b) In a job-order cost system, only one work in process account is used, whereas in a process cost system, multiple work in process accounts are used.
(c) Manufacturing costs are accumulated the same way in a job-order system as in a process cost system.
(d) Manufacturing costs are assigned the same way in a job-order and in a process cost system.

(SO 3) 3. In a process cost system, costs are assigned only:
(a) to one work in process account.
(b) to Work in Process and Finished Goods Inventory.
(c) to Work in Process, Finished Goods Inventory, and Cost of Goods Sold.
(d) to work in process accounts.

(SO 4) 4. In making the journal entry to assign raw materials costs:
(a) the debit is to Finished Goods Inventory.
(b) the debit is often to two or more work in process accounts.
(c) the credit is generally to two or more work in process accounts.
(d) the credit is to Finished Goods Inventory.

(SO 5) 5. The mixing department's output during the period consists of 20,000 units completed and transferred out, and 5,000 units in ending work in process that are 60% complete as to materials and conversion costs. Beginning inventory is 1,000 units, 40% complete as to materials and conversion costs. The equivalent units of production are:
(a) 22,600.   (c) 24,000.
(b) 23,000.   (d) 25,000.

(SO 6) 6. In RYZ Company, there are no units in beginning work in process, 7,000 units started into production, and 500 units in ending work in process that are 20% completed. The physical units to be accounted for are:
(a) 7,000.   (c) 7,600.
(b) 7,360.   (d) 7,340.

(SO 6) 7. Mora Company has 2,000 units in beginning work in process, 20% complete as to conversion costs; 23,000 units transferred out to finished goods; and 3,000 units in ending work in process, $33^1/_3$% complete as to conversion costs. The beginning and ending inventory is fully complete as to materials costs. Equivalent units for materials and conversion costs are, respectively:
(a) 22,000 and 24,000.   (c) 26,000 and 24,000.
(b) 24,000 and 26,000.   (d) 26,000 and 26,000.

(SO 6) 8. Fortner Company has no beginning work in process; 9,000 units are transferred out and 3,000 units in ending work in process are one-third finished as to conversion costs and fully complete as to materials cost. If the total materials cost is $60,000, the unit materials cost is:
(a) $5.00.
(b) $5.45 rounded.
(c) $6.00.
(d) No correct answer is given.

(SO 6) 9. Largo Company has unit costs of $10 for materials and $30 for conversion costs. If there are 2,500 units in ending work in process, 40% complete as to conversion costs, and fully complete as to materials cost, the total cost assigned to the ending work in process inventory is:
(a) $45,000.   (c) $75,000.
(b) $55,000.   (d) $100,000.

(SO 7)   10. A production cost report:
(a) is an external report.
(b) shows the costs charged to a department and costs accounted for.
(c) shows equivalent units of production but not physical units.
(d) contains six sections.

(SO 9)   *11. Hollins Company uses the FIFO method to calculate equivalent units. It has 2,000 units in beginning work in process, 20% complete as to conversion costs; 25,000 units started and completed; and 3,000 units in ending work in process, 30% complete as to conversion costs. All units are 100% complete as to materials. The equivalent units for materials and conversion costs are, respectively:
(a) 28,000 and 26,600.   (c) 27,000 and 26,200.
(b) 28,000 and 27,500.   (d) 27,000 and 29,600.

*12. KSM Company uses the FIFO method to calculate equivalent units. It has no beginning work in process; 9,000 units are started and completed and 3,000 units in ending work in process are one-third completed. If the total materials cost is $60,000, the unit materials cost is: (SO 9)
(a) $5.00.   (c) $6.67 (rounded).
(b) $6.00.   (d) No correct answer is given.

*13. Toney Company uses the FIFO method to calculate equivalent units. It has unit costs of $10 for materials and $30 for conversion costs. If there are 2,500 units in ending work in process, 100% complete as to materials and 40% complete as to conversion costs, the total cost to assign to the ending work in process inventory is: (SO 9)
(a) $45,000.   (c) $75,000.
(b) $55,000.   (d) $100,000.

Questions

1. Identify which costing system—job-order or process cost—the following companies would use: (a) Imperial Oil, (b) Quebecor, (c) Ganong, and (d) CBC.
2. Contrast the main focus of job-order cost accounting and of process cost accounting.
3. What are the similarities between a job-order and a process cost system?
4. Your roommate is confused about the features of process cost accounting. Identify and explain the distinctive features for your roommate.
5. Zoë Turner believes there are no significant differences in the flow of costs between job-order cost accounting and process cost accounting. Is Turner correct? Explain.
6. (a) What source documents are used in assigning (1) materials and (2) labour to production?
(b) What criterion and basis are commonly used to allocate overhead to processes?
7. At Cale Company, overhead is assigned to production departments at the rate of $15 per machine hour. In July, machine hours were 3,000 in the machining department and 2,400 in the assembly department. Prepare the entry to assign overhead to production.
8. Judy Mastine is uncertain about the steps used to prepare a production cost report. State the procedures that are required, in the sequence in which they are performed.
9. Julien Gauthier is confused about calculating physical units. Explain to Julien how physical units to be accounted for and physical units accounted for are determined.
10. What is meant by the term "equivalent units of production"?

11. How are equivalent units of production calculated?
12. Clay Company had no units of beginning work in process. During the period, 9,000 units were completed, and there were 600 units of ending work in process. What were the units started into production?
13. Gia Co. has no units of beginning work in process. During the period 12,000 units were completed, and there were 600 units of ending work in process that were one-fifth complete as to conversion costs and 100% complete as to materials costs. What were the equivalent units of production for (a) materials costs and (b) conversion costs?
14. Hall Co. started 3,000 units for the period. Its beginning inventory was 800 units that were one-fourth complete as to conversion costs and 100% complete as to materials costs. Its ending inventory is 400 units that are one-fifth complete as to conversion costs and 100% complete as to materials costs. How many units were transferred out during this period?
15. Grace Company transfers out 14,000 units and has 2,000 units of ending work in process that are 25% complete. Materials are entered at the beginning of the process and there is no beginning work in process. Assuming unit materials costs of $3 and unit conversion costs of $9, what are the costs to be assigned to units (a) transferred out and (b) in ending work in process?
16. (a) Jim Jain believes the production cost report is an external report for stockholders. Is Jim correct? Explain.
(b) Identify the sections in a production cost report.
17. What purposes are served by a production cost report?

18. At Adan Company, there are 800 units of ending work in process that are 100% complete as to materials and 40% complete as to conversion costs. If the unit cost of materials is $4 and the costs assigned to the 800 units is $6,600, what is the per-unit conversion cost?

19. What is the difference between operations costing and a process costing system?

20. How does a company decide whether to use a job-order or a process cost system?

*21. Silva Co. started and completed 2,000 units for the period. Its beginning inventory was 600 units that were one-fourth complete and its ending inventory is 400 units that are one-fifth complete. Silva uses the FIFO method to calculate equivalent units. How many units were transferred out during this period?

*22. Ortiz Company transfers out 12,000 units and has 2,000 units of ending work in process that are 25% complete. Materials are entered at the beginning of the process and there is no beginning work in process. Ortiz uses the FIFO method to calculate equivalent units. Assuming unit materials costs of $3 and unit conversion costs of $9, what are the costs to be assigned to units (a) transferred out and (b) in ending work in process?

Brief Exercises

BE3–1 Turner Manufacturing purchases $60,000 of raw materials on account, and it incurs $40,000 of factory labour costs. Journalize the two transactions on May 31, assuming the labour costs are not paid until June.

Journalize entries for accumulating costs. (SO 4)

BE3–2 Data for Turner Manufacturing are given in BE3–1. Supporting records show that (a) the assembly department used $29,000 of raw materials and $28,000 of factory labour, and (b) the finishing department used the remainder. Journalize the assignment of the costs to these processing departments on May 31.

Journalize assignment of materials and labour costs. (SO 4)

BE3–3 Factory labour data for Turner Manufacturing are given in BE3–2. Manufacturing overhead is assigned to departments on the basis of 150% of the labour costs. Journalize the assignment of overhead to the assembly and finishing departments.

Journalize assignment of overhead costs. (SO 4)

BE3–4 Barclay Manufacturing Company has the following production data for selected months:

Calculate physical units of production. (SO 6)

Month	Beginning Work in Process	Units Transferred Out	Ending Work in Process Units	% Complete as to Conversion Costs
January	0	20,000	5,000	40%
March	0	30,000	4,000	75
July	0	50,000	10,000	25

Calculate the physical units for each month.

BE3–5 Using the data in BE3–4, calculate the equivalent units of production for materials costs and conversion costs, assuming materials are entered at the beginning of the process.

Calculate equivalent units of production. (SO 5)

BE3–6 In Cuthbert Company, total material costs are $52,000, and total conversion costs are $60,000. Equivalent units of production are 10,000 for materials and 20,000 for conversion costs. Calculate the unit costs for materials, conversion costs, and the total manufacturing cost.

Calculate unit costs of production. (SO 6)

BE3–7 Sosa Company has the following production data for March: units transferred out, 40,000; ending work in process, 5,000 units that are 100% complete for materials and 40% complete for conversion costs. If the unit materials cost is $8 and the unit conversion cost is $15, determine the costs to be assigned to the units transferred out and the units in ending work in process.

Assign costs to units transferred out and in process. (SO 6)

BE3–8 Production costs that are chargeable to the finishing department in Murdock Company in July are materials $9,000; labour $23,800; and overhead $18,000. The equivalent units of production are 20,000 for materials and 19,000 for conversion costs. Calculate the unit costs for materials and conversion costs.

Calculate unit costs. (SO 6)

BE3–9 Data for Murdock Company are given in BE3–8. Production records indicate that 15,000 units were transferred out, and 2,000 units in ending work in process were

Prepare cost reconciliation schedule. (SO 6)

50% complete as to conversion costs and 100% complete as to materials. Prepare a cost reconciliation schedule.

Calculate equivalent units of production.
(SO 5)

BE3–10   The smelting department of Dewey Manufacturing Company has the following production and cost data for October: beginning work in process, 2,000 units that are 100% complete as to materials and 20% complete as to conversion costs; units transferred out, 8,000 units; and ending work in process, 3,000 units that are 100% complete as to materials and 40% complete as to conversion costs.

Calculate the equivalent units of production for (a) materials and (b) conversion costs for the month of October.

Assign costs to units transferred out and in process.
(SO 6, 9)

*BE3–11   Mora Company has the following production data for March: units started and completed, 30,000; and ending work in process, 5,000 units that are 100% complete for materials and 40% complete for conversion costs. Mora uses the FIFO method to calculate equivalent units. If the unit materials cost is $8 and the unit conversion cost is $12, determine the costs to be assigned to the units transferred out and the units in ending work in process. The total cost to be assigned is $664,000.

Prepare partial production cost report.
(SO 7, 9)

*BE3–12   Using the data in BE3–11, prepare the cost section of the production cost report for Mora Company.

Calculate unit costs.
(SO 9)

*BE3–13   Production costs that are chargeable to the finishing department in May in Brown Company are materials $8,000; labour $20,000; overhead $18,000; and transferred-in costs $62,000. The equivalent units of production are 20,000 for materials and 19,000 for conversion costs. Brown uses the FIFO method to calculate equivalent units. Calculate the unit costs for materials and conversion costs. Transferred-in costs are considered to be materials costs.

Exercises

Journalize transactions.
(SO 3, 4)

E3–1   Sally May Company manufactures pizza sauce through two production departments: cooking and canning. In each department, materials and conversion costs are incurred evenly throughout the process. For the month of March, the work in process accounts show the following debits:

	Cooking	Canning
Beginning work in process	$ 0	$ 4,000
Materials	14,000	6,000
Labour	8,500	7,000
Overhead	29,500	22,000
Costs transferred in	0	45,000

Instructions

Journalize the March transactions.

Journalize transactions for two processes.
(SO 4)

E3–2   Greenleaf Manufacturing Company has two production departments: cutting and assembly. August 1 inventories are Raw Materials $4,200; Work in Process—Cutting $3,900; Work in Process—Assembly $10,600; and Finished Goods $31,900. During August, the following transactions occurred:

1. Purchased $56,300 of raw materials on account.
2. Incurred $55,000 of factory labour. (Credit Wages Payable.)
3. Incurred $70,000 of manufacturing overhead; $36,000 was paid and the remainder is unpaid.
4. Requisitioned materials for cutting $15,700; and for assembly, $8,900.
5. Used factory labour for cutting; $28,000; and for assembly, $27,000.
6. Applied overhead at the rate of $20 per machine hour. Machine hours were 1,640 for cutting and 1,720 for assembly.
7. Transferred goods costing $77,600 from cutting to assembly.
8. Transferred goods costing $135,000 from assembly to finished goods.
9. Sold goods costing $130,000 for $200,000 on account.

Instructions

Journalize the transactions. (Omit explanations.)

E3–3 In Bing Company, materials are entered at the beginning of each process. Bing's work in process inventories—with the percentage of conversion costs completed—and the production data for Bing's sterilizing department in selected months during 2005 are as follows:

Calculate physical units and equivalent units of production.
(SO 5, 6)

	Beginning Work in Process		Units	Ending Work in Process	
Month	Units	Conversion Cost %	Transferred Out	Units	Conversion Cost %
January	0	—	7,000	2,000	70
March	0	—	12,000	3,000	30
May	0	—	16,000	5,000	80
July	0	—	10,000	1,500	40

Instructions

(a) Calculate the physical units for January and May.
(b) Calculate the equivalent units of production for (1) materials and (2) conversion costs for each month.

E3–4 The cutting department of Behan Manufacturing has the following production and cost data for August:

Determine equivalent units, unit costs, and assignment of costs.
(SO 5, 6)

Production	Costs	
1. Transferred out 9,000 units.	Beginning work in process	$ 0
2. Started 1,000 units that are 40% complete as to conversion costs and 100% complete as to materials at August 31.	Materials	45,000
	Labour	14,940
	Manufacturing overhead	18,900

Materials are entered at the beginning of the process. Conversion costs are incurred evenly during the process.

Instructions

(a) Determine the equivalent units of production for (1) materials and (2) conversion costs.
(b) Calculate the unit costs and prepare a cost reconciliation schedule.

E3–5 The sanding department of Han Furniture Company has the following production and manufacturing cost data for April 2005:

Prepare production cost report.
(SO 5, 6, 7)

Production: 12,000 units finished and transferred out; 3,000 units started that are 100% complete as to materials and 40% complete as to conversion costs

Manufacturing costs: Materials $36,000; labour $30,000; overhead $37,320

Instructions

Prepare a production cost report.

E3–6 The blending department of Ceja Company has the following cost and production data for the month of May:

Determine equivalent units, unit costs, and assignment of costs.
(SO 5, 6)

Work in process, May 1		
Direct materials: 100% complete	$100,000	
Conversion costs: 20% complete	75,000	
Cost of work in process, May 1	$175,000	
Costs incurred during production in May		
Direct materials	$ 800,000	
Conversion costs	350,000	
Costs incurred in May	$1,150,000	

Units transferred out totalled 8,000. Ending work in process was 2,000 units that are 100% complete as to materials and 25% complete as to conversion costs.

Instructions

(a) Calculate the equivalent units of production for (1) materials and (2) conversion costs for the month of May.
(b) Calculate the unit costs for the month.
(c) Determine the costs to be assigned to the units transferred out and in ending work in process.

Answer questions on costs and production.
(SO 3, 5, 6)

E3–7   The ledger of Lui Company has the following work in process account data for July:

Work in Process—Painting

July	1	Balance	4,450	July 31	Transferred out	?
	31	Materials	6,100			
	31	Labour	2,500			
	31	Overhead	1,650			
	31	Balance	?			

Production records show that there were 700 units in the beginning inventory, 30% complete; 1,100 units started; and 1,300 units transferred out. The beginning work in process had materials costs of $2,900 and conversion costs of $1,550. The units in ending inventory were 40% complete. Materials are entered at the beginning of the painting process.

Instructions

(a) How many units are in process at July 31?
(b) What is the unit materials cost for July?
(c) What is the unit conversion cost for July?
(d) What is the total cost of units transferred out in July?
(e) What is the cost of the July 31 inventory?

Answer questions on costs and production.
(SO 3, 5, 6)

E3–8   The polishing department of Pimetry Manufacturing Company has the following production and manufacturing cost data for October. Materials are entered at the beginning of the process.

Production: Beginning inventory, 1,600 units that are 100% complete as to materials and 30% complete as to conversion costs; units started during the period, 11,000; ending inventory, 2,000 units that are 10% complete as to conversion costs.

Manufacturing costs: Beginning inventory costs, $20,000 of materials and $43,180 of conversion costs; materials costs added in polishing during the month, $162,700; labour and overhead applied in polishing during the month, $100,080 and $250,940, respectively.

Instructions

(a) Calculate the equivalent units of production for materials and conversion costs for the month of October.
(b) Calculate the unit costs for materials and conversion costs for the month.
(c) Determine the costs to be assigned to the units transferred out and in process.

Explain production cost report.
(SO 7)

E3–9   Mary Mahr has recently been promoted to production manager, and has just started to receive various managerial reports. One of the reports she has received is the production cost report that you prepared. It showed that her department had 1,000 equivalent units in ending inventory. Her department has had a history of not keeping enough inventory on hand to meet demand. She has come to you, very angry, and wants to know why you credited her with only 1,000 units when she knows she had at least twice that many on hand.

Instructions

▭▭▭▷ Explain to her why her production cost report showed only 1,000 equivalent units in ending inventory. Write an informal memo. Be kind and explain very clearly why she is mistaken.

Prepare production cost report.
(SO 5, 6, 7)

E3–10   The welding department of Marlin Manufacturing Company has the following production and manufacturing cost data for February 2005. All materials are added at the beginning of the process.

Manufacturing Costs			Production Data	
Beginning work in process			Beginning work in process	15,000 units,
Materials	$15,000			10% complete
Conversion costs	30,435	$ 45,435	Units transferred out	49,000
Materials		180,000	Units started	60,000
Labour		35,100	Ending work in process	26,000 units,
Overhead		64,545		20% complete

Instructions

Prepare a production cost report for the welding department for the month of February.

E3–11 Container Shipping, Inc. is thinking of using process costing to track its operations. The operations consist of three segments (departments): receiving, shipping, and delivery. Containers are received at Container Shippings' docks and sorted according to the ship they will be carried on. The containers are loaded onto a ship, which carries them to the appropriate port of destination. The containers are then off-loaded and delivered to the receiving company.

Calculate physical units and equivalent units of production.
(SO 5, 6)

Container Shipping wants to begin using process costing in the shipping department. Direct materials are the fuel costs to run the ship, and "Containers in transit" are considered work in process. Listed below is the shipping department's activity for the first month:

Containers in transit, April 1   0
Containers loaded   800
Containers in transit, April 30   350 (40% of direct materials and 30% of conversion costs)

Instructions

(a) Determine the physical flow of containers for the month.
(b) Calculate the equivalent units for direct materials and conversion costs.

E3–12 Hi-Tech Mortgage Company uses a process costing system to accumulate costs in its loan application department. When an application is completed, it is forwarded to the loan department for final processing. The following processing and cost data are for September:

Determine equivalent units, unit costs, and assignment of costs.
(SO 5, 6)

Production	Costs	
1. Applications in process on September 1, 100	Beginning WIP:	
2. Applications started in September, 900	Direct materials	$ 1,000
3. Completed applications during September, 800	Conversion costs	4,000
4. Applications still in process at September 30	September costs:	
were 100% complete as to materials (forms) and	Direct materials	4,000
60% complete as to conversion costs.	Direct labour	12,000
	Overhead	9,400

Materials are the forms used in the application process and are incurred at the beginning of the process. Conversion costs are incurred evenly during the process.

Instructions

(a) Determine the equivalent units of service (production) for materials and conversion costs.
(b) Calculate the unit costs and prepare a cost reconciliation schedule.

*E3–13 Using the data in Exercise E3–12, assume Hi-Tech Mortgage Company uses the FIFO method. Also assume that the applications in process on September 1 were 100% complete as to materials (forms) and 40% complete as to conversion costs.

Calculate equivalent units, unit costs, and costs assigned.
(SO 5, 6, 9)

Instructions

(a) Determine the equivalent units of service (production) for materials and conversion costs.
(b) Calculate the unit costs and prepare a cost reconciliation schedule.

*E3–14 The cutting department of Chan Manufacturing has the following production and cost data for August:

Determine equivalent units, unit costs, and assignment of costs.
(SO 5, 6, 9)

Production	Costs	
1. Started and completed 8,000 units.	Beginning work in process	$ 0
2. Started 1,000 units that are 40%	Materials	45,000
completed at August 31.	Labour	14,700
	Manufacturing overhead	18,900

Materials are entered at the beginning of the process. Conversion costs are incurred evenly during the process. Chan Manufacturing uses the FIFO method to calculate equivalent units.

Instructions

(a) Determine the equivalent units of production for (1) materials and (2) conversion costs.
(b) Calculate the unit costs and show the assignment of manufacturing costs to units transferred out, and in work in process.

Answer questions on costs and production.
(SO 5, 6, 9)

*E3–15 The smelting department of Amber Manufacturing Company has the following production and manufacturing cost data for September:

Production: Beginning work in process, 2,000 units that are 100% complete as to materials and 20% complete as to conversion costs; units started and finished, 11,000; ending work in process, 1,000 units that are 100% complete as to materials and 40% complete as to conversion costs

Manufacturing costs: Work in process, September 1, $15,200; materials added, $60,000; labour and overhead, $143,000.

Amber uses the FIFO method to calculate equivalent units.

Instructions

(a) Calculate the equivalent units of production for (1) materials and (2) conversion costs for the month of September.
(b) Calculate the unit costs for the month.
(c) Determine the costs to be assigned to the units transferred out, and in work in process.

Calculate equivalent units, unit costs, and costs assigned.
(SO 5, 6, 9)

*E3–16 The ledger of Platt Company has the following work in process account data for March:

Work in Process—Painting				
March 1	Balance	3,680	March 31 Transferred out	?
31	Materials	6,600		
31	Labour	2,500		
31	Overhead	1,280		
31	Balance	?		

Production records show that there were 800 units in the beginning inventory, 30% complete; 1,100 units started; and 1,300 units transferred out. The units in ending inventory were 40% complete. Materials are entered at the beginning of the painting process. Platt uses the FIFO method to calculate equivalent units.

Instructions

Answer the following questions.

(a) How many units are in process at March 31?
(b) What is the unit materials cost for March?
(c) What is the unit conversion cost for March?
(d) What is the total cost of units started in February and completed in March?
(e) What is the total cost of units started and finished in March?
(f) What is the cost of the March 31 inventory?

Prepare production cost report for second process.
(SO 8, 9)

*E3–17 The welding department of Hirohama Manufacturing Company has the following production and manufacturing costs data for February 2005. All materials are added at the beginning of the process. Hirohama uses the FIFO method to calculate equivalent units.

Manufacturing Costs		Production Data	
Beginning work in process	$ 32,175	Beginning work in process	15,000 units, 10% complete
Costs transferred in	135,000	Units transferred out	50,000
Materials	57,000	Units transferred in	60,000
Labour	35,100	Ending work in process	25,000 units, 20% complete
Overhead	71,900		

Instructions

Prepare a production cost report for the welding department for February. Transferred-in costs are considered to be materials costs.

Problems: Set A

P3–18A Vargas Company manufactures the nutrient Everlife through two manufacturing processes: blending and packaging. All materials are entered at the beginning of each process. On August 1, 2005, inventories consisted of Raw Materials $5,000; Work in Process— Blending $0; Work in Process—Packaging $3,945; and Finished Goods $7,500. The beginning inventory for packaging consisted of 500 units, two-fifths complete as to conversion costs and fully complete as to materials. During August, 9,000 units were started into production in blending, and the following transactions were completed:

Journalize transactions. (SO 3, 4)

1. Purchased $25,000 of raw materials on account.
2. Issued raw materials for production: $16,800 for blending and $7,200 for packaging.
3. Incurred labour costs of $18,770.
4. Used factory labour: $12,230 for blending and $6,540 for packaging.
5. Incurred $41,300 of manufacturing overhead on account.
6. Applied manufacturing overhead at the rate of $35 per machine hour. Machine hours were 900 for blending and 300 for packaging.
7. Transferred 8,200 units from blending to packaging at a cost of $54,940.
8. Transferred 8,600 units from packaging to finished goods at a cost of $74,490.
9. Sold goods costing $62,000 for $85,000 on account.

Instructions

Journalize the August transactions.

P3–19A Newton Inc. manufactures electronic switching mechanisms on a highly automated assembly line. Its costing system uses two cost categories: direct materials and conversion costs. Each product must pass through the assembly department and the testing department. Direct materials are added at the beginning of the production process. Conversion costs are incurred evenly throughout the process. Newton Inc. uses a weighted-average process costing system. Production and cost data for the assembly department for June follow:

Calculate equivalent units, unit costs, and costs assigned. (SO 5, 6, 7)

Work in process, beginning inventory (conversion costs 50% complete)	250 units
Units started during June	800 units
Work in process, ending inventory (conversion costs 75% complete)	150 units
Work in process, beginning inventory costs	
Direct materials	$ 180,000
Conversion costs	270,000
Direct material costs added in June	1,000,000
Conversion costs incurred in June	1,000,000

Instructions

(a) What is the total cost debited to the work in process account during June?
(b) What is the direct material cost (rounded to the nearest dollar) per equivalent unit during June?
(c) What is the amount (rounded to the nearest dollar) of conversion costs assigned to ending work in process in June?

P3–20A Zion Corporation manufactures water skis through two processes: moulding and packaging. In the moulding department, fibreglass is heated and shaped into the form of a ski. In the packaging department, the skis are placed in cartons and sent to the finished goods warehouse. Materials are entered at the beginning of both processes. Labour and manufacturing overhead are incurred uniformly throughout each process. Production and cost data for the moulding department for January 2005 follow.

Complete four necessary steps to prepare a production cost report. (SO 5, 6, 7)

Production Data	January
Beginning work in process units	0
Units started into production	43,000
Ending work in process units	3,000
Percent complete—ending inventory	40%

Cost Data	January
Materials	$550,400
Labour	126,640
Overhead	170,000
Total	$847,040

Instructions

(a) Calculate the physical units of production.
(b) Determine the equivalent units of production for materials and conversion costs.
(c) Calculate the unit costs of production.
(d) Determine the costs to be assigned to the units transferred out, and in work in process.
(e) Prepare a production cost report for the moulding department for the month of January.

Complete four necessary steps to prepare production cost report. (SO 5, 6, 7)

P3–21A   Stein Corporation uses separate processes to manufacture refrigerators and freezers for homes. In each process, materials are entered at the beginning and conversion costs are incurred evenly. Production and cost data for the first process in making these two products are as follows in two different manufacturing plants:

	Stamping Department	
	Plant A	Plant B
Production Data—June	R12 Refrigerators	F24 Freezers
Work in process units, June 1	0	0
Units started into production	20,000	20,000
Work in process units, June 30	2,000	3,000
Work in process percent complete	70%	50%

Cost Data—June		
Work in process, June 1	$ 0	$ 0
Materials	840,000	700,000
Labour	200,800	236,000
Overhead	420,000	319,000
Total	$1,460,800	$1,255,000

Instructions

(a) For each plant:
    1. Calculate the physical units of production.
    2. Calculate the equivalent units of production for materials and for conversion costs.
    3. Determine the unit costs of production.
    4. Show the assignment of costs to units transferred out, and in work in process.
(b) Prepare the production cost report for Plant A for June 2005.

Assign costs and prepare production cost report. (SO 5, 6, 7)

P3–22A   Elite Company has several processing departments. Costs charged to the assembly department for October 2005 totalled $1,328,400, as follows:

Work in process, October 1		
Materials	$ 9,000	
Conversion costs	27,400	$ 36,400
Materials added		1,071,000
Labour		90,000
Overhead		131,000

Production records show that 35,000 units were in beginning work in process and were 40% complete as to conversion cost; 415,000 units were started into production; and 45,000 units were in ending work in process and were 20% complete as to conversion costs. Materials are entered at the beginning of each process.

Instructions

(a) Determine the equivalent units of production and the unit costs for the assembly department.
(b) Determine the assignment of costs to goods transferred out, and in work in process.
(c) Prepare a production cost report for the assembly department.

P3–23A Sprague Company manufactures bicycles and tricycles. For both products, materials are added at the beginning of the production process, and conversion costs are incurred evenly. Production and cost data for the month of July are as follows:

Determine equivalent units and unit costs, and assign costs.
(SO 5, 6, 7)

Production Data—Bicycles	Units	Percent Complete
Work in process units, July 1	400	80%
Units started in production	1,100	
Work in process units, July 31	500	10%

Cost Data—Bicycles		
Work in process, July 1		
Materials	$10,000	
Conversion costs	9,300	$19,300
Direct materials		50,000
Direct labour		23,700
Manufacturing overhead		30,000

Instructions

(a) Calculate the following:
   1. The equivalent units of production for materials and conversion
   2. The unit costs of production for materials and conversion costs
   3. The assignment of costs to units transferred out and to work in process at the end of the accounting period
(b) Prepare a production cost report for the month of July for the bicycles segment.

P3–24A Taylor Cleaner Company uses a weighted-average process costing system and manufactures a single product—an all-purpose liquid cleaner. The manufacturing activity for the month of March has just been completed. A partially completed production cost report for the month of March for the mixing and blending department is shown below:

Calculate equivalent units and complete production cost report.
(SO 5, 7)

TAYLOR CLEANER COMPANY
Mixing and Blending Department
Production Cost Report
Month Ended May 31

Quantities	Physical Units	Equivalent Units Materials	Conversion Costs	Total
Units to be accounted for				
Work in process, May 1 (40% materials, 20% conversion costs)	7,000			
Started into production	100,000			
Total units	107,000			
Units accounted for				
Transferred out	95,000	(a)	(b)	
Work in process, May 31 (75% materials, 25% conversion costs)	12,000	(c)	(d)	
Total units accounted for	107,000	(e)	(f)	

Costs				
Unit costs				
Costs in May		$166,400	$98,000	$264,400
Equivalent units		(g)	(h)	
Unit costs		$ (i) +	$ (j) =	$ (k)
Costs to be accounted for				
Work in process, May 1				$ 12,000
Started into production				252,400
Total costs				$264,400

Cost Reconciliation Schedule

Costs accounted for		
Transferred out		$ (l)
Work in process, May 31		
Materials	$ (m)	
Conversion costs	(n)	(o)
Total cost		$ (p)

Instructions

(a) Prepare a schedule that shows how the equivalent units were calculated so that you can complete the "Quantities: Units accounted for" equivalent units section shown in the production cost report above, and calculate the unit costs for May.

(b) Complete the "Cost Reconciliation Schedule" part of the production cost report above.

Calculate equivalent units, unit costs, and costs assigned.
(SO 5, 6, 7)

P3–25A　Montreal Leather Company manufactures high-quality leather goods. One of the company's main products is a fine leather belt. The belts are produced in a single, continuous process in its Quebec plant. During the process, leather strips are sewn, punched, and dyed. The belts then enter a final finishing stage to conclude the process. Labour and overhead are applied continuously during the manufacturing process. All materials, leather strips, and buckles are introduced at the beginning of the process. The firm uses the weighted-average method to calculate its unit costs.

The leather belts produced at the Quebec plant are sold wholesale for $9.85 each. Management wants to compare the current manufacturing cost per unit to the market prices for leather belts. Top management has asked the Quebec plant controller to submit data on the cost of manufacturing the leather belts for the month of October. These cost data will be used to determine whether modifications in the production process should be initiated or whether an increase in the selling price of the belts is justified. The cost per belt used for planning and control is $4.85.

The work in process inventory consisted of 1,200 partially completed units on October 1. The belts were 25 percent complete as to conversion costs. The costs included in the inventory on October 1 were as follows:

Leather strips	$3,000
Buckles	750
Conversion costs	900
Total	$4,650

During October, 22,800 leather strips were placed into production. A total of 21,000 leather belts were completed. The work-in-process inventory on October 31 consisted of 13,000 belts, which were 50 percent complete as to conversion costs.

The costs charged to production during October were as follows:

Leather strips	$ 61,800
Buckles	13,650
Conversion costs	62,100
Total	$137,550

Instructions

In order to provide cost data on the manufacture of leather belts in the Quebec plant to the top management of Montreal Leather Company, calculate the following amounts for the month of October:

(a) The equivalent units for material and conversion

(b) The assignment of production costs to the October 31 work in process inventory and to goods transferred out

(c) The weighted-average unit cost of the leather belts completed and transferred to finished goods. Comment on the cost per belt that the company uses for planning and control

(CMA Canada-adapted)

Determine equivalent units and unit costs, and prepare production cost report.
(SO 5, 6, 7, 9)

***P3–26A**　Nicholas Company manufactures bicycles and tricycles. For both products, materials are added at the beginning of the production process, and conversion costs are incurred evenly. Nicholas Company uses the FIFO method to calculate equivalent units. Production and cost data for the month of March are as follows:

Production Data—Bicycles	Units	Percent Complete
Work in process units, March 1	200	80%
Units started into production	1,000	
Work in process units, March 31	200	40%

Cost Data—Bicycles		
Work in process, March 1	$19,280	
Direct materials	50,000	
Direct labour	25,200	
Manufacturing overhead	30,000	

Production Data—Tricycles	Units	Percent Complete
Work in process units, March 1	100	75%
Units started into production	800	
Work in process units, March 31	60	25%

Cost Data—Tricycles		
Work in process, March 1	$ 6,125	
Direct materials	38,400	
Direct labour	15,100	
Manufacturing overhead	20,000	

Instructions

(a) Calculate the following for both the bicycles and the tricycles segments:

1. The equivalent units of production for materials and conversion
2. The unit costs of production for materials and conversion costs
3. The assignment of costs to units transferred out and in work in process at the end of the accounting period

(b) Prepare a production cost report for the month of March for the bicycles only.

*P3–27A   The following information is for production activities in the refining department of Petro Pure Corporation. All units in work in process (WIP) were costed using the FIFO cost system.

Calculate equivalent units, unit costs, and costs assigned.
(SO 5, 6, 9)

Refining Department	Units	Percentage of Completion	Conversion Costs
WIP, February 1	25,000	80%	$ 22,000
Units started and cost incurred during February	135,000		143,000
Units completed and transferred to the mixing department	100,000		
WIP, February 28	?	50%	?

Instructions

(a) What were the conversion costs per equivalent unit of production last period and this period?

(b) What was the conversion cost in the work in process inventory account at February 28?

(c) What was the per-unit conversion cost of the units started last period and completed this period?

*P3–28A   Petro Pure Corporation manufactures chemical additives for industrial applications. As the new cost accountant, you have been assigned the task of completing the production cost report for the most recent period. The company uses the FIFO method of process costing. The following information is for the most recent period:

Prepare production cost report using FIFO.
(SO 5, 6, 7, 9)

Production Data—Units	
Beginning WIP inventory (75% complete as to materials; 70% complete as to conversion costs)	16,000
Units started into production this period	27,000
Units completed and transferred out	33,000
Ending WIP inventory (60% complete as to materials; 50% complete as to conversion costs)	10,000

Cost Data	
Beginning inventory:	
Materials	$ 32,000
Conversion costs	64,000
Current period:	
Materials	252,000
Conversion costs	440,000

Instructions

Prepare a complete production report for the period using the FIFO method. (Round the cost per equivalent unit to three decimal places; round the costs in the cost report to the nearest dollar.)

(CGA-adapted)

Problems: Set B

Journalize transactions.
(SO 3, 4)

P3–29B   Peppy Company manufactures its product Vitadrink through two manufacturing processes: mixing and packaging. All materials are entered at the beginning of each process. On October 1, 2005, inventories consisted of Raw Materials $26,000; Work in Process—Mixing $0; Work in Process—Packaging $250,000; and Finished Goods $89,000. The beginning inventory for packaging consisted of 10,000 units that were 50% complete as to conversion costs and fully complete as to materials. During October, 50,000 units were started into production in the mixing department and the following transactions were completed:

1. Purchased $500,000 of raw materials on account.
2. Issued raw materials for production: $210,000 for mixing and $45,000 for packaging.
3. Incurred labour costs of $238,900.
4. Used factory labour: $182,000 for mixing and $56,900 for packaging.
5. Incurred $800,000 of manufacturing overhead on account.
6. Applied manufacturing overhead on the basis of $24 per machine hour. Machine hours were 28,000 in mixing and 7,000 in packaging.
7. Transferred 45,000 units from mixing to packaging at a cost of $999,000.
8. Transferred 53,000 units from packaging to finished goods at a cost of $1,455,000.
9. Sold goods costing $1,600,000 for $2,500,000 on account.

Instructions

Journalize the October transactions.

Calculate equivalent units, unit costs, and costs assigned.
(SO 5, 6)

P3–30B   Toronto Timers Inc.'s costing system uses two cost categories: direct materials and conversion costs. Each of its products must go through the assembly department and the testing department. Direct materials are added at the beginning of production. Conversion costs are allocated evenly throughout production. Data for the assembly department for June 2005 are as follows:

Production Data—Units	
Work in process, beginning inventory	400 units
(50% complete as to conversion costs)	
Units started during June	1,200 units
Work in process, ending inventory	200 units

Cost Data	
Work in process, beginning inventory costs	
Direct materials	$ 200,000
Conversion costs	200,000
Direct materials costs added during June	2,000,000
Conversion costs added during June	2,500,000

Instructions

(a) What unit cost can be calculated from the information provided for work in process beginning inventory?

(b) How many units were completed and transferred out of the assembly department during June 2005?

P3–31B Aquatic Company manufactures bowling balls through two processes: moulding and packaging. In the moulding department, the urethane, rubber, plastics, and other materials are moulded into bowling balls. In the packaging department, the balls are placed in cartons and sent to the finished goods warehouse. All materials are entered at the beginning of each process. Labour and manufacturing overhead are incurred evenly throughout each process. Production and cost data for the moulding department during June 2005 are presented below:

Complete four necessary steps to prepare production cost report.
(SO 5, 6, 7)

Production Data	June
Beginning work in process units	0
Units started into production	20,000
Ending work in process units	5,000
Percent complete—ending inventory	40%

Cost Data	
Materials	$286,000
Labour	114,000
Overhead	101,900
Total	$501,900

Instructions

(a) Prepare a schedule showing the physical units of production.

(b) Determine the equivalent units of production for materials and conversion costs.

(c) Calculate the unit costs of production.

(d) Determine the costs to be assigned to the units transferred, and in work in process for June.

(e) Prepare a production cost report for the moulding department for the month of June.

P3–32B Freedo Industries Inc. uses separate processes to manufacture furniture for homes. In each process, materials are entered at the beginning, and conversion costs are incurred evenly. Production and cost data for the first process in making these two products in two different manufacturing plants are as follows:

Complete four necessary steps to prepare production cost report.
(SO 5, 6, 7)

	Cutting Department	
	Plant 1	Plant 2
Production Data—August	T12 Tables	C10 Chairs
Work in process units, August 1	0	0
Units started into production	20,000	15,000
Work in process units, August 31	2,000	500
Work in process percent complete	50%	80%

Cost Data—August		
Work in process, August 1	$ 0	$ 0
Materials	380,000	225,000
Labour	190,000	118,100
Overhead	76,000	60,700
Total	$646,000	$403,800

Instructions

(a) For each plant:
   1. Calculate the physical units of production.
   2. Calculate the equivalent units of production for materials and for conversion costs.
   3. Determine the unit costs of production.
   4. Show the assignment of costs for units transferred out and for work in process.

(b) Prepare the production cost report for Plant 1 for August 2005.

Assign costs and prepare production cost report.
(SO 5, 6, 7)

P3–33B Wang Company has several processing departments. Costs charged to the assembly department for November 2005 totalled $2,126,000, as follows:

Work in process, November 1		
Materials	$70,000	
Conversion costs	48,000	$ 118,000
Materials added		1,270,000
Labour		358,000
Overhead		380,000

Production records show that 30,000 units were in beginning work in process and were 30% complete as to conversion costs; 640,000 units were started into production; and 25,000 units were in ending work in process and were 40% complete as to conversion costs. Materials are entered at the beginning of each process.

Instructions

(a) Determine the equivalent units of production and the unit costs for the assembly department.
(b) Determine the assignment of costs to goods transferred out, and in work in process.
(c) Prepare a production cost report for the assembly department.

Determine assignment of costs.
(SO 4, 5, 6, 7, 8)

P3–34B The following is partial information for the month of March for Macmillan International Inc., a two-department manufacturer that uses process costing:

Work in process, beginning (67% converted)	12,000 units
Costs of beginning work in process:	
Transferred in from Department A	$ 9,500
Materials	0
Conversion	$11,200
Units completed and transferred out during March	44,000 units
Units transferred in during March from Department A	? units
Work in process, ending (37.5% converted)	16,000 units
Materials costs added during March	$13,200
Conversion costs added during March	$63,000

Other information:

1. Material is introduced at the beginning of Department A and additional material is added at the very end of Department B.
2. Conversion costs are incurred evenly throughout both processes.
3. As the process in Department A is completed, goods are immediately transferred to Department B; as goods are completed in Department B, they are transferred to finished goods.
4. Unit costs of production in Department A in March were:

Materials	$0.55
Conversion	0.40
Total	$0.95

5. The company uses the weighted-average method.

Instructions

(a) Calculate the cost of goods transferred out of Department B in March.
(b) Calculate the cost of the March ending work in process inventory in Department B.

(CGA-adapted)

Calculate equivalent units, unit costs, costs assigned and prepare cost report
(SO 5, 6, 7)

P3–35B Clemente Company manufactures basketballs. Materials are added at the beginning of the production process and conversion costs are incurred evenly. Production and cost data for the month of July 2005 are as follows:

Production Data—Basketballs	Units	Percent Complete
Work in process units, July 1	500	60%
Units started into production	1,600	
Work in process units, July 31	600	40%

Cost Data—Basketballs		
Work in process, July 1		
Materials	$540	
Conversion costs	500	$1,040
Direct materials		2,400
Direct labour		1,600
Manufacturing overhead		1,380

Instructions

(a) Calculate the following:

1. The equivalent units of production for materials and conversion costs
2. The unit costs of production for materials and conversion costs
3. The assignment of costs to units transferred out and to work in process at the end of the accounting period

(b) Prepare a production cost report for the month of July.

P3–36B Magic Manufacturing Company uses a weighted-average process costing system and manufactures a single product—a premium rug shampoo and cleaner. The manufacturing activity for the month of November has just ended. A partially completed production cost report for the month of November for the mixing department follows.

Calculate equivalent units and complete production cost report.
(SO 5, 7)

MAGIC MANUFACTURING COMPANY
Mixing Department
Production Cost Report
Month Ended November 30

Quantities	Physical Units	Equivalent Units — Materials	Conversion Costs	Total
Units to be accounted for				
Work in process, November 1 (100% materials, 70% conversion costs)	10,000			
Started into production	160,000			
Total units	170,000			
Units accounted for				
Transferred out	130,000	(a)	(b)	
Work in process, November 30 (50% materials, 25% conversion costs)	40,000	(c)	(d)	
Total units accounted for	170,000	(e)	(f)	

Costs				
Unit costs				
Costs in November		$240,000	$98,000	$338,000
Equivalent units		(g)	(h)	
Unit costs		$ (i) +	$ (j) =	$ (k)
Costs to be accounted for				
Work in process, November 1				$ 38,000
Started into production				300,000
Total costs				$338,000

Cost Reconciliation Schedule			
Costs accounted for			
Transferred out			$ (l)
Work in process, November 30			
Materials		$ (m)	
Conversion costs		(n)	(o)
Total cost			$ (p)

Instructions

(a) Prepare a schedule that shows how the equivalent units were calculated so that you can complete the "Quantities: Units accounted for" equivalent units section shown in the production cost report above, and calculate the November unit costs.

(b) Complete the "Cost Reconciliation Schedule" part of the production cost report above.

Determine assignment of costs.
(SO 5, 6, 7)

P3-37B Alberta Instrument Company uses a process costing system. A unit of product passes through three departments—moulding, assembly, and finishing—before it is completed. The following activity took place in the finishing department during May:

	Units
Work in process inventory, May 1	1,400
Transferred in from the assembly department	14,000
Transferred out to finished goods inventory	11,900

Raw material is added at the beginning of processing in the finishing department. The work in process inventory was 70 percent complete as to conversion costs on May 1 and 40 percent complete as to conversion costs on May 31. Alberta Instrument Company uses the weighted-average method of process costing. The equivalent units and current period costs per equivalent unit of production for each cost factor are as follows for the finishing department.

	Equivalent Units	Current Period Costs per Equivalent Unit
Transferred-in costs	15,400	$5.00
Raw materials	15,400	1.00
Conversion costs	13,300	3.00
Total		$9.00

Instructions

Calculate the following amounts:

(a) The cost of units transferred to finished goods inventory during May

(b) The cost of the finishing department's work in process inventory on May 31

(CMA Canada-adapted)

Determine assignment of costs using FIFO.
(SO 6, 8, 9)

*P3-38B** Below is information about ABC Ltd., a chemical producer, for the month of June:

Work in process, beginning inventory	50,000 units
Transferred-in units—100% complete	
Direct materials—0% complete	
Conversion costs—80% complete	
Transferred in during June	200,000 units
Completed and transferred out during June	210,000 units
Work in process, ending inventory	? units
Transferred-in units—100% complete	
Direct materials—0% complete	
Conversion costs—40% complete	

Instructions

(a) How many units are in ending work in process inventory?

(b) Under FIFO, what are the equivalent units of production for the month of June for materials?

(c) Under FIFO, what are the equivalent units of production for the month of June for conversion costs?

Determine assignment of costs using FIFO.
(SO 6, 7, 9)

*P3-39B** The Allbright BrickWorks, in Winnipeg, Manitoba, manufactures high-quality bricks used in residential and commercial construction. The firm is small but highly automated and typically produces about 300,000 bricks per month. A brick is created in a continuous production operation. In the initial step, the raw material, a mixture of soils and water, is forced into a brick mould moving along a conveyer belt. No other materials are actually required in the manufacture of a brick. Each brick takes about three days to complete. Approximately the last 36 hours on the conveyer belt are spent in an oven that removes moisture from the product. The conveyer belt speed is monitored and controlled by computer. The firm uses a process costing system based on actual costs in three cost pools—direct materials, direct labour, and factory overhead—to assign production costs to output. Cost and production data for October 2005 follow:

Production Data

Beginning work in process inventory	
(100% complete as to direct materials;	
60% complete as to direct labour; 36%	
complete as to factory overhead)	25,000 bricks
Started this period	305,000 bricks
Ending work in process inventory	
(100% complete as to direct materials;	
50% complete as to direct labour; 40%	
complete as to factory overhead)	30,000 bricks

Cost Data

	Materials	Direct Labour	Overhead
Beginning inventory	$ 1,330	$ 435	$ 852
Cost in October	12,200	15,000	18,180

Instructions

Determine the cost of bricks transferred to finished goods inventory and the cost of bricks in ending work in process inventory for October 2005. Assume the company uses the FIFO method.

(CGA-adapted)

*P3–40B Jessica Company manufactures basketballs and soccer balls. For both products, materials are added at the beginning of the production process and conversion costs are incurred evenly. Jessica uses the FIFO method to calculate equivalent units. Production and cost data for the month of August are as follows:

Determine equivalent units and unit cost, and prepare production cost report, using FIFO.
(SO 6, 7, 9)

Production Data—Basketballs	Units	Percent Complete
Work in process units, August 1	500	60%
Units started into production	1,600	
Work in process units, August 31	600	40%

Cost Data—Basketballs	
Work in process, August 1	$1,125
Direct materials	1,600
Direct labour	1,160
Manufacturing overhead	1,000

Production Data—Soccer Balls	Units	Percent Complete
Work in process units, August 1	200	80%
Units started into production	2,000	
Work in process units, August 31	150	70%

Cost Data—Soccer balls	
Work in process, August 1	$ 450
Direct materials	2,500
Direct labour	1,000
Manufacturing overhead	995

Instructions

(a) Calculate the following for both the basketballs and the soccer balls:

1. The equivalent units of production for materials and conversion
2. The unit costs of production for materials and conversion costs
3. The assignment of costs to units transferred out and to work in process at the end of the accounting period

(b) Prepare a production cost report for the month of August for the basketballs only.

Analyze a process costing
system and calculate
equivalent units, unit costs.
(SO 6, 8, 9)

*P3–41B   United Dominion Manufacturing Co. produces a wood refinishing kit that sells for $17.95. The final processing of the kits occurs in the packaging department. A quilted wrap is applied at the beginning of the packaging process. A compartmented outside box printed with instructions and the company's name and logo is added when units are 60 percent through the process. Conversion costs, consisting of direct labour and applied overhead, occur evenly throughout the packaging process. Conversion activities after the completion of the box include package sealing, testing for leakage, and final inspection. The following data are for the packaging department's activities during the month of October:

1. Beginning work-in-process inventory was 10,000 units, 40 percent complete as to conversion costs.
2. During the month, 40,000 units were transferred to packaging.
3. There were 10,000 units in ending work in process, 80 percent complete as to conversion costs.

The packaging department's October costs were as follows:

Quilted wrap	$80,000
Outside boxes	50,000
Direct labour	22,000
Applied overhead ($3.00/per direct-labour dollar)	66,000

The costs transferred in from prior processing were $3.00 per unit. The cost of goods sold for the month was $240,000, and the ending finished goods inventory was $84,000. United Dominion Manufacturing Co. uses the first-in, first-out (FIFO) method for process costing.

Instructions

(a) Prepare a schedule of equivalent units for the October activity in the packaging department.

(b) Determine the cost per equivalent unit for the October production.

(CMA Canada-adapted)

Additional Cases

Cases

C3–42   British Beach Company manufactures suntan lotion, called Surtan, in 350-ml plastic bottles. Surtan is sold in a competitive market. As a result, management is very cost-conscious. Surtan is manufactured through two processes: mixing and filling. Materials are entered at the beginning of each process, and labour and manufacturing overhead are incurred evenly throughout each process. Unit costs are based on the cost per litre of Surtan using the weighted-average costing approach.

On June 30, 2005, Sara Simmons, the chief accountant for the past 20 years, decided to take early retirement. Her replacement, Joe Jacobs, had extensive accounting experience with motels in the area, but only limited contact with manufacturing accounting.

During July, Joe correctly accumulated the following production quantity and cost data for the mixing department:

Production quantities: Work in process, July 1, 32,000 litres, 75% complete; started into production, 400,000 litres; work in process, July 31, 20,000 litres, 20% complete. Materials are added at the beginning of the process.

Production costs: Beginning work in process $88,000, comprising $21,000 of materials costs and $67,000 of conversion costs; costs incurred in July: materials $600,000, conversion costs $785,800

Joe then prepared a production cost report on the basis of physical units started into production. His report showed a production cost of $3.685 per litre of Surtan. The management of British Beach Company was surprised at the high unit cost. The president comes to you, as Sara's top assistant, to review Joe's report and prepare a correct report if necessary.

Instructions

With the class divided into groups, answer the following questions:

(a) Show how Joe arrived at the unit cost of $3.685 per litres of Surtan.

(b) What error(s) did Joe make in preparing his production cost report?
(c) Prepare a correct production cost report for July.

C3–43 You have recently been appointed as the cost accountant for Silky Hair Co. Ltd., a manufacturer of hair shampoo. Your first task is to clear up the production records of the mixing department for November 2005.

You learn that the mixing department is the last stage of the shampoo production process. Units transferred from the previous department use direct labour and overhead inputs evenly in mixing. A secret ingredient is also added to each unit at the halfway point of processing.

You also find out that the beginning inventory for the month of November was 3,000 units (60% complete) with the following costs:

Transferred-in costs	$12,000
Direct materials	5,100
Conversion costs	12,825

In addition, during November 13,000 units were transferred to mixing at a $4 unit cost. The ending inventory consisted of 4,000 units that were 40% complete. During the month, direct materials of $15,300 were added and 8,850 hours of direct labour were used at a wage rate of $7.00 per hour.

The overhead rate for 2005, applied on a basis of direct labour hours, was based on a predicted annual usage of 120,000 hours and a cost function derived from the following overhead equation $Y = 60,000 + 2X$, where Y total overhead costs, X direct labour hour.

Instructions

Using weighted-average process costing techniques, calculate the following for the mixing department for November 2005:

(a) The predetermined overhead rate for 2005
(b) The number of equivalent units in ending inventory
(c) The unit cost of items transferred to finished goods
(d) The value assigned to ending inventory

(CGA-adapted)

C3–44 Passera Inc. manufactures a single product in a continuous processing environment. All materials are added at the beginning of the process, and conversion costs are applied evenly throughout the process. To assign costs to inventories, the company uses weighted average process costing.

The following information was available for 2005:

Sales (selling price per unit, $40)	$4,080,000
Actual manufacturing overhead	660,000
Selling and administrative expenses	328,000
Unit costs of production:	
Direct materials (1 kilogram)	$ 5.00
Direct labour (1/2 hour)	6.00
Overhead	9.00
Total	$20.00
Units transferred to finished goods	140,000 units
Materials purchased	125,000 kilograms
Materials used in process	136,000 kilograms

An inventory count at year end (December 31, 2005) revealed that the inventories had the following balances:

Raw materials	8,000 kilograms
Work in process (35% complete)	22,000 units
Finished goods	45,000 units

The January 1, 2005, work in process units are 60 percent complete. The unit cost of production was the same in 2005 as it was in 2004.

Instructions

Calculate the following amounts for Passera Inc.:

(a) The opening (January 1, 2005) balance in units and costs of (1) raw materials, (2) work in process, and (3) finished goods
(b) The equivalent units for 2005 for (1) materials and (2) conversion costs
(c) The total cost for 2005 for (1) materials used and (2) conversion applied
(d) The cost of ending work in process for 2005
(e) The cost of units completed and transferred to finished goods

(CMA Canada-adapted)

*C3–45   Icy Delight Company, which manufactures quality ice cream sold at premium prices, uses a single production department. Production begins with the blending of various ingredients, which are added at the beginning of the process, and ends with the packaging of the ice cream. Packaging occurs when the mixture reaches the 90 percent stage of completion. The two-litre cartons are then transferred to the shipping department for shipment. Labour and overhead are added continuously throughout the process. Manufacturing overhead is applied on the basis of direct-labour hours at the rate of $3.00 per hour.

The company has always used the weighted-average method to determine equivalent units of production and unit costs. Now, production management is considering changing from the weighted-average method to the first-in, first-out method. The following data relate to actual production during the month of May:

Costs

Work in process inventory, May 1 (16,000 litres; 25% complete)	
Direct materials (ingredients)	$ 45,600
Direct labour ($10 per hour)	6,250
Manufacturing overhead	1,875

Costs Incurred	
Direct materials (ingredients)	$228,400
Direct materials (cartons)	7,000
Direct labour ($10 per hour)	35,000
Manufacturing overhead	10,500

Production Units	Litres
Work in process inventory, May 1 (25% complete)	16,000
Started in May	84,000
Sent to shipping department	80,000
Work in process inventory, May 31 (80% complete)	20,000

Instructions

(a) Prepare a schedule of equivalent units for each cost element for the month of May using (1) the weighted-average method, and 2) the first-in, first-out method.
(b) Calculate the cost (to the nearest cent) per equivalent unit for each cost element for the month of May using (1) the weighted-average method, and (2) the first-in, first-out method.
(c) Discuss the advantages and disadvantages of the weighted-average method versus the first-in, first-out method.

(CMA Canada-adapted)

*C3–46   The Saunders Paint Co. uses a process costing system. You have been given the following selected information for July 2005:

	Units	Percent Complete
Beginning work in process	6,000	60%
Units started	24,000	
Ending work in process	10,000	40%

The total cost of the beginning work in process was $37,000, of which $7,000 was for direct labour costs. Overhead is applied on the basis of direct labour costs.

During July, the company added $69,400 of direct materials, $50,500 of direct labour, and $60,600 of overhead to work in process.

All direct materials are added at the beginning of the process, and the conversion costs are incurred evenly throughout the process.

Instructions

(a) Calculate the overhead rate.
(b) Calculate the direct materials, the direct labour, and the overhead cost components of the beginning work in process.
(c) Calculate the number of equivalent units that would be used to establish the weighted-average costs for direct materials, direct labour, and overhead.
(d) Calculate the number of equivalent units that would be used to establish the FIFO costs for direct materials, direct labour, and overhead.
(e) Assuming weighted-average is used, calculate the cost of goods completed and transferred out.
(f) Assuming FIFO is used, calculate the cost of ending work in process inventory for direct materials, direct labour, and overhead. Show each component separately.

(CGA-adapted)

C3–47 C. C. Daibo Company manufactures a high-tech component that passes through two production processing departments: moulding and assembly. The department managers' earnings are based partially on the units of product completed and transferred out compared to the units of product put into production. This practice was intended as encouragement to be efficient and to minimize waste.

Barb Crusmer is the department head in the moulding department, and Wayne Terrago is her quality control inspector. During the month of June, Barb had three new employees who were not yet technically skilled. As a result, many of the units produced in June had minor moulding defects. In order to maintain the department's normal high rate of completion, Barb told Wayne to pass through inspection and on to the assembly department all units that had defects that were nondetectable to the human eye. "Company and industry tolerances on this product are too high anyway," Barb said. "Less than 2 percent of the units we produce are subjected in the market to the stress tolerance we've designed into them. The odds of those 2 percent being any of this month's units are even lower. Anyway, we're saving the company money."

Instructions

(a) Who are the potential stakeholders in this situation?
(b) What alternatives does Wayne have in this situation? What could the company do to prevent this kind of situation from occurring?

Answers to Self-Study Questions

1. b   2. d   3. c   4. b   5. b   6. a   7. c   8. a   9. b   10. b   11. b   12. a   13. b

Remember to go back to the Navigator Box at the beginning of the chapter to check off your completed work.

CHAPTER 4
Activity-Based Costing

Storage Solutions

RONA Inc. was having difficulty accounting for the costs of its warehousing and distribution. So the Boucherville, Quebec–based distributor and retailer of hardware, home improvement, and gardening supplies introduced an activity-based costing system to keep better track of its route-to-market costs.

"The costs are reallocated to the product based on the characteristics of each product and the activities required to complete an order," says RONA's controller for distribution, Martin Beauregard, CMA. The value of the product inside a carton has little bearing on the cost to ship it; it depends on the process required. For example, electric saws are stored at 40 cases per pallet, which takes up one cubic metre of space. With its new system, RONA can determine that it costs, say, $40 per cubic metre per year—or $1 per case—to store this product.

But with 40,000 SKUs, 28 separate processes in its warehouses, more than 3,000 vendors, and 535 stores, the task of allocating costs this specifically was not accomplished easily. RONA divided its storage options into several sectors, with the activities for each sector having different costs. For example, storage in the yard is cheaper than in the warehouse. Also some products require more labour and take more time to handle than others. By breaking down this information and assigning costs to it, the company was able to determine the actual cost requirements for each product.

"In the past, we allocated the costs on a general basis," Mr. Beauregard explains. "We knew our average costs for every sector. Every product was X percent, so we were using that percentage." But, since some products require more manipulation than others, the company knew these averages were not accurate measures.

With value-chain analytics software, RONA can run simulations that push the products through different supply channels and then decide which is the most cost-effective. Usually suppliers prefer to ship their products through their warehouse, but it may be less costly to send products directly to retail outlets. The software will confirm this. This information allows RONA to instruct suppliers on the best way to ship and package their goods. "Now, people in merchandising have better information to negotiate the appropriate allocation with suppliers," Mr. Beauregard says.

the navigator

RONA Inc.: www.rona.ca

THE NAVIGATOR

- [ ] Scan *Study Objectives*
- [ ] Read *Feature Story*
- [ ] Read *Chapter Preview*
- [ ] Read text and answer *Before You Go On* p. 150, p. 156, p. 159
- [ ] Work *Using the Decision Toolkit*
- [ ] Review *Summary of Study Objectives*
- [ ] Review *Using the Decision Toolkit—A Summary*
- [ ] Work *Demonstration Problem*
- [ ] Answer *Self-Study Questions*
- [ ] Complete assignments

STUDY OBJECTIVES

After studying this chapter, you should be able to:

1. Recognize the difference between traditional costing and activity-based costing.
2. Identify the steps in the development of an activity-based costing system.
3. Know how companies identify the activity cost pools used in activity-based costing.
4. Know how companies identify and use the activity cost drivers in activity-based costing.
5. Understand the benefits and limitations of activity-based costing.
6. Differentiate between value-added and non–value-added activities.
7. Understand the value of using activity levels in activity-based costing.
8. Apply activity-based costing to service industries.

the navigator

As indicated in our feature story about RONA, the traditional costing systems described in earlier chapters are not the best answer for every company. Because RONA suspected that the traditional system was hiding significant differences in its real cost structure, it looked for a new method of assigning costs. Similar searches by other companies for ways to improve operations and gather more accurate data for decision-making have resulted in the development of powerful new management tools, including **activity-based costing (ABC)**, which this chapter explains and illustrates.

The chapter is organized as follows:

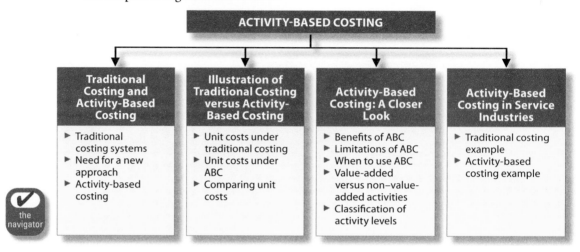

Traditional Costing and Activity-Based Costing

Traditional Costing Systems

study objective 1

Recognize the difference between traditional costing and activity-based costing.

It is probably impossible to determine the **exact** cost of a product or service. However, for decision-makers to make better management decisions, they must have the most accurate cost estimates possible. A product's cost can be estimated most accurately when this cost can be traced directly to the product produced or the service provided. Direct material and direct labour costs are the easiest to determine, because these can be traced directly to the product by examining material requisition forms and payroll time sheets. Overhead costs, on the other hand, are an indirect or common cost that generally cannot be easily or directly traced to individual products or services. Instead, we use estimates to assign overhead costs to products and services.

Often the most difficult part of calculating accurate unit costs is determining the proper amount of **overhead cost** to assign to each product, service, or job. In our coverage of job order costing in Chapter 2 and of process costing in Chapter 3, we used a single or plantwide overhead rate throughout the year for the entire factory operation. That rate was called the **predetermined overhead rate**. For job order costing, we assumed that **direct labour cost** was the relevant activity base for assigning all overhead costs to jobs. For process costing, we assumed that **machine hours** was the relevant activity base for assigning all overhead to the process or department.

The use of direct labour as the activity base made sense when overhead cost allocation systems were first developed. At that time, direct labour made up a large portion of the total manufacturing cost. Therefore, it was widely accepted that there was a high correlation between direct labour and overhead costs. As a result, direct labour became the most popular basis for allocating overhead.

Even in today's increasingly automated environment, direct labour is sometimes the appropriate basis for assigning overhead costs to products. It is appropriate to use direct labour when (a) direct labour is a significant part of the total product cost, and (b) there is a high correlation between direct labour and changes in the amount of overhead costs. A simplified (one-stage) traditional costing system that uses direct labour to assign overhead costs is shown in Illustration 4-1.

Illustration 4-1 ◀

Traditional one-stage costing system

The Need for a New Approach

The last decade brought tremendous change to manufacturers and service providers. Advances in computerized systems, technological innovation, global competition, and automation have changed the manufacturing environment dramatically. As a result, the amount of direct labour that is used in many industries has greatly decreased, and total overhead costs from depreciation on expensive equipment and machinery, and from utilities, repairs, and maintenance have significantly increased. When there is no correlation between direct labour and overhead, it is inappropriate to use plantwide, predetermined overhead rates that are based on direct labour. When this correlation does not exist, companies that use overhead rates based on direct labour have significant product cost distortions.

To avoid such distortions, many companies now use machine hours as the basis for allocating overhead in an automated manufacturing environment. But machine hours can be inadequate as the only plantwide basis for allocating all overhead. If the manufacturing process is complex, multiple allocation bases are needed for more accurate product-cost calculations. In such situations, managers need to consider an overhead cost-allocation method that uses multiple bases. That method is **activity-based costing**.

Activity-Based Costing

Broadly, **activity-based costing (ABC)** is an approach for allocating overhead costs. More specifically, ABC allocates overhead to multiple activity cost pools, and it then assigns the activity cost pools to products and services by using cost drivers. To understand more clearly what that means, you need new meanings for the rather common-sounding words that make up the definition. In activity-based costing, an **activity** is any event, action, transaction, or work sequence that incurs a cost when producing a product or providing a service. An **activity cost pool** is a distinct type of activity (e.g., ordering materials or setting up machines). A **cost driver** is any factor or activity that has a direct cause-effect relationship with the resources consumed. The reasoning behind ABC cost allocation is simple: **Products consume activities, and activities consume resources**.

These definitions of terms will become clearer as we look more closely at how ABC works. ABC allocates overhead in a two-stage process. In the first stage, overhead costs are allocated to activity cost pools. (In traditional costing systems, in contrast, these costs are allocated to departments or to jobs.) Examples of overhead activity cost pools are ordering materials, setting machines, assembling products, and inspecting product.

In the second stage, cost drivers are used to assign the overhead allocated to the activity cost pools to specific products. The cost drivers measure the number of individual activities that are performed to produce products or provide services. Examples are the number of purchase orders, number of setups, labour hours, or number of inspections. Illustration 4-2 shows examples of activities, and the possible cost drivers that measure them, for a company that manufactures two products—axles and steering wheels.

Illustration 4-2 ▶

Activities and related cost
drivers

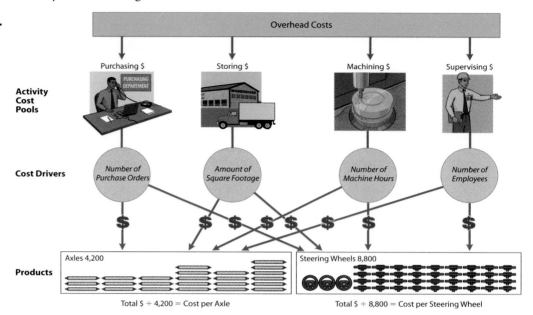

In the first step (as shown at the top of the illustration), the company's overhead costs are allocated to activity cost pools. In this simplified example, four activity cost pools have been identified: purchasing, storing, machining, and supervising. After the costs are allocated to the activity cost pools, the company uses cost drivers to measure the costs to be assigned to the individual products (either axles or steering wheels) based on each product's use of each activity. For example, if axles require more activity by the purchasing department, as measured by the number of required purchase orders, then more of the overhead cost from the purchasing pool will be allocated to the axles.

Alternative Terminology
Product costs are also
called *inventory costs*.

Not all products or services share equally in these activities. When a product's manufacturing operation is more complex, it is likely to have more activities and cost drivers. If there is little or no correlation between changes in the cost driver and the consumption of the overhead cost, inaccurate **product costs** will result. The design of a more complex activity-based costing system with seven activity cost pools is shown in Illustration 4-3 for Lift Jack Company. Lift Jack Company manufactures two automotive jacks—an automobile scissors jack and a truck hydraulic jack.

Illustration 4-3 ▼

ABC system design—Lift
Jack Company

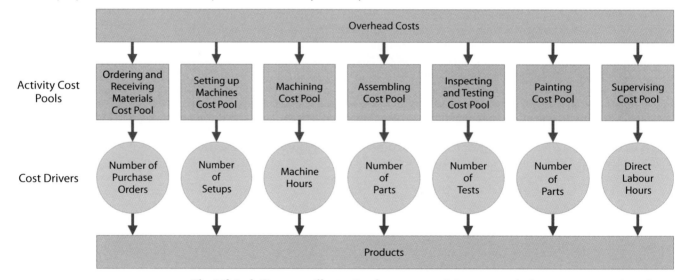

The Lift Jack Company illustration has seven activity cost pools. In some companies, a large number of activities can be related to a cost pool. For example, at Clark-Hurth (a division of Clark Equipment Company), a manufacturer of axles and transmissions, over 170 activities were identified; at Compumotor (a division of Parker Hannifin), over 80 activities were identified in just the procurement function of its Material Control department.

Helpful Hint Computers lessen the problem of having huge numbers of activities and are helping ABC reach its potential for improving product costing.

Illustration of Traditional Costing versus ABC

In this section, we present a simple case that compares traditional costing and activity-based costing. This example shows how ABC eliminates the distortion that can occur in traditional overhead cost allocation. You should understand that ABC generally does not replace an existing job order or process costing system. ABC simply segregates overhead into various cost pools in an effort to provide more accurate cost information. Thus, ABC supplements the traditional cost systems; it does not replace them.

Assume that Atlas Company produces two automobile antitheft devices: The Boot and The Club. The Boot is a high-volume item totalling 25,000 units annually. The Club is a low-volume item totalling only 5,000 units per year. Each product requires one hour of direct labour for completion. Total annual direct labour hours are therefore 30,000 (25,000 + 5,000). Expected annual manufacturing overhead costs are $900,000. Thus, the predetermined overhead rate is $30 ($900,000 ÷ 30,000) per direct labour hour. In addition, the direct materials cost per unit is $40 for The Boot and $30 for The Club. The direct labour cost is $12 per unit for each product.

Unit Costs under Traditional Costing

The calculation of the unit cost for The Boot and The Club under traditional costing is shown in Illustration 4-4.

	Products	
Manufacturing Costs	The Boot	The Club
Direct materials	$40	$30
Direct labour	12	12
Overhead	30*	30*
Total unit cost	$82	$72

* Predetermined overhead rate times direct labour hours ($30 × 1 hr = $30).

Illustration 4-4 ◀

Calculation of unit costs—traditional costing

Unit Costs under ABC

Now let's calculate the unit costs under ABC in order to compare activity-based costing with a traditional costing system. Activity-based costing involves the following four steps:

1. Identify and classify the major activities involved in the manufacture of specific products, and allocate the manufacturing overhead costs to the appropriate cost pools.
2. Identify the cost driver that has a strong correlation to the costs accumulated in the cost pool.
3. For each cost pool, calculate the overhead rate per cost driver.
4. Using the overhead rates (cost per driver), assign the manufacturing overhead costs for each cost pool to the products.

study objective 2

Identify the steps in the development of an activity-based costing system.

Identify and Classify Activities and Allocate Overhead to Cost Pools (Step 1)

A well-designed activity-based costing system starts with an analysis of the activities that are performed to manufacture a product or provide a service. This analysis should identify all activities that consume resources. It requires a detailed, step-by-step walk-through of each operation, in order to document every activity done to accomplish a task. Atlas Company identified three activity cost pools: setting up machines, machining, and inspecting.

Next, overhead costs are assigned directly to the appropriate activity cost pool. For example, all overhead costs that are directly associated with Atlas Company's machine setups

study objective 3

Know how companies identify the activity cost pools used in activity-based costing.

(such as salaries, supplies, and depreciation) would be assigned to the machine setup cost pool. These cost pools, along with the estimated overhead allocated to each one, are shown in Illustration 4-5.

Illustration 4-5 ▶

Activity cost pools and estimated overhead

Activity Cost Pools	Estimated Overhead
Setting up machines	$300,000
Machining	500,000
Inspecting	100,000
Total	$900,000

Identify Cost Drivers (Step 2)

study objective 4

Know how companies identify and use the activity cost drivers in activity-based costing.

After costs are allocated to the activity cost pools, the cost drivers for each cost pool must be identified. The cost driver must accurately measure the actual consumption of the activity by the various products. For costing to be accurate, there has to be a high degree of correlation between the cost driver and the actual consumption of the overhead costs in the cost pool.

The cost drivers identified by Atlas and their total expected use per activity cost pool are shown in Illustration 4-6.

Illustration 4-6 ▶

Cost drivers and their expected use

Activity Cost Pools	Cost Drivers	Expected Use of Cost Drivers per Activity
Setting up machines	Number of setups	1,500 setups
Machining	Machine hours	50,000 machine hours
Inspecting	Number of inspections	2,000 inspections

The availability of data on the cost driver and how easy it is to get these data are important factors that must be considered in selecting which drivers to use.

Calculate Overhead Rates (Step 3)

Next, an **activity-based overhead rate** per cost driver is calculated by dividing the estimated overhead per activity by the number of cost drivers expected to be used per activity. The formula for this calculation is shown in Illustration 4-7.

Illustration 4-7 ▶

Formula for calculating activity-based overhead rate

$$\text{Estimated Overhead per Activity} \div \text{Expected Use of Cost Drivers per Activity} = \text{Activity-Based Overhead Ratio}$$

Atlas Company calculates its activity-based overhead rates by using the total estimated overhead per activity cost pool, shown in Illustration 4-5, and the total expected use of cost drivers per activity, shown in Illustration 4-6. The calculations are in Illustration 4-8.

Illustration 4-8 ▶

Calculation of activity-based overhead rates

Activity Cost Pools	Estimated Overhead	÷ Expected Use of Cost Drivers per Activity	= Activity-Based Overhead Rates
Setting up machines	$300,000	1,500 setups	$200 per setup
Machining	500,000	50,000 machine hours	$10 per machine hour
Inspecting	100,000	2,000 inspections	$50 per inspection
Total	$900,000		

Assign Overhead Costs to Products under ABC (Step 4)

In assigning overhead costs, it is necessary to know the expected use of cost drivers **for each product**. Because of its low volume, The Club requires more setups and inspections than The Boot. The expected use of cost drivers per product for each of Atlas's products is shown in Illustration 4-9.

Illustration 4-9 ◄

Expected use of cost drivers per product

Activity Cost Pools	Cost Drivers	Expected Use of Cost Drivers per Activity	Expected Use of Cost Drivers per Product	
			The Boot	The Club
Setting up machines	Number of setups	1,500 setups	500	1,000
Machining	Machine hours	50,000 machine hours	30,000	20,000
Inspecting	Number of inspections	2,000 inspections	500	1,500

To assign overhead costs to each product, the activity-based overhead rates per cost driver (Illustration 4-8) are multiplied by the number of cost drivers expected to be used per product (Illustration 4-9). The amount of overhead cost assigned to each product for Atlas Company is shown in Illustration 4-10.

Illustration 4-10 ▼

Assignment of activity cost pools to products

	The Boot			The Club		
Activity Cost Pools	Expected Use of Cost Drivers per Product	× Activity-Based Overhead Rates =	Cost Assigned	Expected Use of Cost Drivers per Product	× Activity-Based Overhead Rates =	Cost Assigned
Setting up machines	500	$200	$100,000	1,000	$200	$200,000
Machining	30,000	$10	300,000	20,000	$10	200,000
Inspecting	500	$50	25,000	1,500	$50	75,000
Total assigned costs [(a)]			$425,000			$475,000
Units produced [(b)]			25,000			5,000
Overhead cost per unit [(a) ÷ (b)]			$17			$95

These data show that under ABC, overhead costs are shifted from the high-volume product (The Boot) to the low-volume product (The Club). This shift results in more accurate costing for two reasons:

1. Low-volume products often require more special handling, such as more machine set-ups and inspections, than high-volume products. This is true for Atlas Company. Thus, a low-volume product is frequently responsible for more overhead costs per unit than a high-volume product.[1]
2. Assigning overhead using ABC will usually increase the cost per unit for low-volume products. Therefore, a traditional overhead allocation such as direct labour hours is usually a poor cost driver for assigning overhead costs to low-volume products.

Comparing Unit Costs

A comparison of unit manufacturing costs under traditional costing and ABC reveals that there are significant differences, as shown in Illustration 4-11.

Illustration 4-11 ◄

Comparison of unit product costs

Manufacturing Costs	The Boot		The Club	
	Traditional Costing	ABC	Traditional Costing	ABC
Direct materials	$40	$40	$30	$ 30
Direct labour	12	12	12	12
Overhead	30	17	30	95
Total cost per unit	$82	$69	$72	$137
	Overstated $13		Understated $65	

The comparison shows that unit costs under traditional costing are significantly distorted. The cost of producing The Boot is overstated by $13 per unit ($82 − $69), and the cost of producing The Club is understated by $65 per unit ($137 − $72). These differences are entirely due to how manufacturing overhead is assigned. A likely consequence of the differences in assigning over-

---

[1] Robin Cooper and Robert S. Kaplan, "How Cost Accounting Distorts Product Costs," *Management Accounting* 69, No. 10 (April 1988), pp. 20-27.

head is that Atlas Company has been overpricing The Boot and possibly losing market share to competitors. Moreover, it has been sacrificing profitability by underpricing The Club.

BUSINESS INSIGHT ▶ International Perspective

The use of activity-based costing has been less popular in Europe than in North America, but there have been success stories in both the public and private sectors.

Laporte, a British specialty chemicals and materials producer, developed an ABC spreadsheet package in order to help its sales team prioritize accounts. The sales force had a variety of clients, but tended to focus on winning big-name customers, such as large food and drink producers, at the expense of smaller ones, such as farmers. Using the ABC spreadsheet, salespeople entered the product they were selling, the customer they were selling it to, the number of support visits required, and the free-on-loan equipment the customer needed. They discovered that the margins on business involving farmers were actually larger than those on sales to big-name companies. Farmers simply placed orders on the telephone when they needed to restock, so support costs were small. However, clinching deals with clients in areas where Laporte had competition was relatively expensive. To keep clients happy, sales executives had to visit them regularly. Laporte was also expected to lend them dispensing equipment and provide 24-hour technical support. With this information, Laporte's sales staff were able to negotiate more favourable prices and service agreements.

In the 1990s, the German army, which employs almost half a million people, rolled out ABC across the entire force. The army had been struggling with heavy budget cuts. With the help of a consulting firm, the army documented every activity in each unit as part of a huge savings drive. It identified potential savings in running costs and logistics that amounted to around 10% of the army's DM50 billion (US$30.5 billion) annual budget. For example, an air force equipment depot was able to spot logistical inefficiencies and reduce the average time needed to process routine equipment delivery from 3.5 days to 1.2 days. ABC also helped the depot save DM156,000 each year on transportation costs by determining that it was more cost-effective to use trucks than trains to transport materials. More than 200 units have since adopted ABC.

Source: Christopher Watts, "Not as easy as ABC," *CFO Europe.com*, October 1998.

BEFORE YOU GO ON . . .

▶ Review It

1. Historically, why has direct labour hours been the most popular basis for allocating overhead costs to products?
2. What changes in the industrial environment have made traditional volume-based overhead allocation systems less attactive?
3. What four steps are involved in developing an ABC system?

▶ Do It

Lift Jack Company, as shown in Illustration 4-3, page 148, has seven activity cost pools and two products. It expects to produce 200,000 units of its automobile scissors jack, and 80,000 units of its truck hydraulic jack. Having identified its activity cost pools and the cost drivers for each cost pool, Lift Jack Company accumulated the following data on those activity cost pools and cost drivers.

Annual Overhead Data				Expected Use of Cost Drivers per Product	
Activity Cost Pools	Cost Drivers	Estimated Overhead	Expected Use of Cost Drivers per Activity	Scissors Jacks	Hydraulic Jacks
Ordering and receiving	Purchase orders	$ 200,000	2,500 orders	1,000	1,500
Machine setup	Setups	600,000	1,200 setups	500	700
Machining	Machine hours	2,000,000	800,000 hours	300,000	500,000
Assembling	Parts	1,800,000	3,000,000 parts	1,800,000	1,200,000
Inspecting and testing	Tests	700,000	35,000 tests	20,000	15,000
Painting	Parts	300,000	3,000,000 parts	1,800,000	1,200,000
Supervising	Labour hours	1,200,000	200,000 hours	130,000	70,000
		$6,800,000			

Using the above data, do the following:

(a) Prepare a schedule that shows the calculations of the activity-based overhead rates per cost driver.
(b) Prepare a schedule for assigning each activity's overhead cost to the two products.
(c) Calculate the overhead cost per unit for each product.
(d) Comment on the comparative overhead cost per unit.

Action Plan

- Determine the activity-based overhead rate by dividing the estimated overhead per activity by the expected use of cost drivers per activity.
- Assign the overhead of each activity cost pool to the individual products by multiplying the expected use of the cost drivers per product by the activity-based overhead rate.
- Determine the overhead cost per unit by dividing the overhead assigned to each product by the number of units of that product.

Solution

(a) Calculations of activity-based overhead rates per cost driver:

Activity Cost Pools	Estimated Overhead ÷	Expected Use of Cost Drivers per Activity =	Activity-Based Overhead Rates
Ordering and receiving	$ 200,000	2,500 purchase orders	$80 per order
Machine setup	600,000	1,200 setups	$500 per setup
Machining	2,000,000	800,000 machine hours	$2.50 per machine hour
Assembling	1,800,000	3,000,000 parts	$0.60 per part
Inspecting and testing	700,000	35,000 tests	$20 per tests
Painting	300,000	3,000,000 parts	$0.10 per part
Supervising	1,200,000	200,000 labour hours	$6 per labour hour
	$6,800,000		

(b) Assignment of each activity's overhead cost to products, using ABC:

	Scissors Jacks			Hydraulic Jacks		
Activity Cost Pools	Expected Use of Cost Drivers per Product ×	Activity-Based Overhead Rates =	Cost Assigned	Expected Use of Cost Drivers per Product ×	Activity-Based Overhead Rates =	Cost Assigned
Ordering and receiving	1,000	$80	$ 80,000	1,500	$80	$ 120,000
Machine setup	500	$500	250,000	700	$500	350,000
Machining	300,000	$2.50	750,000	500,000	$2.50	1,250,000
Assembling	1,800,000	$0.60	1,080,000	1,200,000	$0.60	720,000
Inspecting and testing	20,000	$20	400,000	15,000	$20	300,000
Painting	1,800,000	$0.10	180,000	1,200,000	$0.10	120,000
Supervising	130,000	$6	780,000	70,000	$6	420,000
Total assigned costs			$3,520,000			$3,280,000

(c) Calculation of overhead cost per unit:

	Scissors Jack	Hydraulic Jack
Total costs assigned	$3,520,000	$3,280,000
Total units produced	200,000	80,000
Overhead cost per unit	$17.60	$41.00

(d) These data show that the total overhead assigned to 80,000 hydraulic jacks is nearly as great as the overhead assigned to 200,000 scissors jacks. However, the overhead cost per hydraulic jack is $41.00. It is only $17.60 per scissors jack.

Related exercise material: BE4–1, BE4–2, BE4–3, BE4–4, BE4–5, E4–1, E4–2, E4–3, E4–4, E4–5, E4–6, E4–7, and E4–8.

Activity-Based Costing: A Closer Look

As the use of activity-based costing has grown, both its practical benefits and its limitations have become apparent.

Benefits of ABC

study objective 5

Understand the benefits and limitations of activity-based costing.

The primary benefit of ABC is **more accurate product costing**. Here's why:

1. **ABC leads to more cost pools** for assigning overhead costs to products. Instead of one plantwide pool (or even departmental pools) and a single cost driver, numerous activity cost pools with more relevant cost drivers are used. Costs are also assigned more directly based on the number of cost drivers used to produce each product.
2. **ABC leads to better control over overhead costs.** Under ABC, many overhead costs can be traced directly to activities; some indirect costs can even be identified as direct costs. As a result, managers become more aware of their responsibility to control the activities that generate those costs.
3. **ABC leads to better management decisions.** More accurate product costing should contribute to setting selling prices that can help achieve desired profitability levels for each product. In addition, the more accurate cost data could be helpful in deciding whether to make or buy a product part or component, and sometimes even whether to eliminate a product.

As mentioned, the identification of which activities drive costs can result in some indirect costs being accounted for as direct costs. This is because under ABC these costs can be traced to specific activities.

Activity-based costing does not change the amount of overhead costs. It simply assigns those overhead costs more accurately. Furthermore, if the score-keeping is more realistic and more accurate, managers should be able to better understand cost behaviour and overall profitability.

Limitations of ABC

Although ABC systems often provide better product cost data than traditional volume-based systems, there are limitations:

1. **ABC can be expensive to use.** Many companies are discouraged from using ABC because of the increased cost of identifying multiple activities and applying numerous cost drivers. Activity-based costing systems are more complex than traditional costing systems—sometimes significantly more complex. So companies must ask whether the cost of implementation is greater than the benefits of increased accuracy. Sometimes it may be. For some companies, there may be no need to consider ABC at all because their existing system is sufficient. If the costs of ABC outweigh the benefits, then the company should not use ABC.
2. **Some arbitrary allocations continue.** Even though more overhead costs can be assigned directly to products through ABC's multiple activity cost pools, certain overhead costs still need to be allocated using some arbitrary volume-based cost driver, such as labour or machine hours.

BUSINESS INSIGHT ▶ Management Perspective

These days, investors and regulators are demanding more transparent financial information, so companies must find ways to improve their internal monitoring and control systems. For example, the *Financial Market Act* requires companies to disclose material changes as quickly as possible, sometimes within 48 hours. BAM (business activity monitoring), the buzzword coined in the early 2000s by U.S. consultants Gartner Inc., is the automated monitoring of business-related activities in as close to real time as possible. It calls for sophisticated software and systems that can focus on data from disparate areas in real time. This involves an added burden and cost, but the benefits include improved processes and better performance.

Source: Bertrand Marotte, "BAM Is Like Having Eyes Everywhere," *The Globe and Mail*, May 14, 2004.

When to Use ABC

How does a company know when to use ABC? The presence of one or more of the following factors indicates that using ABC could be worthwhile:

1. Product lines differ greatly in volume and manufacturing complexity.
2. Product lines are numerous and diverse, and require differing degrees of support services.
3. Overhead costs are a significant portion of total costs.
4. The manufacturing process or the number of products has changed significantly—for example, from labour-intensive to capital-intensive due to automation.
5. Production or marketing managers are ignoring data provided by the existing system and are instead using "bootleg" costing data or other alternative data when pricing or making other product decisions.

The redesign and installation of a product-costing system is a significant decision that requires considerable expense and a major effort to accomplish. Therefore, financial managers need to be very expense and deliberate when making changes in costing systems. A key factor in implementing a successful ABC system is the support of top management.

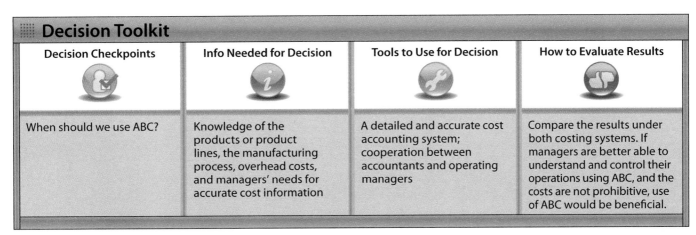

Decision Toolkit

Decision Checkpoints	Info Needed for Decision	Tools to Use for Decision	How to Evaluate Results
When should we use ABC?	Knowledge of the products or product lines, the manufacturing process, overhead costs, and managers' needs for accurate cost information	A detailed and accurate cost accounting system; cooperation between accountants and operating managers	Compare the results under both costing systems. If managers are better able to understand and control their operations using ABC, and the costs are not prohibitive, use of ABC would be beneficial.

Value-Added versus Non–Value-Added Activities

Some companies that have experienced the benefits of activity-based costing have applied it to a broader range of management activities. **Activity-based management (ABM)** is an extension of ABC from a product costing system to a management function. The focus is on reducing costs and improving processes and decision-making. A refinement of activity-based costing that is used in ABM is the classification of activities as either value-added or non–value-added.

study objective 6

Differentiate between value-added and non–value-added activities.

Value-added activities **increase the worth of a product or service** to customers; they involve resource usage and related costs that customers are willing to pay for. Value-added activities are the activities related to actually manufacturing a product or performing a service—they increase the worth of the product or service. Examples of value-added activities in a manufacturing operation are engineering design, machining, assembly, painting, and packaging. Examples of value-added activities in a service company would be performing surgery, providing legal research for legal services, or delivering packages by a delivery service.

Non–value-added activities are production- or service-related activities that simply **add cost to, or increase the time spent on, a product or service without increasing its market value**. Examples of non–value-added activities in a manufacturing operation include the repair of machines; the storage of inventory; the moving of raw materials, assemblies, and finished product within the factory; building maintenance; inspections; and inventory control. Examples of non–value-added activities in service enterprises might include taking appointments, reception, bookkeeping, billing, travelling, ordering supplies, advertising, cleaning, and computer repair.

Activity flowcharts are often used to help identify the activities that will be used in ABC costing. Illustration 4-12 shows an activity flowchart. In the top part of this flowchart, activities are identified as value-added or non–value-added. The value-added activities are highlighted in red.

In the lower part of the flowchart, there are two rows that show the number of days spent on each activity. The first row shows the number of days spent on each activity under the current manufacturing process. The second row shows the number of days expected to be spent on each activity under management's proposed re-engineered manufacturing process. The proposed changes would reduce time spent on non–value-added activities by 17 days. This 17-day improvement would be due entirely to moving inventory more quickly through the non–value-added processes—that is, by reducing inventory time in moving, storage, and waiting.

Illustration 4-12 ▼

Flowchart showing value-added and non–value-added activities

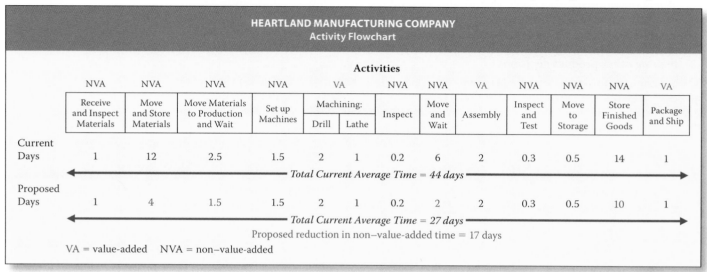

						Activities							
	NVA	NVA	NVA	NVA	VA		NVA	NVA	VA	NVA	NVA	NVA	VA
	Receive and Inspect Materials	Move and Store Materials	Move Materials to Production and Wait	Set up Machines	Machining: Drill	Machining: Lathe	Inspect	Move and Wait	Assembly	Inspect and Test	Move to Storage	Store Finished Goods	Package and Ship
Current Days	1	12	2.5	1.5	2	1	0.2	6	2	0.3	0.5	14	1

◀ ——————— *Total Current Average Time = 44 days* ——————— ▶

	Receive and Inspect Materials	Move and Store Materials	Move Materials to Production and Wait	Set up Machines	Drill	Lathe	Inspect	Move and Wait	Assembly	Inspect and Test	Move to Storage	Store Finished Goods	Package and Ship
Proposed Days	1	4	1.5	1.5	2	1	0.2	2	2	0.3	0.5	10	1

◀ ——————— *Total Current Average Time = 27 days* ——————— ▶

Proposed reduction in non–value-added time = 17 days

VA = value-added   NVA = non–value-added

Not all activities that are labelled non–value-added are totally wasteful. Nor can they be totally eliminated. For example, although inspection time is a non–value-added activity from a customer's perspective, few companies would eliminate their quality control functions. Similarly, moving and waiting time is non–value-added, but it would be impossible to completely eliminate it. Nevertheless, when managers recognize the non–value-added nature of these activities, they are motivated to minimize them as much as possible. Attention to such matters is part of the growing practice of activity-based management which helps managers concentrate on **continuous improvement** of operations and activities.

BUSINESS INSIGHT ▶ Management Perspective

Often the best way to improve a process is to learn from observing a different process. At the giant food producer General Mills, production line technicians were flown to North Carolina to observe first-hand how race-car pit crews operate. In a NASCAR race, the value-added activity is driving toward the finish-line; any time spent in the pit is non–value-added. Every split second saved in the pit increases the chances of winning. From what the General Mills technicians learned at the race track, as well as other efforts, they were able to reduce setup time from five hours to just 20 minutes.

Decision Toolkit

Decision Checkpoints	Info Needed for Decision	Tools to Use for Decision	How to Evaluate Results
How can ABC help managers manage the business?	Activities classified as value-added and non–value-added	The activity analysis flowchart extended to identify each activity as value-added or non–value-added	The flowchart should motivate managers to minimize non–value-added activities. Managers should better understand the relationship between activities and the resources they consume.

Classification of Activity Levels

As mentioned earlier, traditional costing systems are volume-driven—that is, they are driven by unit-based cost drivers such as direct labour or machine hours. These activity costs are variable and are caused by the production or acquisition of a single unit of product or the performance of a single unit of service. However, because other activity costs are not driven by unit-based cost drivers, a classification of ABC activities into four levels has been developed.

study objective 7

Understand the value of using activity levels in activity-based costing.

The four levels of activities are classified and defined as follows:

1. **Unit-level activities:** Activities performed for each unit of production
2. **Batch-level activities:** Activities performed for each batch of products rather than each unit
3. **Product-level activities:** Activities performed in support of an entire product line, but not always performed every time a new unit or batch of products is produced
4. **Facility-level activities:** Activities required to support or sustain an entire production process

Greater accuracy in overhead cost allocation may be achieved by recognizing these four different levels of activities and, from them, developing specific activity cost pools and their related cost drivers. Illustration 4-13 presents this four-level activity hierarchy, along with the types of activities and examples of costs that are traceable to those activities at each level.

Illustration 4-13 ▼

Hierarchy of activity levels

Four Levels	Types of Activities	Examples of Cost Drivers
Unit-Level Activities		
	Machine-related:	Machine hours
	Drilling, cutting, milling, trimming, pressing	
	Labour-related:	Direct labour hours or cost
	Assembling, painting, sanding, sewing	
Batch-Level Activities		
	Equipment setup	Number of setups or setup time
	Purchase ordering	Number of purchase orders
	Inspection	Number of inspections or inspection time
	Material handling	Number of material moves
Product-Level Activities		
	Product design	Number of product designs
	Engineering changes	Number of changes
Facility-Level Activities		
	Plant management salaries	Number of employees managed
	Plant amortization	Square footage
	Property taxes	Square footage
	Utilities	Square footage

This classification gives managers a structured way of thinking about the relationships between activities and the resources they consume. In contrast, traditional volume-based costing recognizes only unit-level costs. **The failure to recognize this classification of activities is one of the reasons that volume-based cost allocation causes distortions in product costing.**

As indicated earlier, allocating all overhead costs by unit-based cost drivers can send false signals to managers: Dividing batch-level, product-level, or facility-level costs by the number of units produced gives the mistaken impression that these costs vary with the number of units. **The resources consumed by batch-, product-, and facility-level supporting activities do not vary at the unit level.** And they cannot be controlled at the unit level either. The number of activities performed at the batch level goes up as the number of batches rises—not as the number of units in the batches changes. Similarly, the number of product-level activities performed depends on the number of different products—not on how many units or batches are produced. Furthermore, facility-level activity costs do not depend on the number of products, batches, or units produced. Batch-, product-, and facility-level costs can be controlled only by modifying batch-, product-, and facility-level activities.

BEFORE YOU GO ON . . .

▶ Review It

1. What are the benefits of activity-based costing?
2. What are the limitations of activity-based costing?
3. What company factors indicate that ABC would be a better costing system?
4. What is the benefit of classifying activities as value-added and non–value-added?
5. How is the classification of activities into the unit-level, batch-level, product-level, and facility-level categories important to managers?

▶ Do It

Morgan Toy Company manufactures six primary product lines in its Morganville plant. As a result of an activity analysis, the accounting department has identified eight activity cost pools. Each of the toy products is produced in large batches, with the whole plant devoted to one product at a time. Classify each of the following activities as either unit-level, batch-level, product-level, or facility-level: (a) engineering design, (b) machine setup, (c) inventory management, (d) plant cafeteria, (e) inspections after each setup, (f) polishing parts, (g) assembling parts, (h) health and safety.

Action Plan

• Recall that:
  Unit-level activities are performed for each individual unit of product.
  Batch-level activities are performed each time a batch of a product is produced.
  Product-level activities are performed to support an entire product line.
  Facility-level activities support the production process across the entire range of products.

Solution

(a) Product-level, (b) batch-level, (c) product-level, (d) facility-level, (e) batch-level, (f) unit-level, (g) unit-level, (h) facility-level.

Related exercise material: BE4–9, BE4–10, E4–12, and E4–13.

Activity-Based Costing in Service Industries

study objective 8

Apply activity-based costing to service industries.

Although it was initially developed and used by manufacturers, activity-based costing has been widely adopted in service industries as well. ABC has been a useful tool in such diverse industries as airlines, railroads, hotels, hospitals, banks, insurance companies, telephone companies, and financial services firms. The overall objective of ABC in service firms is the same as it is in a manufacturing company. That objective is to identify the key activities that generate costs and to keep track of how many of those activities are performed for each service provided (by job, service, contract, or customer).

The general approach to identifying activities, activity cost pools, and cost drivers is the same for service companies and for manufacturers. Also, the labelling of activities as value-added and non–value-added, and the attempt to reduce or eliminate non–value-added activities as much as possible, is just as valid in service industries as in manufacturing operations. What sometimes makes it harder to use activity-based costing in service industries is that **a larger proportion of the overhead costs are company-wide costs** that cannot be directly traced to specific services provided by the company.

To illustrate the use of activity-based costing instead of traditional costing in a service enterprise, we use a public accounting firm. This illustration is equally applicable to a law firm, consulting firm, architectural firm, or any service firm that performs numerous services for a client as part of a job.

Traditional Costing Example

Assume that the public accounting firm of Castle and Field prepares the condensed annual budget in Illustration 4-14.

Illustration 4-14 ◄

Condensed annual budget of a service firm under traditional costing

CASTLE AND FIELD, CAs
Annual Budget

Revenue		$2,000,000
Direct labour	$ 600,000	
Overhead (expected)	1,200,000	
Total costs		1,800,000
Operating income		$ 200,000

$$\frac{\text{Estimated overhead}}{\text{Direct labour cost}} = \text{Predetermined overhead rate}$$

$$\frac{\$1,200,000}{\$600,000} = 200\%$$

Under traditional costing, direct labour is the professional service performed, and it is the basis for applying overhead to each audit job. To determine the operating income earned on any job, Castle and Field applies overhead at the rate of 200 percent of the actual direct professional labour costs incurred. For example, assume that Castle and Field records $70,000 of actual direct professional labour cost during its audit of Plano Moulding Company, which was billed an audit fee of $260,000. Under traditional costing, using 200 percent as the rate for applying overhead to the job, applied overhead and operating income related to the Plano Moulding Company audit would be calculated as shown in Illustration 4-15.

Illustration 4-15 ◄

Overhead applied under traditional costing system

CASTLE AND FIELD, CAs
Plano Moulding Company Audit

Revenue		$260,000
Less: Direct professional labour	$ 70,000	
Applied overhead (200% × $70,000)	140,000	210,000
Operating income		$ 50,000

In this example, only one direct cost item and one overhead application rate are used under traditional costing.

Activity-Based Costing Example

Illustration 4-16 ▼

Condensed annual budget of a service firm under activity-based costing

Under activity-based costing, Castle and Field's estimated annual overhead costs of $1.2 million are distributed to several activity cost pools. Activity-based overhead rates per cost driver are calculated by dividing each activity overhead cost pool by the expected number of cost drivers used per activity. Illustration 4-16 shows an annual overhead budget using an ABC system.

CASTLE AND FIELD, CAs
Annual Overhead Budget

Activity Cost Pools	Cost Drivers	Estimated Overhead	÷ Expected Use of Cost Drivers per Activity	= Activity-Based Overhead Rates
Secretarial support	Direct professional hours	$ 210,000	30,000	$7 per hour
Direct-labour fringe benefits	Direct labour cost	240,000	$600,000	$0.40 per $1 labour cost
Printing and photocopying	Working paper pages	20,000	20,000	$1 per page
Computer support	CPU minutes	200,000	50,000	$4 per minute
Telephone and postage	None (traced directly)	71,000	$71,000	Based on usage
Legal support	Hours used	129,000	860	$150 per hour
Insurance (professional liability, etc.)	Revenue billed	120,000	$2,000,000	$0.06 per $1 revenue
Recruiting and training	Direct professional hours	210,000	30,000	$7 per hour
		$1,200,000		

Illustration 4-17 ▼

Assigning overhead in a service company

Note that some of the overhead costs can be directly assigned (see telephone and postage).

The assignment of the individual overhead activity rates to the actual number of activities used in the performance of the Plano Moulding audit results in total overhead assigned of $165,100, as shown in Illustration 4-17.

CASTLE AND FIELD, CAs
Plano Moulding Company Audit

Activity Cost Pools	Cost Drivers	Actual Use of Drivers	Activity-Based Overhead Rates	Costs Assigned
Secretarial support	Direct professional hours	3,800	$ 7.00	$ 26,600
Direct-labour fringe benefits	Direct labour cost	$70,000	0.40	28,000
Printing and photocopying	Working paper pages	1,800	1.00	1,800
Computer support	CPU minutes	8,600	4.00	34,400
Telephone and postage	None (traced directly)	0	0	8,700
Legal support	Hours used	156	150.00	23,400
Insurance (professional liability, etc.)	Revenue billed	$260,000	0.06	15,600
Recruiting and training	Direct professional hours	3,800	7.00	26,600
				$165,100

Under activity-based costing, overhead costs of $165,100 are assigned to the Plano Moulding Company audit, as compared to $140,000 under traditional costing. A comparison of the total costs and operating margins is shown in Illustration 4-18.

CASTLE AND FIELD, CAs Plano Moulding Company Audit				
	Traditional Costing		ABC	
Revenue		$260,000		$260,000
Expenses				
Direct professional labour	$ 70,000		$ 70,000	
Applied overhead	140,000		165,100	
Total expenses		210,000		235,100
Operating income		$ 50,000		$ 24,900
Profit margin		19.2%		9.6%

The comparison shows that the assignment of overhead costs under traditional costing is distorted. The total cost assigned to performing the audit of Plano Moulding Company is greater under activity-based costing by $25,100, or 18 percent, and the profit margin is only half as much. Traditional costing gives the false impression of an operating profit of $50,000. This is more than double the operating income of $24,900 using ABC.

BEFORE YOU GO ON . . .

▶ Review It

1. What is the main barrier to effectively using ABC in a service-company environment?
2. What is the main advantage to be gained by using ABC in a service-company environment?

Using the Decision Toolkit

Preece Company manufactures a line of high-end exercise equipment of commercial quality. Assume that the chief accountant has proposed changing from a traditional costing system to an activity-based costing system. The financial vice-president is not convinced, so she requests that the next large order for equipment be costed under both systems for purposes of comparison and analysis. An order from Slim-Way Salons, Inc., for 150 low-impact treadmills is received and is identified as the order to be used for dual costing. The following cost data relate to the Slim-Way order:

Data Relevant to Both Costing Systems:

Direct materials	$55,500
Direct labour hours	820
Direct labour rate per hour	$18.00

Data Relevant to the Traditional Costing System:

Predetermined overhead rate is 300% of direct labour cost.

Data Relevant to the Activity-Based Costing System:

Activity Cost Pools	Cost Drivers	Activity-Based Overhead Rate	Expected Use of Cost Drivers per Treadmill
Engineering design	Engineering hours	$30 per hour	330
Machine setup	Setups	$200 per setup	22
Machining	Machine hours	$25 per hour	732
Assembly	Number of subassemblies	$8 per subassembly	1,450
Packaging and shipping	Packaging/shipping hours	$15 per hour	152
Building occupancy	Machine hours	$6 per hour	732

Instructions

Calculate the total cost of the Slim-Way Salons, Inc., order under (a) the traditional costing system and (b) the activity-based costing system. (c) As a result of this comparison, which costing system is Preece likely to adopt? Why?

Solution

(a) Traditional costing system:

Direct materials	$ 55,500
Direct labour (820 × $18)	14,760
Overhead assigned ($14,760 × 300%)	44,280
Total costs assigned to Slim-Way order	$114,540
Number of low-impact treadmills	150
Cost per unit	$763.60

(b) Activity-based costing system:

Direct materials		$ 55,500
Direct labour (820 × $18)		14,760
Overhead activity costs:		
Engineering design (330 hours @ $30)	$ 9,900	
Machine setup (22 setups @ $200)	4,400	
Machining (732 machine hours @ $25)	18,300	
Assembly (1,450 subassemblies @ $8)	11,600	
Packaging and shipping (152 hours @ $15)	2,280	
Building occupancy (732 hours @ $6)	4,392	50,872
Total costs assigned to Slim-Way order		$121,132
Number of low-impact treadmills		150
Cost per unit		$807.55

(c) Preece Company will likely adopt ABC because of the difference in the cost per unit (which ABC found to be higher). More importantly, ABC provides greater insight into the sources and causes of the cost per unit. Managers have a better understanding of which activities to control in order to reduce costs. ABC will provide better product costing and greater profitability for the company.

the navigator

Summary of Study Objectives

1. **Recognize the difference between traditional costing and activity-based costing.** A traditional costing system allocates overhead to products based on a predetermined plantwide or department-wide volume of unit-based output rates, such as direct labour or machine hours. An ABC system allocates overhead to identified activity cost pools, and costs are then assigned to products using related cost drivers that measure the activities (resources) consumed.

2. **Identify the steps in the development of an activity-based costing system.** The development of an activity-based costing system involves four steps: (1) Identify and classify the major activities that pertain to the manufacture of specific products, and allocate manufacturing overhead costs to the appropriate cost pools. (2) Identify the cost driver that has a strong correlation to the costs accumulated in each activity cost pool.

(3) Calculate the activity-based overhead rate per cost driver. (4) Use the cost drivers to assign overhead costs for each activity cost pool to products or services.

3. **Know how companies identify the activity cost pools used in activity-based costing.** To identify activity cost pools, a company must perform an analysis of each operation or process, documenting and timing every task, action, or transaction.

4. **Know how companies identify and use the activity cost drivers in activity-based costing.** Cost drivers that are identified for activity cost pools must (a) accurately measure the actual consumption of the activity by the various products, and (b) have data on them that is easily available.

5. **Understand the benefits and limitations of activity-based costing.** What makes ABC a more accurate

product costing system is (1) the increased number of cost pools used to assign overhead, (2) the enhanced control over overhead costs, and (3) the better management decisions it makes possible. The limitations of ABC are (1) the higher analysis and measurement costs that accompany multiple activity centres and cost drivers, and (2) the need to still allocate some costs arbitrarily.

6. **Differentiate between value-added and non–value-added activities.** Value-added activities increase the worth of a product or service. Non–value-added activities simply add cost to, or increase the time spent on, a product or service without increasing its market value. Being aware of these classifications helps managers reduce or eliminate the time spent on the non–value-added activities.

7. **Understand the value of using activity levels in activity-based costing.** Activities may be classified as unit-level, batch-level, product-level, and facility-level. Overhead costs at unit, batch, product, and facility levels are controlled by modifying unit-, batch-, product-, and facility-level activities, respectively. Failure to recognize this classification of levels can result in distorted product costing.

8. **Apply activity-based costing to service industries.** The overall objective of using ABC in service industries is the same as in manufacturing industries, that is, improved costing of the services provided (by job, service, contract, or customer). The general approach to costing is the same: analyze operations, identify activities, accumulate overhead costs by activity cost pools, and identify and use cost drivers to assign the cost pools to the services.

Decision Toolkit—A Summary

Decision Checkpoints	Info Needed for Decision	Tools to Use for Decision	How to Evaluate Results
When should we use ABC?	Knowledge of the products or product lines, the manufacturing process, overhead costs, and managers' needs for accurate cost information	A detailed and accurate cost accounting system; cooperation between accountants and operating managers	Compare the results under both costing systems. If managers are better able to understand and control their operations using ABC, and the costs are not prohibitive, the use of ABC would be beneficial.
How can ABC help managers manage the business?	Activities classified as value-added and non–value-added	The activity analysis flowchart extended to identify each activity as value-added or non–value-added	The flowchart should motivate managers to minimize non–value-added activities. Managers should better understand the relationship between activities and the resources they consume.

Glossary

Activity   Any event, action, transaction, or work sequence that causes a cost to be incurred in producing a product or providing a service. (p. 145)

Activity-based costing (ABC)   An overhead cost allocation system that allocates overhead to multiple activity cost pools and assigns the activity cost pools to products or services by using cost drivers that represent the activities used. (p. 145)

Activity-based management (ABM)   An extension of ABC from a product costing system to a management function that focuses on reducing costs and improving processes and decision-making. (p. 153)

Activity cost pool   The overhead cost allocated to a distinct type of activity or related activities. (p. 145)

Batch-level activities   Activities performed for each batch of products. (p. 155)

Cost driver   Any factor or activity that has a direct cause–effect relationship with the resources consumed. In ABC, cost drivers are used to assign activity cost pools to products or services. (p. 145)

Facility-level activities   Activities required to support or sustain an entire production process and not dependent on the number of products, batches, or units produced. (p. 155)

Non–value-added activity   An activity that adds cost to, or increases the time spent on, a product or service without increasing its market value. (p. 153)

Product-level activities   Activities performed for and identifiable with an entire product line. (p. 155)

Unit-level activities   Activities performed for each unit of production. (p. 155)

Value-added activity   An activity that increases the worth of a product or service. (p. 153)

Demonstration Problem

Animated
Demonstration
Problem

Spreadwell Paint Company manufactures two high-quality base paints: an oil-based paint and a latex paint. Both paints are housepaints and are manufactured in a neutral white colour only. The white base paints are sold to franchised retail paint and decorating stores where pigments are added to tint (colour) the paint as desired by the customer. The oil-based paint is made from petroleum products, and is thinned and cleaned with organic solvents such as mineral spirits or turpentine. The latex paint is made from water, and thinned and cleaned with it; synthetic resin particles that are suspended in the water dry and harden when exposed to the air.

Spreadwell uses the same processing equipment to produce both paints in different production runs. Between batches, the vats and other processing equipment must be washed and cleaned.

After analyzing the company's entire operations, Spreadwell's accountants and production managers have identified activity cost pools and have accumulated annual budgeted overhead costs for each pool as follows:

Activity Cost Pools	Estimated Overhead
Purchasing	$ 240,000
Processing (weighing and mixing, grinding, thinning and drying, straining)	1,400,000
Packaging (quarts, gallons and 5 gallons)	580,000
Testing	240,000
Storage and inventory control	180,000
Washing and cleaning equipment	560,000
Total annual budgeted overhead	$3,200,000

With further analysis, activity cost drivers were identified and their expected use by product and activity were scheduled as follows:

Activity Cost Pools	Cost Drivers	Expected Cost Drivers per Activity	Expected Use of Drivers per Product	
			Oil-Based	Latex
Purchasing	Purchase orders	1,500 orders	800	700
Processing	Gallons processed	1,000,000 gals.	400,000	600,000
Packaging	Containers filled	400,000 containers	180,000	220,000
Testing	Number of tests	4,000 tests	2,100	1,900
Storing	Avg. gals. on hand	18,000 gals.	10,400	7,600
Washing	Number of batches	800 batches	350	450

Spreadwell has budgeted 400,000 gallons of oil-based paint and 600,000 gallons of latex paint for processing during the year.

Instructions

(a) Prepare a schedule showing the calculations of the activity-based overhead rates.
(b) Prepare a schedule that assigns each activity's overhead cost pool to each product.
(c) Calculate the overhead cost per unit for each product.
(d) Classify each activity cost pool as value-added or non–value-added.

Solution to Demonstration Problem

(a) Calculations of activity-based overhead rates:

Activity Cost Pools	Extimated Overhead	Expected Use of Cost Drivers	Activity-Based Overhead Rates
Purchasing	$ 240,000	1,500 orders	$160 per order
Processing	1,400,000	1,000,000 gallons	$1.40 per gallon
Packaging	580,000	400,000 containers	$1.45 per container
Testing	240,000	4,000 tests	$60 per test
Storing	180,000	18,000 gallons	$10 per gallon
Washing	560,000	800 batches	$700 per batch
	$3,200,000		

(b) Assignment of activity cost pools to products:

Activity Cost Pools	Oil-Based Paint			Latex Paint		
	Expected Use of Drivers	Overhead Rates	Cost Assigned	Expected Use of Drivers	Overhead Rates	Cost Assigned
Purchasing	800	$160	$ 128,000	700	$160	$ 112,000
Processing	400,000	$1.40	560,000	600,000	$1.40	840,000
Packaging	180,000	$1.45	261,000	220,000	$1.45	319,000
Testing	2,100	$60	126,000	1,900	$60	114,000
Storing	10,400	$10	104,000	7,600	$10	76,000
Washing	350	$700	245,000	450	$700	315,000
Total overhead assigned			$1,424,000			$1,776,000

(c) Calculation of overhead cost assigned per unit:

	Oil-Based Paint	Latex Paint
Total overhead cost assigned	$1,424,000	$1,776,000
Total gallons produced	400,000	600,000
Overhead cost per gallon	$3.56	$2.96

(d) Value-added activities: processing and packaging
Non–value-added activities: purchasing, testing, storing, and washing

Action Plan

• Identify the major activities that pertain to the manufacture of specific products and allocate manufacturing overhead costs to activity cost pools.

• Identify the cost drivers that accurately measure each activity's contribution to the finished product.

• Calculate the activity-based overhead rates.

• Assign manufacturing overhead costs for each activity cost pool to products, using the activity-based overhead rates.

the navigator

Self-Study Questions

Additional Self-Study Questions

Answers are at the end of the chapter.

(SO 1) 1. Activity-based costing (ABC):
   (a) can be used only in a process cost system.
   (b) focuses on units of production.
   (c) focuses on activities that are performed to produce a product.
   (d) uses only a single basis of allocation.

(SO 1) 2. Activity-based costing:
   (a) is the initial phase of converting to a just-in-time operating environment.
   (b) can be used only in a job-order costing system.
   (c) is a two-stage overhead cost allocation system that identifies activity cost pools and cost drivers.
   (d) uses direct labour as its main cost driver.

(SO 3) 3. Any activity that causes resources to be consumed is called a:
   (a) just-in-time activity.
   (b) facility-level activity.
   (c) cost driver.
   (d) non–value-added activity.

(SO 4) 4. The overhead rate for machine setups is $100 per setup. Products A and B have 80 and 60 setups, respectively. The overhead assigned to each product is:
   (a) product A $8,000, product B $8,000.
   (b) product A $8,000, product B $6,000.
   (c) product A $6,000, product B $6,000.
   (d) product A $6,000, product B $8,000.

(SO 4) 5. Donna Crawford Co. has identified an activity cost pool and has allocated estimated overhead of $1,920,000 to it. It has determined the expected use of cost drivers for that activity to be 160,000 inspections. Widgets require 40,000 inspections; gadgets, 30,000 inspections; and targets, 90,000 inspections. The overhead assigned to each product is:
   (a) widgets $40,000, gadgets $30,000, targets $90,000.
   (b) widgets $480,000, gadgets $360,000, targets $108,000.
   (c) widgets $360,000, gadgets $480,000, targets $1,080,000.
   (d) widgets $480,000, gadgets $360,000, targets $1,080,000.

(SO 6) 6. An activity that adds costs to the product but does not increase its market value is a:
   (a) value-added activity.
   (b) cost driver.
   (c) cost-benefit activity.
   (d) non–value-added activity.

(SO 6) 7. The following activity is value-added:
   (a) storage of raw materials.
   (b) moving parts from machine to machine.
   (c) shaping a piece of metal on a lathe.
   (d) All of the above

(SO 7) 8. A relevant facility-level cost driver for heating costs is:
   (a) machine hours.   (c) floor space.
   (b) direct material.   (d) direct labour cost.

Questions

1. Under what conditions is direct labour a valid basis for allocating overhead?

2. What has happened in recent industrial history to reduce the usefulness of direct labour as the main basis for allocating overhead to products?

3. In an automated manufacturing environment, what basis of overhead allocation is often more relevant than direct labour hours?

4. What is generally true about overhead allocation to high-volume products versus low-volume products under a traditional costing system?

5. (a) What are the principal differences between activity-based costing (ABC) and traditional product costing?
   (b) What assumptions must be met for ABC costing to be useful?

6. What is the formula for calculating activity-based overhead rates?

7. What are the steps in developing an activity-based costing system?

8. Explain the preparation and use of an activity flowchart in an ABC system.

9. What is an activity cost pool?

10. What is a cost driver?

11. What makes a cost driver accurate and appropriate?

12. What is the formula for assigning activity cost pools to products?

13. What are the benefits of activity-based costing?

14. What are the limitations of activity-based costing?

15. Under what conditions is ABC generally the better overhead costing system?

16. What refinement has been made to increase the efficiency and effectiveness of ABC for use in managing costs?

17. What is the benefit of classifying activities as value-added and non–value-added?

18. In what ways is the application of ABC to service industries the same as its application to manufacturing companies?

19. How is the classification of levels of activity relevant to ABC?

Brief Exercises

BE4–1 Infortrac Inc. sells a high-speed retrieval system for mining information. It provides the following information for the year:

	Budgeted	Actual
Overhead cost	$1,000,000	$950,000
Machine hours	50,000	45,000
Direct labour hours	100,000	90,000

Identify differences between costing systems. (SO 1)

Overhead is applied based on direct labour hours. (a) Calculate the predetermined overhead rate. (b) Determine the amount of overhead applied for the year. (c) Explain how an activity-based costing system might differ in terms of calculating a predetermined overhead rate.

BE4–2 Sassafras Inc. has conducted an analysis of overhead costs for one of its product lines using a traditional cost system (volume-based) and an activity-based costing system. Here are its results:

Identify differences between costing systems. (SO 1)

	Traditional Costing	ABC
Sales revenues	$600,000	$600,000
Overhead costs:		
Product RX3	$34,000	$50,000
Product Y12	36,000	20,000
	$70,000	$70,000

Explain how a difference in the overhead costs between the two systems may have occurred.

BE4–3 Altex Co. identifies the following activities that pertain to manufacturing overhead: materials handling, machine setups, factory machine maintenance, factory supervision, and quality control. For each activity, identify an appropriate cost driver.

Identify cost drivers. (SO 4)

BE4–4 Ayala Company manufactures four products in a single production facility. The company uses activity-based costing. The following activities have been identified through the company's activity analysis: (a) inventory control, (b) machine setups, (c) employee training, (d) quality inspections, (e) material ordering, (f) drilling operations, and (g) building maintenance.

For each activity, name a cost driver that might be used to assign overhead costs to products.

Identify cost drivers. (SO 4)

BE4–5 Gomez Company identifies three activities in its manufacturing process: machine setups, machining, and inspections. The estimated annual overhead cost for each activity is $180,000, $325,000, and $87,500, respectively. The cost driver for each activity and the expected annual usage are as follows: number of setups 2,500, machine hours 25,000, and number of inspections 1,750. Calculate the overhead rate for each activity.

Calculate activity-based overhead rates. (SO 4)

BE4–6 Coats Galore, Inc. uses activity-based costing as the basis for information to set prices for its six lines of seasonal coats. Calculate the activity-based overhead rates using the following budgeted data for each of the activity cost pools:

Calculate activity-based overhead rates. (SO 4)

Activity Cost Pools	Estimated Overhead	Expected Use of Cost Drivers per Activity
Designing	$ 450,000	12,000 designer hours
Sizing and cutting	4,000,000	160,000 machine hours
Stitching and trimming	1,440,000	80,000 labour hours
Wrapping and packing	336,000	32,000 finished units

Calculate activity-based overhead rates.
(SO 4)

BE4–7   Computer Parts, Inc., a manufacturer of computer chips, uses activity-based costing. The following budgeted data for each of the activity cost pools are provided for the year 2005:

Activity Cost Pools	Estimated Overhead	Expected Use of Cost Drivers per Activity
Ordering and receiving	$ 90,000	15,000 orders
Etching	480,000	60,000 machine hours
Soldering	1,760,000	440,000 labour hours

For 2005, the company had 11,000 orders and used 50,000 machine hours, and labour hours totalled 500,000. What is the total overhead applied?

Classify activities as value-added or non–value-added.
(SO 6)

BE4–8   Newman Novelty Company identified the following activities in its production and support ope rations. Classify each of these activities as either value-added or non–value-added.

(a) purchasing
(b) receiving
(c) design engineering
(d) storing inventory

(e) cost accounting
(f) moving work-in-process
(g) inspecting and testing
(h) painting and packing

Classify service company activities as value-added or non–value-added.
(SO 6, 8)

BE4–9   R & M is an architectural firm that is contemplating the installation of activity-based costing. The following activities are performed daily by staff architects: (1) designing and draft-ing, 3 hours; (2) staff meetings, 1 hour; (3) on-site supervision, 2 hours; (4) lunch, 1 hour; (5) con-sultation with client on specifications, 1.5 hours; (6) entertaining a prospective client for dinner, 2 hours. Classify these activities as value-added or non–value-added.

Classify activities according to level.
(SO 7, 8)

BE4–10   Quick Pix is a large film developing and processing centre that serves 130 out-lets in grocery stores, service stations, camera and photo shops, and drugstores in 16 nearby towns. Quick Pix operates 24 hours a day, 6 days a week. Classify each of the following activ-ity costs as either unit-level, batch-level, product-level, or facility-level:

(a) developing fluids
(b) photocopy paper
(c) depreciation of machinery
(d) setups for enlargements
(e) supervisor's salary

(f) ordering materials
(g) pickup and delivery
(h) commission to dealers
(i) insurance on building
(j) loading developing machines

Classify activities according to level.
(SO 7)

BE4–11   Tool Time, Inc. operates 20 injection molding machines in the production of tool boxes of four different sizes, named the Apprentice, the Handyman, the Journeyman, and the Professional. Classify each of the following costs as unit-level, batch-level, product-level, or facility-level:

(a) first-shift supervisor's salary
(b) powdered raw plastic
(c) dies for casting plastic components
(d) depreciation on injection molding machines
(e) changing dies on machines
(f) moving components to assembly department
(g) engineering design
(h) employee health and medical insurance coverage

Calculate rates and activity levels.
(SO 4, 7)

BE4–12   Trek Cycle Company uses three activity pools to apply overhead to its products. Each activity has a cost driver that is used to allocate the overhead costs to the product. The activities and related overhead costs are as follows: product design $50,000; machining $300,000; and material handling $100,000. The cost drivers and expected use are as follows:

Activity	Cost Driver	Expected Use of Cost Drivers per Activity
Product design	Number of product changes	10
Machining	Machine hours	150,000
Material handling	Number of setups	100

(a) Calculate the predetermined overhead rate for each activity. (b) Classify each of these activities as unit-level, batch-level, product-level, or facility-level.

Exercises

E4–1 Elle Inc. makes two types of handbags: standard and custom. The controller has decided to use a plantwide overhead rate based on direct labour costs. The president has heard of activity-based costing and wants to see how the results would differ if this system were used. Two activity cost pools were developed: machining and setup. Presented below is information related to the company's operations:

Assign overhead using traditional costing and ABC. (SO 1, 4)

	Standard	Custom
Direct labour costs	$50,000	$100,000
Machine hours	1,000	1,000
Setup hours	100	400

Total estimated overhead costs are $300,000. The overhead cost allocated to the machining activity cost pool is $200,000, and $100,000 is allocated to the machine setup activity cost pool.

Instructions

(a) Calculate the overhead rate using the traditional (plantwide) approach.
(b) Calculate the overhead rates using the activity-based costing approach.
(c) Determine the difference in allocation between the two approaches.

E4–2 Perdon Inc. has conducted the following analysis related to its product lines, using a traditional cost system (volume-based) and an activity-based costing system. Both the traditional and the activity-based costing systems include direct materials and direct labour costs.

Explain difference between traditional and activity-based costing. (SO 1)

		Total Costs	
Product	Sales Revenue	Traditional	ABC
Product 540X	$200,000	$55,000	$50,000
Product 137Y	160,000	50,000	35,000
Product 249S	80,000	15,000	35,000

Instructions

(a) For each product line, calculate the operating income using the traditional costing system.
(b) For each product line, calculate the operating income using the activity-based costing system.
(c) Using the following formula, calculate the percentage difference in operating income for each of Perdon's product lines: Operating Income (ABC) less Operating Income (traditional cost) divided by Operating Income (traditional cost). Round the percentage to two decimals.
(d) Explain why the costs for Product 540X are approximately the same using either the traditional or activity-based costing system.

E4–3 International Fabrics has budgeted overhead costs of $900,000. It has allocated overhead on a plantwide basis to its two products (wool and cotton) using direct labour hours which are estimated to be 450,000 for the current year. The company has decided to experiment with activity-based costing and has created two activity cost pools and related activity cost drivers. These two cost pools are as follows: cutting (cost driver is machine hours) and design (cost driver is number of setups). Overhead allocated to the cutting cost pool is $300,000 and $600,000 is allocated to the design cost pool. Additional information related to these pools is as follows:

Assign overhead using traditional costing and ABC. (SO 1, 4)

	Wool	Cotton	Total
Machine hours	100,000	100,000	200,000
Number of setups	1,000	500	1,500

Instructions

(a) Determine the amount of overhead allocated to the wool product line and the cotton product line using activity-based costing.
(b) What is the difference between the allocation of overhead to the wool and cotton product lines using activity-based costing versus the traditional approach, assuming direct labour hours were incurred evenly between the cutting and design activities?

Assign overhead using
traditional costing and ABC.
(SO 1, 4)

E4−4   Alonzo Inc. manufactures two products: car and truck wheels. To determine the amount of overhead to assign to each product line, the controller, YuYu Ortega, has developed the following information:

	Car	Truck
Estimated wheels produced	40,000	10,000
Direct labour hours per wheel	1	3

The total estimated overhead costs for the two product lines are $700,000.

Instructions

(a) Calculate the overhead cost assigned to the car and truck wheels, assuming that direct labour hours is used to allocate overhead costs.

(b) Ortega is not satisfied with the traditional method of allocating overhead because he believes that most of the overhead costs relate to the truck wheel product line because of its complexity. He therefore develops the following three activity cost pools and related cost drivers to better understand these costs:

Activity Cost Pools	Expected Use of Cost Drivers	Estimated Overhead Costs
Setting up machines	1,000 setups	$180,000
Assembling	70,000 labour hours	280,000
Inspection	1,200 inspections	240,000

Calculate the activity-based overhead rates for these three cost pools.

(c) Calculate the cost that is assigned to the car and truck product lines using an activity-based cost system, given the following information:

	Expected Use of Cost Drivers per Product	
	Car	Truck
Number of setups	200	800
Direct labour hours	40,000	30,000
Number of inspections	100	1,100

(d) What do you believe Ortega should do?

Assign overhead using
traditional costing and ABC.
(SO 1, 4)

E4−5   Shady Lady sells window coverings to both commercial and residential customers. The following information is for its budgeted operations for the current year:

	Commercial		Residential	
Revenues		$300,000		$480,000
Direct material costs	$ 30,000		$ 50,000	
Direct labour costs	100,000		300,000	
Overhead costs	50,000	180,000	150,000	500,000
Operating income (loss)		$120,000		$ (20,000)

The controller, Wanda Lewis, is concerned about the residential product line. She cannot understand why this line is not more profitable as window coverings are less complex to install for residential customers. In addition, the residential client base lives close to the company office, so travel costs are not as expensive on a per client visit for residential customers. As a result, she has decided to take a closer look at the overhead costs assigned to the two product lines. She hopes to determine whether a more accurate product costing model can be developed. Here are the three activity cost pools and related information she developed:

Activity Cost Pools	Estimated Overhead	Cost Drivers
Scheduling and travel	$90,000	Hours of travel
Setup time	70,000	Number of setups
Supervision	40,000	Direct labour cost

	Expected Use of Cost Drivers per Product	
	Commercial	Residential
Scheduling and travel	1,000	500
Setup time	450	250

Instructions

(a) Calculate the activity-based overhead rates for both the commercial and residential product lines, and determine the overhead cost assigned to each line.

(b) Calculate the operating income for each product line, using the activity-based overhead rates.

(c) What do you believe Wanda Lewis should do?

E4–6 Wilkins Corporation manufactures safes—large mobile safes, and large walk-in stationary bank safes. As part of its annual budgeting process, Wilkins is analyzing the profitability of its two products. Part of this analysis involves estimating the amount of overhead to be allocated to each product line. The following information relates to overhead:

Assign overhead using traditional costing and ABC. (SO 1, 4)

	Mobile Safes	Walk-In Safes
Units planned for production	200	50
Material moves per product line	300	200
Purchase orders per product line	450	350
Direct labour hours per product line	800	1,700

Instructions

(a) The total estimated manufacturing overhead was $235,000. Under traditional costing (which assigns overhead on the basis of direct-labour hours), what amount of manufacturing overhead costs is assigned to (1) one mobile safe, and (2) one walk-in safe? Do not round your answers.

(b) The total estimated manufacturing overhead of $235,000 comprised $150,000 for material-handling costs and $85,000 for purchasing activity costs. Under activitybased costing (ABC):

1. What amount of material handling costs is assigned to (a) one mobile safe, and (b) one walk-in safe?

2. What amount of purchasing activity costs is assigned to (a) one mobile safe, and (b) one walk-in safe?

(c) Compare the amount of overhead allocated to one mobile safe and to one walk-in safe under the traditional costing approach versus under ABC.

E4–7 Quik Prints Company is a small printing and copying firm with three high-speed offset printing presses, five copiers (two colour and three black and white), one collator, one cutting and folding machine, and one fax machine. To improve its pricing practices, owner-manager Damon Hastings is installing activity-based accounting. Damon also has five employees: two printer/designers, one receptionist/bookkeeper, one sales person and copy-machine operator, and one janitor/delivery clerk. Damon can operate any of the machines and, in addition to managing the entire operation, he performs the training, designing, selling, and marketing functions.

Identify activity cost pools. (SO 3)

Instructions

As Quik Prints' independent accountant who prepares tax forms and quarterly financial statements, you have been asked to identify the activities that would be used to accumulate overhead costs to assign to jobs and customers. Using your knowledge of a small printing and copying firm (and some imagination), identify at least twelve activity cost pools as the start of an activity-based costing system for Quik Prints Company.

E4–8 Galavic Corporation manufactures snowmobiles in its, Ontario, plant. The following costs are budgeted for the first quarter's operations:

Identify activity cost pools and cost drivers. (SO 3, 4)

Machine setup—indirect materials	$ 4,000
Inspections	16,000
Tests	4,000
Insurance—plant	110,000
Engineering design	140,000
Amortization—machinery	520,000
Machine setup—indirect labour	20,000
Property taxes	29,000
Oil—heating	19,000
Electricity—plant lighting	21,000
Engineering prototypes	60,000
Amortization—plant	210,000
Electricity—machinery	36,000
Custodial (machine maintenance) wages	19,000

Instructions

Classify the above costs of Galavic Corporation into activity cost pools using the following categories: engineering, machinery, machine setup, quality control, factory utilities, and maintenance. Next, identify a cost driver that may be used to assign each cost pool to each line of snowmobiles.

Identify activity cost drivers.
(SO 4)

E4–9   Peter Catalano's Verde Vineyard produces three varieties of wine: Merlot, Viognier, and Pinot Noir. His winemaster, Kyle Ward, has identified the following activities as cost pools for accumulating overhead and assigning it to products:

1. Culling and replanting. Dead or overcrowded vines are culled, and new vines are planted or relocated. (There are separate vineyards for each variety.)
2. Tying. The posts and wires are reset, and vines are tied to the wires for the dormant season.
3. Trimming. At the end of the harvest, the vines are cut and trimmed back in preparation for the next season.
4. Spraying. The vines are sprayed with chemicals for protection against insects and fungi.
5. Harvesting. The grapes are hand-picked, placed in carts, and transported to the crushers.
6. Stemming and crushing. Cartfuls of bunches of grapes of each variety are separately loaded into machines which remove stems and gently crush the grapes.
7. Pressing and filtering. The crushed grapes are transferred to presses which mechanically remove the juices and filter out bulk and impurities.
8. Fermentation. The grape juice, by variety, is fermented in either stainless-steel tanks or oak barrels.
9. Aging. The wines are aged in either stainless-steel tanks or oak barrels for one to three years depending on variety.
10. Bottling and corking. Bottles are machine-filled and corked.
11. Labelling and boxing. Each bottle is labelled, as is each nine-bottle case, with the name of the vintner, vintage, and variety.
12. Storing. Packaged and boxed bottles are stored awaiting shipment.
13. Shipping. The wine is shipped to distributors and private retailers.
14. Heating and air-conditioning of plant and offices.
15. Maintenance of buildings and equipment. Printing, repairs, replacements, and general maintenance are performed in the off-season.

Instructions

For each of Verde's fifteen activity cost pools, identify a probable cost driver that is used to assign overhead costs to the three wine varieties.

Identify activity cost drivers.
(SO 4)

E4–10   Anna Bellatorre, Inc. manufactures five models of kitchen appliances at its Alberta plant. The company is installing activity-based costing and has identified the following activities performed at its Alberta plant:

1. Designing new models
2. Purchasing raw materials and parts
3. Storing and managing inventory

4. Receiving and inspecting raw materials and parts
5. Interviewing and hiring new personnel
6. Machine-forming sheet steel into appliance parts
7. Manually assembling parts into appliances
8. Training all employees of the company
9. Insuring all tangible fixed assets
10. Supervising production
11. Maintaining and repairing machinery and equipment
12. Painting and packaging finished appliances

Having analyzed its Alberta plant operations for purposes of installing activity-based cost-ing, Anna Bellatorre, Inc. identified its activity cost centres. It now needs to identify rel-evant activity cost drivers in order to assign overhead costs to its products.

Instructions

Using the activities listed above, identify for each activity one or more cost drivers that might be used to assign overhead to Anna Bellatorre's five products.

E4–11 Fontillas Instruments, Inc. manufactures two products: missile range instruments and space pressure gauges. During April, 50 range instruments and 300 pressure gauges were produced, and overhead costs of $89,000 were estimated. An analysis of estimated overhead costs reveals the following activities:

Calculate overhead rates and assign overhead using ABC.
(SO 4, 5)

Activity	Cost Driver	Total Cost
Materials handling	Number of requisitions	$35,000
Machine setups	Number of setups	27,500
Quality inspections	Number of inspections	27,000

The cost driver volume for each product was as follows:

Cost Driver	Instruments	Gauges	Total
Number of requisitions	400	600	1,000
Number of setups	200	300	500
Number of inspections	200	400	600

Instructions

(a) Determine the overhead rate for each activity.
(b) Assign the manufacturing overhead costs for April to the two products using activity-based costing.
(c) ▭▭▭▷ Write a memorandum to the president of Fontillas Instruments to explain the benefits of activity-based costing.

E4–12 Lim Clothing Company manufactures its own designed and labelled sports attire and sells its products through catalogue sales and retail outlets. While Lim has for years used activity-based costing in its manufacturing activities, it has always used traditional costing in assigning its selling costs to its product lines. Selling costs have traditionally been assigned to Lim's product lines at a rate of 70% of direct material costs. Its direct material costs for the month of March for its "high-intensity" line of attire are $400,000. The com-pany has decided to extend activity-based costing to its selling costs. Data relating to the "high-intensity" line of products for the month of March are as follows:

Assign overhead using traditional costing and ABC; classify activities as value- or non–value-added and by level.
(SO 1, 4, 6)

Activity Cost Pools	Cost Drivers	Overhead Rates	Number of Cost Drivers Used per Activity
Sales commissions	Dollar sales	$0.05 per dollar sales	$930,000
Advertising—TV/Radio	Minutes	$300 per minute	250
Advertising—Newspaper	Column inches	$10 per column inch	3,000
Catalogues	Catalogues mailed	$2.50 per catalogue	60,000
Cost of catalogue sales	Catalogue orders	$1 per catalogue order	9,000
Credit and collection	Dollar sales	$0.03 per dollar sales	$930,000

Instructions

(a) Calculate the selling costs to be assigned to the "high-intensity" line of attire for the month of March: (1) using the traditional product costing system (direct material cost is the cost driver), and (2) using activity-based costing.

(b) By what amount does the traditional product costing system undercost or overcost the "high-intensity" product line?

(c) Classify each of the activities as value-added or non–value-added.

Assign overhead using traditional costing and ABC; classify activities as value- or non–value-added.
(SO 1, 4, 6)

E4–13   Healthy Products, Inc., uses a traditional product costing system to assign overhead costs uniformly to all products. To meet government regulations and to assure its customers of safe, sanitary, and nutritious food, Healthy engages in a high level of quality control. Healthy assigns its quality-control overhead costs to all products at a rate of 17% of direct labour costs. Its direct labour cost for the month of June for its low-calorie dessert line is $55,000. In response to repeated requests from its financial vice-president, Healthy's management agrees to adopt activity-based costing. Data relating to the low-calorie dessert line for the month of June are as follows:

Activity Cost Pools	Cost Drivers	Overhead Rates	Number of Cost Drivers Used per Activity
Inspections of material received	Number of kilograms	$0.60 per kilogram	6,000 kilograms
In-process inspections	Number of servings	$0.33 per serving	10,000 servings
Government certification	Customer orders	$12.00 per order	420 orders

Instructions

(a) Calculate the quality-control overhead cost to be assigned to the low-calorie dessert product line for the month of June: (1) using the traditional product costing system (direct labour cost is the cost driver), and (2) using activity-based costing.

(b) By what amount does the traditional product costing system undercost or overcost the low-calorie dessert line?

(c) Classify each of the activities as value-added or non–value-added.

Classify activities as value-added or non–value-added.
(SO 6)

E4–14   In an effort to expand the usefulness of its activity-based costing system, Peter Catalano's Verde Vineyards decides to adopt activity-based management techniques. One of these ABM techniques is classifying its activities as either value-added or non–value-added.

Instructions

Using Verde's list of fifteen activity cost pools in Exercise 4–9, classify each of the activities as either value-added or non–value-added.

Classify activities as value-added or non–value-added.
(SO 6)

E4–15   Anna Bellatorre, Inc. is interested in using its activity-based costing system to improve its operating efficiency and its profit margins by using activity-based management techniques. As part of this undertaking, you have been asked to classify its Alberta plant activities as value-added or non–value-added.

Instructions

Using the list of activities identified in Exercise 4–10, classify each activity as either value-added or non–value-added.

Classify service company activities by level.
(SO 6, 8)

E4–16   D & G is a law firm that is initiating an activity-based costing system. Jim Dewey, the senior partner and a strong supporter of ABC, has prepared the following list of activities typically performed by a lawyer in a day at the firm:

Activities	Hours
Writing contracts and letters	1.0
Attending staff meetings	0.5
Taking depositions	1.0
Doing research	1.0
Travelling to/from court	1.0
Contemplating legal strategy	1.0
Eating lunch	1.0
Litigating a case in court	2.5
Entertaining a prospective client	2.0

Instructions

Classify each of the activities listed by Jim Dewey as value-added or non–value-added; be able to defend your classification. How much of the time was value-added and how much was non–value-added?

E4–17 Having itemized its costs for the first quarter of next year's budget, Galavic Corporation wants to install an activity-based costing system. First it identified the activity cost pools in which to accumulate factory overhead; second, it identified the relevant cost drivers. (This was done in E4–8.)

Classify activities by level. (SO 7)

Instructions

Using the activity cost pools identified in E4–8, classify each of those cost pools as either unit-level, batch-level, product-level, or facility-level.

E4–18 Otto Dieffenbach & Sons, Inc. is a small manufacturing company that uses activity-based costing. Dieffenbach & Sons accumulates overhead in the following activity cost pools:

Classify activities by level. (SO 7)

1. Hiring personnel
2. Managing parts inventory
3. Purchasing
4. Testing prototypes
5. Designing products
6. Setting up equipment
7. Training employees
8. Inspecting machined parts
9. Machining
10. Assembling

Instructions

For each activity cost pool, indicate whether the activity cost pool would be unit-level, batch-level, product-level, or facility-level.

Problems: Set A

P4–19A FireOut, Inc. manufactures steel cylinders and nozzles for two models of fire extinguishers: (1) a home fire extinguisher, and (2) a commercial fire extinguisher. The home model is a high-volume (54,000 units), two-litre cylinder that holds 1 kilogram of multi-purpose dry chemical at 480 PSI. The commercial model is a low-volume (10,200 units), four-litre cylinder that holds five kilograms of multi-purpose dry chemical at 390 PSI. Both products require 1.5 hours of direct labour for completion. Therefore, total annual direct labour hours are 96,300 or [1.5 hrs × (54,000 + 10,200)]. Expected annual manufacturing overhead is $1,502,280. Thus, the predetermined overhead rate is $15.60 ($1,502,280 ÷ 96,300) per direct labour hour. The direct materials cost per unit is $18.50 for the home model and $26.50 for the commercial model. The direct labour cost is $19 per unit for both the home and the commercial models.

Assign overhead using traditional costing and ABC; calculate unit costs; classify activities as value- or non–value-added. (SO 1, 4, 6)

The company's managers identified six activity cost pools and related cost drivers, and accumulated overhead by cost pool as follows.

Activity Cost Pools	Cost Drivers	Estimated Overhead	Expected Use of Cost Drivers	Expected Use of Drivers by Product	
				Home	Commercial
Receiving	Kilograms	$ 70,350	335,000	215,000	120,000
Forming	Machine hours	150,500	35,000	27,000	8,000
Assembling	Number of parts	390,600	217,000	165,000	52,000
Testing	Number of tests	51,000	25,500	15,500	10,000
Painting	Litres	52,580	5,258	3,680	1,578
Packing and shipping	Kilograms	787,250	335,000	215,000	120,000
		$1,502,280			

Instructions

(a) Under traditional product costing, calculate the total unit cost of both products. Prepare a simple schedule that compares the individual costs by product (similar to Illustration 4-4).
(b) Under ABC, prepare a schedule that shows the calculations of the activity-based overhead rates (per cost driver).
(c) Prepare a schedule that assigns each activity's overhead cost pool to each product based on the use of cost drivers. (Include a calculation of the overhead cost per unit, rounding to the nearest cent.)
(d) Calculate the total cost per unit for each product under ABC.
(e) Classify each of the activities as a value-added activity or a non–value-added activity.
(f) Comment on (1) the comparative overhead cost per unit for the two products under ABC, and (2) the comparative total costs per unit under traditional costing and ABC.

Assign overhead costs using traditional costing and ABC; compare results.
(SO 1, 4)

P4–20A Mars Company has four categories of overhead: purchasing and receiving materials; machine operating costs; materials handling; and shipping. The costs expected for these categories for the coming year are as follows:

Purchasing and receiving materials	$200,000
Machine operating costs	450,000
Materials handling	80,000
Shipping	170,000
Total	$900,000

The plant currently applies overhead using machine hours and expected annual capacity. Expected capacity is 150,000 machine hours. Robert, the financial controller, has been asked to submit a bid on job #287, on which he has assembled the following data:

Direct materials per unit	$0.35
Direct labour per unit	$0.85
Applied overhead	$?
Number of units produced	6,000
Number of purchases and receipts	2
Number of machine hours	1,500
Number of material moves	300
Number of kilometres to ship to the customer	2,300

Robert has been told that Arrow Company, a major competitor, is using activity-based costing and will bid on job #287 with a price of $2.95 per unit. Before submitting his bid, Robert wants to assess the effects of this alternative costing approach. He estimates that 850,000 units will be produced next year, 2,500 purchases and receipts will be made, 400,000 moves will be performed plantwide, and the delivery of finished goods will require 300,000 kilometres. The bid price policy is full manufacturing cost plus 25%.

Instructions

(a) Calculate the bid price per unit of job #287 using machine hours to assign overhead.
(b) Using an activity-based approach, determine whether Mars or Arrow will produce the most competitive bid and obtain the contract. Show all your calculations.

(CGA-adapted)

Assign overhead to products using ABC and evaluate decision.
(SO 4)

P4–21A Jacobson Electronics manufactures two large-screen television models: the Royale, which sells for $1,600, and a new model, the Majestic, which sells for $1,300. The production costs per unit under traditional costing for each model in 2005 were as follows:

Traditional Costing	Royale	Majestic
Direct materials	$ 700	$420
Direct labour ($20 per hour)	120	100
Manufacturing overhead ($38 per DLH)	228	190
Total per unit cost	$1,048	$710

In 2005, Jacobson manufactured 25,000 units of the Royale and 10,000 units of the Majestic. The overhead rate of $38 per direct labour hour (DLH) was determined by dividing total expected manufacturing overhead of $7.6 million by the total direct labour hours (200,000) for the two models.

Under traditional costing, the gross profit on the models was as follows: Royale $552 ($1,600 − $1,048), and Majestic $590 ($1,300 − $710). Because of this difference, management is considering phasing out the Royale model and increasing the production of the Majestic model.

Before finalizing its decision, management asks Jacobson's controller to prepare an analysis using activity-based costing (ABC). The controller accumulates the following information about overhead for the year ended December 31, 2005:

Activities	Cost Drivers	Estimated Overhead	Expected Use of Cost Drivers	Activity-Based Overhead Rate
Purchasing	Number of orders	$1,200,000	40,000	$30
Machine setups	Number of setups	900,000	18,000	50
Machining	Machine hours	4,800,000	120,000	40
Quality control	Number of inspections	700,000	28,000	25

The cost drivers used for each product were:

Cost Drivers	Royale	Majestic	Total
Purchase orders	15,000	25,000	40,000
Machine setups	5,000	13,000	18,000
Machine hours	75,000	45,000	120,000
Inspections	9,000	19,000	28,000

Instructions

(a) Assign the total 2005 manufacturing overhead costs to the two products using activity-based costing (ABC).
(b) What were the cost per unit and gross profit of each model using ABC costing?
(c) ▭▭▭▭► Are management's future plans for the two models reasonable? Explain.

P4–22A   Quality Paints Inc. uses a traditional cost accounting system to apply quality-control costs uniformly to all its products at a rate of 25 percent of the direct labour cost. The monthly direct labour cost for the varnish paint line is $100,000. The company is considering activity-based costing to apply quality-control costs. The monthly data have been gathered for the varnish paint line as follows:

Assign overhead costs using traditional costing and ABC; compare results.
(SO 1, 4)

Activity Cost Pools	Cost Drivers	Unit Rates	Use of Drivers for Varnish Paint
Incoming material inspection	Type of material	$ 25.00 per type	20 types
In-process inspection	Number of units	0.30 per unit	25,000 units
Product certification	Per order	150.00 per order	75 orders

Instructions

(a) Calculate the monthly quality-control cost to be assigned to the varnish paint line using a traditional costing system that allocates overhead based on the direct labour cost.
(b) Calculate the monthly quality-control cost to be assigned to the varnish paint line using an activity-based costing system.
(c) Comment on the results.

(CMA Canada-adapted)

P4–23A   Stellar Stairs Co. designs and builds factory-made premium wooden staircases for homes. The manufactured staircase components (spindles, risers, hangers, handrails) permit installations of staircases of varying lengths and widths. All are of white oak. The company's budgeted manufacturing overhead costs for the year 2003 were as follows:

Assign overhead costs using traditional costing and ABC; compare results.
(SO 1, 4, 6)

Overhead Cost Pools	Amount
Purchasing	$ 57,000
Handling materials	82,000
Production (cutting, milling, finishing)	210,000
Setting up machines	85,000
Inspecting	90,000
Inventory control (raw materials and finished goods)	126,000
Utilities	180,000
Total budgeted overhead costs	$830,000

For the last four years, Stellar Stairs Co. has been charging overhead to products on the basis of machine hours. For the year 2006, 100,000 machine hours are budgeted. Heather Fujar, owner-manager of Stellar Stairs Co., recently directed her accountant, Lindsay Baker, to implement the activity-based costing system that she has repeatedly proposed. At Heather Fujar's request, Lindsay and the production foreman identify the following cost drivers and their usage for the previously budgeted overhead cost pools:

Overhead Cost Pools	Activity Cost Drivers	Expected Use of Cost Drivers
Purchasing	Number of orders	600
Handling materials	Number of moves	8,000
Production (cutting, milling, finishing)	Direct labour hours	100,000
Setting up machines	Number of setups	1,250
Inspecting	Number of inspections	6,000
Inventory control (raw materials and finished goods)	Number of components	168,000
Utilities	Square feet occupied	90,000

Jason Dion, sales manager, has received an order for 280 staircases from Community Builders, Inc., a large housing development contractor. At Jason's request, Lindsay prepares cost estimates for producing components for 280 staircases so Jason can submit a contract price per staircase to Community Builders. She accumulates the following data for the production of the staircases:

Direct materials	$103,600
Direct labour	$112,000
Machine hours	14,500
Direct labour hours	5,000
Number of purchase orders	60
Number of material moves	800
Number of machine setups	100
Number of inspections	450
Number of components	16,000
Number of square feet occupied	8,000

Instructions

(a) Calculate the predetermined overhead rate using traditional costing with machine hours as the basis.
(b) What is the manufacturing cost per staircase under traditional costing?
(c) What is the manufacturing cost per staircase under the proposed activity-based costing? (Prepare all of the necessary schedules.)
(d) ✏▷Which of the two costing systems is better to use in pricing decisions? Why?

Assign overhead costs using traditional costing and ABC; compare results.
(SO 1, 4)

P4–24A   Scalar Manufacturing produces automobile parts. The parts are produced in batches in one continuous manufacturing process. The company uses direct labour hours to assign overhead to each part. Shanon, the financial controller, is wondering what the reasons are for the low profits in 2004 and why the gear product line did not attain Scalar's 20% net profit margin target (net profit per unit on sale price). The 2004 net profit per unit has been calculated as follows:

	Brake Disk	Gear
Sales price per unit	$35.00	$43.00
Manufacturing costs per unit:		
Direct materials	10.00	7.50
Direct labour		
(0.1 hour × $12/hour)	1.20	
(0.5 hour × $12/hour)		6.00
Overhead		
(0.1 hour × $50/hour)	5.00	
(0.5 hour × $50/hour)		25.00
Total manufacturing costs per unit	$16.20	$38.50
Net profit per unit	$18.80	$ 4.50
Net profit margin percentage	53.7%	10.5%

Shanon intends to implement activity-based costing at Scalar. Each part requires engineering design activity. Once the design is completed, the equipment can be set up for batch production. Once the batch is completed, a sample is taken and inspected to see if the parts are within the tolerances allowed. The manufacturing process has five activities: engineering, setups, machining, inspection, and processing. Overhead has been assigned to each activity using direct attribution and resource drivers:

Engineering	$ 80,000
Setups	45,000
Machining	130,000
Inspection	63,000
Processing	35,000
Total overhead	$353,000

Activity drivers for each activity have been identified and their practical capacities listed:

Engineering Hours	Number of Setups	Machine Hours	Number of Inspections	Direct Labour Hours
4,000	250	20,000	1,500	7,000

These are the production data in 2004 for brake disks and gears:

	Brake Disk	Gear
Number of units produced	5,000	3,000
Engineering hours per unit	0.05	0.15
Number of setups	25	9
Machine hours per unit	2.5	1
Number of inspections	250	125

Instructions

(a) Using the activity-based approach, calculate the activity rates, the net profit per unit, and the net profit margin percentage for both the brake disk and the gear.
(b) Explain why the new profit margin percentages for the brake disk and the gear are different compared to what they were originally.

(CGA-adapted)

P4–25A Mendocino Corporation produces two grades of wine from grapes that it buys from California growers. It produces and sells roughly 3 million litres per year of a low-cost, high-volume product called CoolDay. It sells 600,000 five-litre jugs of this each year. Mendocino also produces and sells roughly 300,000 litres per year of a low-volume, high-cost product called LiteMist. LiteMist is sold in one-litre bottles. Based on recent data, the CoolDay product has not been as profitable as LiteMist. Management is considering dropping the inexpensive CoolDay line so it can focus more attention on the LiteMist product. The LiteMist product already demands considerably more attention than the CoolDay line.

Tyler Silva, president and founder of Mendocino, is skeptical about this idea. He points out that for many decades the company produced only the CoolDay line, and that it was always quite profitable. It wasn't until the company started producing the more complicated LiteMist wine that the profitability of CoolDay declined. Prior to the introduction of

Assign overhead costs using traditional costing and ABC; compare results. (SO 1, 4)

LiteMist, the company had simple equipment, simple growing and production procedures, and virtually no need for quality control. Because LiteMist is bottled in one-litre bottles, it requires considerably more time and effort both to bottle and to label and box than does CoolDay. The company must bottle and handle five times as many bottles of LiteMist to sell the same quantity as CoolDay. CoolDay requires one month of aging; LiteMist requires one year. CoolDay requires cleaning and inspection of equipment every 10,000 litres; LiteMist requires such maintenance every 600 litres.

Tyler has asked the accounting department to prepare an analysis of the cost per litre using the traditional costing approach and using activity-based costing. The following information was collected:

	CoolDay	LiteMist
Direct materials per litre	$0.40	$1.20
Direct labour cost per litre	$0.25	$0.50
Direct labour hours per litre	0.05	0.09
Total direct labour hours	120,000	25,000

Activity Cost Pools	Cost Drivers	Estimated Overhead	Expected Use of Cost Drivers	Expected Use of Cost Drivers per Product CoolDay	LiteMist
Grape processing	Cart of grapes	$ 145,860	6,600	6,000	600
Aging	Total months	396,000	6,600,000	3,000,000	3,600,000
Bottling and corking	Number of bottles	270,000	900,000	600,000	300,000
Labelling and boxing	Number of bottles	189,000	900,000	600,000	300,000
Maintaining and inspecting equipment	Number of inspections	240,800	800	350	450
		$1,241,660			

Instructions

Answer each of the following questions. (Round all calculations to three decimal places.)

(a) Under traditional product costing using direct labour hours, calculate the total manufacturing cost per litre of both products.

(b) Under ABC, prepare a schedule that shows the calculation of the activity-based overhead rates (per cost driver).

(c) Prepare a schedule that assigns each activity's overhead cost pool to each product, based on the use of cost drivers. Include a calculation of the overhead cost per litre.

(d) Calculate the total manufacturing cost per litre for both products under ABC.

(e) ◁▦▦▦▷ Write a memo to Tyler Silva discussing the implications of your analysis for the company's plans. In this memo, provide a brief description of ABC, as well as an explanation of how the traditional approach can result in distortions.

Assign overhead costs using ABC.
(SO 4, 5)

P4–26A　ProDriver Inc. (PDI) recently started operations to obtain a share of the growing market for golf equipment. PDI manufactures two models of specialty drivers: the Thunderbolt model and the Earthquake model. Two professional engineers and a professional golfer, none of whom had any accounting background, formed the company as a partnership. The business has been very successful, and to cope with the increased level of activity, the partners have hired a CGA as their controller. One of the first improvements that the controller wants to make is to update the costing system by changing from a single overhead application rate using direct labour hours to activity-based costing. The controller has identified the following three activities as cost drivers, along with the related cost pools:

Model	Number of Material Requisitions	Number of Product Inspections	Number of Orders Shipped
Thunderbolt	46	23	167
Earthquake	62	31	129
Costs per pool	$54,000	$8,200	$103,000

Instructions

(a) Using activity-based costing, prepare a schedule that shows the allocation of the costs of each cost pool to each model. Show your calculations.

(b) Identify three conditions which should be present in PDI in order for the implementation of activity-based costing to be successful.

(CGA-adapted)

P4–27A Huang and Lowe is a public accounting firm that offers two primary services: auditing and tax return preparation. A controversy has developed between the partners of the two service lines as to who is contributing the greater amount to the bottom line. The area of disagreement is the assignment of overhead. The tax partners want overhead assigned on the basis of 40% of direct labour dollars, while the audit partners want to implement activity-based costing. The partners agree to use next year's budgeted data for purposes of analysis and comparison. The following overhead data are collected to develop the comparison:

Assign overhead costs to services using traditional costing and ABC; calculate overhead rates and unit cost; compare results. (SO 1, 4, 6, 8)

Activity Cost Pools	Cost Drivers	Estimated Overhead	Expected Use of Cost Drivers	Expected Use of Cost Drivers per Service	
				Audit	Tax
Employee training	Direct labour dollars	$216,000	$1,800,000	$1,000,000	$800,000
Typing and secretarial	Number of reports/forms	76,200	2,500	600	1,900
Calculating	Number of minutes	204,000	60,000	25,000	35,000
Facility rental	Number of employees	142,500	40	22	18
Travel	Per expense reports	127,000	Direct	86,000	41,000
		$765,700			

Instructions

(a) Using traditional product costing, as proposed by the tax partners, calculate the total overhead cost assigned to both services (audit and tax) of Huang and Lowe.

(b) 1. Using activity-based costing, prepare a schedule that shows the calculations of the activity-based overhead rates (per cost driver).

    2. Prepare a schedule that assigns each activity's overhead cost pool to each service based on the use of the cost drivers.

(c) Classify each of the activities as a value-added activity or a non–value-added activity.

(d) Comment on the comparative overhead cost for the two services under both traditional costing and ABC.

Problems: Set B

P4–28B Allen Inc. is a manufacturer of quality shoes. The company has always used a plantwide allocation rate for allocating manufacturing overhead to its products. The plant manager believes it is time to change to a better method of cost allocation. The accounting department has established the following relationships between production activities and manufacturing overhead costs:

Assign overhead costs using traditional costing and ABC; compare results. (SO 1, 4)

Activities	Cost Drivers	Allocation Rate
Material handling	Number of parts	$8 per part
Assembly	Labour hours	$80 per hour
Inspection	Time spent by item at inspection station	$12 per minute

The previous plantwide allocation rate method was based on direct manufacturing labour hours, and if that method is used, the allocation rate is $800 per labour hour.

Instructions

(a) Assume that a batch of 1,000 pairs of shoes requires 4,000 parts, 40 direct manufacturing labour hours, and 60 minutes of inspection time. What are the indirect manufacturing costs per pair of shoes to produce a batch of 1,000 pairs of shoes, assuming the previous plantwide allocation rate method is used?

(b) What are the indirect manufacturing costs per pair of shoes to produce a batch of 1,000 pairs of shoes, assuming the activity-based method of allocation is used?

(c) Comment on the results.

(CMA Canada-adapted)

Assign overhead using traditional costing and ABC; calculate unit costs; classify activities as value- or non–value-added.
(SO 1, 4, 6)

P4–29B   Waves Galore, Inc. manufactures hair curlers and blow-dryers. The hand-held hair curler is Waves Galore's high-volume product (80,000 units annually). It is a "large-barrel," 20-watt, triple-heat appliance designed to appeal to the teenage market segment with its glow-in-the-dark handle. The hand-held blow-dryer is Waves Galore's lower-volume product (40,000 units annually). It is a three-speed, 2,000-watt appliance with a "cool setting" and a removable filter. It also is designed for the teen market.

Both products require one hour of direct labour for completion. Therefore, total annual direct labour hours are 120,000 (80,000 + 40,000). Expected annual manufacturing overhead is $438,000. Thus, the predetermined overhead rate is $3.65 per direct labour hour. The direct materials cost per unit is $5.25 for the hair curler and $9.75 for the blow-dryer. The direct labour cost is $8.00 per unit for both the hair curler and the blow-dryer.

Waves Galore purchases most of the parts from suppliers and assembles the finished product at its plant. It recently adopted activity-based costing, which after this year end will totally replace its traditional direct labour–based cost accounting system. Waves Galore has identified six activity cost pools and related cost drivers and has gathered the following information:

Activity Cost Pools	Cost Drivers	Estimated Overhead	Expected Use of Cost Drivers	Expected Use of Cost Drivers per Product Curlers	Expected Use of Cost Drivers per Product Dryers
Purchasing	Orders	$ 57,500	500	170	330
Receiving	Kilograms	42,000	140,000	58,000	82,000
Assembling	Parts	166,000	830,000	415,000	415,000
Testing	Tests	52,000	130,000	82,000	48,000
Finishing	Units	60,000	120,000	80,000	40,000
Packing and shipping	Cartons	60,500	12,100	8,040	4,060
		$438,000			

Instructions

(a) Under traditional product costing, calculate the total unit cost of both products. Prepare a simple comparative schedule of the individual costs for each product (similar to Illustration 4-4).

(b) Under ABC, prepare a schedule that shows the calculations of the activity-based overhead rates (per cost driver).

(c) Prepare a schedule that assigns each activity's overhead cost pool to each product based on the use of cost drivers. (Include a calculation of the overhead cost per unit, rounding to the nearest cent.)

(d) Calculate the total cost per unit for each product under ABC.

(e) Classify each of the activities as a value-added activity or a non–value-added activity.

(f) Comment on (1) the comparative overhead cost per unit for the two products under ABC, and (2) the comparative total costs per unit under traditional costing and ABC.

Assign overhead costs using traditional costing and ABC; compare results.
(SO 1, 4)

P4–30B   Kiddy Company manufactures bicycles. It recently received a request to manufacture 10 units of a mountain bike at a price lower than it normally accepts. Bruce, the sales manager, indicated that if the order were accepted at that price, the company could expect additional orders from the same client. Bruce believes that if Kiddy could offer this price in the market generally, sales of this bike would increase by 30%. Melany, president of Kiddy, is skeptical about accepting the order. The company has a policy of not accepting any order that does not provide a markup of 20% on full manufacturing costs. The price offered is $575 per bike.

The controller, Sanjay, has recently researched the possibility of using activity-based multiple overhead rates instead of the single rate currently in use. He has promised more accurate product costing, and Melany is curious about how this approach would affect product costing and pricing of the mountain bike.

The plantwide overhead rate is based on an expected volume of 15,000 direct labour hours and the following budgeted overhead:

Machine operating costs	$ 75,000
Rework labour	45,000
Inspection	25,000
Scrap costs	35,000
General factory overhead	120,000
Total	$300,000

Expected activities for selected cost drivers for 2005:

Machine hours	25,000
Units reworked	600
Inspection hours	500
Units scrapped	140
Direct labour hours	12,000

Estimated data for the production of one mountain bike:

Direct materials	$160
Direct labour (7.5 hours/unit)	$180
Number of machine hours	6
Number of units reworked	0.25
Number of inspection hours	0.10
Number of units scrapped	0.05

Instructions

(a) Using the single-rate method to assign overhead on a plantwide basis, determine whether or not Kiddy should accept the order for the 10 mountain bikes. Explain your decision.

(b) Using activity-based costing to assign overhead, determine whether or not Kiddy should accept the order for the 10 mountain bikes. Explain your decision.

(CGA-adapted)

P4–31B Tough Thermos, Inc. manufactures two plastic thermos containers at its plastic moulding facility. Its large container, called the Ice House, has a volume of 20 litres, side carrying handles, a snap-down lid, and a side drain and plug. Its smaller container, called the Cool Chest, has a volume of eight litres, an over-the-top carrying handle which is part of a tilting lid, and a removable shelf. Both containers and their parts are made entirely of hard-moulded plastic. The Ice House sells for $35 and the Cool Chest sells for $24. The production costs calculated per unit under traditional costing for each model in 2005 were as follows:

Assign overhead to products using ABC and evaluate decision.
(SO 4)

Traditional Costing	Ice House	Cool Chest
Direct materials	$ 9.50	$ 6.00
Direct labour ($10 per hour)	8.00	5.00
Manufacturing overhead ($17.08 per DLH)	13.66	8.54
Total per unit cost	$31.16	$19.54

In 2005, Tough Thermos manufactured 50,000 units of the Ice House and 20,000 units of the Cool Chest. The overhead rate of $17.08 per direct labour hour was determined by dividing total expected manufacturing overhead of $854,000 by the total direct labour hours (50,000) for the two models.

Under traditional costing, the gross profit on the two containers was as follows: Ice House $3.84 ($35 − $31.16), and Cool Chest $4.46 ($24 − $19.54). The gross margin rates on cost were 12% for the Ice House ($3.84 ÷ $31.16), and 23% for the Cool Chest ($4.46 ÷ $19.54).

Because Tough Thermos can earn a gross margin rate on the Cool Chest that is nearly twice as great as that earned on the Ice House, and with less investment in inventory and labour costs, its management is urging its sales staff to put its efforts into selling the Cool Chest over the Ice House.

Before finalizing its decision, management asks the controller, Sven Meza, to prepare a product costing analysis using activity-based costing (ABC). Meza accumulates the following information about overhead for the year ended December 31, 2005:

Activities	Cost Drivers	Estimated Overhead	Total Expected Cost Drivers	Activity-Based Overhead Rate
Purchasing	Number of orders	$179,000	4,475	$40 per order
Machine setups	Number of setups	195,000	780	$250 per setup
Extruding	Machine hours	320,000	80,000	$4 per machine hour
Quality control	Tests and inspections	160,000	8,000	$20 per test

The cost drivers used for each product were:

Cost Drivers	Ice House	Cool Chest	Total
Purchase orders	2,500	1,975	4,475
Machine setups	480	300	780
Machine hours	60,000	20,000	80,000
Tests and inspections	5,000	3,000	8,000

Instructions

(a) Assign the total 2005 manufacturing overhead costs to the two products using activity-based costing (ABC).

(b) What was the cost per unit and gross profit of each model using ABC costing?

(c) ▭▭▭▶ Are management's future plans for the two models reasonable?

P4–32B   Kitchen Kabinets Company designs and builds upscale kitchen cabinets for luxury homes. Many of the kitchen cabinet and counter arrangements are custom-made, but occasionally the company does mass production on order. Its budgeted manufacturing overhead costs for the year 2006 are as follows:

Assign overhead costs using traditional costing and ABC; compare results.
(SO 1, 4)

Overhead Cost Pools	Amount
Purchasing	$ 114,400
Handling materials	164,320
Production (cutting, milling, finishing)	500,000
Setting up machines	174,480
Inspecting	184,800
Inventory control (raw materials and finished goods)	252,000
Utilities	360,000
Total budget overhead costs	$1,750,000

For the last three years, Kitchen Kabinets Company has been charging overhead to products on the basis of machine hours. For the year 2006, 100,000 machine hours are budgeted.

Ben Chen, the owner-manager, recently directed his accountant, John Kandy, to implement the activity-based costing system he has repeatedly proposed. At Ben's request, John and the production foreman identify the following cost drivers and their usage for the previously budgeted overhead cost pools:

Overhead Cost Pools	Activity Cost Drivers	Total Drivers
Purchasing	Number of orders	650
Handling materials	Numbers of moves	8,000
Production (cutting, milling, finishing)	Direct labour hours	100,000
Setting up machines	Number of setups	1,200
Inspecting	Number of inspections	6,000
Inventory control (raw materials and finished goods)	Number of components	36,000
Utilities	Square feet occupied	90,000

Sara Sosa, sales manager, has received an order for 50 kitchen cabinet arrangements from Bitty Builders, a housing development contractor. At Sara's request, John prepares cost estimates for producing components for 50 cabinet arrangements so Sara can submit a contract price per kitchen arrangement to Bitty Builders. He accumulates the following data for the production of 50 kitchen cabinet arrangements:

Direct materials	$180,000
Direct labour	$200,000
Machine hours	15,000
Direct labour hours	12,000
Number of purchase orders	50
Number of material moves	800
Number of machine setups	100
Number of inspections	450
Number of components (cabinets and accessories)	3,000
Number of square feet occupied	8,000

Instructions

(a) Calculate the predetermined overhead rate using traditional costing with machine hours as the basis. (Round to the nearest cent.)

(b) What is the manufacturing cost per complete kitchen arrangement under traditional costing?

(c) What is the manufacturing cost per kitchen arrangement under the proposed activity-based costing? (Prepare all of the necessary schedules.)

(d) ⬛▭▭▭▷ Which of the two costing systems is better to use in pricing decisions? Why?

P4–33B GoGo Ltd. manufactures three models of children's swing sets: Standard, Deluxe, and Super. The Standard set is made of steel, the Deluxe set is made of aluminum, and the Super set is made of a titanium-aluminum alloy. Because of the different materials used, production requirements differ significantly across models in terms of machine types and time requirements. However, once the parts are produced, assembly time per set for the three models is similar. For this reason, GoGo has adopted the practice of allocating overhead costs on the basis of machine hours. Last year, the company produced 5,000 Standard sets, 500 Deluxe sets, and 2,000 Super sets. The company had the following revenues and expenses for the year:

Assign overhead costs using traditional costing and ABC; compare results.
(SO 1, 4)

GOGO LTD.
Income Statement
Year Ended December 31, 2005

	Standard	Deluxe	Super	Total
Sales	$475,000	$380,000	$560,000	$1,415,000
Direct costs:				
Direct materials	200,000	150,000	240,000	590,000
Direct labour	54,000	14,400	24,000	92,400
Variable overhead costs:				
Machine setups	?	?	?	26,000
Order processing	?	?	?	64,000
Warehouse	?	?	?	93,000
Shipping	?	?	?	36,000
Contribution margin	?	?	?	513,600
Fixed overhead costs:				
Plant administration				88,000
Other				182,000
Gross profit				$243,600

The chief financial officer of GoGo has hired a consultant to recommend cost allocation bases. The consultant has recommended the following:

Activities	Cost Drivers	Activity Level Standard	Deluxe	Super	Total
Machine setups	No. of production runs	22	11	17	50
Sales order processing	No. of sales orders received	300	200	300	800
Warehouse costs	No. of units held in inventory	200	100	100	400
Shipping	No. of units shipped	5,000	500	2,000	7,500

The consultant found no basis for allocating the plant administration and other fixed overhead costs, and recommended that they not be applied to products.

Instructions

(a) Complete the income statement using the bases recommended by the consultant. Do not allocate any fixed overhead costs.
(b) Explain how activity-based costing might result in better decisions by GoGo's management.

(CGA-adapted)

Assign overhead costs using traditional costing and ABC; compare results.
(SO 1, 4)

P4–34B   Vino Verite Corporation produces two grades of wine from grapes that it buys from California growers. It produces and sells, in four-litre jugs, roughly 3.2 million litres per year of a low-cost, high-volume product called StarDew. It also produces and sells roughly 800,000 litres per year of a low-volume, high-cost product called VineRose. VineRose is sold in one-litre bottles; thus 800,000 litres results in 800,000 bottles. Based on recent data, the StarDew product has not been as profitable as VineRose. Management is considering dropping the inexpensive StarDew so it can focus more attention on the VineRose line. VineRose already demands considerably more attention than StarDew.

Jorge Rojo, president and founder of Vino Verite, is skeptical about this idea. He points out that for many decades the company produced only the StarDew line, and that it was always quite profitable. It wasn't until the company started producing the more complicated VineRose wine that the profitability of StarDew declined. Prior to the introduction of VineRose the company had simple equipment, simple production procedures, and virtually no need for quality control. Because VineRose is bottled in 1-litre bottles it requires considerably more time and effort, both to bottle and to label and box, than does StarDew. (There are four litres in a jug; thus the company must bottle and handle four bottles of VineRose to sell the same amount of wine as StarDew.) StarDew requires one month of aging; VineRose requires one year. StarDew requires cleaning and inspection of equipment every 20,000 litres; VineRose requires such maintenance every 500 litres.

Jorge has asked the accounting department to prepare an analysis of the cost per litre using the traditional costing approach and using activity-based costing. The following information was collected:

	StarDew	VineRose
Direct materials per litre	$1.10	$2.40
Direct labour cost per litre	$0.50	$1.00
Direct labour hours per litre	0.075	0.15
Total direct labour hours	60,000	30,000

Activity Cost Pools	Cost Drivers	Estimated Overhead	Expected Use of Cost Drivers	Expected Use of Cost Drivers per Product StarDew	Expected Use of Cost Drivers per Product VineRose
Grape processing	Cart of grapes	$ 180,000	10,000	8,000	2,000
Aging	Total months	416,000	10,400,000	800,000	9,600,000
Bottling and corking	Number of bottles	360,000	1,600,000	800,000	800,000
Labelling and boxing	Number of bottles	240,000	1,600,000	800,000	800,000
Maintaining and inspecting equipment	Number of inspections	280,000	560	160	400
		$1,476,000			

Instructions

Answer each of the following questions. (Round all calculations to three decimal places.)

(a) Under traditional product costing using direct labour hours, calculate the total manufacturing cost per litre for each product.
(b) Under ABC, prepare a schedule that shows the calculation of the activity-based overhead rates (per cost driver).
(c) Prepare a schedule that assigns each activity's overhead cost pool to each product, based on the use of cost drivers. Include a calculation of the overhead cost per unit.
(d) Calculate the total manufacturing cost per litre for each product under ABC.
(e) ◁▭▭▷ Write a memo to Jorge Rojo discussing the implications of your analysis for the company's plans. In this memo, provide a brief description of ABC, as well as an explanation of how the traditional approach can result in distortions.

P4–35B Farm and Home Veterinary Clinic is a small-town partnership that offers two primary services: farm animal services and pet care services. Providing veterinary care to farm animals requires travel to the farm animal (house calls), while veterinary care to pets generally requires that the pet be brought into the clinic. As part of an investigation to determine the contribution that each of these two types of services makes to overall profit, one partner argues for allocating overhead using activity-based costing while the other partner argues for a more simple overhead cost allocation on the basis of direct labour hours. The partners agree to use next year's budgeted data, as prepared by their public accountant, for analysis and comparison purposes. The following overhead data are collected to develop the comparison:

Assign overhead costs to services using traditional costing and ABC; calculate overhead rates and unit costs; compare results. (SO 1, 4, 6, 8)

Activity Cost Pools	Cost Drivers	Estimated Overhead	Total Expected Cost Drivers	Expected Use of Drivers by Service	
				Farm Animals	Pets
Drug treatment	Treatments	$ 64,000	4,000	1,700	2,300
Surgery	Operations	70,000	800	200	600
Travel	Kilometres	28,000	28,000	26,000	2,000
Consultation	Appointments/Calls	33,000	3,000	600	2,400
Accounting/office	Direct labour hours	30,000	5,000	2,000	3,000
Boarding and grooming	100% pets	40,000			
		$265,000			

Instructions

(a) Using traditional product costing, as proposed by one partner, calculate the total overhead cost assigned to both services of Farm and Home Veterinary Clinic.

(b) 1. Using activity-based costing, prepare a schedule that shows the calculations of the activity-based overhead rates (per cost driver).
   2. Prepare a schedule assigning each activity's overhead cost pool to each service based on the use of the cost drivers.

(c) Classify each of the activities as a value-added activity or a non–value-added activity.

(d) ◖▭▭▭▭▷ Comment on the comparative overhead cost for the two services under both traditional costing and ABC.

Cases

C4–36 For the past five years, Collins Ltd. has been running a consulting practice in which it provides two major services: general management consulting and executive training seminars. The CFO is not quite sure that he is charging accurate fees for the different services he provides. He has recently read an article about activity-based costing that convinced him he could use ABC to improve the accuracy of his costing. He has gathered the following selected information concerning the consulting practice during the previous year:

Overhead Activities	Cost Pools	Activities	Cost Drivers
Planning and review	$ 300,000	60,000 hours	Billable hours
Research	48,000	200 journals	Journals purchased
General administration	600,000	300 clients	Number of clients
Building and equipment	84,000	1,200 square metres	Square metres
Clerical	85,000	17 professionals	Professional staff
	$1,117,000		

In addition, the CFO gathered the following statistics for each of the two types of services provided to clients during the year:

	Management Consulting	Executive Training
Direct labour costs	$900,000	$450,000
Billable hours	45,000	15,000
Research—journals purchased	140	60
Number of clients	120	180
Square metres	800	400
Professional staff	10	7

Instructions

(a) In the past, the CFO took the total overhead costs and divided them by the total billable hours to determine an average rate. To this amount he would then add the direct labour costs per hour and double this total amount to establish his average hourly charge-out rate. What was the CFO's average hourly charge-out rate using this method?

(b) Using ABC, what would the CFO's charge-out rate be? Note that he will continue to add the overhead to the direct labour costs per hour on a service basis and then double this amount to set an average hourly charge-out rate.

(c) Identify and discuss three ways in which ABC leads to more accurate product costs.

(d) Identify and discuss two limitations of ABC.

(e) After reviewing the ABC methodology described in part (b), identify one significant flaw in how the overhead costs will be allocated by the CFO in the ABC system. Discuss how this flaw would affect the average hourly charge-out rates (i.e., increase or decrease the rates) for management consulting and executive training. You do not have to calculate the new rates to answer this part of the question.

(CGA-adapted)

C4–37   R & R Inc. of Montreal, Quebec, has supported a research and development (R&D) department that has for many years been the sole contributor to the company's new products. The R&D activity is an overhead cost centre that provides services only to in-house manufacturing departments (four different product lines), all of which produce aerospace-related products.

The department has never sold its services outside, but because of its long history of success, larger manufacturers of aerospace products have approached R & R to hire its R&D department for special projects. Because the costs of operating the R&D department have been spiralling uncontrollably, R & R's management is considering taking on these outside contracts to absorb the increasing costs. However, management doesn't have any cost basis for charging R&D services to outsiders, and it needs to gain control of its R&D costs. Management decides to implement an activity-based costing system in order to determine the charges for both outsiders and the in-house users of the department's services.

R&D activities fall into four pools with the following annual costs:

Market analysis	$1,050,000
Product design	2,280,000
Product development	3,600,000
Prototype testing	1,400,000

Analysis determines that the appropriate cost drivers and their usage for the four activities are as follows:

Activities	Cost Drivers	Total Estimated Drivers
Market analysis	Hours of analysis	15,000 hours
Product design	Number of designs	2,500 designs
Product development	Number of products	90 products
Prototype testing	Number of tests	700 tests

Instructions

(a) Calculate the activity-based overhead rate for each activity cost pool.

(b) How much cost would be charged to an in-house manufacturing department that consumed 1,800 hours of market analysis time, was provided with 280 designs relating to 10 products, and requested 92 engineering tests?

(c) How much cost would serve as the basis for pricing an R&D bid with an outside company on a contract that would consume 800 hours of analysis time, require 178 designs relating to three products, and result in 70 engineering tests?

(d) What is the benefit to R & R Inc. of applying activity-based costing to its R&D activity for both in-house and outside charging purposes?

C4–38   B & B Electronics Company manufactures two large-screen television models, the Deluxe, which has been produced for many years and sells for $900, and the Flat, a new model introduced in early 2004, which sells for $1,260. Based on the following income statement for 2005, the CFO at B & B has made a decision to concentrate the marketing resources on the Flat model and to begin to phase out the Deluxe model:

B & B ELECTRONICS COMPANY
Income Statement
Year Ended December 31, 2005

	Flat	Deluxe	Total
Sales	$5,040,000	$19,800,000	$24,840,000
Cost of goods sold	3,760,000	15,840,000	19,600,000
Gross margin	1,280,000	3,960,000	5,240,000
Selling and administrative expenses	780,000	2,640,000	3,420,000
Net profit	$ 500,000	$ 1,320,000	$ 1,820,000
Units produced and sold	4,000	22,000	
Net profit per unit sold	$125.00	$60.00	

The standard unit costs for the Flat and Deluxe models are as follows:

	Flat	Deluxe
Direct materials	$650	$250
Direct labour:		
Flat (3.5 hrs × $20/hr)	70	
Deluxe (1.5 hrs × $20/hr)		30
Machine usage:		
Flat (4 hrs × $25/hr)	100	
Deluxe (8 hrs × $25/hr)		200
Manufacturing overhead	120	240
Standard cost	$940	$720

Manufacturing overhead was applied on the basis of machine hours at a predetermined rate of $30 per hour. B & B Electronics Company's CFO is in favour of the use of an activity-based costing system and has gathered the following information about the company's manufacturing overhead costs for 2005:

		Units of the Cost Driver		
Activity Centres and Cost Drivers	Activity Costs	Flat	Deluxe	Total
Soldering (number of solder joints)	$ 900,000	300,000	1,200,000	1,500,000
Shipments (number of shipments)	800,000	4,800	15,200	20,000
Quality control (number of inspections)	1,200,000	21,000	59,000	80,000
Purchase orders (number of orders)	800,000	110,000	50,000	160,000
Machine power (machine hours)	37,500	15,000	135,000	150,000
Machine setups (number of setups)	1,000,000	4,000	6,000	10,000
Total traceable costs	$4,737,500			

Instructions

Using activity-based costing, determine whether B & B Electronics should continue to emphasize the Flat model and phase out the Deluxe model.

(CMA Canada-adapted)

C4–39 Wet Ride Inc. manufactures and distributes three types of water skis: beginner, intermediate, and advanced. Production is highly automated for the beginner model, whereas the intermediate and advanced models require increasing degrees of labour, depending on the shaping and finishing processes. Wet Ride applies all indirect costs to production using a single predetermined overhead (OH) rate based on direct labour hours (DLH). A consultant recently suggested that Wet Ride switch to an activity-based costing system, and assembled the following information:

Activities	Recommended Cost Drivers	Estimated OH Cost	Cost Drivers
Order processing	Number of orders	$ 52,500	100 orders
Materials handling	Kilograms of materials used	585,000	122,385 kilograms
Machine amortization and maintenance	Machine hours	322,000	16,000 hours
Quality control	Number of inspections	94,000	40 inspections
		$1,053,500	

In addition, management estimates that 30,000 direct labour hours will be used in the up-coming year, at a rate of $14 per hour.

Assume that the following activity took place in the first month of the new year:

	Beginner	Intermediate	Advanced
Number of units produced	20,000	8,000	3,000
Direct material costs	$20,800	$13,000	$8,000
Direct labour hours	500	1,000	2,000
Number of orders	6	4	3
Number of production runs	2	2	3
Kilograms of material used	8,000	3,200	1,500
Machine hours	1,200	300	200
Number of inspections	3	3	3
Number of units shipped	18,000	7,500	2,500

Instructions

(a) Calculate the production costs for each product in the first month of the upcoming year, using direct labour hours as the allocation base. (Round calculations to the nearest cent.)

(b) Calculate the production costs for each product in the first month of the upcoming year, using activity-based costing. (Round calculations to the nearest cent.)

(c) Compare your answers in parts (a) and (b). Is the overhead charged to each product the same under each method? Explain.

(CGA-adapted)

C4–40   The CEO of Walker Ltd. is currently investigating ways to modernize the company's manufacturing process. At the first staff meeting, the chief engineer presented a proposal for automating the assembly department. He recommended that the company purchase two robots that would have the capability of replacing the eight direct labour employees in the department. The cost savings outlined in the chief engineer's proposal include the elimination of the direct labour cost in the assembly department and a reduction of the manufacturing overhead cost in the department to zero, because the company charges manufacturing overhead on the basis of direct labour dollars using a plantwide rate. The CEO of Walker Ltd. is puzzled by the chief engineer's explanation: "This just doesn't make any sense. How can a department's overhead rate drop to zero by adding expensive, high-tech manufacturing equipment? If anything, it seems like the rate ought to go up."

The chief engineer responds by saying, "I'm an engineer, not an accountant. But if we're charging overhead on the basis of direct labour, and we eliminate the labour, then we elimi-nate the overhead."

The CFO explains that as firms become more automated, they should rethink their prod-uct-costing systems. The CEO asks the CFO to look into the matter and prepare a report for the next staff meeting. The CFO gathers the following data on the manufacturing overhead rates experienced by Walker Ltd. over the last five years. The CFO also estimates the following annual averages for each manufacturing department over the past several years:

		Historical Plantwide Data	
Year	Average Annual Direct Labour Cost	Average Annual Manufacturing Overhead Cost	Average Manufacturing Overhead Application Rate
2000	$ 500,000	$ 1,000,000	200%
2001	600,000	3,000,000	500%
2002	1,000,000	7,000,000	750%
2003	1,500,000	12,000,000	800%
2004	2,000,000	20,000,000	1,000%

	Annual Averages during a Recent Year		
	Moulding Department	Component Department	Assembly Department
Direct labour costs	$ 1,000,000	$ 875,000	$ 125,000
Manufacturing overhead costs	11,000,000	7,000,000	2,000,000

Instructions

(a) Evaluate Walker Ltd.'s current product-costing system of charging manufacturing overhead on the basis of direct labour dollars using a plantwide rate.

(b) Comment on the chief engineer's statement that the manufacturing overhead cost in the assembly department would be reduced to zero if the automation proposal was implemented.

(c) How might Walker Ltd. find the ABC information useful in applying manufacturing overhead and revising its product-costing system to accommodate automation in the assembly department?

(CMA Canada-adapted)

C4–41 The Canadian Motorcycle Company (CMC) produces two models of motorcycles: Faster and Slower. The company has five categories of overhead costs: purchasing, receiving, machine operating costs, handling, and shipping. Each category represents the following percentages of total overhead costs, which amount to $4.2 million:

Purchasing	25.0%
Receiving	12.5%
Machine operating	37.5%
Handling	10.0%
Shipping	15.0%

Current capacity is 200,000 machine hours, and the current production uses 100% of the available hours. The sales mix is 45% Faster and 55% Slower. The overhead costs are applied to each model based on machine hours.

The production costs for each model of motorcycle and other relevant information are as follows:

	Faster	Slower
Directs materials per unit	$8,000	$6,500
Direct labour per unit	$1,750	$1,850
Applied overhead	?	?
Number of units produced	450	550
Number of purchases	5	4
Number of shipments received	3	3
Percentage of machine hours consumed by each product	50%	50%
Number of moves in handling	75	100
Number of kilometres to ship to customers	4,000	4,250

Instructions

(a) CMC determines its prices by adding 40% to the cost of direct materials and direct labour. Is this pricing policy appropriate? Show all calculations to support your answer.

(b) Use an activity-based approach to determine whether CMC can make a profit if it sells the Faster model for $15,000. Show all supporting calculations. (Round all answers to the nearest dollar.)

(CGA-adapted)

C4–42 Java Inc. is a distributor and processor of a variety of different blends of coffee. The company buys coffee beans from around the world and roasts, blends, and packages them for resale. Java Inc. currently offers 10 different coffees to gourmet shops in 500-gram bags. The major cost is raw materials; however, there is a substantial amount of manufacturing overhead in the mostly automated roasting and packing process. The company uses relatively little direct labour.

Some of the coffees are very popular and sell in large volumes, while a few of the newer blends have very low volumes. Java Inc. prices its coffee at total product costs, including allocated overhead, plus a markup of 25%. If prices for certain coffees are significantly higher than market, the prices are adjusted lower.

Data for the 2005 budget include manufacturing overhead of $3.5 million, which has been allocated in the existing costing system based on each product's budgeted direct labour cost. The budgeted direct labour cost for 2005 totals $700,000. Purchases and use of materials (mostly coffee beans) are budgeted to total $6 million.

The budgeted prime costs for 500-gram bags of two of the company's products are as follows:

	Mocha	Vanilla
Direct Materials	$3.20	$2.80
Direct Labour	$0.25	$0.25

Java's controller believes the traditional costing system may be providing misleading cost information. He has developed an activity-based analysis of the 2005 budgeted manufacturing overhead costs shown in the following table:

Activity Pools	Cost Drivers	Budgeted Units	Budgeted Cost
Purchasing	Purchase orders	1,150	$ 575,000
Materials handling	Setups	1,750	612,500
Quality control	Batches	500	150,000
Roasting	Roasting hours	100,000	950,000
Blending	Blending hours	23,125	462,500
Packaging	Packaging hours	30,000	750,000
Total manufacturing overhead cost			$3,500,000

Data for the 2005 production of Mocha and Vanilla coffee are as follows. There will be no beginning or ending materials inventory for either of these coffees.

	Mocha	Vanilla
Expected sales	50,000 kilograms	1,000 kilograms
Batch size	55,000 kilograms	250 kilograms
Setups	3 per batch	3 per batch
Purchase order size	12,500 kilograms	250 kilograms
Roasting time	1 hour/50 kg	1 hour/50 kg
Blending time	0.5 hour/50 kg	0.5 hour/50 kg
Packaging time	0.1 hour/50 kg	0.1 hour/50 kg

Instructions

(a) Calculate the company's 2005 budgeted manufacturing overhead rate using direct labour cost as the single rate and the 2005 budgeted costs and selling prices of 500 gram of Mocha coffee and 500 gram of Vanilla coffee.

(b) Use the controller's activity-based approach to estimate the 2005 budgeted cost for one kilogram of Mocha coffee and one kilogram of Vanilla coffee.

(c) Comment on the results.

(CMA Canada-adapted)

C4–43   Marcus Lim, the cost accountant for Hi-Power Mower Company, recently installed activity-based costing at its western lawn tractor (riding mower) plant where three models are manufactured: the 8-horsepower Bladerunner, the 12-horsepower Quickcut, and the 18-horsepower Supercut. Marcus's new product costs for these three models show that the company's traditional costing system had been significantly undercosting the 18-horsepower Supercut. This was due primarily to the lower sales volume of the Supercut compared to the Bladerunner and the Quickcut.

Before completing his analysis and reporting these results to management, Marcus is approached by his friend Ray Pon, who is the production manager for the 18-horsepower Supercut model. Ray has heard from one of Marcus's staff about the new product costs and is upset and worried for his job because the new costs show the Supercut to be losing, rather than making, money.

At first Ray condemns the new cost system, so Marcus explains the practice of activity-based costing and why it is more accurate than the company's present system. Even more worried now, Ray begs Marcus, "Massage the figures just enough to save the line from being discontinued. You don't want me to lose my job, do you? Anyway, nobody will know." Marcus holds firm but agrees to recalculate all his calculations for accuracy before submitting his costs to management.

Instructions

(a) Who are the stakeholders in this situation?
(b) What, if any, are the ethical considerations in this situation?
(c) What are Marcus's ethical obligations to the company? To his friend?

Answers to Self-Study Questions

1. c   2. c   3. c   4. b   5. d   6. d   7. c   8. c

 Remember to go back to the Navigator Box at the beginning of the chapter to check off your completed work.

CHAPTER 5

Decision-Making: Cost-Volume-Profit

Balancing Profits and Losses

The Delta Chelsea in downtown Toronto is Canada's largest hotel, with 1,590 guestrooms and six restaurants and lounges. To operate a hotel of this size, the management team must deal with a variety of both fixed costs and those that are variable, that is, costs that vary according to the number of guests staying at the hotel at any given time.

The hotel's labour costs have both a fixed and a variable nature, explains Joe Pisani, Delta Chelsea's regional controller. Fixed labour costs include salaries for management and full-time staff. The number of part-time housekeeping or food and beverage staff scheduled, and therefore paid, depends on how many rooms are occupied or how busy the restaurants are. For example, the hotel schedules room attendants based on the number of rooms rented at a standard ratio of one attendant for 16 rooms.

While labour costs can increase or decrease depending on how many people are in the hotel, expenses like property taxes or the cable bill are fixed. "We pay X number of dollars per room regardless of whether the rooms are occupied or empty," Mr. Pisani says. "When the hotel is at full occupancy, these fixed costs, when considered as a percentage of total revenue, actually decrease while the hotel's profit increases."

Unexpected reductions in the volume of guests or customers could have a negative effect on profits; however, the hotel takes steps to minimize this. During the Severe Acute Respiratory Syndrome (SARS) crisis in 2003, travellers avoided Toronto, leaving hotels virtually empty during the height of the summer season. To offset revenue reductions, the Delta Chelsea avoided scheduling part-time staff and encouraged salaried staff to take vacations, Mr. Pisani explains. "When an employee takes vacation, they are paid from the vacation accrual account, so this impacts the cash on hand, but it does not actually impact your profit and loss statement." In addition, some employees received employment benefits through the federal Workshare Program while working reduced hours. By minimizing its variable costs, the Delta Chelsea came close to breaking even despite the unexpected loss in revenue during the SARS crisis.

the navigator

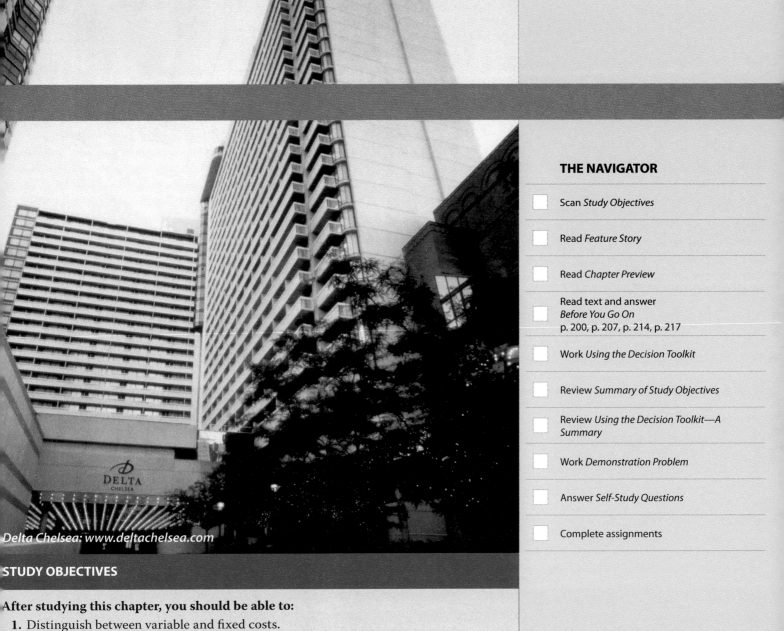

Delta Chelsea: www.deltachelsea.com

THE NAVIGATOR

	Scan *Study Objectives*
	Read *Feature Story*
	Read *Chapter Preview*
	Read text and answer *Before You Go On* p. 200, p. 207, p. 214, p. 217
	Work *Using the Decision Toolkit*
	Review *Summary of Study Objectives*
	Review *Using the Decision Toolkit—A Summary*
	Work *Demonstration Problem*
	Answer *Self-Study Questions*
	Complete assignments

STUDY OBJECTIVES

After studying this chapter, you should be able to:

1. Distinguish between variable and fixed costs.
2. Explain the significance of the relevant range.
3. Explain the concept of mixed costs.
4. List the five components of cost-volume-profit analysis.
5. Explain what the contribution margin is and how it can be expressed.
6. Identify the three ways to determine the break-even point.
7. State the formulas for determining the sales required to earn the target net income.
8. State the formulas for determining the sales required to earn the target net income after tax.
9. Define margin of safety, and state the formulas for calculating it.
10. Understand how operating leverage affects profitability.
11. Explain the term "sales mix" and its effect on break-even sales (Appendix 5A).

the navigator

As the feature story about Delta Chelsea indicates, to manage any business, whatever its size, you must understand how changes in sales volume affect costs, and how costs and revenues affect profits. But before you can understand cost-volume-profit (CVP) relationships, you first need to understand how costs behave. In this chapter, we therefore first explain cost behaviour analysis, and then discuss and illustrate CVP analysis and contribution margin analysis.

The chapter is organized as follows:

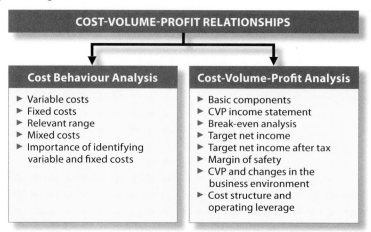

the navigator

Cost Behaviour Analysis

Cost behaviour analysis is the study of how specific costs are affected by changes in the level of business activity. As you might expect, some costs change and others remain the same. For example, for an airline company such as Air Canada or WestJet, the longer the flight, the higher the fuel costs. On the other hand, Montreal General Hospital's employee costs to run the emergency room on any particular night are relatively constant regardless of the number of patients treated. A knowledge of cost behaviour helps management plan activities and decide between alternative courses of action. Cost behaviour analysis applies to all types of entities, as the feature story about Delta Chelsea indicates.

The starting point in cost behaviour analysis is measuring the key business activities. Activity levels may be expressed in terms of sales dollars (in a retail company), kilometres driven (in a trucking company), room occupancy (in a hotel), or dance classes taught (by a dance studio). Many companies use more than one measurement base. A manufacturer, for example, may use direct labour hours or units of output for manufacturing costs, and sales revenue or units sold for selling expenses.

For an activity level to be useful in cost behaviour analysis, changes in the level or volume of activity should be correlated with changes in costs. The activity level selected is referred to as the activity (or volume) index. The **activity index** identifies the activity that causes changes in the behaviour of costs. With an appropriate activity index, it is possible to classify the behaviour of costs in response to changes in activity levels into three categories: variable, fixed, or mixed.

Variable Costs

study objective 1

Distinguish between variable and fixed costs.

Variable costs are costs that vary **in total** directly and proportionately with changes in the activity level. If the level increases by 10 percent, total variable costs will increase by 10 percent. If the level of activity decreases by 25 percent, variable costs will decrease by 25 percent. Examples of variable costs include direct materials and direct labour for a manufacturer; cost of goods sold, sales commissions, and freight out for a merchandiser; and gasoline for an airline or trucking company. A variable cost may also be defined as a cost that **remains the same *per unit* at every level of activity**.

To illustrate the behaviour of a variable cost, assume that Damon Company manufactures radios that contain a $10 digital clock. The activity index is the number of radios produced. As each radio is manufactured, the total cost of the clocks increases by $10. As shown in part (a) of Illustration 5-1, the total cost of the clocks will be $20,000 if 2,000 radios are produced, and $100,000 when 10,000 radios are produced. We can also see that a variable cost remains the same per unit as the level of activity changes. As shown in part (b) of Illustration 5-1, the unit cost of $10 for the clocks is the same whether 2,000 or 10,000 radios are produced.

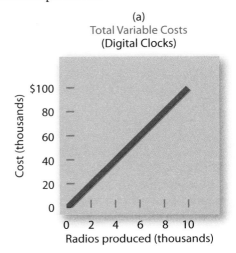

(a)
Total Variable Costs
(Digital Clocks)

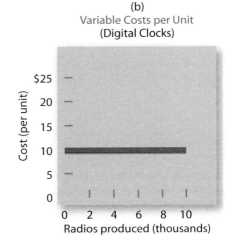

(b)
Variable Costs per Unit
(Digital Clocks)

Illustration 5-1 ◄

Behaviour of total and unit variable costs

Helpful Hint True or false: The variable cost per unit changes directly and proportionately with changes in activity. Answer: False. The cost per unit remains constant at all levels of activity.

Companies that rely heavily on labour to manufacture a product, such as Nike or Reebok, or to provide a service, such as Delta Chelsea or Marriott, are likely to have many variable costs. In contrast, companies that use a high proportion of machinery and equipment in producing revenue, such as BCE Inc. or Alberta Energy Co. Ltd., may have few variable costs.

Fixed Costs

Fixed costs are costs that **remain the same in total within the relevant range** regardless of changes in the activity level. Examples include property taxes, insurance, rent, supervisory salaries, and amortization on buildings and equipment. Because total fixed costs remain constant as activity changes, it follows that **fixed costs *per unit* vary inversely with activity**: in other words **as volume increases, unit cost declines, and vice versa**.

To illustrate the behaviour of fixed costs, assume that Damon Company leases its productive facilities at a cost of $10,000 per month. The total fixed costs of the facilities will remain constant at every level of activity, as shown in part (a) of Illustration 5-2. But, on a per unit basis, the cost of rent will decline as activity increases, as shown in part (b) of Illustration 5-2. At 2,000 units, the unit cost is $5 ($10,000 ÷ 2,000). When 10,000 radios are produced, the unit cost is only $1 ($10,000 ÷ 10,000).

Illustration 5-2 ▶

Behaviour of total and unit
fixed costs

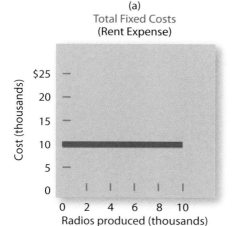

(a)
Total Fixed Costs
(Rent Expense)

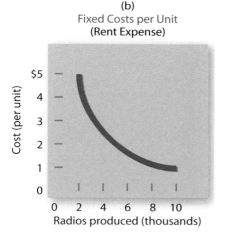

(b)
Fixed Costs per Unit
(Rent Expense)

Currently, the trend for many manufacturers is to have more fixed costs and fewer variable costs. This trend is the result of an increased use of automation and less use of employee labour. As a result, amortization and lease charges (fixed costs) increase, whereas direct labour costs (variable costs) decrease.

BUSINESS INSIGHT ▶ International Perspective

The slump in the export market following the Asian financial crisis in the late 1990s and the terrorist attacks of September 11, 2001, began to level off in 2004 with a return in export growth. This was good news for Canadian businesses that deliver products internationally; surplus trade with the world for these companies was at the highest level in three years. However, the Canadian dollar rose as the U.S. dollar fell, making Canadian products more expensive. Many companies that price their products in U.S. dollars chose to take a hit by freezing their prices. While some business sectors experienced a profit squeeze, many export companies offset this with increases in volume and price. "If demand has increased the price people are willing to pay for a product 100 percent while the dollar is down 20 percent, you're still up 80," said Stephen Poloz, chief economist at Export Development Canada.

Source: Jeff Sanford, "How to Cash in on Global Trade," *Canadian Business*, June 7, 2004.

Relevant Range

study objective 2

Explain the significance of the relevant range.

In Illustration 5-1, a straight line was drawn throughout the entire range of the activity index for total variable costs. Basically, the assumption was made that the costs were **linear**. If a relationship is linear (that is, straight-line), then changes in the activity index will result in a direct, proportional change in the variable cost. For example, if the activity level doubles, the cost will double.

It is now necessary to ask: Is the straight-line relationship realistic? Does the linear assumption produce useful data for CVP analysis?

In most business situations, a straight-line relationship **does not exist** for variable costs throughout the entire range of possible activity. At abnormally low levels of activity, it may be impossible to be cost-efficient. Small-scale operations may not allow the company to obtain quantity discounts for raw materials or to use specialized labour. In contrast, at abnormally high levels of activity, labour costs may increase sharply because of overtime pay. Also, at high activity levels, materials costs may jump significantly because of excess spoilage caused by worker fatigue. As a result, in the real world, the relationship between the behaviour of a variable cost and changes in the activity level is often **curvilinear**, as shown in part (a) of Illustration 5-3. In the curved sections of the line, a change in the activity index will not result in a direct, proportional change in the variable cost. That is, a doubling of the activity index will not result in an exact doubling of the variable cost. The variable cost may be more than double, or it may be less than double.

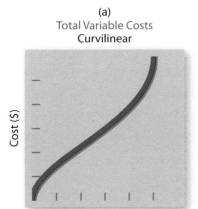

(a)
Total Variable Costs
Curvilinear

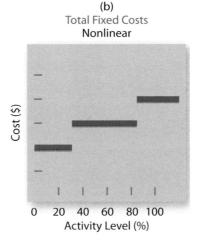

(b)
Total Fixed Costs
Nonlinear

Illustration 5-3 ◀

Nonlinear behaviour of
variable and fixed costs

Total fixed costs also do not have a straight-line relationship over the entire range of activity. Some fixed costs will not change. But it is possible for management to change other fixed costs. For example, a dance studio's rent might start out variable and then become fixed at a certain amount. It could then increase to a new fixed amount when the size of the studio increases beyond a certain point. An example of the behaviour of total fixed costs through all potential levels of activity is shown in part (b) of Illustration 5-3.

For most companies, operating at almost zero or at 100 percent capacity is the exception rather than the rule. Instead, companies often operate over a narrower range, such as 40 to 80 percent of capacity. The range that a company expects to operate in during a year is called the **relevant range** of the activity index. Within the relevant range, as shown in both diagrams in Illustration 5-4, there is usually a straight-line relationship for both variable and fixed costs.

Helpful Hint Fixed costs that may be changeable include research, such as new product development, and management training programs.

Alternative Terminology The relevant range is also called the *normal* or *practical range*.

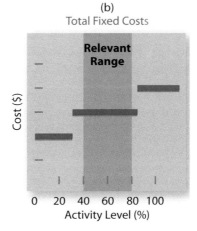

(a)
Total Variable Costs

Relevant Range

(b)
Total Fixed Costs

Relevant Range

Illustration 5-4 ◀

Linear behaviour within
relevant range

As you can see, although the linear (straight-line) relationship may not be completely realistic, **the linear assumption produces useful data for CVP analysis as long as the level of activity stays in the relevant range**.

Mixed Costs

Mixed costs are costs that have both a variable element and a fixed element. They are sometimes called semi variable costs. **Mixed costs change in total but not proportionately with changes in the activity level.**

The rental of a U-Haul truck is a good example of a mixed cost. Assume that local rental terms for a five-metre truck, including insurance, are $50 per day plus 25 cents per kilometre. When the cost of a one-day rental is being determined, the per day charge is a fixed cost (with respect to kilometres driven), whereas the mileage charge is a variable cost. Illustration 5-5 shows the rental cost for a one-day rental.

study objective 3

Explain the concept of mixed costs.

Illustration 5-5 ▶

Behaviour of a mixed cost

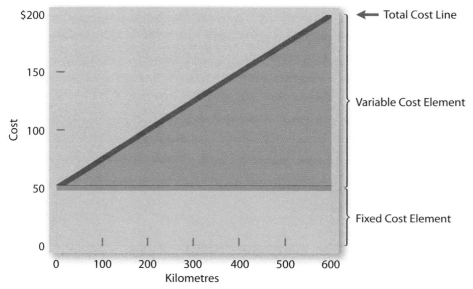

In this case, the fixed cost element is the cost of having the service available. The variable cost element is the cost of actually using the service. Another example of a mixed cost is utility costs (electricity, telephone, and so on), where there is a flat service fee plus a usage charge.

For CVP analysis, **mixed costs must be classified into their fixed and variable elements**. How does management make the classification? One possibility is to determine the variable and fixed components each time a mixed cost is incurred. But because of time and cost constraints, this approach is rarely used. Instead, the usual approach is to determine the variable and fixed cost components of the total cost **at the end of a period of time**. The company does this by using its past experience with the behaviour of the mixed cost at various levels of activity. Management may use any of several methods in making the determination. We will explain the **high-low method** here. Other methods include the scatter diagram method and least squares regression analysis. These other methods are explained in cost accounting courses.

High-Low Method

The **high-low method** uses the total costs incurred at the high and low levels of activity. The difference in costs between the high and low levels represents variable costs, since only the variable cost element can change as activity levels change. The steps in calculating fixed and variable costs under this method are as follows:

1. **Determine the variable cost per unit by using the formula in Illustration 5-6.**

Illustration 5-6 ▶

Formula for variable cost per unit using high-low method

To illustrate, assume that Metro Transit Company has the following maintenance costs and mileage data for its fleet of buses over a four-month period:

Illustration 5-7 ▶

Assumed maintenance costs and mileage data

Month	Kilometres Driven	Total Cost	Month	Kilometres Driven	Total Cost
January	40,000	$30,000	March	70,000	$49,000
February	80,000	48,000	April	100,000	63,000

The high and low levels of activity are 100,000 kilometres in April and 40,000 kilometres in January. The maintenance costs at these two levels are $63,000 and $30,000, respectively. The difference in maintenance costs is $33,000 ($63,000 − $30,000) and the difference in kilometres is 60,000 (100,000 − 40,000). Therefore, for Metro Transit, the variable cost per unit is $0.55, calculated as follows:

$$\$33,000 \div 60,000 = \$0.55$$

2. **Determine the fixed cost by subtracting the total variable cost at either the high or the low activity level from the total cost at that activity level.**

For Metro Transit, the calculations are shown in Illustration 5-8.

Illustration 5-8 ◄

Calculation of fixed costs using high-low method

	Activity Level	
	High	Low
Total cost	$63,000	$30,000
Less: Variable costs		
100,000 × $0.55	55,000	
40,000 × $0.55		22,000
Total fixed costs	$ 8,000	$ 8,000

Maintenance costs are therefore $8,000 per month plus $0.55 per kilometre. This is represented by the following formula:

$$\text{Maintenance costs} = \text{Fixed costs} + \$0.55 \text{ (kilometres driven)}$$

For example, at 90,000 kilometres, estimated maintenance costs would be $8,000 fixed and $49,500 variable (90,000 × $0.55) for a total of $57,500.

The high-low method generally produces a reasonable estimate for analysis. However, it does not produce a precise measurement of the fixed and variable elements in a mixed cost, because other activity levels are ignored in the calculation.

Importance of Identifying Variable and Fixed Costs

Why is it important to segregate costs into variable and fixed elements? The answer may become clear if we look at the following four business decisions:

1. If Air Canada is to make a profit when it reduces all domestic fares by 30 percent, what reduction in costs or increase in passengers will be required? Answer: To make a profit when it cuts domestic fares by 30 percent, Air Canada will have to increase the number of passengers or cut its variable costs for those flights. Its fixed costs will not change.
2. If Ford Motor Company Ltd. of Canada meets the Canadian Auto Workers' demands for higher wages, what increase in sales revenue will be needed to maintain current profit levels? Answer: Higher wages to CAW members at Ford Motor Company will increase the variable costs of manufacturing automobiles. To keep present profit levels, Ford will have to cut other variable costs or increase the price of its automobiles.
3. If Dofasco Inc.'s program to modernize plant facilities through significant equipment purchases reduces the workforce by 50 percent, what will the effect be on the cost of producing one tonne of steel? Answer: The modernizing of plant facilities changes the proportion of fixed and variable costs of producing one ton of steel. Fixed costs increase because of higher amortization charges, whereas variable costs decrease due to the reduction in the number of steelworkers.
4. What happens if Kellogg Company increases its advertising expenses but cannot increase prices because of competitive pressure? Answer: Its sales volume must be increased to cover three items: (1) the increase in fixed advertising costs, (2) the variable cost of the increased sales volume, and (3) the desired additional net income.

BEFORE YOU GO ON . . .

▶Review It

1. What are the effects of a change in activity on (a) a variable cost and (b) a fixed cost?
2. What is the relevant range, and how do costs behave within this range?
3. What steps are used in applying the high-low method to mixed costs?

▶Do It

Helena Company reports the following total costs at two levels of production:

	10,000 units	20,000 units
Direct materials	$20,000	$40,000
Maintenance	8,000	10,000
Amortization	4,000	4,000

Classify each cost as either variable, fixed, or mixed.

Action Plan

- Recall that a variable cost varies in total directly and proportionately with each change.
- Recall that a fixed cost remains the same in total with each change.
- Recall that a mixed cost changes in total but not proportionately with each change.

Solution

Direct materials is a variable cost. Maintenance is a mixed cost. Amortization is a fixed cost.

Related exercise material: BE5–1, BE5–2, BE5–3, E5–1, E5–2, and E5–3.

Cost-Volume-Profit Analysis

---

study objective 4

List the five components of cost-volume-profit analysis.

Cost-volume-profit (CVP) analysis is the study of the effects that changes in costs and volume have on a company's profits. CVP analysis is important in profit planning. It is also a critical factor in such management decisions as setting selling prices, determining product mix, and maximizing the use of production facilities.

Basic Components

CVP analysis considers the interrelationships among the components shown in Illustration 5-9.

Illustration 5-9 ▶

Components of CVP analysis

| Volume or level of activity | Unit selling prices | Variable cost per unit | Total cost per unit | Sales mix |

The following assumptions underlie each CVP analysis:

1. The behaviour of both costs and revenues is linear throughout the relevant range of the activity index.
2. All costs can be classified with reasonable accuracy as either variable or fixed.
3. Changes in activity are the only factors that affect costs.
4. All units that are produced are sold.
5. When more than one type of product is sold, the sales mix will remain constant. That is, the percentage that each product represents of total sales will stay the same. The sales mix complicates CVP analysis because different products will have different cost relationships. In this chapter, we assume a single product is being sold. Sales mix issues are addressed in Appendix 5A.

When these five assumptions are not valid, the results of CVP analysis may be inaccurate.

CVP Income Statement

Because CVP is so important for decision-making, management often wants this information reported in a *CVP income statement format*. The **CVP income statement** classifies costs as variable or fixed and calculates a *contribution margin*. **Contribution margin (CM)** is the amount of revenue that remains after variable costs have been deducted. It is often stated both as a total amount and on a per unit basis.

We will use Vargo Video Company to illustrate a CVP income statement. Vargo Video produces a high-end, progessive-scan DVD player/recorder with up to 160 hours of recording capacity and MP3 playback capability. Relevant data for the DVD players made by this company are given in Illustration 5-10.

Unit selling price of DVD player	$500
Unit variable costs	$300
Total monthly fixed costs	$200,000
Units sold	1,600

Illustration 5-10 ◄

Assumed selling and cost data for Vargo Video

The CVP income statement for Vargo Video therefore would be reported as in the following illustration:

VARGO VIDEO COMPANY
CVP Income Statement
Month Ended June 30, 2005

	Total	Per Unit
Sales (1,600 DVD players)	$800,000	$500
Variable costs	480,000	300
Contribution margin	320,000	$200
Fixed costs	200,000	
Net income	$120,000	

Illustration 5-11 ◄

CVP income statement, with net income

A traditional income statement and a CVP income statement both report the same bottom-line net income of $120,000. However, a traditional income statement does not classify costs as variable or fixed, and therefore a contribution margin would not be reported. In addition, both a total and a per unit amount are often shown on a CVP income statement to help CVP analysis.

In the examples of CVP analysis that follow, we will assume that the term "cost" includes all costs and expenses for the production and sale of the product. That is, cost includes manufacturing costs plus selling and administrative expenses.

Contribution Margin per Unit

From Vargo Video's CVP income statement, we can see that the contribution margin is $320,000, and the contribution margin per unit is $200 ($500 − $300). The formula for calculating the **contribution margin per unit** using data for Vargo Video is shown in Illustration 5-12:

Unit Selling Price	−	Unit Variable Costs	=	Contribution Margin per Unit
$500	−	$300	=	$200

Illustration 5-12 ◄

Formula for contribution margin per unit

The contribution margin per unit indicates that for every DVD player sold, Vargo will have $200 to cover its fixed costs and contribute to net income. Because Vargo Video has fixed costs of $200,000, it must sell 1,000 DVD players ($200,000 ÷ $200) before it earns any net income. Vargo's CVP income statement, assuming a zero net income, appears in Illustration 5-13.

Illustration 5-13 ▶

CVP income statement, with
zero net income

VARGO VIDEO COMPANY
CVP Income Statement
Month Ended June 30, 2005

	Total	Per Unit
Sales (1,000 DVD players)	$500,000	$500
Variable costs	300,000	300
Contribution margin	200,000	$200
Fixed costs	200,000	
Net income	$ 0	

It follows that for every DVD player sold above 1,000 units, net income is increased by $200. For example, assume that Vargo sold one more DVD player, for a total of 1,001 DVD players sold. In this case, it would report net income of $200 as shown in Illustration 5-14.

Illustration 5-14 ▶

CVP income statement, with
net income

VARGO VIDEO COMPANY
CVP Income Statement
Month Ended June 30, 2005

	Total	Per Unit
Sales (1,001 DVD players)	$500,500	$500
Variable costs	300,300	300
Contribution margin	200,200	$200
Fixed costs	200,000	
Net income	$ 200	

Contribution Margin Ratio

Some managers prefer to use a contribution margin ratio in CVP analysis. The **contribution margin ratio** is the contribution margin per unit divided by the unit selling price. Illustration 5-15 shows the ratio for Vargo Video.

Illustration 5-15 ▶

Formula for contribution
margin ratio

Contribution Margin per Unit	÷	Unit Selling Price	=	Contribution Margin Ratio
$200	÷	$500	=	40%

The contribution margin ratio of 40 percent means that $0.40 of each sales dollar ($1 × 40%) can be applied to fixed costs and contribute to net income.

This expression of the contribution margin is very helpful in determining the effect of changes in sales on net income. For example, if sales increase by $100,000, net income will increase by $40,000 (40% × $100,000) above the break-even level. Thus, by using the contribution margin ratio, managers can quickly determine what increases in net income will result from any increase in sales.

We can also see this effect through a CVP income statement. Assume that Vargo Video's current sales are $500,000 and it wants to know the effect of a $100,000 increase in sales. It could prepare the comparative CVP income statement shown in Illustration 5-16.

Illustration 5-16 ◀

Comparative CVP income statements

VARGO VIDEO COMPANY
CVP Income Statements
Month Ended June 30, 2005

	No Change		With Change	
	Total	Per Unit	Total	Per Unit
Sales	$500,000	$ 500	$600,000	$ 500
Variable costs	300,000	300	360,000	300
Contribution margin	200,000	$200	240,000	$200
Fixed costs	200,000		200,000	
Net income	$ 0		$ 40,000	

Study these CVP income statements carefully. The concepts used in these statements will be used often in this and later chapters.

Decision Toolkit

Decision Checkpoints	Info Needed for Decision	Tools to Use for Decision	How to Evaluate Results
What was the contribution toward fixed costs and income from each unit sold?	Selling price per unit and variable cost per unit	Contribution margin per unit = Unit selling price − Unit variable cost	Every unit sold will increase income by the contribution margin.
What was the increase in income as a result of an increase in sales?	Contribution margin per unit and unit selling price	Contribution margin ratio = Contribution margin per unit ÷ Unit selling price	Every dollar of sales will increase income by the contribution margin ratio.

Break-Even Analysis

A key relationship in CVP analysis is the level of activity at which total revenues equal total costs (both fixed and variable). This level of activity is called the **break-even point**. At this volume of sales, the company will realize no income and will suffer no loss. The process of finding the break-even point is called **break-even analysis**. Knowledge of the break-even point is useful to management when it decides whether to introduce new product lines, change sales prices on established products, or enter new market areas.

study objective 6

Identify the three ways to determine the break-even point.

The break-even point can be:

1. Calculated with a mathematical equation
2. Calculated by using contribution margin
3. Derived from a cost-volume-profit (CVP) graph

The break-even point can be expressed **in either sales units or sales dollars**.

Mathematical Equation

A common equation that is used for CVP analysis is shown in Illustration 5-17.

Sales = Variable Costs + Fixed Costs + Net Income

Illustration 5-17 ◀

Basic CVP equation

Identifying the break-even point is a special case of CVP analysis. Because net income is zero at the break-even point, **break-even occurs when total sales equal variable costs plus fixed costs**.

The break-even point in units can be calculated directly from the equation by **using unit selling prices** and **unit variable costs**. Illustration 5-18 shows the calculation for Vargo Video.

Illustration 5-18 ▶

Calculation of break-even point in units

Sales	=	Variable Costs	+	Fixed Costs	+	Net Income
$500Q	=	$300Q	+	$200,000	+	$0

$$200Q = \$200,000$$
$$Q = 1,000 \text{ units}$$

where:

$$Q = \text{sales volume}$$
$$\$500 = \text{selling price}$$
$$\$300 = \text{variable cost per unit}$$
$$\$200,000 = \text{total fixed costs}$$

Thus, Vargo Video must sell 1,000 units to break even.

To find the **sales dollars** required to break even, we multiply the units sold at the break-even point by the selling price per unit, as shown below:

$$1,000 \times \$500 = \$500,000 \text{ (break-even sales in dollars)}$$

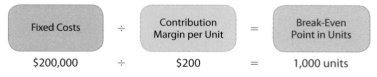

BUSINESS INSIGHT ▶ @-Business Perspective

Despite the increase in Internet radio and music downloading, conventional radio actually flourished in 2003, Statistics Canada reported. Sales for airtime for private radio broadcasters increased for the second year in a row, by 8.4% or $1.2 billion. Radio stations did not simply break even; profits were up, since operating expense growth, at 3.7%, was less than half the 8.2% revenue increase. The FM radio sector had its highest growth in airtime sales since 1998, while AM stations' sales experienced a profit margin of 1.6%. The profit margin for stations in the five largest metropolitan areas was 23.3%, compared with 15.3% for those operating outside these areas. Calgary and Ottawa-Gatineau were the most profitable markets. These results show that old-fashioned radio has survived the impact of technological advances in recent years, as the number of listeners continues to attract advertising sales and generate profits.

Source: "Conventional Radio Flourishes in 2003," *The Globe and Mail*, July 5, 2004.

Contribution Margin Technique

We know that the contribution margin equals total revenues less variable costs. It follows that at the break-even point, **the contribution margin must equal total fixed costs**. On the basis of this relationship, the we can calculate the break-even point using either the contribution margin per unit or the contribution margin ratio.

When the contribution margin per unit is used, the formula to calculate the break-even point in units is fixed costs divided by the contribution margin per unit. For Vargo Video, the calculation is shown in Illustration 5-19.

Illustration 5-19 ▶

Formula for break-even point in units using contribution margin

Fixed Costs	÷	Contribution Margin per Unit	=	Break-Even Point in Units
$200,000	÷	$200	=	1,000 units

One way to interpret this formula is to state that Vargo Video generates $200 of contribution margin with each unit that it sells. As this $200 is used to pay off fixed costs, the company must therefore sell 1,000 units to pay off $200,000 in fixed costs.

For Vargo Video, the contribution margin per unit is $200, as explained earlier. This means that each unit sold generates $200 of contribution margin to pay off fixed costs. Thus, the break-even point in units is:

$$\$200,000 \div \$200 = 1,000 \text{ units}$$

When the contribution margin ratio is used, the formula to calculate the break-even point in dollars is fixed costs divided by the contribution margin ratio. We know that the contribution margin ratio for Vargo Video is 40 percent ($200 ÷ $500). This means that every dollar of sales generates $0.40 to pay off fixed costs.

Illustration 5-20 shows the calculation of the break-even point in dollars.

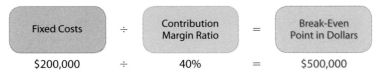

| Fixed Costs | ÷ | Contribution Margin Ratio | = | Break-Even Point in Dollars |
| $200,000 | ÷ | 40% | = | $500,000 |

Illustration 5-20 ◀

Formula for break-even point in dollars using contribution margin ratio

Graphic Presentation

An effective way to find the break-even point is to prepare a break-even graph. Because this graph also shows costs, volume, and profits, it is referred to as a **cost-volume-profit (CVP) graph**.

As shown in the CVP graph in Illustration 5-21, the sales volume is recorded along the horizontal axis. This axis should extend to the maximum level of expected sales. Both the total revenues (sales) and total costs (fixed plus variable) are recorded on the vertical axis.

Using the data for Vargo Video, the steps to construct the graph are as follows:

1. Plot the total-revenue line, starting at the zero activity level. For every DVD player sold, total revenue increases by $500. For example, at 200 units, sales are $100,000. At the upper level of activity (1,800 units), sales are $900,000. Note that the revenue line is assumed to be linear throughout the full range of activity.
2. Plot the total fixed cost using a horizontal line. For the DVD players, this line is plotted at $200,000. The fixed cost is the same at every level of activity.
3. Plot the total cost line. This starts at the fixed-cost line at zero activity. It increases by the variable cost at each level of activity. For each DVD player, variable costs are $300. Thus, at 200 units, the total variable cost is $60,000, and the total cost is $260,000. At 1,800 units the total variable cost is $540,000, and the total cost is $740,000. On the graph, the amount of the variable cost can be derived from the difference between the total cost and fixed cost lines at each level of activity.
4. Determine the break-even point from the intersection of the total cost line and the total revenue line. The break-even point in dollars is found by drawing a horizontal line from the break-even point to the vertical axis. The break-even point in units is found by drawing a vertical line from the break-even point to the horizontal axis. For the DVD players, the break-even point is $500,000 of sales, or 1,000 units. At this sales level, Vargo Video will cover costs but make no profit.

The CVP graph also shows both the net income and net loss areas. Thus, the amount of income or loss at each level of sales can be derived from the total sales and total cost lines.

Illustration 5-21 ▶

CVP graph

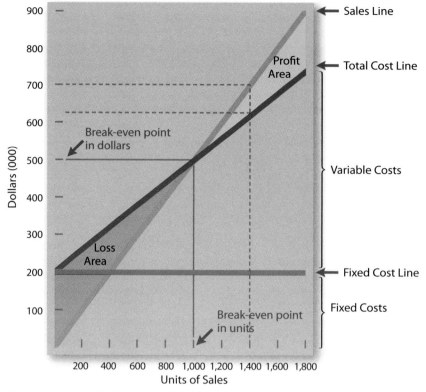

A CVP graph is useful because the effects of a change in any element in the CVP analysis can be quickly seen. For example, a 10-percent increase in the selling price will change the location of the total revenue line. Likewise, the effects on total costs of wage increases can be quickly observed.

BUSINESS INSIGHT ▶ Management Perspective

Computer graphics are a valuable component of many computer software packages. Colour graphs can be instantly changed to provide visual "what if" analyses. Current technology allows for stunning graphs in a variety of different formats (pie chart, bar, stacked bar, two-dimensional, three-dimensional, etc.). In the appropriate situation, a graph can truly be worth a thousand words.

▦ Decision Toolkit

Decision Checkpoints	Info Needed for Decision	Tools to Use for Decision	How to Evaluate Results
At what amount of sales does a company cover its costs?	Unit selling price, unit variable cost, and total fixed costs	Break-even point analysis *In units:* $\text{Break-even point} = \dfrac{\text{Fixed costs}}{\text{Unit contribution margin}}$ *In dollars:* $\text{Break-even point} = \dfrac{\text{Fixed costs}}{\text{Contribution margin ratio}}$	Below the break-even point—the point at which total sales equal total costs—the company is unprofitable.

the
navigator

BEFORE YOU GO ON . . .

►Review It

1. What are the assumptions that underlie each CVP application?
2. What is the contribution margin, and how can it be expressed?
3. How can the break-even point be determined?

►Do It

Lombardi Company has a unit selling price of $400, variable costs per unit of $240, and fixed costs of $160,000. Calculate the break-even point in units using (a) a mathematical equation and (b) the contribution margin per unit.

Action Plan

- Apply the formula: sales = variable costs + fixed costs + net income.
- Apply the formula: fixed costs = contribution margin per unit ÷ break-even point in units.

Solution

(a) The formula is $400Q = $240Q + $160,000. The break-even point in units is 1,000 ($160,000 ÷ $160Q).
(b) The contribution margin per unit is $160 ($400 − $240). The formula is $160,000 ÷ $160, and the break-even point in units is 1,000.

Related exercise material: BE5–6, BE5–8, BE5–9, E5–4, E5–5, E5–6, E5–9, and E5–10.

Target Net Income

Rather than simply "breaking even," management usually sets an income objective for individual product lines. This objective is called the **target net income**. It indicates the sales that are needed in order to achieve a specified level of income. The sales necessary to achieve the target net income can be determined from each of the approaches that are used to determine the break-even sales.

study objective 7

State the formulas for determining the sales required to earn the target net income.

Mathematical Equation

We know that at the break-even point there is no profit or loss for the company. By instead adding an amount for the target net income to the same basic equation, we obtain the formula for determining required sales that is shown in Illustration 5-22.

Illustration 5-22 ◄

Formula for required sales to meet target net income

Required sales may be expressed in **either sales units or sales dollars**. Assuming that the target net income is $120,000 for Vargo Video, Illustration 5-23 shows the calculation of required sales in units:

Illustration 5-23 ◄

Calculation of required sales

$$
\begin{aligned}
\$500Q &= 300Q + \$200,000 + \$120,000 \\
\$200Q &= \$320,000 \\
Q &= 1,600
\end{aligned}
$$

where:

$$
\begin{aligned}
Q &= \text{sales volume} \\
\$500 &= \text{selling price} \\
\$300 &= \text{variable costs per unit} \\
\$200,000 &= \text{total fixed costs} \\
\$120,000 &= \text{target net income}
\end{aligned}
$$

The sales dollars required to achieve the target net income is found by multiplying the units sold by the unit selling price [(1,600 × $500) = $800,000].

Contribution Margin Technique

As in the case of break-even sales, the sales required to meet the target net income can be calculated in either units or dollars. Illustration 5-24 shows the formula to calculate the required sales in units for Vargo Video using the contribution margin per unit.

Illustration 5-24 ▶

Formula for required sales in units using contribution margin per unit

(\$200,000 + \$120,000)   ÷   \$200   =   1,600 units

This calculation tells us that to achieve its desired target net income of $120,000, the company must sell 1,600 DVD players.

The formula to calculate the required sales in dollars for Vargo Video using the contribution margin ratio is shown in Illustration 5-25.

Illustration 5-25 ▶

Formula for required sales in dollars using contribution margin ratio

(\$200,000 + \$120,000)   ÷   40%   =   \$800,000

This calculation tells us that to achieve its desired target net income of $120,000, the company must generate sales of $800,000.

Graphic Presentation

The CVP graph in Illustration 5-21 (on page 206) can also be used to find the sales required to meet target net income. In the profit area of the graph, the distance between the sales line and the total cost line at any point equals net income. The required sales amount is found by analyzing the differences between the two lines until the desired net income is found.

For example, suppose Vargo Video sells 1,400 DVD players. Illustration 5-21 shows that a vertical line drawn at 1,400 units intersects the sales line at $700,000 and the total cost line at $620,000. The difference between the two amounts represents the net income (profit) of $80,000.

Target Net Income after Tax

So far, we have ignored the effect of income taxes in our CVP analysis.

However, management may want to know the effect of taxes on net income and to set targets for net income after taxes. In general, income taxes can be calculated by multiplying the tax rate by net income before taxes. While the net income after taxes can then be calculated by subtracting the tax amount from income before taxes, another calculation may also be used: net income after taxes is equal to net income before taxes times the difference between 1 and the tax rate (1 − tax rate):

Net income after taxes = net income before taxes × (1 − tax rate)

To figure out what the net income before taxes needs to be in order to reach a specific target net income after taxes, we divide the desired net income after taxes by the difference between 1 and the tax rate (1 − tax rate):

Net income before taxes = net income after taxes ÷ (1 − tax rate)

Using the previous example, assume that the tax rate is 40 percent and the target net income is $120,000 after taxes for Vargo Video. The calculation of the required sales in units is as follows:

$$\$500Q \;=\; 300Q + \$200,000 + \frac{\$120,000}{(1 - 0.4)}$$
$$\$200Q \;=\; \$200,000 + \$200,000 \text{ target net income before tax}$$
$$Q \;=\; \$400,000 \div \$200$$
$$Q \;=\; 2,000$$

where:
$$Q \;=\; \text{sales volume}$$
$$\$500 \;=\; \text{selling price}$$
$$\$300 \;=\; \text{variable costs per unit}$$
$$\$200,000 \;=\; \text{total fixed costs}$$
$$\$120,000 \;=\; \text{target net income}$$
$$40\% \;=\; \text{tax rate}$$

The sales dollars amount that is needed to reach the target net income after taxes is found by multiplying the required sales in units by the unit-selling price [(2,000 × $500) = $1,000,000].

Contribution Margin Technique

The required sales to meet a target net income after taxes can also be calculated in either units or dollars using the contribution margin per unit, as shown in Illustration 5-26.

Illustration 5-26 ◀

Formula for required sales in units using contribution margin per unit

The calculation for Vargo Video is as follows:

[$200,000 + ($120,000 ÷ (1 − 0.4))] ÷ $200 = 2,000 units

The formula using the contribution margin ratio is shown in Illustration 5-27.

Illustration 5-27 ◀

Formula for required sales in dollars using contribution margin per unit

The calculation for Vargo Video is as follows:

$400,000 ÷ 40% = $1,000,000

Margin of Safety

The margin of safety is another relationship that may be calculated in CVP analysis. **Margin of safety** is the difference between actual or expected sales and sales at the break-even point. This relationship measures the "cushion" that management has, allowing it to still break even if expected sales fail to be reached. The margin of safety may be expressed in dollars or as a ratio.

The formula for stating the **margin of safety in dollars** is actual (or expected) sales minus break-even sales. Assuming that actual (expected) sales for Vargo Video are $750,000, the calculation is given in Illustration 5-28.

study objective 9

Define margin of safety, and state the formulas for calculating it.

Illustration 5-28 ◀

Formula for margin of safety in dollars

Actual (Expected) Sales	−	Break-Even Sales	=	Margin of Safety in Dollars
$750,000	−	$500,000	=	$250,000

This means that the company's sales could fall by $250,000 before it would be operating at a loss.

The margin of safety ratio is calculated by dividing the margin of safety in dollars by actual (or expected) sales. Illustration 5-29 provides the formula and calculation for determining the **margin of safety ratio**:

Illustration 5-29 ▶

Formula for margin of safety ratio

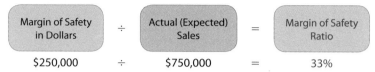

Margin of Safety in Dollars	÷	Actual (Expected) Sales	=	Margin of Safety Ratio
$250,000	÷	$750,000	=	33%

This means that the company's sales could fall by 33 percent before it would be operating at a loss.

The higher the dollars or the percentage, the greater the margin of safety. Based on such factors as how vulnerable the product is to competitive pressures and to downturns in the economy, management should evaluate whether or not the margin of safety is adequate.

BUSINESS INSIGHT ▶ Management Perspective

Calculating break-even and the margin of safety is important in all industries, including the entertainment world. The multi-channel universe of the 21st century has reduced the profitability of producing television dramas. This fact led Toronto-based Alliance Atlantis to abandon the film and television production side of its business in 2003. Over the previous few years, the number of television channels per country skyrocketed, from an average of about a dozen to more than 100. Meanwhile, average viewing times per person have remained unchanged since the 1960s, at about 22 hours per week. The pieces of the broadcast "pies" (for audience and revenue) have become much smaller, forcing channel owners to reduce programming costs by buying cheaper reality shows and scheduling more reruns. Alliance Atlantis saw no alternative but to cancel production, except for its profitable *CSI: Crime Scene Investigation* franchise. It decided instead to concentrate on growing its ownership of specialty channels. Although digital channels have been losing money, they are poised to break even, the company said. In the multi-channel universe, the more specific the subject matter is, the better its ability to attract viewers and thus profits.

Source: Richard Blackwell, "It's Here! Alliance Atlantis, the Sequel," *The Globe and Mail*, July 3, 2004.

CVP and Changes in the Business Environment

When the IBM personal computer (PC) was introduced, it sold for around $3,000. Today the same type of computer sells for much less. Recently, when oil prices rose, the break-even point for airline companies rose dramatically. Because of lower prices for imported steel, the demand for domestic steel dropped significantly. The point should be clear: business conditions change rapidly, and management must respond intelligently to these changes. CVP analysis can help.

To show how CVP analysis can be used in responding to change, we will look at three independent situations that might occur at Vargo Video. Each case is based on the original DVD player sales and cost data, shown here again in Illustration 5-30:

Illustration 5-30 ▶

Original DVD player sales and cost data

Unit selling price	$500
Unit variable cost	$300
Total fixed costs	$200,000
Break-even sales	$500,000 or 1,000 units

CASE 1. A competitor is offering a 10-percent discount on the selling price of its DVD players. Vargo Video's management must decide whether to offer a similar discount. Question: What effect will a 10-percent discount on the selling price have on the break-even point for DVD players? Answer: A 10-percent discount on the selling price reduces the selling price per unit to $450 [$500 − ($500 × 10%)]. Variable costs per unit remain unchanged at $300. Thus, the contribution margin per unit is $150. Assuming no change in fixed costs, break-even sales are 1,333 units, calculated as in Illustration 5-31.

Illustration 5-31 ◄

Calculation of break-even sales in units

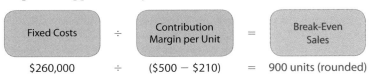

$$\text{Fixed Costs} \div \text{Contribution Margin per Unit} = \text{Break-Even Sales}$$

$$\$200{,}000 \div \$150 = 1{,}333 \text{ units (rounded)}$$

For Vargo Video, this change would thus require monthly sales to increase by 333 units, or 33⅓ percent, in order to break even. In reaching a conclusion about offering a 10-percent discount to customers, management must determine how likely it is to achieve the increased sales. Also, management should estimate the possible loss of sales if the competitor's discount price is not matched.

CASE 2. To meet the threat of foreign competition, management invests in new robotic equipment that will lower the amount of direct labour required to make DVD players. It is estimated that total fixed costs will increase by 30 percent and that the variable cost per unit will decrease by 30 percent. Question: What effect will the new equipment have on the sales volume required to break even? Answer: Total fixed costs become $260,000 [$200,000 + (30% × $200,000)]. The variable cost per unit becomes $210 [$300 − (30% × $300)]. The new break-even point is approximately 900 units, calculated as in Illustration 5-32.

Illustration 5-32 ◄

Calculation of break-even sales in units

$$\text{Fixed Costs} \div \text{Contribution Margin per Unit} = \text{Break-Even Sales}$$

$$\$260{,}000 \div (\$500 - \$210) = 900 \text{ units (rounded)}$$

These changes appear to be advantageous for Vargo Video. The break-even point is reduced by 10 percent, or 100 units.

CASE 3. Vargo Video's principal supplier of raw materials has just announced a price increase. The higher cost is expected to increase the variable cost of DVD players by $25 per unit. Management would like to keep the same selling price for the DVD players. It plans a cost-cutting program that will save $17,500 in fixed costs per month. Vargo Video is currently realizing monthly net income before taxes of $80,000 on sales of 1,400 DVD players. Question: What increase in units sold will be needed to maintain the same level of net income? Answer: The variable cost per unit increases to $325 ($300 + $25). Fixed costs are reduced to $182,500 ($200,000 − $17,500). Because of the change in variable cost, the contribution margin per unit becomes $175 ($500 − $325). The required number of units sold to achieve the target net income is calculated as in Illustration 5-33.

Illustration 5-33 ◄

Calculation of required sales

$$\text{Fixed Costs + Target Net Income} \div \text{Contribution Margin per Unit} = \text{Required Sales in Units}$$

$$(\$182{,}500 + \$80{,}000) \div \$175 = 1{,}500$$

To achieve the required sales, 1,500 DVD players will have to be sold, an increase of 100 units. If this does not seem to be a reasonable expectation, management will either have to make further cost reductions or accept less net income if the selling price remains unchanged.

BUSINESS INSIGHT ▶ @-Business Perspective

When analyzing an Internet business, the conversion rate is key. The conversion rate is calculated by dividing the number of people who buy something on a website by the total number of people who visit the site. Canadian Mark Fox, of Novator Systems Ltd., has been very successful at improving the conversion rates for some high-profile clients like FTD and Warner Bros., Novator designs, builds, and manages consumer-targeted websites, applying traditional merchandising techniques like pricing strategies, up-selling, and co-brand management to on-line storefronts. Its site architecture and software make it easy for retailers to implement these strategies—with great success. After using Novator's tools, the average order-basket size goes up 20 percent year-over-year, and conversion rates are 12 to 15 percent, compared to industry norms of between 0.5 and 7 percent.

Source: Andrew Wahl, "The Lord of Ka-Chings," *Canadian Business*, Sept. 15, 2003.

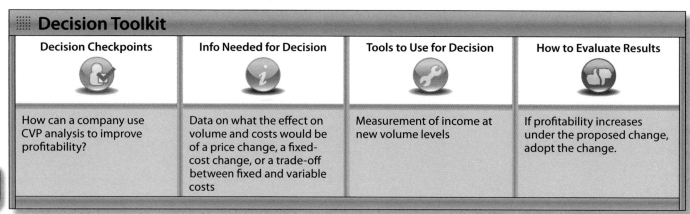

the navigator

Cost Structure and Operating Leverage

study objective 10

Understand how operating leverage affects profitability.

Cost structure refers to the proportion of fixed costs versus variable costs that a company incurs.

Operating leverage measures how sensitive net income is to a specific percentage change in sales volume. In highly leveraged firms—those with high fixed costs and low variable costs—small changes in the sales volume result in large changes in net profit. Firms with low leverage—those with low fixed costs and high variable costs—are not affected as much by changes in the sales volume.

Cost structure can have a significant effect on profitability. Consider two different firms as an example. To produce the same product line of wooden croquet mallets, one firm is labour-intensive and the other is capital-intensive. Old English Mallet Company uses a traditional, labour-intensive approach to form, sand, and apply a protective finish to the mallets. New Wave Mallet Company has invested in a completely automated system to do the same thing. Its factory employees are involved only in setting, adjusting, and maintaining the machinery. The CVP income statements for each company are shown in Illustration 5-34.

Illustration 5-34 ▶

Variable cost CVP income statements for two companies

	Old English Mallet	New Wave Mallet
Sales revenue	$300,000	$300,000
Variable costs	255,000	120,000
Contribution margin	45,000	180,000
Fixed costs	15,000	150,000
Net income	$ 30,000	$ 30,000

Both companies have the same sales and the same net income. However, because of the differences in their cost structures, they differ greatly in the way they would be managed. Let's evaluate the impact of cost structure on the profitability of the two companies.

Effect on Contribution Margin Ratio

We start with the contribution margin ratio. Illustration 5-35 shows the calculation of the contribution margin ratio for each company.

Illustration 5-35 ▶

Contribution margin ratio for two companies

	Contribution Margin	÷	Sales Revenue	=	Contribution Margin Ratio
Old English Mallet	$45,000	÷	$300,000	=	0.15
New Wave Mallet	$180,000	÷	$300,000	=	0.60

New Wave Mallet has a contribution margin ratio of 60 percent versus only 15 percent for Old English Mallet. That means that with every dollar of sales, New Wave Mallet generates 60 cents of contribution margin (and thus a 60-cent increase in net income), versus only 15 cents for Old English Mallet. However, it also means that for every dollar that sales decline, New Wave Mallet loses 60 cents in net income, whereas Old English Mallet will only lose 15 cents. New Wave Mallet's cost structure, which relies more heavily on fixed costs, makes it more sensitive to changes in sales revenue.

Degree of Operating Leverage

How can we compare the operating leverage of two companies? The **degree of operating leverage** provides a measure of a company's earnings volatility and can be used to compare companies. The degree of operating leverage is calculated by dividing the total contribution margin by net income. This formula is presented in Illustration 5-36, and applied to our two mallet manufacturers.

	Contribution Margin	÷	Net Income	=	Degree of Operating Leverage
Old English Mallet	$45,000	÷	$30,000	=	1.5
New Wave Mallet	$180,000	÷	$30,000	=	6

Illustration 5-36 ◄

Calculation of degree of operating leverage

New Wave Mallet's earnings would go up (or down) by 4.0 times (6 ÷ 1.5) as much as Old English Mallet's would with an equal increase (or decrease) in sales. For example, suppose both companies experience a 5-percent decrease in sales. Old English Mallet's net income will decrease by 7.5 percent (1.5 × 5%), while New Wave Mallet's will decrease by 30 percent (6 × 5%). Thus, New Wave Mallet's higher operating leverage exposes it to greater earnings volatility risk.

Effect on Break-Even Point

The difference in operating leverage also affects the break-even point. The break-even point for each company is calculated in Illustration 5-37.

	Fixed Costs	÷	Contribution Ratio	=	Break-Even Point in Dollars
Old English Mallet	$15,000	÷	0.15	=	$100,000
New Wave Mallet	$150,000	÷	0.60	=	$250,000

Illustration 5-37 ◄

Calculation of break-even point for two companies

New Wave Mallet needs to generate $150,000 ($250,000 − $100,000) more in sales than Old English Mallet before it breaks even. This makes New Wave Mallet riskier than Old English Mallet because a company cannot survive for very long unless it at least breaks even.

Effect on Margin of Safety Ratio

We can also evaluate the relative impact that changes in sales would have on the two companies by calculating the margin of safety ratio. Illustration 5-38 shows this calculation for the two companies.

	Actual Sales − Break-Even Sales	÷	Actual Sales	=	Margin of Safety Ratio
Old English Mallet	($300,000 − $100,000)	÷	$300,000	=	0.67
New Wave Mallet	($300,000 − $250,000)	÷	$300,000	=	0.17

Illustration 5-38 ◄

Calculation of margin of safety for two companies

The difference in the margin of safety ratio also reflects the difference in risk between the two companies. Old English Mallet could sustain a 67-percent decline in sales before it would be operating at a loss. New Wave Mallet could sustain only a 17-percent decline in sales before it would be "in the red."

You should be careful not to conclude from this analysis that a cost structure that relies on higher fixed costs, and consequently has higher operating leverage, is necessarily bad. When it is used carefully, operating leverage can make a company much more profitable. Computer equipment manufacturer Komag enjoyed a 66-percent increase in net income when its sales increased by only eight percent. As one commentator noted, "Komag's fourth quarter illustrates the company's significant operating leverage; a small increase in sales leads to a big profit rise." However, as our illustration demonstrates, an increased reliance on fixed costs also increases a company's risk. In recent years, computer equipment manufacturer Cisco Systems has substantially reduced its operating leverage by choosing to outsource much of its production. While this has made the company less susceptible to economic swings, it has also reduced its ability to experience the incredible profitability that it used to have during economic booms.

The choice of cost structure must be carefully considered. There are many ways in which companies can influence their cost structure. For example, by acquiring sophisticated robotic equipment, many companies have reduced their use of manual labour. Similarly, some brokerage firms, such as ETrade, have reduced their reliance on human brokers and have instead invested heavily in computers and on-line technology. In so doing, they have increased their reliance on fixed costs (through amortization on the robotic equipment or computer equipment) and reduced their reliance on variable costs (the variable employee labour cost). Alternatively, some companies, such as Cisco Systems, have reduced their fixed costs and increased their variable costs by outsourcing their production. Nike does very little manufacturing, but instead outsources the manufacture of nearly all of its shoes. It has consequently converted many of its fixed costs into variable costs and therefore reduced its operating leverage.

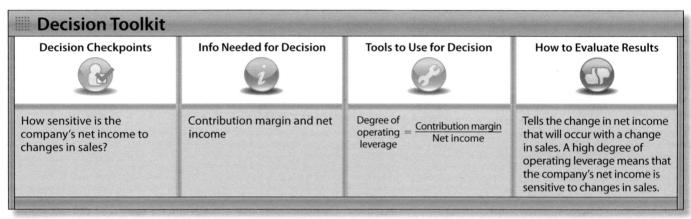

Decision Toolkit

Decision Checkpoints	Info Needed for Decision	Tools to Use for Decision	How to Evaluate Results
How sensitive is the company's net income to changes in sales?	Contribution margin and net income	$\text{Degree of operating leverage} = \dfrac{\text{Contribution margin}}{\text{Net income}}$	Tells the change in net income that will occur with a change in sales. A high degree of operating leverage means that the company's net income is sensitive to changes in sales.

BEFORE YOU GO ON . . .

▶Review It

1. What is the formula for calculating the margin of safety (a) in dollars and (b) as a ratio?
2. What is the equation to calculate target net income?

APPENDIX 5A ▶ CVP ANALYSIS: MULTIPLE–PRODUCT SETTING (SALES MIX)

Sales Mix

study objective 11

Explain the term "sales mix" and its effect on break-even sales.

The term **sales mix** means the proportions that a company's products are sold in, relative to each other. Most companies have several products with differing contribution margins. Thus, changes in the sales mix can cause variations in a company's profits. As a result, the break-even point in a multi-product firm depends on the mix in which the various products are sold. For example, if two units of Product A are sold for every unit of Product B that is sold, the sales mix of the products is 2:1. The sales mix affects management's decision-making in a number of ways. For example, Ford Motor Company Ltd. of Canada's SUVs and F150 pickups have traditionally had very high contribution margins compared to its economy cars. Similarly, first-class tickets sold by WestJet provided substantially higher contribution margins than coach-class tickets.

In this section, we discuss how sales mix affects break-even analysis, and in Chapter 6 we discuss how restrictions on a company's resources can affect the decision about the best sales mix. The information that we need for this analysis comes from a contribution margin analysis. This analysis is illustrated below for both sales in units and sales in dollars.

Break-Even Sales in Units

Break-even sales can be calculated for a mix of two or more products by determining the weighted-average unit contribution margin of all the products. To illustrate, we will assume that Vargo Video Company sells both DVD players and television sets, with the per unit data shown in Illustration 5A-1. It also incurs $200,000 in fixed costs.

Unit Data	DVD Players	TVs
Selling price	$500	$800
Variable costs	300	400
Contribution margin	$200	$400
Sales mix	75%	25%

Illustration 5A-1 ◄

Per unit data—sales mix

The weighted-average unit contribution margin for the sales mix of 75 percent DVD players and 25 percent TVs is $250, which is calculated as in Illustration 5A-2.

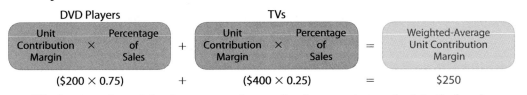

($200 × 0.75) + ($400 × 0.25) = $250

Illustration 5A-2 ◄

Weighted-average unit contribution margin calculation

We then use the weighted-average unit contribution margin to calculate the break-even point in unit sales. Illustration 5A-3 shows the calculation of break-even sales in units for Vargo Video, assuming $200,000 of fixed costs.

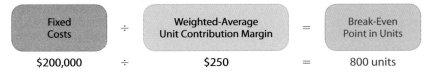

$200,000 ÷ $250 = 800 units

Illustration 5A-3 ◄

Break-even point in units calculation

Note that with the sales mix of 75 percent to 25 percent, 75 percent of the units sold will be DVD players and 25 percent will be TVs. Therefore, in order to break even, Vargo Video must sell 600 DVD players (0.75 × 800) and 200 TVs (0.25 × 800). This can be verified by the proof shown in Illustration 5A-4.

Product	Unit Sales	×	Unit Contribution Margin	=	Total Contribution Margin
DVD players	600	×	$200	=	$120,000
TVs	200	×	400	=	80,000
	800				$200,000

Illustration 5A-4 ◄

Break-even proof—sales mix

Management should continually review the company's sales mix. At any level of units sold, **net income will be greater if more high-contribution-margin units are sold than low-contribution-margin units**. For Vargo Video, the television sets produce the higher contribution margin. Consequently, if 300 TVs and 500 DVD players were sold, net income would be higher than in the current sales mix, even though the total units sold has not changed.

An analysis of these relationships shows that a shift from low-margin sales to high-margin sales may increase net income, even if there is a decline in the total units sold. Likewise, a shift from high- to low-margin sales may result in a decrease in net income, even if there is an increase in the total units sold.

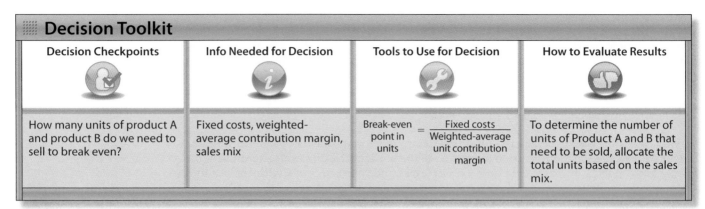

Decision Toolkit

Decision Checkpoints	Info Needed for Decision	Tools to Use for Decision	How to Evaluate Results
How many units of product A and product B do we need to sell to break even?	Fixed costs, weighted-average contribution margin, sales mix	$$\text{Break-even point in units} = \frac{\text{Fixed costs}}{\text{Weighted-average unit contribution margin}}$$	To determine the number of units of Product A and B that need to be sold, allocate the total units based on the sales mix.

Break-Even Sales in Dollars

The calculation of the break-even point presented for Vargo Video in the previous section works well if the company has only a small number of products. However, take 3M, the maker of such things as Post-it Notes. It has more than 30,000 products. In order to calculate the break-even point for 3M using the weighted-average unit contribution margin, we would need to calculate 30,000 different contribution margins. That is not realistic. For a company like 3M, we instead calculate the break-even point by using sales information for divisions or product lines, rather than for individual products.

To illustrate, suppose that Kale Garden Supply Company has two divisions—Indoor Plants and Outdoor Plants. Each division has hundreds of different types of plants and plant-care products. During the last year, 20 percent of the company's sales were in the Indoor Plant Division, and 80 percent were in the Outdoor Plant Division. The Indoor Plant Division has a contribution margin ratio of 40 percent, while the Outdoor Plant Division has a contribution margin ratio of 30 percent. Total fixed costs are $300,000.

The formula for calculating the break-even point in dollars is fixed costs divided by the weighted-average contribution margin ratio. To calculate the company's weighted-average contribution margin ratio, we multiply each division's contribution margin ratio by its percentage of total sales and then sum these amounts, as shown in Illustration 5A-5.

Illustration 5A-5 ▶

Calculation of weighted-average contribution margin ratio

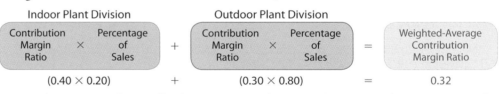

We then can use the weighted-average contribution margin ratio of 32 percent to calculate the company's break-even point in dollars, as shown in Illustration 5A-6.

Illustration 5A-6 ▶

Calculation of break-even point in dollars

This break-even point is based on the sales mix of 20 percent to 80 percent. Of the company's total break-even sales of $937,500, a total of $187,500 (0.20 × $937,500) will come from the Indoor Plant Division and $750,000 (0.80 × $937,500) will come from the Outdoor Plant Division.

What would be the impact on the break-even point if a higher percentage of the company's sales were to come from the Indoor Plant Division? Because the Indoor Plant Division enjoys a higher contribution margin ratio, this change in the sales mix would result in a higher weighted-average contribution margin ratio, and consequently a lower break-even point in dollars. The opposite would occur if a higher percentage of sales were expected from the Outdoor Plant Division. As you can see, understanding and managing the sales mix is highly important to the company's success.

Decision Toolkit

Decision Checkpoints	Info Needed for Decision	Tools to Use for Decision	How to Evaluate Results
How many dollars of sales are required from Division A versus Division B in order to break even?	Fixed costs, weighted-average contribution margin ratio, sales mix	$\text{Break-even point in dollars} = \dfrac{\text{Fixed costs}}{\text{Weighted-average contribution margin ratio}}$	To determine the sales dollars required from each division, allocate the total break-even sales using the sales mix.

BEFORE YOU GO ON . . .

▶ Review It

1. Explain what is meant by the term sales mix.
2. Why is the sales mix important for break-even analysis?
3. Explain how the number of products that a company sells affects the method that is used to determine the break-even point.
4. What information is needed to calculate the break-even sales in units? Break-even sales in dollars?

Using the Decision Toolkit

B.T. Hernandez Company, maker of high-quality flashlights, has experienced steady growth over the last six years. However, increased competition has led Mr. Hernandez, the president, to believe that an aggressive campaign is needed next year to maintain the company's present growth. The company's accountant has presented Mr. Hernandez with the following data for the current year, 2005. The data are to be used in preparing next year's advertising campaign.

Cost Schedules

Variable costs	
Direct labour per flashlight	$ 8.00
Direct materials	4.00
Variable overhead	3.00
Variable cost per flashlight	$15.00
Fixed costs	
Manufacturing	$ 25,000
Selling	40,000
Administrative	70,000
Total fixed costs	$135,000
Selling price per flashlight	$25.00
Expected sales, 2005 (20,000 flashlights)	$500,000

Mr. Hernandez has set the sales target for the year 2006 at a level of $550,000 (22,000 flashlights).

Instructions

(Ignore any income tax considerations.)

  (a) What is the projected operating income for 2005?
  (b) What is the contribution margin per unit for 2005?
  (c) What is the break-even point in units for 2005?
  (d) Mr. Hernandez believes that to attain the sales target in the year 2006, the company must incur an additional selling expense of $10,000 for advertising in 2006, with all other costs remaining constant. What will be the break-even point in dollar sales for 2006 if the company spends the additional $10,000?
  (e) If the company spends the additional $10,000 for advertising in 2006, what is the sales level in dollars will be required to equal the 2005 operating income?

Solution

(a)

Expected sales	$500,000
Less: Variable cost (20,000 flashlights × $15)	300,000
Fixed costs	135,000
Projected operating income	$ 65,000

(b) $500,000 ÷ 20,000 = $25 selling price per flashlight

Selling price per flashlight	$25
Variable cost per flashlight	15
Contribution margin per unit	$10

(c) Fixed costs ÷ contribution margin per unit = break-even point in units
$135,000 ÷ $10 = 13,500 units

(d) Fixed costs ÷ contribution margin ratio = break-even point in dollars
$145,000 ÷ 40% = $362,500

Fixed costs (from 2005)	$135,000
Additional advertising expense	10,000
Fixed costs (2006)	$145,000

Contribution margin = sales − variable costs

Expected sales	$550,000
Variable costs (22,000 × $15)	330,000
Contribution margin	$220,000

Contribution margin ratio = contribution margin ÷ sales
40% = $220,000 ÷ $550,000

(e) Required sales = (fixed costs + target net income) ÷ contribution margin ratio
$525,000 = ($145,000 + $65,000) ÷ 40%

the navigator

Summary of Study Objectives

1. *Distinguish between variable and fixed costs.* Variable costs are costs that vary in total directly and proportionately with changes in the activity index. Fixed costs are costs that remain the same in total regardless of changes in the activity index.

2. *Explain the significance of the relevant range.* The relevant range is the range of activity in which a company expects to operate during a year. It is important in CVP analysis because the behaviour of costs is linear throughout the relevant range.

3. *Explain the concept of mixed costs.* Mixed costs increase in total but not proportionately with changes in the activity level. For CVP analysis, mixed costs must be classified into their fixed and variable elements. One method that management may use is the high-low method.

4. *List the five components of cost-volume-profit analysis.* The five components of CVP analysis are (a) volume or level of activity, (b) unit selling prices, (c) variable cost per unit, (d) total fixed costs, and (e) sales mix.

5. *Explain what the contribution margin is and how it can be expressed.* Contribution margin is the amount of revenue remaining after deducting variable costs. It is identified in a CVP income statement, which classifies costs as variable or fixed. It can be expressed as a per unit amount or as a ratio.

6. *Identify the three ways to determine the break-even point.* The break-even point can be (a) calculated with a mathematical equation, (b) calculated by using a contribution margin technique, and (c) derived from a CVP graph.

7. *State the formulas for determining the sales required to earn the target net income.* One formula is: required sales = variable costs + fixed costs + target net income. Another formula is: fixed costs + target net income ÷ contribution margin ratio = required sales.

8. *State the formulas for determining the sales required to earn the target net income after tax.* One formula is: required sales = variable costs + fixed costs + target net income before tax. Another formula is: (fixed costs + target net income before tax) ÷ contribution margin ratio = required sales.

9. *Define margin of safety, and state the formulas for calculating it.* Margin of safety is the difference between actual or expected sales and sales at the break-even point. The formulas for margin of safety are: actual (expected) sales − break-even sales = margin of safety in dollars; margin of safety in dollars ÷ actual (expected) sales = margin of safety ratio.

10. *Understand how operating leverage affects profitability.* Operating leverage is how much a company's net income reacts to a change in sales. Operating leverage is determined by a company's relative use of fixed versus variable costs. Companies with high fixed costs relative to variable costs have a high operating leverage. A company with a high operating leverage will experience a sharp increase (decrease) in net income with an increase (decrease) in sales. The degree of operating leverage can be measured by dividing the contribution margin by net income.

11. *Explain the term "sales mix" and its effect on break-even sales (Appendix 5A).* The sales mix is the relative proportion in which each product is sold when a company sells more than one product. For a multi-product company, break-even sales in units is determined by using the weighted-average unit contribution margin of all the products. If the company sells many different products, calculating the break-even point using unit information is not practical. Instead, in a company with many products, break-even sales in dollars is calculated using the weighted-average contribution margin ratio.

▦ Decision Toolkit—A Summary

Decision Checkpoints	Info Needed for Decision	Tools to Use for Decision	How to Evaluate Results
What was the contribution toward fixed costs and income from each unit sold?	Selling price per unit and variable cost per unit	$\text{Contribution margin per unit} = \text{Unit selling price} - \text{Unit variable cost}$	Every unit sold will increase income by the contribution margin.
What was the increase in income as a result of an increase in sales?	Contribution margin per unit and unit selling price	$\text{Contribution margin ratio} = \text{Contribution margin per unit} \div \text{Unit selling price}$	Every dollar of sales will increase income by the contribution margin ratio.
At what amount of sales does a company cover its costs?	Unit selling price, unit variable cost, and total fixed costs	Break-even point analysis *In units:* $\text{Break-even point} = \dfrac{\text{Fixed costs}}{\text{Unit contribution margin}}$ *In dollars:* $\text{Break-even point} = \dfrac{\text{Fixed costs}}{\text{Contribution margin ratio}}$	Below the break-even point—the point at which total sales equal total costs—the company is unprofitable.
How can a company use CVP analysis to improve profitability?	Data on what the effect on volume and costs would be of a price change, a fixed-cost change, or a trade-off between fixed and variable costs	Measurement of income at new volume levels	If profitability increases under the proposed change, adopt the change.
How sensitive is the company's net income to changes in sales?	Contribution margin and net income	$\text{Degree of operating leverage} = \dfrac{\text{Contribution margin}}{\text{Net income}}$	Tells the change in net income that will occur with a change in sales. A high degree of operating leverage means that the company's net income is sensitive to changes in sales.
How many units of product A and product B do we need to sell to break even?	Fixed costs, weighted-average contribution margin, sales mix	$\text{Break-even point in units} = \dfrac{\text{Fixed costs}}{\text{Weighted-average unit contribution margin}}$	To determine the number of units of Product A and B that need to be sold, allocate the total units based on the sales mix.
How many dollars of sales are required from Division A versus Division B in order to break even?	Fixed costs, weighted-average contribution margin ratio, sales mix	$\text{Break-even point in dollars} = \dfrac{\text{Fixed costs}}{\text{Weighted-average contribution margin ratio}}$	To determine the sales dollars required from each division, allocate the total break-even sales using the sales mix.

the navigator

www.wiley.com/canada/managerial

Key Term Matching Activity

Glossary

Activity index   The activity that causes changes in the behaviour of costs. (p. 194)

Break-even point   The level of activity at which total revenues equal total costs. (p. 203)

Contribution margin (CM)   The amount of revenue remaining after deducting variable costs. (p. 201)

Contribution margin per unit   The amount of revenue remaining per unit after deducting variable costs;

calculated as the unit selling price minus the unit variable cost. (p. 201)

Contribution margin ratio   The percentage of each dollar of sales that is available to contribute to net income; calculated as the contribution margin per unit divided by the unit selling price. (p. 202)

Cost behaviour analysis   The study of how specific costs respond to changes in the level of business activity. (p. 194)

Cost structure The proportion of fixed costs versus variable costs that a company incurs. (p. 212)

Cost-volume-profit (CVP) analysis The study of the effects of changes in costs and volume on a company's profits. (p. 200)

Cost-volume-profit (CVP) graph A graph showing the relationship between costs, volume, and profits. (p. 205)

Cost-volume-profit (CVP) income statement A statement for internal use that classifies costs and expenses as fixed or variable, and reports contribution margin in the body of the statement. (p. 201)

Degree of operating leverage Provides the percentage effect on profits of a specific percentage increase in sales volume. Calculated by dividing the total contribution margin by net profit. (p. 213)

Fixed costs Costs that remain the same in total regardless of changes in the activity level. (p. 195)

High-low method A mathematical method that uses the total costs incurred at the high and low levels of activity. (p. 198)

Margin of safety The difference between actual or expected sales and sales at the break-even point. (p. 209)

Mixed costs Costs that contain both a variable and a fixed cost element and change in total but not proportionately with changes in the activity level. (p. 197)

Operating leverage Measures the effect that fixed costs have on operating profit as a result of a specific percentage change in the sales volume. (p. 212)

Relevant range The range of the activity index over which the company expects to operate during the year. (p. 197)

Sales mix The relative percentage in which each product is sold when a company sells more than one product. (p. 214)

Target net income The income objective for individual product lines. (p. 207)

Variable costs Costs that vary in total directly and proportionately with changes in the activity level. (p. 194)

the navigator

Demonstration Problem

Mabo Company makes calculators that sell for $20 each. For the coming year, management expects fixed costs to total $220,000 and variable costs to be $9 per unit.

Instructions

(a) Calculate the break-even point in units using the mathematical equation.
(b) Calculate the break-even point in dollars using the contribution margin ratio.
(c) Calculate the margin of safety percentage, assuming actual sales are $500,000.
(d) Calculate the sales required in dollars to earn a net income of $165,000.

www.wiley.com/canada/managerial

Animated Demonstration Problem

Solution to Demonstration Problem

(a) Sales = variable costs + fixed costs + net income
$20Q = $9Q + $220,000 + $0
$11Q = $220,000
Q = 20,000 units

(b) Contribution margin per unit = unit selling price − unit variable costs
$11 = $20 − $9
Contribution margin ratio = contribution margin per unit ÷ unit selling price
55% = $11 ÷ $20
Break-even point in dollars = fixed cost ÷ contribution margin ratio
= $220,000 ÷ 55%
= $400,000

(c) Margin of safety = $\dfrac{\text{actual sales} - \text{break-even sales}}{\text{actual sales}}$

$= \dfrac{\$500,000 - \$400,000}{\$500,000}$

$= 20\%$

(d) Required sales = variable costs + fixed costs + net income
$20Q = $9Q + $220,000 + $165,000
$11Q = $385,000
Q = 35,000 units
35,000 units × $20 = $700,000 required sales

Action Plan

• Know the formulas.

• Recognize that variable costs change with the sales volume; fixed costs do not.

• Avoid calculation errors.

• Prove your answers.

the navigator

Note: All questions, exercises, and problems below with an asterisk (*) relate to material in Appendix 5A.

Self-Study Questions

Additional Self-Study Questions

Answers are at the end of the chapter.

(SO 1)   1. Variable costs are costs that:
(a) vary in total directly and proportionately with changes in the activity level.
(b) remain the same per unit at every activity level.
(c) Neither of the above
(d) Both (a) and (b) above

(SO 2)   2. The relevant range is:
(a) the range of activity in which variable costs will be curvilinear.
(b) the range of activity in which fixed costs will be curvilinear.
(c) the range that the company expects to operate in during a year.
(d) usually from zero to 100% of operating capacity.

(SO 3)   3. Mixed costs consist of a:
(a) variable cost element and a fixed cost element.
(b) fixed cost element and a controllable cost element.
(c) relevant cost element and a controllable cost element.
(d) variable cost element and a relevant cost element.

(SO 3)   4. Kendra Corporation's total utility costs during the past year were $1,200 during its highest month and $600 during its lowest month. These costs corresponded to 10,000 units of production during the high month and 2,000 units during the low month. What are the fixed and variable components of its utility costs using the high-low method?
(a) $0.075 variable and $450 fixed
(b) $0.120 variable and $0 fixed
(c) $0.300 variable and $0 fixed
(d) $0.060 variable and $600 fixed

(SO 10)   5. Which of the following is not involved in CVP analysis?
(a) Sales mix
(b) Unit selling prices
(c) Fixed costs per unit
(d) Volume or level of activity

6. Contribution margin: (SO 10)
(a) is revenue remaining after deducting variable costs.
(b) may be expressed as contribution margin per unit.
(c) is the selling price less cost of goods sold.
(d) Both (a) and (b) above

7. Cournot Company sells 100,000 wrenches for $12   (SO 11)
a unit. Fixed costs are $300,000, and net income is $200,000. What should be reported as variable expenses in the CVP income statement?
(a) $700,000   (c) $500,000
(b) $900,000   (d) $1,000,000

8. Marshall Company had actual sales of $600,000   (SO 5)
when break-even sales were $420,000. What is the margin of safety ratio?
(a) 25%   (c) 33⅓%
(b) 30%   (d) 45%

9. The degree of operating leverage: (SO 6)
(a) can be calculated by dividing total contribution margin by net income.
(b) provides a measure of the company's earnings volatility.
(c) affects a company's break-even point.
(d) All of the above

*10. Sales mix is: (SO 5)
(a) important to sales managers but not to accountants.
(b) easier to analyze on traditional income statements.
(c) a measure of the relative percentage of a company's variable costs to its fixed costs.
(d) a measure of the relative percentage in which a company's products are sold.

Questions

1. (a) What is cost behaviour analysis?
   (b) Why is cost behaviour analysis important to management?

2. (a) Jenny Beason asks for your help in understanding the term "activity index." Explain the meaning and importance of this term for Jenny.
   (b) State the two ways that variable costs may be defined.

3. Contrast the effects of changes in the activity level on total fixed costs and on unit fixed costs.

4. E.L. Dion claims that the relevant range concept is important only for variable costs.
   (a) Explain the relevant range concept.
   (b) Do you agree with E.L.'s claim? Explain.

5. "The relevant range is indispensable in cost behaviour analysis." Is this true? Why or why not?

6. Shawn Grace is confused. He does not understand why rent on his apartment is a fixed cost and rent on a Hertz rental truck is a mixed cost. Explain the difference to Shawn.

7. How should mixed costs be classified in CVP analysis? What approach is used to make the appropriate classification?

8. At the high and low levels of activity during the month, direct labour hours are 90,000 and 40,000, respectively. The related costs are $185,000 and $100,000. What are the fixed and variable costs at any level of activity?

9. "Cost-volume-profit (CVP) analysis is based entirely on unit costs." Do you agree? Explain.

10. Andrea Dubois defines contribution margin as the amount of profit available to cover operating expenses. Is there any truth in this definition? Discuss.

11. The traditional income statement for Rice Company shows sales of $900,000, cost of goods sold of $500,000, and operating expenses of $200,000. Assuming all costs and expenses are 70% variable and 30% fixed, prepare a CVP income statement through to the contribution margin.

12. Darosa Company's Speedo pocket calculator sells for $40. Variable costs per unit are estimated to be $25. What are the contribution margin per unit and the contribution margin ratio?

13. "Break-even analysis is of limited use to management because a company cannot survive by just breaking even." Do you agree? Explain.

14. Total fixed costs are $22,000 for Forrest Inc. It has a contribution margin per unit of $15, and a contribution margin ratio of 25%. Calculate the break-even sales in dollars.

15. Cynthia Andrade asks for your help in constructing a CVP graph. Explain to Cynthia
    (a) how the break-even point is plotted, and
    (b) how the level of activity and dollar sales at the break-even point are determined.

16. (a) Define the term "margin of safety."
    (b) If Harold Company expects to sell 1,600 units of its product at $12 per unit, and break-even sales for the product are $13,440, what is the margin of safety ratio?

17. Singh Company's break-even sales are $600,000. Assuming fixed costs are $240,000, what sales volume is needed to achieve a target net income of $60,000?

18. What is meant by "cost structure?" Explain how a company's cost structure affects its break-even point.

19. What is operating leverage? How does a company increase its operating leverage?

20. How does the replacement of manual labour by automated equipment affect a company's cost structure? What implications does this have for its operating leverage and break-even point?

21. What is a measure of operating leverage, and how is it calculated?

22. Acorn Company has a degree of operating leverage of eight. Oak Company has a degree of operating leverage of four. Explain the significance of these measures.

*23. What is meant by the term "sales mix"? How does the sales mix affect the calculation of the break-even point?

*24. Radial Company sells two types of radial tires. The lower-priced model is guaranteed for only 40,000 kilometres; the higher-priced model is guaranteed for 100,000 kilometres. The unit contribution margin on the higher-priced tire is twice as high as that of the lower-priced tire. If the sales mix shifts so that the company begins to sell more units of the lower-priced tire, explain how the company's break-even point will change.

*25. What approach should be used to calculate the break-even point of a company that has many products?

Brief Exercises

Classify costs as variable, fixed, or mixed.
(SO 1, 3)

BE5–1   Monthly production costs in Ogden Company for two levels of production are as follows:

Cost	2,000 Units	4,000 Units
Indirect labour	$10,000	$20,000
Supervisory salaries	5,000	5,000
Maintenance	2,500	4,000

Indicate which costs are variable, fixed, and mixed, and give the reason for each answer.

Diagram behaviour of costs within relevant range.
(SO 1, 2)

BE5–2   For Leahy Company, the relevant range of production is 40 to 80% of capacity. At 40% of capacity, a specific variable cost is $2,000 and a specific fixed cost is $5,000. Diagram the behaviour of each cost within the relevant range, assuming their behaviour is linear.

Diagram behaviour of mixed cost.
(SO 3)

BE5–3   For Stork Company, a specific mixed cost is $40,000 plus $6 per direct labour hour. Diagram the behaviour of the cost using increments of 1,000 hours up to 5,000 hours on the horizontal axis and increments of $10,000 up to $70,000 on the vertical axis.

Determine variable and fixed cost elements using high-low method.
(SO 3)

BE5–4   Nesterenko Company accumulates the following data concerning a mixed cost, using kilometres as the activity level:

	Kilometres Driven	Total Cost		Kilometres Driven	Total Cost
January	8,000	$14,100	March	8,500	$15,000
February	7,500	13,500	April	8,200	14,400

Calculate the variable and fixed cost elements using the high-low method.

Determine variable and fixed cost elements using high-low method.
(SO 3)

BE5–5   Westerville Corp. has collected the following data concerning its maintenance costs for the past six months:

	Units Produced	Total Cost
July	18,000	$32,000
August	32,000	48,000
September	36,000	55,000
October	22,000	38,000
November	40,000	65,000
December	38,000	62,000

Calculate the variable and fixed cost elements using the high-low method.

Determine missing amounts for contribution margin.
(SO 5)

BE5–6   Determine the missing amounts:

	Unit Selling Price	Unit Variable Costs	Contribution Margin per Unit	Contribution Margin Ratio
1.	$260	$160	(a)	(b)
2.	500	(c)	$140	(d)
3.	(e)	(f)	360	30%

Prepare CVP income statement.
(SO 5)

BE5–7   Fontillas Manufacturing Inc. has sales of $1.8 million for the first quarter of 2005. In making the sales, the company incurred the following costs and expenses:

	Variable	Fixed
Cost of goods sold	$750,000	$540,000
Selling expenses	95,000	60,000
Administrative expenses	79,000	70,000

Prepare a CVP income statement for the quarter ended March 31, 2005.

Calculate break-even point.
(SO 6)

BE5–8   Panciuk Company has a unit selling price of $400, variable costs per unit of $250, and fixed costs of $150,000. Calculate the break-even point in units using (a) the mathematical equation and (b) the contribution margin per unit.

Calculate break-even point.
(SO 6)

BE5–9   Shantz Corp. had total variable costs of $170,000, total fixed costs of $120,000, and total revenues of $250,000. Calculate the required sales in dollars to break even.

BE5–10 For Biswell Company, variable costs are 75% of sales, and fixed costs are $180,000. Calculate the required sales in dollars that are needed to achieve management's target net income of $70,000. (Use the contribution margin approach.)

BE5–11 For Korb Company, actual sales are $1.2 million and break-even sales are $840,000. Calculate (a) the margin of safety in dollars and (b) the margin of safety ratio.

BE5–12 Vu Corporation has fixed costs of $480,000. It has a unit selling price of $6, unit variable cost of $4.50, and a target net income of $1.5 million. Calculate the required sales in units to achieve its target net income.

BE5–13 The degrees of operating leverage for Delta Corp. and Epsilon Co. are 1.4 and 5.6, respectively. Both have net incomes of $50,000. Determine their respective contribution margins.

BE5–14 Sanjay's Shingle Corporation is considering the purchase of a new automated shingle-cutting machine. The new machine will reduce variable labour costs but will increase amortization expense. The contribution margin is expected to increase from $160,000 to $240,000. Net income is expected to be the same at $40,000. Calculate the degree of operating leverage before and after the purchase of the new equipment. Interpret your results.

BE5–15 Presented below are the CVP income statements for Finch Company and Sparrow Company. They are in the same industry, with the same net incomes, but different cost structures.

	Finch Co.	Sparrow Co.
Sales	$150,000	$150,000
Variable costs	60,000	15,000
Contribution margin	90,000	135,000
Fixed costs	50,000	95,000
Net income	$ 40,000	$ 40,000

Calculate the break-even point in dollars for each company and comment on your findings.

BE5–16 Family Furniture Co. has two divisions: Bedroom Division and Dining Room Division. The results of operations for the most recent quarter are:

	Bedroom Division	Dining Room Division
Sales	$500,000	$750,000
Variable costs	250,000	450,000
Contribution margin	$250,000	$300,000

Determine the company's weighted-average contribution margin ratio.

*BE5–17 Russell Corporation sells three different models of mosquito "zapper." Model A12 sells for $50 and has variable costs of $40. Model B22 sells for $100 and has variable costs of $70. Model C124 sells for $400 and has variable costs of $300. The sales mix of the three models is as follows: A12, 60%; B22, 25%; and C124, 15%. What is the weighted-average unit contribution margin?

*BE5–18 Information for Russell Corporation is given in BE5-14. If the company has fixed costs of $199,500, how many units of each model must the company sell in order to break even?

*BE5–19 Presto Candle Supply makes candles. The sales mix (as a percentage of total dollar sales) of its three product lines is birthday candles 30%, standard tapered candles 50%, and large scented candles 20%. The contribution margin ratio of each candle type is as follows:

Candle Type	Contribution Margin Ratio
Birthday	10%
Standard tapered	20%
Large scented	45%

If the company's fixed costs are $440,000 per year, what is the dollar amount of each type of candle that must be sold to break even?

Exercises

Define and classify variable, fixed, and mixed costs.
(SO 1, 3)

E5–1   Vergados Company manufactures a single product. Annual production costs incurred in the manufacturing process are shown below for two levels of production:

	Costs Incurred			
Production in Units:	5,000		10,000	
Production Costs	Total Cost	Cost/Unit	Total Cost	Cost/Unit
Direct materials	$8,250	$1.65	$16,500	$1.65
Direct labour	9,400	1.88	18,800	1.88
Utilities	1,400	0.28	2,300	0.23
Rent	4,000	0.80	4,000	0.40
Maintenance	800	0.16	1,200	0.12
Supervisory salaries	1,000	0.20	1,000	0.10

Instructions

(a) Define these terms: variable costs, fixed costs, and mixed costs.
(b) Classify each cost above as either variable, fixed, or mixed.

Determine fixed and variable costs using high-low method, and use cost equation.
(SO 1, 3)

E5–2   The owner/operator of Medicine Hat Taxi Company is interested in determining the cost equation for his one-vehicle taxi service, based on the number of kilometres driven. To that end, he has collected the following volume and cost data:

Month	Total Operating Costs	Kilometres Driven
July	$16,000	13,000
August	17,800	14,250
September	12,400	9,750
October	15,100	12,500
November	13,250	10,500
December	11,500	9,000

Instructions

(a) Determine the company's operating cost equation, using the high-low method to calculate the variable and fixed cost components.
(b) The owner feels that the maximum level of operating costs that the company can sustain, because of cash flow concerns, is $14,500. Determine the number of kilometres that corresponds to that level of costs.

Determine fixed and variable costs using high-low method, and prepare graph.
(SO 1, 3)

E5–3   The controller of Gutierrez Industries has collected the following monthly expense data for use in analyzing the cost behaviour of maintenance costs:

Month	Total Maintenance Costs	Total Machine Hours
January	$2,800	3,000
February	3,000	4,000
March	3,600	6,000
April	4,500	7,900
May	3,200	5,000
June	5,000	8,000

Instructions

(a) Determine the fixed and variable cost components using the high-low method.
(b) Prepare a graph showing the behaviour of the maintenance costs, and identify the fixed and variable cost elements. Use 2,000 unit increments and $1,000 cost increments.

Calculate break-even point and margin of safety.
(SO 5, 6, 9)

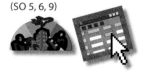

E5–4   The Richibouctou Inn is trying to determine its break-even point. The inn has 50 rooms that are rented at $50 a night. Operating costs are as follows:

Salaries	$8,500 per month	Maintenance	$500 per month
Utilities	2,000 per month	Maid service	5 per room
Amortization	1,000 per month	Other costs	33 per room

Instructions

(a) Determine the inn's break-even point in (1) the number of rented rooms per month and (2) dollars.

(b) If the inn plans on renting an average of 50 rooms per day (assuming a 30-day month), what is (1) the monthly margin of safety in dollars and (2) the margin of safety ratio?

E5–5 In 2005, Demuth Company had a break-even point of $320,000 based on a selling price of $8 per unit and fixed costs of $140,000. In 2006, the selling price and the variable cost per unit did not change, but the break-even point increased to $450,000.

Calculate variable cost per unit, contribution margin ratio, and increase in fixed costs.
(SO 1, 5)

Instructions

(a) Calculate the variable cost per unit and the contribution margin ratio for 2005.

(b) Calculate the increase in fixed costs for 2006.

E5–6 In the month of June, Kwami's Beauty Salon gave 3,500 haircuts, shampoos, and permanents at an average price of $30. During the month, fixed costs were $16,800 and variable costs were 80% of sales.

Calculate contribution margin, break-even point, and margin of safety.
(SO 5, 6, 9)

Instructions

(a) Determine the contribution margin in dollars, per unit, and as a ratio.

(b) Using the contribution margin technique, calculate the break-even point in dollars and in units.

(c) Calculate the margin of safety in dollars and as a ratio.

E5–7 Johansen Company had $150,000 of net income in 2005 when the selling price per unit was $150, the variable costs per unit were $100, and the fixed costs were $750,000. Management expects per unit data and total fixed costs to remain the same in 2006. The president of Johansen Company is under pressure from shareholders to increase net income by $90,000 in 2006.

Calculate various components to derive target net income under different assumptions.
(SO 6, 7)

Instructions

(a) Calculate the number of units sold in 2005.

(b) Calculate the number of units that would have to be sold in 2006 to reach the shareholders' desired profit level.

(c) Assume that Johansen Company sells the same number of units in 2006 as it did in 2005. What would the selling price have to be in order to reach the shareholders' desired profit level?

E5–8 Ger Company reports the following operating results for the month of August: sales $300,000 (units 5,000); variable costs $210,000; and fixed costs $70,000. Management is considering the following independent courses of action to increase net income:

Calculate net income under different alternatives.
(SO 7)

1. Increase selling price by 10% with no change in total variable costs.
2. Reduce variable costs to 58% of sales.
3. Reduce fixed costs by $20,000.

Instructions

Calculate the net income to be earned under each alternative. Which course of action will produce the highest net income?

E5–9 Peter David, owner of Regional Airways, Inc., a small two-plane passenger airline, has asked you to help him with some basic analysis of his operations. Both planes seat 10 passengers, and they fly commuters from Regional's base airport to the major city in the region, Bridgeland. Each month, 40 round-trip flights are made. A recent month's activity in the form of a cost-volume-profit income statement follows:

Calculate break-even point and prepare CVP income statement.
(SO 5, 6, 7)

Fare revenues (300 fares)		$45,000
Variable expenses		
Fuel	$14,000	
Snacks and drinks	800	
Landing fees	2,000	
Supplies and forms	1,200	18,000
Contribution margin		27,000
Fixed expenses		
Amortization	3,000	
Salaries	15,000	
Advertising	500	
Airport hangar fees	1,750	20,250
Net income		$ 6,750

Instructions

(a) Calculate the break-even point in (1) dollars and (2) the number of fares.

(b) Without calculations, determine the contribution margin at the break-even point.

(c) If fares were decreased by 10%, an additional 100 fares could be generated. However, variable costs would increase by 35%. Should the fare decrease be adopted? Support your answer with a CVP income statement.

Prepare CVP graph, and calculate break-even point and margin of safety.
(SO 6, 9)

E5–10   Embleton Company estimates that variable costs will be 40% of sales, and fixed costs will total $900,000. The selling price of the product is $5.

Instructions

(a) Prepare a CVP graph, assuming maximum sales of $4 million. (*Note:* Use $500,000 increments for sales and costs, and 100,000 increments for units.)

(b) Calculate the break-even point in (1) units and (2) dollars.

(c) Assuming actual sales are $2 million, calculate the margin of safety in (1) dollars and (2) as a ratio.

Prepare CVP income statement before and after changes in business environment.
(SO 5)

E5–11   Volmar Company had sales in 2005 of $1.5 million on 60,000 units. Variable costs totalled $576,000, and fixed costs totalled $400,000.

A new raw material is available that will decrease the variable costs per unit by 25% (or $2.40). However, to process the new raw material, fixed operating costs will increase by $50,000. Management feels that one-half of the decline in the variable costs per unit should be passed on to customers in the form of a sales price reduction. The marketing department expects that this sales price reduction will result in a 5% increase in the number of units sold.

Instructions

Prepare a CVP income statement for 2005, assuming the changes are made as described.

Calculate degree of operating leverage and impact on net income of alternative cost structures.
(SO 10)

E5–12   An investment banker is analyzing two companies that specialize in the production and sale of candied apples. Old-Fashion Apples uses a labour-intensive approach, and Mech-Apple uses a mechanized system. Variable costing income statements for the two companies are shown below:

	Old-Fashion Apples	Mech-Apple
Sales	$400,000	$400,000
Variable costs	320,000	160,000
Contribution margin	80,000	240,000
Fixed costs	20,000	180,000
Net income	$ 60,000	$ 60,000

The investment banker wants to acquire one of these companies. However, she is concerned about the impact that each company's cost structure might have on its profitability.

Instructions

(a) Determine which company's cost structure makes it more sensitive to changes in its sales volume. Present your answer in terms of the contribution margin ratio.

(b) Calculate each company's degree of operating leverage.

(c) Determine the effect on each company's net income (1) if sales decrease by 10% and (2) if sales increase by 5%. Do not prepare income statements.

(d) Which company should the investment banker acquire? Explain.

*E5-13   Grass King manufactures lawn mowers, weed-trimmers, and chainsaws. Its sales mix and contribution margin per unit are as follows:

Calculate break-even point in units for company with more than one product. (SO 11)

	Sales Mix	Contribution Margin per Unit
Lawn mowers	30%	$30
Weed-trimmers	50%	$20
Chainsaws	20%	$40

Grass King has fixed costs of $4.86 million.

Instructions

Calculate the number of units of each product that Grass King must sell in order to break even under this product mix.

*E5-14   Rapid Auto has over 200 auto-maintenance service outlets nationwide. It provides two main lines of service: oil changes and brake repair. Oil change–related services represent 65% of its sales and provide a contribution margin ratio of 20%. Brake repair represents 35% of its sales and provides a 60% contribution margin ratio. The company's fixed costs are $17 million (that is, $85,000 per service outlet).

Calculate product line, break-even point, and target net income in dollars for company with more than one product. (SO 11)

Instructions

(a) Calculate the dollar amount of each type of service that the company must provide in order to break even.

(b) The company has a desired net income of $63,750 per service outlet. What is the dollar amount of each type of service that must be provided by each service outlet to meet the company's target net income per outlet?

*E5-15   Blazer Delivery is a rapidly growing delivery service. Last year, 80% of its revenue came from the delivery of mailing "pouches" and small, standardized delivery boxes (which provides a 10% contribution margin). The other 20% of its revenue came from delivering non-standardized boxes (which provides a 60% contribution margin). With the rapid growth of Internet retail sales, Blazer believes that there are great opportunities for growth in the delivery of non-standardized boxes. The company has fixed costs of $12 million.

Calculate product line break-even point in dollars for company with more than one product. (SO 11)

Instructions

(a) What is the company's break-even point in total sales dollars? At the break-even point, how much of the company's sales are provided by each type of service?

(b) The company's management would like to keep its fixed costs constant, but shift its sales mix so that 60% of its revenue comes from the delivery of non-standardized boxes and the remainder from pouches and small boxes. If this were to occur, what would be the company's break-even sales, and what amount of sales would be provided by each service type?

*E5-16   Veejay Golf Accessories sells golf shoes, gloves, and a laser-guided range-finder that measures distance. Shown below are unit cost and sales data:

Calculate break-even point in units for company with multiple products. (SO 11)

	Pairs of Shoes	Pairs of Gloves	Range-Finder
Unit sales price	$100	$30	$250
Unit variable costs	60	10	200
Unit contribution margin	$ 40	$20	$ 50
Sales mix	40%	50%	10%

Fixed costs are $620,000.

Instructions

(a) Calculate the break-even point in units for the company.

(b) Determine the number of units to be sold at the break-even point for each product line.

(c) Verify that the mix of sales units determined in (b) will generate a zero net income.

Determine break-even point in dollars for two divisions.
(SO 11)

*E5–17   Mega Electronix sells television sets and DVD players. The business is divided into two divisions along product lines. A variable cost income statement for a recent quarter's activity is presented below:

	TV Division	DVD Division	Total
Sales	$600,000	$400,000	$1,000,000
Variable costs	450,000	240,000	690,000
Contribution margin	$150,000	$160,000	310,000
Fixed costs			124,000
Net income			$ 186,000

Instructions

(a) Determine the percentage of sales and contribution margin for each division.

(b) Calculate the company's weighted-average contribution margin ratio.

(c) Calculate the company's break-even point in dollars.

(d) Determine the sales level in dollars for each division at the break-even point.

Problems: Set A

Determine variable and fixed costs, calculate break-even point, prepare CVP graph, and determine net income.
(SO 1, 3, 5, 6)

P5–18A   The Peace Barber Shop employs four barbers. One barber, who also serves as the manager, is paid a salary of $1,800 per month. The other barbers are paid $1,300 per month. In addition, each barber is paid a commission of $4 per haircut. Other monthly costs are as follows: store rent $800 plus 60 cents per haircut; amortization on equipment $500; barber supplies 40 cents per haircut; utilities $300; and advertising $200. The price of a haircut is $11.

Instructions

(a) Determine the variable cost per haircut and the total monthly fixed costs.

(b) Calculate the break-even point in units and dollars.

(c) Prepare a CVP graph, assuming a maximum of 1,500 haircuts in a month. Use increments of 300 haircuts on the horizontal axis and $3,300 increments on the vertical axis.

(d) Determine the net income, assuming 1,500 haircuts are given in a month.

Determine contribution margin ratio, break-even point in dollars, and margin of safety.
(SO 5, 6, 7, 9)

P5–19A   Montreal Seating Co., a manufacturer of chairs, had the following data for 2005:

Sales	2,400 units
Sales price	$40 per unit
Variable costs	$14 per unit
Fixed costs	$19,500

Instructions

(a) What is the contribution margin ratio?

(b) What is the break-even point in dollars?

(c) What is the margin of safety in units and dollars?

(d) If the company wishes to increase its total dollar contribution margin by 40% in 2006, by how much will it need to increase its sales if all other factors remain constant?

(CGA-adapted)

Prepare CVP income statement; calculate break-even point, contribution margin ratio, margin of safety ratio, and sales for target net income.
(SO 5, 6, 7, 9)

P5–20A   Boisclair Company bottles and distributes LO-KAL, a fruit drink. The beverage is sold for $1.00 per 500-ml bottle to retailers, who charge customers $1.29 per bottle. Management estimates the following revenues and costs:

Net sales	$2,500,000	Selling expenses—variable	$ 90,000
Direct materials	360,000	Selling expenses—fixed	200,000
Direct labour	650,000	Administrative expenses—variable	30,000
Manufacturing overhead—variable	370,000	Administrative expenses—fixed	140,000
Manufacturing overhead— fixed	260,000		

Instructions

(a) Prepare a CVP income statement for 2005 based on management's estimates.
(b) Calculate the break-even point in (1) units and (2) dollars.
(c) Calculate the contribution margin ratio and the margin of safety ratio.
(d) Determine the sales required to earn a net income of $240,000.

P5–21A   Dias Manufacturing had a bad year in 2005. For the first time in its history, it operated at a loss. The company's income statement showed the following results from selling 80,000 units of product: net sales $1.6 million; total costs and expenses $1.74 million; and net loss $240,000. Costs and expenses consisted of the following:

Calculate break-even point under alternative courses of action.
(SO 5, 6)

	Total	Variable	Fixed
Cost of goods sold	$1,200,000	$780,000	$420,000
Selling expenses	420,000	75,000	345,000
Administrative expenses	120,000	45,000	75,000
	$1,740,000	$900,000	$840,000

Management is considering the following independent alternatives for 2006:

1. Increase the unit selling price by 25% with no change in costs and expenses.
2. Change the compensation of salespersons from fixed annual salaries totalling $200,000 to total salaries of $40,000 plus a 5% commission on net sales.
3. Purchase new high-tech factory machinery that will change the proportion between variable and fixed costs of goods sold to 50:50.

Instructions

(a) Calculate the break-even point in dollars for 2005.
(b) Calculate the break-even point in dollars under each of the alternative courses of action. Which course of action do you recommend? Explain.

P5–22A   The vice-president of marketing, Alice Chow, thinks that her firm can increase sales by 10,000 units for each $3 per unit reduction in its selling price. The company's current selling price is $90 per unit and variable expenses are $60 per unit. Fixed expenses are $810,000 per year. The current sales volume is 30,000 units.

Determine break-even point in dollars and units, and target income.
(SO 5, 6, 7)

Instructions

(a) What is the current yearly net income?
(b) What is the current break-even point in units and in dollar sales?
(c) Assuming that Chow is correct, what is the maximum profit that the firm could generate yearly? At how many units and at what selling price(s) per unit would this profit be generated? Assume that capacity is not a problem and total fixed expenses will be the same regardless of volume.
(d) What would be the break-even point(s) in units and in dollar sales using the selling price(s) you have determined?

(CGA-adapted)

P5–23A   Lois Baiser is the advertising manager for Value Shoe Store. She is currently working on a major promotional campaign. Her ideas include the installation of a new lighting system and increased display space that will add $27,000 in fixed costs to the $225,000 currently spent. In addition, Lois is proposing that a 6⅔% price decrease (from $30 to $28) will produce an increase in the sales volume from 17,000 to 20,000 units. Variable costs will remain at $10 per pair of shoes. Management is impressed with Lois's ideas but concerned about the effects that these changes will have on the break-even point and the margin of safety.

Calculate break-even point and margin of safety ratio, and prepare CVP income statement before and after changes in business environment.
(SO 5, 6, 7, 9)

Instructions

(a) Calculate the current break-even point in units, and compare it to the break-even point in units if Lois's ideas are used.
(b) Calculate the margin of safety ratio for current operations and after Lois's changes are introduced. (Round to nearest full percent.)
(c) Prepare a CVP income statement for current operations and after Lois's changes are introduced. Would you make the changes suggested?

Calculate break-even point
and margin of safety ratio,
and prepare CVP income
statement before and after
changes in business
environment.
(SO 5, 6, 7, 9)

P5–24A   Poole Corporation has collected the following information after its first year of sales. Net sales were $1.6 million on 100,000 units; selling expenses $240,000 (40% variable and 60% fixed); direct materials $511,000; direct labour $285,000; administrative expenses $280,000 (20% variable and 80% fixed); manufacturing overhead $360,000 (70% variable and 30% fixed). Top management has asked you to do a CVP analysis so that it can make plans for the coming year. It has projected that unit sales will increase by 10% next year.

Instructions

(a) Prepare a CVP income statement with the current-year numbers in one column and next year's projected numbers in the next column. (Assume that fixed costs will remain the same.)
(b) Calculate the break-even point in units and sales dollars.
(c) The company has a target net income of $310,000. What is the required sales in dollars for the company to meet its target?
(d) If the company meets its target net income number, by what percentage could its sales fall before it is operating at a loss? That is, what is its margin of safety ratio?
(e) The company is considering a purchase of equipment that would reduce its direct labour costs by $104,000 and would change its manufacturing overhead costs to 30% variable and 70% fixed (assume total cost is $360,000, as above). It is also considering switching to a pure commission basis for its sales staff. This would change selling expenses to 90% variable and 10% fixed (assume total cost is $240,000, as above). Prepare a new CVP income statement, then recalculate the break-even point in sales dollars. Comment on the effect that each of the proposed changes has on the break-even point.

Determine contribution
margin ratio, break-even
point, and margin of safety.
(SO 1, 5, 7, 9)

P5–25A   Kosinksi Manufacturing carries no inventories. Its product is manufactured only when a customer's order is received. It is then shipped immediately after it is made. For its fiscal year ended October 31, 2004, Kosinksi's break-even point was $1.35 million. On sales of $1.2 million, its full cost income statement showed a gross profit of $100,000, direct materials cost of $400,000, and direct labour costs of $500,000. The contribution margin was $100,000, and variable manufacturing overhead was $100,000.

Instructions

(a) Calculate the following:

  1. Variable selling and administrative expenses
  2. Fixed manufacturing overhead
  3. Fixed selling and administrative expenses

(b) Ignoring your answer to part (a), assume that fixed manufacturing overhead was $100,000 and the fixed selling and administrative expenses were $80,000. The marketing vice-president feels that if the company increased its advertising, sales could be increased by 20%.
(c) What is the maximum increased advertising cost the company can incur and still report the same income as before the advertising expenditure?

(CGA-adapted)

Determine contribution
margin, break-even point,
and target sales after taxes.
(SO 5, 6, 8)

P5–26A   Newton Cellular Ltd. manufactures and sells the TopLine Cell phone. For its 2005 business plan, Newton Cellular estimated the following:

Selling price	$600
Variable cost per cell phone	$300
Annual fixed costs	$150,000
Net (after-tax) income	$360,000
Tax rate	25%

The March financial statements reported that sales were not meeting expectations. For the first three months of the year, only 400 units had been sold at the established price. With variable costs staying as planned, it was clear that the 2005 after-tax profit projection would not be reached unless some action was taken. A management committee presented the following mutually exclusive alternatives to the president:

  1. Reduce the selling price by $60. The sales team forecasts that, with the significantly reduced selling price, 2,700 units can be sold during the remainder of the year. Total fixed and variable unit costs will stay as budgeted.
  2. Lower variable costs per unit by $20 through the use of less expensive direct materials and slightly modified manufacturing techniques. The selling price will also be reduced by $40, and sales of 2,500 units for the remainder of the year are forecast.

3. Cut fixed costs by $20,000 and lower the selling price by 5%. Variable costs per unit will be unchanged. Sales of 2,200 units are expected for the remainder of the year.

Instructions

(a) Under the current production policy, determine the number of units that the company must sell to break even and to achieve its desired net income.
(b) Determine which alternative the company should select to achieve its desired net income.

(CMA Canada-adapted)

P5–27A Olin Beauty Corporation manufactures cosmetic products that are sold through a network of sales agents. The agents are paid a commission of 18% of sales. The income statement for the year ending December 31, 2005, is as follows:

Determine contribution margin, break-even point, target sales, and degree of operating leverage.
(SO 5, 6, 7, 10)

OLIN BEAUTY CORPORATION
Income Statement
Year Ending December 31, 2005

Sales		$78,000,000
Cost of goods sold		
Variable	$35,100,000	
Fixed	8,610,000	43,710,000
Gross margin		34,290,000
Selling and marketing expenses		
Commissions	$14,040,000	
Fixed costs	10,260,000	24,300,000
Operating income		$ 9,990,000

The company is considering hiring its own sales staff to replace the network of agents. It will pay its salespeople a commission of 8% and incur fixed costs of $7.8 million.

Instructions

(a) Under the current policy of using a network of sales agents, calculate the Olin Beauty Corporation's break-even point in sales dollars for the year 2005.
(b) Calculate the company's break-even point in sales dollars for the year 2005 if it hires its own sales force to replace the network of agents.
(c) Calculate the degree of operating leverage at sales of $78 million if (1) Olin Beauty uses sales agents, and (2) Olin Beauty employs its own sales staff. Describe the advantages and disadvantages of each alternative.
(d) Calculate the estimated sales volume in sales dollars that would generate an identical net income for the year ending December 31, 2005, regardless of whether Olin Beauty Corporation employs its own sales staff and pays them a 10% commission or continues to use the independent network of agents.

(CMA Canada-adapted)

P5–28A Martin Footwear Co. produces high quality shoes. To prepare for next year's marketing campaign, the company's controller has prepared the following information for the current year, 2005:

Determine contribution margin, break-even point in dollars, and target income.
(SO 5, 6, 8)

Variable costs (per pair of shoes)	
Direct materials	$16.25
Direct manufacturing labour	8.75
Variable overhead (manufacturing, marketing, distribution, customer service, and administration)	25.00
Total variable costs	$50.00
Fixed costs	
Manufacturing	$2,500,000
Marketing, distribution, and customer service	250,000
Administrative	750,000
Total fixed costs	$3,750,000
Selling price per pair of shoes	$150
Expected revenues, 2005 (50,000 units)	$7,500,000
Income tax rate	40%

Instruction

(a) What is the projected net income before tax for 2005?
(b) What is the break-even point in units for 2005?
(c) The controller of the company has set the revenue target for 2006 at $8.25 million (or 55,000 pairs). He believes an additional marketing cost of $500,000 for advertising in 2006, with all other costs remaining constant, will be necessary to attain the revenue target. What will be the net income for 2006 if the additional $250,000 is spent and the revenue target is met?

(CMA Canada-adapted)

Calculate degree of operating leverage and evaluate its impact on financial results.
(SO 5, 7, 11)

*P5−29A   The following CVP income statements are available for Old Company and New Company:

	Old Company	New Company
Sales revenue	$400,000	$400,000
Variable costs	180,000	80,000
Contribution margin	220,000	320,000
Fixed costs	170,000	270,000
Net income	$ 50,000	$ 50,000

Instructions

(a) Calculate the break-even point in dollars and the margin of safety ratio for each company.
(b) Calculate the degree of operating leverage for each company and interpret your results.
(c) Assuming that sales revenue increases by 20%, prepare a variable cost income statement for each company.
(d) Assuming that sales revenue decreases by 20%, prepare a variable cost income statement for each company.
(e) ◁▭▭▭▷ Discuss how the cost structure of these two companies affects their operating leverage and profitability.

Determine break-even sales under alternative sales strategies and evaluate.
(SO 6, 9, 10)

*P5−30A   The Creekside Inn is a restaurant that specializes in southwestern style meals in a moderate price range. Terry Wilson, the manager of Creekside, has determined that during the last two years the sales mix and contribution margin ratio of its offerings have been as follows:

	Percent of Total Sales	Contribution Margin Ratio
Appetizers	10%	60%
Main entrees	60%	30%
Desserts	10%	50%
Beverages	20%	80%

Terry is considering a variety of options to try to improve the profitability of the restaurant. Her goal is to generate a target net income of $150,000. The company has fixed costs of $1.2 million per year.

Instructions

(a) Calculate the total restaurant sales and the sales of each product line that would be necessary in order to achieve the desired target net income.
(b) Terry believes the restaurant could greatly improve its profitability by reducing the complexity and selling price of its entrees to increase the number of clients that it serves, and by more heavily marketing its appetizers and beverages. She is proposing to drop the contribution margin ratio on the main entrees to 10% by dropping the average selling price. She envisions an expansion of the restaurant that would increase fixed costs by 50%. At the same time, she is proposing to change the sales mix to the following:

	Percent of Total Sales	Contribution Margin Ratio
Appetizers	20%	60%
Main entrees	30%	10%
Desserts	10%	50%
Beverages	40%	80%

Calculate the total restaurant sales and the sales of each product line that would be necessary in order to achieve the desired target net income if Terry's changes are implemented.

(c) Suppose that Terry drops the selling price on entrees and increases fixed costs as proposed in part (b), but customers are not swayed by the marketing efforts and the product mix remains what it was in part (a). Calculate the total restaurant sales and the sales of each product line that would be necessary in order to achieve the desired target net income. Comment on the potential risks and benefits of this strategy.

Problems: Set B

P5–31B Hung Van owns the College Barber Shop. He employs five barbers and pays each a base rate of $1,200 per month. One of the barbers serves as the manager and receives an extra $600 per month. In addition to the base rate, each barber also receives a commission of $3.50 per haircut. Hung currently charges $12 per haircut.

Determine variable and fixed costs, calculate break-even point, prepare CVP graph, and determine net income. (SO 1, 3, 5, 6)

Other costs are as follows.

Advertising	$200 per month
Rent	$1,000 per month
Barber supplies	$0.30 per haircut
Utilities	$175 per month plus $0.20 per haircut
Magazines	$25 per month

Instructions

(a) Determine the variable cost per haircut and the total monthly fixed costs.
(b) Calculate the break-even point in units and dollars.
(c) Prepare a CVP graph, assuming a maximum of 2,000 haircuts in a month. Use increments of 250 haircuts on the horizontal axis and $4,000 on the vertical axis.
(d) Determine the net income, assuming 1,500 haircuts are given in a month.

P5–32B Maritime Manufacturing Company produces and sells a high-quality handbag. During the year 2005, handbag sales were $500,000, the contribution margin was 20%, and the margin of safety was $200,000.

Determine variable and fixed costs and net income. (SO 1, 3, 5, 6, 7)

Instructions

(a) What are the break-even sales?
(b) What are the variable costs?
(c) What are the fixed costs?
(d) What are the profits at $500,000 of sales?

(CGA-adapted)

P5–33B Corbin Company bottles and distributes NO-KAL, a diet softdrink. The beverage is sold for 80 cents per 500-ml bottle to retailers, who charge customers 99 cents per bottle. Management estimates the following revenues and costs:

Prepare CVP income statement, and calculate break-even point, contribution margin ratio, margin of safety ratio, and sales for target net income. (SO 5, 6, 7, 9)

Net sales	$1,500,000	Selling expenses—variable	$80,000
Direct materials	400,000	Selling expenses—fixed	65,000
Direct labour	250,000	Administrative expenses—variable	20,000
Manufacturing overhead—variable	300,000	Administrative expenses—fixed	52,000
Manufacturing overhead—fixed	93,000		

Instructions

(a) Prepare a CVP income statement for 2005 based on management's estimates.
(b) Calculate the break-even point in (1) units and (2) dollars.
(c) Calculate the contribution margin ratio and the margin of safety ratio. (Round to full percents.)
(d) Determine the sales required to earn net income of $120,000.

P5–34B Delgado Manufacturing's sales slumped badly in 2005. For the first time in its history, it operated at a loss. The company's income statement showed the following results from selling 500,000 units of product: net sales $2.5 million; total costs and expenses $2.6 million; and net loss $100,000. Costs and expenses were as follows:

Calculate break-even point under alternative courses of action. (SO 5, 6)

	Total	Variable	Fixed
Cost of goods sold	$2,100,000	$1,440,000	$ 660,000
Selling expenses	300,000	72,000	228,000
Administrative expenses	200,000	48,000	152,000
	$2,600,000	$1,560,000	$1,040,000

Management is considering the following independent alternatives for 2006:

1. Increase the unit selling price by 20% with no change in costs and expenses.
2. Change the compensation of salespersons from fixed annual salaries totalling $210,000 to total salaries of $70,000 plus a 4% commission on net sales.
3. Purchase new automated equipment that will change the proportion of variable and fixed costs of goods sold to 60% variable and 40% fixed.

Instructions

(a) Calculate the break-even point in dollars for 2005.
(b) Calculate the break-even point in dollars under each of the alternative courses of action. (Round to nearest full percent.) Which course of action do you recommend?

Determine break-even point in dollars, and target income.
(SO 5, 6, 9)

P5–35B   John, now retired, owns the Campus Cutter Barber Shop. He employs five barbers and pays each a base salary of $1,500 per month. One of the barbers serves as the manager and receives an extra $500 per month. In addition to the base salary, each barber receives a commission of $6 per haircut. Each barber can do as many as 20 haircuts a day, but the average is 14 haircuts each day. The Campus Cutter Barber Shop is open an average of 24 days per month and charges $15 per haircut.

Other costs are incurred as follows:

Advertising	$500 per month
Rent	$1,000 per month
Supplies	$1.50 per haircut
Utilities	$300 per month plus $0.50 per haircut
Magazines	$50 per month
Cleaning supplies	$0.25 per haircut

Instructions

(a) Calculate the monthly break-even point for the following:
    1. Number of haircuts
    2. Total sales dollars
    3. As a percentage of maximum capacity
(b) In February, 1,500 haircuts were given. Calculate the net income for February.
(c) If John would like a $4,000 monthly profit, calculate the number of haircuts that must be given per month to achieve this profit.
(d) In March, 1,600 haircuts were given. Assuming demand is sufficient, would it be possible to give enough haircuts in April to bring the total for the two months combined to the target profit of $4,000 for each month?

(CGA-adapted)

Calculate break-even point and margin of safety ratio, and prepare CVP income statement before and after changes in business environment.
(SO 5, 6, 9)

P5–36B   Barb Tsai is the advertising manager for Thrifty Shoe Store. She is currently working on a major promotional campaign. Her ideas include the installation of a new lighting system and increased display space that will add $45,000 in fixed costs to the $280,000 currently spent. In addition, Barb is proposing that a 5% price decrease ($40 to $38) will produce a 20% increase in sales volume (30,000 to 36,000). Variable costs will remain at $25 per pair of shoes. Management is impressed with Barb's ideas but concerned about the effects that these changes will have on the break-even point and the margin of safety.

Instructions

(a) Calculate the current break-even point in units, and compare it to the break-even point in units if Barb's ideas are used.
(b) Calculate the margin of safety ratio for current operations and after Barb's changes are introduced. (Round to nearest full percent.)
(c) Prepare a CVP income statement for current operations and after Barb's changes are introduced. Would you make the changes suggested?

P5–37B Regina Enterprises, Ltd., has estimated the following costs for producing and selling 8,000 units of its product:

Direct materials	$32,000
Direct labour	40,000
Variable overhead	20,000
Fixed overhead	30,000
Variable selling and administrative expenses	24,000
Fixed selling and administrative expenses	33,000

Determine break-even point and target income.
(SO 5, 6, 7, 8)

Regina Enterprises's income tax rate is 30%.

Instructions

(a) Given that the selling price of one unit is $35, how many units would Regina Enterprises have to sell in order to break even?

(b) At a selling price of $37.50 per unit, how many units would Regina Enterprises have to sell in order to produce a profit of $22,000 before taxes?

(c) If 7,500 units were produced and sold, what price would Regina Enterprises have to charge in order to produce a profit of $28,000 after taxes?

(d) If 9,000 units were produced and sold, what price would Regina Enterprises have to charge in order to produce a before-tax profit equal to 30% of sales?

(CGA-adapted)

P5–38B Axelle Corporation has collected the following information after its first year of sales. Net sales were $2.4 million on 200,000 units; selling expenses $360,000 (30% variable and 70% fixed); direct materials $626,500; direct labour $507,500; administrative expenses $420,000 (40% variable and 60% fixed); manufacturing overhead $540,000 (50% variable and 50% fixed). Top management has asked you to do a CVP analysis so that it can make plans for the coming year. It has projected that unit sales will increase by 20% next year.

Calculate break-even point and margin of safety ratio, and prepare CVP income statement before and after changes in business environment.
(SO 5, 6, 7, 9)

Instructions

(a) Prepare a CVP income statement with the current-year numbers in one column and next year's projected numbers in the next column. (Assume that fixed costs will remain the same.)

(b) Calculate the break-even point in units and sales dollars.

(c) The company has a target net income of $620,000. What is the required sales in dollars for the company to meet its target?

(d) If the company meets its target net income number, by what percentage could its sales fall before it is operating at a loss? That is, what is its margin of safety ratio?

(e) The company is considering a purchase of equipment that would reduce its direct labour costs by $240,000 and would change its manufacturing overhead costs to 20% variable and 80% fixed (assume total cost is $540,000, as above). It is also considering switching to a pure commission basis for its sales staff. This would change selling expenses to 75% variable and 25% fixed (assume total cost is $360,000, as above). Prepare a new CVP income statement, then recalculate the break-even point in sales dollars. Comment on the effect each of these changes has on the break-even point.

P5–39B The company you work for as a managerial accountant uses independent agents to sell its products. These agents are currently being paid a commission of 15% of the sales price but are asking for an increase to 20% of sales made during the coming year. You had already prepared the following pro forma income statement for the company based on the 15% commission:

Determine contribution margin ratio, break-even point in dollars, and target sales.
(SO 5, 6, 7)

Pro Forma Income Statement
Year Ending April 30, 2005

Sales		$1,000,000
Cost of goods sold (all variable)		600,000
Gross profit		400,000
Selling and administrative		
Variable (commission only)	$150,000	
Fixed	10,000	160,000
Income before taxes		240,000
Income tax expense (25%)		60,000
Net income		$ 180,000

Management wants to examine the possibility of employing the company's own salespeople. The company would need a sales manager at an annual salary of $60,000 and three sales people at an annual salary of $30,000 each plus a commission of 5% of sales. All other fixed costs as well as the variable cost percentages would remain the same as in the above pro forma income statement.

Instructions

(a) Based on the pro forma income statement you have already prepared, what is the break-even point in sales dollars for the company for the year ending April 30, 2005?

(b) If the company uses its own salespeople, what would be the break-even point in sales dollars for the year ending April 30, 2005?

(c) What would be the volume of sales dollars required for the year ending April 30, 2005, to have the same net income as projected in the pro forma income statement if the company continues to use the independent sales agents and agrees to their demand for a 20% sales commission?

(d) Calculate the estimated sales volume in sales dollars that would generate an identical net income for the year ending April 30, 2005, regardless of whether the company employs its own salespeople or continues to use the independent sales agents and pays them a 20% commission.

(CGA-adapted)

Determine contribution margin, break-even point in dollars, and sales.
(SO 5, 6, 7)

P5–40B High Quality Toy's projected operating income for 2005 is $500,000, based on a sales volume of 87,500 units. High Quality sells The Toy for $32 per unit. Variable costs consist of the $15 purchase price and a $1 shipping and handling cost. High Quality's annual fixed costs are $900,000.

Instructions

(a) Calculate the company's break-even point in units.

(b) Calculate the company's operating income in 2005 if there is a 10% increase in projected unit sales.

(c) For 2006, management expects that the unit purchase price of The Toy will increase by 30%. Calculate the sales revenue the company must generate in 2006 to maintain the current year's operating income if the selling price remains unchanged.

(CMA Canada-adapted)

Calculate degree of operating leverage and evaluate its impact on financial results.
(SO 10)

P5–41B The following CVP income statements are available for Retro Company and Modern Company:

	Retro Company	Modern Company
Sales revenue	$500,000	$500,000
Variable costs	300,000	100,000
Contribution margin	200,000	400,000
Fixed costs	140,000	340,000
Net income	$ 60,000	$ 60,000

Instructions

(a) Calculate the break-even point in dollars and the margin of safety ratio for each company.

(b) Calculate the degree of operating leverage for each company and interpret your results.

(c) Assuming that sales revenue increases by 25%, prepare a variable cost income statement for each company.

(d) Assuming that sales revenue decreases by 25%, prepare a variable cost income statement for each company.

(e) ◖▭▭▭▭▷ Discuss how the cost structure of these two companies affects their operating leverage and profitability.

*P5–42B   The Bricktown Pub is a restaurant that specializes in classic East Coast fare in a moderate price range. Debbie MacNeil, the manager of Bricktown, has determined that during the last two years the sales mix and contribution margin of its offerings are as follows:

Determine break-even sales under alternative sales strategies and evaluate. (SO 5, 6, 9, 11)

	Percent of Total Sales	Contribution Margin Ratio
Appetizers	10%	50%
Main entrees	55%	30%
Desserts	10%	60%
Beverages	25%	75%

Debbie is considering a variety of options to try to improve the profitability of the restaurant. Her goal is to generate a target net income of $155,000. The company has fixed costs of $400,000 per year.

Instructions

(a) Calculate the total restaurant sales and the sales of each product line that would be necessary in order to achieve the desired target net income.

(b) Debbie believes the restaurant could greatly improve its profitability by reducing the complexity and selling price of its entrees to increase the number of clients that it serves, and by then more heavily marketing its appetizers and beverages. She is proposing to reduce the contribution margin on the main entrees to 15% by dropping the average selling price. She envisions an expansion of the restaurant that would increase fixed costs by 50%. At the same time, she is proposing to change the sales mix to the following:

	Percent of Total Sales	Contribution Margin Ratio
Appetizers	15%	50%
Main entrees	30%	15%
Desserts	15%	60%
Beverages	40%	75%

Calculate the total restaurant sales, and the sales of each product line that would be necessary in order to achieve the desired target net income.

(c) Suppose that Debbie drops the selling price on entrees, and increases fixed costs as proposed in part (b), but customers are not swayed by her marketing efforts, and the product mix remains what it was in part (a). Calculate the total restaurant sales and the sales of each product line that would be necessary to achieve the desired target net income. Comment on the potential risks and benefits of this strategy.

Cases

Additional Cases

C5–43   Clay Company has decided to introduce a new product. The new product can be manufactured by either a capital-intensive method or a labour-intensive method. The manufacturing method will not affect the quality of the product. The estimated manufacturing costs under the two methods are as follows:

	Capital-Intensive	Labour-Intensive
Direct materials	$5 per unit	$5.50 per unit
Direct labour	$6 per unit	$7.20 per unit
Variable overhead	$3 per unit	$4.80 per unit
Fixed manufacturing costs	$2,440,000	$1,390,000

Clay's market research department has recommended an introductory unit sales price of $30. The incremental selling expenses are estimated to be $500,000 annually plus $2 for each unit sold, regardless of the manufacturing method.

Instructions

With the class divided into groups, answer the following:

(a) Calculate the estimated break-even point in annual unit sales of the new product if Clay Company uses the (1) capital-intensive manufacturing method, and (2) labour-intensive manufacturing method.

(b) Determine the annual unit sales volume at which it would not make any difference if Clay Company used one method or the other.

(c) For each method, explain the circumstance under which Clay should use it.

(CMA-adapted)

C5–44   Production cost and price data for Kempinski Company are as follows:

Maximum capacity per year	200,000 units
Variable manufacturing costs	$12/unit
Fixed factory overhead costs	$600,000/year
Variable selling and administrative costs	$5/unit
Fixed selling and administrative costs	$300,000/year
Current sales price	$23/unit

The company's sales for the year just ended totalled 185,000 units. However, a strike at a major supplier has caused a shortage in raw materials, and as a result, the current year's sales will reach only 160,000 units. Top management is planning to reduce fixed costs this year by $59,000 compared to last year.

Management is also thinking of either increasing the selling price or reducing the variable costs, or both, in order to earn a target net income that will be the same dollar amount as last year's. The company has already sold 30,000 units this year at $23 per unit, with the variable costs remaining unchanged from last year.

Instructions

(a) Calculate the contribution margin per unit that is required on the remaining 130,000 units in order to reach the target net income.

(b) The president of the company is considering a significant change in the manufacturing process for next year. This change would increase the capacity to 225,000 units. The change would increase fixed factory overhead to $2.2 million, while reducing the variable manufacturing cost per unit to $3.35. All other costs and revenues would remain unchanged.

(c) Draft a brief memo to the president explaining the potential benefits and risks of a move to this cost structure. Support your explanation with an analysis of the numbers. (*Hint:* Use the previous year's sales and costs as a point of reference to compare the effects on net income of a 19% increase or a 20% decrease in sales volume under the current and proposed cost structures.)

(CGA-adapted)

C5–45   The condensed income statement for the Phan and Nguyen partnership for 2005 is as follows:

PHAN AND NGUYEN LLP
Income Statement
Year Ended December 31, 2005

Sales (200,000 units)		$1,200,000
Cost of goods sold		800,000
Gross profit		400,000
Operating expenses		
Selling	$320,000	
Administrative	160,000	480,000
Net loss		$ (80,000)

A cost behaviour analysis indicates that 75% of the cost of goods sold is variable, 50% of the selling expenses are variable, and 25% of the administrative expenses are variable.

Instructions

(Round to nearest unit, dollar, and percentage, where necessary. Use the CVP income statement format in calculating profits.)

(a) Calculate the break-even point in total sales dollars and in units for 2002.

(b) Phan has proposed a plan to get the partnership "out of the red" and improve its profitability. She feels that the quality of the product could be substantially improved by spending $0.55 more per unit on better raw materials. The selling price per unit could be increased to only $6.50 because of competitive pressures. Phan estimates that sales volume will increase by 30%. What effect would Phan's plan have on the profits and the break-even point in dollars of the partnership?

(c) Nguyen was a marketing major in college. He believes that the sales volume can be increased only by intensive advertising and promotional campaigns. He therefore proposed the following plan as an alternative to Phan's: (1) increase variable selling expenses to $0.85 per unit, (2) lower the selling price per unit by $0.20, and (3) increase fixed selling expenses by $20,000. Nguyen quoted an old marketing research report that said that sales volume would increase by 50% if these changes were made. What effect would Nguyen's plan have on the profits and the break-even point in dollars of the partnership?

(d) Which plan should be accepted? Explain your answer.

C5–46   All-Day Candy Company is a wholesale distributor of candy. The company services grocery, convenience, and drug stores in a large metropolitan area.

All-Day Candy Company has achieved small but steady growth in sales over the past few years, but prices have also been increasing. The company is formulating its plans for the coming fiscal year. The following data were used to project the current year's after-tax net income of $110,400:

Average selling price	$8.00 per box
Average variable costs	
Cost of candy	$4.00 per box
Selling expenses	0.80 per box
Total	$4.80 per box
Annual fixed costs	
Selling	$320,000
Administrative	560,000
Total	$880,000

The expected annual sales volume (780,000 boxes) is $6.24 million and the tax rate is 40%.

Manufacturers of candy have announced that they will increase prices of their products by an average of 15% in the coming year because of increases in raw material (sugar, cocoa, peanuts, and so on) and labour costs. All-Day Candy Company expects that all other costs will remain at the same rates or levels as during the current year.

Instruction

(a) What is All-Day Candy Company's break-even point in boxes of candy for the current year?

(b) What selling price per box must All-Day Candy Company charge to cover the 15% increase in the variable cost of candy and still maintain the current contribution margin ratio?

(c) What volume of sales in dollars must All-Day Candy Company achieve in the coming year to keep the same net income after taxes that was projected for the current year if the selling price of candy remains at $8 per box and the cost of candy increases by 15%?

(CMA Canada-adapted)

C5–47   Labrador Company produces a single product. It sold 75,000 units last year with the following results:

Sales		$1,875,000
Variable costs	$750,000	
Fixed costs	300,000	1,050,000
Net income before taxes		825,000
Income taxes (45%)		371,250
Net income		$ 453,750

In an attempt to improve its product, Labrador is considering replacing a component part in its product that has a cost of $5 with a new and better part costing $10 per unit during the coming year. A new machine would also be needed to increase plant capacity. The machine would cost $90,000, with a useful life of six years and no salvage value. The company uses straight-line amortization on all plant assets.

Instruction

(a) What was Labrador's break-even point in units last year?
(b) How many units of product would Labrador have had to sell in the past year to earn $247,500 in net income after taxes?
(c) If it holds the sales price constant and makes the suggested changes, how many units of product must the company sell in the coming year to break even?
(d) If it holds the sales price constant and makes the suggested changes, how many units of product will Labrador have to sell to make the same net income before taxes as last year?
(e) If Labrador wishes to maintain the same contribution margin ratio, what selling price per unit of product must it charge next year to cover the increased materials costs?

(CMA Canada-adapted)

C5–48   Ronnie Drake is an accountant for Benson Company. Early this year, Ronnie made a highly favourable projection of sales and profits over the next three years for Benson's hot-selling computer PLEX. As a result of the projections Ronnie presented to senior management, management decided to expand production in this area. This decision led to dislocations of some plant personnel, who were reassigned to one of the company's newer plants in another province. However, no one was fired, and in fact the company expanded its workforce slightly.

Unfortunately, Ronnie rechecked his calculations on the projections a few months later and found that he had made an error that would have reduced his projections substantially. Luckily, sales of PLEX have exceeded projections so far, and management is satisfied with its decision. Ronnie, however, is not sure what to do. Should he confess his honest mistake and jeopardize his possible promotion? He suspects that no one will catch the error because sales of PLEX have exceeded his projections, and it appears that profits will materialize close to his projections.

Instructions

(a) Who are the stakeholders in this situation?
(b) Identify the ethical issues involved in this situation.
(c) What are the possible alternative actions for Ronnie? What would you do in Ronnie's position?

Answers to Self-Study Questions

1. d   2. c   3. a   4. a   5. c   6. d   7. a   8. b   9. d   10. d

Remember to go back to the Navigator Box at the beginning of the chapter to check off your completed work.

CHAPTER 6

Incremental Analysis

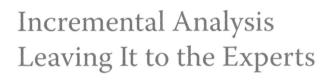

Incremental Analysis
Leaving It to the Experts

When is a manufacturer not a manufacturer? When it outsources. An extension of the classic "make or buy" decision, outsourcing involves hiring other companies to make all or part of a product or to perform services. And performing specific services is just what Toronto-based Consumer Impact Marketing (CIM) Ltd. does. CIM provides sales, merchandising, experiential marketing, and events and promotions management services to companies from across North America, including H.J.Heinz, Microsoft, QTG (Quaker Tropicana Gatorade), Pepsi, Abbott Labs, Schick, FujiFilm and HP.

"CIM is an expert in these areas," says Hesham Shafie, vice president, finance and administration. "We have developed great people, tools, and technologies that enable us to deliver high-quality results to our clients. CIM's expertise allows clients to focus on their core business, whether it's manufacturing a product or developing the strategy for the product."

CIM is the driving force behind events and promotions for the Xbox brand in Canada, including sending Xbox vehicles across the country to provide game aficionados with the chance to try new Xbox game software. Its staff also take care of the Pepsi Taste Patrol's tasting challenges that take place throughout Canada. For QTG, CIM provides sales and merchandising support, which includes visiting retailers to promote new products and ensure that QTG products have prime locations on the store shelves. CIM has also developed sales force automation solutions that provide the tools and technologies to allow salespeople to communicate with their head offices, collect data, process orders, and transmit them to warehouses to ensure that their products are in stores.

The reason companies outsource these services to CIM isn't only about cost, Mr. Shafie points out. "Cost is definitely a factor, but it's not the deciding factor." Other important considerations are quality, reputation, and technology, he says. "We invest heavily in our people, sales force automation solutions, reporting tools, and analytical tools. Manufacturers don't really want to put millions of dollars into this technology because it's not their expertise. Specialization is one of the reasons that companies look to outsource. You know that if you give it to the experts, they're going to do it more effectively, more efficiently, and more economically."

the
navigator

Consumer Impact Marketing: www.cimweb.com

THE NAVIGATOR

☐ Scan *Study Objectives*

☐ Read *Feature Story*

☐ Read *Chapter Preview*

☐ Read text and answer
Before You Go On
p. 254, p. 257

☐ Work *Using the Decision Toolkit*

☐ Review *Summary of Study Objectives*

☐ Review *Using the Decision Toolkit—A Summary*

☐ Work *Demonstration Problem*

☐ Answer *Self-Study Questions*

☐ Complete assignments

STUDY OBJECTIVES

After studying this chapter, you should be able to:

1. Identify the steps in management's decision-making process.
2. Describe the concept of incremental analysis.
3. Identify the relevant costs in accepting an order at a special price.
4. Identify the relevant costs in a make-or-buy decision.
5. Identify the relevant costs in deciding whether to sell or process materials further.
6. Identify the relevant costs in deciding whether to keep or replace equipment.
7. Identify the relevant costs in deciding whether to eliminate an unprofitable segment.
8. Determine the sales mix when a company has limited resources.

the navigator

An important purpose of management accounting is to provide managers with relevant information for decision-making. Companies of all sorts must make product decisions. Philip Morris decided to cut prices to raise its market share. Oral-B Laboratories chose to produce a new, higher-priced toothbrush. General Motors of Canada discontinued the Buick Riviera and announced the closure of its Oldsmobile Division. Quaker Oats decided to sell a line of beverages, at a price more than one billion dollars lower than what it paid for that product line only a few years before. Aircraft manufacturer Bombardier Inc., in Quebec, had to decide whether to continue making snowmobiles or eliminate that segment from its business. As our feature story indicated, many companies decide to outsource the marketing and sales of their products to CIM Ltd.

This chapter explains management's decision-making process and a decision-making approach called incremental analysis. The use of incremental analysis is demonstrated in a variety of situations.

The chapter is organized as follows:

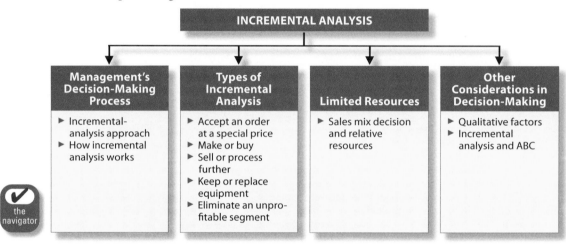

INCREMENTAL ANALYSIS			
Management's Decision-Making Process	**Types of Incremental Analysis**	**Limited Resources**	**Other Considerations in Decision-Making**
▶ Incremental-analysis approach ▶ How incremental analysis works	▶ Accept an order at a special price ▶ Make or buy ▶ Sell or process further ▶ Keep or replace equipment ▶ Eliminate an unprofitable segment	▶ Sales mix decision and relative resources	▶ Qualitative factors ▶ Incremental analysis and ABC

the navigator

Management's Decision-Making Process

study objective 1

Identify the steps in management's decision-making process.

Making decisions is an important management function. Management's decision-making process does not always follow the same pattern, however, because decisions vary significantly in their scope, urgency, and importance. It is possible, though, to identify some steps that are frequently used in the process. These steps are shown in Illustration 6-1.

Accounting's contribution to the decision-making process occurs mostly in Steps 2 and 4—evaluating the possible courses of action, and reviewing results. In Step 2, for each possible course of action, relevant revenue and cost data are provided. These show the expected overall effect on net income. In Step 4, internal reports are prepared that review the actual impact of the decision.

Illustration 6-1 ▼

Management's decision-making process

1. Identify the problem and assign responsibility.

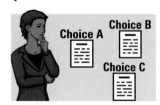

2. Determine and evaluate possible courses of action.

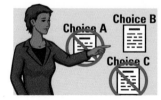

3. Make a decision.

4. Review the results of the decision.

In making business decisions, management ordinarily considers both financial and non-financial information. **Financial** information is about revenues and costs and their effect on the company's overall profitability. **Non-financial** information is about such factors as the effect of the decision on employee turnover, the environment, or the overall image of the company in the community. Although non-financial information can be as important as financial information, we will focus mainly on financial information that is relevant to the decision.

Incremental-Analysis Approach

Decisions involve a choice among alternative courses of action. Suppose that you were deciding whether to buy or lease a computer for doing your accounting homework. The financial data would be the cost of leasing versus the cost of purchasing. For example, leasing would involve periodic lease payments; purchasing would require "up-front" payment of the purchase price. In other words, the financial data that are relevant to the decision relate to the expense that would vary in the future among the possible alternatives. The process used to identify the financial expense that change under alternative courses of action is called **incremental analysis**. In some cases, you will find that when you use incremental analysis, both costs **and** revenues will vary. In other cases, only costs **or** revenues will vary.

Just as your decision to buy or lease a PC will affect your future, similar decisions on a larger scale will affect a company's future. Incremental analysis identifies the probable effects of those decisions on future earnings. This type of analysis always involves estimates and uncertainty. Data for incremental analyses may be gathered from market analysts, engineers, and accountants. In quantifying the data, the accountant is expected to produce the most reliable information available when the decision must be made.

> **study objective 2**
> Describe the concept of incremental analysis.

Alternative Terminology
Incremental analysis is also called *differential analysis* because the analysis focuses on differences.

How Incremental Analysis Works

The basic approach in incremental analysis is shown in the example in Illustration 6-2.

	Alternative A	Alternative B	Net Income Increase (Decrease)
Revenues	$125,000	$110,000	$(15,000)
Costs	100,000	80,000	20,000
Net income	$ 25,000	$ 30,000	$ 5,000

Illustration 6-2 ◄
Basic approach in incremental analysis

In this example, alternative B is being compared with alternative A. The net income column shows the differences between the alternatives. In this case, incremental revenue will be $15,000 less under alternative B than under alternative A. But a $20,000 incremental cost saving will also be realized under alternative B.[1] Thus, alternative B will produce $5,000 more net income than alternative A.

In the following pages, you will learn about three important cost concepts that are used in incremental analysis. They are defined and discussed in Illustration 6-3.

Illustration 6-3 ◄
Key cost concepts in incremental analysis

- **Relevant cost** In incremental analysis, the only factors to be considered are (1) those costs and revenues that are different for each alternative, and (2) those costs and revenues that will occur in the future. These factors are called **relevant costs**. Costs and revenues that do not differ across alternatives and will not occur in the future can be ignored when trying to choose between alternatives.

- **Opportunity cost** In choosing to take one action, the company must often give up the opportunity to benefit from some other action. For example, if a machine is used to make one type of product, the benefit of making another type of product with that machine is lost. This lost benefit is called an **opportunity cost**.

- **Sunk cost** Costs that have already been incurred and will not be changed or avoided by any future decision are called **sunk costs**. For example, if you have already purchased a machine, and now a new, more efficient machine is available, the book value of the original machine is a sunk cost. It should not affect your decision about whether to buy the new machine. **Sunk costs are not relevant costs.**

---

[1] Although income taxes are sometimes important in incremental analysis, they are ignored in the chapter in order to keep the explanation simpler and clearer.

Incremental analysis sometimes involves changes that at first might go against your intuition. For example, sometimes variable costs **do not** change under the alternative courses of action. Also, sometimes fixed costs **do** change. For example, direct labour, normally a variable cost, is not an incremental cost in deciding between two new factory machines if each asset requires the same amount of direct labour. In contrast, rent expense, normally a fixed cost, is an incremental cost in a decision about whether to stay in the current building or to purchase or lease a new building.

Types of Incremental Analysis

study objective 3

Identify the relevant costs in accepting an order at a special price.

Several types of decisions involve incremental analysis. The more common ones are whether to:

1. Accept an order at a special price
2. Make or buy component parts or finished products
3. Sell products or process them further
4. Keep or replace equipment
5. Eliminate or keep an unprofitable business segment

We will consider each of these types of incremental analysis in the following pages.

Accept an Order at a Special Price

Sometimes a company may have an opportunity to obtain additional business if it is willing to make a major price concession to a specific customer (i.e., lower its price for the customer). To illustrate, assume that Sunbelt Company produces 100,000 automatic blenders per month, which is 80 percent of plant capacity. Variable manufacturing costs are $8 per unit. Fixed manufacturing costs are $400,000, or $4 per unit. The blenders are normally sold directly to retailers at $20 each. Sunbelt has an offer from Mexico Co. (a foreign wholesaler) to purchase an additional 2,000 blenders at $11 per unit. Accepting the offer would not affect normal sales of the product, and the additional units can be manufactured without increasing plant capacity. What should management do?

Helpful Hint This is a good example of different costs for different purposes. In the long run, all costs are relevant, but for this decision only costs that change are relevant.

If management makes its decision based on the total cost per unit of $12 ($8 + $4), the order would be rejected, because costs ($12) would exceed revenues ($11) by $1 per unit. However, since the units can be produced within existing plant capacity, the special order **will not increase fixed costs**. Let's identify the relevant data for the decision. First, the variable manufacturing costs will increase by $16,000 ($8 × 2,000). Second, the expected revenue will increase by $22,000 ($11 × 2,000). Thus, as shown in Illustration 6-4, Sunbelt will increase its net income by $6,000 by accepting this special order.

Illustration 6-4 ▶

Incremental analysis—accepting an order at a special price

	Reject Order	Accept Order	Net Income Increase (Decrease)
Revenues	$0	$22,000	$ 22,000
Costs	0	16,000	(16,000)
Net income	$0	$ 6,000	$ 6,000

Two points should be emphasized: First, it is assumed that sales of the product in other markets **would not be affected by this special order**. If other sales will be lost, then Sunbelt would have to consider the lost sales in making the decision. Second, if Sunbelt was operating **at full capacity**, it is likely that the special order would be rejected. Under such circumstances, the company would have to expand plant capacity. In that case, the special order would have to absorb these additional fixed manufacturing costs, as well as the variable manufacturing costs.

Make or Buy

When a manufacturer assembles component parts in producing a finished product, management must decide whether to make or buy the components. The decision to buy parts or services is often called outsourcing. For example, a company such as General Motors Corporation of Canada may either make or buy the batteries, tires, and radios used in its cars. Similarly, Hewlett-Packard Corporation may make or buy the electronic circuitry, cases, and printer heads for its printers. The decision to make or buy components should be made on the basis of incremental analysis.

study objective 4

Identify the relevant costs in a make-or-buy decision.

To illustrate the analysis, assume that Baron Company incurs the annual costs in Illustration 6-5 in producing 25,000 ignition switches for motor scooters.

Direct materials	$ 50,000
Direct labour	75,000
Variable manufacturing overhead	40,000
Fixed manufacturing overhead	60,000
Total manufacturing costs	$225,000
Total cost per unit ($225,000 ÷ 25,000)	$9.00

Illustration 6-5 ◀

Annual product cost data

Or, instead of making its own switches, Baron Company might purchase the ignition switches from Ignition, Inc. at a price of $8 per unit. The question again is, "What should management do?"

At first glance, it appears that management should purchase the ignition switches for $8, rather than make them at a cost of $9. However, a review of operations indicates that if the ignition switches are purchased from Ignition, Inc., *all* of Baron's variable costs but only $10,000 of its fixed manufacturing costs will be eliminated. Thus, $50,000 of the fixed manufacturing costs will remain if the ignition switches are purchased. The relevant costs for incremental analysis, therefore, are as in Illustration 6-6.

	Make	Buy	Net Income Increase (Decrease)
Direct materials	$ 50,000	$ 0	$ 50,000
Direct labour	75,000	0	75,000
Variable manufacturing costs	40,000	0	40,000
Fixed manufacturing costs	60,000	50,000	10,000
Purchase price (25,000 × $8)	0	200,000	(200,000)
Total annual cost	$225,000	$250,000	$ (25,000)

Illustration 6-6 ◀

Incremental analysis—make or buy

This analysis shows that Baron Company will incur $25,000 of additional costs by buying the ignition switches. Therefore, Baron should continue to make the ignition switches even though the total manufacturing cost is $1 higher than the purchase price. The reason is that if the company purchases the ignition switches, it will still have fixed costs of $50,000 to absorb.

Opportunity Cost

The make-or-buy analysis we just did is complete only if it is assumed that the productive capacity that is used to make the ignition switches cannot be used for another purpose. If there is an opportunity to use this productive capacity in some other manner, then this opportunity cost must be considered. As indicated earlier, an **opportunity cost** is the potential benefit that may be obtained by following an alternative course of action.

To illustrate, assume that if it buys the switches, Baron Company can use the released productive capacity to generate additional income of $28,000 by producing a different product. This lost income is an additional cost of continuing to make the switches in the make-or-buy decision. This opportunity cost therefore is added to the "Make" column, for comparison. As Illustration 6-7 shows, it is now advantageous to buy the ignition switches.

Helpful Hint In the make-or-buy decision, it is important for management to take into account the social impact of the choice. For instance, buying may be the most economically feasible solution, but it could result in the closure of a manufacturing plant that employs many good workers.

Illustration 6-7 ▶

Incremental analysis—make
or buy, with opportunity
cost

	Make	Buy	Net Income Increase (Decrease)
Total annual cost	$225,000 [1]	$250,000 [1]	$(25,000)
Opportunity cost	28,000	0	28,000
Total cost	$253,000	$250,000	$ 3,000

[1] From Illustration 6-6.

The qualitative factors in this decision include the possible loss of jobs for employees who produce the ignition switches. In addition, management must assess how long the supplier will be able to satisfy the company's quality control standards at the quoted price per unit.

BUSINESS INSIGHT ▶ Management Perspective

For some companies, supplying others with the components that they need can be a lucrative prospect. Take, for example, Canadian auto-parts manufacturer Magna International, which started in 1957 as a one-man shop in a Toronto garage called Multimatic. It soon had its first auto-part contract to make sun visors for General Motors. After the 1969 merger with aerospace and defence manufacturer Magna Electronics, sales jumped to $10 million and continued to grow through the 1970s, eventually topping $150 million. In the 1980s, Magna sold off its aerospace and defence divisions to focus on auto parts and systems. Sales hit $1 billion. The 1990s saw the company spin off its engine and metal-stamping units and expand into vehicle manufacturing in Europe. It also divested its horseracing venture and interior-systems group. By 2003, Magna was designing and manufacturing auto systems, assemblies, modules, and components, as well as complete vehicles, at 247 sites in 22 countries. Annual revenue is expected to hit US$20 billion by 2006, a more than 192-million percent increase from Multimatic's first-year revenue of $13,000. By expanding operations at opportune times, and knowing when to divest and focus on its key operations, the company experienced exponential revenue growth.

Source: Thomas Watson, "The Countdown Continues," *Canadian Business*, July 7, 2003.

Sell or Process Further

study objective 5

Identify the relevant costs in deciding whether to sell or process materials further.

Many manufacturers have the option of selling products at a particular point in the production cycle or continuing to process the products in order to sell them later at a higher price. For example, a bicycle manufacturer such as Schwinn could sell its 10-speed bicycles to retailers either unassembled or assembled. A furniture manufacturer such as Ethan Allen could sell its dining room sets to furniture stores either unfinished or finished. The sell-or-process-further decision should be made on the basis of incremental analysis. The basic decision rule is as follows: **Process further as long as the incremental revenue from the processing is more than the incremental processing costs.**

Single-Product Case

Assume, for example, that Woodmasters Inc. makes tables. The cost to manufacture an unfinished table is $35, calculated as in Illustration 6-8.

Illustration 6-8 ▶

Per unit cost of unfinished
table

Direct material	$15
Direct labour	10
Variable manufacturing overhead	6
Fixed manufacturing overhead	4
Manufacturing cost per unit	$35

The selling price per unfinished unit is $50. Woodmasters currently has unused productive capacity that is expected to continue indefinitely. What are the relevant costs? Management concludes that some of this capacity can be used to finish the tables and sell them at $60 per unit. For a finished table, direct materials will increase by $2 and direct labour costs will increase by $4. Variable manufacturing overhead costs will increase by $2.40 (60% of direct labour). No increase is anticipated in fixed manufacturing overhead. Illustration 6-9 shows the incremental analysis on a per unit basis.

	Sell	Process Further	Net Income Increase (Decrease)
Sales per unit	$50.00	$60.00	$ 10.00
Cost per unit			
Direct materials	15.00	17.00	(2.00)
Direct labour	10.00	14.00	(4.00)
Variable manufacturing overhead	6.00	8.40	(2.40)
Fixed manufacturing overhead	4.00	4.00	0
Total	35.00	43.40	(8.40)
Net income per unit	$15.00	$16.60	$ 1.60

Illustration 6-9 ◄

Incremental analysis—sell or process further

Helpful Hint Current net income is known. Net income from processing further is an estimate. In making its decision, management could add a "risk" factor for the estimate.

It would be advantageous for Woodmaster to process the tables further. The incremental revenue of $10.00 from the additional processing is $1.60 higher than the incremental processing costs of $8.40.

Multiple-Product Case

Sell-or-process-further decisions are especially relevant to production processes that produce multiple products simultaneously. In many industries, several end products are produced from a single raw material and a common production process. These multiple end products are commonly called **joint products**. For example, in the meat-packing industry, a single sheep produces meat, internal organs, hides, wool, bones, and fat. In the petroleum industry, crude oil is refined to produce gasoline, lubricating oil, kerosene, paraffin, and ethylene.

Illustration 6-10 presents a joint product situation for Marais Creamery, which must decide whether **to sell or process further cream and skim milk**. Both of these products result from the processing of raw milk.

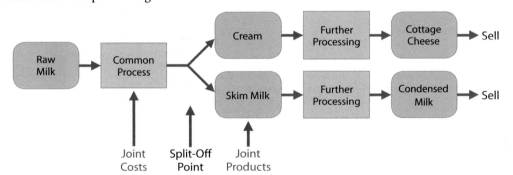

Illustration 6-10 ◄

Joint production process—Creamery

Marais Creamery incurs many costs before it manufactures cream and skim milk. All costs that are incurred before the point at which the two products are separately identifiable (the *split-off point*) are called **joint costs**. To determine the cost of each product, joint product costs must be allocated to the individual products. This is frequently done based on the relative sales value of the joint products. Although this allocation is important for determining the product cost, it is irrelevant in sell-or-process-further decisions. This is because these joint product costs are **sunk costs**. That is, they have already been incurred, and they cannot be changed or avoided by any later decision.

The daily cost and revenue data for Marais Creamery are shown in Illustration 6-11.

Illustration 6-11 ▶

Cost and revenue data per day

Costs (per day)	
Joint cost allocated to cream	$ 9,000
Joint cost allocated to skim milk	5,000
Processing cream into cottage cheese	10,000
Processing skim milk into condensed milk	8,000
Expected Revenues from Products (per day)	
Cream	$19,000
Skim milk	11,000
Cottage cheese	27,000
Condensed milk	26,000

From this information, we can determine whether the company should simply sell the cream and skim milk, or process them further into cottage cheese and condensed milk. Illustration 6-12 shows the analysis that is needed for deciding whether to sell the cream or process it further into cottage cheese.

	Sell	Process Further	Net Income Increase (Decrease)
Sales per day	$19,000	$27,000	$ 8,000
Cost per day			
Processing cream into cottage cheese	0	10,000	(10,000)
	$19,000	$17,000	$ (2,000)

From this analysis, we can see that Marais Creamery should not process the cream further, because it will sustain an incremental loss of $2,000. Illustration 6-13, however, shows that Marais Creamery should process the skim milk into condensed milk, as it will increase net income by $7,000.

	Sell	Process Further	Net Income Increase (Decrease)
Sales per day	$11,000	$26,000	$15,000
Cost per day			
Processing skim milk into condensed milk	0	8,000	(8,000)
	$11,000	$18,000	$ 7,000

Note that the amount of joint costs allocated to each product ($9,000 to the cream and $5,000 to the skim milk) is irrelevant in deciding whether to sell or process further. Why? The joint costs remain the same whether or not there is further processing.

Keep or Replace Equipment

study objective 6

Identify the relevant costs to be considered in deciding whether to keep or replace equipment.

Management often has to decide whether to continue using an asset or replace it. To illustrate, assume that Jeffcoat Company has a factory machine with a book value of $40,000 and a remaining useful life of four years. It is considering replacing this machine with a new one. The new machine costs $120,000 and is expected to have zero salvage value at the end of its four-year useful life. If the new machine is acquired, variable manufacturing costs are expected to decrease from $160,000 to $125,000 annually, and the old unit will be scrapped. Illustration 6-14 shows the incremental analysis for the four-year period.

Illustration 6-14 ◄

Incremental analysis—keep or replace equipment

	Keep Equipment	Replace Equipment	Net Income Increase (Decrease)
Variable manufacturing costs	$640,000[1]	$500,000[2]	$ 140,000
New machine cost	0	120,000	(120,000)
Total	$640,000	$620,000	$ 20,000

[1] (4 years × $160,000)
[2] (4 years × $125,000)

In this case, it would be to the company's advantage to replace the equipment. The lower variable manufacturing costs due to the replacement more than cover the cost of the new equipment.

One other point should be mentioned regarding Jeffcoat's decision: **The book value of the old machine does not affect the decision.** Book value is a **sunk cost**—a cost that cannot be changed by any present or future decision. **Sunk costs are not relevant in incremental analysis.** In this example, if the asset is kept, the book value will be amortized over its remaining useful life. Or, if the new unit is acquired, the book value will be recognized as a loss of the current period. Thus, the effect of book value on current and future earnings is the same regardless of the replacement decision. **Any trade-in allowance or cash disposal value of the existing asset, however, is relevant** to the decision, because this value will not be realized if the asset continues to be used.

Eliminate an Unprofitable Segment

Management must sometimes decide whether to eliminate an unprofitable business segment. Again, the key is to **focus on the relevant costs—the data that change under the alternative courses of action.** To illustrate, assume that Martina Company manufactures tennis racquets in three models: Pro, Master, and Champ. Pro and Master are profitable lines. Champ (highlighted in colour in the table below) operates at a loss. Condensed income statement data are given in Illustration 6-15.

study objective 7

Identify the relevant costs in deciding whether to eliminate an unprofitable segment.

Illustration 6-15 ◄

Segment income data

Helpful Hint A decision to discontinue a segment based solely on the bottom line—net loss—is inappropriate.

	Pro	Master	Champ	Total
Sales	$800,000	$300,000	$100,000	$1,200,000
Variable expenses	520,000	210,000	90,000	820,000
Contribution margin	280,000	90,000	10,000	380,000
Fixed expenses	80,000	50,000	30,000	160,000
Net income	$200,000	$ 40,000	$ (20,000)	$ 220,000

It might be expected that total net income will increase by $20,000, to $240,000, if the unprofitable Champ line of racquets is eliminated. However, **net income may actually decrease if the Champ line is discontinued.** This is because the fixed expenses allocated to the Champ racquets will have to be absorbed by the other products. To illustrate, assume that the $30,000 of fixed costs applicable to the unprofitable segment are allocated two-thirds to the Pro model and one-third to the Master model if the Champ model is eliminated. Fixed expenses will increase to $100,000 ($80,000 + $20,000) in the Pro line and to $60,000 ($50,000 + $10,000) in the Master line. Illustration 6-16 presents the revised income statement:

Illustration 6-16 ◄

Income data after eliminating unprofitable product line

	Pro	Master	Total
Sales	$800,000	$300,000	$1,100,000
Variable expenses	520,000	210,000	730,000
Contribution margin	280,000	90,000	370,000
Fixed expenses	100,000	60,000	160,000
Net income	$180,000	$ 30,000	$ 210,000

Total net income has decreased by $10,000 ($220,000 − $210,000). This result is also obtained in the incremental analysis of the Champ racquets in Illustration 6-17.

	Continue	Eliminate	Net Income Increase (Decrease)
Sales	$100,000	$ 0	$(100,000)
Variable expenses	90,000	0	90,000
Contribution margin	10,000	0	(10,000)
Fixed expenses	30,000	30,000	0
Net income	$ (20,000)	$(30,000)	$ (10,000)

The loss in net income is attributable to the Champ line's contribution margin ($10,000), which will not be realized if the segment is discontinued.

In deciding on the future status of an unprofitable segment, management should consider the effect of elimination on related product lines. Product lines that continue may be able to get some or all of the sales lost by the discontinued product line. In some businesses, services or products may be linked—for example, free chequing accounts at a bank, or coffee at a doughnut shop. In addition, management should consider the effect of eliminating the product line on employees who may have to be laid off or retrained.

BUSINESS INSIGHT ▶ Management Perspective

In 2003, Montreal's Bombardier Inc. sold off its recreational products business, ending its production of the product that most Canadians would identify with the company—Ski-Doos. But, with the $960-million sale to Bombardier Recreational Products Inc.—a corporation formed by Bain Capital, members of the Bombardier family, and the Caisse de dépôt et placement du Québec—Bombardier would continue to own certain trademarks. The sale was part of an action plan presented in April 2003, designed to restore the corporation's balance sheet and liquidity profile and to focus on the aerospace and transportation businesses. The plan also included divestures of the company's Defence Services unit, Belfast City Airport, and Bombardier Capital's business aircraft portfolio. It was expected to generate more than $2.5 billion.

Source: Bombardier Inc. news releases, Dec. 18, 2003, Aug. 27. 2003, and April 28, 2003.

▦ Decision Toolkit

Decision Checkpoints	Info Needed for Decision	Tools to Use for Decision	How to Evaluate Results
Which alternative should the company choose?	All relevant costs and opportunity costs	Compare the relevant cost of each alternative.	Choose the alternative that maximizes net income.

the navigator

BEFORE YOU GO ON . . .

▶Review It

1. Give three examples of how incremental analysis might be used.
2. What is the decision rule in deciding to sell or process products further?
3. How may the elimination of an unprofitable segment decrease the overall net income of a company?

▶Do It

Cobb Company incurs a cost of $28 per unit, of which $18 is variable, to make a product that normally sells for $42. A foreign wholesaler offers to buy 5,000 units at $25 each. Cobb will incur shipping costs of $1 per unit. Calculate the increase or decrease in net income that Cobb will realize by accepting the special order, assuming Cobb has excess operating capacity.

Action Plan

• Identify all revenues that will change as a result of accepting the order.
• Identify all costs that will change as a result of accepting the order, and net this amount against the change in revenues.

Solution

	Reject	Accept	Net Income Increase (Decrease)
Revenues	$0	$125,000	$125,000
Costs	0	95,000*	(95,000)
Net income	$0	$ 30,000	$ 30,000

* (5,000 × $18) + (5,000 × $1)

Given the result of the analysis, Cobb Company should accept the special order.

Related exercise material: BE6–3, E6–1, and E6–2.

Limited Resources

In our break-even analysis in Chapter 5 (Appendix 5A), we assumed a certain sales mix. But management must constantly evaluate its sales mix to determine whether it is as good as it can be. One factor that affects the sales mix decision is how much of the available resources each product uses.

Everyone's resources are limited. For a company, the limited resource may be floor space in a retail department store, or raw materials, direct labour hours, or machine capacity in a manufacturing company. When a company has limited resources, management must decide which products to make and sell in order to maximize net income.

To illustrate, assume that Collins Company manufactures deluxe and standard pen-and-pencil sets. The limiting resource is machine capacity, which is 3,600 hours per month. Relevant data appear in Illustration 6-18.

study objective 8

Determine the sales mix when a company has limited resources.

	Deluxe Sets	Standard Sets
Contribution margin per unit	$8	$6
Machine hours required per unit	0.4	0.2

Illustration 6-18 ◄

Contribution margin and machine hours

The deluxe sets may appear to be more profitable since they have a higher contribution margin ($8) than the standard sets ($6). However, note that the standard sets take fewer machine hours to produce than the deluxe sets. Therefore, it is necessary to find the **contribution margin per unit of the limited resource**, in this case, the contribution margin per machine hour. This is obtained by dividing the contribution margin per unit of each product by the number of units of the limited resource required for each product, as shown in Illustration 6-19.

Helpful Hint Contribution margin (CM) alone is not enough to make this decision. The key factor is CM per limited resource.

	Deluxe Sets	Standard Sets
Contribution margin per unit (a)	$8	$6
Machine hours required (b)	÷0.4	÷0.2
Contribution margin per unit of limited resource [(a) ÷ (b)]	$ 20	$ 30

Illustration 6-19 ◄

Contribution margin per unit of limited resource

The calculation shows that the standard sets have a higher contribution margin per unit of the limited resource. This would suggest that, if there is enough demand for standard sets, the company should shift the sales mix to standard sets or increase its machine capacity.

If Collins Company is able to increase machine capacity from 3,600 hours to 4,200 hours, the additional 600 hours could be used to produce either the standard or deluxe pen-and-pencil sets. The total contribution margin under each alternative is found by multiplying the machine hours by the contribution margin per unit of the limited resource, as shown in Illustration 6-20.

Illustration 6-20 ▶

**Incremental analysis—
calculation of total
contribution margin**

	Produce Deluxe Sets	Produce Standard Sets
Machine hours (a)	600	600
Contribution margin per unit of limited resource (b)	× $20	× $30
Contribution margin [(a) × (b)]	$12,000	$18,000

From this analysis, we can see that to maximize net income, all of the increased capacity should be used to make and sell the standard sets. When there are multiple limited resources, solving the product mix requires the use of a specialized mathematical technique called linear programming, which is covered in production management or operation research courses.

As indicated in Illustration 6-19, the constraint on the production of the deluxe sets is the larger number of machine hours needed to produce these items. In addressing this problem, we have not questioned the limited number of machine hours, and have simply tried to maximize the contribution margin under this constraint. One question that Collins should ask, however, is whether this constraint can be minimized. For example, the constraint might be due to a bottleneck in production or to poorly trained machine operators. In addition, other possible solutions, such as outsourcing part of the production, acquiring additional new equipment (discussed in Chapter 12), or striving to eliminate any non–value-added activities, should be considered.

As discussed in Chapter 1, this approach to evaluating constraints is referred to as the theory of constraints. The **theory of constraints** is a specific approach to constraints in which they are managed to improve the overall goals of the company. According to this theory, a company must continually identify its constraints and find ways to reduce or eliminate them, where appropriate.

BUSINESS INSIGHT ▶ Management Perspective

When fragrance sales recently went flat, retailers turned up the heat on fragrance manufacturers. The amount of floor space devoted to fragrances was reduced, leaving fragrance manufacturers fighting each other for a smaller space. The retailer doesn't just choose the fragrance with the highest contribution margin. Instead, it chooses the fragrance with the highest contribution margin per square foot. In this game, a product with a lower contribution margin but a higher turnover could well be the winner.

▦ Decision Toolkit

Decision Checkpoints	Info Needed for Decision	Tools to Use for Decision	How to Evaluate Results
How many units of products A and B should we produce with a limited resource?	Contribution margin per unit, limited resource required per unit	$\dfrac{\text{Contribution margin per unit of limited resource}} {} = \dfrac{\text{Contribution margin per unit}}{\text{Limited resource per unit}}$	Any additional capacity of the limited resource should be applied toward the product with the higher contribution margin per unit of the limited resource.

the navigator

Other Considerations in Decision-Making

Qualitative Factors

In this chapter, we have focused mainly on the quantitative factors that affect a decision—those attributes that can be easily expressed in numbers or dollars. However, many of the decisions that use incremental analysis have important qualitative features. Although they are not easy to measure, these factors should not be ignored.

Consider, for example, the potential effects of the make-or-buy decision, or of the decision to eliminate a line of business, on existing employees and the community in which the plant is located. The cost savings that may result from outsourcing or from eliminating a plant should be weighed against these qualitative factors. One factor would be the cost of lost morale that might result. Albert "Chainsaw #A1" Dunlap was a so-called "turnaround" artist who went into many companies, identified inefficiencies (using incremental analysis techniques), and tried to correct these problems to improve corporate profitability. Along the way, he laid off thousands of employees at many companies. As head of Sunbeam, it was Al Dunlap who lost his job because his draconian approach failed to improve Sunbeam's profitability. It was widely reported that Sunbeam's employees openly rejoiced for days after his departure. Clearly, qualitative factors can matter.

Relationship of Incremental Analysis and Activity-Based Costing

In Chapter 4, we noted that many companies have shifted to activity-based costing to allocate overhead costs to products. The main reason for using activity-based costing is that it results in a more accurate allocation of overhead. That is, activity-based costing better associates the actual increase in overhead costs that results from the manufacture of each product. The concepts presented in this chapter are completely consistent with the use of activity-based costing. In fact, activity-based costing will result in a better identification of relevant costs and, therefore, a better incremental analysis.

BUSINESS INSIGHT ▶ Management Perspective

When selecting pension and health-care products and plan-administration vendors, companies have several important goals, including improving transaction accuracy and integrity, improving customer service, and reducing costs. However, a Watson Wyatt survey has found that very few companies are actually aware of or able to evaluate the cost of outsourcing these functions in a meaningful way. Of the 127 Canadian companies surveyed, approximately 70 to 80 percent of those who outsourced the administration of their benefit plans were successful in reducing costs. However, more than half were not aware of ongoing costs for these outsourced plans, and nearly all were not aware of the total service-centre costs per participant. The study also found that few Canadian companies completely outsource their employee benefits administration. Instead, most firms use internal and external resources to administer these plans.

Source: Watson Wyatt news release, March 25, 2004.

BEFORE YOU GO ON . . .

▶ Review It

1. What is the critical factor in allocating limited resources to various product lines?
2. What are some qualitative factors that should be considered in an incremental-analysis decision?
3. What is the theory of constraints?

Using the Decision Toolkit

Suppose Canadian Communications Company must decide whether to make some of its components or buy them from Xenia Corp. The cost of producing 50,000 electrical connectors for its network is $110,000, broken down as follows:

Direct materials	$60,000	Variable overhead	$12,000
Direct labour	30,000	Fixed overhead	8,000

Instead of making the electrical connectors at an average cost per unit of $2.20 ($110,000 ÷ 50,000), the company has an opportunity to buy the connectors at $2.15 per unit. If the connectors are purchased, all variable costs and one-half of the fixed costs will be eliminated.

Instructions

(a) Prepare an incremental analysis showing whether the company should make or buy the electrical connectors.
(b) Will your answer be different if the productive capacity that becomes available because of the purchase of the connectors will generate additional income of $25,000?

Solution

(a)

	Make	Buy	Net Income Increase (Decrease)
Direct materials	$ 60,000	$ 0	$ 60,000
Direct labour	30,000	0	30,000
Variable manufacturing costs	12,000	0	12,000
Fixed manufacturing costs	8,000	4,000	4,000
Purchase price	0	107,500	(107,500)
Total cost	$110,000	$111,500	$ (1,500)

This analysis indicates that Canadian Communications Company will incur $1,500 of additional costs if it buys the electrical connectors. Canadian Communications would therefore choose to make the connectors.

(b)

	Make	Buy	Net Income Increase (Decrease)
Total cost	$110,000	$111,500	$ (1,500)
Opportunity cost	25,000	0	25,000
Total cost	$135,000	$111,500	$23,500

Yes, the answer is different. The analysis shows that if additional capacity is released by purchasing the electrical connectors, net income will be increased by $23,500. In this case, Canadian Communications would choose to purchase the connectors.

the navigator

Summary of Study Objectives

1. **Identify the steps in management's decision-making process.** Management's decision-making process consists of (a) identifying the problem and assigning responsibility for the decision, (b) determining and evaluating possible courses of action, (c) making the decision, and (d) reviewing the results of the decision.

2. **Describe the concept of incremental analysis.** Incremental analysis is the process that is used to identify financial data that change under alternative courses of action. These data are relevant to the decision because they will vary in the future among the possible alternatives.

3. **Identify the relevant costs in accepting an order at a special price.** The relevant information in accepting an order at a special price is the difference between the variable manufacturing costs to produce the special order and expected revenues.

4. *Identify the relevant costs in a make-or-buy decision.* In a make-or-buy decision, the relevant costs are (a) the variable manufacturing costs that will be saved, (b) the purchase price, and (c) opportunity costs.

5. *Identify the relevant costs in deciding whether to sell or process materials further.* The decision rule for whether to sell or process materials further is as follows: Process further as long as the incremental revenue from processing is more than the incremental processing costs.

6. *Identify the relevant costs in deciding whether to keep or replace equipment.* The relevant costs to be considered in determining whether equipment should be kept or replaced are the effects on variable costs and the cost of the new equipment. Also, any disposal value of the existing asset must be considered.

7. *Identify the relevant costs in deciding whether to eliminate an unprofitable segment.* In deciding whether to eliminate an unprofitable segment, the relevant information is the contribution margin, if any, produced by the segment and the disposition of the segment's fixed expenses.

8. *Determine the sales mix when a company has limited resources.* When a company has limited resources, it is necessary to find the contribution margin per unit of the limited resource. This amount is then multiplied by the units of limited resource to determine which product maximizes net income.

Decision Toolkit—A Summary

Decision Checkpoints	Info Needed for Decision	Tools to Use for Decision	How to Evaluate Results
Which alternative should the company choose?	All relevant costs and opportunity costs	Compare the relevant cost of each alternative.	Choose the alternative that maximizes net income.
How many units of products A and B should we produce with a limited resource?	Contribution margin per unit, limited resource required per unit	$\dfrac{\text{Contribution margin per unit of limited resource}}{} = \dfrac{\text{Contribution margin per unit}}{\text{Limited resource per unit}}$	Any additional capacity of the limited resource should be applied toward the product with the higher contribution margin per unit of the limited resource.

www.wiley.com/canada/managerial

Key Term Matching Activity

Glossary

Incremental analysis The process of identifying the financial data that change under alternative courses of action. (p. 247)

Joint costs For joint products, all costs incurred before the point at which the two products are separately identifiable. This point is known as the split-off point. (p. 251)

Joint products Multiple end products produced from a single raw material and a common process. (p. 251)

Opportunity cost The potential benefit that may be obtained from following an alternative course of action. (p. 247)

Relevant costs Those costs and revenues that differ across alternatives. (p. 247)

Sunk cost A cost that cannot be changed by any present or future decision. (p. 247)

Theory of constraints A specific approach that is used to identify and manage constraints in order to achieve the company's goals. (p. 256)

Demonstration Problem

**Animated
Demonstration
Problem**

Canada Bearings Corporation manufactures and sells three different types of high-quality sealed ball bearings. The bearings vary in their quality specifications—mainly in terms of their smoothness and roundness. They are referred to as Fine, Extra-Fine, and Super-Fine bearings. Machine time is limited. More machine time is required to manufacture the Extra-Fine and Super-Fine bearings. Additional information follows:

	Product		
	Fine	Extra-Fine	Super-Fine
Selling price	$6.00	$10.00	$16.00
Variable costs and expenses	4.00	6.50	11.00
Contribution margin	$2.00	$ 3.50	$ 5.00
Machine hours required	0.02	0.04	0.08

Total fixed costs: $234,000

Instructions

Answer each of the following questions.

(a) Ignoring the machine-time constraint, what strategy would be the best?
(b) What is the contribution margin per unit of the limited resource for each type of bearing?
(c) If additional machine time could be obtained, how should the additional capacity be used?

Action Plan

• To determine how best to use a limited resource, calculate the contribution margin per unit of the limited resource for each product type.

Solution to Demonstration Problem

(a) The Super-Fine bearings have the highest contribution margin per unit. Thus, ignoring any manufacturing constraints, it would appear that the company should shift toward production of more Super-Fine units.

(b) The contribution margin per unit of the limited resource is calculated as follows:

	Fine	Extra-Fine	Super-Fine
Contribution margin per unit ÷	$2	$3.5	$5
Limited resource consumed per unit	÷ 0.02	÷ 0.04	÷ 0.08
	$100.00	$87.50	$62.50

the navigator

5. The Fine bearings have the highest contribution margin per limited resource, even though they have the lowest contribution margin per unit. Because of this resource constraint, any additional capacity should be used to make Fine bearings.

Self-Study Questions

Additional Self-Study Questions

Answers are at the end of the chapter.

(SO 1) 1. Three of the steps in management's decision-making process are to (1) review the results of the decision, (2) determine and evaluate possible courses of action, and (3) make the decision. The steps are prepared in the following order:
(a) 1, 2, 3.   (c) 2, 1, 3.
(b) 3, 2, 1.   (d) 2, 3, 1.

(SO 2) 2. Incremental analysis is the process of identifying the financial data that:
(a) do not change under alternative courses of action.
(b) change under alternative courses of action.
(c) are mixed under alternative courses of action.
(d) No correct answer is given.

3. It costs a company $14 of variable costs and $6 of   (SO 3)
fixed costs to produce product A that sells for $30. A foreign buyer offers to purchase 3,000 units at $18 each. If the special offer is accepted and produced with unused capacity, net income will:
(a) decrease by $6,000.   (c) increase by $12,000.
(b) increase by $6,000.   (d) increase by $9,000.

4. It costs a company $14 of variable costs and $6   (SO 3)
of fixed costs to produce product A that sells for $30. A foreign buyer offers to purchase 3,000 units at $18 each. If the special offer is accepted and produced when capacity is already fully used, net income will:
(a) increase by $6,000.   (c) decrease by $6,000.
(b) increase by $36,000.   (d) decrease by $36,000.

(SO 4) 5. In a make-or-buy decision, the relevant costs are:
    (a) the manufacturing costs that will be saved.
    (b) the purchase price of the units.
    (c) opportunity costs.
    (d) All of the above

(SO 5) 6. The decision rule in a sell-or-process-further decision is to process further as long as the incremental revenue from processing is more than the:
    (a) incremental processing costs.
    (b) variable processing costs.
    (c) fixed processing costs.
    (d) No correct answer is given.

(SO 6) 7. In a decision to keep or replace equipment, the book value of the old equipment is a (an):
    (a) opportunity cost. (c) incremental cost.
    (b) sunk cost. (d) marginal cost.

8. If an unprofitable segment is eliminated: (SO 7)
    (a) net income will always increase.
    (b) the variable expenses of the eliminated segment will have to be absorbed by other segments.
    (c) fixed expenses allocated to the eliminated segment will have to be absorbed by other segments.
    (d) net income will always decrease.

9. If the contribution margin per unit is $15 and it takes three machine hours to produce the unit, the contribution margin per unit of the limited resource is: (SO 8)
    (a) $25.
    (b) $5.
    (c) $4.
    (d) No correct answer is given.

Questions

1. What steps are frequently used in management's decision-making process?

2. Your roommate, Mark Myer, contends that accounting contributes to most of the steps in management's decision-making process. Is your roommate correct? Explain.

3. "Incremental analysis involves the accumulation of information about a single course of action." Do you agree? Explain.

4. Sara Gura asks for your help in understanding the relevance of variable and fixed costs in incremental analysis. Explain this to her.

5. What data are relevant in deciding whether to accept an order at a special price?

6. Son Ly Company has an opportunity to buy parts at $7 each that currently cost $10 to make. What manufacturing costs are relevant to this make-or-buy decision?

7. Define the term "opportunity cost." How may this cost be relevant in a make-or-buy decision?

8. What is the decision rule in deciding whether to sell a product or process it further?

9. What are joint products? What accounting issue results from the production process that creates joint products?

10. How are allocated joint costs treated when a sell-or-process-further decision is being made?

11. Your roommate, Vanessa Hunt, is confused about sunk costs. Explain to your roommate the meaning of sunk costs and their relevance to a decision to keep or replace equipment.

12. Erm Paris Inc. has one product line that is unprofitable. What circumstances may cause the company's overall net income to be lower if the unprofitable product line is eliminated?

13. How is the contribution margin per unit of a limited resource calculated?

14. What is the theory of constraints? Provide some examples of possible constraints for a manufacturer.

Brief Exercises

Identify the steps in management's decision-making process.
(SO 1)

BE6–1   The steps in management's decision-making process are listed in random order below. Indicate the order in which the steps should be executed.

_____ Make decision.
_____ Identify the problem and assign responsibility.
_____ Review the results of the decision.
_____ Determine and evaluate possible courses of action.

Determine incremental changes.
(SO 2)

BE6–2   Anna Company is considering two alternatives. Alternative A will have sales of $150,000 and costs of $100,000. Alternative B will have sales of $185,000 and costs of $125,000. Compare alternative A to alternative B showing incremental revenues, costs, and net income.

Determine whether to accept special order.
(SO 3)

BE6–3   In Rajasthan Company, it costs $30 per unit ($20 variable and $10 fixed) to make a product that normally sells for $45. A foreign wholesaler offers to buy 3,000 units at $24 each. Rajasthan will incur special shipping costs of $2 per unit. Assuming that Rajasthan has excess operating capacity, indicate the net income (loss) Rajasthan would realize by accepting the special order.

Determine whether to accept special order.
(SO 3)

BE6–4   Assume the same information as in BE6–3, except that Rajasthan has no excess capacity. Indicate the net income (loss) that Rajasthan would realize by accepting the special order.

Determine whether to make or buy part.
(SO 4)

BE6–5   Emil Manufacturing incurs unit costs of $7.50 ($4.50 variable and $3 fixed) in making a sub-assembly part for its finished product. A supplier offers to make 10,000 of the parts at $5 per unit. If the offer is accepted, Emil will save all variable costs but no fixed costs. Prepare an analysis showing the total cost saving, if any, that Emil will realize by buying the part.

Determine whether to sell or process further.
(SO 5)

BE6–6   Green Inc. makes unfinished bookcases that it sells for $60. Production costs are $35 variable and $10 fixed. Because it has unused capacity, Green is considering finishing the bookcases and selling them for $70. Variable finishing costs are expected to be $8 per unit with no increase in fixed costs. Prepare an analysis on a per unit basis that shows whether Green should sell unfinished or finished bookcases.

Determine whether to sell or process further—joint products.
(SO 5)

BE6–7   Each day, Iwaniuk Corporation processes one tonne of a secret raw material into two resulting products, AB1 and XY1. When it processes one tonne of the raw material, the company incurs joint processing costs of $60,000. It allocates $25,000 of these costs to AB1 and $35,000 to XY1. The resulting AB1 can be sold for $90,000. Alternatively, it can be processed further to make AB2 at an additional processing cost of $50,000, and sold for $150,000. Each day's batch of XY1 can be sold for $90,000. Alternatively, it can be processed further to create XY2, at an additional processing cost of $50,000, and sold for $130,000. Discuss what products Iwaniuk Corporation should make.

Determine whether to keep or replace equipment.
(SO 6)

BE6–8   Chudzick Company has a factory machine with a book value of $90,000 and a remaining useful life of four years. A new machine is available at a cost of $250,000. This machine will have a four-year useful life with no salvage value. The new machine will lower annual variable manufacturing costs from $600,000 to $500,000. Prepare an analysis that shows whether the old machine should be kept or replaced.

Determine whether to eliminate unprofitable segment.
(SO 7)

BE6–9   Bitterman, Inc., manufactures golf clubs in three models. For the year, the Big Bart line has a net loss of $10,000 from sales of $200,000, variable expenses of $175,000, and fixed expenses of $30,000. If the Big Bart line is eliminated, $15,000 of fixed costs will remain. Prepare an analysis that shows whether the Big Bart line should be eliminated.

Determine allocation of limited resources.
(SO 8)

BE6–10   In Lebeau Company, data for the contribution margin per unit and machine hours per unit for two products are as follows: Product A, $10 and two hours; Product B, $12 and three hours. Calculate the contribution margin per unit of the limited resource for each product.

Exercises

E6–1 Quick Company manufactures toasters. For the first eight months of 2005, the company reported the following operating results while operating at 75% of plant capacity:

Prepare incremental analysis for special order decision.
(SO 3)

Sales (350,000 units)	$4,375,000
Cost of goods sold	2,500,000
Gross profit	1,875,000
Operating expenses	875,000
Net income	$1,000,000

The cost of goods sold was 70% variable and 30% fixed; operating expenses were also 70% variable and 30% fixed.

In September, Quick Company receives a special order for 15,000 toasters at $7.50 each from Ortiz Company of Mexico City. Accepting the order would result in $3,000 of shipping costs but no increase in fixed operating expenses.

Instructions

(a) Prepare an incremental analysis for the special order.
(b) ▦▦▦▶ Should Quick Company accept the special order? Why or why not?

E6–2 Hardy Fibre is the creator of Y-Go, a technology that weaves silver into fabrics to kill bacteria and odour on clothing while managing heat. Y-Go has become very popular in undergarments for sports activities. Operating at capacity, the company can produce one million Y-Go undergarments each year. The per unit and total costs for the undergarment are as follows:

Prepare incremental analysis for special order decision.
(SO 3)

	Per Undergarment	Total
Direct materials	$2.00	$2,000,000
Direct labour	0.50	500,000
Variable manufacturing overhead	1.00	1,000,000
Fixed manufacturing overhead	1.50	1,500,000
Variable selling expenses	0.25	250,000
Totals	$5.25	$5,250,000

The Canadian Forces (CF) has approached Hardy Fibre and expressed an interest in purchasing 200,000 Y-Go undergarments for soldiers in extremely warm climates. The CF would pay the unit cost for direct materials, direct labour, and variable manufacturing overhead costs. In addition, the CF has agreed to pay an additional $1 per undergarment to cover all other costs and provide a profit. Presently, Hardy Fibre is operating at 70% capacity and does not have any other potential buyers for Y-Go. If Hardy Fibre accepts the CF's offer, it will not incur any variable selling expenses for this order.

Instructions

(a) Using incremental analysis, determine whether Hardy Fibre should accept the CF's offer.
(b) Assume Hardy Fibre can now sell one million undergarments in the open market at $8 per unit. Using incremental analysis, determine whether Hardy Fibre should accept the CF's offer for the 200,000 garments.

E6–3 Young Mi Inc. has been manufacturing its own shades for its table lamps. The company is currently operating at 100% of capacity, and variable manufacturing overhead is charged to production at the rate of 60% of direct labour costs. The direct materials and direct labour cost per unit to make the lampshades are $5 and $6, respectively. Normal production is 30,000 table lamps per year.

Prepare incremental analysis for the make or buy decision.
(SO 4)

A supplier offers to make the lampshades at a price of $15.50 per unit. If Young Mi Inc. accepts the supplier's offer, all variable manufacturing costs will be eliminated, but the $45,000 of fixed manufacturing overhead currently being charged to the lampshades will have to be absorbed by other products.

Instructions

(a) Prepare the incremental analysis for the decision to make or buy the lampshades.
(b) ▭▭▭▷ Should Young Mi Inc. buy the lampshades?
(c) ▭▭▭▷ Would your answer be different in (b) if the productive capacity released by not making the lampshades could be used to produce income of $35,000?

Prepare incremental analysis for the make or buy decision.
(SO 4)

E6–4   SY Telc has recently started to manufacture RecRobo, a three-wheeled robot that can scan a home for fires and gas leaks and then transmit this information to a mobile phone. The cost structure to manufacture 20,000 RecRobos is as follows:

	Cost
Direct materials ($40 per robot)	$ 800,000
Direct labour ($30 per robot)	600,000
Variable overhead ($6 per robot)	120,000
Allocated fixed overhead ($25 per robot)	500,000
Total	$2,020,000

SY Telc is approached by Chen Inc., which offers to make RecRobo for $90 per unit or $1.8 million.

Instructions

(a) Using incremental analysis, determine whether SY Telc should accept this offer under each of the following independent assumptions:
   1. Assume that $300,000 of the fixed overhead cost is avoidable.
   2. Assume that none of the fixed overhead is avoidable. However, if the robots are purchased from Chen Inc., SY Telc can use the released productive resources to generate additional income of $300,000.
(b) Describe the qualitative factors that might affect the decision to buy the robots from an outside supplier.

Prepare incremental analysis for decision to further process material.
(SO 5)

E6–5   Josée Chabot recently opened her own basket-weaving studio. She sells finished baskets in addition to the raw materials needed by customers to weave baskets of their own. Josée has put together a variety of raw material kits, with each kit including materials at various stages of completion. Unfortunately, because of space limitations, Josée is unable to carry all the varieties of kits she originally assembled and must choose between two basic packages.

The basic introductory kit includes undyed, uncut reeds (with dye included) for weaving one basket. This basic package costs Josée $14 and sells for $28. The second kit, called Stage 2, includes cut reeds that have already been dyed. With this kit, the customer only has to soak the reeds and weave the basket. Josée is able to produce the second kit by using the basic materials included in the first kit and adding one hour of her own time, which she values at $20 per hour. Because she is more efficient at cutting and dyeing reeds than her average customer, Josée is able to make two kits of the dyed reeds, in one hour, from one kit of undyed reeds. The kit of dyed and cut reeds sells for $35.

Instructions

Determine whether Josée's basket-weaving shop should carry the basic introductory kit with undyed and uncut reeds or the Stage 2 kit with reeds already dyed and cut. Prepare an incremental analysis to support your answer.

Determine whether to sell or process further—joint products.
(SO 5)

E6–6   Benson, Inc. produces three separate products from a common process costing $100,000. Each of the products can be sold at the split-off point or can be processed further and then sold for a higher price. The cost and selling price data for a recent period follow:

	Sales Value at Split-off Point	Cost to Process Further	Sales Value After Further Processing
Product 12	$50,000	$100,000	$190,000
Product 14	10,000	30,000	35,000
Product 16	60,000	150,000	220,000

Instructions

(a) Determine the total net income if all products are sold at the split-off point.
(b) Determine the total net income if all products are sold after further processing.

(c) Using incremental analysis, determine which products should be sold at the split-off point and which should be processed further.
(d) Determine the total net income using the results from (c) and explain why the net income is different from that determined in (b).

E6–7 Shynee Minerals processes materials extracted from mines. The most common raw material that it processes results in three joint products: Sarco, Barco, and Larco. Each of these products can be sold as is, or it can be processed further and sold for a higher price. The company incurs joint costs of $180,000 to process one batch of the raw material that produces the three joint products. The following cost and selling price information is available for one batch of each product:

Determine whether to sell or process further—joint products.
(SO 5)

	Selling Price at Split-off Point	Allocated Joint Costs	Cost to Process Further	Selling Price of Processed Product
Sarco	$200,000	$40,000	$120,000	$300,000
Barco	300,000	60,000	89,000	400,000
Larco	400,000	80,000	250,000	800,000

Instructions

Determine whether each of the three joint products should be sold as is, or processed further.

E6–8 On January 2, 2006, Riverside Hospital purchased a $100,000 special radiology scanner from Faital Inc. The scanner has a useful life of five years and will have no disposal value at the end of its useful life. The straight-line method of amortization is used on this scanner. Annual operating costs with this scanner are $105,000.

Prepare incremental analysis for decision to keep or replace equipment.
(SO 6)

Approximately one year later, the hospital is approached by Alliant Technology salesperson Becky Bishop, who indicates that purchasing the scanner in 2006 from Faital was a mistake. She points out that Alliant has a scanner that will save Riverside Hospital $27,000 a year in operating expenses over its four-year useful life. She notes that the new scanner will cost $120,000 and has the same capabilities as the scanner purchased last year. The hospital agrees that both scanners are of equal quality. The new scanner will have no disposal value. Bishop agrees to buy the old scanner from Riverside Hospital for $30,000.

Instructions

(a) If Riverside Hospital sells its old scanner on January 2, 2007, calculate the gain or loss on the sale.
(b) Using incremental analysis, determine whether Riverside Hospital should purchase the new scanner on January 2, 2007.
(c) Explain why the hospital might be reluctant to purchase the new scanner, regardless of the results indicated by the incremental analysis in (b).

E6–9 Twyla Enterprises uses a word-processing computer to handle its sales invoices. Lately, business has been so good that it takes an extra three hours per night, plus every third Saturday, to keep up with the volume of sales invoices. Management is considering updating its computer with a faster model that would eliminate all of the overtime processing. Data for the two computers are as follows:

Prepare incremental analysis for decision to keep or replace equipment.
(SO 6)

	Current Computer	New Computer
Original purchase cost	$15,000	$25,000
Accumulated amortization	$6,000	$0
Estimated operating costs	$24,000	$18,000
Useful life	5 years	5 years

If sold now, the current computer would have a salvage value of $5,000. If it is used for the remainder of its useful life, the current computer would have zero salvage value. The new computer is expected to have zero salvage value after five years.

Instructions

Should the current computer be replaced? (Ignore the time value of money.)

Prepare incremental analysis concerning elimination of divisions. (SO 7)

E6–10   Nicole Filippas, a recent graduate of Rolling's accounting program, evaluated the operating performance of Poway Company's six divisions. Nicole made the following presentation to Poway's board of directors and suggested the Erie Division be eliminated. "If the Erie Division is eliminated," she said, "our total profits would increase by $15,500."

	The Other Five Divisions	Erie Division	Total
Sales	$1,664,200	$100,000	$1,764,200
Cost of goods sold	978,520	76,500	1,055,020
Gross profit	685,680	23,500	709,180
Operating expenses	527,940	48,000	575,940
Net income	$ 157,740	$ (24,500)	$ 133,240

In the Erie Division, the cost of goods sold is $60,000 variable and $16,500 fixed, and operating expenses are $25,000 variable and $23,000 fixed. None of the Erie Division's fixed costs will be eliminated if the division is discontinued.

Instructions

Is Nicole right about eliminating the Erie Division? Prepare a schedule to support your answer.

Calculate contribution margin and determine product to be manufactured. (SO 8)

E6–11   Spencer Company manufactures and sells three products. Relevant per unit data for each product follow:

	Product		
	A	B	C
Selling price	$9	$12	$14
Variable costs and expenses	$3	$9.50	$12
Machine hours to produce	2	1	2

Instructions

(a) Calculate the contribution margin per unit of the limited resource (machine hours) for each product.
(b) Assuming 1,500 additional machine hours are available, which product should be manufactured?
(c) Prepare an analysis that shows the total contribution margin if the additional hours are (1) divided equally among the products, and (2) allocated entirely to the product identified in (b) above.

Calculate contribution margin and determine products to be manufactured. (SO 8)

E6–12   Moctezuma Inc. produces and sells three products. Unit data for each product follow:

	Product		
	D	E	F
Selling price	$200	$300	$250
Direct labour	25	75	30
Other variable costs	105	90	148

The company has 2,000 hours of labour available to build inventory in anticipation of the company's peak season. Management is trying to decide which product should be produced. The direct labour hourly rate is $10.

Instructions

(a) Determine the number of direct labour hours per unit.
(b) Determine the cost per contribution margin per direct labour hour.
(c) Determine which product should be produced and the total contribution margin for that product.

E6–13 The costs listed below relate to a variety of different decision situations:

Cost	Decision
1. Unavoidable fixed overhead	• Eliminate an unprofitable segment.
2. Direct labour	• Make or buy.
3. Original cost of old equipment	• Replace equipment.
4. Joint production costs	• Sell or process further.
5. Opportunity cost	• Accept a special order.
6. Segment manager's salary	• Eliminate an unprofitable segment; manager will be terminated.
7. Cost of new equipment	• Replace equipment.
8. Incremental production costs	• Sell or process further.
9. Direct material	• Replace equipment. The amount of material required does not change.
10. Rent expense	• Purchase or lease a building.

Identify relevant costs for different decisions.
(SO 3, 4, 5, 6, 7)

Instructions

For each cost listed above, indicate whether it is relevant or not to the decision in the column beside it. For each cost that you consider irrelevant, briefly explain your reasoning.

Problems: Set A

P6–14A Pro Sports Inc. manufactures basketballs for professional basketball associations. For the first six months of 2005, the company reported the following operating results while operating at 90% of plant capacity:

Prepare incremental analysis for special order and identify non-financial factors in decision.
(SO 3)

	Amount	Per Unit
Sales	$4,500,000	$40.00
Cost of goods sold	3,600,000	30.00
Selling and administrative expenses	450,000	5.00
Net income	$ 450,000	$ 5.00

Fixed costs for the period were cost of goods sold $1,080,000, and selling and administrative expenses $225,000.

In July, normally a slack manufacturing month, Pro Sports receives a special order for 10,000 basketballs at $28 each from the Italian Basketball Association. Accepting the order would increase variable selling and administrative expenses by $0.50 per unit because of shipping costs but would not increase fixed costs and expenses.

Instructions

(a) Prepare an incremental analysis for the special order.
(b) Should Pro Sports Inc. accept the special order?
(c) What is the minimum selling price on the special order to produce net income of $4.10 per ball?
(d) ⬤▭▭▭▭▷ What non-financial factors should management consider in making its decision?

P6–15A The management of Borealis Manufacturing Company is trying to decide whether to continue manufacturing a part or to buy it from an outside supplier. The part, called WISCO, is a component of the company's finished product.

The following information was collected from the accounting records and production data for the year ending December 31, 2005:

Prepare incremental analysis related to make-or-buy decision; consider opportunity cost; and identify non-financial factors.
(SO 4)

1. The machining department produced 7,000 units of WISCO during the year.
2. Variable manufacturing costs applicable to the production of each WISCO unit were direct materials $4.80, direct labour $4.30, indirect labour $0.43, and utilities $0.40.
3. Fixed manufacturing costs applicable to the production of WISCO were as follows:

Cost Item	Direct	Allocated
Amortization	$2,100	$ 900
Property taxes	500	200
Insurance	900	600
	$3,500	$1,700

All variable manufacturing and direct fixed costs will be eliminated if WISCO is purchased. Allocated costs will have to be absorbed by other production departments.

4. The lowest quotation for 7,000 WISCO units from a supplier is $70,000.
5. If WISCO units are purchased, freight and inspection costs would be $0.40 per unit, and receiving costs totalling $1,250 per year would be incurred by the machining department.

Instructions

(a) Prepare an incremental analysis for WISCO. Your analysis should have columns for (1) Make WISCO, (2) Buy WISCO, and (3) Net Income Increase/Decrease.
(b) Based on your analysis, what decision should management make?
(c) Would the decision be different if Borealis has the opportunity to produce $5,000 of net income with the facilities currently being used to manufacture WISCO? Show calculations.
(d) ▰▰▰▶ What non-financial factors should management consider in making its decision?

Calculate contribution margin and prepare differential analysis for make-or-buy decision.
(SO 4)

P6–16A   Harmon Company purchases sails and produces sailboats. It currently produces 1,200 sailboats per year, operating at normal capacity, which is about 80% of full capacity. Harmon purchases sails at $260 each, but the company is considering using the excess capacity to manufacture the sails instead. The manufacturing cost per sail would be $100 for materials, $80 for direct labour, and $100 for overhead. The $100 overhead is based on $72,000 of annual fixed overhead that is allocated using normal capacity.

The president of Harmon has come to you for advice. "It would cost me $280 to make the sails," she says, "but only $260 to buy them. Should I continue buying them or have I missed something?"

Instructions

(a) Prepare a per unit analysis of the differential costs. Briefly explain whether Harmon should make or buy the sails.
(b) If Harmon suddenly finds an opportunity to rent out the unused capacity of its factory for $80,000 per year, would your answer to part (a) change? Briefly explain.
(c) Identify three qualitative factors that should be considered by Harmon in this make-or-buy decision.

(CGA-adapted)

Calculate contribution margin and prepare incremental analysis concerning make-or-buy decision.
(SO 4)

P6–17A   Interdesign uses 1,000 units of the component IMC2 every month to manufacture one of its products. The unit costs incurred to manufacture the component are as follows:

Direct materials	$ 65.00
Direct labour	48.00
Overhead	126.50
Total	$239.50

Overhead costs include variable material handling costs of $6.50 which are applied to products on the basis of direct material costs. The remainder of the overhead costs are applied on the basis of direct labour dollars and consist of 50% variable costs and 50% fixed costs.

A vendor has offered to supply the IMC2 component at a price of $200 per unit.

Instructions

(a) Should Interdesign purchase the component from the outside vendor if Interdesign's capacity remains idle?
(b) Should Interdesign purchase the component from the outside vendor if it can use its facilities to manufacture another product? What information will Interdesign need to make an accurate decision? Show your calculations.
(c) What are the qualitative factors that Interdesign will have to consider when making this decision?

(CGA-adapted)

P6–18A Miramichi Industrial Products Co. is a diversified industrial-cleaner processing company. The company's main plant produces two products: a table cleaner and a floor cleaner. They are made from a common set of chemical inputs (CDG). Each week, 27,000 litres of chemical input are processed at a cost of $210,000 into 18,000 litres of floor cleaner and 9,000 litres of table cleaner. The floor cleaner has no market value until it is converted into a polish with the trade name FloorShine. The additional processing costs for this conversion total $250,000.

FloorShine sells at $20 per one-litre bottle. The table cleaner can be sold for $25 per one-litre bottle. However, the table cleaner can be converted into two other products by adding 9,000 litres of another compound (TCP) to the 9,000 litres of table cleaner. This joint process will yield 9,000 litres each of table stain remover (TSR) and table polish (TP). The additional processing costs for this process are $120,000. Both table products can be sold for $18 per one-litre bottle.

The company decided not to process the table cleaner into TSR and TP based on the following analysis:

Determine whether product should be sold or processed further.
(SO 5)

	Table Cleaner	Process Further Stain Remover (TSR)	Process Further Table Polish (TP)	Total
Production in litres	(9,000)	9,000	9,000	
Revenue	$250,000	$180,000	$180,000	$360,000
Costs				
CDG costs	70,000[1]	52,500	52,500	105,000[2]
TCP costs	0	50,000	50,000	100,000
Total costs	70,000	102,500	102,500	205,000
Weekly gross profit	$180,000	$ 77,500	$ 77,500	$155,000

[1] If table cleaner is not processed further, it is allocated one-third of the $210,000 of CDG cost, which is equal to one-third of the total physical output.

[2] If table cleaner is processed further, the total physical output is 36,000 litres. TSR and TP combined account for 50% of the total physical output and are each allocated 25% of the CDG cost.

Instructions

(a) Do the following to determine whether management made the correct decision by not processing the table cleaner further.
  1. Calculate the company's total weekly gross profit assuming the table cleaner is not processed further.
  2. Calculate the company's total weekly gross profit assuming the table cleaner is processed further.
  3. Compare the resulting net incomes and comment on management's decision.
(b) Using incremental analysis, determine whether the table cleaner should be processed further.

(CMA-adapted)

P6–19A Last year (2005), Calway Condos installed a mechanized elevator for its tenants. The owner of the company, Cab Calway, recently returned from an industry equipment exhibition where he watched a computerized elevator demonstrated. He was impressed with the elevator's speed, comfortable ride, and cost efficiency. Upon returning from the exhibition, he asked his purchasing agent to collect price and operating cost data on the new elevator. In addition, he asked the company's accountant to provide him with cost data on the company's elevator. The information is presented below:

Calculate gain or loss, and determine whether equipment should be replaced.
(SO 6)

	Old Elevator	New Elevator
Purchase price	$150,000	$180,000
Estimated salvage value	0	0
Estimated useful life	6 years	5 years
Amortization method	Straight-line	Straight-line
Annual operating expenses other than amortization:		
Variable	$35,000	$12,000
Fixed	23,000	8,400

Annual revenues are $240,000, and selling and administrative expenses are $29,000, regardless of which elevator is used. If the old elevator is replaced now, at the beginning of 2006, Calway Condos will be able to sell it for $25,000.

Instructions

(a) Determine any gain or loss if the old elevator is replaced.
(b) Prepare a five-year summarized income statement for each of the following assumptions:
    1. The old elevator is kept.
    2. The old elevator is replaced.
(c) Using incremental analysis, determine whether the old elevator should be replaced.
(d) ◁▤▤▤▷ Write a memo to Cab Calway explaining why any gain or loss should be ignored in the decision to replace the old elevator.

Calculate contribution margin and prepare incremental analysis for elimination of divisions.
(SO 7)

P6–20A Ribeiro Manufacturing Company has four operating divisions. During the first quarter of 2005, the company reported aggregate income from operations of $176,000 and the following divisional results:

	Division			
	I	II	III	IV
Sales	$250,000	$200,000	$500,000	$400,000
Cost of goods sold	200,000	189,000	300,000	250,000
Selling and administrative expenses	65,000	60,000	60,000	50,000
Income (loss) from operations	$ (15,000)	$ (49,000)	$140,000	$100,000

Analysis reveals the following percentages of variable costs in each division:

	I	II	III	IV
Cost of goods sold	70%	90%	80%	75%
Selling and administrative expenses	40	70	50	60

Discontinuance of any division would save 50% of the fixed costs and expenses for that division.
    Top management is very concerned about the unprofitable divisions (I and II). Consensus is that one or both of the divisions should be discontinued.

Instructions

(a) Calculate the contribution margin for divisions I and II.
(b) Prepare an incremental analysis for the possible discontinuance of (1) division I and (2) division II. What course of action do you recommend for each division?
(c) Prepare a condensed income statement in columns for Ribeiro Manufacturing, assuming division II is eliminated. Use the CVP format. Division II's unavoidable fixed costs are allocated equally to the continuing divisions.
(d) Reconcile the total income from operations ($176,000) with the total income from operations without division II.

Prepare incremental analysis for whether to sell or process materials further.
(SO 5)

P6–21A A company manufactures three products using the same production process. The costs incurred up to the split-off point are $200,000. These costs are allocated to the products on the basis of their sales value at the split-off point. The number of units produced, the selling prices per unit of the three products at the split-off point and after further processing, and the additional processing costs are as follows:

Product	Number of Units Produced	Selling Price at Split-Off	Selling Price after Processing	Additional Processing Costs
A	3,000	$10.00	$15.00	$14,000
B	6,000	11.60	16.20	16,000
C	2,000	19.40	21.60	9,000

Instructions

(a) Which information is relevant to the decision on whether or not to process the products further? Explain why this information is relevant.
(b) Which product(s) should be processed further and which should be sold at the split-off point?
(c) Would your decision be different if the company was using the quantity of output to allocate joint costs? Explain.

(CGA-adapted)

P6–22A Straus Company operates a small factory in which it manufactures two products: A and B. Production and sales results for last year were as follows:

	A	B
Units sold	8,000	20,000
Selling price per unit	$95	$78
Variable costs per unit	50	45
Fixed costs per unit	22	22

For purposes of simplicity, the firm averages total fixed costs over the total number of units of A and B produced and sold.

The research department has developed a new product (C) as a replacement for product B. Market studies show that Straus Company could sell 11,000 units of C next year at a price of $120; the variable costs per unit of C are $42. The introduction of product C will lead to a 10% increase in demand for product A and discontinuation of product B. If the company does not introduce the new product, it expects next year's results to be same as last year's.

Instructions

Should Straus Company introduce product C next year? Explain why or why not. Show calculations to support your decision.

(CMA Canada-adapted)

P6–23A The Kamloops Outdoors Corporation, which produces a highly successful line of summer lotions and insect repellents and sells them to wholesalers, has decided to diversify in order to stabilize its sales throughout the year. A natural area for the company to consider is the production of winter lotions and creams to prevent dry and chapped skin.

After considerable research, a winter products line has been developed. However, because of the conservative nature of company management, the president has decided to introduce only one of the new products for this coming winter. If the product is a success, there will be further expansion in future years.

The product selected is a lip balm to be sold in a lipstick-type tube. The product will be sold to wholesalers in boxes of 24 tubes for $16.00 per box. Because of available capacity, no additional fixed charges will be incurred to produce the product. However, to allocate a fair share of the company's present fixed costs to the new product, the product will absorb a $150,000 fixed charge.

Using the estimated sales and production of 100,000 boxes of lip balm as the standard volume, the accounting department has developed the following costs per box of 24 tubes:

Direct labour	$ 4.00
Direct materials	6.00
Total overhead	3.00
Total	$13.00

Kamloops Outdoors has approached a cosmetics manufacturer to discuss the possibility of purchasing the tubes for the new product. The purchase price of the empty tubes from the cosmetics manufacturer would be $1.90 per 24 tubes. If Kamloops Outdoors accepts the purchase proposal, it is estimated that direct labour and variable overhead costs would be reduced by 10% and direct materials costs would be reduced by 20%.

Instructions

(a) Should Kamloops Outdoors make or buy the tubes? Show calculations to support your answer.

(b) What would be the maximum purchase price acceptable to Kamloops Outdoors for the tubes? Support your answer with an appropriate explanation.

(c) Instead of sales of 100,000 boxes, revised estimates show a sales volume of 125,000 boxes. At this new volume, additional equipment, at an annual rental charge of $10,000, must be acquired to manufacture the tubes. However, this incremental cost would be the only additional fixed cost, even if sales increased to 300,000 boxes. (The 300,000 level is the goal for the third year of production.) Under these circumstances, should Kamloops Outdoors make or buy the tubes? Show calculations to support your answer.

(d) The company has the option of making and buying at the same time. What would be your answer to (c) if this alternative was considered? Show calculations to support your answer.

(e) What qualitative factors should Kamloops Outdoors Corporation consider in determining whether it should make or buy the lip balm tubes?

(CMA Canada-adapted)

Problems: Set B

Prepare incremental analysis for special order and identify non-financial factors in decision.
(SO 3)

P6–24B   Oakbrook Company is currently producing 18,000 units per month, which is 80% of its production capacity. Variable manufacturing costs are currently $13.20 per unit, and fixed manufacturing costs are $72,000 per month. Oakbrook pays a 9% sales commission to its salespeople, has $30,000 in fixed administrative expenses per month, and is averaging $432,000 in sales per month.

A special order received from a foreign company would enable Oakbrook Company to operate at 100% capacity. The foreign company offered to pay 80% of Oakbrook's current selling price per unit. If the order is accepted, Oakbrook will have to spend an extra $2.00 per unit to package the product for overseas shipping. Also, Oakbrook would need to lease a new stamping machine to imprint the foreign company's logo on the product, at a monthly cost of $5,000. The special order would require a sales commission of $4,000.

Instructions

(a) Calculate the number of units involved in the special order and the foreign company's offered price per unit.

(b) What is the manufacturing cost of producing one unit of Oakbrook's product for regular customers?

(c) Prepare an incremental analysis of the special order. Should management accept the order?

(d) What is the lowest price that Oakbrook could accept for the special order to earn net income of $1.20 per unit?

(e) ▭▭▭▷ What non-financial factors should management consider in making its decision?

Calculate contribution margin and prepare incremental analysis for maximizing operating income and replacing equipment.
(SO 6)

P6–25B   Sharp Aerospace has a five-year contract to supply North Plane with four specific spare parts for its fleet of airplanes. The following table provides information on selling prices, costs, and the number of units of each part that the company needs to produce annually according to the contract with North Plane:

	A10	A20	A30	A40
Sales	$1,500,000	$875,000	$450,000	$2,400,000
Variables costs	1,235,000	425,000	187,000	1,875,000
Contribution margin	$ 265,000	$450,000	$263,000	$ 525,000
Production in units	1,000	250	750	600
Machine hours/unit	2	4	1.5	3

Fixed overhead costs amount to $820,000 and are allocated based on the number of units produced. The company has a maximum annual capacity of 6,000 machine hours.

Instructions

(a) If Sharp Aerospace could manufacture only one of the four parts, which spare part should it produce, based on the contribution margin? Explain why.

(b) Polaris Airline wants to buy 200 units of part A10 at 110% of the price currently paid by North Plane. Assume that for any of the four parts, Sharp Aerospace has to supply North Plane with at least 90% of the number of units specified in the contract. Should Sharp Aerospace accept the order for 200 units of part A10?

(c) A new technology is available that costs $2.5 million and would increase Sharp Aerospace's annual capacity by 25%. Should the company purchase the new technology? Assume that the technology has an estimated life of four years and that Sharp Aerospace can sell, at the same prices paid by North Plane, all the units it can produce of any of the four parts. Show all your calculations.

(CGA-adapted)

P6–26B The management of Dunham Manufacturing Company has asked for your assistance in deciding whether to continue manufacturing a part or to buy it from an outside supplier. The part, called Tropica, is a component of Dunham's finished product.

Prepare incremental analysis related to make-or-buy decision, consider opportunity cost; and identify non-financial factors.
(SO 3, 4)

An analysis of the accounting records and the production data revealed the following information for the year ending December 31, 2005:

1. The machinery department produced 35,000 units of Tropica.
2. Each Tropica unit requires 10 minutes to produce. Three people in the machinery department work full-time (2,000 hours per year each) producing Tropica. Each person is paid $12 per hour.
3. The cost of materials per Tropica unit is $2.20.
4. Manufacturing costs directly applicable to the production of Tropica are as follows: indirect labour, $6,000; utilities, $1,500; amortization, $1,800; property taxes and insurance, $1,000. All of the costs will be eliminated if Tropica is purchased.
5. The lowest price for a Tropica from an outside supplier is $4 per unit. Freight charges would be $0.50 per unit, and a part-time receiving clerk at $8,500 per year would be required.
6. If Tropica is purchased, the excess space that becomes available will be used to store Dunham's finished product. Currently, Dunham rents storage space at approximately $0.80 per unit stored per year. Approximately 5,000 units per year are stored in the rented space.

Instructions

(a) Prepare an incremental analysis for the make-or-buy decision. Should Dunham make or buy the part? Why?
(b) Prepare an incremental analysis, assuming the released facilities (freed-up space) can be used to produce $12,000 of net income in addition to the savings on the rental of storage space. What decision should now be made?
(c) ▭▭▭▶ What non-financial factors should be considered in the decision?

P6–27B Bonita Household Products Co. is a diversified household-cleaner processing company. The company's St. Lawrence plant produces two products from a common set of chemical inputs (TLC): a glass cleaner and a metal cleaner. Each week 30,000 litres of chemical input are processed at a cost of $200,000 into 20,000 litres of metal cleaner and 10,000 litres of glass cleaner. The metal cleaner has no market value until it is converted into a polish with the trade name MetalShine. The additional processing costs for this conversion total $270,000. MetalShine sells at $15 per 750-ml bottle.

Determine whether product should be sold or processed further.
(SO 5)

The glass cleaner can be sold for $24 per 750-ml bottle. However, the glass cleaner can be converted into two other products by adding 10,000 litres of another compound (MST) to the 10,000 litres of glass cleaner. This joint process will yield 10,000 litres each of plastic cleaner (PC) and plastic polish (PP). The additional processing costs for this process total $140,000. Both plastic products can be sold for $20 per 750-ml bottle.

The company decided not to process the glass cleaner into PC and PP based on the following analysis:

| | Glass Cleaner | Process Further | | |
		Plastic Cleaner (PC)	Plastic Polish (PP)	Total
Production in litres	(10,000)	10,000	10,000	
Revenue	$240,000	$200,000	$200,000	$400,000
Costs				
TLC costs	50,000[1]	40,000	40,000	80,000[2]
MST costs	0	70,000	70,000	140,000
Total costs	50,000	110,000	110,000	220,000
Weekly gross profit	$190,000	$ 90,000	$ 90,000	$180,000

[1] If glass cleaner is not processed further, it is allocated one-quarter of the $200,000 of TLC cost, because it represents one quarter of the total physical output.
[2] If glass cleaner is processed further, the total physical output is 40,000 litres. PC and PP combined account for 40% of the total physical output and are each allocated 20% of the TLC cost.

Instructions

(a) Do the following to determine whether management made the correct decision by not processing the glass cleaner further:
  1. Calculate the company's total weekly gross profit assuming the glass cleaner is not processed further.
  2. Calculate the company's total weekly gross profit assuming the glass cleaner is processed further.
  3. Compare the resulting net incomes and comment on management's decision.
(b) Using incremental analysis, determine whether the glass cleaner should be processed further.

(CMA-adapted)

Calculate gain or loss, and determine whether equipment should be replaced.
(SO 6)

P6–28B   Quik Press Inc. offers one-day dry cleaning. At the beginning of 2005, the company purchased a mechanized pressing machine. The owner of the company, Jill Jabowski, recently returned from an industry equipment exhibition where she saw a computerized pressing machine demonstrated. She was impressed with the machine's speed, efficiency, and quality of output. Upon returning from the exhibition, she asked her purchasing agent to collect price and operating cost data on the new pressing machine. In addition, she asked the company's accountant to provide her with cost data on the company's pressing machine. This information is presented below:

	Old Pressing Machine	New Pressing Machine
Purchase price	$120,000	$150,000
Estimated salvage value	0	0
Estimated useful life	6 years	5 years
Amortization method	Straight-line	Straight-line
Annual operating expenses other than amortization:		
Variable	$30,000	$10,000
Fixed	20,000	7,000

Annual revenues are $200,000, and selling and administrative expenses are $24,000, regardless of which pressing machine is used. If the old machine is replaced now, at the beginning of 2006, Quik Press will be able to sell it for $10,000.

Instructions

(a) Determine any gain or loss if the old pressing machine is replaced.
(b) Prepare a five-year summarized income statement for each of the following assumptions:
  1. The old machine is kept.
  2. The old machine is replaced.
(c) Using incremental analysis, determine whether the old pressing machine should be replaced.
(d) ▭▭▭▷ Write a memo to Jill Jabowski explaining why any gain or loss should be ignored in the decision to replace the old pressing machine.

Calculate contribution margin and prepare incremental analysis for make-or-buy decision.
(SO 4, 6)

P6–29B   Quincy Inc. manufactures and sells bakery products and has decided to put a new product on the market: an ice cream cake. The product will be sold in boxes of 24. The price of each box will be $8. The company will use its excess capacity to manufacture the product. The accounting department has decided that $100,000 worth of fixed overhead costs should be allocated to the product.

The accounting department has budgeted the following costs (based on production of 100,000 boxes):

Direct materials (per box)	$3.00
Direct labour (per box)	2.00
Fixed and variable overhead (per box)	1.50
Total	$6.50

Quincy can purchase ice cream units, one of the ingredients, from a dairy company. The dairy company would sell the ice cream units for $0.90 for 24 units. If Quincy buys the ice cream units from the dairy company, direct labour and variable overhead costs would be reduced by 10%. The direct materials cost would be 20% lower than the original budgeted amount and would not include the cost of the ice cream units purchased from the dairy company.

Instructions

(a) Should Quincy make or buy the ice cream units? Explain your decision.

(b) Calculate the maximum amount that Quincy should pay for the ice cream units.

(c) Suppose that sales projections are revised and that Quincy could sell 125,000 boxes instead of 100,000. In such a case, to produce ice cream, it would need to lease a new machine for $10,000 a year. Under these conditions, should Quincy make the ice cream units or buy them from the dairy company? Explain your decision.

(d) Suppose that sales projections are revised and that Quincy could sell 125,000 boxes instead of 100,000, and that it would need to lease the machine. Would it be better off if it makes the ice cream for the first 100,000 boxes and buys the remainder from the dairy company? Explain your decision. Assume the $0.90 price is available for any volume.

(e) List four qualitative factors that Quincy should consider when determining whether it should make or buy the ice cream units.

(CGA-adapted)

P6-30B Laos Manufacturing Company has four operating divisions. During the first quarter of 2005, the company reported total income from operations of $36,000 and the following results for the divisions:

Calculate contribution margin and prepare incremental analysis for elimination of divisions. (SO 7)

	Division			
	Kelowna	Brandon	Sherbrooke	Moncton
Sales	$405,000	$730,000	$920,000	$500,000
Cost of goods sold	400,000	480,000	576,000	390,000
Selling and administrative expenses	100,000	207,000	246,000	120,000
Income (loss) from operations	$ (95,000)	$ 43,000	$ 98,000	$ (10,000)

Analysis reveals the following percentages of variable costs in each division.

	Kelowna	Brandon	Sherbrooke	Moncton
Cost of goods sold	90%	80%	90%	95%
Selling and administrative expenses	60	60	70	80

Closing any division would save 70% of the fixed costs and expenses for that division.

Top management is deeply concerned about the unprofitable divisions (Kelowna and Moncton). The consensus is that one or both of them should be eliminated.

Instructions

(a) Calculate the contribution margin for the two unprofitable divisions.

(b) Prepare an incremental analysis for the possible elimination of (1) the Kelowna division and (2) the Moncton division. What course of action do you recommend for each division?

(c) Prepare a condensed income statement in columns using the CVP format for Laos Manufacturing Company, assuming (1) the Kelowna division is eliminated, and (2) the unavoidable fixed costs and expenses of the Kelowna division are allocated 30% to Brandon, 50% to Sherbrooke, and 20% to Moncton.

(d) Compare the total income from operations with the Kelowna division ($36,000) to total income from operations without this division.

P6-31B Benkhadour Co. manufactures four different products. Because the quality of its products is high, the demand for the products is more than the company can produce.

Based on the enquiries made by current and potential customers, you have estimated the following for the coming year:

Calculate contribution margin and prepare incremental analysis for maximizing operating income. (SO 8)

Product	Estimated Demand in Units	Selling Price per Unit	Direct Materials Cost per Unit	Direct Labour Cost per Unit
A	8,000	$ 50	$ 5	$ 5
B	24,000	60	10	9
C	20,000	150	25	30
D	30,000	100	15	20

The following information is also available:

1. The direct labour rate is $15 per hour and the factory has a capacity of 80,000 hours. For the next year, Benkhadour is unable to expand this capacity.

2. Benkhadour is unwilling to increase its selling prices.

3. Apart from direct materials and direct labour, the only other variable expense is variable overhead. The variable overhead is 50% of the direct labour cost.
4. Fixed manufacturing overhead is estimated to be $1 million for the coming year. Fixed marketing and administrative expenses are estimated to be $750,000 for the coming year.

Instructions

Which products and how many units of each should Benkhadour produce in the coming year in order to maximize its operating income?

(CGA-adapted)

Prepare incremental analysis for whether to sell or process materials further. (SO 5)

P6−32B The following information is for a company that produces four types of microprocessors using the same production process. The common costs of these products, up to the split-off point, are $550,000. Common costs are allocated based on the quantity of output. The following information includes additional processing costs, the selling price of each product at the split-off point, and the selling price of each product after further processing:

Microprocessor	Number of Units Produced	Selling Price at Split-off Point	Selling Price after Further Processing	Additional Costs for Further Processing
1	3,000	$10.00	$15.00	$14,800
2	4,000	9.50	12.25	8,500
3	2,500	11.00	15.70	12,000
4	500	7.75	10.25	1,250

Instructions

(a) If only one product can be processed further, which one should the company choose? Briefly explain why.
(b) Referring to your answer in part (a), identify which information is relevant to the decision to process this product further.
(c) If common costs up to the split-off point were allocated on the basis of the market values at the split-off point, would your decision in part (a) be different? Briefly explain why.

(CGA-adapted)

Calculate contribution margin and prepare incremental analysis for maximizing operating income and replacing equipment. (SO 6)

P6−33B ATI Teck manufactures an electronic component for a high-end computer. The company currently sells 50,000 units a year at a price of $180 per unit. These units are produced using a machine that was purchased five years ago at a cost of $1.2 million. It currently has a book value of $600,000; however, due to its specialized nature, it has a market value today of only $70,000. The machine, which is expected to last another five years, will have no salvage value. The costs to produce an electronic component are as follows:

Direct materials	$ 15.00
Direct labour (4 hours × $30.00/hour)	120.00
Variable overhead (4 hours × $2.40/hour)	9.60
Fixed overhead (4 hours × $3.20/hour)[1]	12.80
Total cost per unit	$157.40

[1] Based on an annual activity of 100,000 direct labour hours.

The company expects the following changes for next year:

• The unit selling price will increase by 10 percent.
• Direct labour rates will increase by 15 percent.
• Sales are expected to increase to 52,000 units (within the capacity of present facilities) and remain at that level.

Management is currently considering the replacement of the company's old machine with a new one that would cost $2.5 million. The new machine is expected to last five years and to have a salvage value of $60,000 (straight-line amortization is used). By using the new machine, management expects to cut variable direct labour hours to 3.5 hours per unit, but the company will have to hire an operator for the machine at $90,000 per year.

Instructions

(Ignore income taxes.)

(a) Determine whether or not the company should purchase the new machine.

(b) How many units would the company have to sell to earn annual profits of $460,000 (before taxes) if it were to purchase the new machine? Ignore any gain or loss on the sale of the old machine.

(CMA Canada-adapted)

P6–34B Furniture Shop Co. manufactures three types of computer desks. The income statement for the three products and the whole company is shown below:

Calculate contribution margin and prepare incremental analysis for elimination of product and special order.
(SO 7, 8)

	Product A	Product B	Product C	Total
Sales	$50,000	$60,000	$65,000	$175,000
Variable costs	25,000	40,000	60,000	125,000
Fixed costs	16,000	12,000	8,000	36,000
Total costs	41,000	52,000	68,000	161,000
Operating income	$ 9,000	$ 8,000	$ (3,000)	$ 14,000

The company produces 1,000 units of each product. The company's capacity is 9,000 labour hours. The labour for each product is four hours for Product A, three hours for Product B, and two hours for Product C. Fixed costs are allocated based on labour hours.

Instructions

(a) If the current production levels are maintained, should the company eliminate Product C? Explain your reasoning.

(b) If the company can sell unlimited quantities of any of the three products, which product should be produced?

(c) Suppose the company can sell unlimited quantities of any of the three products. If a customer wanted to purchase 500 units of Product C, what would the minimum sale price per unit be for this order?

(d) The company has a contract that requires it to supply 500 units of each product to a customer. The total market demand for a single product is limited to 1,500 units. How many units of each product should the company manufacture to maximize its total contribution margin?

(CGA-adapted)

Cases

Additional Cases

C6–35 Castle Company is considering the purchase of a new machine. The invoice price of the machine is $125,000, freight charges are estimated to be $4,000, and installation costs are expected to be $6,000. The salvage value of the new equipment is expected to be zero after a useful life of four years. Existing equipment could be kept and used for an additional four years if the new machine is not purchased. At that time, the salvage value of the equipment would be zero. If the new machine is purchased now, the existing machine would have to be scrapped. Castle's accountant, Shaida Fang, has accumulated the following data for annual sales and expenses, with and without the new machine:

1. Without the new machine, Castle can sell 12,000 units of product annually at a per unit selling price of $100. If the new machine is purchased, the number of units produced and sold would increase by 20%, and the selling price would remain the same.

2. The new machine is faster than the old machine, and it is more efficient in its usage of materials. With the old machine, the gross profit rate is 25% of sales, whereas the rate will be 30% of sales with the new machine.

3. Annual selling expenses are $180,000 with the current machine. Because the new machine would produce a greater number of units to be sold, annual selling expenses are expected to increase by 10% if it is purchased.

4. Annual administrative expenses are expected to be $100,000 with the old machine, and $113,000 with the new machine.

5. The current book value of the existing machine is $36,000. Castle uses straight-line amortization.

Instructions

Prepare an incremental analysis for the four years that shows whether Castle should keep the existing machine or buy the new one. (Ignore income tax effects.)

C6–36   Axia Inc. manufactures two electronic products, widgets and gadgets, and has a capacity of 1,000 machine hours. Prices and costs for each product are as follows:

	Widget	Gadget
Selling price per unit	$200	$280
Variable costs per unit		
Direct materials	$25	$30
Other direct costs	$6	$10
Indirect manufacturing costs[1]	$30	$44

[1] Variable indirect manufacturing costs are applied at a rate of $40 per machine hour.

Bromont Industries, a potential client, has offered $240 per unit to Axia for 250 special units. These 250 units would incur the following production costs and time:

Direct materials	$7,000
Other direct costs	$2,000
Machine hours	200

Instructions

(a) Assume that Axia has enough excess capacity to produce the special order. Calculate what the total contribution would be if the special order from Bromont were accepted.
(b) Assume that Axia is currently operating at full capacity. Determine whether Axia should produce the units for the special order instead of widget or gadget units. Show your calculations.
(c) Assume that Axia is actually operating at 95% of full capacity. Calculate what the opportunity cost would be if Bromont's special order were accepted. Show your calculations.
(d) Assume that Axia is actually operating at 95% of full capacity, and additional machines can be rented at a cost of $33,000 to produce Bromont's special order. If the special order is accepted, calculate its effect on Axia's profit. Show your calculations.

(CGA-adapted)

C6–37   Technology Plus manufactures small private-label electronic products, such as alarm clocks, stopwatches, kitchen timers, calculators, and automatic pencil sharpeners. Some of the products are sold as sets, and others are sold individually. Products are studied for their sales potential, and then cost estimates are made. The engineering department develops production plans, and then production begins. The company has generally had very successful product introduction. Only two products introduced by the company have been discontinued.

One of the products currently sold is a multi-alarm alarm clock. The clock has four alarms that can be programmed to sound at various times and for varying lengths of time. The company has had a lot of trouble making the circuit boards for the clocks. The production process has never operated smoothly. The product is unprofitable at the present time, mainly because of warranty repairs and product recalls. Two models of the clocks were recalled, for example, because they sometimes caused an electric shock when the alarms were being shut off. The engineering department is trying to revise the manufacturing process, but the revision will take another six months at least.

The clocks were very popular when they were introduced, and since they are private label, the company has not suffered much from the recalls. Presently, the company has a very large order for several items from a major retailer with locations across Canada. The order includes 5,000 of the multi-alarm clocks. When the company suggested that the retailer purchase the clocks from another manufacturer, the retailer threatened to cancel the entire order unless the clocks were included.

The company has therefore investigated the possibility of having another company make the clocks for it. The clocks were bid for the retailer's order based on an estimated $6.65 cost to manufacture, broken down as follows:

Circuit board, 1 each @ $2.00	$2.00
Plastic case, 1 each @ $0.75	0.75
Alarms, 4 @ $0.10 each	0.40
Labour, 15 minutes @ $12/hour	3.00
Overhead, $2.00 per labour hour	0.50

Technology Plus could purchase clocks to fill the retailer's order for $11 from Silver Star, a Korean manufacturer with a very good quality record. Silver Star has offered to reduce the price to $7.50 after Technology Plus has been a customer for six months and agrees to order at least 1,000 units per month. If Technology Plus becomes a "preferred customer" by purchasing 15,000 units per year, the price would be reduced still further to $4.50.

Alpha Products, a local manufacturer, has also offered to make clocks for Technology Plus. It has offered to sell 5,000 clocks for $4 each. However, Alpha Products has been in business for only six months. It has had significant turnover in its labour force, and the local press has reported that the owners may face tax evasion charges soon. The owner of Alpha Products is an electronics engineer, however, and the quality of the clocks is likely to be good.

If Technology Plus decides to purchase the clocks from either Silver Star or Alpha, all of its current costs to manufacture the alarm clock could be avoided, except a total of $5,000 in overhead costs for machine amortization. The machinery is fairly new, and has no alternative use.

Instructions

(a) What is the difference in profit under each of the alternatives if the clocks are to be sold for $14.50 each to the retailer?

(b) What are the most important non-financial factors that Technology Plus should consider when making this decision?

(c) What do you think Technology Plus should do about the retailer's order? What should it do with regard to continuing to manufacture the multi-alarm alarm clocks? Be prepared to defend your answer.

C6−38 La Mode Design Inc., a high-fashion women's dress manufacturer, is planning to market a new cocktail dress for the coming season. La Mode Design Inc. supplies retailers in Toronto, Montreal, and the Atlantic provinces.

Four metres of material are laid out for the dress pattern. After cutting, some material remains, which can be sold as remnants. The leftover material could also be used to manufacture a matching cape and handbag. However, if the leftover material is to be used for the cape and handbag, more care will be needed in the cutting, and the cutting costs will therefore increase.

The company expects to sell 1,250 dresses if a matching cape and handbag are not available. La Mode Design's market research reveals, however, that dress sales will be 20% higher if a matching cape and handbag are available. The market research indicates that the cape and/or handbag could not be sold individually but only as accessories with the dress. The various combinations of dresses, capes, and handbags that will be sold by retailers are as follows:

Complete sets of dress, cape, and handbag	70%
Dress and cape	6
Dress and handbag	15
Dress only	9
Total	100%

The material used in the dress costs $12.50 a metre, or $50.00 for each dress. The cost of cutting the dress if the cape and handbag are not manufactured is estimated at $20.00 a dress, and the resulting remnants can be sold for $5.00 for each dress cut out. If the cape and handbag are to be manufactured, the cutting costs will be increased by $9.00 per dress. There will be no saleable remnants if the capes and handbags are manufactured in the quantities estimated.

The selling prices and the costs to complete the three items once they are cut are as follows:

	Selling Price per Unit	Unit Cost to Complete[1]
Dress	$200.00	$80.00
Cape	27.50	19.50
Handbag	9.50	6.50

[1] Excludes cost of material and cutting.

Instructions

(a) Prepare La Mode Design's incremental analysis for manufacturing the capes and hand-bags with the dresses.
(b) Based on your analysis, what decision should management make?
(c) Identify any qualitative factors that could influence the company's decision to manu-facture the capes and handbags that match the dresses.

(CMA Canada-adapted)

C6–39   John Bourcier operates a small machine shop. He manufactures one standard prod-uct that is also available from many other similar businesses, and he also manufactures deluxe products to order. His accountant prepared the following annual income statement:

	Deluxe Sales	Standard Sales	Total
Sales	$50,000	$25,000	$75,000
Costs			
Material	10,000	8,000	18,000
Labour	20,000	9,000	29,000
Amortization	6,300	3,600	9,900
Power	700	400	1,100
Rent	6,000	1,000	7,000
Heat and light	600	100	700
Other	400	900	1,300
Total costs	44,000	23,000	67,000
Net income	$ 6,000	$ 2,000	$ 8,000

The amortization charges are for machines used in the product lines. The power charge is apportioned based on an estimate of the power consumed by each line. The rent is for the building space, which has been leased for 10 years at $7,000 per year. The rent and the heat and light costs are apportioned to the product lines based on the amount of floor space oc-cupied by each line. All other costs are current expenses that are identified with the product line causing them.

A valued customer has asked Mr. Bourcier if he would manufacture 5,000 of the deluxe products for him. Mr. Bourcier is working at capacity and would have to give up some other business in order to take this order. He cannot cancel deluxe orders he has already agreed to, so he would have to reduce the output of his standard product by about one-half for a year while producing the requested deluxe product. The customer is willing to pay $7.00 for each unit. The material cost will be about $2.00 per unit and the labour will be $3.60 per unit. Mr. Bourcier will have to spend $2,000 for a special device that will be discarded when the job is done.

Instructions

(a) Calculate the incremental cost of the order.
(b) Calculate the full cost of the order.
(c) Calculate the opportunity cost of taking the order.
(d) Determine the sunk costs related to the order.
(e) Should Mr. Bourcier accept the order? Explain your answer.

(CMA Canada-adapted)

C6–40   Robert Buey became chief executive officer of Phelps Manufacturing two years ago. At the time, the company was reporting lagging profits, and Robert was brought in to "stir things up." The company has three divisions: electronics, fibre optics, and plumb-ing supplies. Robert has no interest in plumbing supplies, and one of the first things he did was to put pressure on his accountants to reallocate some of the company's fixed costs away from the other two divisions to the plumbing division. This had the effect of causing the plumbing division to report losses during the last two years; in the past it had always reported low, but acceptable, net income. Robert felt that this reallocation would shine a favourable light on him in front of the board of directors because it meant that the electronics and fibre optics divisions would appear to be improving. Since these are "businesses of the future," he believed that the stock market would react favourably to these increases, and not penalize the poor results of the plumbing division.

Without this shift in the allocation of fixed costs, the profits of the electronics and fibre optics divisions would not have improved. But now the board of directors has suggested that the plumbing division be closed because it is reporting losses. This would mean that nearly 500 employees, many of whom have worked for Phelps their whole lives, would lose their jobs.

Instructions

(a) If a division is reporting losses, does that necessarily mean that it should be closed?
(b) Was the reallocation of fixed costs across divisions unethical?
(c) What should Robert do?

Answers to Self-Study Questions

1. d   2. b   3. c   4. d   5. d   6. a   7. b   8. c   9. b

Remember to go back to the Navigator Box at the beginning of the chapter to check off your completed work.

CHAPTER 7

Variable Costing: A Decision-Making Perspective

No Fishy Business in Tracking Costs

High Liner Foods Incorporated, the processor and marketer of seafood and frozen pasta products with a head office and food processing plant in Lunenburg, Nova Scotia, has one of the largest prepared seafood processing operations in North America. It produces a wide range of products, the raw materials for which come from around the world, including Europe, the Far East, South America, and Alaska.

For the most part, High Liner uses absorption costing, says CFO Kelly Nelson. Costs are classified into three categories: direct costs, including direct labour, packaging, ingredients, seafood, and the energy to run the fryers; manufacturing overhead, including service labour (forklift drivers and people who are moving product), repair and maintenance, other energy costs, such as heat and electricity, and sanitation and garbage removal; and fixed overhead, such as rent, depreciation, insurance, property taxes, administrative expenses, and salaried employees.

"We use full standard costs for tracking our profitability," says Mr. Nelson. "We fully allocate the cost both for inventory and cost of sales purposes."

However, there are occasions when the food processor uses variable costing to assess operations internally, such as when analyzing variances between variable and absorbed costs. High Liner produces a number of individual variances—for seafood, bread and batter, packaging, manufacturing overhead, etc.—and does a variance analysis for each component. "Yield is very important on the seafood raw material because we've got expensive raw material, throughput is very important on our labour, and waste is important on the other ingredients," says Mr. Nelson. "We're looking to make sure that we're working within standard, or else we have to re-engineer the standard."

Also, on the rare occasions High Liner decides to move one product line from one plant to another, it uses variable costing since much of the overhead stays. "Part of the manufacturing overheads we deem to be variable—about 35 percent of them—so what we do is take the direct cost plus 35 percent of the manufacturing overhead and compare that from plant to plant," says Mr. Nelson.

High Liner Foods Incorporated: www.highlinerfoods.com

THE NAVIGATOR

☐ Scan *Study Objectives*

☐ Read *Feature Story*

☐ Read *Chapter Preview*

☐ Read text and answer *Before You Go On* p. 293

☐ Review *Summary of Study Objectives*

☐ Review *Using the Decision Toolkit—A Summary*

☐ Work *Demonstration Problem*

☐ Answer *Self-Study Questions*

☐ Complete assignments

STUDY OBJECTIVES

After studying this chapter, you should be able to:

1. Explain the difference between absorption costing and variable costing.
2. Discuss the effect that changes in the production level and sales level have on net income measured under absorption costing versus under variable costing.
3. Discuss the advantages of absorption costing versus variable costing for management decision-making.

the navigator

As the opening story about High Liner Food Incorporated suggests, the relationship between a company's fixed and variable costs can have a huge impact on its profitability. In particular, the trend toward cost structures that have mostly fixed costs has significantly increased the volatility of many companies' net income. In order to better track and understand the impact of cost structure on corporate profitability, some companies use an approach called *variable costing*. The purpose of this chapter is to show how variable costing can be helpful in making solid business decisions.

The chapter is organized as follows:

Absorption Costing versus Variable Costing

study objective 1

Explain the difference between absorption costing and variable costing.

In the earlier chapters, both variable and fixed manufacturing costs were classified as product costs. In job order costing, for example, a job is assigned the costs of direct materials, direct labour, and **both** variable and fixed manufacturing overhead. This costing approach is referred to as **full** or **absorption costing**. It is so named because all manufacturing costs are charged to, or absorbed by, the product. Absorption costing is the approach used for external reporting under generally accepted accounting principles.

An alternative approach is to use variable costing. Under **variable costing**, only direct materials, direct labour, and variable manufacturing overhead costs are considered product costs. Fixed manufacturing overhead costs are recognized as period costs (expenses) when incurred. The difference between absorption costing and variable costing is shown graphically as follows.

Illustration 7-1 ▶

Difference between absorption costing and variable costing

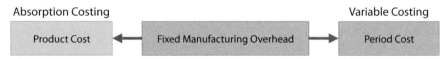

Selling and administrative expenses are period costs under both absorption and variable costing.

Illustration Comparing Absorption Costing and Variable Costing

To illustrate absorption and variable costing, assume that Premium Products Corporation manufactures a polyurethane sealant called Fix-it for car windshields. Relevant data for Fix-it in January 2005, the first month of production, are as follows:

Selling price: $20 per unit

Units: produced 30,000; sold 20,000; beginning inventory zero

Variable unit costs: manufacturing $9 (direct materials $5, direct labour $3, and variable overhead $1); selling and administrative expenses $2

Fixed costs: manufacturing overhead $120,000; selling and administrative expenses $15,000

The per unit manufacturing cost under each costing approach is calculated in Illustration 7-3.

Illustration 7-3 ◀

Calculation of per unit manufacturing cost

Type of Cost	Absorption Costing	Variable Costing
Direct materials	$ 5	$5
Direct labour	3	3
Variable manufacturing overhead	1	1
Fixed manufacturing overhead ($120,000 ÷ 30,000 units produced)	4	0
Manufacturing cost per unit	$13	$9

The manufacturing cost per unit is $4 ($13 − $9) higher for absorption costing. This occurs because fixed manufacturing costs are a product cost under absorption costing. Under variable costing, in contrast, they are a period cost, and are therefore expensed. Based on these data, each unit sold and each unit remaining in inventory is costed at $13 under absorption costing and at $9 under variable costing.

Absorption Costing Illustration

The income statement for Premium Products using absorption costing is shown in Illustration 7-4. It shows that the cost of goods manufactured is $390,000, calculated by multiplying the 30,000 units produced by the manufacturing cost of $13 per unit (see Illustration 7-3). Also, both the variable and fixed selling and administrative expenses are treated as period costs and are therefore expensed in 2005. Under absorption costing, $40,000 of the fixed overhead costs (10,000 × $4) is deferred to a future period as part of the cost of ending inventory.

Helpful Hint The income statement in Illustration 7-4 is the same as the one used under generally accepted accounting principles and the same as that used previously in Chapter 2.

Illustration 7-4 ◀

Absorption-costing income statement

PREMIUM PRODUCTS CORPORATION
Income Statement
Month Ended January 31, 2005
Absorption Costing

Sales (20,000 units × $20)		$400,000
Cost of goods sold		
Inventory, January 1	$ 0	
Cost of goods manufactured (30,000 units × $13)	390,000	
Cost of goods available for sale	390,000	
Inventory, January 31 (10,000 units × $13)	130,000	
Cost of goods sold (20,000 units × $13)		260,000
Gross profit		140,000
Variable selling and administrative expenses (20,000 × $2)		40,000
Fixed selling and administrative expenses		15,000
Net income		$ 85,000

Helpful Hint This is the traditional statement that would result from job-order and processing costing, as explained in Chapters 2 and 3.

Variable Costing Illustration

As shown in Illustration 7-5, the cost-volume-profit format is used in preparing a variable-costing income statement. The variable manufacturing cost of $270,000 is calculated by multiplying the 30,000 units produced by the variable manufacturing cost of $9 per unit (see Illustration 7-3). As in absorption costing, both variable and fixed selling and administrative expenses are treated as period costs.

Illustration 7-5 ▶

Variable-costing income statement

Helpful Hint Note the difference in the calculation of the ending inventory: $9 per unit here, $13 per unit above.

PREMIUM PRODUCTS CORPORATION Income Statement Month Ended January 31, 2005 Variable Costing		
Sales (20,000 units × $20)		$400,000
Variable cost of goods sold		
Inventory, January 1	$ 0	
Variable manufacturing costs (30,000 units × $9)	270,000	
Cost of goods available for sale	270,000	
Inventory, January 31 (10,000 units × $9)	90,000	
Variable cost of goods sold	180,000	
Variable selling and administrative expenses (20,000 units × $2)	40,000	220,000
Contribution margin		180,000
Fixed manufacturing overhead		120,000
Fixed selling and administrative expenses		15,000
Net income		$ 45,000

Conceptually, there is one major difference between variable and absorption costing: Under variable costing, the fixed manufacturing overhead is charged as an expense in the current period. Fixed overhead costs of the current period, therefore, are not deferred to future periods through the ending inventory. As a result, absorption costing will show a higher net income than variable costing whenever there are more units produced than sold. This difference can be seen in the two income statements for our example (Illustrations 7-4 and 7-5). There is a $40,000 difference in the ending inventories ($130,000 under absorption costing, but $90,000 under variable costing). Under absorption costing, $40,000 of the fixed overhead costs ($10,000 × $4) has been deferred to a future period as a product cost. In contrast, under variable costing, all the fixed manufacturing costs are expensed in the current period.

In summary, therefore, when there are more units produced than sold, income under absorption costing is higher. When fewer units are produced than sold, income under absorption costing is lower. When units produced and sold are the same, net income will be equal under the two costing approaches. In this case, there is no increase in ending inventory. So fixed overhead costs of the current period are not deferred to future periods through the ending inventory.

BUSINESS INSIGHT ▶ Service Company Perspective

Although most service companies have no inventory, the distinction between absorption costing and variable costing is still important for them. For example, many shipping companies have begun to rely more on variable costing for decision-making, especially for pricing decisions. For a shipping company, the problems with absorption costing are easier to see when operations are below full capacity. If it sets its price based on absorption costs, it will spread its full fixed costs over its existing jobs—resulting in a high fixed cost charge per shipment. This will make its price too high relative to competitors, and it will lose business—thus operating even further below capacity, and consequently charging an even higher fixed charge per job. This cycle continues until it is out of business. If, instead, it sets its prices using variable costing, it can avoid this dangerous cycle.

An Extended Example

To further illustrate the concepts underlying absorption and variable costing, we will now work through an extended example using Overbay Inc., a manufacturer of small airplane drones. We assume that the production volume stays the same over the three-year period, but that the number of units sold varies.

2005 Results

As indicated in Illustration 7-6, the manufacturing cost per drone is $300,000, which comprises variable manufacturing costs of $240,000 per drone and fixed manufacturing costs of $60,000 per drone. Overbay also has variable and fixed selling and administrative expenses ($50,000 and $80,000, respectively), which are expensed in 2005. The absorption-costing income statement for Overbay Inc. in Illustration 7-7 shows that the company reports net income of $870,000 under absorption costing.

study objective 2

Discuss the effect that changes in the production level and sales level have on net income measured under absorption costing versus under variable costing.

	2005	2006	2007
Volume information			
Drones in beginning inventory	0	0	2
Drones produced	10	10	10
Drones sold	10	8	12
Drones in ending inventory	0	2	0
Financial information			
Selling price per drone	$400,000		
Variable manufacturing costs per drone	240,000		
Fixed manufacturing costs for the year	600,000		
Fixed manufacturing costs per drone	60,000	($600,000 ÷ 10)	
Variable selling and administrative expenses per drone	5,000		
Fixed selling and administrative expenses	80,000		

Illustration 7-6 ◄

Information for Overbay Inc.

Illustration 7-7 ◄

Absorption-costing income statement—2005

OVERBAY INC.
Income Statement
Year Ended January 31, 2005
Absorption Costing

Sales (10 drones × $400,000)		$4,000,000
Cost of goods sold (10 drones × $300,000)		3,000,000
Gross profit		1,000,000
Variable selling and administrative expenses (10 drones × $5,000)	$50,000	
Fixed selling and administrative expenses	80,000	130,000
Net income		$ 870,000

As indicated earlier, under a variable-costing system the income statement follows a cost-volume-profit (CVP) format. In this case, the manufacturing cost is composed solely of the variable manufacturing costs of $240,000 per drone. The fixed manufacturing costs of $600,000 for the year are expensed in 2005. As in absorption costing, the fixed and variable selling and administrative expenses are period costs expensed in 2005. A variable-costing income statement for Overbay Inc. for 2005 is shown in Illustration 7-8.

Illustration 7-8 ▶

Variable-costing income
statement—2005

OVERBAY INC. Income Statement Year Ended January 31, 2005 Variable Costing		
Sales (10 drones × $400,000)		$4,000,000
Variable cost of goods sold (10 drones × $240,000)	$2,400,000	
Variable selling and administrative expenses (10 drones × $5,000)	50,000	2,450,000
Contribution margin		1,550,000
Fixed manufacturing overhead	600,000	
Fixed selling and administrative expenses	80,000	680,000
Net income		$ 870,000

As shown in Illustration 7-8, the variable-costing net income of $870,000 is the same as the absorption-costing net income calculated in Illustration 7-7. **When the number of units produced and sold is the same, net income is equal under the two costing approaches.** Because there is no increase in ending inventory, no fixed manufacturing costs in 2005 are deferred to future periods.

2006 Results

In 2006, Overbay produced 10 drones but sold only eight of them. As a result, there are two drones in ending inventory. The absorption-costing income statement for 2006 is shown in Illustration 7-9.

Illustration 7-9 ▶

Absorption-costing income
statement—2006

OVERBAY INC. Income Statement Year Ended January 31, 2006 Absorption Costing		
Sales (8 drones × $400,000)		$3,200,000
Cost of goods sold (8 drones × $300,000)		2,400,000
Gross profit		800,000
Variable selling and administrative expenses (8 drones × $5,000)	$40,000	
Fixed selling and administrative expenses	80,000	120,000
Net income		$ 680,000

Under absorption costing, the ending inventory of two drones is $600,000 ($300,000 × 2). Each unit of ending inventory includes $60,000 of fixed manufacturing overhead. Therefore, fixed manufacturing costs of $120,000 ($60,000 × 2 drones) are deferred until a future period.

The variable-costing income statement for 2006 is shown in Illustration 7-10.

Illustration 7-10 ◄

Variable-costing income
statement—2006

OVERBAY INC.
Income Statement
Year Ended January 31, 2006
Variable Costing

Sales (8 drones × $400,000)		$3,200,000
Variable cost of goods sold (8 drones × $240,000)	$1,920,000	
Variable selling and administrative expenses		
(8 drones × $5,000)	40,000	1,960,000
Contribution margin		1,240,000
Fixed manufacturing overhead	600,000	
Fixed selling and administrative expenses	80,000	680,000
Net income		$ 560,000

As shown, when more units are produced (10) than sold (8), net income under absorption costing ($680,000) is higher than net income under variable costing ($560,000). This is because cost of the ending inventory is higher under absorption costing than under variable costing. In 2006, under absorption costing, fixed manufacturing overhead of $120,000 is deferred and carried to future periods as part of the inventory. Under variable costing, the $120,000 is expensed in the current period and, therefore, the difference in the two net income numbers is $120,000 ($680,000 − $560,000).

2007 Results

In 2007, Overbay produced 10 drones and sold 12 (10 drones from the current year's production and two drones from the beginning inventory). As a result, there are no drones in ending inventory. The absorption-costing income statement for 2007 is shown in Illustration 7-11.

Illustration 7-11 ◄

Absorption-costing income
statement—2007

OVERBAY INC.
Income Statement
Year Ended January 31, 2007
Absorption Costing

Sales (12 drones × $400,000)		$4,800,000
Cost of goods sold (12 drones × $300,000)		3,600,000
Gross profit		1,200,000
Variable selling and administrative expenses		
(12 drones × $5,000)	$60,000	
Fixed selling and administrative expenses	80,000	140,000
Net income		$1,060,000

Fixed manufacturing costs of $720,000 are expensed in 2007—$120,000 of fixed manufacturing costs incurred during 2006 and included in beginning inventory, plus $600,000 of fixed manufacturing costs incurred during 2007. Having now seen the result for the absorption-costing statement, what would you expect the result to be under variable costing? Let's take a look.

The variable-costing income statement for 2007 is shown in Illustration 7-12.

Illustration 7-12 ►

Variable-costing income statement—2007

OVERBAY INC.
Income Statement
Year Ended January 31, 2007
Variable Costing

Sales (12 drones × $400,000)		$4,800,000
Variable cost of goods sold (12 drones × $240,000)	$2,880,000	
Variable selling and administrative expenses		
(12 drones × $5,000)	60,000	2,940,000
Contribution margin		1,860,000
Fixed manufacturing overhead	600,000	
Fixed selling and administrative expenses	80,000	680,000
Net income		$1,180,000

When fewer drones are produced (10) than sold (12), net income under absorption costing ($1,060,000) is less than net income under variable costing ($1,180,000). This difference of $120,000 ($1,180,000 − $1,060,000) occurs because $120,000 of fixed manufacturing overhead costs in the beginning inventory is charged to 2007 under absorption costing. Under variable costing, there is no fixed manufacturing overhead cost in the beginning inventory.

The results for the three years are summarized in Illustration 7-13.

Illustration 7-13 ►

Comparison of net income under both costing approaches

	Net Income under Both Costing Approaches		
	2005	2006	2007
	Production = Sales	Production > Sales	Production < Sales
Absorption costing	$870,000	$680,000	$1,060,000
Variable costing	870,000	560,000	1,180,000
Difference	$ 0	$120,000	$ (120,000)

This relationship between production and sales and its effect on net income under the two costing approaches is shown graphically in Illustration 7-14.

Illustration 7-14 ►

Summary of income effects

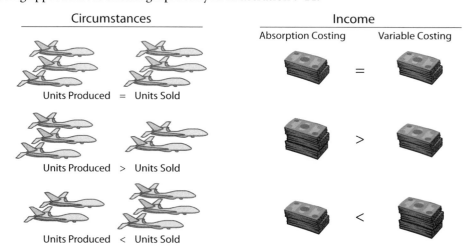

Circumstances	Income
	Absorption Costing Variable Costing
Units Produced = Units Sold	=
Units Produced > Units Sold	>
Units Produced < Units Sold	<

Decision-Making Concerns

For external reporting purposes, companies must report their financial information using generally accepted accounting principles (GAAP). **GAAP requires that absorption costing be used for the costing of inventory.** Net income measured under GAAP (absorption costing) is often used internally to evaluate performance, justify cost reductions, or evaluate new projects.

Some companies, however, have recognized that net income calculated using GAAP does not highlight the differences between variable and fixed costs, and may lead to poor business decisions. Consequently, some companies have decided that it is better to use variable costing for their internal reporting. The following discussion and example highlight a significant problem that can happen when absorption costing is used for decision-making.

When production exceeds sales, absorption costing reports a higher net income than variable costing. As noted earlier, the reason is that some fixed manufacturing costs are not expensed in the current period, but are deferred to future periods as part of the inventory. As a result, management may be tempted to overproduce in a period in order to increase net income. Although net income will increase, this decision to overproduce may not be in the company's best interest.

Suppose, for example, that a division manager's compensation is based on the division's net income. In such a case, the manager may decide to meet the net income targets by increasing production. While this overproduction may increase the manager's compensation, the build-up of inventories will lead to additional costs to the company. This situation is avoided under variable costing, because net income under variable costing is not affected by changes in production levels. The example that follows shows this point.

Warren Lund, a division manager of Walker Enterprises, is under pressure to boost the performance of the Lighting Division in 2005. Unfortunately, recent profits have not met expectations. The expected sales for this year are 20,000 units. As he plans for the year, he has to decide whether to produce 20,000 or 30,000 units. Illustration 7-15 provides the facts that are available for the division.

Illustration 7-15 ◄

Facts on Lighting Division—2005

Beginning inventory	0	
Expected sales in units	20,000	
Selling price per unit	$15	
Variable manufacturing costs per unit	$6	
Fixed manufacturing costs (total)	$60,000	
Fixed manufacturing costs per unit		
Based on 20,000 units		$3 per unit ($60,000 ÷ 20,000)
Based on 30,000 units		$2 per unit ($60,000 ÷ 30,000)
Manufacturing costs per unit		
Based on 20,000 units		$9 per unit ($6 variable + $3 fixed)
Based on 30,000 units		$8 per unit ($6 variable + $2 fixed)
Variable selling and administrative expenses per unit	$1	
Fixed selling and administrative expenses	$15,000	

The division's results for the two possible levels of output under absorption costing are presented in Illustration 7-16.

Illustration 7-16 ◄

Absorption-costing income statement—2005

LIGHTING DIVISION
Income Statement
Year Ended January 31, 2005
Absorption Costing

	20,000 Produced		30,000 Produced	
Sales (20,000 units × $15)	$300,000		$300,000	
Cost of goods sold	180,000	(20,000 × $9)	160,000	(20,000 × $8)
Gross profit	120,000		140,000	
Variable selling and administrative expenses (20,000 × $1)	20,000		20,000	
Fixed selling and administrative expenses	15,000		15,000	
Net income	$ 85,000		$105,000	

If the Lighting Division produces 20,000 units, its net income is $85,000. If it produces 30,000 units, its net income is $105,000. By producing 30,000 units, the division will have an inventory of 10,000 units. This excess inventory causes net income to increase by $20,000 because $20,000 of fixed costs (10,000 × $2) are not charged to the current year, but are deferred to future periods. What do you think Warren Lund might do in this situation? Given his concern about the profit numbers of the Lighting Division, he may be tempted to increase production. Although this increased production will increase 2005 net income, it may be costly to the company in the long run.

Now let's evaluate the same situation under variable costing. Illustration 7-17 shows the variable-costing income statement for production at both 20,000 and 30,000 units, using the information in Illustration 7-15.

Illustration 7-17 ▶

Variable-costing income statement—2005

LIGHTING DIVISION **Income Statement** **Year Ended 2005** **Variable Costing**		
	20,000 Produced	30,000 Produced
Sales (20,000 × $15)	$300,000	$300,000
Less: Variable cost of goods sold (20,000 × $6)	120,000	120,000
Variable selling and administrative expenses (20,000 × $1)	20,000	20,000
Contribution margin	160,000	160,000
Less: Fixed manufacturing overhead	60,000	60,000
Fixed selling and administrative expenses	15,000	15,000
Net income	$ 85,000	$ 85,000

From this example, we see that, under variable costing, net income is not affected by the number of units produced. Net income is $85,000 whether 20,000 or 30,000 units are produced. Why? Because fixed manufacturing overhead is treated as a period expense. Unlike absorption costing, no fixed manufacturing overhead is deferred through inventory build-up.

Potential Advantages of Variable Costing

study objective 3

Discuss the advantages of absorption costing versus variable costing for management decision-making.

Variable costing has the following potential advantages compared to absorption costing:

1. The use of variable costing is consistent with the cost-volume-profit material presented in Chapter 5 and the incremental analysis material presented in Chapter 6.
2. Net income calculated under variable costing is not affected by changes in production levels. As a result, it is much easier to understand the impact of fixed and variable costs on the calculation of net income when variable costing is used.
3. Net income calculated under variable costing is greatly affected by changes in sales levels (not production levels), and it therefore provides a more realistic assessment of the company's success or failure during a period.
4. Because the fixed and variable cost components are shown in the variable-costing income statement, it is easier to identify these costs and understand their effect on the business. Under absorption costing, the allocation of fixed costs to inventory makes it difficult to evaluate the impact of fixed costs on the company's results.

BUSINESS INSIGHT ▶ Management Perspective

Nortel Networks announced in June 2004 that it was moving toward a 100% variable cost structure for manufacturing by divesting certain operations to Flextronics, a Singapore-based electronics manufacturing services (EMS) provider. As part of Nortel's five-year plan to divest its manufacturing activities to EMS companies, Flextronics will take over product integration, testing, and repair operations, as well as supply chain, related suppliers and third-party logistics, in Calgary, Montreal, and Campinas, Brazil. It will also acquire Nortel's global repair services and certain design assets in Ottawa and Monsktown, Northern Ireland. With the move toward a complete variable cost structure, Nortel expects to have more control over costs and increase the efficiency of its inventory management. Any manufacturing-related expenses would be expensed when incurred rather than deferred to a future period as a product cost.

Decision Toolkit

Decision Checkpoints	Info Needed for Decision	Tools to Use for Decision	How to Evaluate Results

What is the company's composition of fixed versus variable costs?	Variable cost of goods sold, variable selling and administrative expenses, fixed manufacturing overhead, fixed selling and administrative expenses	**Variable-costing income statement**
		Sales
		Less:
		   Variable cost of goods sold
		   Variable selling and administrative expenses
		Contribution margin
		Less:
		   Fixed manufacturing overhead
		   Fixed selling and administrative expenses
		Net income
			The variable-costing income statement provides information about variable and fixed costs that is needed for CVP analysis and incremental analysis.

the navigator

BEFORE YOU GO ON . . .

► Review It

1. What is the main difference between absorption costing and variable costing?
2. Explain how a difference between the amount produced and amount sold creates a difference between net income under absorption costing and net income under variable costing.
3. What are the potential advantages of variable costing for decision-making?

► Do It

Justin and Andrea Doll Company produces and sells tennis balls. The following costs are available for the year ended December 31, 2005. The company has no beginning inventory. In 2005, 8 million units were produced, but only 7.5 million units were sold. The unit selling price was $0.50 per ball. Costs and expenses were:

Variable costs per unit	
Direct materials	$0.10
Direct labour	0.05
Variable manufacturing overhead	0.08
Variable selling and administrative expenses	0.02
Annual fixed costs and expenses	
Manufacturing overhead	$500,000
Selling and administrative expenses	100,000

(a) Calculate the manufacturing cost of one unit of product using variable costing.
(b) Prepare a 2005 income statement for Justin and Andrea Doll Company using variable costing.

Action Plan

• Remember that under variable costing, only variable manufacturing costs are treated as manufacturing costs.

• Subtract all fixed costs as period costs. This includes both manufacturing overhead and selling and administrative expenses.

Solution

(a) The cost of one unit of product under variable costing would be as follows:

Direct materials	$0.10
Direct labour	0.05
Variable manufacturing overhead	0.08
	$0.23

(b) The variable-costing income statement would be as follows:

JUSTIN AND ANDREA DOLL COMPANY
Income Statement
Year Ended December 31, 2005
Variable Costing

Sales		$3,750,000
Variable cost of goods sold	$1,725,000	
Variable selling and administrative expenses	150,000	1,875,000
Contribution margin		1,875,000
Fixed manufacturing overhead	500,000	
Fixed selling and administrative expenses	100,000	600,000
Net income		$1,275,000

Summary of Study Objectives

1. *Explain the difference between absorption costing and variable costing.* Under absorption costing, fixed manufacturing costs are product costs. Under variable costing, fixed manufacturing costs are period costs.

2. *Discuss the effect that changes in the production level and sales level have on net income measured under absorption costing versus under variable costing.* If the production volume is greater than the sales volume, net income under absorption costing will be greater than net income under variable costing by the amount of fixed manufacturing costs included in the ending inventory that results from the units produced but not sold during the period. If the production volume is less than the sales volume, net income under absorption costing will be less than it is under variable costing

by the amount of fixed manufacturing costs included in the units sold during the period that were not produced during the period.

3. *Discuss the advantages of absorption costing versus variable costing for management decision-making.* The use of variable costing is consistent with cost-volume-profit analysis and incremental analysis. Net income under variable costing is not affected by changes in production levels. Instead, it is closely tied to changes in sales. The presentation of fixed costs in the variable costing approach makes it easier to identify fixed costs and to evaluate their impact on the company's profitability.

▦ Decision Toolkit—A Summary

Decision Checkpoints	Info Needed for Decision	Tools to Use for Decision	How to Evaluate Results

What is the company's composition of fixed versus variable costs?	Variable cost of goods sold, variable selling and administrative expenses, fixed manufacturing overhead, fixed selling and administrative expenses	**Variable-costing income statement**
		Sales
		Less:
		  Variable cost of goods sold
		  Variable selling and administrative expenses
		Contribution margin
		Less:
		  Fixed manufacturing overhead
		  Fixed selling and administrative expenses
		Net income
			The variable-costing income statement provides information about variable and fixed costs that is needed for CVP analysis and incremental analysis.

Glossary

 www.wiley.com/canada/managerial

Key Term Matching Activity

Absorption costing A costing approach in which all manufacturing costs are charged to the product. (p. 284)

Variable costing A costing approach in which only variable manufacturing costs are product costs. Fixed manufacturing costs are period costs (expenses). (p. 284)

Demonstration Problem

Taylor Enterprises produces birdhouses. In 2005, it began the year with no beginning inventory. During the year, it produced 10,000 birdhouses and sold 8,000 for $30 per house. Variable manufacturing costs were $9 per house produced; variable selling and administrative expenses were $4 per unit sold; fixed manufacturing costs were $70,000 in total and $7 per unit ($70,000 ÷ 10,000); fixed selling and administrative costs were $20,000.

Instructions

(a) Prepare an income statement using absorption costing.
(b) Prepare an income statement using variable costing.
(c) Show a calculation that explains the difference in net income under the two costing approaches.

 www.wiley.com/canada/managerial

Animated Demonstration Problem

Action Plan

• Recall that under variable costing, only variable manufacturing costs are treated as manufacturing costs.

• For variable costing, subtract all fixed costs—both manufacturing overhead and selling and administrative expenses—as period costs.

• For absorption costing, manufacturing costs include variable materials and labour and overhead, as well as an allocated per unit charge for the fixed manufacturing overhead.

Solution to Demonstration Problem

(a)

TAYLOR ENTERPRISES
Income Statement
Year Ended 2005
Absorption Costing

Sales (8,000 units × $30)	$240,000
Cost of goods sold [8,000 units × ($9 + $7)]	128,000
Gross profit	112,000
Variable selling and administrative expenses (8,000 × $4)	32,000
Fixed selling and administrative expenses	20,000
Net income	$ 60,000

(b)

TAYLOR ENTERPRISES
Income Statement
Year Ended 2005
Variable Costing

Sales (8,000 × $30)		$240,000
Variable cost of goods sold (8,000 × $9)	$72,000	
Variable selling and administrative expenses (8,000 × $4)	32,000	104,000
Contribution margin		136,000
Fixed manufacturing overhead	70,000	
Fixed selling and administrative expenses	20,000	90,000
Net income		$ 46,000

(c) The difference in net income of $14,000 can be explained by the 2,000-unit difference between the number of units sold (8,000) versus the number of units produced (10,000). Under absorption costing, the company defers $7 per unit of fixed manufacturing costs in the 2,000 units of ending inventory. This represents the total difference of $14,000 ($7 × 2,000 units) between the net income under variable costing ($46,000) and under absorption costing ($60,000).

Self-Study Questions

Additional Self-Study Questions

(SO 1) 1. Fixed manufacturing overhead costs are recognized as:
  (a) period costs under absorption costing.
  (b) product costs under absorption costing.
  (c) product costs under variable costing.
  (d) part of the ending inventory costs under both absorption and variable costing.

(SO 1, 2) 2. Net income calculated under absorption costing will be:
  (a) higher than net income under variable costing in all cases.
  (b) equal to net income under variable costing in all cases.

  (c) higher than net income under variable costing when more units are produced than sold.
  (d) higher than net income under variable costing when fewer units are produced than sold.

3. A company will be in compliance with GAAP when   (SO 2)
  it prepares financial statements in accordance with:
  (a) cost-volume-profit principles.
  (b) absorption-costing principles.
  (c) variable-costing principles.
  (d) all of the above methods.

(SO 2) 4. A manager can increase reported income by:
 (a) producing more units than are sold under absorption costing.
 (b) producing fewer units than are sold under absorption costing.
 (c) producing more units than are sold under variable costing.
 (d) producing fewer units than are sold under variable costing.

(SO 2) 5. Gross profit is disclosed on an income statement prepared using:
 (a) CVP analysis.   (c) variable costing.
 (b) absorption costing. (d) all costing methods.

(SO 3) 6. When preparing internal reports, service companies:
 (a) cannot benefit from variable costing, because they have no inventory.
 (b) cannot use variable costing.

 (c) can benefit from variable costing, because they have both fixed and variable costs.
 (d) Both (b) and (c) are correct.

7. Using variable costing rather than absorption (SO 3) costing is an advantage to a company because:
 (a) variable costing is consistent with cost-volume-profit and incremental analysis used by managers for decision-making.
 (b) it agrees with the income information released to external users under GAAP.
 (c) it always produces higher net income.
 (d) it focuses on gross profit, which is the best indicator of a company's ability to meet income goals.

Questions

1. What is variable costing? What is absorption costing?

2. What costs are considered as product costs in a variable-costing system?

3. How are fixed manufacturing costs treated in a variable-costing system?

4. Under absorption costing, what happens to fixed overhead costs if ending inventories increase during the period?

5. What is the main difference between the absorption and variable costing approaches?

6. Flygt Corporation sells one product, its waterproof hiking boot. It began operations in the current year and had an ending inventory of 10,500 units. The company sold 20,000 units throughout the year. Fixed overhead is $5 per unit, and the total manufacturing cost per unit is $20 (including fixed costs). What is the difference in net income under absorption costing and variable costing?

7. If production equals sales, what, if any, is the difference between net income under absorption costing versus under variable costing?

8. If production is greater than sales, how does absorption-costing net income differ from variable-costing net income?

9. In the long run, will net income be higher or lower under variable costing than under absorption costing?

10. Brunow Company uses an absorption-costing system for internal reporting. If its production exceeds sales by 5,000 units, how will fixed manufacturing overhead be affected?

11. Can variable costing be used for external financial statements? Why or why not?

12. What are some of the benefits to a manager of using variable costing instead of absorption costing?

13. How might the use of just-in-time inventory techniques affect the difference in net income calculated under variable costing and under absorption costing?

14. Which method, absorption costing or variable costing, is better for a company to use as its costing system for internal decision-making? Explain why. Why do firms that use variable costing also use absorption-costing systems?

Brief Exercises

Identify costs as product costs or period costs under variable costing.
(SO 1)

BE7–1   Determine whether each of the following costs would be classified as product costs or period costs under a variable-costing system:

	Product Cost	Period Cost
Commission fees for salespersons		
Glue for wooden chairs—variable		
Fabric for T-shirts		
Labour costs for producing TVs		
Factory rent expense—fixed		
Factory utility costs—variable		
Car mileage for salespersons		
Administrative expenses—fixed		
Administrative Internet connection fees		
Wages—assembly line		

Identify costs as product costs or period costs under absorption costing.
(SO 1)

BE7–2   Using the costs from BE7–1, determine how those same costs would be classified under an absorption-costing system.

	Product Cost	Period Cost
Commission fees for salespersons		
Glue for wooden chairs—variable		
Fabric for T-shirts		
Labour costs for producing TVs		
Factory rent expense—fixed		
Factory utility costs—variable		
Car mileage for salespersons		
Administrative expenses—fixed		
Administrative Internet connection fees		
Wages—assembly line		

Calculate product cost under variable costing.
(SO 1)

BE7–3   Large Orange Company produces basketballs. It incurred the following costs during the year:

Direct materials	$14,490
Direct labour	25,530
Fixed manufacturing overhead	10,000
Variable manufacturing overhead	32,420
Selling costs	21,000

What is the total product cost for the company under variable costing?

Calculate product costs under absorption costing.
(SO 1)

BE7–4   Information for Large Orange Company is given in BE7–3. What is the total product cost for the company under absorption costing?

Determine manufacturing cost per unit under absorption and variable costing.
(SO 1)

BE7–5   Burns Manufacturing incurred the following costs during the year: direct materials, $20 per unit; direct labour, $12 per unit; variable manufacturing overhead, $15 per unit; variable selling and administrative costs, $8 per unit; fixed manufacturing overhead, $120,000; and fixed selling and administrative costs, $150,000. Burns produced 12,000 units and sold 10,000 units. Determine the manufacturing cost per unit under (a) absorption costing and (b) variable costing.

Prepare variable-costing income statement.
(SO 1)

BE7–6   During 2005, Rafael Corp. produced 40,000 units and sold 30,000 for $12 per unit. Variable manufacturing costs were $4 per unit. Annual fixed manufacturing overhead was $80,000 ($2 per unit). Variable selling and administrative costs were $1 per unit sold, and fixed selling and administrative expenses were $10,000. Prepare a variable-costing income statement.

Prepare absorption-costing income statement and reconcile difference between variable-costing and absorption-costing net income.
(SO 1, 2)

BE7–7   Information for Rafael Corp. is given in BE7–6. (a) Prepare an absorption-costing income statement. (b) Reconcile the difference between the net income under variable costing and the net income under absorption costing. That is, show a calculation that explains what causes the difference in net income between the two approaches.

BE7–8 Caspian Company produced 20,000 units and sold 18,000 during the current year. Under absorption costing, net income was $25,000. Fixed overhead was $190,000. Determine the net income under variable costing.

Determine net income under variable costing. (SO 1, 2)

Exercises

E7–1 Wu Equipment Company manufactures and distributes industrial air compressors. The following data are available for the year ended December 31, 2005. The company had no beginning inventory. In 2005, 1,500 units were produced, but only 1,200 units were sold. The unit selling price was $4,500. Costs and expenses were as follows:

Calculate total product cost, and prepare income statement using variable costing. (SO 1)

Variable costs per unit	
Direct materials	$ 800
Direct labour	1,500
Variable manufacturing overhead	300
Variable selling and administrative expenses	70
Annual fixed costs and expenses	
Manufacturing overhead	$1,200,000
Selling and administrative expenses	100,000

Instructions

(a) Calculate the manufacturing cost of one unit of product using variable costing.
(b) Prepare a 2005 income statement for Wu Company using variable costing.

E7–2 Asian Windows manufactures a hand-painted bamboo window shade for standard-size windows. Production and sales data for 2005 are as follows:

Prepare income statements under absorption costing and variable costing. (SO 1)

Variable manufacturing costs	$40 per shade
Fixed manufacturing costs	$100,000
Variable selling and administrative expenses	$9 per shade
Fixed selling and administrative expenses	$250,000
Selling price	$90 per shade
Units produced	10,000 shades
Units sold	8,500 shades

Instructions

(a) Prepare an income statement using absorption costing.
(b) Prepare an income statement using variable costing.

E7–3 Bob's Company builds custom fishing lures for sporting goods stores. In its first year of operations, 2005, the company incurred the following costs:

Calculate product cost; prepare income statements under variable costing and absorption costing, and compare usefulness of each for decisions. (SO 1, 3)

Variable cost per unit	
Direct materials	$7.50
Direct labour	2.45
Variable manufacturing overhead	5.75
Variable selling and administrative expenses	3.90
Fixed costs for year	
Fixed manufacturing overhead	$235,000
Fixed selling and administrative expenses	240,100

Bob's Company sells the fishing lures for $25. During 2005, the company sold 80,000 lures and produced 95,000 lures.

Instructions

(a) Assuming the company uses variable costing, calculate Bob's manufacturing cost per unit for 2005.
(b) Prepare a variable-costing income statement for 2005.

Calculate product cost and
prepare income statement
under absorption costing.
(SO 1)

Calculate product cost
under absorption costing
and variable costing;
prepare absorption-costing
income statement; compare
usefulness of variable-
costing format versus
absorption-costing format.
(SO 1, 2, 3)

E7–4 Information for Bob's Company is provided in E7–3.

Instructions

(a) Assuming the company uses absorption costing, calculate Bob's manufacturing cost per unit for 2005.
(b) Prepare an absorption-costing income statement for 2005.

E7–5 Empey Manufacturing produces towels to be sold as souvenirs at sporting events throughout the world. Assume that units produced equalled units sold in 2005. The company's variable-costing income statement is as follows

EMPEY MANUFACTURING
Income Statement
Year Ended December 31, 2005
Variable Costing

Sales (260,700 units)		$521,400
Variable cost of goods sold	$255,486	
Variable selling expenses	31,284	
Variable administrative expenses	36,498	323,268
Contribution margin		198,132
Fixed manufacturing overhead	96,459	
Fixed selling expenses	38,500	
Fixed administrative expenses	42,625	177,584
Net income		$ 20,548
Unit selling price	$2.00	
Variable costs per unit		
Direct material	$0.26	
Direct labour	$0.34	
Variable overhead	$0.38	
Variable selling expenses	$0.12	
Variable administrative expenses	$0.14	

Instructions

(a) Under variable costing, what was the manufacturing cost per towel?
(b) Under absorption costing, what was the manufacturing cost per towel?
(c) Prepare an absorption-costing income statement for Empey Manufacturing.
(d) Can you explain why there is or is not a difference in the net income amounts in the two income statements?
(e) Why might Empey Manufacturing Company want to prepare both an absorption-costing income statement and a variable-costing income statement?

Determine ending inventory
under variable costing;
determine whether
absorption or variable
costing would result in
higher net income.
(SO 1, 2)

E7–6 Ortiz Company produced 10,000 units during the past year, but only 9,000 of the units were sold. The following additional information is also available:

Direct materials used	$90,000
Direct labour incurred	30,000
Variable manufacturing overhead	24,000
Fixed manufacturing overhead	50,000
Fixed selling and administrative expenses	70,000
Variable selling and administrative expenses	10,000

There was no work in process inventory at the beginning of the year. Ortiz did not have any beginning finished goods inventory either.

Instructions

(a) What would Ortiz Company's finished goods inventory cost on December 31 be under variable costing?
(b) Which costing method, absorption or variable, would show a higher net income for the year? By what amount?

E7–7   Hardwood Inc. mostly produces wooden crates used for shipping products by ocean freighter. In 2005, Hardwood incurred the following costs:

Wood used	$54,000
Nails (considered insignificant and a variable expense)	$340
Direct labour	$37,000
Utilities for the plant:	
$2,000 each month, plus $0.45 for each kilowatt	
hour used each month	
Rent expense for plant for year	$21,400

Calculate manufacturing cost under absorption and variable costing and explain difference.
(SO 1, 2)

Assume Hardwood used an average of 500 kilowatt hours per month over the past year.

Instructions

(a) What is Hardwood's total manufacturing cost if it uses a variable-costing approach?
(b) What is Hardwood's total manufacturing cost if it uses an absorption-costing approach?
(c) What is the reason for the difference between manufacturing costs under these two costing approaches?

Problems: Set A

P7–8A   Blue Mountain Products manufactures and sells a variety of camping products. Recently, the company opened a new plant to manufacture a lightweight, self-standing tent. Cost and sales data for the first month of operations follow:

Calculate product cost; prepare income statement under variable costing and absorption costing and reconcile difference.
(SO 1, 2)

Manufacturing costs	
Fixed overhead	$200,000
Variable overhead	$4 per tent
Direct labour	$16 per tent
Direct material	$40 per tent
Beginning inventory	0 tents
Tents produced	10,000
Tents sold	9,000
Selling and administrative costs	
Fixed	$400,000
Variable	$6 per tent sold

The tent sells for $150. Management is interested in the opening month's results and has asked for an income statement.

Instructions

(a) Assuming the company uses absorption costing, do the following:
   1. Calculate the manufacturing cost per unit.
   2. Prepare an absorption-costing income statement for the month of June 2005.
(b) Assuming the company uses variable costing, do the following:
   1. Calculate the manufacturing cost per unit.
   2. Prepare a variable-costing income statement for the month of June 2005.
(c) Reconcile the difference in net income between the two methods.

P7–9A   AFN produces plastic that is used for injection-moulding applications such as gears for small motors. In 2005, the first year of operations, AFN produced 4,000 tonnes of plastic and sold 3,000 tonnes. In 2006, the production and sales results were exactly reversed. In each year, the selling price per tonne was $2,000; variable manufacturing costs were 15% of the sales price for the units produced; variable selling expenses were 10% of the selling price of the units sold; fixed manufacturing costs were $2.4 million; and fixed administrative expenses were $600,000.

Prepare income statements under absorption costing and variable costing for company with beginning inventory.
(SO 1, 2, 3)

Instructions

(a) Prepare comparative income statements for each year using variable costing. (Use the format from Illustration 7-5.)
(b) Prepare comparative income statements for each year using absorption costing. (Use the format from Illustration 7-4.)
(c) Reconcile the differences each year in the income from operations under the two costing approaches.
(d) ◁▭▭▷ Comment on the effects that the production and sales levels have on net income under the two costing approaches.

Prepare absorption- and variable-costing income statements; reconcile differences between absorption- and variable-costing income statements when sales and production levels change; discuss usefulness of absorption costing versus variable costing.
(SO 1, 2, 3)

P7–10A Basic Electric Motors is a Division of Basic Electric Products Corporation. The division manufactures and sells an electric motor used in a wide variety of applications. During the coming year, it expects to sell 50,000 units for $30 per unit. Ester Madden is the division manager. She is considering producing either 50,000 or 80,000 units during the period. Other information is as follows:

Division Information for 2005

Beginning inventory	0
Expected sales in units	50,000
Selling price per unit	$30
Variable manufacturing cost per unit	$12
Fixed manufacturing cost (total)	$400,000

Fixed manufacturing overhead costs per unit
Based on 50,000 units	$8 per unit ($400,000 ÷ 50,000)
Based on 80,000 units	$5 per unit ($400,000 ÷ 80,000)

Manufacturing cost per unit
Based on 50,000 units	$20 per unit ($12 variable + $8 fixed)
Based on 80,000 units	$17 per unit ($12 variable + $5 fixed)
Variable selling and administrative expense	$2 per unit
Fixed selling and administrative expenses (total) $40,000	

Instructions

(a) Prepare an absorption-costing income statement, with one column showing the results if 50,000 units are produced and one column showing the results if 80,000 units are produced.
(b) Prepare a variable-costing income statement, with one column showing the results if 50,000 units are produced and one column showing the results if 80,000 units are produced.
(c) Reconcile the difference in the net incomes under the two approaches and explain what causes this difference.
(d) ◁▭▭▷ Discuss the usefulness of the variable-costing income statements versus the absorption-costing income statements for decision-making and for evaluating the manager's performance.

Prepare income statement under variable costing and absorption costing and reconcile difference; discuss usefulness of absorption costing versus variable costing.
(SO 1, 2, 3)

P7–11A Alta Products Ltd. has just created a new division to manufacture and sell DVD players. The facility is highly automated and thus has high monthly fixed costs, as shown in the following schedule of budgeted monthly costs. This schedule was prepared based on an expected monthly production volume of 1,500 units.

Manufacturing costs	
Variable cost per unit	
Direct materials	$25
Direct labour	30
Variable overhead	5
Total fixed overhead	$60,000
Selling and administrative costs	
Variable	6% of sales
Fixed	$45,000

During August 2005, the following activity was recorded:

Units produced	1,500
Units sold	1,200
Selling price per unit	$150

Instructions

(a) Prepare an income statement for the month ended August 31, 2005, under absorption costing.

(b) Prepare an income statement for the month ended August 31, 2005, under variable costing.

(c) Reconcile the absorption costing and variable costing income figures for the month.

(d) What are some of the arguments in favour of using variable costing? What are some of the arguments in favour of using absorption costing?

(CGA-adapted)

P7–12A Amanjeet Chinmayi left her job as the production manager of a medium-sized firm two years ago to join a new firm that was manufacturing a revolutionary type of fitness equipment. Amanjeet was made the general manager at the start of operations, and the firm seemed to be doing extremely well. The president was extremely pleased with the company's first-year performance and at the beginning of the second year promised Amanjeet a $20,000 bonus if the company's net income were to increase by 25% in year 2.

Calculate product cost; prepare income statement under variable costing and absorption costing and reconcile difference when sales and production levels change. (SO 1, 2, 3)

During year 2, Amanjeet sold 25% more units than she had in year 1 and was so confident that she would receive her bonus that she bought non-refundable airline tickets to Europe for her husband Leo, her three sons, and herself.

At the end of year 2, Amanjeet received the income statement, and it showed that the company's income had decreased from year 1 even though it had sold considerably more units. Amanjeet did not get along very well with the accountant and felt that he had deliberately distorted the financial statements for year 2.

Amanjeet received the following reports:

	Year 1	Year 2
Production (in units)	6,000	3,000
Sales (in units)	4,000	5,000
Unit selling price	$500	$500
Unit costs		
Variable manufacturing	$ 300	$ 300
Variable selling	20	20
Fixed manufacturing	180,000	210,000
Fixed selling	100,000	140,000
Income Statement—(FIFO)		
Sales	$2,000,000	$2,500,000
Cost of goods sold	1,320,000	1,770,000
Gross margin	680,000	730,000
Selling	180,000	240,000
Net income	$ 500,000	$ 490,000

Instructions

(a) Prepare variable-costing income statements for years 1 and 2.

(b) For years 1 and 2, reconcile the differences between the net income as determined by the income statements you have prepared in part (a) and the income statements prepared by the accountant.

(c) Explain to Amanjeet why she lost her $20,000 bonus. Which income statement more accurately measures performance? Why?

(CGA-adapted)

P7–13A Xantra Corp. is a manufacturer of specialty in-line skates. The operating results for 2005 follow:

Calculate product cost; prepare income statement under variable costing and absorption costing and reconcile difference. (SO 1, 2, 3)

Units produced	20,000 pairs
Units sold	18,000 pairs
Selling price	$200 per pair

Production information:

Direct materials	$1,000,000
Direct labour	750,000
Variable manufacturing overhead	450,000
Fixed manufacturing overhead	800,000
Variable marketing	180,000
Fixed marketing	200,000

There was no beginning finished goods inventory.

Instructions

(a) Prepare an absorption-costing income statement.
(b) Prepare a variable-costing income statement.
(c) Reconcile the net incomes under absorption costing and variable costing.
(d) Calculate the break-even point in sales units (pairs of skates) under the current cost structure.

(CGA-adapted)

Explain variable costing and absorption costing and reconcile difference when sales and production levels change.
(SO 1, 2, 3)

P7–14A   Sun Company, a wholly owned subsidiary of Guardian, Inc., produces and sells three main product lines. At the beginning of 2004, the president of Sun Company presented the budget to the parent company and accepted a commitment to contribute $15,800 to Guardian's consolidated profit in 2005. The president was confident that the year's profit would exceed the budget target, since the monthly sales reports had shown that sales for the year would be 10% more than what was predicted in the budget. The president is both disturbed and confused when the controller presents an adjusted forecast as at November 30, 2005, indicating that profits will be 11% under budget. The two forecasts are presented below:

SUN COMPANY
Forecasts of Operating Results

	January 1, 2005	November 30, 2005
Sales	$268,000	$294,800
Cost of sales	212,000[1]	233,200
Gross margin	56,000	61,600
Overapplied (underapplied) fixed manufacturing overhead	0	(6,000)
Actual gross margin	56,000	55,600
Selling expenses	13,400	14,740
Administrative expenses	26,800	26,800
Total operating expenses	40,200	41,540
Earnings before tax	$ 15,800	$ 14,060

[1] Includes fixed manufacturing overhead of $30,000.

There have been no sales price changes or product-mix shifts since the January 1, 2005, forecast. Variable costs have remained constant throughout the year. The only cost that has varried in the income statement is the underapplied manufacturing overhead. This happened because the company worked only 16,000 machine hours (budgeted machine hours were 20,000) during 2005 as a result of a shortage of raw materials when its main supplier was closed by a strike. Fortunately, Sun Company's finished goods inventory was large enough to fill all sales orders received.

Instructions

(a) Analyze and explain why the profit has declined in spite of increased sales and control over costs.
(b) What plan, if any, could Sun Company adopt during December to improve the reported profit at year end? Explain your answer.
(c) Explain and illustrate how Sun Company could use a different internal cost reporting procedure that would not result in the confusing effect of the procedure it currently uses.

(CMA Canada-adapted)

P7–15A The Daniels Tool & Die Corporation has been in existence for a little over three years. The company's sales have been increasing each year as it builds a reputation. The company manufactures dies to its customers' specifications and therefore uses a job-order cost system. Factory overhead is applied to the jobs based on direct labour hours—the absorption-costing (full) method. Overapplied or underapplied overhead is treated as an adjustment to Cost of Goods Sold. The company's income statements and other data for the last two years are as follows:

Prepare income statement under variable costing and absorption costing and reconcile difference when sales and production levels change; discuss usefulness of absorption costing versus variable costing.
(SO 1, 2, 3)

DANIELS TOOL & DIE CORPORATION
2004–2005 Comparative Income Statements

	2004	2005
Sales	$840,000	$1,015,000
Cost of goods sold		
Finished goods, January 1	25,000	18,000
Cost of goods manufactured	548,000	657,600
Total available	573,000	675,600
Finished goods, December 31	18,000	14,000
Cost of goods sold before overhead adjustment	555,000	661,600
Underapplied factory overhead	36,000	14,400
Cost of goods sold	591,000	676,000
Gross profit	249,000	339,000
Selling expenses	82,000	95,000
Administrative expenses	70,000	75,000
Total operating expenses	152,000	170,000
Operating income	$ 97,000	$ 169,000

Daniels Tool & Die Corporation Inventory Balances

	January 1, 2004	December 31, 2004	December 31, 2005
Raw material	$22,000	$30,000	$10,000
Work in process			
Costs	$40,000	$48,000	$64,000
Direct labour hours	1,335	1,600	2,100
Finished goods			
Costs	$25,000	$18,000	$14,000
Direct labour hours	1,450	1,050	820

Daniels used the same predetermined overhead rate in applying overhead to its production orders in both 2004 and 2005. The rate was based on the following estimates:

Fixed factory overhead	$ 25,000
Variable factory overhead	$155,000
Direct labour hours	25,000
Direct labour costs	$150,000

In 2004 and 2005, the actual direct labour hours used were 20,000 and 23,000, respectively. Raw materials put into production were $292,000 in 2004 and $370,000 in 2005. The actual fixed overhead was $42,300 for 2004, and $37,400 for 2005, and the planned direct labour rate was the direct labour achieved.

For both years, all of the administrative costs were fixed. The variable portion of the selling expenses results from a commission that is paid as a percentage of the sales revenue. The variable portion of the selling expenses results from a 5% commission that is paid as a percentage of the sales revenue.

Instructions

(a) For the year ended December 31, 2005, prepare a revised income statement for Daniels Tool & Die Corporation using the variable-costing method.

(b) Reconcile the difference in operating income between Daniels Tool & Die Corporation's 2005 absorption-costing income statement and the revised 2005 income statement prepared under variable costing.

(c) Describe both the advantages and disadvantages of using variable costing.

(CMA Canada-adapted)

Problems: Set B

Calculate product cost; prepare income statement under variable costing and absorption costing and reconcile difference.
(SO 1, 2)

P7–16B SpongeFun Products manufactures and sells a variety of swimming products. Recently, the company opened a new plant to manufacture a lightweight, inflatable boat. Cost and sales data for the first month of operations are shown below:

Manufacturing costs	
Fixed overhead costs	$150,000
Variable overhead	$5 per boat
Direct labour	$10 per boat
Direct materials	$10 per boat
Beginning inventory	0 boats
Boats produced	50,000
Boats sold	46,000
Selling and administrative costs	
Fixed	$300,000
Variable	$8 per boat sold

The boat sells for $60. Management is interested in the opening month's results and has asked for an income statement.

Instructions

(a) Assuming the company uses absorption costing, do the following:
  1. Calculate the production cost per unit.
  2. Prepare an income statement for the month of July 2005.
(b) Assuming the company uses variable costing, do the following:
  1. Calculate the production cost per unit.
  2. Prepare an income statement for the month of July 2005.
(c) Reconcile the difference in net income between the two methods.

Prepare income statements under absorption costing and variable costing for company with beginning inventory.
(SO 1, 2, 3)

P7–17B Zaki Metal Company produces the steel wire that is used for the production of paper clips. In 2005, the first year of operations, Zaki produced 40,000 kilometres of wire and sold 30,000 kilometres. In 2006, the production and sales results were exactly reversed. In each year, the selling price per kilometre was $80; variable manufacturing costs were 25% of the sales price of the units produced; variable selling expenses were $6 per kilometre sold; fixed manufacturing costs were $1.2 million; and fixed administrative expenses were $200,000.

Instructions

(a) Prepare comparative income statements for each year using variable costing. (Use the format from Illustration 7-5.)
(b) Prepare comparative income statements for each year using absorption costing. (Use the format from Illustration 7-4.)
(c) Reconcile the differences for each year in income from operations under the two costing approaches.
(d) ◁▭▭▷ Comment on the effects that the production and sales levels have on net income under the two costing approaches.

Prepare absorption- and variable-costing income statements; reconcile differences between absorption- and variable-costing income statements when sales and production levels change; discuss usefulness of absorption costing versus variable costing.
(SO 1, 2)

P7–18B Harrison Pumps is a division of Liverpool Controls Corporation. The division manufactures and sells a pump that is used in a wide variety of applications. During the coming year, it expects to sell 60,000 units for $20 per unit. Richard Strong manages the division. He is considering producing either 60,000 or 100,000 units during the period. Other information follows:

Division Information for 2005

Beginning inventory	0
Expected sales in units	60,000
Selling price per unit	$20.00
Variable manufacturing cost per unit	$9.00
Fixed manufacturing overhead cost (total)	$240,000

Fixed manufacturing overhead costs per unit

Based on 60,000 units	$4.00 per unit ($240,000 ÷ 60,000)
Based on 100,000 units	$2.40 per unit ($240,000 ÷ 100,000)

Manufacturing costs per unit

Based on 60,000 units	$13.00 per unit ($9.00 variable + $4.00 fixed)
Based on 100,000 units	$11.40 per unit ($9.00 variable + $2.40 fixed)
Variable selling and administrative expenses	$1 per unit
Fixed selling and administrative expenses	
(total)	$30,000

Instructions

(a) Prepare an absorption-costing income statement, with one column showing the results if 60,000 units are produced and one column showing the results if 100,000 units are produced.

(b) Prepare a variable-costing income statement, with one column showing the results if 60,000 units are produced and one column showing the results if 100,000 units are produced.

(c) Reconcile the difference in net incomes under the two approaches and explain what causes this difference.

(d) ◁▦▦▶ Discuss the usefulness of the variable-costing income statements versus the absorption-costing income statements for decision-making and for evaluating the manager's performance.

P7–19B Allerdyce Corporation Ltd. (ACL) prepares external financial statements using absorption costing and internal financial statements using variable costing. You have the following information for the operations of ACL for the past two years:

	2004	2005
Sales in units (@ $35 per unit)	25,000	35,000
Production in units	30,000	30,000
Variable production costs per unit	$20.00	$20.00
Fixed production costs	$120,000	$120,000
Fixed marketing costs	$50,000	$50,000
Beginning inventory	0	

Calculate product cost; prepare income statement under variable costing and absorption costing and reconcile difference when sales and production levels change.
(SO 1, 2, 3)

Instructions

(a) Prepare absorption-costing income statements for the years ended December 31, 2004 and 2005. Include a column for totals for the two years.

(b) Prepare variable-costing income statements for the years ended December 31, 2004 and 2005. Include a column for totals for the two years.

(c) Reconcile the year-to-year differences in net income under the two methods.

(CGA-adapted)

P7–20B The vice-president of Abscorp Ltd. is not happy. Sales have been rising steadily, but profits have been falling. In September 2005, Abscorp had record sales, but the lowest profits ever. The results for the months of July, August, and September 2005 follow:

Calculate product cost; prepare income statement under variable costing and absorption costing and reconcile difference when sales and production levels change.
(SO 1, 2, 3)

ABSCORP LTD.
Comparative Monthly Income Statements
(in thousands)

	July	August	September
Sales (@ $25 per unit)	$1,750	$1,875	$2,000
Less cost of goods sold			
Opening inventory	80	320	400
Costs applied to production			
Variable manufacturing (@ $9 per unit)	765	720	540
Fixed manufacturing overhead	595	560	420
Cost of goods manufactured	1,360	1,280	960
Goods available for sale	1,440	1,600	1,360
Less ending inventory	320	400	80
Cost of goods sold	1,120	1,200	1,280
Under applied (overapplied) fixed overhead	(35)	0	140
Adjusted cost of goods sold	1,085	1,200	1,420
Gross margin	665	675	580
Less selling and administrative expenses	620	650	680
Net income (loss)	$ 45	$ 25	$ (100)

You have been asked to explain to the vice-president that the problem is more a matter of appearance than reality, by reinterpreting the results in a variable-costing format. You obtain the following information that will help you:

	July	August	September
Production	85,000 units	80,000 units	60,000 units
Sales	70,000	75,000	80,000

Additional information about the company's operations is as follows:

- There were 5,000 units of finished goods in the opening inventory on July 1, 2005.
- Fixed manufacturing overhead costs totalled $1,680,000 per quarter and were incurred evenly throughout the quarter. The fixed manufacturing overhead cost is applied to the units of production based on a budgeted production volume of 80,000 units per month.
- Variable selling and administrative expenses are $6 per unit sold. The remaining selling and administrative expenses on the comparative monthly income statements are fixed.
- The company uses a FIFO cost flow assumption. Work in process inventories are small enough to be ignored.

Instructions

(a) Calculate the monthly break-even point under variable costing.
(b) 1. Calculate the net income for each month under variable costing.
    2. Reconcile the variable-costing and absorption-costing net incomes for each month.
    3. Explain why profits have not been more closely related to changes in the sales volume.

(CGA-adapted)

Calculate product cost, contribution margin under variable costing, and gross margin under absorption costing.
(SO 1, 2, 3)

P7–21B   Boat Refit Inc. produces and sells custom parts for powerboats. The company uses a costing system based on actual costs. Selected accounting and production information for fiscal 2005 is as follows:

Net income (under absorption costing)	$400,000
Sales	$3,400,000
Fixed factory overhead	$600,000
Fixed selling and administrative costs	
(all costs are fixed)	$400,000
Net income (under variable costing)	$310,000
Units produced	2,000
Units sold	?

Boat Refit had no work in process inventory at either the beginning or the end of fiscal 2005. The company also did not have any finished goods inventory at the beginning of the fiscal year.

Instructions

(a) Calculate the units sold in fiscal 2005.
(b) Calculate the total contribution margin under variable costing.
(c) Calculate the gross margin under absorption costing.
(d) Calculate the cost per unit sold under variable costing.
(e) Calculate the cost per unit sold under absorption costing.

(CGA-adapted)

P7–22B Wingfoot Co. began operations on July I, 2004. By the end of its first fiscal year, ended June 30, 2005, Wingfoot had sold 10,000 wingers. Selected data on operations for the year ended June 30, 2005, follow. Any balance sheet figures are as at June 30, 2005.

Prepare income statement under variable costing. (SO 1)

Selling price per unit	$100
Wingers produced	18,000
Ending work in process	0
Total manufacturing overhead	$15,000
Wage rate	$8.00 per hour
Machine hours used	9,000
Wages payable	$20,000
Direct materials costs	$10 per kilogram
Selling and administrative expenses	$40,000

Additional information:

1. Each winger requires two kilograms of direct materials, 0.5 machine hours, and one direct labour hour.
2. Except for machinery amortization of $5,000 and a $1,000 miscellaneous fixed cost, all manufacturing overhead is variable.
3. Except for $4,000 in advertising expenses, all selling and administrative expenses are variable.
4. The tax rate is 40%.

Instructions

Assume that variable costing is used and prepare a contribution-method income statement in good form for the year ended June 30, 2005.

(CGA-adapted)

P7–23B Portland Optics, Inc., specializes in manufacturing lenses for large telescope cameras used in space exploration. As the specifications for the lenses are determined by the customer and vary considerably, the company uses a job-order costing system. Factory overhead is applied to jobs based on direct labour hours using the absorption (full) costing method. Portland's predetermined overhead rates for 2004 and 2005 were based on the following estimates:

Calculate product cost; prepare income statement under variable costing and absorption costing and reconcile difference when sales and production levels change; discuss usefulness of absorption costing versus variable costing. (SO 1, 2, 3)

	2004	2005
Direct labour hours	32,500	44,000
Direct labour cost	$325,000	$462,000
Fixed factory overhead	$130,000	$176,000
Variable factory overhead	$162,500	$198,000

Marie-Michelle David, Portland's controller, would like to use variable costing for internal reporting as she believes statements prepared using variable costing are more appropriate for making product decisions. In order to explain the benefits of variable costing to the other members of Portland's management team, Marie-Michelle plans to convert the company's income statement from absorption costing to variable costing. She has gathered the following information, along with a copy of Portland's comparative income statement for the years 2004 and 2005.

PORTLAND OPTICS, INC.
Comparative Income Statement
Years 2004–2005

	2004	2005
Net sales	$1,140,000	$1,520,000
Cost of goods sold		
Finished goods at January 1	16,000	25,000
Cost of goods manufactured	720,000	976,000
Total available	736,000	1,001,000
Finished goods at December 31	25,000	14,000
Cost of goods sold before overhead adjustment	711,000	987,000
Overhead adjustment	12,000	7,000
Cost of goods sold	723,000	994,000
Gross profit	417,000	526,000
Selling expenses	150,000	190,000
Administrative expenses	160,000	187,000
Total operating expenses	310,000	377,000
Operating income	$ 107,000	$ 149,000

Portland's actual manufacturing data for the two years are as follows:

	2004	2005
Direct labour hours	30,000	42,000
Direct labour cost	$300,000	$435,000
Raw materials used	140,000	210,000
Fixed factory overhead	132,000	175,000

The company's actual inventory balances were as follows:

	Dec. 31, 2003	Dec. 31, 2004	Dec. 31, 2005
Raw materials	$32,000	$36,000	$18,000
Work in process			
Costs	$44,000	$34,000	$60,000
Direct labour hours	1,800	1,400	2,500
Finished goods			
Costs	$16,000	$25,000	$14,000
Direct labour hours	700	1,080	550

For both years, all administrative costs were fixed. A portion of the selling expenses was variable as it resulted from an 8% commision paid on net sales. Portland reports any over- or underapplied overhead as an adjustment to Cost of Goods Sold.

Instructions

(a) For the year ended December 31, 2005, prepare the revised income statement for Portland Optics, Inc., using the variable-costing method. Be sure to include the contribution margin on the revised income statement.

(b) Describe two advantages of using variable costing rather than absorption costing.

(CMA Canada-adapted)

Additional Cases

Cases

C7–24   ComfortCraft manufactures swivel seats for customized vans. It currently manufactures 10,000 seats per year, which it sells for $480 per seat. It incurs variable costs of $180 per seat and fixed costs of $2.2 million. It is considering automating the upholstery process, which is now largely manual. It estimates that if it does this, its fixed costs will be $3.2 million, and its variable costs will drop to $80 per seat.

Instructions

With the class divided into groups, do the following:

(a) Prepare a variable-costing income statement based on current activity.
(b) Calculate the contribution margin ratio, break-even point in dollars, margin of safety ratio, and degree of operating leverage based on current activity.
(c) Prepare a variable-costing income statement assuming that the company invests in the automated upholstery system.
(d) Calculate the contribution margin ratio, break-even point in dollars, margin of safety ratio, and degree of operating leverage assuming the new upholstery system is implemented.
(e) Discuss the implications of adopting the new system.

C7–25 Big Sports Manufacturing produces basketballs used for indoor or outdoor games. The company has been having significant troubles over the past few years, as the number of competitors in the basketball market has increased dramatically. Recently, the company was forced to cut back production in order to decrease its rising inventory level. The following is a list of costs for the company in 2005:

Variable costs per unit	
Rubber	$2.75
Other materials—indirect	1.40
Ball makers—direct labour	5.60
Factory electricity usage	0.50
Factory water usage	0.15
Other labour—indirect	0.27
Selling and administrative expenses	0.40
Fixed costs per year	
Factory property taxes	$120,000
Factory sewer usage	50,000
Factory electricity usage	40,000
Selling and administrative expenses	83,000

Big Sports Manufacturing had ending inventories of 85,000 basketballs in 2004. For these units, the fixed manufacturing overhead included a unit cost of $4.00 and variable manufacturing costs per unit of $9.67. In 2005, the company produced 35,000 basketballs, sold 72,500 basketballs, and had an ending inventory of 47,500 units. The basketballs sold for $18 each.

Instructions

(a) Calculate Big Sports' manufacturing cost per unit under a variable-costing system.
(b) Prepare a variable-costing income statement for 2005.
(c) Calculate Big Sports' manufacturing cost per unit under absorption costing.
(d) Prepare an absorption-costing income statement for 2005.
(e) Big Sports' chief financial officer, Mr. Swetkowski, is contemplating the benefits of using the absorption- and variable-costing approaches. He has asked you to perform a variety of tasks to help him analyze the differences between the two approaches:
  1. Reconcile the differences between the income values of the two approaches.
  2. Mr. Swetkowski has heard that some basic managerial tasks can be better performed when variable costing is used. Calculate the break-even point in units for the company in 2005 using the variable-costing data.
  3. Mr. Swetkowski has been very impressed with the variable-costing techniques that he has seen so far. He has been thinking of eliminating absorption costing for the company. What do you think of this idea?

C7–26 The Wei Nan Company manufactures and sells personal organizers. The following are the operating data for the company for 2004 and 2005:

	2004	2005
Units produced	60,000	50,000
Units sold	54,000	54,000
Selling price per unit	$250	$250
Variable costs per unit		
Direct materials	$80	$80
Direct labour	40	40
Variable overhead	35	35
Selling expenses	30	30
Fixed manufacturing overhead (total)	$2,500,000	$2,500,000
Fixed selling and administrative expenses (total)	$300,000	$300,000

There was no beginning inventory on January 1, 2004. The FIFO method was used to calculate the cost of inventories. Ignore income taxes.

Instructions

(a) Prepare income statements for 2004 and 2005 using the absorption-costing method.
(b) Prepare income statements for 2004 and 2005 using the variable-costing method.
(c) Reconcile the absorption-costing and variable-costing net income figures for 2004 and 2005.

(CGA-adapted)

C7–27 DDD Golf Ltd. produces and sells special golf balls for $20 for a pack of three. In May 2005, the company manufactured 30,000 packs (its normal volume) and sold 28,000 packs. The beginning inventory on May 1, 2005, was 5,000 packs. Production information for May 2005 is as follows:

Direct manufacturing labour per pack	15 minutes
Fixed selling and administrative costs	$40,000
Fixed manufacturing overhead	$132,000
Direct materials costs per pack	$2
Direct labour rate per hour	$24
Variable manufacturing overhead per pack	$4
Variable selling expenses per unit	$2

Instructions

(a) Calculate the total cost per pack under both absorption and variable costing.
(b) Prepare income statements in good form for the month ended May 31, 2005, under absorption and variable costing.
(c) Reconcile the operating income calculated under absorption costing with the operating income calculated under variable costing.

(CGA-Adapted)

C7–28 The vice-president for sales of Huber Corporation has received the following income statement for November, which was prepared on a variable-costing system. The firm has just adopted variable costing for its internal reporting:

HUBER CORPORATION
Income Statement
For the Month of November
(in thousands)

Sales	$2,400
Less variable cost of goods sold	1,200
Contribution margin	1,200
Less fixed manufacturing costs at budget	600
Gross margin	600
Less fixed selling and administrative costs	400
Net income before taxes	$ 200

The controller attached the following notes to the statements:

1. The unit sales price for November averaged $24.
2. The unit manufacturing costs for the month were as follows:

Variable costs	$12
Fixed costs applied	4
Total cost	$16

3. The unit rate for fixed manufacturing costs is a predetermined rate based on a monthly production of 150,000 units.
4. The variable costs per unit have been stable all year.
5. Production for November was 45,000 units in excess of sales.
6. The inventory at November 30 was 80,000 units.

Instruction

(a) The vice-president for sales is not comfortable with the variable-costing system and wonders what the net income would have been under the prior absorption-costing system.
  1. Present the November income statement on an absorption-costing basis.
  2. Reconcile and explain the difference between the variable-costing and absorption-costing net income figures.
(b) Explain the features of variable-cost income measurement that should be attractive to the vice-president for sales.

(CMA Canada-adapted)

C7–29 The following data relate to a year's budgeted activity for Rickuse Limited, a company that manufactures one product:

	Units
Beginning inventory	30,000
Production	120,000
Available for sale	150,000
Sales	110,000
Ending inventory	40,000

	Per unit
Selling price	$5.00
Variable manufacturing costs	1.00
Variable selling, general, and administrative expenses	2.00
Fixed manufacturing costs (based on 100,000 units)	0.25
Fixed selling, general, and administrative expenses (based on 100,000 units)	0.65

Total fixed costs and expenses remain unchanged within the relevant range of 25,000 units to a total capacity of 160,000 units.

Instructions

(a) Calculate the projected annual break-even sales in units.
(b) Calculate the projected net income for the year under variable costing.
(c) Determine the company's net income for the year under absorption (full) costing, assuming the fixed overhead adjustment is closed to Cost of Goods Sold.

(CMA Canada-adapted)

C7–30 BBG Corporation manufactures a synthetic element, pixie dust. Management was surprised to learn that income before taxes had dropped even though the sales volume had increased. Steps had been taken during the year to improve profitability. The steps included raising the selling price by 12% because of a 10% increase in production costs and instructing the selling and administrative departments to spend no more this year than last year. Both changes were implemented at the beginning of the year.

BBG's accounting department prepared and distributed to top management the comparative income statements and related financial information that follow. BBG uses the FIFO inventory method for finished goods.

BBG CORPORATION
Comparative Statements of Operating Income
(in thousands)

	2004	2005
Sales revenue	$9,000	$11,200
Cost of goods sold	$7,200	$ 8,320
Manufacturing volume variance	(600)	495
Adjusted cost of goods sold	6,600	8,815
Gross margin	2,400	2,385
Selling and administrative expenses	1,500	1,500
Income before taxes	$ 900	$ 885

BBG CORPORATION
Selected Operating and Financial Data

	2004	2005
Sales price	$10.00/kg	$11.20/kg
Material costs	$1.50/kg	$1.65/kg
Direct labour cost	$2.50/kg	$2.75/kg
Variable overhead costs	$1.00/kg	$1.10/kg
Fixed overhead costs	$3.00/kg	$3.30/kg
Total fixed overhead costs	$3,000,000	$3,300,000
Selling and administrative expenses (all fixed)	$1,500,000	$1,500,000
Sales volume	900,000 kg	1,000,000 kg
Beginning inventory	300,000 kg	600,000 kg

Instructions

(a) Explain for management why net income decreased despite the sales price and sales volume increases.

(b) It has been proposed that the company use variable costing for its internal reporting. Prepare the variable-costing income statement for 2005.

(c) Reconcile the difference in income before taxes using the absorption-costing method currently used by BBG and the variable-costing method proposed for 2005.

(CMA Canada-adapted)

C7–31   Scott Wadzicki was hired in January 2005 to manage the home products division of Advanced Techno. As part of his employment contract, he was told that he would get an extra $5,000 bonus for every 1% increase by which the division's profits exceeded the previous year's profits.

Soon after coming on board, Scott met with his plant managers and explained that he wanted the plants to be run at full capacity. Previously, the plant had employed just-in-time inventory practices and had consequently produced units only as they were needed. Scott stated that under the previous management the company had missed out on too many sales opportunities because it did not have enough inventory on hand. Because the previous management had employed just-in-time inventory practices, when Scott came on board there was virtually no beginning inventory. The selling price and variable cost per unit remained the same from 2004 to 2005. Additional information follows:

	2004	2005
Net income	$400,000	$600,000
Units produced	20,000	25,000
Units sold	20,000	20,000
Fixed manufacturing costs	$1,000,000	$1,000,000
Fixed manufacturing costs per unit	$50	$40

Instructions

(a) Calculate Scott's bonus based on the net income figures shown.
(b) Recalculate the 2004 and 2005 results using variable costing.
(c) Recalculate Scott's 2005 bonus under variable costing.
(d) Were Scott's actions unethical? Do you think any actions need to be taken by the company?

Answers to Self-Study Questions

1. b   2. c   3. b   4. a   5. b   6. c   7. a

 Remember to go back to the Navigator Box at the beginning of the chapter to check off your completed work.

CHAPTER 8
Pricing

Strategy in the Skies

In 1996, Canada's airline industry included two big players—Air Canada and Canadian Airlines. There seemed to be little room for a third. Enter WestJet, calling itself "Canada's low-fare airline," with a new formula on service and convenience. Over the past eight years, Calgary-based WestJet has grown from three planes serving short-haul routes between five Western cities, to almost 50 planes touching down in 24 cities across the country.

The secret to its success? Low-cost airfares that have made air travel more accessible to more people. "Before we came along, Canadians found that it was cheaper to fly abroad or into the U.S. than it was to fly in Canada," says Sandy Campbell, CGA, WestJet's CFO and senior vice-president, finance. "Air travel had become elitist, with most Canadians either having never flown before or flying infrequently."

WestJet was able to cover its costs while also setting lower prices than its competitors by following a precise business plan. This plan included starting small, following a low-cost structure, having a highly productive workforce, being well capitalized, and not spending too much, too soon. This isn't to say that WestJet cut corners; it made "considerable and appropriate investments in technology," Campbell says, which included state-of-the-art reservation systems. Many travellers have since taken advantage of the online reservation system and ticketless travel, as well as basic flights without meals or movies.

The airline's formula worked, as more Canadians chose WestJet, increasing sales and allowing the company to grow. Meanwhile, its competitors floundered. Canadian no longer flies and Air Canada sought bankruptcy protection in 2003. By 2004, WestJet served 25 percent of the domestic Canadian air-travel market and had enjoyed 29 consecutive quarters of profitability.

"Other airlines with higher costs have attempted to price their product like ours, but with terrible financial results," Campbell explains. "While it's great to have low prices, you must also have the low costs to go along with them. Air Canada's difficulty is its high-cost structure." For example, Air Canada's salaries were higher while employee and fleet productivity was lower than at WestJet. When the larger airlines tried to match WestJet's prices, they simply couldn't cover their overhead costs.

THE NAVIGATOR

- Scan *Study Objectives*
- Read *Feature Story*
- Read *Chapter Preview*
- Read text and answer
  Before You Go On
  p. 323, p. 326, p. 336
- Work *Using the Decision Toolkit*
- Review *Summary of Study Objectives*
- Review *Using the Decision Toolkit—A Summary*
- Work *Demonstration Problem*
- Answer *Self-Study Questions*
- Complete assignments

Air Canada: www.aircanada.com
WestJet: www.westjet.com

STUDY OBJECTIVES

After studying this chapter, you should be able to:

1. Calculate a target cost when the product's price is determined by the market.
2. Calculate a target selling price using cost-plus pricing.
3. Use time and material pricing to determine the cost of services provided.
4. Define "transfer price" and its role in an organization.
5. Determine a transfer price using the negotiated, cost-based, and market-based approaches.
6. Explain the issues that arise when goods are transferred between divisions that are located in countries with different tax rates.
7. Determine prices using the absorption cost approach and the contribution (variable cost) approach (Appendix 8A).

the
navigator

As the feature story about WestJet indicates, few management decisions are more important than setting prices. WestJet was able to cover its costs while also setting lower prices than its competitors by following a precise business plan. In this chapter, two types of pricing situations are examined. The first part of the chapter explains pricing for goods sold or services provided to external parties. The second part of the chapter examines pricing decisions that need to be made when goods are sold to other divisions within the same company.

The chapter is organized as follows.

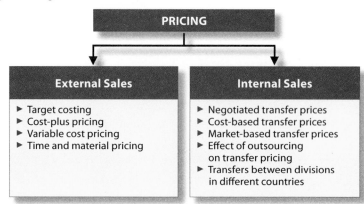

the navigator

PRICING

External Sales
- Target costing
- Cost-plus pricing
- Variable cost pricing
- Time and material pricing

Internal Sales
- Negotiated transfer prices
- Cost-based transfer prices
- Market-based transfer prices
- Effect of outsourcing on transfer pricing
- Transfers between divisions in different countries

Section 1: External Sales

Decisions that set the price for any good or service are affected by many factors. Take the pharmaceutical industry as an example. Its approach to profitability has been to spend heavily on research and development in an effort to find and patent a few new drugs, price them high, and market them aggressively. Due to the AIDS crisis in Africa, the drug industry has been under great pressure recently to lower its prices on drugs that are used to treat AIDS. For example, Merck Co. lowered the price of its AIDS drug Crixivan to $600 per patient in these countries. This compares with the $6,016 it typically charges in the United States.[1] One consequence of the lower price for Africa is that individuals in the United States are now questioning whether prices in the U.S. market are too high. The drug companies say, however, that to cover the large financial risks they take in order to develop these products, they need to set the prices high. Illustration 8-1 presents the many factors that can affect pricing decisions.

Illustration 8-1 ▶

Pricing factors

Pricing Objectives		Environment
Gain market share		Political reaction to prices
Achieve a target rate of return		Patent or copyright protection

What price should we charge?

Demand		Cost Considerations
Price sensitivity		Fixed and variable costs
Demographics		Short-run or long-run

Ideally, a company must price its product to cover the product's costs and eventually earn a reasonable profit. But to price its product appropriately, the company must have a good understanding of the market forces that will influence the price. In most cases, a company does not set its own prices. Instead the price is set by the competitive market (the laws of supply and demand). For example, a company such as Canadian Ultramar Co. or Petro-Canada cannot set the price of gasoline by itself. These companies are called **price takers** because the price of gasoline is set by market forces (the supply of oil and the demand

---

[1] "AIDS Gaffes in Africa Come Back to Haunt Drug Industry at Home," *Wall Street Journal*, April 23, 2001, p. 1.

by customers). This happens with any product that appears to be identical to competing products, such as farm products (corn or wheat) or minerals (coal or sand).

In other situations, the company sets its own prices. This occurs when the product is specially made for a customer, as in a one-of-a-kind product, such as a designer dress by Zoran or Armani. This also occurs when there are few or no other producers who can manufacture a similar item. An example would be a company that has a patent or copyright on a unique process, such as computer chips by Intel. However, a company also becomes able to set the price when it has been successful at making its product or service seem different from others. Even in a competitive market like coffee, Starbucks has been able to differentiate its product and charge more for a cup of java.

BUSINESS INSIGHT ▶ @-Business Perspective

What effect has e-business had on pricing? For one, it has reduced haggling over car prices. After joining the rush to on-line sales in 2000, Toronto-based used-car dealer, Cars4u.com Inc. has turned its attention back to its bricks and mortar operations. The company, which spent $1.5 million to launch an e-dealership in September 2000, announced in February 2002 that it would spend another $1.6 million for two Toronto-area Mazda dealerships, which will join its leasing operation, Lease-Win Ltd., used-car wholesaler, Carriage Motor Sales Inc., and two other Toronto dealerships. However, the company isn't abandoning its on-line presence. The website, which reported losses of about $10,000 a month, has provided insight into purchaser preferences. The company discovered that some people prefer the fixed prices found on the website, something that may become more common at its regular dealerships. The renewed focus on the bricks and mortar stores is part of Cars4u.com's strategy to become an automobile dealer consolidator, like U.S.-based AutoNation Inc. Many of AutoNation's land-based dealers offer fixed pricing. Cars4u.com sees standardized pricing as inevitable if it is to become a major consolidator.

Source: Andy Holloway, "There and Back Again," *Canadian Business*, March 18, 2002.

Target Costing

Automobile manufacturers like Ford Motor Company of Canada Ltd. or Toyota Canada Ltd. face a competitive market. The price of an automobile is affected greatly by the laws of supply and demand, so no company in this industry can affect the price to a significant degree. Therefore, to earn a profit, companies in the auto industry must focus on controlling their costs. This requires setting a **target cost** that gives a desired profit. The relationship of the target cost to the price and desired profit is shown in Illustration 8-2.

study objective 1

Calculate a target cost when the product's price is determined by the market.

Illustration 8-2 ◀

Target cost as related to price and profit

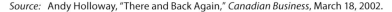

$$\boxed{\text{Market Price}} - \boxed{\text{Desired Profit}} = \boxed{\text{Target Cost}}$$

If General Motors of Canada Ltd., for example, can produce its automobiles for the target cost (or less), it will meet its profit goal. If it cannot achieve its target cost, it will fail to produce the desired profit (and will most likely "get hammered" by shareholders and the market).

In a competitive market, a company goes through several stages as it chooses its product and sets its price. It begins by choosing the segment of the market that it wants to compete in—that is, it finds its market niche. For example, it may choose between selling luxury goods or economy goods in order to focus its efforts on one segment or the other.

Once the company has identified its segment of the market, it then does market research to determine the target price. This target price is the price that the company believes would place it in the best position for its target audience (its customers).

Once the company has determined this target price, it can next determine its target cost by setting a desired profit. The difference between the target price and the desired profit is the target cost of the product. (This calculation was shown in Illustration 8-2.)

After the company determines the target cost, a team of employees with expertise in a variety of areas (production and operations, marketing, and finance) is assembled. The team's task is to design and develop a product that can meet quality specifications without costing more than the target cost. The target cost includes all the product and period costs that are necessary in order to make and market the product or service.

BUSINESS INSIGHT ▶ Management Perspective

"And the price should be $19 per set of jeans instead of $23," said the retailer Wal-Mart to jeans-maker Levi Strauss. What happened to Levi Strauss is what happens to many manufacturers who deal with Wal-Mart. Wal-Mart often sets the price, and the manufacturer has to find out how to make a profit, given that price. In Levi Strauss's case, it revamped its distribution and production to serve Wal-Mart and improve its overall record of timely deliveries. Producing a season of new jeans styles, from conception to store shelves, used to take Levi Strauss 12 to 15 months. Today it takes just 10 months for Levi Strauss signature jeans, while for regular Levi's, the time is down to seven and a half months. As the chief executive of Levi Strauss noted, "We had to change people and practice. It's been somewhat of a D-Day invasion approach."

Source: "In Bow to Retailers' New Clout, Levi Strauss Makes Alterations," *Wall Street Journal*, June 17, 2004, p. A1.

▦ Decision Toolkit

Decision Checkpoints	Info Needed for Decision	Tools to Use for Decision	How to Evaluate Results
How does management use target costs to make decisions about manufacturing a product or providing a service?	Target selling price, desired profit, target cost	Target selling price less desired profit equals target cost.	If the target cost is too high, the company will not earn its desired profit. If the desired profit is not achieved, the company must evaluate whether or not to manufacture the product or provide the service.

the navigator

Cost-Plus Pricing

study objective 2

Calculate a target selling price using cost-plus pricing.

As we just saw, in a competitive, common-product environment the market price is already set, and the company instead must set a target cost. But, in a less competitive or noncompetitive environment, the company may have to set its own price. When the price is set by the company, the price usually depends on the cost of the product or service. That is, the typical approach is to use **cost-plus pricing**. In this approach, a cost base is determined and a **markup** is added to the cost base to determine a **target selling price**. The size of the markup (the "plus") depends on the desired operating income or return on investment (ROI) for the product line, product, or service. To determine the proper markup, the company must also consider competitive and market conditions, political and legal issues, and other relevant risk factors. Illustration 8-3 shows the cost-plus pricing formula.

Illustration 8-3 ▶

Cost-plus pricing formula

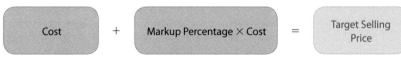

Cost + Markup Percentage × Cost = Target Selling Price

To illustrate, assume that Cleanmore Products, Inc. is in the process of setting a selling price on its new top-of-the-line, three-horsepower, 65-litre, variable-speed wet/dry shop vacuum. The variable-cost estimates per unit for the new shop vacuum are given in Illustration 8-4.

Illustration 8-4 ◀

Variable costs per unit

	Per Unit
Direct materials	$23
Direct labour	17
Variable manufacturing overhead	12
Variable selling and administrative expenses	8
Variable cost per unit	$60

Cleanmore also has the fixed costs per unit shown in Illustration 8-5, at a budgeted sales volume of 10,000 units.

Illustration 8-5 ◀

Fixed costs per unit—10,000 units

	Total Costs	÷	Budgeted Volume	=	Cost Per Unit
Fixed manufacturing overhead	$280,000	÷	10,000	=	$28
Fixed selling and administrative expenses	240,000	÷	10,000	=	24
Fixed cost per unit					$52

Cleanmore has decided to price its new shop vacuum to earn a 20-percent return on its investment (ROI) of $1 million. Therefore, Cleanmore expects to receive income of $200,000 (20% × $1,000,000) on its investment. On a per unit basis, the desired ROI is $20 ($200,000 ÷ 10,000). Using the per unit costs shown above, we then calculate the sales price to be $132, as shown in Illustration 8-6.

Illustration 8-6 ◀

Calculation of selling price—10,000 units

	Per Unit
Variable cost	$ 60
Fixed cost	52
Total cost	112
Desired ROI	20
Selling price per unit	$132

In most cases, companies like Cleanmore will use a percentage markup on the product's cost to determine the selling price. Illustration 8-7 presents the formula to calculate the markup percentage to achieve a desired ROI of $20 per unit.

Illustration 8-7 ◀

Calculation of markup percentage

Desired ROI per Unit	÷	Total Unit Cost	=	Markup Percentage
$20	÷	$112	=	17.86%

Using a 17.86-percent markup on cost, Cleanmore Products would next calculate the target selling price as in Illustration 8-8.

Illustration 8-8 ◀

Calculation of selling price—markup approach

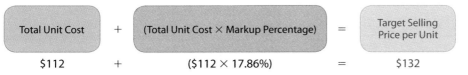

Total Unit Cost	+	(Total Unit Cost × Markup Percentage)	=	Target Selling Price per Unit
$112	+	($112 × 17.86%)	=	$132

As indicated, then, Cleanmore should set the price for its wet/dry vacuum at $132 per unit.

Limitations of Cost-Plus Pricing

The cost-plus pricing approach has a major advantage: it is simple to calculate. However, this cost model does not consider the demand side. That is, will customers pay the price Cleanmore calculated for its vacuums? In addition, sales volume plays a large role in determining per unit costs. The lower the sales volume, for example, the higher the price Cleanmore must charge to meet its desired ROI. To illustrate, if the budgeted sales volume was 8,000 instead of 10,000, Cleanmore's variable cost per unit would remain the same. However, its fixed cost per unit would change as shown in Illustration 8-9.

Illustration 8-9 ▶

Fixed cost per unit—8,000 units

	Total Costs	÷	Budgeted Volume	=	Cost Per Unit
Fixed manufacturing overhead	$280,000	÷	8,000	=	$35
Fixed selling and administrative expenses	240,000	÷	8,000	=	30
Fixed cost per unit					$65

As indicated in Illustration 8-5, the fixed costs per unit for 10,000 units added up to $52. However, at a lower sales volume of 8,000 units, the fixed cost per unit increases to $65. Cleanmore's desired 20-percent ROI now results in a $25 ROI per unit [(20% × 1,000,000) ÷ 8,000]. The selling price can be calculated in Illustration 8-10.

Illustration 8-10 ▶

Fixed cost per unit, 8,000 units

	Per Unit
Variable cost	$ 60
Fixed cost	65
Total cost	125
Desired ROI	25
Selling price per unit	$150

As shown, the lower the budgeted volume, the higher the per unit price. The reason: fixed costs and ROI are spread over fewer units, and therefore the fixed cost and ROI per unit increase. In this case, at 8,000 units, Cleanmore would have to mark up its total unit costs 20 percent to earn a desired ROI of $25 per unit, as shown below:

$$20\% = \frac{\$25 \text{ (desired ROI)}}{\$125 \text{ (total unit cost)}}$$

The target selling price would then be $150, as indicated earlier, and calculated again here:

$$\$125 + (\$125 \times 20\%) = \$150$$

The opposite effect will occur if the budgeted volume is higher (for example, at 12,000 units) because the fixed costs and ROI can be spread over more units. As a result, the cost-plus model of pricing will achieve its desired ROI only when Cleanmore sells the quantity that it budgeted. If the actual sales volume is much less than the budgeted sales volume, Cleanmore will lose money unless it can raise its prices.

Variable-Cost Pricing

Instead of using both fixed and variable costs to set prices, some companies simply add a markup to their variable costs. Using variable costs as the basis for setting prices avoids the problem of using poor cost information for the fixed cost per unit calculations (as shown in Illustration 8-9). Variable-cost pricing is also very helpful in pricing special orders or when there is excess capacity.

The major disadvantage of variable-cost pricing is that managers may set the price too low and not cover their fixed costs. In the long run, failure to cover fixed costs will lead to losses. As a result, companies that use variable-cost pricing must use higher markups to make sure that the price they set will give a fair return. An example of how variable costs are used as the basis for setting prices is discussed in the appendix to this chapter.

BUSINESS INSIGHT ▶ Management Perspective

If a company plans to sell its product or service in another country, it needs an effective pricing strategy. Assessing your export price, cost mix (variable and fixed), and price competitiveness is crucial. First, do lots of market research to identify which markets would give you the best possible price. Then determine how potential customers view your product and what specific criteria lead them to purchase a product. Knowing preferences in size, colour, model, useful life, celebrity spokesperson, etc., will help in setting prices. Consider what your product's major advantages are over your competitors' products.

Another important consideration is production cost. It is better to use only variable costs when you consider the product's cost for the export market, says marketing specialist Pierre Trudel. These costs will include expenses for adapting, manufacturing, and selling a product, as well as any export-related costs.

A company must find a balance between the purchaser's cost and the product's intrinsic value. Differentiation (showing how your product is different) allows you to distinguish your product from similar ones in your target market. By tailoring your product to the selected market (optimizing attributes that are valuable for your target market and abandoning the less attractive features), you can sell it at the highest price possible (as long as you do not create a loss from excessive costs), rather than at the price it sells for in Canada. A company will not necessarily sell more export items at a lower price, so it might as well set the highest price that the foreign market will accept.

Source: Julie Demers, "Enhanced Export Pricing Strategies," *CMA Management Magazine*, June/July 2003.

Decision Toolkit

Decision Checkpoints	Info Needed for Decision	Tools to Use for Decision	How to Evaluate Results
What factors should be considered in determining the selling price in a less competitive environment?	The total cost per unit and desired profit (cost-plus pricing)	Total cost per unit plus desired profit equals target selling price.	Does the company make its desired profit? If not, is it because of a lower sales volume?

BEFORE YOU GO ON . . .

▶ Review It

1. What is a target cost, and how is it used by management?
2. What is the general formula for determining the target selling price with cost-plus pricing?
3. How is the per unit return on investment determined?

▶ Do It

Air Corporation produces air purifiers. The following cost information per unit is available: direct materials $16; direct labour $18; variable manufacturing overhead $11; fixed manufacturing overhead $10; variable selling and administrative expenses $6; and fixed selling and administrative expenses $10. Using a 45-percent markup percentage on the total cost per unit, calculate the target selling price.

Action Plan

- Calculate the total cost per unit.
- Multiply the total cost per unit by the markup percentage. Then add this amount to the total cost per unit to determine the target selling price.

Solution

Direct materials	$16
Direct labour	18
Variable manufacturing overhead	11
Fixed manufacturing overhead	10
Variable selling and administrative expenses	6
Fixed selling and administrative expenses	10
Total unit cost	$71

Total unit cost + (total unit cost × markup percentage) = target selling price

$$\$71 \quad + \quad (\$71 \quad \times \quad 45\%) \quad = \quad \$102.95$$

Related exercise material: BE8–2, BE8–3, BE8–4, BE8–5, E8–3, E8–4, E8–5, E8–6, and E8–7.

Time and Material Pricing

Another variation on cost-plus pricing is called **time and material pricing**. Under this approach, the company sets two pricing rates—one for the **labour** used on a job and another for the **material**. The labour rate includes direct labour time and other employee costs. The material charge is based on the cost of direct parts and materials used and a **material loading charge** for related overhead costs. Time and material pricing is widely used in service industries, especially professional firms such as public accounting, law, engineering, and consulting firms, as well as construction companies, repair shops, and printers.

To illustrate time and material pricing, assume the data in Illustration 8-11 for Lake Holiday Marina, a boat and motor repair shop.

Illustration 8-11 ▶

Total annual budgeted time and material costs

LAKE HOLIDAY MARINA Budgeted Costs for the Year 2005		
	Time Charges	Material Loading Charges[1]
Mechanics' wages and benefits	$103,500	$ 0
Parts manager's salary and benefits	0	11,500
Office employee's salary and benefits	20,700	2,300
Other overhead (supplies, amortization, property taxes, advertising, utilities)	26,800	14,400
Total budgeted costs	$151,000	$28,200

[1] The invoice cost of the materials is not included in the material loading charges.

There are three steps in time and material pricing: (1) calculate the labour charge per hour, (2) calculate the charge for obtaining and holding materials, and (3) calculate the charges for a particular job.

Step 1: Calculate the labour charge. The first step for time and material pricing is to determine a charge for labour time. The charge for labour time is expressed as a rate per hour of labour. This rate includes (1) the direct labour cost of the employee, including the hourly rate or salary and fringe benefits; (2) selling, administrative, and similar overhead costs; and (3) an allowance for a desired profit or ROI per hour of employee time. In some industries, such as auto, boat, and farm equipment repair shops, the same hourly labour rate is charged regardless of which employee performs the work. In other industries, the rate charged depends on the classification or level of the employee. In a public accounting firm, for example, the services of an assistant, senior manager, or partner would be charged at different rates, as would those of a paralegal, associate, or partner in a law firm.

The calculation of the hourly charges for Lake Holiday Marina during 2005 is shown in Illustration 8-12. The marina budgets 5,000 hours of repair time in 2005, and it wants a profit margin of $8 per hour of labour.

Illustration 8-12 ◄

Calculation of hourly time-charge rate

Per Hour	Total Cost	÷	Total Hours	=	Per Hour Charge
Hourly labour rate for repairs					
Mechanics' wages and benefits	$103,500	÷	5,000	=	$20.70
Overhead costs					
Office employee's salaries and benefits	20,700	÷	5,000	=	4.14
Office overhead	26,800	÷	5,000	=	5.36
Total hourly cost	$151,000	÷	5,000	=	30.20
Profit margin					8.00
Rate charged per hour of labour					$38.20

This rate of $38.20 is multiplied by the number of hours of labour used on any particular job to determine the labour charge for that job.

Step 2: Calculate the material loading charge. The charge for materials typically includes the invoice price of any materials used on the job plus a **material loading charge**. The material loading charge covers the costs of purchasing, receiving, handling, and storing materials, plus any desired profit margin on the materials themselves. The material loading charge is expressed as a percentage of the total estimated costs of parts and materials for the year. To determine this percentage, the company does the following: (1) It estimates its total annual costs for purchasing, receiving, handling, and storing materials. (2) It divides this amount by the total estimated cost of parts and materials. And (3) it adds a desired profit margin on the materials themselves.

The calculation of the material loading charge used by Lake Holiday Marina during 2005 is shown in Illustration 8-13. The marina estimates that the total invoice cost of parts and materials used in 2005 will be $120,000. The marina wants a 20-percent profit margin on the invoice cost of parts and materials.

Illustration 8-13 ◄

Calculation of material loading charge

Per Hour	Material Loading Charges	÷	Total Invoice Costs, Parts and Materials	=	Material Loading Percentage
Overhead costs					
Parts manager's salary and benefits	$11,500				
Office employee's salary	2,300				
	13,800	÷	$120,000	=	11.50%
Other overhead	14,400	÷	120,000	=	12.00%
	$28,200	÷	120,000	=	23.50%
Profit margin					20.00%
Material loading percentage					43.50%

The material loading charge on any particular job is 43.50 percent multiplied by the cost of materials used on the job. For example, if $100 of parts were used, the additional material loading charge would be $43.50.

Step 3: Calculate Charges for a Particular Job. The charges for any particular job are the sum of (1) the labour charge, (2) the charge for the materials, and (3) the material loading charge. For example, suppose that Lake Holiday Marina prepares a price quotation to estimate the cost to refurbish a used 28-foot pontoon boat. Lake Holiday Marina estimates the job will require 50 hours of labour and $3,600 in parts and materials. The marina's price quotation is shown in Illustration 8-14.

Illustration 8-14 ▶

Price quotation for time and material

LAKE HOLIDAY MARINA		
Time and Material Price Quotation		

Job: Marianne Perino, repair of 28-foot pontoon boat		
Labour charges: 50 hours @ $38.20		$1,910
Material charges		
Cost of parts and materials	$3,600	
Material loading charge (43.5% × $3,600)	1,566	5,166
Total price of labour and material		$7,076

Included in the $7,076 price quotation for the boat repair and refurbishment are charges for labour costs, overhead costs, materials costs, materials handling and storage costs, and a profit margin on both labour and parts. Lake Holiday Marina used labour hours as a basis for calculating the time rate. Other companies—such as machine shops, plastic moulding shops, and printers—might use machine hours.

Decision Toolkit

Decision Checkpoints	Info Needed for Decision	Tools to Use for Decision	How to Evaluate Results
How do we set prices when it is difficult to estimate the total cost per unit?	Two pricing rates needed: one for labour use and another for materials	Calculate the labour rate charge and material rate charge. In each of these calculations, add a profit margin.	Is the company profitable under this pricing approach? Are employees earning reasonable wages?

BEFORE YOU GO ON . . .

▶ Review It

1. What is time and material pricing? Where is it often used?
2. What is a material loading charge?

▶ Do It

Presented below are data for Harmon Electrical Repair Shop for next year:

Repair-technicians' wages	$130,000
Fringe benefits	30,000
Overhead	20,000

The desired profit margin per labour hour is $10. The material loading charge is 40 percent of the invoice cost. It is estimated that 8,000 labour hours will be worked next year. If Harmon repairs a TV that takes four hours to repair and uses parts costing $50, calculate the bill for this job.

Action Plan

• Calculate the labour charge.
• Calculate the material loading charge.
• Calculate the bill for the specific repair.

Solution

	Total Cost	÷	Total Hours	=	Per Hour Charge
Repair-technicians' wages	$130,000	÷	8,000	=	$16.25
Fringe benefits	30,000	÷	8,000	=	3.75
Overhead	20,000	÷	8,000	=	2.50
	$180,000	÷	8,000	=	22.50
Profit margin					10.00
Rate charged per hour of labour					$32.50
Materials cost					$50
Material loading charge ($50 × 40%)					20
Total materials cost					$70
Cost of TV repair					
Labour costs ($32.50 × 4)					$130
Materials cost					70
Total repair cost					$200

Related exercise material: BE8–6, E8–8, E8–9, and E8–10.

Section 2: Internal Sales

In today's global economy, growth is vital to survival. Frequently, growth is "vertical," which means that the company expands in the direction of either its suppliers or its customers. For example, a manufacturer of bicycles, like Trek, may acquire a chain of bicycle shops. A movie production company like Walt Disney or a broadcaster like CTV Inc. might acquire a movie theatre chain or a cable television company.

> **study objective 4**
>
> Define "transfer price" and its role in an organization.

A division in a vertically integrated company normally transfers goods or services to other divisions in the same company, in addition to making sales to customers outside the company. When goods are transferred internally, the price used to record the transfer between the two divisions is the **transfer price**. Illustration 8-15 highlights these transactions for Aerobic Bicycle Company.

Aerobic Bicycle has two divisions: a bicycle assembly division and a bicycle components manufacturing division. The price charged for intermediate goods is the cost of goods sold to the buying division (assembly division) and revenue to the selling division (manufacturing division). A high transfer price results in high revenue for the selling division and high costs for the buying division. A low transfer price has the reverse outcome and therefore affects the selling division's performance. Thus, transfer prices can be a point of serious disagreement for division managers and can lead to actions that benefit a division but hurt the company as a whole.

Illustration 8-15 ◀

Transfer pricing illustration

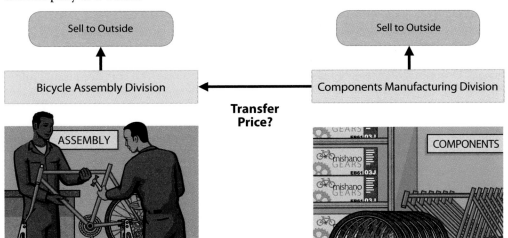

A firm's transfer pricing policy should accomplish three objectives:

1. **Promote goal congruence.** The policy should motivate division managers to choose actions that maximize company earnings as a whole and it should allow each division manager to make decisions that maximize his or her own division's earnings.
2. **Maintain divisional autonomy.** Top management should not interfere with the decision-making process of division managers.
3. **Provide accurate performance evaluation.** The policy should make it possible to accurately evaluate the division managers involved in the transfer.

A general approach to transfer pricing which achieves the above objectives uses the variable costs per unit of product and the opportunity cost for the company as a whole to determine the transfer price. Illustration 8-16 provides the formula.

Illustration 8-16 ▶

General transfer-pricing formula

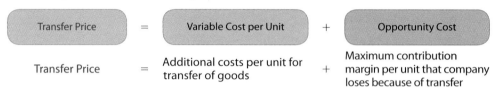

| Transfer Price | = | Additional costs per unit for transfer of goods | + | Maximum contribution margin per unit that company loses because of transfer |

Other key elements in this approach are the minimum price that the selling division is willing to accept and the maximum price that the buying division is willing to pay. For the selling division, the minimum price is the price that it needs to charge the buying division so that the selling division would not be better off if it sold the product to an outside buyer. For the buying division, the maximum price is determined by the outside market. That is, the maximum price is how much the buying division would have to pay an outside seller for the product.

With these minimum and maximum prices known, the division managers can now decide if a transfer should occur. In general, the goods should be transferred internally if the selling division's minimum price is less than or equal to the buying division's maximum price.

To illustrate this general approach to transfer pricing, we will continue with our example of Aerobic Bicycle Company. The manufacturing division transfers some of its products to the company's assembly division, and it sells some of its products under different labels to other companies. As each division manager is compensated based on whether or not his or her division has achieved its target profit amount, the managers are motivated to get the best possible price, from each manager's perspective, for any transfers of goods. Illustration 8-17 provides the data for the two divisions.

Illustration 8-17 ▼

Basic data for Aerobic Bicycle Company

Assembly Division		Components Manufacturing Division	
Selling price of Aerobic Bicycle	$290	Wholesale selling price of components per bicycle	$130
Variable cost of assembly (not including cost of manufacturing components)	70	Variable cost of manufacturing components per bicycle	95
Cost of bicycle components	130		
Contribution margin per unit	$ 90	Contribution margin per unit	$ 35

The above information indicates that the assembly division has a contribution margin per unit of $90 and the manufacturing division has a contribution margin of $35. The total contribution margin per bicycle is $125 ($90 + $35) for the Aerobic Bicycle Company as a whole. Using this data, we will now apply the general approach to transfer pricing under two different situations: first, when the manufacturing division has no excess capacity and, second, when it has excess capacity.

First Situation: No Excess Capacity

Assume the manufacturing division can sell to outside buyers all the bicycle components it can produce, and that it sells them at the wholesale price of $130 per unit and has no excess capacity remaining. Now let's ask the question, "What would be a fair transfer price if top management wants the company's manufacturing division to transfer all its production to the company's assembly division?"

As indicated in Illustration 8-17, the manufacturing division charges $130 and has a contribution margin of $35 per unit. The division has no excess capacity and produces and sells all its production to outside customers. Therefore, from the perspective of the division, it must receive from the assembly division a payment that will at least cover its variable cost per unit plus the contribution margin per unit it would lose (often called the opportunity cost). Otherwise, it makes no sense for the manufacturing division to sell its products to the assembly division. The minimum transfer price that would be acceptable to the manufacturing division, therefore, is $130, as shown in Illustration 8-18.

	Variable Cost	+	Opportunity Cost	=	Minimum Transfer Price
	$95	+	$35	=	$130

Illustration 8-18 ◀

Minimum transfer price—no excess capacity

Goal Congruence. If the transfer price is charged at $130, according to the general approach, goal congruence is achieved. The manufacturing division is willing to transfer its products to the assembly division at the price of $130, which is equal to the external market price. The assembly division is willing to buy the bicycle components from the internal division because the assembly division will have a contribution margin of $90 on each bicycle component purchased from the manufacturing division ($290 sales price minus the $70 of variable assembly costs and the transfer price of $130). Thus, the total contribution margin per unit is $125 ($90 + $35) for the Aerobic Bicycle Company.

Second Situation: Excess Capacity

Now assume the manufacturing division has excess capacity. The demand from all sources—internal sales and external market sales—is less than the division's production capacity. In this setting of excess capacity, let's ask the question, as before, "What would be a fair transfer price under the general transfer-price approach?" Because the division has excess capacity and cannot sell all its production to outside customers, from the perspective of the division, it must receive from the assembly division a payment that will at least cover the manufacturing division's variable cost per unit. Otherwise, it makes no sense for the division to sell its products to the assembly division. The minimum transfer price that would be acceptable to the manufacturing division is $95, as shown in Illustration 8-19.

	Variable Cost	+	Opportunity Cost	=	Minimum Transfer Price
	$95	+	$0	=	$95

Illustration 8-19 ◀

Minimum transfer price—excess capacity

Goal Congruence. If the transfer price is charged at $95, according to the general approach, goal congruence is achieved. The goal is achieved because the total contribution margin per unit is still $125 ($125 + $0) for the Aerobic Bicycle Company as a whole. It is in the company's best interest for the bicycle components to be purchased internally from the manufacturing division as long as the variable cost to produce and transfer the bicycle components is less than the outside price of $130. In this situation, it is beneficial for the assembly division to buy the bicycle components from the internal division because the assembly division will have a contribution margin that is greater than $90 on the components for each bicycle that are purchased from the internal division ($290 sales price minus the $70 of variable assembly costs and the transfer price up to a maximum market price of $130).

In summary, the pricing issues presented above for transfer pricing are similar to pricing issues for outside buyers. The objective is to maximize the return to the whole company. In the transfer-pricing situation, it is also important, however, that divisional performance not decline because of internal transfers. This means that setting a transfer price is often more complicated because of competing interests among divisions within the company. It is not suprising, therefore, that no single transfer-pricing policy will suit every organization's needs.[1] In the following section, we will discuss three possible approaches for determining a transfer price:

1. Negotiated transfer prices
2. Cost-based transfer prices
3. Market-based transfer prices

In theory, a negotiated transfer price should work best, but due to practical considerations, the other two methods are often used.

Negotiated Transfer Prices

<table>
<tr><td>

study objective 5

Determine a transfer price using the negotiated, cost-based, and market-based approaches.

</td></tr>
</table>

The **negotiated transfer price** is determined through an agreement by division managers. To illustrate the negotiated transfer-pricing approach, we will examine Alberta Boot Company. Until recently, Alberta Boot focused exclusively on making rubber soles for work boots and hiking boots. These rubber soles were sold to boot manufacturers. However, last year the company decided to take advantage of its strong reputation by expanding into the business of making hiking boots. Because of this expansion, the company is now structured as two independent divisions, the boot division and the sole division. The manager of each division is compensated based on how well his or her division achieves its profitability targets.

The sole division continues to make rubber soles for both hiking boots and work boots and to sell these soles to other boot manufacturers. The boot division manufactures leather uppers for hiking boots and attaches these uppers to rubber soles. During its first year, the boot division purchased its rubber soles from outside suppliers so as not to disrupt the operations of the sole division. However, top management now wants the sole division to provide at least some of the soles used by the boot division. Illustration 8-20 shows the calculation of the contribution margin per unit for each division when the boot division buys soles from an outside supplier.

Illustration 8-20 ▶

Basic data for Alberta Boot Company

Boot Division		Sole Division	
Selling price of hiking boots	$90	Selling price of sole	$18
Variable cost of manufacturing boot (not including sole)	35	Variable cost per sole	11
Cost of sole purchased from outside suppliers	17	Contribution margin per unit	$ 7
Contribution margin per unit	$38		
Total contribution margin per unit: $38 + $7 = $45			

This information indicates that the boot division has a contribution margin per unit of $38 and the sole division has one of $7. The total contribution margin per unit for the company is $45 ($38 + $7). Now let's ask the question, "What would be a fair transfer price if the sole division sold 10,000 soles to the boot division?"

No Excess Capacity

As indicated in Illustration 8-21, the sole division charges $18 and gets a contribution margin of $7 per sole. The sole division has no excess capacity and produces and sells 80,000 units (soles) to outside customers. Therefore, the sole division must receive from the boot division a payment that will at least cover its variable cost per sole **plus** its lost contribution margin per sole (the **opportunity cost**). Otherwise, the sole division should not sell its soles to the boot division. The minimum transfer price that would be acceptable to the sole division is $18, as shown in Illustration 8-21.

---

[1] Manmohan Rai Kapoor, "Dueling Divisions: A New Dual Transfer Pricing Method," *CMA Magazine*, March 1998, p. 23.

Illustration 8-21 ◄

Minimum transfer price—no excess capacity

From the perspective of the boot division (the buyer), the most it will pay is what the sole would cost from an outside supplier, which in this case is $17. As shown in Illustration 8-22, therefore, an acceptable transfer price is not available in this situation.

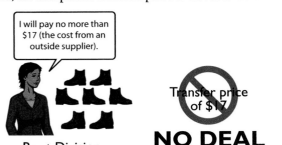

Illustration 8-22 ◄

Transfer-pricing illustration—no deal

Excess Capacity

What happens if the sole division has excess capacity? For example, assume the sole division can produce 80,000 soles but can sell only 70,000 soles in the open market. As a result, it has available capacity of 10,000 units. In this situation, the sole division does not lose its contribution margin of $7 per unit and, therefore, the minimum price it would now accept is $11, as shown in Illustration 8-23.

Illustration 8-23 ◄

Minimum transfer price formula—excess capacity

In this case, the boot division and the sole division should negotiate a transfer price within the range of $11 to $17, as shown in illustration 8-24.

Illustration 8-24 ◄

Transfer-pricing negotiations—deal

Because of the excess capacity, Alberta Boot Company will increase its overall net income if the 10,000 soles are purchased internally. This is true as long as the sole division's variable cost is less than the outside price of $17. The sole division will receive a positive contribution margin from any transfer price above its variable cost of $11. The boot division will benefit from any price below $17. At any transfer price above $17, the boot division will go to an outside supplier, a solution that would be undesirable to both divisions, as well as to the company as a whole.

Variable Costs

In the minimum transfer price formula, **variable cost is defined as the variable cost of units sold *internally*.** In some instances, the variable cost of units sold internally will differ from the variable cost of units sold externally. For example, variable selling expenses are often lower when units are sold internally. In this case, the variable cost of units sold internally will be lower than the cost of units sold externally.

Alternatively, the variable cost of units sold internally could be higher if the internal division requests a special order that requires more expensive materials or additional labour. For example, assume that the boot division would like to make 5,000 new high-margin, heavy-duty boots. The sole required for this boot will be made of a denser rubber and will have an intricate lug design. Alberta Boot Company is not aware of any supplier that currently makes such a sole, and it doubts that any other supplier can meet the quality expectations. As a result, there is no available market price to use as the transfer price.

We can, however, still use the formula for the minimum transfer price to help find a reasonable solution. After evaluating the special sole, the sole division determines that its variable cost would be $19 per sole. The sole division is already at full capacity, however. The sole division's opportunity cost at full capacity is the $7 per sole ($18 − $11) that it earns producing the standard sole and selling it to an outside customer. Therefore, the minimum transfer price that the sole division would be willing to accept would be as shown in Illustration 8-25:

Illustration 8-25 ►

Minimum transfer price formula—special order

Variable Cost	+	Opportunity Cost	=	Minimum Transfer Price
$19	+	$7	=	$26

The transfer price of $26 gives the sole division enough revenue to cover its increased variable cost and its opportunity cost (the contribution margin on its standard sole).

Summary of Negotiated Transfer Pricing Approach

Using the negotiated transfer-pricing approach, a minimum transfer price is established by the selling division, and a maximum transfer price is established by the purchasing division. If used appropriately, this system provides a sound basis for establishing a transfer price because both divisions are better off if the proper decision rules are used by both. However, negotiated transfer pricing often is not used because of the following factors:

- Market price information is sometimes not easily obtainable.
- A lack of trust between the two negotiating divisions may lead to a breakdown in the negotiations.
- Negotiations often lead to different pricing strategies from division to division, which is difficult to work with and sometimes costly to implement.

Many companies, therefore, use more objective and simple systems that are based on cost or market information to develop transfer prices.

Cost-Based Transfer Prices

One way of determining transfer-prices is to base the transfer price on the costs of the division that produces the goods or services. If a **cost-based transfer price** is used, the transfer price may be based on variable costs alone, or on variable costs plus fixed costs. A markup may be added to these cost numbers.

Unfortunately, under a cost-based approach, divisions sometimes use improper transfer prices. This leads to a loss of profitability for the company and unfair evaluations of division performance. To illustrate, assume that Alberta Boot Company requires the division to use a transfer price based on the variable cost of the sole. Illustration 8-26 shows what happens to the contribution margin per unit of the two divisions when there is no excess capacity.

Illustration 8-26 ◀

Cost-based transfer price—
10,000 units

Boot Division		Sole Division	
Selling price of hiking boots	$90	Selling price of sole	$11
Variable cost of manufacturing boot (not including sole)	35	Variable cost per sole	11
Cost of sole purchased from Sole Division	11	Contribution margin per unit	$ 0
Contribution margin per unit	$44		
Total contribution margin per unit	$44 ($44 + $0)		

This cost-based transfer system is a bad deal for the sole division, as it reports no profit on the transfer of 10,000 soles to the boot division. If the sole division had sold the 10,000 soles externally, it would have made $70,000 [10,000 × ($18 − $11)]. The boot division, on the other hand, is delighted, as its contribution margin per unit increases from $38 to $44, or $6 more per boot. Overall, Alberta Boot Company loses $10,000 (10,000 units × $1). The sole division lost a contribution margin per unit of $7 (illustration 8-26), and the boot division experienced only a $6 increase in its contribution margin per unit. Illustration 8-27 shows this deficiency.

The overall results change if the sole division **has excess capacity**. In this case, the sole division continues to report a zero profit on these 10,000 units but does not lose the $7 per unit (because it had excess capacity). The boot division gains $6. So overall, the company is better off by $60,000 (10,000 × $6). However, with a cost-based system, the sole division continues to report a zero profit on these 10,000 units.

What happened? We were earning $45 per unit and now it is only $44.

This is great. We now earn $6 more per unit.

Boot Division

Hey, we lost $7 per unit and earned no profit.

Sole Division

Illustration 8-27 ◀

Cost-based transfer price—
no excess capacity

From this analysis, we can see that a cost-based system does not reflect the division's true profitability. Moreover, it does not even provide enough incentive for the sole division to control costs. Whatever the division's costs are, they are passed on to the next division. One way that some companies try to overcome this problem is to base the transfer price on **standard costs**, rather than actual costs. Although it has these disadvantages, the cost system is simple to understand and easy to use because the information is already available in the accounting system. In addition, market information is sometimes not available, so the only alternative is some type of cost-based system. As a result, it is the method that most companies use in order to establish transfer prices.

Market-Based Transfer Prices

The **market-based transfer price** is based on the actual market prices of competing goods or services. A market-based system is often considered the best approach because it is objective and generally provides the proper economic incentives. For example, if the sole division can charge the market price, it will not care if soles are sold to outside customers or internally to the boot division—it does not lose any contribution margin. Similarly, the boot division will be satisfied because it is paying a price for the good or service that is at or reasonably close to market.

When the sole division has no excess capacity, the market-based system works reasonably well. The sole division receives the market price and the boot division pays the market price. If the sole division has excess capacity, however, the market-based system can lead to actions that are not the best ones for the company.

For example, the minimum transfer price that the sole division should receive is its variable cost plus opportunity cost. Because the sole division has excess capacity, its opportunity cost is zero. However, under the market-based system, the sole division transfers the goods at the market price of $18, for a contribution margin per unit of $7. The boot division manager then has to accept the $18 sole price. The boot division needs to know, however, that this price is not the cost of the sole when the sole division has excess capacity. If it does not know this, the boot division may overprice its boots in the market if it uses the market price of the sole plus a markup in setting the price of the boot. This action can lead to losses for Alberta Boot overall.

Another problem, as indicated earlier, is that in many cases there simply is not a well-defined market for the good or service being transferred. As a result, a reasonable market value cannot be determined, and companies may therefore use a cost-based system.

Effect of Outsourcing on Transfer Pricing

More and more companies rely on **outsourcing**. Outsourcing involves contracting with an external party to obtain a good or service, rather than doing the work internally. Some companies have taken outsourcing to the extreme by outsourcing all of their production. These so-called virtual companies have well-established brand names, but they do not manufacture any of their own products. Incremental analysis (Chapter 6) is used to determine whether outsourcing is profitable. As companies increasingly rely on outsourcing, it means that fewer components are transferred internally between divisions.

Transfers between Divisions in Different Countries

study objective 6

Explain the issues that arise when goods are transferred between divisions that are located in countries with different tax rates.

As more companies "globalize" their operations, more transfers are happening between divisions that are in different countries. For example, one estimate suggests that 60 percent of the trade between countries is simply transfers between divisions. Differences in tax rates in different countries can complicate the determination of the right transfer price.

Companies must pay income tax in the country where income is generated. In order to increase income and pay less income tax, many companies prefer to report more income in countries with low tax rates, and less income in countries with high tax rates. This is done by adjusting the transfer prices they use on internal transfers between divisions located in different countries. The division in the country with the lower tax rate is allocated more contribution margin, and the division in the country with the higher tax rate is allocated less.

To illustrate, suppose that Alberta Boot's boot division is in a country with a corporate tax rate of 10 percent, and the sole division is in a country with a tax rate of 30 percent. Illustration 8-28 shows the after-tax contribution margin to the company as a whole assuming, first, that the soles are transferred at a transfer price of $18, and second, that the soles are transferred at a transfer price of $11.

$18 Transfer Price

Boot Division		Sole Division	
Selling price of hiking boots	$90.00	Selling price of sole	$18.00
Variable cost of manufacturing boot (not including sole)	35.00	Variable cost per sole	11.00
Cost of sole purchased internally	18.00		
Before-tax contribution margin	37.00	Before-tax contribution margin	7.00
Tax at 10%	3.70	Tax at 30%	2.10
After-tax contribution margin	$33.30	After-tax contribution margin	$ 4.90

Before-tax total contribution margin to company $37 + $7 = $44
After-tax total contribution margin to company $33.30 + $4.90 = $38.20

$11 Transfer Price

Boot Division		Sole Division	
Selling price of hiking boots	$90.00	Selling price of sole	$11.00
Variable cost of manufacturing boot (not including sole)	35.00	Variable cost per sole	11.00
Cost of sole purchased internally	11.00		
Before-tax contribution margin	44.00	Before-tax contribution margin	0.00
Tax at 10%	4.40	Tax at 30%	0.00
After-tax contribution margin	$39.60	After-tax contribution margin	$ 0.00

Before-tax total contribution margin to company $44 + $0 = $44
After-tax total contribution margin to company $39.60 + $0 = $39.60

Note that the before-tax total contribution margin to Alberta Boot Company is $44 whether the transfer price is $18 or $11. However, the after-tax total contribution margin to Alberta Boot Company is $38.20 using the $18 transfer price, and $39.60 using the $11 transfer price. The reason: when the $11 transfer price is used, more of the contribution margin goes to the division that is in the country with the lower tax rate.

As this analysis shows, Alberta Boot Company would be better off using the $11 transfer price. However, this creates some concerns. First, the sole division manager will not be happy with an $11 transfer price. This price may lead to unfair evaluations of the sole division's manager. Second, the company must ask whether it is legal and ethical to use an $11 transfer price when the market price clearly is higher than that. International transfer pricing is presented further in more advanced accounting courses.

BUSINESS INSIGHT ► International Perspective

International transfer-pricing issues can create headaches for both companies and taxing authorities. In 2004, Swiss watch manufacturer Swatch Group Ltd. found itself fighting charges that it evaded millions of dollars in taxes through its use of transfer pricing in its Asia-Pacific operations. In denying the charges, Swatch said it used the practice of profit transfers, a financial mechanism that allows the movement of profits from high-tax locations to offshore locations with lower taxes. Swatch claimed the practice is simply part of managing 18 different brands and ensuring harmonized prices across markets when taxation levels vary according to segment, category, and price. The U.S. Labor Department rejected the complaint, and there was no public investigation in Switzerland.

Source: Edward Taylor, "Consumer Products," *The Globe and Mail*, August 25, 2004.

Decision Toolkit

Decision Checkpoints	Info Needed for Decision	Tools to Use for Decision	How to Evaluate Results
What price should be charged for the transfer of goods between divisions of a company?	Variable costs, opportunity costs, market prices	Variable costs plus opportunity costs should provide a minimum transfer price for the seller.	If the income of the division provides for a fair evaluation of managers, then the transfer price is useful. Also, the income of the company overall should not be reduced by the transfer-pricing approach.

BEFORE YOU GO ON . . .

▶ Review It

1. What are the objectives of transfer pricing?
2. What are the three approaches to transfer pricing? What are the advantages and disadvantages of each approach?
3. How do some companies reduce their tax payments through their transfer price?

APPENDIX 8A ▶ OTHER COST APPROACHES TO PRICING

study objective 7

Determine prices using the absorption cost approach and the contribution (variable cost) approach.

In calculating the target price of $132 for Cleanmore's shop vacuum in the chapter, we calculated the cost base by **including all costs incurred (the full cost approach)**. Using total cost as the basis of the markup makes sense in theory because the price must eventually cover all costs and provide a reasonable profit. However, total cost is difficult to determine in reality. This is because period costs (selling and administrative expenses) are difficult to trace to a specific product. Activity-based costing can be used to overcome this difficulty to some extent.

In practice, two other cost approaches are used: (1) the absorption cost approach, and (2) the contribution (variable cost) approach. The absorption cost approach is more popular than the contribution approach.[1] We will illustrate both of them, though, because both have their strengths.

Absorption Cost Approach

The **absorption cost approach** is consistent with generally accepted accounting principles (GAAP) because it defines the cost base as the manufacturing cost. **Both the variable and fixed selling and administrative costs are excluded from this cost base.** Thus, the markup needs to be high enough to cover the selling and administrative costs plus the target ROI.

---

[1] For a discussion of cost-plus pricing, see Eunsup Shim and Ephraim F. Sudit, "How Manufacturers Price Products," *Management Accounting* (February 1995), pp. 37–39; and V. Govindarajan and R.N. Anthony, "How Firms Use Cost Data in Pricing Decisions," *Management Accounting* (July 1983), pp. 30–36.

The **first step** in the absorption cost approach is to calculate the **manufacturing cost per unit**. For Cleanmore Products, Inc., this amounts to $80 per unit at a volume of 10,000 units, as shown in Illustration 8-1A.

	Per Unit
Direct materials	$23
Direct labour	17
Variable manufacturing overhead	12
Fixed manufacturing overhead ($280,000 ÷ 10,000)	28
Total manufacturing cost per unit (absorption cost)	$80

Illustration 8-1A ◀

Calculation of manufacturing cost per unit

In addition, Cleanmore provided the following information on selling and administrative expenses per unit and the desired ROI per unit.

Variable selling and administrative expenses	$ 8
Fixed selling and administrative expenses ($240,000 ÷ 10,000)	24
Desired ROI per unit	20

Illustration 8-2A ◀

Other information

The **second step** in the absorption cost approach is to calculate the markup percentage using the formula in Illustration 8-3A. Note that when the manufacturing cost per unit is used as the cost base to calculate the markup percentage, the **percentage must cover the desired ROI and also the selling and administrative expenses.**

Illustration 8-3A ◀

Markup percentage—absorption approach

Desired ROI per Unit + Selling and Administrative Expenses per Unit = Markup Percentage × Manufacturing Cost per Unit

$20 + $32 = MP × $80

Solving the equation we find:

$$MP = (\$20 + \$32) \div \$80 = 65\%$$

The **third** and final **step** is to set the target selling price. Using a markup percentage of 65 percent and the absorption approach, we calculate the target selling price as shown in Illustration 8-4A.

Illustration 8-4A ◀

Calculation of target price—absorption approach

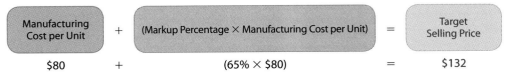

Manufacturing Cost per Unit + (Markup Percentage × Manufacturing Cost per Unit) = Target Selling Price

$80 + (65% × $80) = $132

Using a target price of $132 will produce the desired 20-percent return on investment for Cleanmore Products on its three-horsepower, wet/dry shop vacuum at a sales volume level of 10,000 units, as proved in Illustration 8-5A.

Illustration 8-5A ▶

Proof of 20% ROI—
absorption approach

CLEANMORE PRODUCTS, INC.
Budgeted Absorption-Cost Income Statement

Revenue (10,000 units × $132)	$1,320,000
Less: Cost of goods sold (10,000 units × $80)	800,000
Gross profit	520,000
Less: Selling and administrative expenses [10,000 units × ($8 + $24)]	320,000
Net income	$ 200,000

Budgeted ROI

$$\frac{\text{Net income}}{\text{Invested assets}} = \frac{\$200,000}{\$1,000,000} = \underline{20\%}$$

Markup Percentage

$$\frac{\text{Net income + Selling and administrative expenses}}{\text{Cost of goods sold}} = \frac{\$200,000 + \$320,000}{\$800,000} = \underline{65\%}$$

Because of the fixed cost element, if more than 10,000 units are sold, the ROI will be greater than 20 percent. If fewer than 10,000 units are sold, the ROI will be less than 20 percent. The markup percentage is also verified by adding $200,000 (the net income) and $320,000 (the selling and administrative expenses) and then dividing by $800,000 (the cost of goods sold or the cost base).

Most companies that use cost-plus pricing use either the absorption cost or the full cost as the basis. The reasons are as follows:

1. Absorption cost information is provided most easily by a company's cost accounting system. Because absorption cost data already exist in general ledger accounts, it is cost-effective to use them for pricing.
2. Basing the cost-plus formula on only variable costs could encourage managers to set too low a price in order to boost sales. There is the fear that if only variable costs are used, they will be substituted for full costs and this can lead to suicidal price-cutting.
3. The absorption cost or full cost is the easiest basis to defend when prices need to be justified to all interested parties—managers, customers, and governments.

Contribution (Variable Cost) Approach

Under the **contribution approach**, the cost base consists of all of the variable costs associated with a product, including the variable selling and administrative costs. **Because fixed costs are not included in the base, the markup must cover fixed costs (manufacturing, and selling and administrative) and the target ROI.** The contribution approach is more useful for making short-term decisions because it considers variable cost and fixed cost behaviour patterns separately.

The **first step** in the contribution approach to cost-plus pricing is to calculate the variable cost per unit. For Cleanmore Products, Inc., this amounts to $60 per unit, as shown in Illustration 8-6A.

Illustration 8-6A ▶

Calculation of variable cost
per unit

	Per Unit
Direct materials	$23
Direct labour	17
Variable manufacturing overhead	12
Variable selling and administrative expenses	8
Total variable cost per unit	$60

The **second step** in the contribution approach is to calculate the markup percentage. The formula for the markup percentage is shown in Illustration 8-7A. For Cleanmore, the fixed costs include fixed manufacturing overhead of $28 per unit ($280,000 ÷ 10,000) and fixed selling and administrative expenses of $24 per unit ($240,000 ÷ 10,000).

Desired ROI per Unit	+	Fixed Cost per Unit	=	Markup Percentage	×	Variable Cost per Unit
$20	+	($28 + $24)	=	MP	×	$60

Illustration 8-7A ◄

Calculation of markup percentage—contribution approach

Solving the equation, we find:

$$MP = \frac{\$20 + (\$28 + \$24)}{\$60} = 120\%$$

The **third step** is to set the target selling price. Using a markup percentage of 120 percent and the contribution approach, the selling price is calculated as in Illustration 8-8A.

Variable Cost per Unit	+	(Markup Percentage × Variable Cost per Unit)	=	Target Selling Price
$60	+	(120% × $60)	=	$132

Illustration 8-8A ◄

Calculation of target price—contribution approach

Using a target price of $132 will produce the desired 20-percent return on investment for Cleanmore Products on its three-horsepower, wet/dry shop vacuum at a sales volume level of 10,000 units, as proved in Illustration 8-9A.

Illustration 8-9A ◄

Proof of 20% ROI—contribution approach

CLEANMORE PRODUCTS, INC.
Budgeted Contribution-Based Income Statement

Revenue (10,000 units × $132)		$1,320,000
Less: Variable costs (10,000 units × $60)		600,000
Contribution margin		720,000
Less: Fixed costs		
Manufacturing (10,000 × $28)	$280,000	
Selling and administrative (10,000 × $24)	240,000	520,000
Net income		$ 200,000

Budgeted ROI

$$\frac{\text{Net income}}{\text{Invested assets}} = \frac{\$200,000}{\$1,000,000} = \underline{20\%}$$

Markup Percentage

$$\frac{\text{Net income} + \text{Fixed costs}}{\text{Cost of goods sold}} = \frac{\$200,000 + \$520,000}{\$600,000} = \underline{120\%}$$

Under any of the three approaches we have looked at (full cost, absorption cost, and contribution), the desired ROI will be reached only if the budgeted sales volume for the period is reached. None of these approaches guarantees a profit or a desired ROI. Achieving a desired ROI is the result of many factors, and some of these are beyond the company's control, such as market conditions, political and legal issues, customers' tastes, and competitive actions.

Because the absorption cost includes allocated fixed costs, it does not make clear how the company's costs will change as the sales volume changes. To avoid blurring the effects of cost behaviour on operating income, some managers therefore prefer the contribution approach. The specific reasons for using the contribution approach, even though the basic accounting data are less accessible, are as follows:

1. The contribution approach, being based on variable cost, is more consistent with the cost-volume-profit analysis that is used by managers to measure the profit implications of changes in price and volume.
2. The contribution approach provides the type of data that managers need for pricing special orders. It shows the incremental cost of accepting one more order.

3. The contribution approach avoids an arbitrary allocation of common fixed costs (such as executive salary) to individual product lines.

Using the Decision Toolkit

Cedarburg Lumber specializes in building "high-end" playhouses for kids. It builds the components in its factory, then ships the parts to the customer's home. It has contracted with carpenters across the country to do the final assembly. Each year, it comes out with a new model. This year's model looks like a miniature castle, complete with spires and drawbridge. The following cost estimates for this new product have been provided by the accounting department for a budgeted sales volume of 1,000 units:

	Per Unit	Total
Direct materials	$840	
Direct labour	$1,600	
Variable manufacturing overhead	$400	
Fixed manufacturing overhead		$540,000
Variable selling and administrative expenses	$510	
Fixed selling and administrative expenses		$320,000

Cedarburg Lumber uses cost-plus pricing to set its selling price. Management also wants the target price to provide a 25% return on investment (ROI) on invested assets of $4.2 million.

Instructions

(a) Calculate the markup percentage and target selling price on this new playhouse.
(b) Assuming that the sales volume is 1,500 units instead of 1,000 units, calculate the markup percentage and target selling price that will allow Cedarburg Lumber to earn its desired ROI of 25%.

Solution

(a)
Variable cost per unit

	Per Unit
Direct materials	$ 840
Direct labour	1,600
Variable manufacturing overhead	400
Variable selling and administrative expenses	510
Variable cost per unit	$3,350

Fixed cost per unit

	Total Costs	÷	Budgeted Volume	=	Cost per Unit
Fixed manufacturing overhead	$540,000	÷	1,000	=	$540
Fixed selling and administrative expenses	320,000	÷	1,000	=	320
Fixed cost per unit	$860,000				$860

Calculation of selling price (1,000 units)

Variable cost per unit	$3,350
Fixed cost per unit	860
Total cost per unit	4,210
Desired ROI per unit [1]	1,050
Selling price	$5,260

[1] ($4,200,000 × 0.25) ÷ 1,000

The markup percentage is:

$$\frac{\text{Desired ROI per unit}}{\text{Total unit cost}} = \frac{\$1,050}{\$4,210} = 24.9\%$$

(b) If the company produces 1,500 units, its selling price and markup percentage would be as follows:

Calculation of selling price (1,500 units)

Variable cost per unit	$3,350
Fixed cost per unit ($860,000 ÷ 1,500)	573
Total cost per unit	3,923
Desired ROI per unit[2]	700
Selling price	$4,623

[2] ($4,200,000 × 0.25) ÷ 1,500

The markup percentage is:

$$\frac{\text{Desired ROI per unit}}{\text{Total unit cost}} = \frac{\$700}{\$3,923} = 17.8\%$$

Summary of Study Objectives

1. Calculate a target cost when the product's price is determined by the market. To calculate a target cost, the company determines its target selling price. Once the target selling price is set, it determines its target cost by setting a desired profit. The difference between the target price and the desired profit is the target cost of the product.

2. Calculate a target selling price using cost-plus pricing. In cost-plus pricing, a cost base is determined and a markup is added to it to determine a target selling price. The cost-plus pricing formula is as follows: cost + (markup percentage × cost) = target selling price.

3. Use time and material pricing to determine the cost of services provided. Under time and material pricing, two pricing rates are set—one for the labour used on a job and another for the material. The labour rate includes direct labour time and other employee costs. The material charge is based on the cost of the direct parts and materials that are used and a material loading charge for related overhead costs.

4. Define "transfer price" and its role in an organization. The transfer price is the amount charged for goods that are transferred between two divisions of the same company. Transfer-pricing policy should achieve goal congruence, accurate performance evaluation among division managers, and division autonomy.

5. Determine a transfer price using the negotiated, cost-based, and market-based approaches. The negotiated price is determined by an agreement between division managers. A cost-based transfer price may be based on full cost, variable cost, or some modification including a markup. The cost-based approach often leads to poor performance evaluations and purchasing decisions. The advantage of the cost-based system is its simplicity. A market-based transfer price is based on actual market prices for products and services. A market-based system is often considered the best approach because it is objective and generally creates good economic incentives.

6. Explain the issues that arise when goods are transferred between divisions that are located in countries with different tax rates. Companies must pay income tax in the country where the income is generated. In order to increase income and pay less income tax, many companies prefer to report more income in countries with low tax rates, and less income in countries with high tax rates. This is done by adjusting the transfer prices they use on internal transfers between divisions that are located in different countries.

7. Determine prices using the absorption cost approach and the contribution (variable cost) approach. The absorption cost approach uses the manufacturing cost as the cost base and covers the selling and administrative costs plus the target ROI through the markup. The target selling price is calculated as follows: manufacturing cost per unit + (markup percentage × manufacturing cost per unit). The contribution (variable cost) approach uses all of the variable costs, including selling and administrative costs, as the cost base and covers the fixed costs and target ROI through the markup. The target selling price is calculated as follows: variable cost per unit + (markup percentage × variable cost per unit).

▦ Decision Toolkit—A Summary

Decision Checkpoints	Info Needed for Decision	Tools to Use for Decision	How to Evaluate Results
How does management use target costs to make decisions about manufacturing a product or providing a service?	Target selling price, desired profit, target cost	Target selling price less desired profit equals target cost.	If the target cost is too high, the company will not earn its desired profit. If the desired profit is not achieved, the company must evaluate whether or not to manufacture the product or provide the service.
What factors should be considered in determining the selling price in a less competitive environment?	The total cost per unit and desired profit (cost-plus pricing)	Total cost per unit plus desired profit equals target selling price.	Does the company make its desired profit? If not, is it because of a lower sales volume?
How do we set prices when it is difficult to estimate the total cost per unit?	Two pricing rates needed: one for labour use and another for materials	Calculate the labour rate charge and material rate charge. In each of these calculations, add a profit margin.	Is the company profitable under this pricing approach? Are employees earning reasonable wages?
What price should be charged for the transfer of goods between divisions of a company?	Variable costs, opportunity costs, market prices	Variable costs plus opportunity costs should provide a minimum transfer price for the seller.	If the income of the division provides for a fair evaluation of managers, then the transfer price is useful. Also, the income of the company overall should not be reduced by the transfer-pricing approach.

Glossary

Key Term Matching Activity

Absorption cost approach   An approach to pricing that defines the cost base as the manufacturing cost; it excludes both variable and fixed selling and administrative costs. (p. 336)

Contribution approach   An approach to pricing that defines the cost base as all variable costs; it excludes both the fixed manufacturing and fixed selling and administrative costs. (p. 338)

Cost-based transfer price   A transfer price that is based on the costs of the division producing the goods. (p. 332)

Cost-plus pricing   A process in which a product's selling price is determined by adding a markup to a cost base. (p. 320)

Market-based transfer price   A transfer price that is based on the actual market prices of products. (p. 333)

Markup   The percentage applied to a product's cost to determine the product's selling price. (p. 320)

Material loading charge   A charge added to cover the cost of purchasing, receiving, handling, and stor-ing materials, plus any desired profit margin on the materials themselves. (p. 325)

Negotiated transfer price   A transfer price that is determined by the agreement of the division managers when no external market price is available. (p. 330)

Outsourcing   Contracting with an external party to provide a good or service rather than performing the work internally. (p. 334)

Target cost   The cost that will provide the desired profit on a product when the seller does not have con-trol over the product's price. (p. 319)

Target selling price   The selling price that will pro-vide the desired profit on a product when the seller can determine the product's price. (p. 320)

Time and material pricing   An approach to cost-plus pricing in which the company uses two pricing rates: one for the labour used on a job and another for the material. (p. 324)

Transfer price   The price used to record the transfer of goods between two divisions of a company. (p. 327)

Demonstration Problem

Animated
Demonstration
Problem

Revco Electronics is a division of International Motors, an automobile manufacturer. Revco produces car radio/CD players. Revco sells its products to International Motors, and to other car manufacturers and electronics distributors. The following information is for the car radio/CD player:

Selling price of car radio/CD player to external customers	$49
Variable cost per unit	$28
Capacity	200,000 units

Instructions

Determine whether the goods should be transferred internally or purchased externally and what the appropriate transfer price should be under each of the following independent situations:

(a) Revco Electronics is operating at full capacity. There is a saving of $4 per unit for variable costs if the car radio is made for internal sale. International Motors can purchase a similar car radio from an outside supplier for $47.

(b) Revco Electronics has enough capacity to satisfy the needs of International Motors. International Motors can purchase a similar car radio from an outside supplier for $47.

(c) International Motors wants to purchase a special-order car radio/CD player that also includes a tape deck. It needs 15,000 units. Revco Electronics has determined that the additional variable cost would be $12 per unit. Revco Electronics has no unused capacity. It will have to lose sales of 15,000 units to external parties in order to provide this special order.

Solution to Demonstration Problem

(a) Revco Electronics' opportunity cost (its lost contribution margin) would be $21 ($49 − $28). Using the formula for minimum transfer price, we determine:

Minimum transfer price	=	variable cost	+	opportunity cost
$45	=	($28 − $4)	+	$21

Since this minimum transfer price is less than the $47 it would cost if International Motors purchases from an external party, an internal transfer should take place. Revco Electronics and International Motors should negotiate a transfer price between $45 and $47.

(b) Since Revco Electronics has available capacity, its opportunity cost (its lost contribution margin) would be $0. Using the formula for minimum transfer price, we determine the following:

Minimum transfer price	=	variable cost	+	opportunity cost
$28	=	$28	+	$0

Since International Motors can purchase the unit for $47 from an external party, the most it would be willing to pay would be $47. It is in the best interest of the company as a whole, as well as the two divisions, for a transfer to take place. The two divisions must reach a negotiated transfer price between $28 and $47 that recognizes the costs and benefits to each party and is acceptable to both.

(c) Revco Electronics' opportunity cost (its lost contribution margin per unit) would be $21 ($49 − $28). Its variable cost would be $40 ($28 + $12). Using the formula for minimum transfer price, we determine the following:

Minimum transfer price	=	variable cost	+	opportunity cost
$61	=	$40	+	$21

Note that in this case Revco Electronics has no available capacity. Its management may decide that it does not want to provide this special order because this would force the company to cut off the supply of the standard unit to some of its existing customers. This may anger those customers and result in the company's losing them.

Action Plan

- Determine whether the company is at full capacity or not.
- Find the minimum transfer price, using formulas.
- Compare the maximum price the buyer would pay to the minimum price for the seller.
- Determine if a deal can be made.

the navigator

Note: All questions, exercises, and problems below with an asterisk (*) relate to material in Appendix 8A.

Self-Study Questions

www.wiley.com/canada/managerial

Additional Self-Study Questions

Answers are at the end of the chapter.

(SO 2)   1. Cost-plus pricing means that:
(a) selling price = variable cost + (markup percentage + variable cost).
(b) selling price = cost + (markup percentage × cost).
(c) selling price = manufacturing cost + (markup percentage + manufacturing cost).
(d) selling price = fixed cost + (markup percentage × fixed cost).

(SO 1)   2. When there is a target cost in terms of the price and profit, this means that:
(a) the cost and desired profit must be determined before the selling price is determined.
(b) the cost and selling price must be determined before the desired profit is determined.
(c) the price and desired profit must be determined before the costs are determined.
(d) costs can be covered only if the company is at full capacity.

(SO 1)   3. Classic Toys has examined the market for toy train locomotives. It believes there is a market niche in which it can sell locomotives at $80 each. It estimates that 10,000 of these locomotives could be sold annually. Variable costs to make a locomotive are expected to be $25. Classic anticipates a profit of $15 per locomotive. The target cost for the locomotive is:
(a) $80.   (c) $40.
(b) $65.   (d) $25.

(SO 2)   4. Adler Company is considering developing a new product. The company has gathered the following information on this product:

Expected total unit cost	$25
Estimated investment for new product	$500,000
Desired ROI	10%
Expected number of units to be produced and sold	1,000

The desired markup percentage and selling price are:
(a) markup percentage 10%; selling price $55.
(b) markup percentage 200%; selling price $75.
(c) markup percentage 10%; selling price $50.
(d) markup percentage 100%; selling price $55.

(SO 2)   5. The following information is for Mystique Co. concerning the new product it recently introduced:

Total unit cost	$30
Desired ROI per unit	$10
Target selling price	$40

Mystique Co.'s percentage markup on cost would be:
(a) 125%.   (c) 33⅓%.
(b) 75%.   (d) 25%.

(SO 3)   6. Crescent Electrical Repair has decided to price its work on a time and materials basis. It estimates the following costs for the year for labour:

Technician wages and benefits	$100,000
Office employee's salary and benefits	40,000
Other overhead	80,000

Crescent wants a profit margin of $10 per labour hour and budgets 5,000 hours of repair time for the year. The office employee's salary and benefits, and other overhead costs should be divided evenly between the time charges and material loading charges. Crescent's labour charge per hour would be:
(a) $42.   (c) $32.
(b) $34.   (d) $30.

(SO 4)   7. The plastics division of Weston Company manufactures plastic moulds and then sells them to customers for $70 per unit. Its variable cost is $30 per unit, and its fixed cost is $10 per unit. Management would like the division to transfer 10,000 of these moulds to another division within the company at a price of $40. The plastics division is operating at full capacity. What is the minimum transfer price that the plastics division should accept?
(a) $10.   (c) $40.
(b) $30.   (d) $70.

(SO 4)   8. Assume the same information as question 7, except that the plastics division has available capacity of 10,000 units for plastic mouldings. What is the minimum transfer price that the plastics division should accept?
(a) $10.   (c) $40.
(b) $30.   (d) $70.

(SO 7)   *9. AST Electrical provides the following cost information for its production of electronic circuit boards:

	Per Unit
Variable manufacturing cost	$40
Fixed manufacturing cost	$30
Variable selling and administrative expenses	$8
Fixed selling and administrative expenses	$12
Desired ROI per unit	$15

What is its markup percentage, assuming that AST Electrical uses the absorption cost approach?
(a) 16.67%.　　　　(c) 54.28%.
(b) 50%.　　　　　(d) 118.75%.

*10. Assume the same information as question 9. What is AST Electrical's markup percentage using the contribution approach? (SO 7)
(a) 16.67%.　　　　(c) 54.28%.
(b) 50%.　　　　　(d) 118.75%.

Questions

1. What are the two types of pricing environments for sales to external parties?

2. In what situation does a company focus most on its target cost? How is the target cost determined?

3. What is the basic formula to determine the target selling price in cost-plus pricing?

4. Stine Corporation produces a filter that has a per unit cost of $17. The company would like a 30% markup percentage. Using cost-plus pricing, determine the selling price per unit.

5. What is the basic formula for the markup percentage?

6. What are some of the factors that affect a company's target ROI?

7. Livingston Corporation manufactures an electronic switch for dishwashers. The cost base per unit, excluding selling and administrative expenses, is $60. The per unit cost of selling and administrative expenses is $20. The company's desired ROI per unit is $6. Calculate its markup percentage on the total unit cost.

8. Estevan manufactures a standard cabinet for a DVD player. The variable cost per unit is $15. The fixed cost per unit is $9. The desired ROI per unit is $6. Calculate the markup percentage on the total unit cost and the target selling price for the DVD cabinet.

9. Where is time and material pricing most often used?

10. What is the material loading charge? How is it expressed?

11. What is a transfer price? Why is determining a fair transfer price important for division managers?

12. When it is setting a transfer price, what objective(s) should the company have?

13. What are the three approaches for determining transfer prices?

14. Describe the cost-based approach to transfer pricing. What is the strength of this approach? What are the weaknesses of this approach?

15. What is the general formula for determining the minimum transfer price that the selling division should be willing to accept?

16. When determining the minimum transfer price, what is meant by the "opportunity cost"?

17. In what circumstances will a negotiated transfer price be used instead of a market-based price?

18. Explain how transfer pricing between divisions that are located in different countries is used to reduce tax payments, and discuss the correctness of this approach.

*19. What costs are excluded from the cost base when the absorption cost approach is used to determine the markup percentage?

*20. Kay Corporation manufactures a fibre optic connector. The variable cost per unit is $15. The fixed cost per unit is $9. The company's desired ROI per unit is $3. Calculate the markup percentage using the contribution approach.

Brief Exercises

Calculate target cost.
(SO 1)

BE8–1   Podborski Company manufactures computer hard drives. The market for hard drives is very competitive. The current market price for a computer hard drive is $45. Podborski would like a profit of $14 per drive. How can Podborski Company accomplish this objective?

Use cost-plus pricing to determine selling price.
(SO 2)

BE8–2   Gruner Corporation produces snowboards. The following cost information per unit is available: direct materials $12; direct labour $8; variable manufacturing overhead $6; fixed manufacturing overhead $14; variable selling and administrative expenses $4; and fixed selling and administrative expenses $12. Using a 32% markup percentage on the total cost per unit, calculate the target selling price.

Calculate ROI per unit.
(SO 2)

BE8–3   Travis Corporation produces high-performance rotors. It expects to produce 50,000 rotors in the coming year. It has invested $10 million to produce rotors. The company has a required return on investment of 18%. What is its ROI per unit?

Calculate markup percentage.
(SO 2)

BE8–4   Schuman Corporation produces microwave units. The following per unit cost information is available: direct materials $36; direct labour $24; variable manufacturing overhead $18; fixed manufacturing overhead $42; variable selling and administrative expenses $14; and fixed selling and administrative expenses $28. Its desired ROI per unit is $30. Calculate its markup percentage using a total cost approach.

Calculate ROI and markup percentage.
(SO 2)

BE8–5   During the current year, Bierko Corporation expects to produce 10,000 units and has budgeted the following: net income $300,000; variable costs $1.1 million; and fixed costs $100,000. It has invested assets of $1.5 million. What was the company's budgeted ROI? What was its budgeted markup percentage using a total cost approach?

Use time and material pricing to determine bill.
(SO 3)

BE8–6   Swayze Small Engine Repair charges $45 per hour of labour. It has a material loading percentage of 40%. On a recent job to replace the engine of a riding lawnmower, Swayze worked 10.5 hours and used parts with a cost of $700. Calculate Swayze's total bill.

Determine minimum transfer price.
(SO 5)

BE8–7   The heating division of ITA International produces a heating element that it sells to its customers for $42 per unit. Its variable cost per unit is $19, and its fixed cost per unit is $10. Top management of ITA International would like the heating division to transfer 15,000 heating units to another division within the company at a price of $29. The heating division is operating at full capacity. What is the minimum transfer price that the heating division should accept?

Determine minimum transfer price with excess capacity.
(SO 5)

BE8–8   Use the data from BE8–7, but assume that the heating division has enough excess capacity to provide the 15,000 heating units for the other division. What is the minimum transfer price that the heating division should accept?

Determine minimum transfer price for special order.
(SO 5)

BE8–9   Use the data from BE8–7, but assume that the units being requested are special high-performance units, and that the division's variable cost would be $24 per unit. What is the minimum transfer price that the heating division should accept?

Calculate markup percentage using absorption cost approach.
(SO 7)

*BE8–10   Using the data in BE8–4, calculate the markup percentage using the absorption cost approach.

Calculate markup percentage using contribution approach.
(SO 7)

*BE8–11   Using the data in BE8-4, calculate the markup percentage using the contribution approach.

Exercises

E8–1 Culver Cheese Company has developed a new cheese slicer called the Slim Slicer. The company plans to sell this slicer through its monthly catalogue. Given market research, Culver believes that it can charge $15 for the Slim Slicer. Prototypes of the Slim Slicer, however, are costing $22. By using cheaper materials and gaining efficiencies in mass production, Culver believes it can reduce the Slim Slicer's cost substantially. Culver wants to earn a return of 30% of the selling price.

Calculate target cost.
(SO 1)

Instructions

(a) Calculate the target cost for the Slim Slicer.
(b) When is target costing particularly helpful in deciding whether to produce a particular product?

E8–2 Lasik Look produces and sells high-end golf equipment. The company has recently been involved in developing various types of laser guns to measure distances on the golf course. The potential market for one small laser gun, the LittleLasik, appears to be very large. Because of competition, Lasik Look does not believe that it can charge more than $90 for LittleLasik. At this price, Lasik Look believes it can sell 100,000 laser guns. LittleLasik will cost $8.5 million to manufacture, and the company wants an ROI of 20%.

Calculate target cost.
(SO 1)

Instructions

Determine the target cost for one LittleLasik.

E8–3 Mucky Duck makes swimsuits and sells them directly to retailers. Although Mucky Duck has a variety of suits, it does not make the all-body suit used by highly skilled swimmers. The market research department believes that a strong market exists for this type of suit. It says the all-body suit would sell for approximately $110. Given its experience, Mucky Duck believes the all-body suit would have the following manufacturing costs:

Calculate target cost and cost-plus pricing.
(SO 1, 2)

Direct materials	$ 25
Direct labour	30
Manufacturing overhead	45
Total costs	$100

Mucky Duck would like a 25% return on its costs.

Instructions

(a) Assume that Mucky Duck uses cost-plus pricing, and sets the price 25% above the product's costs. (1) What would be the price charged for the all-body swimsuit? (2) Explain whether there are any circumstances where Mucky Duck might consider manufacturing the all-body swimsuit given this approach.
(b) Assume that Mucky Duck uses target costing. What is the price that Mucky Duck would charge the retailer for the all-body swimsuit?
(c) What is the highest acceptable manufacturing cost Mucky Duck would be willing to incur to produce the all-body swimsuit?

E8–4 Selleck Corporation makes a commercial-grade cooking griddle. The following information is available for Selleck Corporation's expected annual volume of 30,000 units:

Use cost-plus pricing to determine selling price.
(SO 2)

	Per Unit	Total
Direct materials	$17	
Direct labour	8	
Variable manufacturing overhead	11	
Fixed manufacturing overhead		$360,000
Variable selling and administrative expenses	4	
Fixed selling and administrative expenses		150,000

The company uses a 40% markup percentage on total cost.

Instructions

(a) Calculate the total cost per unit.
(b) Calculate the target selling price.

Use cost-plus pricing to
determine various amounts.
(SO 2)

E8–5   Ahmed Corporation makes a mechanical stuffed alligator that sings the Martian national anthem. The following information is available for Ahmed Corporation's expected annual volume of 500,000 units:

	Per Unit	Total
Direct materials	$ 7	
Direct labour	9	
Variable manufacturing overhead	15	
Fixed manufacturing overhead		$3,300,000
Variable selling and administrative expenses	14	
Fixed selling and administrative expenses		1,550,000

The company has a desired ROI of 25%. It has invested assets of $24 million.

Instructions

(a) Calculate the total cost per unit.
(b) Calculate the desired ROI per unit.
(c) Calculate the markup percentage using the total cost per unit.
(d) Calculate the target selling price.

Use cost-plus pricing to
determine various amounts.
(SO 2)

E8–6   Caan Corporation produces industrial robots for high-precision manufacturing. The following information is given for Caan Corporation:

	Per Unit	Total
Direct materials	$380	
Direct labour	290	
Variable manufacturing overhead	72	
Fixed manufacturing overhead		$1,800,000
Variable selling and administrative expenses	55	
Fixed selling and administrative expenses		327,000

The company has a desired ROI of 20%. It has invested assets of $49.6 million. It expects to produce 3,000 units each year.

Instructions

(a) Calculate the cost per unit of the fixed manufacturing overhead and the fixed selling and administrative expenses.
(b) Calculate the desired ROI per unit.
(c) Calculate the target selling price.

Use time and material
pricing to determine bill.
(SO 3)

E8–7   Padong Remanufacturing rebuilds spot welders for manufacturers. The following budgeted cost data for 2006 are available for Padong:

	Time Charges	Material Loading Charges
Technicians' wages and benefits	$228,000	
Parts manager's salary and benefits		$42,500
Office employee's salary and benefits	38,000	9,000
Other overhead	15,200	24,000
Total budgeted costs	$281,200	$75,500

The company wants a $35 profit margin per hour of labour and a 25% profit margin on parts. It has budgeted for 7,600 hours of repair time in the coming year, and estimates that the total invoice cost of parts and materials in 2006 will be $400,000.

Instructions

(a) Calculate the rate charged per hour of labour.
(b) Calculate the material loading percentage. (Round to three decimal places.)
(c) Lindy Corporation has asked for an estimate on rebuilding its spot welder. Padong estimates that it would require 40 hours of labour and $2,500 of parts. Calculate the total estimated bill.

Use time and material
pricing to determine bill.
(SO 3)

E8–8   Justin's Custom Electronics (JCE) sells and installs complete security, computer, audio, and video systems for homes. On newly constructed homes, it provides bids using time and material pricing. The following budgeted cost data are available:

	Time Charges	Material Loading Charges
Technicians' wages and benefits	$150,000	
Parts manager's salary and benefits		$34,000
Office employee's salary and benefits	28,000	12,000
Other overhead	15,000	42,000
Total budgeted costs	$193,000	$88,000

The company has budgeted for 6,000 hours of technician time during the coming year. It wants a $38 profit margin per hour of labour and a 100% profit on parts. It estimates the total invoice cost of parts and materials in 2006 will be $700,000.

Instructions

(a) Calculate the rate charged per hour of labour. (Round to two decimal places.)
(b) Calculate the material loading percentage. (Round to two decimal places.)
(c) JCE has just received a request for a bid from R.J. Builders on a $1.2-million new home. The company estimates that it would require 80 hours of labour and $40,000 of parts. Calculate the total estimated bill.

E8–9 Allied Company's small motor division manufactures small motors used in household and office appliances. The household division then assembles and packages such items as blenders and juicers. Both divisions are allowed to buy and sell any of their components internally or externally. The following costs are for the LN233 motor on a per unit basis:

Determine minimum transfer price.
(SO 4, 5)

Fixed cost per unit	$ 5
Variable cost per unit	8
Selling price per unit	30

Instructions

(a) Assuming that the small motor division has excess capacity, calculate the minimum acceptable price for the transfer of the LN233 to the household division.
(b) Assuming that the small motor division does not have excess capacity, calculate the minimum acceptable price for the transfer of the LN233 to the household division.
(c) ▭▭▭▷ Explain why the level of capacity in the small motor division affects the transfer price.

E8–10 The cycle division of TravelFast Company has the following cost data per unit for its most recent cycle, the Roadbuster:

Determine effect of transfer price on income.
(SO 4)

Selling price		$2,200
Variable cost of goods sold		
Body frame	$300	
Other variable costs	900	1,200
Contribution margin		$1,000

The cycle division currently buys its body frames from an outside supplier. However, TravelFast has another division, FrameBody, that makes body frames for other cycle companies. The cycle division believes that FrameBody's product is suitable for its new Roadbuster cycle. FrameBody sells its frames to outside customers for $350 per frame. The variable cost for FrameBody is $250. The cycle division is willing to pay $275 to purchase the frames from FrameBody.

Instructions

(a) Assume that FrameBody has excess capacity and is able to meet all of the cycle division's needs. If the cycle division buys 1,000 frames from FrameBody, determine the following: (1) the effect on the cycle division's income; (2) the effect on FrameBody's income; and (3) the effect on TravelFast's income.
(b) Assume that FrameBody does not have excess capacity and therefore would lose sales if the frames were sold to the cycle division. If the cycle division buys 1,000 frames from FrameBody, determine the following: (1) the effect on the cycle division's income; (2) the effect on FrameBody's income; and (3) the effect on TravelFast's income.

Determine minimum transfer price.
(SO 4, 5)

E8-11   NuVox Corporation manufactures car stereos. It is a division of Lambda Motors, which manufactures vehicles. NuVox sells car stereos to Lambda, as well as to other vehicle manufacturers and retail stores. The following information is available for NuVox's standard unit: variable cost per unit $34; fixed cost per unit $23; and selling price to outside customers $85. Lambda currently purchases a standard unit from an outside supplier for $80. Because of quality concerns and to ensure a reliable supply, the top management of Lambda has ordered NuVox to provide 200,000 units per year at a transfer price of $34 per unit. NuVox is already operating at full capacity. NuVox can avoid $4 per unit of variable selling costs by selling the unit internally.

Instructions

(a) What is the minimum transfer price that NuVox should accept?
(b) What is the potential loss to the corporation as a whole because of this forced transfer?
(c) How should this situation be resolved?

Calculate minimum transfer price.
(SO 4, 5)

E8-12   The faucet division of Korey Plumbing Corporation has recently been approached by the bathtub division. The bathtub division would like to make a special "ivory" tub with gold-plated fixtures for the company's 50-year anniversary. It would make only 5,000 of these units. It would like the faucet division to make the fixtures and provide them to the bathtub division at a transfer price of $160. The estimated variable cost per unit would be $135. However, by selling internally, the faucet division would save $6 per unit on variable selling expenses. The faucet division is currently operating at full capacity. Its standard unit sells for $50 per unit and has variable costs of $29.

Instructions

Calculate the minimum transfer price that the faucet division should be willing to accept, and discuss whether it should accept this offer.

Calculate total cost per unit, ROI, and markup percentages.
(SO 2, 7)

*E8-13   Using the information given in E8–5 for Ahmed Corporation, answer the following.

Instructions

(a) Calculate the total cost per unit.
(b) Calculate the desired ROI per unit.
(c) Using the absorption cost approach, calculate the markup percentage.
(d) Using the contribution approach, calculate the markup percentage.

Calculate markup percentage using absorption cost and contribution approaches.
(SO 7)

*E8-14   Firefly Corporation produces outdoor portable fireplace units. The following cost information per unit is available: direct materials $21; direct labour $26; variable manufacturing overhead $16; fixed manufacturing overhead $22; variable selling and administrative expenses $9; and fixed selling and administrative expenses $15. The company's ROI per unit is $20.

Instructions

Calculate Firefly Corporation's markup percentage using (1) the absorption cost approach and (2) the contribution approach.

Calculate various amounts using the absorption cost and contribution approaches.
(SO 7)

*E8-15   Using the information given in E8–6 for Caan Corporation, answer the following.

Instructions

(a) Calculate the cost per unit of the fixed manufacturing overhead and the fixed selling and administrative expenses.
(b) Calculate the desired ROI per unit.
(c) Calculate the markup percentage and target selling price using the absorption cost approach. (Round to three decimal places.)
(d) Calculate the markup percentage and target selling price using the contribution approach. (Round to three decimal places.)

Problems: Set A

P8–16A Lafleur Corporation needs to set a target price for its newly designed product, M14–M16. The following data relate to it:

Use cost-plus pricing to determine various amounts. (SO 2)

	Per Unit	Total
Direct materials	$20	
Direct labour	42	
Variable manufacturing overhead	10	
Fixed manufacturing overhead		$1,440,000
Variable selling and administrative expenses	5	
Fixed selling and administrative expenses		1,040,000

These costs are based on a budgeted volume of 80,000 units produced and sold each year. Lafleur uses cost-plus pricing to set its target selling price. The markup on the total unit cost is 30%.

Instructions

(a) Calculate the total variable cost per unit, total fixed cost per unit, and total cost per unit for M14–M16.
(b) Calculate the desired ROI per unit for M14–M16.
(c) Calculate the target selling price for M14–M16.
(d) Assuming that 60,000 M14–M16s are sold during the year, calculate the variable cost per unit, fixed cost per unit, and total cost per unit.

P8–17A Berg and Sons Ltd. builds custom-made pleasure boats that range in price from $10,000 to $250,000. For the past 30 years, Mr. Berg Sr. has determined the selling price of each boat by estimating the cost of material, labour, and a prorated portion of overhead, and adding 20% to the estimated costs.

Use cost-plus pricing to determine various amounts. (SO 2, 7)

For example, a recent price quotation was determined as follows:

Direct materials	$ 50,000
Direct labour	80,000
Overhead	20,000
	150,000
Plus 20%	30,000
Selling price	$180,000

Estimating total overhead for the year and allocating it at 25% of the direct labour costs determined the overhead costs.

If a customer rejected the price and business was slow, Mr. Berg Sr. might be willing to reduce his markup to as little as 5% over the estimated costs. Thus, average markup for the year was estimated at 15%.

Mr. Berg Jr. has just completed a managerial accounting course which dealt with pricing, and he believes that the firm could use some of the techniques discussed in the course. The course emphasized the contribution approach to pricing and Mr. Berg Jr. feels that such an approach would be helpful in determining an appropriate price for the boats.

Total overhead, which includes selling and administrative expenses for the year, has been estimated at $1.5 million, of which $900,000 is fixed and the remainder is variable in direct proportion to direct labour.

Instructions

(a) Assume the customer rejected the $180,000 quotation and also rejected a $157,500 (5% markup) quotation during a slack period. The customer countered with a $150,000 offer.
  1. What is the minimum selling price Mr. Berg Sr. could have quoted without reducing or increasing the company's net income?
  2. What is the difference in company net income for the year between accepting or rejecting the customer's offer?
(b) Identify and briefly explain one advantage and one disadvantage of the contribution approach to pricing compared to the approach previously used by Berg and Sons Ltd.

(CGA-adapted)

Use cost-plus pricing to
determine various amounts.
(SO 2)

P8–18A   Bolus Computer Parts Inc. is setting a selling price on a new component it has just designed and developed. The following cost estimates for this new component have been provided by the accounting department for a budgeted volume of 50,000 units:

	Per Unit	Total
Direct materials	$50	
Direct labour	25	
Variable manufacturing overhead	20	
Fixed manufacturing overhead		$600,000
Variable selling and administrative expenses	18	
Fixed selling and administrative expenses		400,000

Management requests that the total cost per unit be used in cost-plus-pricing products. On this particular product, management also directs that the target price be set to provide a 25% return on investment (ROI) on invested assets of $1.2 million.

Instructions

(Round all calculations to two decimal places.)

(a) Calculate the markup percentage and target selling price that will allow Bolus Computer Parts to earn its desired ROI of 25% on this new component.
(b) Assuming that the volume is 40,000 units, calculate the markup percentage and target selling price that will allow Bolus Computer Parts to earn its desired ROI of 25% on this new component.

Use time and material
pricing to determine bill.
(SO 3)

P8–19A   St-Cyr's Electronic Repair Shop has budgeted the following time and material for 2005:

	Time Charges	Material Charges
Shop employees' wages and benefits	$108,000	$ 0
Parts manager's salary and benefits	0	25,400
Office employee's salary and benefits	20,000	13,600
Invoice cost of parts used	0	100,000
Overhead (supplies, amortization, advertising, utilities)	26,000	18,000
Total budgeted costs	$154,000	$157,000

St-Cyr's budgets 5,000 hours of repair time in 2005 and will bill a profit of $5 per labour hour along with a 30% profit markup on the invoice cost of parts.

On January 5, 2005, St-Cyr's is asked to submit a price estimate to fix a 72-inch big-screen TV. St-Cyr's estimates that this job will consume 20 hours of labour and $500 in parts and materials.

Instructions

(a) Calculate the labour rate for St-Cyr's Electronic Repair Shop for the year 2005.
(b) Calculate the material loading-charge percentage for St-Cyr's Electronic Repair Shop for the year 2005.
(c) Prepare a time and material price quotation for fixing the big-screen TV.

Determine minimum
transfer price under
different situations.
(SO 4, 5)

P8–20A   Ampro Inc. has two divisions. Division A makes and sells student desks. Division B manufactures and sells reading lamps.

Each desk has a reading lamp as one of its components. Division A can purchase reading lamps at a cost of $10 from an outside vendor. Division A needs 10,000 lamps for the coming year.

Division B has the capacity to manufacture 50,000 lamps annually. Sales to outside customers are estimated at 40,000 lamps for the next year. Reading lamps are sold at $12 each. Variable costs are $8 per lamp and include $1 of variable sales costs that are not incurred if lamps are sold internally to Division A. The total amount of fixed costs for Division B is $80,000.

Instructions

Consider the following independent situations:

(a) What should be the minimum transfer price accepted by Division B for the 10,000 lamps and the maximum transfer price paid by Division A? Justify your answer.

(b) Suppose Division B could use the excess capacity to produce and sell externally 20,000 units of a new product at a price of $8 per unit. The variable cost for this new product is $6 per unit. What should be the minimum transfer price accepted by Division B for the 10,000 lamps and the maximum transfer price paid by Division A? Justify your answer.

(c) If Division A needs 15,000 lamps instead of 10,000 during the next year, what should be the minimum transfer price accepted by Division B and the maximum transfer price paid by Division A? Justify your answer.

(CGA-adapted)

P8–21A Wordsmith is a publishing company with several different book lines. Each line has contracts with different authors. The company also owns a printing operation called Pronto Press. The book lines and the printing operation each operate as a separate profit centre. The printing operation earns revenue by printing books by authors under contract with the book lines owned by Wordsmith, as well as authors under contract with other companies. The printing operation bills out at $0.01 per page, and a typical book requires 500 pages of print. A manager of Business Books, one of the Wordsmith's book lines, has approached the manager of the printing operation and offers to pay $0.007 per page for 1,200 copies of a 500-page book. The book line pays outside printers $0.009 per page. The printing operation's variable cost per page is $0.006.

Determine minimum transfer price with no excess capacity and with excess capacity. (SO 4, 5)

Instructions

(a) Determine whether the printing should be done internally or externally, and the appropriate transfer price, under each of the following situations:
 1. Assume that the printing operation is booked solid for the next two years, and it would have to cancel an obligation with an outside customer in order to meet the needs of the internal division.
 2. Assume that the printing operation has available capacity.

(b) ⬛▶ The top management of Wordsmith believes that the printing operation should always do the printing for the company's authors. On several occasions, it has forced the printing operation to cancel jobs with outside customers in order to meet the needs of its own lines. Discuss the pros and cons of this approach.

(c) Calculate the change in contribution margin to each division, and to the company as a whole, if top management forces the printing operation to accept the $0.007 per page transfer price when it has no available capacity.

P8–22A Zapp Manufacturing Company makes various electronic products. The company is divided into autonomous divisions that can either sell to internal units or sell externally. All divisions are located in buildings on the same piece of property. The board division has offered the chip division $20 per unit to supply it with chips for 40,000 boards. It has been purchasing these chips for $21 per unit from outside suppliers. The chip division receives $22.50 per unit for sales made to outside customers on this type of chip. The variable cost of chips sold externally by the chip division is $14. It estimates that it will save $4 per unit of selling expenses on units sold internally to the board division. The chip division has no excess capacity.

Determine minimum transfer price with no excess capacity. (SO 4, 5)

Instructions

(a) Calculate the minimum transfer price that the chip division should accept. Discuss whether it is in the chip division's best interest to accept the offer.

(b) Suppose that the chip division decides to reject the offer. What are the financial consequences for each division, and for the company as a whole, of this decision?

P8–23A Wood Inc. manufactures wood poles. Wood has two responsibility centres, harvesting and sawing, which are both evaluated as profit centres. The harvesting division does all the harvesting operations and transfers logs to the sawing division, which converts the wood into poles for external clients. When operating at full capacity, the sawing division can convert 10,000 poles. Management is considering replacing this type of wood pole with

Determine minimum transfer price under different situations. (SO 4, 5)

another type of wood pole that can be sold at a lower price and could allow the firm to operate at full capacity all the time.

The director of the sawing division suggested that the maximum price the division can pay for each log from harvesting is $29.50. Here is the information that supports this suggestion:

Price per pole that the client would pay		$90.00
Direct labour costs	$35.00	
Variable overhead costs	4.50	
Fixed overhead costs	8.50	
Raw material costs (other than logs)	2.50	
	50.50	
Profit margin	10.00	
Total costs		60.50
Maximum price for a log		$29.50

The director of the harvesting division disagrees with selling the logs at a price of $29.50. The division is operating at full capacity and sells logs to external clients for $44.50. Moreover, the director says, "My direct costs of labour are $22.50, my variable overhead costs are $4.50, and my fixed overhead costs are $9.00. I can't cut trees for $36.00 and sell them for $29.50."

Instructions

(a) Assuming production at full capacity, would Wood Inc., as a whole, make a higher profit if logs were transferred to the sawing division for $29.50 per log? Show your calculations.

(b) Explain the effect of transferring the logs at $29.50 per log on each division's profit performance.

(c) Calculate the minimum and maximum transfer prices that could be used, and recommend an appropriate transfer price. Explain your answer.

(CGA-adapted)

Determine minimum transfer price under different situations.
(SO 4, 5)

P8–24A   Commcentre Manufacturing (CM) is a division of Worldwide Communications, Inc. CM produces pagers and other personal communication devices. These devices are sold to other Worldwide divisions, as well as to other communication companies. CM was recently approached by the manager of the personal communications division to make a special pager designed to receive signals from anywhere in the world. Personal communications has requested that CM produce 10,000 units of this special pager. The following facts are for CM:

Selling price of standard pager	$95
Variable cost of standard pager	50
Additional variable costs of special pager	35

Instructions

For each of the following independent situations, calculate the minimum transfer price, and discuss whether the internal transfer should take place or whether personal communications should purchase the pager externally.

(a) Personal communications has offered to pay CM $105 per pager. CM has no available capacity. CM would have to give up sales of 10,000 pagers to existing customers in order to meet the request of personal communications.

(b) Personal communications has offered to pay CM $160 per pager. CM has no available capacity. CM would have to give up sales of 14,000 pagers to existing customers in order to meet the request of personal communications.

(c) Personal communications has offered to pay CM $105 per pager. CM has available capacity.

Determine minimum transfer price under different situations.
(SO 4, 5)

P8–25A   The Atlantic Company is a multidivisional company. Its managers have full responsibility for profits and complete autonomy to accept or reject transfers from other divisions. Division A produces a sub-assembly part that there is a competitive market for. Division B currently uses this sub-assembly for a final product that is sold outside at $2,400. Division A charges division B market price for the part, which is $1,400 per unit. Variable costs are $1,040 and $1,200 for divisions A and B, respectively.

The manager of Division B feels that Division A should transfer the part at a lower price than market because at market Division B is unable to make a profit.

Instructions

(a) Calculate Division B's contribution margin if transfers are made at the market price, and calculate the company's total contribution margin.

(b) Assume that Division A can sell all its production in the open market. Should Division A transfer the goods to Division B? If so, at what price?

(c) Assume that Division A can sell in the open market only 500 units at $1,400 per unit out of the 1,000 units that it can produce every month. Assume also that a 20% reduction in price is necessary to sell all 1,000 units each month. Should transfers be made? If so, how many units should the division transfer and at what price? To support your decision, submit a schedule that compares the contribution margins under three different alternatives.

(CMA Canada-adapted)

P8–26A Lemon Quench manufactures a soft drink. The company is organized into two divisions, glass and filling. The glass division makes bottles and sells them to the filling division. Each division manager receives a bonus based on the division's net income.

Determine transfer price for goal congruence.
(SO 4, 5)

In the open market, bottle producers are charging as follows:

Number of Cases per Month	Total Charge	Average Price per Case
11,000	$135,300	$12.30
12,000	144,000	12.00
13,000	152,750	11.75
14,000	158,900	11.35
15,000	165,000	11.00

The costs per case in the glass division are as follows:

Volume per Month	Glass Division Cost per Case
11,000	$10.71
12,000	10.52
13,000	10.35
14,000	10.18

The filling division's costs (excluding bottle purchases) and selling prices are as follows:

Volume per Month	Selling Price	Cost per Case
11,000	$38.00	$24.32
12,000	37.55	24.09
13,000	37.20	23.91
14,000	36.80	23.76
15,000	36.20	23.57

The current capacities of the divisions are 15,000 cases per month for the filling division and 14,000 cases per month for the glass division.

Instructions

(a) If market prices are used as transfer prices, what is the most profitable volume for each division and for the company as a whole? Show calculations to support your answer. Assume that transfers and sales are made in units of 1,000 and that the glass division is unable to sell its production in the outside market.

(b) Under what conditions should market prices *not* be used in determining the transfer prices?

(CMA Canada-adapted)

Calculate target price
using absorption cost and
contribution approaches.
(SO 7)

*P8–27A   Fast Buck Corporation needs to set a target price for its newly designed product EverRun. The following data relate to this new product:

	Per Unit	Total
Direct materials	$20	
Direct labour	40	
Variable manufacturing overhead	10	
Fixed manufacturing overhead		$1,400,000
Variable selling and administrative expenses	5	
Fixed selling and administrative expenses		1,120,000

The costs above are based on a budgeted volume of 80,000 units produced and sold each year. Fast Buck uses cost-plus pricing to set its target selling price. Because some managers prefer the absorption cost approach and others prefer the contribution approach, the accounting department provides information under both approaches using a markup of 50% on the manufacturing cost per unit and a markup of 75% on the variable cost.

Instructions

(a) Calculate the target price for one unit of EverRun using the absorption cost approach.
(b) Calculate the target price for one unit of EverRun using the contribution approach.

Calculate various amounts
using absorption cost and
contribution approaches.
(SO 7)

*P8–28A   Weather Guard Windows Inc. is setting a target price on its newly designed tinted window. Cost data for the window at a budgeted volume of 4,000 units are as follows.

	Per Unit	Total
Direct materials	$100	
Direct labour	70	
Variable manufacturing overhead	20	
Fixed manufacturing overhead		$120,000
Variable selling and administrative expenses	10	
Fixed selling and administrative expenses		102,000

Weather Guard Windows uses cost-plus pricing to provide the company with a 30% ROI on its tinted window line. A total of $700,000 in assets is committed to production of the new tinted window.

Instructions

(a) Calculate the markup percentage under the absorption cost approach that will allow Weather Guard Windows to realize its desired ROI.
(b) Calculate the target price of the window under the absorption cost approach, and show proof that the desired ROI is realized.
(c) Calculate the markup percentage under the contribution approach that will allow Weather Guard Windows to realize its desired ROI. (Round to three decimal places.)
(d) Calculate the target price of the window under the contribution approach, and show proof that the desired ROI is realized.
(e) Since both the absorption approach and the contribution approach produce the same target price and provide the same ROI, why do both methods exist? Isn't one method clearly better than the other?

Problems: Set B

Use cost-plus pricing to
determine various amounts.
(SO 2)

P8–29B   Wamser Corporation needs to set a target price for its newly designed product, E2-D2. The following data relate to it:

	Per Unit	Total
Direct materials	$18	
Direct labour	30	
Variable manufacturing overhead	9	
Fixed manufacturing overhead		$1,440,000
Variable selling and administrative expenses	4	
Fixed selling and administrative expenses		1,080,000

These costs are based on a budgeted volume of 90,000 units produced and sold each year. Wamser uses cost-plus pricing to set its target selling price. The markup on the total unit cost is 25%.

Instructions

(a) Calculate the total variable cost per unit, total fixed cost per unit, and total cost per unit for E2-D2.
(b) Calculate the desired ROI per unit for E2-D2.
(c) Calculate the target selling price for E2-D2.
(d) Calculate the variable cost per unit, fixed cost per unit, and total cost per unit, assuming that 80,000 E2-D2s are sold during the year. (Round to two decimal places.)

P8–30B Carrier Fabrication Company (CFC) manufactures and sells only one product, a special front-mounting bicycle rack for large vehicles. CFC entered into a one-time contract to produce an additional 1,000 racks for the local public transit authority, at a price of "cost plus 20%." The company has a plant with a capacity of 9,000 units per year, but normal production is 4,000 units per year. The costs each year to produce those 4,000 units are as follows:

Use cost-plus pricing to determine various amounts. (SO 2)

Materials	$192,000
Labour	304,000
Supplies and other variable manufacturing indirect costs	128,000
Fixed indirect costs (allocated based on normal capacity)	176,000
Variable marketing costs	32,000
Administrative costs (all fixed)	64,000

After completing half of the order, the company billed the authority for $134,400. However, the transit authority's purchasing agent then called the president of CFC to dispute the invoice. The purchasing agent stated that the invoice should have been for $93,600.

Instructions

(a) Calculate the components of the "full-cost" unit price charged to the transit authority, as determined by CFC.
(b) Calculate the components of the "variable manufacturing cost" unit price that should have been charged, as determined by the transit authority's purchasing agent.
(c) What price per unit would you recommend? Explain your reasoning. (*Note*: You do not need to limit yourself to the costs selected by the company or by the agent.)

(CGA-adapted)

P8–31B Bosworth Electronics Inc. is setting a selling price on a new CDL component it has just developed. The following cost estimates for this component have been provided by the accounting department for a budgeted volume of 50,000 units:

Use cost-plus pricing to determine various amounts. (SO 2)

	Per Unit	Total
Direct materials	$38	
Direct labour	24	
Variable manufacturing overhead	18	
Fixed manufacturing overhead		$450,000
Variable selling and administrative expenses	12	
Fixed selling and administrative expenses		360,000

Bosworth's management uses cost-plus pricing to set its selling price. Management also directs that the target price be set to provide a 20% return on investment (ROI) on invested assets of $1.5 million.

Instructions

(a) Calculate the markup percentage and target selling price on this new CDL component.
(b) Assuming that the volume is 40,000 units, calculate the markup percentage and target selling price that will allow Bosworth Electronics to earn its desired ROI of 20%.

Use time and material
pricing to determine bill.
(SO 3)

P8−32B   Zip's Auto Body has budgeted the following time and material for 2005:

	Time Charges	Material Charges
Shop employees' wages and benefits	$111,000	$ 0
Parts manager's salary and benefits	0	26,600
Office employee's salary and benefits	21,000	12,000
Invoice cost of parts used	0	200,000
Overhead (supplies, amortization, advertising, utilities)	24,600	15,000
Total budgeted costs	$156,600	$253,600

Zip's budgets 6,000 hours of repair time in 2005. It will bill a profit of $7 per labour hour along with a 50% profit markup on the invoice cost of parts.

On January 10, 2005, Zip's is asked to submit a price estimate for the repair of a 2002 Chevrolet Blazer that was damaged in a head-on collision. Zip's estimates that this repair will consume 61 hours of labour and $4,200 in parts and materials.

Instructions

(a) Calculate the labour rate for Zip's Auto Body for 2005.
(b) Calculate the material loading-charge percentage for Zip's Auto Body for 2005. (Round to three decimal places.)
(c) Prepare a time and material price quotation for the repair of the 2002 Blazer.

Determine minimum
transfer price with no
excess capacity and
with excess capacity.
(SO 4, 5)

P8−33B   Cosmic Sounds is a record company with different record labels. Each record label has contracts with various recording artists. It also owns a recording studio called Blast Off. The record labels and the recording studio operate as separate profit centres. The studio earns revenue by recording artists under contract with the labels owned by Cosmic Sounds, as well as artists under contract with other companies. The studio bills out at $1,100 per hour, and a typical CD requires 80 hours of studio time. A manager from Big Bang, one of Cosmic Sounds' record labels, has approached the manager of the recording studio offering to pay $800 per hour for an 80-hour session. The record label pays outside studios $1,000 per hour. The recording studio's variable cost per hour is $600.

Instructions

(a) Determine whether the recording should be done internally or externally, and the appropriate transfer price, under each of the following situations:
    1. Assume that the recording studio is booked solid for the next three years, and it would have to cancel a contract with an outside customer in order to meet the needs of the internal division.
    2. Assume that the recording studio has available capacity.
(b) The top management of Cosmic Sounds believes that the recording studio should always do the recording for the company's artists. On several occasions, it has forced the recording studio to cancel jobs with outside customers in order to meet the needs of its own labels. Discuss the pros and cons of this approach.
(c) Calculate the change in contribution margin to each division, and to the company as a whole, if top management forces the recording studio to accept the $800 transfer price when it has no available capacity.

Determine minimum
transfer price under
different situations.
(SO 4, 5)

P8−34B   Sun Motors Inc. operates as a decentralized multidivisional car company. Its safety division buys most of its airbags from the airbag division. The airbag division's incremental costs for manufacturing the airbags are $270 per unit. The airbag division is currently working at 75% of capacity. The current market price of the airbags is $300 per unit.

Instructions

(a) Using the general approach to transfer pricing, what is the minimum transfer price for the airbag division?
(b) Sun Motors Inc.'s transfer price rules state that whenever divisions with unused capacity sell products internally, they must transfer the products at incremental costs. Discuss how this transfer-price policy will affect goal congruence, division performance, and autonomy.

(c) The safety and airbag divisions have negotiated a transfer price between $270 and $300 per airbag. Discuss the impact of this transfer price on each division in terms of goal congruence, division performance, and division autonomy.

(CMA Canada-adapted)

P8−35B Chula Vista Pump Company makes irrigation pump systems. The company is divided into several autonomous divisions that can either sell to internal units or sell externally. All divisions are located in buildings on the same piece of property. The pump division has offered the washer division $4 per unit to supply it with the washers for 50,000 units. It has been purchasing these washers for $4.30 per unit from outside suppliers. The washer division receives $4.60 per unit for sales made to outside customers on this type of washer. The variable cost of units sold externally by the washer division is $3.20. It estimates that it will save 50 cents per unit of selling expenses on units sold internally to the pump division. The washer division has no excess capacity.

Determine minimum transfer price with no excess capacity. (SO 4, 5)

Instructions

(a) Calculate the minimum transfer price that the washer division should accept. Discuss whether it is in the washer division's best interest to accept the offer.
(b) Suppose that the washer division decides to reject the offer. What are the financial implications for each division, and the company as a whole, of the decision to reject the offer?

P8−36B Heartland Engines is a division of EverGreen Lawn Equipment Company. Heartland makes engines for lawn mowers, snow blowers, and other types of lawn and garden equipment. It sells its engines to the company's lawn mower division and snow blower division, as well as to other lawn equipment companies. It was recently approached by the manager of the lawn mower division with a request to make a special, high-performance engine for a lawn mower designed to mow heavy brush. The lawn mower division has asked that Heartland produce 8,500 units of this special engine. The following facts are for the Heartland Engines:

Determine minimum transfer price under different situations. (SO 4, 5)

Selling price of standard lawn mower engine	$88
Variable cost of standard lawn mower engine	55
Additional variable costs of special engine	41

Instructions

For each of the following independent situations, calculate the minimum transfer price, and discuss whether the internal transfer should take place or whether the lawn mower division should purchase its goods externally:

(a) The lawn mower division has offered to pay Heartland Engines $110 per engine. Heartland Engines has no available capacity. Heartland Engines would have to cancel sales of 8,500 units to existing customers in order to meet the request of the lawn mower division.
(b) The lawn mower division has offered to pay Heartland Engines $170 per engine. Heartland Engines has no available capacity. It would have to cancel sales of 12,000 units to existing customers in order to meet the request of the lawn mower division.
(c) The lawn mower division has offered to pay Heartland Engines $110 per engine. Heartland Engines has available capacity.

P8−37B Comput Industries is a high-tech company in the United States. Comput Industries has several subsidiaries, including Cancomput, which is located in Canada, and Heavencomput, which is located in another country with very favourable tax laws. Both subsidiaries are considered profit centres. Cancomput manufactures components used by Heavencomput and sells all its production to this subsidiary. The transfer price has been established by the controller at $135 per component, even though Cancomput can sell the same pieces on the external market for $175.

Determine minimum transfer price under different situations. (SO 4, 5)

Instructions

(a) Briefly explain why Comput Industries is fixing a transfer price below the market price. What are the advantages for the company as a whole?
(b) Explain the consequences of the transfer-pricing policy on each subsidiary. Explain what change should be made to improve the situation.
(c) Briefly describe two other transfer-pricing methods that could be used in this situation.

(CGA-adapted)

Determine transfer price
for goal congruence.
(SO 4, 5)

P8–38B   Love, Inc., manufactures a line of men's colognes and aftershave lotions. The manufacturing process is basically a series of mixing operations, with the addition of certain aromatic and colouring ingredients. The finished product is packaged in a company-produced glass bottle and packed in cases of six bottles.

Top management feels that the sale of its product is heavily influenced by the appearance and appeal of the bottle and has therefore had managers focus on the bottle-production process. This has resulted in the development of certain unique bottle-production processes that management is quite proud of.

The two areas (i.e., perfume production and bottle manufacture) have evolved over the years almost independently; in fact, a rivalry has developed between management personnel as to "which division is more important" to the company. This attitude is probably intensified because the bottle manufacturing plant was purchased as a whole company 10 years ago and there has been no real exchange of management personnel or ideas (except at the top corporate level).

Since the acquisition, all bottle production has been used by the perfume manufacturing plant. Each area is considered a separate profit centre and evaluated as such. As the new corporate controller, you are responsible for determining a proper transfer value to use in crediting the bottle production profit centre and in debiting the packaging profit centre.

At your request, the bottle division's general manager has asked certain other bottle manufacturers to quote a price for the quantity and sizes of bottles that the perfume division needs. These competitive prices are as follows:

Volume (equivalent cases)[1]	Total Price	Price per Case
2,000,000	$ 4,000,000	$2.00
4,000,000	7,000,000	1.75
6,000,000	10,000,000	1.67

[1] An "equivalent case" represents 6 bottles.

An analysis of the bottle plant indicates that it can produce bottles at the following costs:

Volume (equivalent cases)	Total Price	Price per Case[2]
2,000,000	$3,200,000	$1.60
4,000,000	5,200,000	1.30
6,000,000	7,200,000	1.20

[2] The analysis indicates that these costs represent fixed costs of $1.2 million and variable costs of $1.00 per equivalent case.

These figures have resulted in a lot of corporate discussion about the proper value to use in the transfer of bottles to the perfume division. Discussions are especially hot because a significant portion of each division manager's income is an incentive bonus that is based on his or her subsidiary's profit. The perfume production division has the following costs in addition to the bottle costs:

Volume (cases)	Total Cost	Cost per Case
2,000,000	$16,400,000	$8.20
4,000,000	32,400,000	8.10
6,000,000	48,400,000	8.07

After considerable analysis, the marketing research department has given you the following price-demand relationship for the finished product:

Sales Volume (cases)	Total Sales Revenue	Sales Price per Case
2,000,000	$25,000,000	$12.50
4,000,000	45,600,000	11.40
6,000,000	63,900,000	10.65

Instructions

(a) Love, Inc. has used market-based transfer prices in the past. Using current market prices and costs, and assuming a volume of 6 million cases, calculate the income for (1) the bottle division, (2) the perfume division, and (3) the corporation.

(b) Are these production and sales levels the most profitable volumes for (1) the bottle division, (2) the perfume division, and (3) the corporation? Explain your answer.

(CMA Canada-adapted)

*P8–39B** Information for Wamser Corporation is given in P8–29B. Assume that instead of the simple 25% markup on the total cost per unit some managers prefer to work with the absorption cost approach and other managers prefer the contribution approach. Assume also that the accounting department provides information under both approaches using a markup of 50% on the manufacturing cost per unit and a markup of 80% on the variable cost.

Calculate target price using absorption cost and contribution approaches. (SO 7)

Instructions

(a) Calculate the target price for one unit of E2-D2 using the absorption cost approach.
(b) Calculate the target price for one unit of E2-D2 using the contribution approach.

*P8–40B** Santana Furniture Inc. is setting a target price on its newly designed leather recliner sofa. Cost data for the sofa at a budgeted volume of 3,000 units are as follows:

Calculate various amounts using absorption cost and contribution approaches. (SO 7)

	Per Unit	Total
Direct materials	$140	
Direct labour	80	
Variable manufacturing overhead	40	
Fixed manufacturing overhead		$180,000
Variable selling and administrative expenses	20	
Fixed selling and administrative expenses		90,000

Santana Furniture uses cost-plus pricing to provide a 30% ROI on its stuffed furniture line. A total of $700,000 in assets has been committed to production of the new leather recliner sofa.

Instructions

(a) Calculate the markup percentage under the absorption cost approach that will allow Santana Furniture to realize its desired ROI.
(b) Calculate the target price of the sofa under the absorption cost approach, and show proof that the desired ROI is realized.
(c) Calculate the markup percentage under the contribution approach that will allow Santana Furniture to realize its desired ROI.
(d) Calculate the target price of the sofa under the contribution approach, and show proof that the desired ROI is realized.
(e) Since both the absorption cost approach and the contribution approach produce the same target price and provide the same ROI, why do both methods exist? Isn't one method clearly better than the other?

Cases

Additional Cases

C8–41 Aurora Manufacturing has multiple divisions that make a wide variety of products. Recently the bearing division and the wheel division got into an argument over a transfer price. The wheel division needed bearings for garden tractor wheels. It normally buys its bearings from an outside supplier for $24 per set. The company's top management recently started a campaign to persuade the different divisions to buy their materials from each other whenever possible. As a result, Maria Hamblin, the purchasing manager for the wheel division, received a letter from the vice-president of purchasing that instructed her to contact the bearing division to discuss buying bearings from it.

To comply with this request, Maria called Terry Tompkin of the bearing division, and asked the price for 15,000 bearings. Terry responded that the bearings normally sell for $35 per set. However, Terry noted that the bearing division would save $3 on marketing costs by selling internally, and would pass this cost savings on to the wheel division. He further commented that his division was at full capacity, and therefore would not be able to provide any bearings right away. In the future, if he had available capacity, he would be happy to provide bearings.

Maria responded indignantly, "Thanks, but no thanks. We can get all the bearings we need from Falk Manufacturing for $24 per set." Terry snorted back, "Falk makes junk. It costs us $22 per set just to make our bearings. Our bearings can withstand heat of 2,000 degrees centigrade, and are good to within .00001 centimetres. If you guys are happy buying junk, then go ahead and buy from Falk."

Two weeks later, Maria's boss from the central office stopped in to find out whether she had placed an order with the bearing division. Maria answered that she would rather buy her bearings from her worst enemy than from the bearing division.

Instructions

(a) Why might the company's top management want the divisions to start doing more business with one another?

(b) Under what conditions should a buying division be forced to buy from an internal supplier? Under what conditions should a selling division be forced to sell to an internal division, rather than to an outside customer?

(c) The vice-president of purchasing thinks that this problem should be resolved by forcing the bearing division to sell to the wheel division at its cost of $22. Is this a good solution for the wheel division? Is this a good solution for the bearing division? Is this a good solution for the company?

(d) Provide at least two other possible solutions to this problem. Discuss the merits and drawbacks of each solution.

C8–42   West-Coast Industries is a decentralized firm. It has two production centres: Vancouver and Kamloops. Each one is evaluated based on its return on investment. Vancouver has the capacity to manufacture 10,000 units of component TR222. Vancouver's variable costs are $140 per unit. Kamloops uses component TR222 in one of its products. Kamloops adds $85 of variable costs to the component and sells the final product for $425.

Instructions

Consider the following independent situations:

(a) Vancouver can sell all 10,000 units of TR222 on the open market at a price of $225 per unit. Kamloops is willing to buy 3,000 of those units. What should the transfer price be? Explain your decision.

(b) Of the 10,000 units of component TR222 it can produce, Vancouver can sell 7,000 units on the open market at a price of $225 per unit. Kamloops is willing to buy an additional 3,000 units. What should the transfer price be? Explain your decision.

(c) Of the 10,000 units of component TR222 it can produce, Vancouver can sell 8,000 units on the open market at a price of $225 per unit. Kamloops is willing to buy an additional 3,000 units. What should the transfer price be? Explain your decision.

(d) The head office of West-Coast has asked the two centres to negotiate a transfer price. List the advantages and disadvantages of negotiated transfer prices.

(CGA-adapted)

C8–43   Solco Industries is a decentralized company with two divisions: mining and processing. They are both evaluated as profit centres. The mining division transfers raw diamonds to the processing division. The processing division is currently operating at 1 million kilograms below its capacity, while the mining division is operating at full capacity. The mining division can sell raw diamonds externally at $75 per kilogram. The unit cost of one kilograms of polished diamonds produced by the processing division is as follows:

Raw diamonds	$ 75
Direct materials	10
Direct labour ($20/hour)	30
Variable manufacturing overhead	20
Fixed manufacturing overhead[1]	50
Total unit cost	$185

[1] Based on a capacity of 5 million kg per year.

The processing division has just received an order from International Diamonds Co. for 300,000 kilograms of polished diamonds at a price of $175 per kilogram. Solco has a policy that prohibits selling any product below full cost. The full cost of a kilogram of raw diamonds in the mining division is $60, which includes 25% of the company's fixed costs.

Instructions

(a) Would Solco as a whole benefit if the raw diamonds were transferred to the processing division at $60 per kilogram to fill the order from International Diamonds? Show all calculations.

(b) Briefly explain whether anything is wrong with Solco's policy that no product should be sold below full cost.

(c) Calculate the minimum and maximum transfer prices that could be used.

(d) Recommend an appropriate transfer price for raw diamonds sold by the mining division to the processing division. Explain your answer.

(e) If the mining division was not operating at full capacity, would your answer in part (d) be different?

(CGA-adapted)

C8–44   National Industries is a diversified corporation with separate operating divisions. Each division's performance is evaluated based on its total dollar profits and return on division investment.

The WindAir division manufactures and sells air conditioners. The coming year's budgeted income statement, based on a sales volume of 15,000 units, is as follows:

WINDAIR DIVISION
Budgeted Income Statement
For the Fiscal Year

	Per Unit	Total (in thousands)
Sales revenue	$400	$6,000
Manufacturing costs		
Compressor	70	1,050
Other raw materials	37	555
Direct labour	30	450
Variable overhead	45	675
Fixed overhead	32	480
Total manufacturing costs	214	3,210
Gross margin	186	2,790
Operating expenses		
Variable selling	18	270
Fixed selling	19	285
Fixed administration	38	570
Total operating expenses	75	1,125
Net income before taxes	$111	$1,665

WindAir's manager believes that sales can be increased if the unit selling price of the air conditioners is reduced. A market research study conducted by an independent firm at the request of the manager indicates that a 5% reduction ($20) in the selling price would increase the sales volume by 16%, or 2,400 units. WindAir has enough production capacity to manage this increased volume with no increase in fixed costs.

Currently, WindAir uses a compressor in its units that it purchases from an outside supplier at a cost of $70 per compressor. The manager of WindAir has approached the manager of National Industries' compressor division about the sale of a compressor unit to WindAir. The compressor division currently manufactures and sells to outside firms a unit that is similar to the compressor used by WindAir. The specifications of the WindAir compressor are slightly different and would reduce the compressor division's raw materials cost by $1.50 per unit. In addition, the compressor division would not incur any variable selling costs for the units sold to WindAir. The manager of WindAir wants all of the compressors it uses to come from one supplier and has offered to pay $50 for each compressor unit.

The compressor division has the capacity to produce 75,000 units. The coming year's budgeted income statement for the compressor division, which follows, is based on a sales volume of 64,000 units without considering WindAir's proposal:

COMPRESSOR DIVISION
Budgeted Income Statement
For The Fiscal Year

	Per Unit	Total (in thousands)
Sales revenue	$100	$6,400
Manufacturing costs		
Raw materials	12	768
Direct labour	8	512
Variable overhead	10	640
Fixed overhead	11	704
Total manufacturing costs	41	2,624
Gross margin	59	3,776
Operating expenses		
Variable selling	6	384
Fixed selling	4	256
Fixed administration	7	448
Total operating expenses	17	1,088
Net income before taxes	$42	$2,688

Instructions

(a) Should WindAir make the 5% price reduction on its air conditioners even if it cannot acquire the compressors internally for $50 each? Support your conclusion with appropriate calculations.

(b) Ignoring your answer to (a), assume that WindAir needs 17,400 units. Should the compressor division be willing to supply the compressor units for $50 each? Support your conclusions with appropriate calculations.

(c) Ignoring your answer to (a), assume that WindAir needs 17,400 units. Would it be in the best interest of National Industries for the compressor division to supply the compressor units at $50 each to the WindAir division? Support your conclusions with appropriate calculations.

(CMA Canada-adapted)

C8–45   Future Industries operates as a decentralized, vertically integrated, multidivisional company. One of its divisions, the systems division, manufactures scientific instruments and uses the products of two of the other divisions. The board division manufactures printed circuit boards (PCBs). One PCB model is made exclusively for the systems division using proprietary designs. Less complex models are sold to outside markets. The products of the transistor division are sold in a well-developed competitive market, and are also sold to the systems division. The costs per unit of the two products used by the systems division follow:

	PCB	Transistor
Direct material	$ 7.50	$1.60
Direct labour	13.50	2.00
Variable overhead	6.00	1.00
Fixed overhead	2.40	1.50
Total cost	$29.40	$6.10

The board division sells its commercial product at full cost plus a 25% markup and believes that the proprietary board made for the systems division would sell for $36.75 per unit on the open market. The market price of the transistor used by the systems division is $7.40 per unit.

Instructions

(a) Using the general approach to transfer pricing, what is the minimum transfer price at which the transistor division would sell the transistor to the systems division?

(b) What is the maximum transfer price at which the systems division would buy the transistor from the internal division?

(c) Assume the systems division is able to purchase a large quantity of transistors from an outside source at $5.80 per unit and that the transistor division has excess capacity. Evaluate this price using the criteria of goal congruence and division performance.

(d) The board and systems divisions have negotiated a transfer price of $33 per printed circuit board. Evaluate this negotiated transfer price in terms of goal congruence, division performance, and division autonomy.

(CMA Canada-adapted)

C8–46 Construction on the Atlantis Full-Service Car Wash is nearing completion. The owner is Jay Leer, a retired accounting professor. The car wash is strategically located on a busy street that separates an affluent suburban community from a middle-class community. It has two state-of-the-art stalls. Each stall can provide anything from a basic two-stage wash and rinse to a five-stage luxurious bath. It is all "touchless," meaning there are no brushes to potentially damage the car. Outside each stall, there is also a 400-horsepower vacuum. Jay likes to joke that these vacuums are so strong that they will pull the carpet right out of your car if you aren't careful.

Jay has some important decisions to make before he can open the car wash. First, he knows that there is one drive-through car wash only a 10-minute drive away. It is attached to a gas station. It charges $5 for a basic wash, and $4 if you also buy at least 30 litres of gas. It is a brush-type wash with rotating brush heads. There is also a self-serve "stand outside your car and spray until you are soaked" car wash a 15-minute drive away from Jay's location. He went over and tried this out. He went through $3 in quarters to get the equivalent of a basic wash. He knows that both of these locations always have long lines, which is one reason why he decided to build a new car wash.

Jay is planning to offer three levels of wash service—Basic, Deluxe, and Premium. The Basic is all automated; it requires no direct intervention by employees. The Deluxe is all automated except that, at the end, an employee will wipe down the car and will put a window treatment on the windshield that reduces glare and allows rainwater to run off more quickly. The Premium level is a "pampered" service. This will include all the services of the Deluxe, plus a special wax after the machine wax, and an employee will vacuum the car, wipe down the entire interior, and wash the inside of the windows. To provide the Premium service, Jay will have to hire a couple of "car wash specialists" to do the additional pampering.

Jay has made the following estimates, based on data he received from the local chamber of commerce and information from a trade association:

	Per Unit	Total
Direct materials per Basic wash	$0.25	
Direct materials per Deluxe wash	0.75	
Direct materials per Premium wash	1.05	
Direct labour per Basic wash	n/a	
Direct labour per Deluxe wash	0.40	
Direct labour per Premium wash	2.40	
Variable overhead per Basic wash	0.10	
Variable overhead per Deluxe or Premium wash	0.20	
Fixed overhead		$112,500
Variable selling and administrative expenses—all washes	0.10	
Fixed selling and administrative expenses		121,500

The total estimated number of washes of any type is 45,000. Jay has invested assets of $324,000. He would like a return on investment (ROI) of 25%.

Instructions

(a) Identify the issues that Jay must consider in deciding on the price of each level of service of his car wash. Also discuss what issues he should consider in deciding on what levels of service to provide.

(b) Jay estimates that of the total 45,000 washes, 20,000 will be Basic, 20,000 will be Deluxe, and 5,000 will be Premium. Using cost-plus pricing, calculate the selling price that Jay should use for each type of wash to achieve his desired ROI of 25%.

(c) During the first year, instead of selling 45,000 washes, Jay sold 43,000 washes. He was quite accurate in his estimate of first-year sales, but he was way off on the types of washes that he sold. He sold 3,000 Basic, 31,000 Deluxe, and 9,000 Premium. His actual total fixed expenses were as he expected, and his variable cost per unit was as estimated. Calculate Jay's net income and his actual ROI.

(d) Jay is using a traditional approach to allocate overhead. As a result, he is allocating overhead equally to all three types of washes, even though the Basic wash is considerably less complicated and uses very little of the technical capabilities of the machinery. What should Jay do to determine more accurate costs per unit? How will this affect his pricing and, consequently, his sales?

C8–47   Giant Airlines operates out of three main "hub" airports in the United States. Recently, Mosquito Airlines began operating a flight from Smallville, into Giant's Metropolis hub for $190. Giant Airlines offers a price of $425 for the same route. The management of Giant is not happy about Mosquito invading its turf. In fact, Giant has driven off nearly every other competing airline from its hub, so that today 90% of flights into and out of Metropolis are Giant Airline flights. Mosquito is able to offer a lower fare because its pilots are paid less, it uses older planes, and it has lower overhead costs. Mosquito has been in business for only six months, and it services only two other cities. It expects the Metropolis route to be its most profitable.

Giant estimates that it would have to charge $210 just to break even on this flight. It estimates that Mosquito can break even at a price of $160. One day after Mosquito's entry into the market, Giant dropped its price to $140, which Mosquito then matched. Both airlines maintained this fare for nine months, until Mosquito went out of business. As soon as Mosquito went out of business, Giant raised its fare back to $425.

Instructions

(a) Who are the stakeholders in this case?
(b) What are some of the reasons why Mosquito's break-even point is lower than Giant's?
(c) What are the likely reasons why Giant was able to offer this price for this period of time, while Mosquito could not?
(d) What are some of the possible courses of action that Mosquito could have followed in this situation?
(e) Do you think that this kind of pricing activity is ethical? What are the implications for the stakeholders in this situation?

Answers to Self-Study Questions

1. b   2. c   3. b   4. b   5. c   6. a   7. d   8. b   9. b   10. d

Remember to go back to the Navigator Box at the beginning of the chapter to check off your completed work.

CHAPTER 9
Budgetary Planning

Turning Trash into Treasure

In 1989, Vancouver teenager Brian Scudamore needed to raise money to pay his way through university. With $700 and a strong desire to do it on his own, he established his own junk removal company. Fifteen years later, 1-800-GOT-JUNK? has 113 franchise partners across Canada and the United States and projected revenues of more than $60 million for 2004.

"It was a high-school business project that was out of control," says Cameron Herold, vice-president, operations, of the business he joined as an adviser in 1995.

While the exponential growth of 1-800-GOT-JUNK? may seem unwieldy (2004 will mark its fifth consecutive year of 100-percent compounded growth), it has in fact involved sound financial planning, budgeting, and cash management. The company follows a "zero-based budget," says Mr. Herold. That is, it only spends money it has; it has no outside investors or debt.

Managing this growth involves forecasting everything by creating a "painted picture" of what the company will look like in three years. The company knows its staffing plans, training requirements, and overhead and office-space needs well in advance. "That filters back to our budgeting process," Mr. Herold says. "We'll sit down and say, 'If this is where we're going, what are all the components of that?'. . . Then we bring it back to zero and say, 'What's it going to cost us? Where does it fit into the budget?'"

Key to the company's growth management was the introduction of franchising in 1999. "We chose franchising because our franchise partners would actually finance our growth," Mr. Herold says. In addition to the initial franchise fee, franchisees pay head office 8 percent of their sales and another 7 percent to run the centralized call centre.

While the company has used franchising to manage growth, a frugal approach to day-to-day costs has also been integral to its budgeting success. "We're always looking for ways to cut costs," Mr. Herold says. This includes establishing strategic relationships with the local coffee shop; doing regular cost analyses of office equipment and changing suppliers when needed; or buying office furniture in bulk from liquidators at 10 cents on the dollar. "All those little things start to really add up," he says.

the navigator

1-800-GOT-JUNK: www.1800gotjunk.com

THE NAVIGATOR

- [ ] Scan *Study Objectives*

- [ ] Read *Feature Story*

- [ ] Read *Chapter Preview*

- [ ] Read text and answer *Before You Go On* p. 374, p. 378, p. 386, p. 388

- [ ] Work *Using the Decision Toolkit*

- [ ] Review *Summary of Study Objectives*

- [ ] Review *Using the Decision Toolkit—A Summary*

- [ ] Work *Demonstration Problem*

- [ ] Answer *Self-Study Questions*

- [ ] Complete assignments

STUDY OBJECTIVES

After studying this chapter, you should be able to:

1. Indicate the benefits of budgeting.
2. State the essentials of effective budgeting.
3. Identify the budgets that comprise the master budget.
4. Describe the sources for preparing the budgeted income statement.
5. Explain the main sections of a cash budget.
6. Indicate how budgeting is done in nonmanufacturing companies.

the navigator

As the feature story about 1-800-GOT-JUNK? indicates, budgeting is critical to financial well-being. As a student, you budget your study time and your money. Families budget income and expenses. Government agencies budget revenues and expenditures. Business enterprises use budgets in planning and controlling their operations.

Our focus in this chapter is budgeting—specifically, how budgeting is used as a **planning tool** by management. Through budgeting, it should be possible for management to have enough cash to pay creditors, to have enough raw materials to meet production requirements, and to have adequate finished goods to meet expected sales.

The chapter is organized as follows:

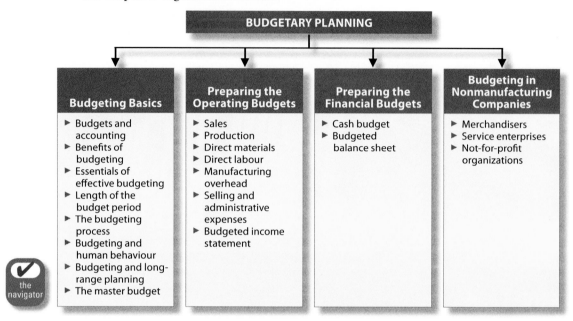

Budgeting Basics

One of management's major responsibilities is planning. As explained in Chapter 1, **planning** is the process of establishing objectives for the whole company. A successful organization makes both long-term and short-term plans. These plans state the objectives of the company and the proposed way of accomplishing them.

A budget is a formal written statement in financial terms of management's plans for a specified future time period. It is normally the main way of communicating agreed-upon objectives throughout the organization. Once adopted, a budget becomes an important basis for evaluating performance. It promotes efficiency and discourages waste and inefficiency. The role of budgeting as a control device is discussed in Chapter 10.

Budgets and Accounting

Accounting information makes major contributions to the budgeting process. From the accounting records, historical data on revenues, costs, and expenses can be obtained. These data are helpful in setting future budget goals.

Normally, accountants have the responsibility for presenting management's budgeting goals in financial terms. In this role, they translate management's plans and communicate the budget to employees throughout the company. Accountants also prepare periodic budget reports that provide the basis for measuring performance and comparing actual results with planned objectives. The budget itself, and the administration of the budget, however, are entirely management's responsibilities.

The Benefits of Budgeting

The main benefits of a budget are as follows:

1. It requires all levels of management to **plan ahead** and to formalize goals on a recurring basis.
2. It provides **definite objectives** for evaluating performance at each level of responsibility.
3. It creates an **early warning system** for potential problems so that management can make changes before things get out of control.
4. It makes it easier to **coordinate activities** within the business. It does this by fitting the goals of each segment with overall company objectives. Thus, production and sales promotion can be integrated with expected sales.
5. It results in greater **management awareness** of the entity's overall operations and the impact on operations of external factors, such as economic trends.
6. It **motivates personnel** throughout the organization to meet planned objectives.

A budget is an aid to management; it is not a substitute for management. A budget cannot operate or enforce itself. Budgeting only provides benefits when budgets are carefully prepared and properly administered by management.

Essentials of Effective Budgeting

Effective budgeting depends on a **sound organizational structure**. In such a structure, authority and responsibility for all phases of operations are clearly defined. Budgets based on **research and analysis** should result in realistic goals that will contribute to a company's growth and profitability. And the effectiveness of a budget program is directly related to how well it is **accepted by all levels of management**.

Once the budget has been adopted, it should be an important tool for evaluating performance. Variations between actual and expected results should be systematically and periodically reviewed to determine their cause(s). However, individuals should not be held responsible for variations that are beyond their control.

Length of the Budget Period

The budget period is not necessarily one year in length. A **budget may be prepared for any period of time**. Various factors influence the length of the budget period. These factors include the type of budget, the type of organization, the need for periodic appraisal, and actual business conditions. For example, cash may be budgeted monthly, whereas a plant expansion budget may cover a 10-year period.

The budget period should be long enough to provide an attainable goal under normal business conditions. Ideally, the time period should be long enough that seasonal or cyclical fluctuations do not have a big impact on it. On the other hand, the budget period should not be so long that reliable estimates are impossible.

The **most common budget period is one year**. The annual budget is then often supplemented by monthly and quarterly budgets. Many companies use **continuous 12-month budgets**. These budgets drop the month just ended and add a future month. One advantage of continuous budgeting is that it keeps management planning a full year ahead.

The Budgeting Process

The development of the budget for the coming year generally starts several months before the end of the current year. The budgeting process usually begins with the collection of data from each organizational unit of the company. Past performance is often the starting point for setting future budget goals.

The budget is developed within the framework of a **sales forecast**. This forecast shows potential sales for the industry and the company's expected share of such sales. In sales forecasting, various factors are considered: (1) general economic conditions, (2) industry trends, (3) market research studies, (4) anticipated advertising and promotion, (5) previous market share, (6) changes in prices, and (7) technological developments. The input of sales personnel and top management is essential to the sales forecast.

In small companies, the budgeting process is often informal. In larger companies, like Petro-Canada, responsibility for coordinating the preparation of the budget is assigned to a **budget committee**. The committee ordinarily includes the president, treasurer, chief accountant (controller), and management personnel from each of the major areas of the company, such as sales, production, and research. The budget committee acts as a review board where managers can defend their budget goals and requests. Differences are reviewed, modified if necessary, and reconciled. The budget is then put in its final form by the budget committee, and is approved and distributed.

Budgeting and Human Behaviour

A budget can have a significant impact on human behavior. It may inspire a manager to higher levels of performance. Or it may discourage additional effort and pull down a manager's morale. Why do these effects occur? The answer is found in how the budget is developed and administered.

In developing the budget, each level of management should be invited to participate. This "bottom-up" approach is called **participative budgeting**. The advantages of participative budgeting are many. First, lower-level managers have more detailed knowledge of their specific area and thus should be able to provide more accurate budgetary estimates. Second, if lower-level managers are invited to participate in the budgeting process, they are more likely to see the resulting budget as fair. The overall goal is to reach agreement on a budget that the managers consider fair and achievable, but which also meets the corporate goals set by top management. When this goal is met, the budget will create positive motivation for the managers. In contrast, if the managers view the budget as being unfair and unrealistic, they may feel discouraged and uncommitted to budget goals. The risk of having unrealistic budgets is generally greater when the budget is developed from top management down to lower management than vice versa.

Participative budgeting does, however, have potential disadvantages. First, it can be far more time-consuming (and thus more costly) than a "top-down" approach, in which the budget is simply dictated to lower-level managers. A second disadvantage of participative budgeting is that it can encourage budgetary "gaming" through budgetary slack. **Budgetary slack** occurs when managers intentionally underestimate budgeted revenues or overestimate budgeted expenses in order to make it easier to achieve budgetary goals. To minimize budgetary slack, higher-level managers must carefully review and thoroughly question the budget projections provided to them by employees who they supervise. Illustration 9-1 shows the appropriate flow of budget data from bottom to top in an organization.

Illustration 9-1 ▶

Flow of budget data from lower levels of management to top levels

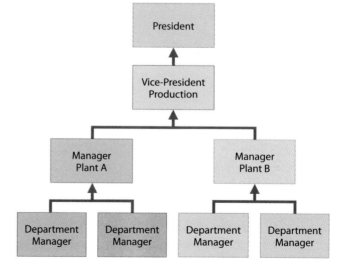

Administering the budget relates to how the budget is used by top management. As explained earlier, the budget should have the complete support of top management. The budget should also be an important basis for evaluating performance. The effect of an evaluation will be positive when top management softens criticism with advice and assistance. In contrast, a manager is likely to respond negatively if the budget is used exclusively to assess blame.

A budget may be used improperly as a pressure device to force improved performance. Or it can be used as a positive aid in achieving projected goals. In sum, a budget can become a manager's friend or foe.

Helpful Hint Unrealistic budgets can lead to unethical employee behaviour, such as cutting corners on the job or distorting internal financial reports.

Budgeting and Long-Range Planning

In business, you may hear talk about the need for long-range planning. Budgeting and long-range planning are not the same. One important difference is the **time period involved**. The maximum length of a budget is usually one year, and budgets are often prepared for shorter periods of time, such as a month or a quarter. In contrast, long-range planning usually covers a period of at least five years.

A second significant difference is in **emphasis**. Budgeting focuses on achieving specific short-term goals, such as meeting annual profit objectives. **Long-range planning**, on the other hand, identifies long-term goals, selects strategies to achieve those goals, and develops policies and plans to implement the strategies. In long-range planning, management also considers anticipated trends in the economic and political environment and how the company should react to them.

The final difference between budgeting and long-range planning pertains to the **amount of detail presented**. Budgets, as you will see in this chapter, can be very detailed. Long-range plans contain much less detail. The data in long-range plans are intended more for a review of progress toward long-term goals than as a basis of control for achieving specific results. The main objective of long-range planning is to develop the best strategy to maximize the company's performance over an extended future period.

Helpful Hint Compare a budget to a long-range plan: (1) Which has more detail? (2) Which is done for a longer period of time? (3) Which is more concerned with short-term goals? Answers: (1) Budget. (2) Long-range plan. (3) Budget.

The Master Budget

The term "budget" is actually a shorthand term to describe several budget documents. All of these documents are combined into a master budget. The **master budget** is a set of interrelated budgets that create a plan of action for a specified time period. The individual budgets included in a master budget are shown in Illustration 9-2.

study objective 3

Identify the budgets that comprise the master budget.

Illustration 9-2 ▶

Components of the master budget

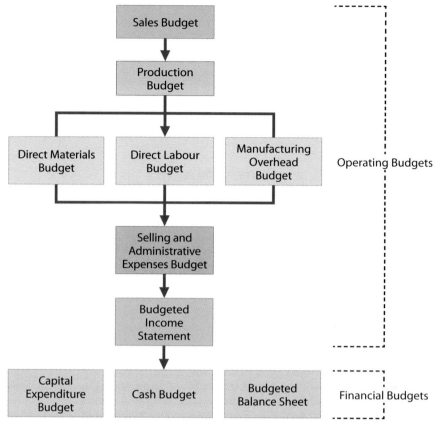

As the illustration shows, the master budget contains two classes of budgets. **Operating budgets** are the individual budgets that are used to prepare the budgeted income statement. These budgets establish goals for the company's sales and production personnel. In contrast, **financial budgets** are the capital expenditure budget, the cash budget, and the budgeted balance sheet. These budgets focus mainly on the cash resources that are needed to fund expected operations and planned capital expenditures.

The master budget is prepared in the sequence shown by the arrows in Illustration 9-2. The operating budgets are developed first, beginning with the sales budget. Then the financial budgets are prepared. We will explain and illustrate each budget shown in Illustration 9-2, except the capital expenditure budget. This last budget is discussed under the topic Capital Budgeting in Chapter 12.

BEFORE YOU GO ON . . .

▶ Review It

1. What are the benefits of budgeting?
2. What factors are essential to effective budgeting?
3. How does the budget process work?
4. How does budgeting differ from long-range planning?
5. What is a master budget?

Preparing the Operating Budgets

A case study of Hayes Company will be used in preparing the operating budgets. Hayes manufactures and sells a single product, Kitchen-mate. The budgets will be prepared by quarters for the year ending December 31, 2005. Hayes Company begins its annual budgeting process on September 1, 2004, and it completes the budget for 2005 by December 1, 2004.

Sales Budget

As shown in the master budget in Illustration 9-2, **the sales budget is the first budget that is prepared.** Each of the other budgets depends on the sales budget. The **sales budget** is based on the sales forecast. It is management's best estimate of sales revenue for the budget period. An inaccurate sales budget may adversely affect net income. For example, an overly optimistic sales budget may result in excessive inventories that may have to be sold at reduced prices. In contrast, an overly conservative budget may result in lost sales revenue due to inventory shortages.

The sales budget is prepared by multiplying the expected sales volume in units for each product by its anticipated selling price per unit. For Hayes Company, the sales volume is expected to be 3,000 units in the first quarter, with 500-unit increments in each quarter after that. Based on a sales price of $60 per unit, the sales budget for the year, by quarters, is shown in Illustration 9-3.

Illustration 9-3 ◄

Sales budget

HAYES COMPANY
Sales Budget
Year Ending December 31, 2005

	Quarter				
	1	2	3	4	Year
Expected unit sales	3,000	3,500	4,000	4,500	15,000
Unit selling price	× $60	× $60	× $60	× $60	× $60
Total sales	$180,000	$210,000	$240,000	$270,000	$900,000

Some companies classify the expected sales revenue as cash or credit sales, and by geographical region, territory, or salesperson.

Production Budget

The **production budget** shows the units that must be produced to meet expected sales. Production requirements are determined with the formula in Illustration 9-4.[1]

Illustration 9-4 ◄

Production requirements formula

A realistic estimate of ending inventory is essential to correctly schedule production requirements. Excessive inventories in one quarter may lead to cutbacks in production and employee layoffs in the next quarter. On the other hand, inadequate inventories may result either in added costs for overtime work or in lost sales. Hayes Company believes it can meet its future sales requirements by maintaining an ending inventory that is equal to 20 percent of the next quarter's budgeted sales volume. For example, the ending finished goods inventory for the first quarter is 700 units (20% × expected second-quarter sales of 3,500 units). The production budget is shown in Illustration 9-5.

---

[1] This formula ignores any work in process inventories, which are assumed to be non-existent in Hayes Company.

Illustration 9-5 ▶

Production budget

HAYES COMPANY Production Budget Year Ending December 31, 2005					
	Quarter				
	1	2	3	4	Year
Expected unit sales (Illustration 9-3)	3,000	3,500	4,000	4,500	
Add: Desired ending finished goods units[a]	700	800	900	1,000[b]	
Total required units	3,700	4,300	4,900	5,500	
Less: Beginning finished goods units	600[c]	700	800	900	
Required production units	3,100	3,600	4,100	4,600	15,400

[a] 20% of next quarter's sales
[b] Expected 2006 first-quarter sales, 5,000 units × 20%
[c] 20% of estimated first-quarter 2005 sales

The production budget, in turn, becomes the basis for determining the budgeted costs for each manufacturing cost element, as explained in the following pages.

BUSINESS INSIGHT ▶ Management Perspective

Great Canadian Bagel began in 1993 with a business model based on large in-store bakeries producing fresh bagels. For a while it was a success; Great Canadian was one of the fastest growing franchises in the country. By 1999, it had more than 150 locations in every province. But high rents and sagging sales forced many outlets to close. By 2003, more than 60 had shut down and the company was advising the remaining franchisees to partner with other food outlets to share rent and cut expenses.

What went wrong? Great Canadian invested very little in marketing, while competitors like McDonald's and Tim Hortons started selling bagels, too. Meanwhile, the in-house bakery required additional staff and more space, resulting in higher labour costs and rents than most sandwich shops. To offset these costs, franchisees tried to sell in bulk to grocery stores and restaurants. But, without a consistent marketing presence, retail customers weren't interested and there were fewer reasons for wholesale customers to pay a premium for Great Canadian's brand. Bulk sales declined, squeezing not only sales, but also margins since bulk sales had lower production and labour costs.

It was a case of too much, too fast.

Source: John Gray, "Sour Dough," *Canadian Business*, June 23, 2003.

Direct Materials Budget

The **direct materials budget** shows both the quantity and cost of direct materials that need to be purchased. The quantities of direct materials to purchase are determined with the formula in Illustration 9-6.

Illustration 9-6 ▶

Formula for direct materials quantities

The budgeted cost of direct materials to be purchased is then calculated by multiplying the required units of direct materials by the expected cost per unit.

The desired ending inventory is again a key component in the budgeting process. For example, inadequate inventories could result in temporary shutdowns of production. Because of its close proximity to suppliers, Hayes Company has found that an ending inventory of raw materials equal to 10 percent of the next quarter's production requirements is enough. The manufacture of each Kitchen-mate requires two kilograms of raw materials, and the expected cost per kilogram is $4. The direct materials budget is shown in Illustration 9-7.

HAYES COMPANY
Direct Materials Budget
Year Ending December 31, 2005

	Quarter				
	1	2	3	4	Year
Units to be produced (Illustration 9-5)	3,100	3,600	4,100	4,600	
Direct materials per unit	× 2	× 2	× 2	× 2	
Total kilograms needed for production	6,200	7,200	8,200	9,200	
Add: Desired ending direct materials (kilograms)[a]	720	820	920	1,020 [b]	
Total materials required	6,920	8,020	9,120	10,220	
Less: Beginning direct materials (kilograms)	620 [c]	720	820	920	
Direct materials purchases	6,300	7,300	8,300	9,300	
Cost per kilogram	× $4	× $4	× $4	× $4	
Total cost of direct materials purchases	$25,200	$29,200	$33,200	$37,200	$124,800

[a] 10% of next quarter's production requirements
[b] Estimated 2006 first-quarter kilograms needed for production, 10,200 × 10%
[c] 10% of estimated first-quarter kilograms needed for production

Illustration 9-7 ▲

Direct materials budget

BUSINESS INSIGHT ► Management Perspective

The successful manufacturers of the twenty-first century will be fully computerized. A crucial step on the way is material-requirements-planning (MRP) systems. Early MRP systems accepted a sales forecast and calculated how much materials, inventory, people, and machinery a company needed to manufacture the product. Current MRP systems link the company's manufacturing resource planning with its financial management. This new capability creates a powerful system of control over the entire business planning and operating process. With MRP, management can make decisions on facts rather than on "hunches" and "instinct."

Direct Labour Budget

Like the direct materials budget, the **direct labour budget** contains the quantity (hours) and cost of direct labour that will be needed to meet production requirements. The total direct labour cost is calculated using the formula in Illustration 9-8.

Units to Be Produced × Direct Labour Time per Unit × Direct Labour Cost per Hour = Total Direct Labour Cost

Illustration 9-8 ◄

Formula for direct labour cost

Direct labour hours are determined from the production budget. At Hayes Company, two hours of direct labour are required to produce each unit of finished goods. The expected hourly wage rate is $10. These data are shown in Illustration 9-9. The direct labour budget is critical in maintaining a labour force that can meet the expected levels of production.

	Quarter				
HAYES COMPANY **Direct Labour Budget** **Year Ending December 31, 2005**					
	1	2	3	4	Year
Units to be produced (Illustration 9-5)	3,100	3,600	4,100	4,600	
Direct labour time (hours) per unit	× 2	× 2	× 2	× 2	
Total required direct labour hours	6,200	7,200	8,200	9,200	
Direct labour cost per hour	× $10	× $10	× $10	× $10	
Total direct labour cost	$62,000	$72,000	$82,000	$92,000	$308,000

Illustration 9-9 ▲

Direct labour budget

BEFORE YOU GO ON . . .

▶ Review It

1. What is the formula to determine required production units?
2. What inputs are necessary to prepare the direct labour budget?
3. Which budget must be prepared before the direct materials budget?

▶ Do It

Becker Company estimates that unit sales will be 12,000 in quarter 1; 16,000 in quarter 2; and 20,000 in quarter 3. The selling price per unit is expected to be $30. Management wants to have ending finished goods inventory that is equal to 15% of the next quarter's expected unit sales. Prepare a production budget by quarters for the first six months of 2005.

Action Plan

- Begin with the budgeted sales in units.
- Add the desired finished goods inventory.
- Subtract the beginning finished goods inventory.

Solution

BECKER COMPANY
Production Budget
Six Months Ending June 30, 2005

	Quarter		
	1	2	Six Months
Expected unit sales	12,000	16,000	28,000
Add: Desired ending finished goods	2,400	3,000	3,000
Total required units	14,400	19,000	31,000
Less: Beginning finished goods inventory	1,800	2,400	1,800
Required production units	12,600	16,600	29,200

Related exercise material: BE9–3, E9–3, and E9–5.

Manufacturing Overhead Budget

The **manufacturing overhead budget** shows the expected manufacturing overhead costs for the budget period. As shown in Illustration 9-10, this budget distinguishes between variable and fixed overhead costs. Hayes Company expects variable costs to fluctuate with the production volume based on the following rates per direct labour hour: indirect materials $1.00; indirect labour $1.40; utilities $0.40; and maintenance $0.20. Thus, for the 6,200 direct labour hours to produce 3,100 units, the budgeted indirect materials cost is $6,200 (6,200 × $1), and the budgeted indirect labour cost is $8,680 (6,200 × $1.40). Hayes also recognizes that some maintenance is fixed. The amounts reported for fixed costs are assumed in our example. The accuracy of budgeted fixed overhead cost estimates can be greatly improved by using activity-based costing.

At Hayes Company, overhead is applied to production based on direct labour hours. Thus, as shown in Illustration 9-10, the annual rate is $8 per hour ($246,400 ÷ 30,800).

HAYES COMPANY
Manufacturing Overhead Budget
Year Ending December 31, 2005

| | Quarter | | | | |
	1	2	3	4	Year
Variable costs					
Indirect materials ($1/hour)	$ 6,200	$ 7,200	$ 8,200	$ 9,200	$ 30,800
Indirect labour ($1.40/hour)	8,680	10,080	11,480	12,880	43,120
Utilities ($0.40/hour)	2,480	2,880	3,280	3,680	12,320
Maintenance ($0.20/hour)	1,240	1,440	1,640	1,840	6,160
Total variable costs	18,600	21,600	24,600	27,600	92,400
Fixed costs					
Supervisory salaries	20,000	20,000	20,000	20,000	80,000
Amortization	3,800	3,800	3,800	3,800	15,200
Property taxes and insurance	9,000	9,000	9,000	9,000	36,000
Maintenance	5,700	5,700	5,700	5,700	22,800
Total fixed costs	38,500	38,500	38,500	38,500	154,000
Total manufacturing overhead	$57,100	$60,100	$63,100	$66,100	$246,400
Direct labour hours (Illustration 9-9)	6,200	7,200	8,200	9,200	30,800
Manufacturing overhead rate per direct labour hour ($246,400 ÷ 30,800)					$8.00

Illustration 9-10 ◄

Manufacturing overhead budget

Selling and Administrative Expenses Budget

Hayes Company combines its operating expenses into one budget, the **selling and administrative expenses budget**. This budget projects selling and administrative expenses for the budget period. In this budget, as in the preceding one, expenses are classified as either variable or fixed. In this case, the variable expense rates per unit of sales are $3 of sales commissions and $1.00 of freight out. Variable expenses per quarter are based on the unit sales from the sales budget (Illustration 9-3). For example, sales in the first quarter are expected to be 3,000 units. Thus, the sales commissions expense is $9,000 (3,000 × $3), and freight out is $3,000 (3,000 × $1). Fixed expenses are based on assumed data. The selling and administrative expenses budget is shown in Illustration 9-11.

Illustration 9-11 ▶

Selling and administrative
expense budget

HAYES COMPANY Selling and Administrative Expenses Budget Year Ending December 31, 2005					
	Quarter				
	1	2	3	4	Year
Budgeted sales in units	3,000	3,500	4,000	4,500	15,000
Variable expenses					
Sales commissions ($3/unit)	$ 9,000	$10,500	$12,000	$13,500	$ 45,000
Freight out ($1/unit)	3,000	3,500	4,000	4,500	15,000
Total variable expenses	12,000	14,000	16,000	18,000	60,000
Fixed expenses					
Advertising	5,000	5,000	5,000	5,000	20,000
Sales salaries	15,000	15,000	15,000	15,000	60,000
Office salaries	7,500	7,500	7,500	7,500	30,000
Amortization	1,000	1,000	1,000	1,000	4,000
Property taxes and insurance	1,500	1,500	1,500	1,500	6,000
Total fixed expenses	30,000	30,000	30,000	30,000	120,000
Total selling and administrative expenses	$42,000	$44,000	$46,000	$48,000	$180,000

BUSINESS INSIGHT ▶ *e*-Business Insight

Good budgeting depends on good information. And good information is what e-business is all about. Businesses looking to integrate the Internet into their business processes have two website models from which to choose: developer and seller.

A developer site collects information to better serve customers and develop personal relations with various stakeholders. Companies that use this model do not sell directly to consumers. Rather, they are in the wholesale trade, manufacturing, or arts, entertainment, and recreation sectors. They gather and analyze information from customers, suppliers, and partners via the Internet in order to improve their processes.

In contrast, a seller website supports on-line ordering and payment transactions. Most companies that adopt this model are in retail trade or the manufacturing sector. They offer a product that can be sold via the Internet. This model is particularly valuable to companies that sell niche products, since it allows businesses to offer the products in places where they are scarce or unavailable. Allowing customers to track orders on-line is another plus. Companies can also cut costs by being able to employ just-in-time inventory management.

Of course, there are website that are combinations of the two models. Generally, these are the result of companies developing their seller websites further.

Source: Hugues Boisvert, CMA, FCMA, "The Next Step: Developer and Seller Sites," *CMA Management Magazine,* May 2003, pp. 28–31.

Budgeted Income Statement

study objective 4

Describe the sources for preparing the budgeted income statement.

The **budgeted income statement** is the important end-product of the operating budgets. This budget indicates the expected profitability of operations for the budget period. The budgeted income statement provides the basis for evaluating company performance.

As you would expect, this budget is prepared from the various operating budgets. For example, to find the cost of goods sold, it is first necessary to determine the total cost per unit of producing one Kitchen-mate. Illustration 9-12 shows this calculation.

Illustration 9-12 ◄

Calculation of total unit cost

Cost of One Kitchen-mate				
Cost Element	Illustration	Quantity	Unit Cost	Total
Direct materials	9-7	2 kilograms	$ 4.00	$ 8.00
Direct labour	9-9	2 hours	$10.00	20.00
Manufacturing overhead	9-10	2 hours	$ 8.00	16.00
Total unit cost				$44.00

The cost of goods sold can then be determined by multiplying the units sold by the unit cost. For Hayes Company, the budgeted cost of goods sold is $660,000 (15,000 × $44). All data for the statement are obtained from the individual operating budgets except the following: (1) interest expense is expected to be $100, and (2) income taxes are estimated to be $12,000. The budgeted income statement is shown in Illustration 9-13.

Illustration 9-13 ◄

Budgeted income statement

HAYES COMPANY
Budgeted Income Statement
Year Ending December 31, 2005

Sales (Illustration 9-3)	$900,000
Cost of goods sold (15,000 × $44)	660,000
Gross profit	240,000
Selling and administrative expenses (Illustration 9-11)	180,000
Income from operations	60,000
Interest expense	100
Income before income taxes	59,900
Income tax expense	12,000
Net income	$ 47,900

Decision Toolkit

Decision Checkpoints	Info Needed for Decision	Tools to Use for Decision	How to Evaluate Results
Has the company met its targets for sales, production expenses, selling and administrative expenses, and net income?	Sales forecasts, inventory levels, and projected materials, labour, overhead, and selling and administrative requirements	Master budget—a set of interrelated budgets including the sales, production, materials, labour, overhead, and selling and administrative budgets	The results are favourable if revenues exceed budgeted amounts, or if expenses are less than budgeted amounts.

Preparing the Financial Budgets

As shown in Illustration 9-2, the financial budgets consist of the capital expenditure budget, the cash budget, and the budgeted balance sheet. The capital expenditure budget is discussed in Chapter 12; the other budgets are explained in the following sections.

Cash Budget

The **cash budget** shows expected cash flows. Because cash is so vital, this budget is often considered to be the most important output in preparing financial budgets. To help the treasurer manage the cash well, a cash budget is typically prepared at least once a month,

study objective 5

Explain the main sections of a cash budget.

and in some companies it is prepared daily. The cash budget contains three sections (cash receipts, cash disbursements, and financing) and the beginning and ending cash balances, as shown in Illustration 9-14.

Illustration 9-14 ▶

Basic form of a cash budget

ANY COMPANY Cash Budget	
Beginning cash balance	$X,XXX
Add: Cash receipts (itemized)	X,XXX
Total available cash	X,XXX
Less: Cash disbursements (itemized)	X,XXX
Excess (deficiency) of available cash over cash disbursements	X,XXX
Financing	X,XXX
Ending cash balance	$X,XXX

Helpful Hint Why is the cash budget prepared after the other budgets are prepared? Answer: Because the information from the other budgets determines the need for inflows and outflows of cash.

The **cash receipts** section includes expected receipts from the company's main source(s) of revenue. These are usually cash sales and collections from customers on credit sales. This section also shows anticipated receipts of interest and dividends, and proceeds from planned sales of investments, plant assets, and the company's capital stock.

The **cash disbursements section** shows expected cash payments. These payments include direct materials, direct labour, manufacturing overhead, and selling and administrative expenses. This section also includes projected payments for income taxes, dividends, investments, and plant assets.

The **financing section** shows expected borrowings and the repayment of the borrowed funds plus interest. This section is needed when there is a cash deficiency or when the cash balance is below management's minimum required balance.

Data in the cash budget must be prepared in sequence. The ending cash balance of one period becomes the beginning cash balance for the next period. Data for preparing the cash budget are obtained from other budgets and from information provided by management. Many companies prepare cash budgets for the year on a monthly basis.

To minimize detail, we will assume that Hayes Company prepares an annual cash budget by quarters. The cash budget for Hayes Company is based on the following assumptions:

1. The January 1, 2005, cash balance is expected to be $38,000.
2. Sales (Illustration 9-3): 60 percent are collected in the quarter sold and 40 percent are collected in the following quarter. Accounts receivable of $60,000 at December 31, 2004, are expected to be collected in full in the first quarter of 2005.
3. Short-term investments are expected to be sold for $2,000 cash in the first quarter.
4. Direct materials (Illustration 9-7): 50 percent are paid for in the quarter purchased and 50 percent are paid for in the following quarter. Accounts payable of $10,600 at December 31, 2004, are expected to be paid in full in the first quarter of 2005.
5. Direct labour (Illustration 9-9): 100 percent is paid in the quarter incurred.
6. Manufacturing overhead (Illustration 9-10) and selling and administrative expenses (Illustration 9-11): All items except amortization are paid in the quarter incurred.
7. Management plans to purchase a truck in the second quarter for $10,000 cash.
8. Hayes makes equal quarterly payments of its estimated annual income taxes.
9. Loans are repaid in the earliest quarter in which there is sufficient cash (i.e., when the cash on hand exceeds the $15,000 minimum required balance).

In preparing the cash budget, it is useful to prepare schedules for collections from customers (assumption No. 2, above) and cash payments for direct materials (assumption No. 4, above). The schedules are shown in Illustrations 9-15 and 9-16.

Illustration 9-15 ◀

Collections from customers

Schedule of Expected Collections From Customers				
	Quarter			
	1	2	3	4
Accounts receivable, December 31, 2004	$ 60,000			
First quarter ($180,000)	108,000	$ 72,000		
Second quarter ($210,000)		126,000	$ 84,000	
Third quarter ($240,000)			144,000	$ 96,000
Fourth quarter ($270,000)				162,000
Total collections	$168,000	$198,000	$228,000	$258,000

Illustration 9-16 ◀

Payments for direct materials

Schedule of Expected Payments for Direct Materials				
	Quarter			
	1	2	3	4
Accounts payable, December 31, 2004	$10,600			
First quarter ($25,200)	12,600	$12,600		
Second quarter ($29,200)		14,600	$14,600	
Third quarter ($33,200)			16,600	$16,600
Fourth quarter ($37,200)				18,600
Total payments	$23,200	$27,200	$31,200	$35,200

The cash budget for Hayes Company is shown in Illustration 9-17. The budget indicates that $3,000 of financing will be needed in the second quarter to keep a minimum cash balance of $15,000. Since there is an excess of available cash over disbursements of $22,500 at the end of the third quarter, the borrowing, plus $100 interest, is repaid in this quarter.

Illustration 9-17 ▼

Cash budget

HAYES COMPANY Cash Budget Year Ending December 31, 2005					
		Quarter			
	Assumption	1	2	3	4
Beginning cash balance	1	$ 38,000	$ 25,500	$ 15,000	$ 19,400
Add: Receipts					
Collections from customers	2	168,000	198,000	228,000	258,000
Sale of securities	3	2,000	0	0	0
Total receipts		170,000	198,000	228,000	258,000
Total available cash		208,000	223,500	243,000	277,400
Less: Disbursements					
Direct materials	4	23,200	27,200	31,200	35,200
Direct labour	5	62,000	72,000	82,000	92,000
Manufacturing overhead	6	53,300 [a]	56,300	59,300	62,300
Selling and administrative expenses	6	41,000 [b]	43,000	45,000	47,000
Purchase of truck	7	0	10,000	0	0
Income tax expense	8	3,000	3,000	3,000	3,000
Total disbursements		182,500	211,500	220,500	239,500
Excess (deficiency) of available cash over disbursements		25,500	12,000	22,500	37,900
Financing					
Borrowings		0	3,000	0	0
Repayments—plus $100 interest	9	0	0	3,100	0
Ending cash balance		$ 25,500	$ 15,000	$ 19,400	$ 37,900

[a] $57,100 − $3,800 amortization
[b] $42,000 − $1,000 amortization

BUSINESS INSIGHT ▶ Management Perspective

The budgeting process has a big impact on hiring decisions since labour obviously takes up a large portion of an organization's budget. Signs of economic growth in Canada have allowed some organizations to move away from the employee-related cost-cutting measures they had implemented in tougher economic times. In fact, a recent Watson Wyatt Worldwide survey found that Canadian companies are now focusing on rebuilding their workforces. More than one-third (34%) of the employers surveyed planned to increase their hiring of "critical-skill" employees in 2004, while only 3% planned to make reductions. Just 12% planned to reduce their salary-increase budgets, compared to 27% in 2003. And 3% planned to eliminate or cut bonuses, down from 12%. Employers also expected a decline in other cost-cutting measures, such as reducing employee benefits or stock option grants. Watson Wyatt surveyed a total of 163 Canadian companies across a broad spectrum of industry sectors for its Canadian Strategic Rewards Survey.

Source: "Canadian Companies Easing Up on Worker-Related Cost-Cutting Measures," Watson Wyatt Worldwide news release, June 9, 2004.

A cash budget contributes to more effective cash management. It can show managers when additional financing will be necessary a long time before the money is needed. And, it can indicate when excess cash will be available for investments or other purposes.

Decision Toolkit

Decision Checkpoints	Info Needed for Decision	Tools to Use for Decision	How to Evaluate Results
Is the company going to need to borrow funds in the coming quarter?	Beginning cash balance, cash receipts, cash disbursements, and desired cash balance	Cash budget	The company will need to borrow money if the cash budget indicates that the available cash will be less than the cash disbursements for the quarter.

Budgeted Balance Sheet

The **budgeted balance sheet** is a projection of the company's financial position at the end of the budget period. This budget is developed from the budgeted balance sheet for the preceding year and the budgets for the current year. Relevant data for Hayes from the budgeted balance sheet at December 31, 2004, are as follows:

Buildings and equipment	$182,000	Common shares	$225,000
Accumulated amortization	28,800	Retained earnings	46,480

Illustration 9-18 shows the budgeted balance sheet at December 31, 2005.

Illustration 9-18 ◀

Budgeted balance sheet

HAYES COMPANY
Budgeted Balance Sheet
December 31, 2005

Assets

Cash		$ 37,900
Accounts receivable		108,000
Finished goods inventory		44,000
Raw materials inventory		4,080
Buildings and equipment	$192,000	
Less: Accumulated amortization	48,000	144,000
Total assets		$337,980

Liabilities and Shareholders' Equity

Accounts payable		$ 18,600
Common shares		225,000
Retained earnings		94,380
Total liabilities and shareholders' equity		$337,980

The calculations and sources of the amounts are as follows:

Cash: Ending cash balance of $37,900, shown in the cash budget (Illustration 9-17).

Accounts receivable: 40 percent of fourth-quarter sales of $270,000, shown in the schedule of expected collections from customers (Illustration 9-15).

Finished goods inventory: Desired ending inventory of 1,000 units, shown in the production budget (Illustration 9-5) times the total cost per unit $44 (shown in Illustration 9-12).

Raw materials inventory: Desired ending inventory of 1,020 kilograms, times the cost per kilogram of $4, shown in the direct materials budget (Illustration 9-7).

Buildings and equipment: December 31, 2004, balance $182,000, plus purchase of truck for $10,000.

Accumulated amortization: December 31, 2004, balance of $28,800, plus $15,200 of amortization shown in the manufacturing overhead budget (Illustration 9-10) and $4,000 of amortization shown in the selling and administrative expenses budget (Illustration 9-11).

Accounts payable: 50 percent of fourth-quarter purchases of $37,200, shown in the schedule of expected payments for direct materials (Illustration 9-16).

Common shares: Unchanged from the beginning of the year.

Retained earnings: December 31, 2004, balance of $46,480, plus net income of $47,900, shown in the budgeted income statement (Illustration 9-13).

After the budgeting data are entered into the company's budgeting software, the various budgets (sales, cash, etc.) can be prepared, as well as the budgeted financial statements. Management can also manipulate the budgets in "what if" (sensitivity) analyses based on different hypothetical assumptions. For example, suppose that sales were budgeted to be 10 percent higher in the coming quarter. What impact would the change have on the rest of the budgeting process and the financing needs of the business? The computer can quickly "play out" the impact on the budgets of the various assumptions. Armed with these analyses, management can make more informed decisions about the impact of various projects. It can also anticipate future problems and business opportunities. Having read this chapter, you may not be surprised to know that budgeting is also one of the top uses of electronic spreadsheets.

BEFORE YOU GO ON . . .

▶ Review It

1. What are the two classifications of the individual budgets in the master budget?
2. What is the sequence for preparing the budgets that comprise the operating budgets?
3. Identify some of the source documents that would be used in preparing each of the operating budgets.
4. What are the three main sections of the cash budget?

▶ Do It

Martian Company's management wants to maintain a minimum monthly cash balance of $15,000. At the beginning of March, the cash balance is $16,500, expected cash receipts for March are $210,000, and cash disbursements are expected to be $220,000. How much cash, if any, must be borrowed to keep the desired minimum monthly balance?

Action Plan

• Write down the basic form of the cash budget, starting with the beginning cash balance. Add cash receipts for the period, deduct cash disbursements, and then identify the needed financing to achieve the desired minimum ending cash balance.
• Insert the data into the outlined form of the cash budget.

Solution

MARTIAN COMPANY
Cash Budget
Month Ending March 31, 2005

Beginning cash balance	$ 16,500
Add: Cash receipts for March	210,000
Total available cash	226,500
Less: Cash disbursements for March	220,000
Excess of available cash over cash disbursements	6,500
Financing	8,500
Ending cash balance	$ 15,000

To keep the desired minimum cash balance of $15,000, Martian Company must borrow $8,500 of cash.

Related exercise material: BE9-9, E9–10, E9–11, and E9-12.

Budgeting in Nonmanufacturing Companies

Budgeting is not limited to manufacturers. Budgets may also be used by merchandisers, service enterprises, and not-for-profit organizations.

Merchandisers

As in manufacturing operations, the sales budget for a merchandiser is both the starting point and the key factor in the development of the master budget. The major differences between the master budgets of a merchandiser and a manufacturer are these: (1) A merchandiser **uses a merchandise purchases budget instead of a production budget.** (2) A merchandiser **does not use the manufacturing budgets (direct materials, direct labour, and manufacturing overhead).** The **merchandise purchases budget** shows the estimated cost of goods to be purchased to meet expected sales. Illustration 9-19 gives the formula for determining budgeted merchandise purchases.

| Budgeted Cost of Goods Sold | + | Desired Ending Merchandise Inventory | − | Beginning Merchandise Inventory | = | Required Merchandise Purchases |

Illustration 9-19 ◄

Merchandise purchases formula

To illustrate, assume that the budget committee of Lima Company is preparing the merchandise purchases budget for July 2005. It estimates that sales will be $300,000 in July and $320,000 in August. The cost of goods sold is expected to be 70 percent of sales—that is, $210,000 in July (0.70 × $300,000) and $224,000 in August (0.70 × $320,000). The company's desired ending inventory is 30 percent of the following month's cost of goods sold. The required merchandise purchases for July are therefore $214,200, calculated as in Illustration 9-20.

Illustration 9-20 ◄

Merchandise purchases budget

LIMA COMPANY
Merchandise Purchases Budget
Month Ending July 31, 2005

Budgeted cost of goods sold ($300,000 × 70%)	$210,000
Plus: Desired ending merchandise inventory ($224,000 × 30%)	67,200
Total	277,200
Less: Beginning merchandise inventory ($210,000 × 30%)	63,000
Budgeted merchandise purchases for July	$214,200

When a merchandiser is organized by department, separate budgets are prepared for each one. For example, a grocery store may start by preparing sales budgets and purchases budgets for each of its major departments, such as meats, dairy, and produce. These budgets are then combined into a master budget for the store. When a retailer has branch stores, separate master budgets are prepared for each store. Then these budgets are incorporated into master budgets for the company as a whole.

Service Enterprises

In a service enterprise, such as a public accounting firm, a law office, or a medical practice, the critical factor in budgeting is **coordinating professional staff needs with expected services**. If a firm is overstaffed, several problems may result: (1) Labour costs will be disproportionately high. (2) Profits will be lower because of the additional salaries. (3) Staff turnover may increase because there is not enough challenging work. In contrast, if an enterprise is understaffed, revenue may be lost because the existing and potential needs of clients for services cannot be met. Also, professional staff may look for other jobs because their workloads are too heavy.

Budget data for service revenue may be obtained from **expected output** or **expected input**. When output is used, it is necessary to determine the expected billings of clients for services provided. In a public accounting firm, for example, output would be the sum of the firm's billings in auditing, tax, and consulting services. When input data are used, each professional staff member is required to project his or her time that will be billed. Billing rates are then applied to this billable time to calculate the expected service revenue.

BUSINESS INSIGHT ► Service Company Perspective

Don Goodison, managing partner of a CGA firm in Vancouver, B.C., uses formal budgets as the principal tool for keeping his firm's cash flow on an even keel throughout the year.

The firm budgets annually for both revenues and expenses on a month-by-month basis. For example, the revenue budget is based on chargeable-hour goals set by the staff. The firm sets a threshold of 1,700 hours for each staff member and manager. This is adjusted for staff who have holidays of more than two weeks and it does not consider tax-season overtime, which can be offset by slow periods in the summer and fall. Each month, the budget is compared with the financial statements, and adjustments are made if necessary.

Not-For-Profit Organizations

Budgeting is just as important for not-for-profit organizations as for profit-oriented enterprises. The budget process, however, is very different. In most cases, not-for-profit entities budget based **on cash flows (expenditures and receipts), rather than on a revenue and expense basis**. Further, the starting point in the process is usually expenditures, not receipts. For the not-for-profit entity, management's task generally is to find the receipts needed to support the planned expenditures. The activity index is also likely to be quite different. For example, in a not-for-profit entity, such as a university, budgeted faculty positions may be based on full-time equivalent students or credit hours expected to be taught in a department.

For some government units, the budget must be approved by voters. In other cases, such as provincial governments and the federal government, legislative approval is required. After the budget is adopted, it must be strictly followed. Overspending is often illegal. In government budgets, authorizations tend to be on a line-by-line basis. That is, the budget for a municipality may have a specified authorization for police and fire protection, garbage collection, street paving, and so on. The line-item authorization of governmental budgets significantly limits how much discretion management has. The city manager often cannot use savings from one line item, such as street paving, to cover increased spending in another line item, such as snow removal.

BEFORE YOU GO ON . . .

▶ Review It

1. What is the formula for calculating required merchandise purchases?
2. How does budgeting in service and not-for-profit organizations differ from budgeting for manufacturers and merchandisers?

▦ Using the Decision Toolkit

The University of Drummondville and its subunits must prepare budgets. One unique subunit of the University of Drummondville is Hilltop Ice Cream, a functioning producer of dairy products (and famous, at least on campus, for its delicious ice cream).

Assume that Hilltop Ice Cream prepares monthly cash budgets. Relevant data from its assumed operating budgets for 2005 are as follows:

	January	February
Sales	$460,000	$412,000
Direct materials purchases	185,000	210,000
Direct labour	70,000	85,000
Manufacturing overhead	50,000	65,000
Selling and administrative expenses	85,000	95,000

Hilltop sells 50% of its ice cream in its shops on campus and the rest to local stores. Collections from local stores are expected to be 75% in the month of sale, and 25% in the month following sale. Sixty percent of direct materials purchases are paid in cash in the month of purchase, and the balance due is paid in the month following the purchase. All other items above are paid in the month incurred. (Amortization has been excluded from manufacturing overhead and selling and administrative expenses.)

Other data:

1. Sales: November 2004, $370,000; December 2004, $320,000
2. Purchases of direct materials: December 2004, $175,000
3. Other receipts: January—donation received, $2,000
   February—sale of used equipment, $4,000

4. Other disbursements: February—purchased equipment, $10,000
5. Repaid debt: January, $30,000

The company's cash balance on January 1, 2005, is expected to be $50,000. The company wants to keep a minimum cash balance of $45,000.

Instructions

(a) Prepare schedules for (1) the expected collections from customers and (2) the expected payments for direct materials purchases.
(b) Prepare a cash budget, with columns, for January and February.

Solution

(a) 1. **Expected Collections from Customers**

	January	February
December ($320,000)	$ 80,000	$ 0
January ($460,000)	345,000	115,000
February ($412,000)	0	309,000
Totals	$425,000	$424,000

2. **Expected Payments for Direct Materials**

	January	February
December ($175,000)	$ 70,000	$ 0
January ($185,000)	111,000	74,000
February ($210,000)	0	126,000
Totals	$181,000	$200,000

(b)

HILLTOP ICE CREAM
Cash Budget
Two Months Ending February 28, 2005

	January	February
Beginning cash balance	$ 50,000	$ 61,000
Add: Receipts		
Collections from customers	425,000	424,000
Donations received	2,000	0
Sale of used equipment	0	4,000
Total receipts	427,000	428,000
Total available cash	477,000	489,000
Less: Disbursements		
Direct materials	181,000	200,000
Direct labour	70,000	85,000
Manufacturing overhead	50,000	65,000
Selling and administrative expenses	85,000	95,000
Purchase of equipment	0	10,000
Total disbursements	386,000	455,000
Excess (deficiency) of available cash over disbursements	91,000	34,000
Financing		
Borrowings	0	11,000
Repayments	30,000	0
Ending cash balance	$ 61,000	$ 45,000

the navigator

Summary of Study Objectives

1. *Indicate the benefits of budgeting.* The main advantages of budgeting are that it (1) requires management to plan ahead, (2) provides definite objectives for evaluating performance, (3) creates an early warning system for potential problems, (4) makes it easier to coordinate activities, (5) results in greater management awareness, and (6) motivates personnel to meet planned objectives.

2. *State the essentials of effective budgeting.* The essentials of effective budgeting are (1) sound organizational structure, (2) research and analysis, and (3) acceptance by all levels of management.

3. *Identify the budgets that comprise the master budget.* The master budget consists of the following budgets: (1) sales, (2) production, (3) direct materials, (4) direct labour, (5) manufacturing overhead, (6) selling and administrative expenses, (7) budgeted income statement, (8) capital expenditure budget, (9) cash budget, and (10) budgeted balance sheet.

4. *Describe the sources for preparing the budgeted income statement.* The budgeted income statement is prepared from (1) the sales budget; (2) the budgets for direct materials, direct labour, and manufacturing overhead; and (3) the selling and administrative expenses budget.

5. *Explain the main sections of a cash budget.* The cash budget has three sections (receipts, disbursements, and financing) and the beginning and ending cash balances.

6. *Indicate how budgeting is done in nonmanufacturing companies.* Budgeting may be used by merchandisers for development of a master budget. In service enterprises budgeting is a critical factor in coordinating staff needs with anticipated services. In not-for-profit organizations, the starting point in budgeting is usually expenditures, not receipts.

Decision Toolkit—A Summary

Decision Checkpoints	Info Needed for Decision	Tools to Use for Decision	How to Evaluate Results
Has the company met its targets for sales, production expenses, selling and administrative expenses, and net income?	Sales forecasts, inventory levels, and projected materials, labour, overhead, and selling and administrative requirements	Master budget—a set of interrelated budgets including the sales, production, materials, labour, overhead, and selling and administrative budgets	The results are favourable if revenues exceed budgeted amounts, or if expenses are less than budgeted amounts.
Is the company going to need to borrow funds in the coming quarter?	Beginning cash balance, cash receipts, cash disbursements, and desired cash balance	Cash budget	The company will need to borrow money if the cash budget indicates that the available cash will be less than the cash disbursements for the quarter.

Glossary

Budget A formal written statement, in financial terms, of management's plans for a specified future time period. (p. 370)

Budgetary slack The amount by which a manager intentionally underestimates budgeted revenues or overestimates budgeted expenses in order to make it easier to achieve budgetary goals. (p. 372)

Budget committee A group responsible for coordinating the preparation of the budget. (p. 372)

Budgeted balance sheet A projection of the company's financial position at the end of the budget period. (p. 384)

Budgeted income statement An estimate of the expected profitability of operations for the budget period. (p. 380)

Cash budget A projection of expected cash flows. (p. 381)

Direct labour budget A projection of the quantity and cost of direct labour to be incurred to meet production requirements. (p. 377)

Direct materials budget An estimate of the quantity and cost of direct materials to be purchased. (p. 376)

Financial budgets Individual budgets that indicate the cash resources that are needed for expected operations and planned capital expenditures. (p. 374)

Long-range planning A formalized process of selecting strategies to achieve long-term goals and developing policies and plans to implement the strategies. (p. 373)

Manufacturing overhead budget An estimate of expected manufacturing overhead costs for the budget period. (p. 378)

Master budget A set of interrelated budgets that becomes a plan of action for a specific time period. (p. 373)

Merchandise purchases budget The estimated cost of goods to be purchased by a merchandiser to meet expected sales. (p. 386)

Operating budgets Individual budgets that result in a budgeted income statement. (p. 374)

Participative budgeting A budgetary approach that starts with input from lower-level managers and works upward so that managers at all levels participate. (p. 372)

Production budget A projection of the units that must be produced to meet expected sales. (p. 375)

Sales budget An estimate of expected sales for the budget period. (p. 375)

Sales forecast The projection of potential sales for the industry and the company's expected share of these sales. (p. 371)

Selling and administrative expenses budget A projection of expected selling and administrative expenses for the budget period. (p. 379)

Demonstration Problem

www.wiley.com/canada/managerial

Animated Demonstration Problem

Soroco Company is preparing its master budget for 2005. Relevant data for its sales and production budgets are as follows:

Sales: Sales for the year are expected to total 1.2 million units. Quarterly sales are expected to be 20%, 25%, 30%, and 25%, respectively, of the total sales. The sales price is expected to be $50 per unit for the first three quarters and $55 per unit beginning in the fourth quarter.

Sales in the first quarter of 2005 are expected to be 10% higher than the budgeted sales volume for the first quarter of 2004.

Production: Management wants to keep ending finished goods inventories at 25% of the next quarter's budgeted sales volume.

Instructions

Prepare the sales budget and production budget by quarters for 2005.

Action Plan

- Know the form and content of the sales budget.
- Prepare the sales budget first, as the basis for the other budgets.
- Determine the units that must be produced to meet expected sales.
- Know how to calculate the beginning and ending finished goods units.

Solution to Demonstration Problem

SOROCO COMPANY
Sales Budget
Year Ending December 31, 2005

	Quarter				
	1	2	3	4	Year
Expected unit sales	240,000	300,000	360,000	300,000	1,200,000
Unit selling price	× $50	× $50	× $50	× $55	—
	$12,000,000	$15,000,000	$18,000,000	$16,500,000	$61,500,000

SOROCO COMPANY
Production Budget
Year Ending December 31, 2005

	Quarter				
	1	2	3	4	Year
Expected unit sales	240,000	300,000	360,000	300,000	
Add: Desired ending finished goods units	75,000	90,000	75,000	66,000 [a]	
Total required units	315,000	390,000	435,000	366,000	
Less: Beginning finished goods units	60,000 [b]	75,000	90,000	75,000	
Units to be produced	255,000	315,000	345,000	291,000	1,206,000

[a] Estimated first-quarter 2005 sales volume, calculate as 240,000 + (240,000 × 10%) = 264,000; 264,000 × 25%
[b] 25% of estimated first-quarter 2004 sales units

the navigator

Self-Study Questions

Additional Self-Study Questions

Answers are at the end of the chapter.

(SO 1) 1. Which of the following is not a benefit of budgeting?
(a) Management can plan ahead.
(b) An early warning system is provided for potential problems.
(c) It makes it possible to take disciplinary action at every level of responsibility.
(d) The coordination of activities is made easier.

(SO 2) 2. The essentials of effective budgeting do not include:
(a) top-down budgeting.
(b) management acceptance.
(c) research and analysis.
(d) sound organizational structure.

(SO 2) 3. Compared to budgeting, long-range planning generally has:
(a) the same amount of detail.
(b) a longer time period.
(c) the same emphasis.
(d) the same time period.

(SO 3) 4. A sales budget is:
(a) derived from the production budget.
(b) management's best estimate of sales revenue for the year.
(c) not the starting point for the master budget.
(d) prepared only for credit sales.

(SO 3) 5. The formula for the production budget is budgeted sales in units plus:
(a) desired ending merchandise inventory less beginning merchandise inventory.
(b) beginning finished goods units less desired ending finished goods units.
(c) desired ending direct materials units less beginning direct materials units.
(d) desired ending finished goods units less beginning finished goods units.

(SO 3) 6. Direct materials inventories are accounted for in kilograms at Byrd Company, and the total kilograms of direct materials needed for production is 9,500. If the beginning inventory is 1,000 kilograms and the desired ending inventory is 2,200 kilograms, the total kilograms to be purchased is:
(a) 9,400.   (c) 9,700.
(b) 9,500.   (d) 10,700.

(SO 3) 7. The formula for calculating the direct labour cost budget is to multiply the direct labour cost per hour by the:
(a) total required direct labour hours.
(b) physical units to be produced.
(c) equivalent units to be produced.
(d) No correct answer is given.

(SO 4) 8. Which of the following budgets is not used in preparing the budgeted income statement?
(a) Sales budget
(b) Selling and administrative budget
(c) Capital expenditure budget
(d) Direct labour budget

(SO 5) 9. Expected direct materials purchases in Read Company are $70,000 in the first quarter and $90,000 in the second quarter. Forty percent of the purchases are paid in cash as incurred, and the rest is paid in the following quarter. The budgeted cash payments for purchases in the second quarter are:
(a) $96,000.   (c) $78,000.
(b) $90,000.   (d) $72,000.

(SO 6) 10. The budget for a merchandiser differs from a budget for a manufacturer because:
(a) a merchandise purchases budget replaces the production budget.
(b) the manufacturing budgets are not applicable.
(c) None of the above
(d) Both (a) and (b) above

the navigator

Questions

1. (a) What is a budget?
   (b) How does a budget contribute to good management?

2. Donna Cox and Tony Carpino are discussing the benefits of budgeting. Identify the main advantages of budgeting for them.

3. Kate Coulter asks for your help in understanding the essentials of effective budgeting. Identify the essentials for Kate.

4. (a) "Accounting plays a relatively unimportant role in budgeting." Do you agree? Explain.

(b) What responsibilities does management have in budgeting?

5. What criteria are helpful in determining the length of the budget period? What is the most common budget period?

6. Cherline Dassamé maintains that the only difference between budgeting and long-range planning is time. Do you agree? Why or why not?

7. What is participative budgeting? What are its potential benefits? What are its potential disadvantages?

8. What is budgetary slack? What incentive do managers have to create budgetary slack?

9. Distinguish between a master budget and a sales forecast.

10. Which budget is the starting point in preparing the master budget? What can happen if this budget is inaccurate?

11. "The production budget shows both unit production data and unit cost data." Is this true? Explain.

12. Alov Company has 10,000 beginning finished goods units. Budgeted sales in units are 160,000. If management wants 20,000 ending finished goods units, what are the required units of production?

13. In preparing the direct materials budget for Quan Company, management concludes that required purchases are 54,000 units. If 52,000 direct materials units are required in production and there are 7,000 units of beginning direct materials, what is the desired number of units of ending direct materials?

14. The production budget of Layden Company calls for 90,000 units to be produced. If it takes 30 minutes to make one unit and the direct labour rate is $16 per hour, what is the total budgeted direct labour cost?

15. Marrero Company's manufacturing overhead budget shows total variable costs of $168,000 and total fixed costs of $162,000. Total production in units is expected to be 160,000. It takes 15 minutes to make one unit, and the direct labour rate is $15 per hour. Express the manufacturing overhead rate as (a) a percentage of the direct labour cost, and (b) an amount per direct labour hour.

16. Ankiel Company's variable selling and administrative expenses are 10% of net sales. Fixed expenses are $60,000 per quarter. The sales budget shows expected sales of $200,000 and $250,000 in the first and second quarters, respectively. What are the total budgeted selling and administrative expenses for each quarter?

17. For Tomko Company, the budgeted cost for one unit of product is direct materials $10, direct labour $20, and manufacturing overhead 80% of the direct labour cost. If 25,000 units are expected to be sold at $69 each, what is the budgeted gross profit?

18. Indicate the supporting schedules that are used in preparing a budgeted income statement through gross profit for a manufacturer.

19. Identify the three sections of a cash budget. What balances are also shown in this budget?

20. Mufti Company has credit sales of $400,000 in January. Past experience suggests that 45% is collected in the month of sale, 50% in the month following the sale, and 4% in the second month following the sale. Calculate the cash collections in January, February, and March from January sales.

21. What is the formula for determining required merchandise purchases for a merchandiser?

22. How may expected revenues in a service enterprise be calculated?

Brief Exercises

Prepare diagram of master budget.
(SO 3)

BE9–1   Russo Manufacturing Company uses the following budgets: balance sheet, capital expenditures, cash, direct labour, direct materials, income statement, manufacturing overhead, production, sales, and selling and administrative expenses. Prepare a diagram that shows the relationships of the budgets in the master budget. Indicate whether each budget is an operating or a financial budget.

Prepare sales budget.
(SO 3)

BE9–2   Maltz Company estimates that unit sales will be 10,000 in quarter 1; 12,000 in quarter 2; 14,000 in quarter 3; and 18,000 in quarter 4. Using a sales price of $70 per unit, prepare the sales budget by quarters for the year ending December 31, 2005.

Prepare production budget for two quarters.
(SO 3)

BE9–3   Sales budget data for Maltz Company are given in BE9–2. Management wants to have an ending finished goods inventory equal to 25% of the next quarter's expected unit sales. Prepare a production budget by quarters for the first six months of 2005.

Prepare direct materials budget for one month.
(SO 3)

BE9–4   Gomez Company has 1,600 kilograms of raw materials in its December 31, 2005, ending inventory. Required production for January and February is 4,000 and 5,000 units, respectively. Two kilograms of raw materials are needed for each unit, and the estimated cost per kilogram is $6. Management wants an ending inventory equal to 20% of next month's materials requirements. Prepare the direct materials budget for January.

Prepare direct labour budget for two quarters.
(SO 3)

BE9–5   For Tracey Company, units to be produced are 5,000 in quarter 1 and 6,000 in quarter 2. It takes 1.8 hours to make a finished unit, and the expected hourly wage rate is $14. Prepare a direct labour budget by quarters for the six months ending June 30, 2005.

BE9-6 For Savage Inc., variable manufacturing overhead costs are expected to be $20,000 in the first quarter of 2005, with $2,000 increments in each of the remaining three quarters. Fixed overhead costs are estimated to be $35,000 in each quarter. Prepare the manufacturing overhead budget by quarters for the year.

Prepare manufacturing overhead budget.
(SO 3)

BE9-7 Rado Company classifies its selling and administrative expenses budget into variable and fixed components. Variable expenses are expected to be $25,000 in the first quarter, and $3,000 increments are expected in the remaining quarters of 2005. Fixed expenses are expected to be $40,000 in each quarter. Prepare the selling and administrative expenses budget by quarters for 2005.

Prepare selling and administrative expenses budget.
(SO 3)

BE9-8 Rajiv Company has completed all of its operating budgets. The sales budget for the year shows 50,000 units and total sales of $2 million. The total cost of making one unit of sales is $24. Selling and administrative expenses are expected to be $300,000. Income taxes are estimated to be $150,000. Prepare a budgeted income statement for the year ending December 31, 2005.

Prepare budgeted income statement for year.
(SO 4)

BE9-9 Chow Industries expects credit sales for January, February, and March to be $200,000, $260,000, and $310,000, respectively. It is expected that 70% of the sales will be collected in the month of sale, and 30% will be collected in the following month. Calculate the cash collections from customers for each month.

Prepare data for cash budget.
(SO 5)

BE9-10 Reebles Wholesalers is preparing its merchandise purchases budget. Budgeted sales are $400,000 for April and $450,000 for May. The cost of goods sold is expected to be 60% of sales. The company's desired ending inventory is 20% of the following month's cost of goods sold. Calculate the required purchases for April.

Determine required merchandise purchases for one month.
(SO 6)

Exercises

E9-1 Vosser Electronics Inc. produces and sells two models of pocket calculators, XQ-103 and XQ-104. The calculators sell for $12 and $25, respectively. Because of the intense competition Vosser faces, management budgets sales semi-annually. Its projections for the first two quarters of 2005 are as follows:

Prepare sales budget for two quarters.
(SO 3)

	Unit Sales	
Product	Quarter 1	Quarter 2
XQ-103	30,000	25,000
XQ-104	12,000	13,000

No changes in selling prices are expected.

Instructions

Prepare a sales budget for the two quarters ending June 30, 2005. For each quarter and for the six months, indicate the number of units, selling price, and total sales for each product and in total.

E9-2 Roche and Young, CAs, are preparing their service revenue (sales) budget for 2005. Their practice is divided into three departments: auditing, tax, and consulting. Billable hours for each department, by quarter, are as follows:

Prepare sales budget for four quarters.
(SO 3)

Department	Quarter 1	Quarter 2	Quarter 3	Quarter 4
Auditing	2,200	1,600	2,000	2,400
Tax	3,000	2,400	2,000	2,500
Consulting	1,500	1,500	1,500	1,500

Average hourly billing rates are $80 for auditing, $90 for tax, and $100 for consulting services.

Instructions

Prepare the service revenue (sales) budget for 2005 by listing the departments and showing for each quarter, and the year in total, the billable hours, billable rate, and total revenue.

Prepare quarterly production budgets.
(SO 3)

E9–3   Wayans Company produces and sells automobile batteries, including the heavy-duty HD-240. The 2005 sales budget is as follows:

Quarter	HD-240
1	5,000
2	7,000
3	8,000
4	10,000

The January 1, 2005, inventory of HD-240 is 2,000 units. Management wants an ending inventory each quarter that is equal to 40% of the next quarter's sales. Sales in the first quarter of 2006 are expected to be 30% higher than sales in the same quarter in 2005.

Instructions

Prepare quarterly production budgets for each quarter for 2005.

Prepare direct materials purchases budget.
(SO 3)

E9–4   Samano Industries has adopted the following production budget for the first four months of 2006:

Month	Units	Month	Units
January	10,000	March	5,000
February	8,000	April	4,000

Each unit requires five kilograms of raw materials costing $2.00 per kilogram. On December 31, 2005, the ending raw materials inventory was 15,000 kilograms. Management wants to have a raw materials inventory at the end of the month equal to 30% of the next month's production requirements.

Instructions

Prepare a direct materials purchases budget by months for the first quarter.

Prepare production and direct materials budgets by quarters for six months.
(SO 3)

E9–5   On January 1, 2006, the Chinlee Company budget committee reached agreement on the following data for the six months ending June 30, 2006:

1. Sales units: First quarter 5,000; second quarter 8,000; third quarter 7,000
2. Ending raw materials inventory: 50% of the next quarter's production requirements
3. Ending finished goods inventory: 30% of the next quarter's expected sales units
4. Third-quarter production: 7,250 units

The ending raw materials and finished goods inventories at December 31, 2005, had the same percentages for production and sales that are budgeted for 2006. Three kilograms of raw materials are needed to make each unit of finished goods. Raw materials purchased are expected to cost $4 per kilogram.

Instructions

(a) Prepare a production budget by quarters for the six-month period ended June 30, 2006.
(b) Prepare a direct materials budget by quarters for the six-month period ended June 30, 2006.

Prepare direct labour budget.
(SO 3)

E9–6   Pacer, Inc. is preparing its direct labour budget for 2005 from the following production budget for a full calendar year:

Quarter	Units	Quarter	Units
1	20,000	3	35,000
2	25,000	4	30,000

Each unit requires 1.2 hours of direct labour.

Instructions

Prepare a direct labour budget for 2005. Wage rates are expected to be $15 for the first two quarters and $16 for the remaining two quarters.

Prepare manufacturing overhead budget for year.
(SO 3)

E9–7   Keyser Company is preparing its manufacturing overhead budget for 2005. Relevant data follow:

1. Units to be produced (by quarters): 10,000, 12,000, 14,000, 16,000
2. Direct labour: 1.5 hours per unit

3. Variable overhead costs per direct labour hour: indirect materials $0.70; indirect labour $1.20; and maintenance $0.30
4. Fixed overhead costs per quarter: supervisory salaries $35,000; amortization $16,000; and maintenance $12,000

Instructions

Prepare the manufacturing overhead budget for the year, showing quarterly data.

E9–8 Lockwood Company combines its operating expenses for budget purposes in a selling and administrative expenses budget. For the first six months of 2005, the following data are available:

1. Sales: 20,000 units in quarter 1; 24,000 units in quarter 2
2. Variable costs per dollar of sales: sales commissions 5%; delivery expense 2%; and advertising 3%
3. Fixed costs per quarter: sales salaries $10,000; office salaries $6,000; amortization $4,200; insurance $1,500; utilities $800; and repairs expense $600
4. Unit selling price: $20.

Prepare selling and administrative expenses budget for two quarters. (SO 3)

Instructions

Prepare a selling and administrative expenses budget by quarters for the first six months of 2005.

E9–9 Haven Company has accumulated the following budget data for the year 2005:

1. Sales: 40,000 units; unit selling price $80
2. Cost of one unit of finished goods: direct materials, two kilograms at $5 per kilogram; direct labour, three hours at $12 per hour; and manufacturing overhead, $6 per direct labour hour
3. Inventories (raw materials only): beginning, 10,000 kilograms; ending, 15,000 kilograms
4. Raw materials cost: $5 per kilogram
5. Selling and administrative expenses: $200,000
6. Income taxes: 30% of income before income taxes

Prepare budgeted income statement for year. (SO 3, 4)

Instructions

(a) Prepare a schedule showing the calculation of the cost of goods sold for 2005.
(b) Prepare a budgeted income statement for 2005.

E9–10 Nunez Company expects to have a cash balance of $46,000 on January 1, 2005. Relevant monthly budget data for the first two months of 2005 are as follows:

1. Collections from customers: January $75,000; February $150,000
2. Payments to suppliers: January $45,000; February $70,000
3. Direct labour: January $30,000; February $45,000. Wages are paid in the month they are incurred.
4. Manufacturing overhead: January $21,000; February $30,000. These costs include amortization of $1,000 per month. All other overhead costs are paid as incurred.
5. Selling and administrative expenses: January $15,000; February $20,000. These costs are exclusive of amortization. They are paid as incurred.
6. Sales of marketable securities in January are expected to realize $10,000 in cash.

Prepare cash budget for two months. (SO 5)

Nunez Company has a line of credit at a local bank. It can borrow up to $25,000. The company wants to keep a minimum monthly cash balance of $20,000.

Instructions

Prepare a cash budget for January and February.

E9–11 Environmental Landscaping Inc. is preparing its budget for the first quarter of 2005. The next step in the budgeting process is to prepare a cash receipts schedule and a cash payments schedule. The following information has been collected:

1. Clients usually pay 60% of their fee in the month when the service is provided, 30% the next month, and 10% in the second month after receiving the service.
2. Actual service revenue for 2004 and expected service revenues for 2005 are as follows: November 2004, $90,000; December 2004, $80,000; January 2005, $100,000; February 2005, $120,000; March 2005, $130,000.

Prepare schedules for cash receipts and cash payments, and determine ending balances for balance sheet. (SO 5, 6)

3. Purchases of landscaping supplies (direct materials) are paid 40% in the month of purchase and 60% the following month. Actual purchases for 2004 and expected purchases for 2005 are as follows: December 2004, $14,000; January 2005, $12,000; February 2005, $15,000; March 2005, $18,000.

Instructions

(a) Prepare the following schedules for each month in the first quarter of 2005 and for the quarter in total: (1) expected collections from clients, and (2) expected payments for landscaping supplies.
(b) Determine the following balances at March 31, 2005: (1) accounts receivable, and (2) accounts payable.

Prepare cash budget for two quarters.
(SO 5, 6)

E9–12   Pisani Dental Clinic is a medium-sized dental service specializing in family dental care. The clinic is currently preparing the budget for the first two quarters of 2005. Only the cash budget still needs to be done. The following information has been collected from parts of the master budget and elsewhere:

Beginning cash balance	$ 30,000
Required minimum cash balance	25,000
Payment of income taxes (2nd quarter)	4,000
Professional salaries:	
1st quarter	140,000
2nd quarter	140,000
Interest from investments (2nd quarter)	5,000
Overhead costs:	
1st quarter	75,000
2nd quarter	100,000
Selling and administrative costs, including	
$3,000 of amortization:	
1st quarter	50,000
2nd quarter	70,000
Purchase of equipment (2nd quarter)	50,000
Sale of equipment (1st quarter)	15,000
Collections from clients:	
1st quarter	230,000
2nd quarter	380,000
Interest on repayments (2nd quarter)	300

Instructions

Prepare a cash budget for each of the first two quarters of 2005.

Prepare purchases budget and budgeted income statement for merchandiser.
(SO 4, 6)

E9–13   In May 2005, the budget committee of Big Jim Stores assembles the following data for preparing the merchandise purchases budget for the month of June:

1. Expected sales: June $550,000; July $600,000.
2. Cost of goods sold is expected to be 70% of sales.
3. Desired ending merchandise inventory is 40% of the following month's cost of goods sold.
4. The beginning inventory at June 1 will be the desired amount.

Instructions

(a) Calculate the budgeted merchandise purchases for June.
(b) Prepare the budgeted income statement for June through gross profit on sales.

Problems: Set A

Prepare budgeted income statement and supporting budgets.
(SO 3, 4)

P9–14A   Tilger Farm Supply Company manufactures and sells a fertilizer called Basic II. The following data are available for preparing budgets for Basic II for the first two quarters of 2005:

1. Sales: quarter 1, 40,000 bags; quarter 2, 55,000 bags. The selling price is $60 per bag.

2. Direct materials: Each bag of Basic II requires six kilograms of Crup at a cost of $3 per kilogram and 10 kilograms of Dert at $1.50 per kilogram.

3. Desired inventory levels:

Type of Inventory	January 1	April 1	July 1
Basic II (bags)	10,000	15,000	20,000
Crup (kilograms)	9,000	12,000	15,000
Dert (kilograms)	15,000	20,000	25,000

4. Direct labour: Direct labour time is 15 minutes per bag at an hourly rate of $12 per hour.

5. Selling and administrative expenses are expected to be 10% of sales plus $150,000 per quarter.

6. Income taxes are expected to be 30% of the income from operations.

Your assistant has prepared two budgets: (1) The manufacturing overhead budget shows the expected costs to be 100% of the direct labour cost. (2) The direct materials budget for Dert shows the expected cost of Dert to be $682,500 in quarter 1 and $907,500 in quarter 2.

Instructions

Prepare the budgeted income statement for the first six months of 2005 and all required supporting budgets by quarters. (*Note*: Use the classifications variable and fixed in the selling and administrative expenses budget.)

P9–15A   Greish Inc. is preparing its annual budgets for the year ending December 31, 2005. Accounting assistants provide the following data:

Prepare sales, production, direct materials, direct labour, and income statement budgets.
(SO 3, 4)

	Product LN 35	Product LN 40
Sales budget:		
Expected volume in units	350,000	180,000
Unit selling price	$20.00	$30.00
Production budget:		
Desired ending finished goods units	30,000	25,000
Beginning finished goods units	20,000	15,000
Direct materials budget:		
Direct materials per unit (kilograms)	2	3
Desired kilograms of ending direct materials	50,000	20,000
Beginning kilograms of direct materials	40,000	10,000
Cost per kilogram	$2.00	$3.00
Direct labour budget:		
Direct labour time per unit (hours)	0.5	0.75
Direct labour rate per hour	$10.00	$10.00
Budgeted income statement:		
Total unit cost	$10.00	$20.00

An accounting assistant has prepared the detailed manufacturing overhead budget and the selling and administrative expenses budget. The latter shows selling expenses of $560,000 for product LN 35 and $440,000 for product LN 40, and administrative expenses of $420,000 for product LN 35 and $380,000 for product LN 40. Income taxes are expected to be 30%.

Instructions

Prepare the following budgets for the year. Show data for each product. Quarterly budgets should not be prepared.

(a) Sales
(b) Production
(c) Direct materials

(d) Direct labour
(e) Income statement (*Note*: Income taxes are not allocated to the products.)

P9–16A   Choo-Foo Company makes and sells artistic frames for pictures. The controller is responsible for preparing the master budget and has accumulated the following information for 2005:

Prepare production and direct labour budgets.
(SO 3)

	January	February	March	April	May
Estimated unit sales	10,000	12,000	8,000	9,000	9,000
Sales price per unit	$50.00	$47.50	$47.50	$47.50	$47.50
Direct labour hours per unit	2.0	2.0	1.5	1.5	1.5
Wage per direct labour hour	$8.00	$8.00	$8.00	$9.00	$9.00

Choo-Foo has a labour contract that calls for a wage increase to $9.00 per hour on April 1. New labour-saving machinery has been installed and will be fully operational by March 1.

Choo-Foo expects to begin the year with 16,000 frames on hand and has a policy of carrying an end-of-month inventory of 100% of the following month's sales plus 50% of the second following month's sales.

Instructions

(a) Prepare a production budget and a direct labour budget for Choo-Foo Company by month and for the first quarter of the year. The direct labour budget should include direct labour hours and show the detail for each direct labour cost category.
(b) For each item used in Choo-Foo's production budget and its direct labour budget, identify the other component(s) of the master budget (budget package) that would also use these data.

(CMA Canada-adapted)

Prepare sales and production budgets and calculate per unit costs under two plans.
(SO 3, 4)

P9–17A Hirsch Industries has sales in 2005 of $5,250,000 (750,000 units) and gross profit of $1,587,500. Management is considering two alternative budget plans to increase gross profit in 2006.

Plan A would increase the selling price per unit from $7.00 to $7.60. The sales volume would decrease by 10% from its 2005 level. Plan B would decrease the selling price per unit by 5%. The marketing department expects that the sales volume would increase by 100,000 units.

At the end of 2005, Hirsch has 75,000 units on hand. If plan A is accepted, the 2006 ending inventory should be equal to 90,000 units. If plan B is accepted, the ending inventory should be equal to 100,000 units. Each unit produced will cost $2.00 in direct materials, $1.50 in direct labour, and $0.50 in variable overhead. The fixed overhead for 2006 should be $965,000.

Instructions

(a) Prepare a sales budget for 2006 under each plan.
(b) Prepare a production budget for 2006 under each plan.
(c) Calculate the cost per unit under each plan. Explain why the cost per unit is different for each of the two plans. (Round to two decimals.)
(d) Which plan should be accepted? (*Hint*: Calculate the gross profit under each plan.)

Calculate cash disbursements for one month.
(SO 3, 5)

P9–18A Lyon Factory Ltd. manufactures two products: chairs and stools. Each chair requires three metres of upholstery and four kilograms of steel. Each stool requires two metres of upholstery and five kilograms of steel. Upholstery costs $2 per metre and steel costs $0.25 per kilogram.

Inventories at January 1, 2005, are expected to be as follows:

Chairs	Stools	Upholstery	Steel
25 units	15 units	75 metres	150 kilograms

Inventories of raw materials should not be allowed to fall below the amounts given as at January 1, 2005. Inventories of finished furniture at the beginning of each month should be enough to cover 25% of the anticipated sales for that month. Upholstery is ordered in units of 100 metres and steel in units of 50 kilograms.

Half of the materials purchased are paid for in the month of purchase and the other half in the following month.

The sales budget for the first three months of the year 2005 is:

	January	February	March
Chairs	100 units	120 units	80 units
Stool	60 units	80 units	60 units

Instructions

Calculate the cash disbursements in February for purchases of steel. Show all your supporting calculations.

(CGA-adapted)

P9–19A Lorch Company prepares monthly cash budgets. Relevant data from operating budgets for 2006 follow:

Prepare cash budget for two months.
(SO 3, 5)

	January	February
Sales	$360,000	$400,000
Direct materials purchases	100,000	110,000
Direct labour	100,000	115,000
Manufacturing overhead	60,000	75,000
Selling and administrative expenses	75,000	80,000

All sales are on account. Collections are expected to be 60% in the month of sale, 30% in the first month following the sale, and 10% in the second month following the sale. Thirty percent of direct materials purchases are paid in cash in the month of purchase, and the balance due is paid in the month following the purchase. All other items above are paid in the month incurred. Amortization is not included in the manufacturing overhead and selling and administrative expenses.

Other data follow:

1. Credit sales: November 2005, $200,000; December 2005, $280,000
2. Purchases of direct materials: December 2005, $90,000
3. Other receipts: January—collection of December 31, 2005, interest receivable $3,000; February—proceeds from sale of securities $5,000
4. Other disbursements: February—payment of $20,000 for land

The company's cash balance on January 1, 2006, is expected to be $60,000. The company wants to maintain a minimum cash balance of $50,000.

Instructions

(a) Prepare schedules for (1) the expected collections from customers and (2) the expected payments for direct materials purchases.
(b) Prepare a cash budget for January and February using columns for each month.

P9–20A The controller of Harrington Company wants to improve the company's control system by preparing a month-by-month cash budget. The following information is for the month ending July 31, 2005:

Prepare cash budget for a month.
(SO 5)

June 30, 2005 cash balance	$45,000
Dividends to be declared on July 15[a]	12,000
Cash expenditures to be paid in July for operating expenses	36,800
Amortization expense in July	4,500
Cash collections to be received in July	89,000
Merchandise purchases to be paid in cash in July	56,200
Equipment to be purchased for cash in July	20,500

[a] Dividends are payable 30 days after declaration to shareholders of record on the declaration date.

Harrington Company wants to keep a minimum cash balance of $25,000.

Instructions

(a) Prepare a cash budget for the month ended July 31, 2005, and indicate how much money, if any, Harrington Company will need to borrow to meet its minimum cash requirement.
(b) Explain how cash budgeting can reduce the cost of short-term borrowing.

(CGA-adapted)

P9–21A The budget committee of Ridder Company collects the following data for its Westwood Store in preparing budgeted income statements for July and August 2005:

Prepare purchases and income statement budgets for merchandiser.
(SO 3, 4, 6)

1. Expected sales: July $400,000; August $450,000; September $500,000.
2. Cost of goods sold is expected to be 60% of sales.
3. Company policy is to maintain ending merchandise inventory at 25% of the following month's cost of goods sold.

4. Operating expenses are estimated as follows:

Sales salaries	$30,000 per month
Advertising	4% of monthly sales
Delivery expense	2% of monthly sales
Sales commissions	3% of monthly sales
Rent expense	$3,000 per month
Amortization	$700 per month
Utilities	$500 per month
Insurance	$300 per month

5. Income taxes are estimated to be 30% of the income from operations.

Instructions

(a) Prepare the merchandise purchases budget, using columns for each month.
(b) Prepare budgeted income statements, using columns for each month. Show details for the cost of goods sold in the statements.

Prepare raw materials purchase budget in dollars.
(SO 3, 5)

P9–22A   Kirkland Ltd. estimates sales for the second quarter of 2005 will be as follows:

April	2,550 units
May	2,475 units
June	2,390 units

The target ending inventory of finished products is as follows:

March 31	2,000
April 30	2,230
May 31	2,190
June 30	2,310

Two units of material are required for each unit of finished product. Production for July is estimated at 2,700 units to start building inventory for the fall sales period. Kirkland's policy is to have an inventory of raw materials at the end of each month equal to 60% of the following month's production requirements.

Raw materials are expected to cost $4 per unit throughout the period.

Instructions

Calculate the May raw materials purchases in dollars.

(CGA-adapted)

P9-23A Kurian Industries' balance sheet at December 31, 2005, follows.

Prepare budgeted income statement and balance sheet.
(SO 3, 4, 5)

KURIAN INDUSTRIES
Balance Sheet
December 31, 2005

Assets

Current assets		
Cash		$ 7,500
Accounts receivable		82,500
Finished goods inventory (2,000 units)		30,000
Total current assets		120,000
Property, plant, and equipment		
Equipment	$40,000	
Less: Accumulated amortization	10,000	30,000
Total assets		$150,000

Liabilities and Shareholders' Equity

Liabilities		
Notes payable		$ 25,000
Accounts payable		45,000
Total liabilities		70,000
Shareholders' equity		
Common shares	$50,000	
Retained earnings	30,000	
Total shareholders' equity		80,000
Total liabilities and shareholders' equity		$150,000

Budgeted data for the year 2006 include the following.

	Q4 of 2006	Year 2006 Total
Sales budget (8,000 units at $30)	$70,000	$240,000
Direct materials used	17,000	69,400
Direct labour	8,500	38,600
Manufacturing overhead applied	10,000	54,000
Selling and administrative expenses	18,000	76,000

To meet sales requirements and to have 3,000 units of finished goods on hand at December 31, 2006, the production budget shows 9,000 required units of output. The total unit cost of production is expected to be $18. Kurian Industries uses the first-in, first-out (FIFO) inventory costing method. Selling and administrative expenses include $4,000 for amortization on equipment. Interest expense is expected to be $3,500 for the year. Income taxes are expected to be 30% of the income before income taxes.

All sales and purchases are on account. It is expected that 60% of the quarterly sales are collected in cash within the quarter and the remainder is collected in the following quarter. Direct materials purchased from suppliers are paid 50% in the quarter incurred and the remainder in the following quarter. Purchases in the fourth quarter were the same as the materials used. In 2006, the company expects to purchase additional equipment costing $14,000. It expects to pay $8,000 on notes payable plus all interest due and payable to December 31 (included in the interest expense of $3,500, above). Accounts payable at December 31, 2006, include amounts due to suppliers (see above) plus other accounts payable of $10,700. In 2006, the company expects to declare and pay a $5,000 cash dividend. Unpaid income taxes at December 31 will be $5,000. The company's cash budget shows an expected cash balance of $9,950 at December 31, 2006.

Instructions

Prepare a budgeted income statement for 2006 and a budgeted balance sheet at December 31, 2006. In preparing the income statement, you will need to calculate the cost of goods manufactured (materials + labour + overhead) and finished goods inventory (December 31, 2006).

Problems: Set B

Prepare budgeted income statement and supporting budgets.
(SO 3, 4)

P9–24B   Wahlen Farm Supply Company manufactures and sells a pesticide called Snare. The following data are for preparing budgets for Snare for the first two quarters of 2006:

1. Sales: quarter 1, 28,000 bags: quarter 2, 40,000 bags. Selling price is $60 per bag.
2. Direct materials: Each bag of Snare requires four kilograms of Gumm at a cost of $3 per kilogram and six kilograms of Tarr at $1.50 per kilogram.
3. Desired inventory levels:

Type of Inventory	January 1	April 1	July 1
Snare (bags)	8,000	12,000	18,000
Gumm (kilograms)	9,000	10,000	13,000
Tarr (kilograms)	14,000	20,000	25,000

4. Direct labour: Direct labour time is 15 minutes per bag at an hourly rate of $14.
5. Selling and administrative expenses are expected to be 15% of sales plus $175,000 per quarter.
6. Income taxes are expected to be 30% of the income from operations.

Your assistant has prepared two budgets: (1) The manufacturing overhead budget shows expected costs to be 150% of the direct labour cost. (2) The direct materials budget for Tarr shows the cost of Tarr to be $297,000 in quarter 1 and $421,500 in quarter 2.

Instructions

Prepare the budgeted income statement for the first six months and all required supporting budgets by quarters. (*Note:* Use the categories variable and fixed in the selling and administrative expenses budget.)

Prepare sales, production, direct materials, direct labour, and income statement budgets.
(SO 3, 4)

P9–25B   Quinn Inc. is preparing its annual budgets for the year ending December 31, 2006. Accounting assistants provide the following data:

	Product JB 50	Product JB 60
Sales budget:		
Anticipated volume in units	450,000	200,000
Unit selling price	$20.00	$25.00
Production budget:		
Desired ending finished goods units	25,000	15,000
Beginning finished goods units	30,000	10,000
Direct materials budget:		
Direct materials per unit (kilograms)	2	3
Desired kilograms of ending direct materials	30,000	15,000
Beginning kilograms of direct materials	40,000	10,000
Cost per kilogram	$3.00	$4.00
Direct labour budget:		
Direct labour time per unit (hours)	0.4	0.6
Direct labour rate per hour	$10.00	$10.00
Budgeted income statement:		
Total unit cost	$12.00	$20.00

An accounting assistant has prepared the detailed manufacturing overhead budget and the selling and administrative expenses budget. The latter shows selling expenses of $660,000 for product JB 50 and $360,000 for product JB 60, and administrative expenses of $540,000 for product JB 50 and $340,000 for product JB 60. Income taxes are expected to be 30%.

Instructions

Prepare the following budgets for the year. Show data for each product. Quarterly budgets should not be prepared.

(a) Sales
(b) Production
(c) Direct materials

(d) Direct labour
(e) Income statement (*Note:* Income taxes are not allocated to the products.)

P9–26B Tick Industries had sales in 2005 of $6 million and gross profit of $1.5 million. Management is considering two alternative budget plans to increase its gross profit in 2006.

Plan A would increase the selling price per unit from $8.00 to $8.40. The sales volume would decrease by 5% from its 2005 level. Plan B would decrease the selling price per unit by $0.50. The marketing department expects that the sales volume would increase by 150,000 units.

At the end of 2005, Tick has 30,000 units of inventory on hand. If plan A is accepted, the 2006 ending inventory should be equal to 4% of the 2006 sales. If plan B is accepted, the ending inventory should be equal to 40,000 units. Each unit produced will cost $1.80 in direct labour, $2.00 in direct materials, and $1.20 in variable overhead. The fixed overhead for 2006 should be $1.8 million.

Prepare sales and production budgets and calculate cost per unit under two plans. (SO 3, 4)

Instructions

(a) Prepare a sales budget for 2006 under each plan.
(b) Prepare a production budget for 2006 under each plan.
(c) Calculate the production cost per unit under each plan. Why is the cost per unit different for each of the two plans? (Round to two decimals.)
(d) Which plan should be accepted? (*Hint*: Calculate the gross profit under each plan.)

P9–27B The following data are for the operations of the Zoë's Fashion Footwear Ltd., a retail store:

Prepare merchandise purchases budget and income statement budget. (SO 3, 4, 6)

1. Sales Forecast—2005	April	$ 70,000
	May	60,000
	June	80,000
	July	100,000
	August	120,000

2. The cost of sales is 40% of sales. Other variable costs are 20% of sales.
3. Inventory is maintained at twice the budgeted sales requirements for the following month.
4. Fixed costs are $20,000 per month.
5. The income tax rate is estimated to be 40%.

Instructions

(a) Prepare a merchandise purchases budget in dollars for June 2005.
(b) Prepare a budgeted income statement for June 2005.

(CGA-adapted)

P9–28B The Big Boy Company is in a seasonal business and prepares quarterly budgets. Its fiscal year runs from July 1 through June 30. Production occurs only in the first quarter (July to September), but sales take place throughout the year. The sales forecast for the coming year shows the following:

Prepare cash budget for a year. (SO 5)

First quarter	$390,000
Second quarter	750,000
Third quarter	390,000
Fourth quarter	390,000

There are no cash sales, and the beginning balance of receivables is expected to be collected in the first quarter. Subsequent collections are two-thirds in the quarter when sales take place and one-third in the following quarter.

Material purchases valued at $360,000 are made in the first quarter and none are made in the last three quarters. Payment is made when the materials are purchased.

Direct labour of $350,000 is incurred and paid only in the first quarter. Factory overhead of $430,000 is also incurred and paid in the first quarter. Factory overhead is at a standby level of $100,000 during the other three quarters. Selling and administrative expenses of $50,000 are paid each quarter throughout the year. Big Boy has an operating line of credit with its bank at an interest rate of 6% per annum. The company plans to keep a cash balance at least $8,000 at all times, and it will borrow and repay in multiples of $5,000. All borrowings are made at the beginning of a quarter, and all payments are made at the end of a quarter. Interest is paid only on the portion of the loan that is repaid in a quarter.

The company plans to purchase equipment in the second and fourth quarters for $150,000 and $50,000, respectively. The cash balance on July 1 is $23,000 and accounts receivable total $130,000.

Instructions

Prepare a cash budget for the year. Show receipts, disbursements, the ending cash balance before borrowing, the amounts borrowed and repaid, interest payments, and the ending cash balance.

(CMA Canada-adapted)

P9–29B　Nigh Company prepares monthly cash budgets. Relevant data from operating budgets for 2006 follow:

	January	February
Sales	$350,000	$400,000
Direct materials purchases	120,000	130,000
Direct labour	80,000	100,000
Manufacturing overhead	70,000	75,000
Selling and administrative expenses	79,000	81,000

All sales are on account. Collections are expected to be 50% in the month of sale, 30% in the first month following the sale, and 20% in the second month following the sale. Sixty percent of direct materials purchases are paid in cash in the month of purchase, and the balance due is paid in the month following the purchase. All other items above are paid in the month incurred, except for selling and administrative expenses, which include $1,000 of amortization per month.

　　Other data:

1. Credit sales: November 2005, $260,000; December 2005, $300,000
2. Purchases of direct materials: December 2005, $100,000
3. Other receipts: January—collection of December 31, 2005, notes receivable, $15,000; February—proceeds from sale of securities, $6,000
4. Other disbursements: February—withdrawal of $5,000 cash for personal use of owner, Dewey Yaeger

The company's cash balance on January 1, 2006, is expected to be $60,000. The company wants to keep a minimum cash balance of $50,000.

Instructions

(a) Prepare schedules for (1) the expected collections from customers and (2) the expected payments for direct materials purchases.
(b) Prepare a cash budget for January and February, with columns for each month.

P9–30B　Raymond Co. began operations in January 2004. The information below is for Raymond Co.'s operations for the three months from January to March (the first quarter) of 2005:

Expenses for Quarter 1	
Amortization	$40,000
Factory overhead	10,000
Income taxes	15,000
Payroll	30,000
Selling costs (2% commision on sales)	8,000
Administrative costs	10,000

Costs are assumed to be incurred evenly throughout the year, with the exception of amortization and income taxes. Amortization on new assets is first taken in the quarter after the quarter in which they are purchased. Income taxes are payable in semi-annual instalments, on the first day of each six-month period, based on last year's actual taxes of $30,000.

　　Other information:

1. Sales (made evenly throughout the quarter):

Quarter 1	(actual)	$400,000
Quarter 2	(forecast)	400,000
Quarter 3	(forecast)	800,000

Collections from sales are as follows: 50% in the quarter of sale; 45% in the following quarter; 5% uncollectible.

2. Purchases (made evenly throughout the quarter):

Quarter 1   (actual) $200,000

The gross margin ratio is constant at 60%.

Cash payments for purchases are as follows: 50% in the quarter of purchase; 50% in the following quarter. Merchandise purchased during a quarter would include 25% of the next quarter's forecasted sales.

3. The company purchased capital equipment for $100,000 in February 2004. The estimated useful life of this equipment is 10 years; it has no estimated scrap value.

4. Dividends of $20,000 are declared on the last day of each quarter, and are paid at the end of the next month.

5. The cash balance in the bank at the end of the first quarter is $25,000.

Instructions

(a) Prepare a cash budget for Raymond Co. for the second quarter of 2005. Show all your supporting calculations.

(b) List three advantages of budgeting.

(CGA-adapted)

P9–31B The budget committee of Wild Things Company collects the following data for its Hamilton store in preparing budgeted income statements for May and June 2006:

Prepare purchases budget and budgeted income statement.
(SO 3, 4, 6)

1. Sales for May are expected to be $600,000. Sales in June and July are expected to be 10% higher than the preceding month.

2. The cost of goods sold is expected to be 75% of sales.

3. Company policy is to maintain ending merchandise inventory at 20% of the following month's cost of goods sold.

4. Operating expenses are estimated as follows:

Sales salaries	$30,000 per month
Advertising	5% of monthly sales
Delivery expense	3% of monthly sales
Sales commissions	4% of monthly sales
Rent expense	$5,000 per month
Amortization	$800 per month
Utilities	$600 per month
Insurance	$500 per month

5. Income taxes are estimated to be 30% of the income from operations.

Instructions

(a) Prepare the merchandise purchases budget, using columns for each month.

(b) Prepare budgeted income statements, using columns for each month. Show details in the statements for the cost of goods sold.

P9–32B Vergados Brothers is trying to estimate the amount of inventory it needs to purchase next month (April). The controller likes to have twice the number of units he expects to sell on hand at the beginning of the month. He always takes the 3/10, net 30 purchase discount on the inventory purchases. Inventory costs $10 per unit. Actual sales for January and February, and the forecast sales for March to June are as follows:

Calculate purchases and disbursements for merchandiser.
(SO 3, 5, 6)

	Units
January	11,000
February	10,000
March	13,000
April	14,000
May	15,000
June	13,000

Cash payments for purchases are as follows: two-thirds in the month of purchase; one-third in the next month. The selling price is $20 per unit, and sales occur evenly throughout the month.

Instructions

(a) Calculate the number of units to be purchased in April.
(b) Calculate the amount of cash that Vergados Brothers will disburse in April for purchases.

(CGA-adapted)

Additional Cases

Cases

C9–33   Peters Corporation operates on a calendar-year basis. It begins the annual budgeting process in late August when the president sets targets for the total dollar sales and net income before taxes for the next year.

The sales target is given first to the marketing department. The marketing manager creates a sales budget for each product line in both units and dollars. From this budget, sales quotas by product line in units and dollars are determined for each of the corporation's sales districts. The marketing manager also estimates the cost of the marketing activities that will be needed to support the target sales volume, and he prepares a tentative marketing expense budget.

The executive vice-president uses the sales and profit targets, the sales budget by product line, and the tentative marketing expense budget to determine the dollar amounts that can be used for manufacturing and corporate office expenses. The executive vice-president prepares the budget for corporate expenses. She then forwards to the production department the product-line sales budget in units and the total dollar amount that can be used for manufacturing.

The production manager meets with the factory managers to develop a manufacturing plan that will produce the required units when they are needed, and within the cost set by the executive vice-president. The budgeting process usually comes to a halt at this point because the production department does not believe that it has been given enough financial resources.

When this standstill occurs, the vice-president of finance, the executive vice-president, the marketing manager, and the production manager meet to determine the final budgets for each of the areas. This normally results in a modest increase in the total amount that is available for manufacturing costs, and cuts are made to the marketing expense and corporate office expense budgets. The total sales and net income figures proposed by the president are almost never changed. Although the participants are usually unhappy about the compromise, these budgets are final. Each executive then develops a new detailed budget for the operations in his or her area.

None of the areas has achieved its budget in recent years. Sales often run below the target. When budgeted sales are not achieved, each area is expected to cut costs so that the president's profit target can be met. However, the profit target is almost never met because costs are not cut enough. In fact, costs often run above the original budget in all functional areas (marketing, production, and corporate office).

The president is disturbed that Peters Corporation has not been able to meet its sales and profit targets. He therefore hired a consultant with considerable experience with companies in Peters' industry. The consultant reviewed the budgets for the past four years. He concluded that the product-line sales budgets were reasonable and that the cost and expense budgets were enough for the budgeted sales and production levels.

Instructions

(a) Discuss how the budgeting process used by Peters Corporation makes failing to achieve the president's sales and profit targets more likely.
(b) Suggest how Peters Corporation's budgeting process could be revised to correct the problems.
(c) Should the functional areas be expected to cut their costs when the sales volume falls below budget forecast? Explain your answer.

(CMA-adapted)

C9–34   Howe Ltd. is trying to decide whether it is going to need to take a loan in January to buy a new microcomputer system. The microcomputer will cost $10,800.

The President, Joan Howe, has collected the following information about her operations as at December 31:

1. Balances of selected general ledger accounts:

Cash	$2,120
Accounts payable	6,667

2. Sales history and forecast (unit selling price, $10):

October	(actual)	$43,000
November	(actual)	35,000
December	(actual)	40,000
January	(forecast)	50,000

3. All sales are on credit and are due 30 days after the sale.
4. Cash payments for purchases are as follows: two-thirds in the month of purchase; one-third in the month after that.
5. Fifty percent of a month's sales are collected one month after the sale; 45% are collected two months after the sale; and 5% are uncollectible.
6. Inventory is purchased as required under terms of 2/10, net 30. Howe Ltd. always takes the 2% discount, but records purchases at gross cost. Accounts payable (shown above) relate solely to inventory purchases. Inventory costs $5 per unit, gross.
7. Other expenses, all paid in cash as required, average about 30% of the sales dollar amount. Amortization is part of these expenses and costs $3,000 per month.
8. Howe Ltd. keeps a minimum cash balance of $1,000.

Instructions

Prepare a cash budget for January, indicating whether Howe Ltd. will need a loan to finance its computer acquisition.

(CGA-adapted)

C9–35 Solid State sells electronic products. The controller is responsible for preparing the master budget and has accumulated the information below for the months of January, February, and March.

Balances at January 1 are expected to be as follows:

Cash	$ 5,500
Accounts receivable	416,100
Inventories	309,400
Accounts payable	133,055

The budget is to be based on the following assumptions:

1. Each month's sales are billed on the last day of the month.
2. Customers are allowed a 3% discount if their payment is made within 10 days after the billing date. Receivables are booked at gross.
3. Sixty percent of the billings are collected within the discount period; 25% are collected by the end of the month after the date of sale; 9% are collected by the end of the second month after the date of sale; and 6% prove uncollectible.
4. Fifty-four percent of all purchases of material and the selling, general, and administrative expenses are paid in the month purchased. The remainder is paid in the following month. Each month's units of ending inventory are equal to 130% of the next month's units of sales.
5. The cost of each unit of inventory is $20.
6. Selling, general, and administrative expenses, of which $2,000 is for amortization, are equal to 15% of the current month's sales.
7. Actual and projected sales are as follows:

Month	Sales	Units
November	354,000	11,800
December	363,000	12,100
January	357,000	11,900
February	342,000	11,400
March	360,000	12,000
April	366,000	12,200

Instructions

(a) What are the budgeted cash disbursements during the month of February?
(b) What are the budgeted cash collections during the month of January?
(c) What is the budgeted number of units of inventory to be purchased during the month of March?

(CMA-adapted)

C9–36 Sports Fanatic is a retail sporting goods store that uses accrual accounting for its records. Facts on Sports Fanatic's operations are as follows:

1. Sales are budgeted at $220,000 for January and $200,000 for February.
2. Collections are expected to be 60% in the month of sale and 38% in the month following the sale. Two percent of sales are expected to be uncollectible.
3. Gross margin is 25% of sales.
4. A total of 80% of the merchandise for resale is purchased in the month before the month of sale and 20% is purchased in the month of sale. Payments for merchandise are made in the month after it is purchased.
5. Other expected monthly expenses to be paid in cash amount to $22,600.
6. Annual amortization is $216,000.
7. Sports Fanatic's balance sheet at the close of business on December 31 follows:

SPORTS FANATIC CO.
Balance Sheet
December 31

Assets

Cash	$ 22,000
Accounts receivable (net of $4,000 allowance for uncollectible accounts)	76,000
Inventory	132,000
Property, plant, and equipment (net of $680,000 of accumulated amortization)	870,000
Total assets	$1,100,000

Liabilities and Shareholders' Equity

Accounts payable	$ 162,000
Common shares	800,000
Retained earnings	138,000
Total liabilities and shareholders' equity	$1,100,000

Instructions

Prepare the pro forma balance sheet and income statement for January.

(CMA Canada-adapted)

C9–37 Prasad & Green Inc. manufactures ergonomic devices for computer users. Some of its more popular products include glare screens (for computer monitors), keyboard stands with wrist rests, and carousels that allow easy access to CDs. Over the past five years, it has experienced rapid growth, with sales of all products increasing 20% to 50% each year.

Last year, some of the big manufacturers of computers also began introducing new products with ergonomic designs, such as glare screens and wrist rests, already built in. As a result, sales of Prasad & Green's accessory devices have dropped a bit. The company believes that the CD carousels will probably continue to show growth, but that the other products will probably continue to decline. When the next year's budget was prepared, increases were given to research and development so that replacement products could be developed or the company could expand into some other product line. Some product lines being considered are general-purpose ergonomic devices, including back supports, foot rests, and sloped writing pads.

The most recent results have shown that sales of the glare screens decreased more than was expected. As a result, the company may have a shortage of funds. Top management has therefore asked that all expenses be reduced by 10% to compensate for these reduced sales. Summary budget information is as follows:

Raw materials	$240,000
Direct labour	110,000
Insurance	50,000
Amortization	90,000
Machine repairs	30,000
Sales salaries	50,000
Office salaries	80,000
Factory salaries (indirect labour)	50,000
Total	$700,000

Instructions

(a) What are the implications of reducing each of the costs? For example, if the company reduces its raw materials costs, it may have to do this by purchasing lower-quality materials. This may affect sales in the long run.

(b) Based on your analysis in (a), what do you think is the best way to obtain the $70,000 in cost savings that top management wants? Be specific. Are there any costs that cannot or should not be reduced? Why?

C9–38 Électronique Instruments, a rapidly expanding electronic parts distributor, is formulating its plans for 2005. John Kedrowski, the firm's director of marketing, has completed his 2005 forecast and is confident that sales estimates will be met or exceeded. The following sales figures show the growth that is expected and are the basis for planning in the other corporate departments:

Month	Forecast Sales	Month	Forecast Sales
January	$1,800,000	July	$3,000,000
February	2,000,000	August	3,000,000
March	1,800,000	September	3,200,000
April	2,200,000	October	3,200,000
May	2,500,000	November	3,000,000
June	2,800,000	December	3,400,000

Samantha Carlson, assistant controller, is responsible for the cash flow projection, a critical element during a period of rapid expansion. She will use the following information in preparing her cash analysis:

1. Électronique has experienced an excellent record in accounts receivable collection and expects this trend to continue. Sixty percent of billings are collected in the month after the sale and 40% in the second month after the sale. Uncollectible accounts are nominal and can be ignored in the analysis.

2. The purchase of electronic parts is Électronique's largest expenditure; the cost of these items is equal to 50% of sales. Sixty percent of the parts are received by Électronique one month before they are sold and 40% are received during the month of sale.

3. Historically, 80% of the accounts payable have been cleared by Électronique one month after it receives its purchases, and the remaining 20% two months after.

4. Hourly wages, including fringe benefits, depend on the sales volume: they are equal to 20% of the current month's sales. These wages are paid in the month incurred.

5. General and administrative expenses are projected to be $2,640,000 for 2005. The composition of these expenses is given below. All of these expenses are incurred uniformly throughout the year, except for property taxes. The property taxes are paid in four equal instalments in the last month of each quarter:

Salaries	$ 480,000
Promotion	660,000
Property taxes	240,000
Insurance	360,000
Utilities	300,000
Amortization	600,000
	$2,640,000

6. Income tax payments are made by Électronique in the first month of each quarter based on income for the prior quarter. Électronique pays a 40% income tax rate. Électronique's net income for the first quarter of 2005 is projected to be $612,000.

7. Électronique has a corporate policy of maintaining an end-of-month cash balance of $100,000. Cash is invested or borrowed monthly, as necessary, to maintain this balance.

8. Électronique uses a calendar-year reporting period.

Instructions

Prepare a pro forma Schedule of Cash Receipts and Disbursements for Électronique Instruments, by month, for the second quarter of 2005. Be sure that all receipts, disbursements, borrowing, and investing amounts are presented on a monthly basis. Ignore the interest expense and income from borrowing and investing.

(CMA Canada-adapted)

C9–39   You are an accountant in the budgetary, projections, and special projects department of Cross Canada, Inc., a large manufacturing company. The president, Brian Doonan, asks you on very short notice to prepare some sales and income projections covering the next two years of the company's much-heralded new product lines. He wants these projections for a series of speeches he is making while on a two-week trip to eight brokerage firms. The president hopes to increase Cross Canada's share sales and price.

You work 23 hours in two days to do the projections and hand deliver them to the president. You are swiftly but graciously thanked as he departs. A week later, you find time to go over some of your calculations and discover a miscalculation that makes the projections grossly overstated. You quickly inquire about the president's itinerary and learn that he has made half of his speeches. You don't know what to do.

Instructions

(a) What are the consequences of telling the president of your gross miscalculation?
(b) What are the consequences of not telling the president of your gross miscalculation?
(c) What are the ethical considerations for you and the president in this situation?

Answers to Self-Study Questions

1. c   2. a   3. b   4. b   5. d   6. d   7. a   8. c   9. c   10. d

Remember to go back to the Navigator Box at the beginning of the chapter to check off your completed work.

CHAPTER 10

Budgetary Control and Responsibility Accounting

Riding High in the Energy Sector

Budgets are critical to an organization's success. To be useful, they must be accurate. In volatile industries like oil and gas, making accurate budgets can be a challenge as prices fluctuate and companies try to keep up with supply and demand.

When setting its budget, Calgary-based Petro-Canada combines outside information with internal expertise to arrive at estimates of future oil and gas prices, explains Craig Chunta, manager of business planning. These estimates are put into a business-planning model, as are production forecasts and estimated royalties and operating costs. The result is profit and loss forecasts.

While it makes its budget annually, Petro-Canada updates its forecasts twice a year or as needed. A change in the industry, such as a significant drop in prices, would trigger a change in forecasts. The company has little control over current prices, which are based on world or market prices rather than set by the company itself.

The company also tests different price scenarios, or "sensitivities," speculating on the impact of a $1 price fluctuation in either direction. "As a result, we are constantly aware of what a change in commodity prices will do to our earnings and ability to finance our spending plans," Mr. Chunta says.

"You pay a lot more attention to that sensitivity when your cash flows are critical," adds Kevin Collins, Petro-Canada's assistant controller, upstream sector, indicating this has not been the case for some time.

Petro-Canada has enjoyed an increasing demand for both crude oil and natural gas over the past few years. This demand—combined with the falling natural gas supply in North America and the political instability in the Middle East that is affecting the worldwide oil supply—has pushed prices up.

Still, the company cannot assume this will continue. "In any commodity market, there's a cycle," Mr. Collins says. "Right now we're riding the high end, and we know that." Instead of using current prices, Petro-Canada's five-year plan looks at longer-term pricing trends.

The company has many investments in multi-year, billion-dollar projects, such as Hibernia, Terra Nova, and White Rose off the East Coast. These capital expenditure commitments require the company to be prudent with its budget estimates. "Budgeting and planning is very critical," says Mr. Collins. "It's the primary control element in an energy company."

the navigator

Petro-Canada: www.petrocanada.ca

THE NAVIGATOR

- [ ] Scan *Study Objectives*
- [ ] Read *Feature Story*
- [ ] Read *Chapter Preview*
- [ ] Read text and answer *Before You Go On* p. 425, p. 432, p. 436
- [ ] Work *Using the Decision Toolkit*
- [ ] Review *Summary of Study Objectives*
- [ ] Review *Using the Decision Toolkit—A Summary*
- [ ] Work *Demonstration Problem*
- [ ] Answer *Self-Study Questions*
- [ ] Complete assignments

STUDY OBJECTIVES

After studying this chapter, you should be able to:

1. Describe the concept of budgetary control.
2. Evaluate the usefulness of static budget reports.
3. Explain the development of flexible budgets and the usefulness of flexible budget reports.
4. Describe the concept of responsibility accounting.
5. Indicate the features of responsibility reports for cost centres.
6. Identify the content of responsibility reports for profit centres.
7. Explain the basis and formula that are used for evaluating performance in investment centres.
8. Explain the difference between ROI and residual income (Appendix 10A).

In Chapter 9, we saw how budgets are developed. It is now the time to see how budgets are used by management to control operations. In the feature story on Petro-Canada, we saw that budgeting must consider factors that management cannot control. This chapter focuses on two aspects of management control: (1) budgetary control and (2) responsibility accounting.

The chapter is organized as follows:

BUDGETARY CONTROL AND RESPONSIBILITY ACCOUNTING

Concept of Budgetary Control	Static Budget Reports	Flexible Budgets	Concept of Responsibility Accounting	Types of Responsibility Centres
	▶ Illustrations ▶ Use and limitations	▶ Why flexible budgets? ▶ Developing the flexible budget ▶ Case study ▶ Flexible budget reports ▶ Management by exception	▶ Controllable versus noncontrollable revenues and costs ▶ Responsibility reporting system	▶ Cost centres ▶ Profit centres ▶ Investment centres ▶ Principles of performance evaluation

the navigator

The Concept of Budgetary Control

study objective 1

Describe the concept of budgetary control.

One of management's major functions is to control company operations. Control consists of the steps that management takes to be sure that planned objectives are met. We will now look at how budgets are used to control operations.

The use of budgets in controlling operations is known as **budgetary control**. This control is achieved by using **budget reports** to compare actual results with planned objectives. Budget reports are used because planned objectives often lose much of their potential value if progress is not monitored along the way. Just as your professors give mid-term exams to evaluate your progress, so top management requires periodic reports on the progress of department managers toward their planned objectives.

Budget reports give management feedback on operations. The feedback for a crucial objective, such as having enough cash on hand to pay bills, may be made daily. For other objectives, such as meeting budgeted annual sales and operating expenses, monthly budget reports may be enough. Budget reports can be prepared as frequently as they are needed. From these reports, management analyzes any differences between actual and planned results and determines their causes. Management may then take corrective action, or it may decide to modify future plans.

Budgetary control involves the activities shown in Illustration 10-1.

Illustration 10-1 ▶

Budgetary control

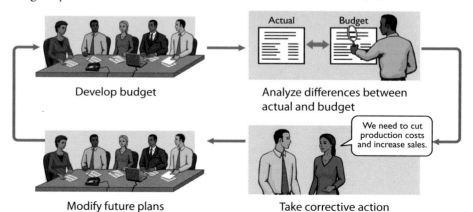

Develop budget

Analyze differences between actual and budget

We need to cut production costs and increase sales.

Modify future plans

Take corrective action

Budgetary control works best when a company has a formalized reporting system. The system should do the following: (1) identify the name of the budget report, such as the sales budget or the manufacturing overhead budget; (2) state the frequency of the report, such as weekly or monthly; (3) specify the purpose of the report; and (4) indicate who the primary recipient(s) of the report are. Illustration 10-2 presents a partial budgetary control system for a manufacturing company. Note the frequency of the reports and their emphasis on control. For example, there is a daily report on scrap and a weekly report on labour.

Illustration 10-2 ▼

Budgetary control

Name of Report	Frequency	Purpose	Primary Recipient(s)
Sales	Weekly	Determine whether sales goals are being met	Top management and sales manager
Labour	Weekly	Control direct and indirect labour costs	Vice-president of production and production department managers
Scrap	Daily	Determine efficient use of materials	Production manager
Departmental overhead costs	Monthly	Control overhead costs	Department manager
Selling expenses	Monthly	Control selling expenses	Sales manager
Income statement	Monthly and quarterly	Determine whether income objectives are being met	Top management

Static Budget Reports

You learned in Chapter 9 that the master budget formalizes management's planned objectives for the coming year. When it is used in budgetary control, each budget in the master budget is viewed as being static. A **static budget** is a projection of budget data **at one level of activity**. Data for different levels of activity are not considered. As a result, actual results are always compared with budget data at the activity level that was used in developing the master budget.

study objective 2

Evaluate the usefulness of static budget reports.

Illustrations

To illustrate the role of a static budget in budgetary control, we will use selected data that were prepared for Hayes Company in Chapter 9. Budget and actual sales data for the Kitchen-mate product in the first and second quarters of 2005 are given in Illustration 10-3.

Illustration 10-3 ◄

Budget and actual sales data

Sales	First Quarter	Second Quarter	Total
Budgeted	$180,000	$210,000	$390,000
Actual	179,000	199,500	378,500
Difference	$ 1,000	$ 10,500	$ 11,500

Illustration 10-4 presents the sales budget report for Hayes Company's first quarter. The right most column reports the difference between the budgeted and actual amounts.

Illustration 10-4 ◄

Sales budget report—first quarter

HAYES COMPANY
Sales Budget Report
Quarter Ended March 31, 2005

Product Line	Budget	Actual	Difference: Favourable (F)/ Unfavourable (U)
Kitchen-mate[a]	$180,000	$179,000	$1,000 U

[a] In practice, each product line would be included in the report.

Alternative Terminology
The difference between budgeted numbers and actual results is sometimes called a budget variance.

Illustration 10-5 ▼

Sales budget report—second quarter

The report shows that sales are $1,000 under budget—an unfavourable result. This difference is less than one percent of the budgeted sales ($1,000 ÷ $180,000 = 56%). Top management's reaction to unfavourable differences is often influenced by the materiality (significance) of the difference. Since the difference of $1,000 is immaterial in this case, we will assume that Hayes Company's management takes no specific corrective action.

The budget report for the second quarter is presented in Illustration 10-5. It has one new feature: cumulative, year-to-date information. This report indicates that sales for the second quarter were $10,500 below budget. This is five percent of budgeted sales ($10,500 ÷ $210,000). Top management may now conclude that the difference between budgeted and actual sales requires investigation.

	HAYES COMPANY **Sales Budget Report** **Quarter Ended June 30, 2005**					
	Second Quarter			Year-to-Date		
Product Line	Budget	Actual	Difference: Favourable (F)/ Unfavourable (U)	Budget	Actual	Difference: Favourable (F)/ Unfavourable (U)
Kitchen-mate	$210,000	$199,500	$10,500 U	$390,000	$378,500	$11,500 U

Management's analysis should start by asking the sales manager the cause(s) of the shortfall. The need for corrective action should be considered. For example, management may decide to help sales by offering sales incentives to customers or by increasing the advertising of Kitchen-mates. Or, if management concludes that a downturn in the economy is responsible for the lower sales, it may modify its planned sales and profit goals for the remainder of the year.

Uses and Limitations

From these examples, you can see that a master sales budget is useful in evaluating the performance of a sales manager. We can now ask if the master budget is appropriate for evaluating a manager's performance in controlling costs. Recall that in a static budget, data are not modified or adjusted, even if there are changes in activity. It follows, then, that a static budget is appropriate in evaluating how well a manager controls costs when (1) the actual activity level is close to the master budget activity level, and/or (2) the costs respond to changes in activity in a fixed way.

A static budget report is, therefore, appropriate for **fixed manufacturing costs** and for **fixed selling and administrative expenses**. But, as you will see shortly, static budget reports may not be a proper basis for evaluating a manager's performance in controlling variable costs.

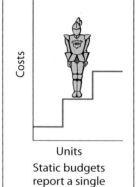

Static budgets report a single level of activity.

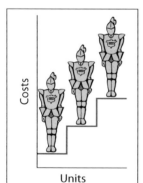

Flexible budgets are static budgets at different levels of activity.

Flexible Budgets

In contrast to a static budget, which is based on one level of activity, a **flexible budget** projects budget data for various levels of activity. **The flexible budget is basically a series of static budgets at different levels of activity.** The flexible budget recognizes that the budgetary process is more useful if it can be adapted to changed operating conditions.

Flexible budgets can be prepared for each of the types of budgets included in the master budget. For example, Choice Hotels Canada can budget revenues and net income on the basis of 60-percent, 80-percent, and 100-percent room occupancy. Similarly, Yanke Expedited Services can budget its operating expenses based on different levels of truck distances driven. Likewise, in the feature story, Petro-Canada can budget revenue and net income based on estimated revenues and expenses from five core businesses: North American Gas, East Coast Oil, Oil Sands, International, and Refining and Marketing. In the following pages, we will illustrate a flexible budget for manufacturing overhead.

Why Flexible Budgets?

Assume that you are the manager in charge of manufacturing overhead in the forging department of Barton Steel. In preparing the manufacturing overhead budget for 2005, you prepare the static budget in Illustration 10-6 based on a production volume of 10,000 units of steel ingots.

study objective 3

Explain the development of flexible budgets and the usefulness of flexible budget reports.

BARTON STEEL
Manufacturing Overhead Budget (static)
Forging Department
Year Ended December 31, 2005

Budgeted production in units (steel ingots)	<u>10,000</u>
Budgeted costs	
Indirect materials	$ 250,000
Indirect labour	260,000
Utilities	190,000
Amortization	280,000
Property taxes	70,000
Supervision	<u>50,000</u>
	<u>$1,100,000</u>

Illustration 10-6 ◄

Static overhead budget

Helpful Hint The static budget is the master budget of Chapter 9.

Fortunately for the company, the demand for steel ingots has increased, and 12,000 units are produced and sold during the year, rather than 10,000. You are elated: increased sales mean increased profitability, which should mean a bonus or a raise for you and the employees in your department. Unfortunately, a comparison of the forging department's actual and budgeted costs has complicated matters for you. The budget report is shown in Illustration 10-7.

Helpful Hint Which of the following is not likely to help much when costs are variable—the static budget or the flexible budget? Answer: The static budget.

BARTON STEEL
Manufacturing Overhead Budget Report (static)
Forging Department
Year Ended December 31, 2005

	Budget	Actual	Difference: Favourable (F)/ Unfavourable (U)
Production in units	<u>10,000</u>	<u>12,000</u>	
Costs			
Indirect materials	$ 250,000	$ 295,000	$ 45,000 U
Indirect labour	260,000	312,000	52,000 U
Utilities	190,000	225,000	35,000 U
Amortization	280,000	280,000	0
Property taxes	70,000	70,000	0
Supervision	<u>50,000</u>	<u>50,000</u>	<u>0</u>
	<u>$1,100,000</u>	<u>$1,232,000</u>	<u>$132,000</u> U

Illustration 10-7 ◄

Static overhead budget report

This comparison uses budget data based on the original activity level (10,000 steel ingots). It indicates that the forging department is significantly **over budget** for three of the six overhead costs. And, there is a total unfavourable difference of $132,000, which is 12 percent over budget ($132,000 ÷ $1,100,000). Your supervisor is very unhappy! Instead of sharing in the company's success, you may find yourself looking for another job. What went wrong?

When you calm down and carefully examine the manufacturing overhead budget, you identify the problem: The budget data are not relevant! At the time the budget was developed, the company anticipated that only 10,000 units of steel ingots would be produced, **not** 12,000

Helpful Hint A static budget will not work if a company has a large amount of variable costs.

ingots. Comparing actual with budgeted variable costs is meaningless. As production increases, the budget allowances for variable costs should increase both directly and proportionately. The variable costs in this example are indirect materials, indirect labour, and utilities.

Analyzing the budget data for these costs at 10,000 units, you arrive at the per unit results in Illustration 10-8.

Illustration 10-8 ▶

Variable costs per unit

Item	Total Cost	Per Unit
Indirect materials	$250,000	$25
Indirect labour	260,000	26
Utilities	190,000	19
	$700,000	$70

Illustration 10-9 shows how you can then calculate the budgeted variable costs at 12,000 units.

Illustration 10-9 ▶

Budgeted variable costs—12,000 units

Item	Calculation	Total
Indirect materials	$25 × 12,000	$300,000
Indirect labour	26 × 12,000	312,000
Utilities	19 × 12,000	228,000
		$840,000

Because fixed costs do not change in total as activity changes, the budgeted amounts for these costs remain the same. The budget report based on the flexible budget for **12,000 units** of production is shown in Illustration 10-10. (Compare this with Illustration 10-7.)

Illustration 10-10 ▶

Variable costs per unit

BARTON STEEL
Manufacturing Overhead Budget Report (flexible)
Forging Department
Year Ended December 31, 2005

	Budget	Actual	Difference: Favourable (F)/ Unfavourable (U)
Production in units	12,000	12,000	
Variable costs			
Indirect materials	$ 300,000	$ 295,000	$5,000 F
Indirect labour	312,000	312,000	0
Utilities	228,000	225,000	3,000 F
Total variable costs	840,000	832,000	8,000 F
Fixed costs			
Amortization	280,000	280,000	0
Property taxes	70,000	70,000	0
Supervision	50,000	50,000	0
Total	400,000	400,000	0
Total costs	$1,240,000	$1,232,000	$8,000 F

This report indicates that the forging department is below budget—a favourable difference. Instead of worrying about being fired, you may be in line for a bonus or a raise after all! As this analysis shows, the only appropriate comparison is between actual costs at 12,000 units of production and budgeted costs at 12,000 units. Flexible budget reports provide this comparison.

Developing the Flexible Budget

The flexible budget uses the master budget as its basis. To develop the flexible budget, management should take the following steps:

1. Identify the activity index and the relevant range of activity.
2. Identify the variable costs, and determine the budgeted variable cost per unit of activity for each cost.
3. Identify the fixed costs, and determine the budgeted amount for each cost.
4. Prepare the budget for selected increments of activity within the relevant range.

The activity index that is chosen should be something that significantly influences the costs that are being budgeted. For manufacturing overhead costs, for example, the activity index is usually the same as the index used in developing the predetermined overhead rate—that is, direct labour hours or machine hours. For selling and administrative expenses, the activity index is usually sales or net sales.

The choice of the increment of activity is largely a matter of judgment. For example, if the relevant range is 8,000 to 12,000 direct labour hours, increments of 1,000 hours may be selected. The flexible budget is then prepared for each increment within the relevant range.

Decision Toolkit

Decision Checkpoints	Info Needed for Decision	Tools to Use for Decision	How to Evaluate Results
Are the increased costs that result from increased production reasonable?	Variable costs projected at different levels of production	Flexible budget	After considering different production levels, results are favourable if expenses are less than the budgeted amounts.

Flexible Budget—A Case Study

To illustrate the flexible budget, we will use Fox Manufacturing Company. Fox's management wants to use a **flexible budget for monthly comparisons** of its finishing department's actual and budgeted manufacturing overhead costs. The master budget for the year ending December 31, 2005, shows an expected annual operating capacity of 120,000 direct labour hours and the overhead costs in Illustration 10-11.

Illustration 10-11 ◀

Master budget data

Variable Costs		Fixed Costs	
Indirect materials	$180,000	Amortization	$180,000
Indirect labour	240,000	Supervision	120,000
Utilities	60,000	Property taxes	60,000
Total	$480,000	Total	$360,000

The four steps for developing the flexible budget are applied as follows:

STEP 1: **Identify the activity index and the relevant range of activity.** The activity index is direct labour hours. Management concludes that the relevant range is 8,000 to 12,000 direct labour hours per month.

STEP 2: **Identify the variable costs, and determine the budgeted variable cost per unit of activity for each cost.** There are three variable costs. The variable cost per unit is found by dividing each total budgeted cost by the direct labour hours that are used in preparing the master budget (120,000 hours). For Fox Manufacturing, the calculations are as in Illustration 10-12:

Illustration 10-12 ▶

Calculation of variable costs per direct labour hour

Variable Cost	Calculation	Variable Cost per Direct Labour Hour
Indirect materials	$180,000 ÷ 120,000	$1.50
Indirect labour	$240,000 ÷ 120,000	2.00
Utilities	$ 60,000 ÷ 120,000	0.50
Total		$4.00

STEP 3: **Identify the fixed costs, and determine the budgeted amount for each cost.** There are three fixed costs. Since Fox wants **monthly budget** data, the budgeted amount is found by dividing each annual budgeted cost by 12. For Fox, the monthly budgeted fixed costs are amortization $15,000, supervision $10,000, and property taxes $5,000.

STEP 4: **Prepare the budget for selected increments of activity within the relevant range.** Management decides to prepare the budget in increments of 1,000 direct labour hours.

Illustration 10-13 shows the resulting flexible budget.

Illustration 10-13 ▶

Flexible monthly overhead budget

FOX MANUFACTURING COMPANY
Flexible Monthly Manufacturing Overhead Budget
Finishing Department
For the Year 2005

Activity level					
Direct labour hours	8,000	9,000	10,000	11,000	12,000
Variable costs					
Indirect materials	$12,000	$13,500	$15,000	$16,500	$18,000
Indirect labour	16,000	18,000	20,000	22,000	24,000
Utilities	4,000	4,500	5,000	5,500	6,000
Total variable costs	32,000	36,000	40,000	44,000	48,000
Fixed costs					
Amortization	15,000	15,000	15,000	15,000	15,000
Supervision	10,000	10,000	10,000	10,000	10,000
Property taxes	5,000	5,000	5,000	5,000	5,000
Total fixed costs	30,000	30,000	30,000	30,000	30,000
Total costs	$62,000	$66,000	$70,000	$74,000	$78,000

Using the budget data, the formula in Illustration 10-14 may be used to determine the total budgeted costs at any level of activity.

Illustration 10-14 ▶

Formula for total budgeted costs

Fixed Costs + Variable Cost [a] = Total Budgeted Costs

[a] Total variable cost per unit times the activity level

Helpful Hint Using the data given for the Fox Manufacturing Company, what amount of total costs would be budgeted for 10,600 direct labour hours?
Answer:

Fixed	$30,000
Variable (10,600 × $4)	42,400
Total	$72,400

For Fox Manufacturing, fixed costs are $30,000, and the total variable cost per unit is $4. Thus, at 9,000 direct labor hours, the total budgeted costs are $66,000 [$30,000 + ($4 × 9,000)]. Similarly, at 8,622 direct labour hours, the total budgeted costs are $64,488 [$30,000 + ($4 × 8,622)].

The total budgeted costs can also be shown graphically, as in Illustration 10-15. In the graph, the activity index is shown on the horizontal axis, and costs are indicated on the vertical axis. The graph highlights two activity levels (10,000 and 12,000). As shown, total budgeted costs at these activity levels are $70,000 [$30,000 + ($4 × 10,000)] and $78,000 [$30,000 + ($4 × 12,000)], respectively.

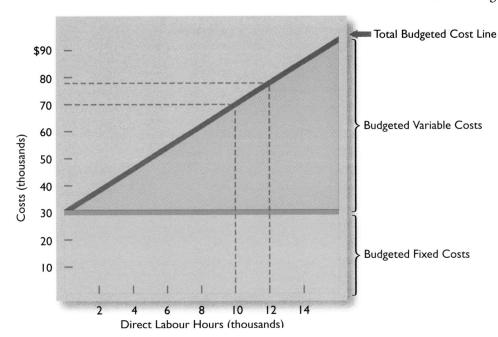

Flexible Budget Reports

Flexible budget reports are another type of internal report. The flexible budget report has two sections: (1) production data for a selected activity index, such as direct labour hours, and (2) cost data for variable and fixed costs. The report provides a basis for evaluating a manager's performance in two areas: production control and cost control. Flexible budget reports are widely used in production and service departments.

A budget report for the finishing department of Fox Company for the month of January is shown in Illustration 10-16. In this month, 9,000 hours were worked. The budget data are therefore based on the flexible budget for 9,000 hours in Illustration 10-13. The actual cost data are assumed.

How appropriate is this report for evaluating the finishing department manager's performance in controlling overhead costs? The report clearly provides a reliable basis. Both the actual and the budget costs are based on the activity level worked during January. Since variable costs are generally incurred directly by the department, the difference between the costs budgeted for those hours and the actual costs is the responsibility of the department manager.

Helpful Hint An assembly department is a production department, and a maintenance department is a service department, as explained on page 429.

Illustration 10-16 ▶

Flexible overhead budget report

FOX MANUFACTURING COMPANY
Flexible Manufacturing Overhead Budget Report
Finishing Department
Month Ended January 31, 2005

	Budget	Actual	Difference: Favourable (F)/ Unfavourable (U)
Direct labour hours	9,000	9,000	
Variable costs			
Indirect materials	$13,500	$14,000	$ 500 U
Indirect labour	18,000	17,000	1,000 F
Utilities	4,500	4,600	100 U
Total variable costs	36,000	35,600	400 F
Fixed costs			
Amortization	15,000	15,000	0
Supervision	10,000	10,000	0
Property taxes	5,000	5,000	0
Total fixed costs	30,000	30,000	0
Total costs	$66,000	$65,600	$ 400 F

Helpful Hint Note that this flexible budget is based on a single cost driver. By using the activity-based costing concepts explained in Chapter 4, a more accurate budget can often be developed.

In subsequent months, other flexible budget reports will be prepared. For each month, the budget data are based on the actual activity level that was reached. In February, that level may be 11,000 direct labour hours, in July it may be 10,000, and so on.

Management by Exception

Management by exception means that top management's review of a budget report is focused either entirely or mostly on differences between actual results and planned objectives. This approach helps top management focus on problem areas. Management by exception does not mean that top management will investigate every difference. For this approach to be effective, there must be guidelines for identifying an exception. The usual criteria are materiality and controllability, as explained next.

Materiality

Without quantitative guidelines, management would have to investigate every budget difference no matter how small it was. Materiality is usually expressed as a percentage difference from the budget. For example, management may set the percentage difference at 5 percent for important items and 10 percent for other items. All differences that are over or under budget by at least the specified percentage will be investigated. Costs that are over budget should be investigated to determine why they were not controlled. Likewise, costs that are under budget should be investigated to determine whether costs that are critical to profitability are being cut too much. For example, if maintenance costs are budgeted at $80,000 but only $40,000 is spent, there could be major, unexpected breakdowns in production facilities in the future.

Alternatively, a company may specify a single percentage difference from budget for all items and add a minimum dollar limit as well. For example, the exception criterion may be stated at 5 percent of budget or more than $10,000.

Controllability of the Item

Exception guidelines are usually more for controllable items than for items that the manager connot control. In fact, there may be no guidelines for noncontrollable items. For example, a large unfavourable difference between the actual and budgeted property tax expense may not be flagged for investigation because the only possible cause is an unexpected increase in the tax rate or in the assessed value of the property. An investigation into the difference will be useless: the manager cannot control the cause.

BEFORE YOU GO ON . . .

► Review It

1. What is the meaning of budgetary control?
2. When is a static budget appropriate for evaluating a manager's effectiveness in controlling costs?
3. What is a flexible budget?
4. How is a flexible budget developed?
5. What criteria are used in management by exception?

► Do It

Your roommate asks for your help in understanding how total budgeted costs are calculated at any level of activity. Calculate the total budgeted costs at 30,000 direct labour hours, assuming that in the flexible budget graph, the fixed cost line and the total budgeted cost line intersect the vertical axis at $36,000 and that the total budget cost line is $186,000 at an activity level of 50,000 direct labour hours.

Action Plan

- Apply the formula: fixed costs + variable costs (total variable costs per unit × activity level) = total budgeted costs.

Solution

Using the graph, fixed costs are $36,000, and variable costs are $3 per direct labour hour [($186,000 − $36,000) ÷ 50,000]. Thus, at 30,000 direct labour hours, the total budgeted costs are $126,000 [$36,000 + ($3 × 30,000)].

Related exercise material: BE10-3, BE10-4, BE10-5, E10-1, E10-2, E10-3, E10-4, E10-5, and E10-6.

the navigator

The Concept of Responsibility Accounting

Like budgeting, responsibility accounting is an important part of management accounting. **Responsibility accounting** involves accumulating and reporting costs (and revenues, where relevant) that involve the manager who has the authority to make the day-to-day decisions about the cost items. Under responsibility accounting, a manager's performance is evaluated based on matters that are directly under that manager's control. Responsibility accounting can be used at every level of management where the following conditions exist:

1. Costs and revenues can be directly associated with the specific level of management responsibility.
2. The costs and revenues are controllable at the level of responsibility that they are associated with.
3. Budget data can be developed for evaluating the manager's effectiveness in controlling the costs and revenues.

Levels of responsibility for controlling costs are shown in Illustration 10-17.

study objective 4

Describe the concept of responsibility accounting.

Illustration 10-17 ◄

Responsibility for controllable costs at varying levels of management

Helpful Hint All companies use responsibility accounting. Without some form of responsibility accounting, there would be chaos in management's control function.

Under responsibility accounting, any individual who has control and is accountable for a specified set of activities can be recognized as a responsibility centre. Thus, responsibility accounting may extend from the lowest level of control to the top layers of management. Once responsibility has been established, the effectiveness of an individual's performance is first measured and reported for the specified activity. It is then reported upward throughout the organization.

Responsibility accounting is especially valuable in a decentralized company. **Decentralization** means that the control of operations is given to many managers throughout the organization. The term **segment** is sometimes used to identify an area of responsibility in decentralized operations. Under responsibility accounting, segment reports are prepared periodically, such as monthly, quarterly, and annually, to evaluate a manager's performance.

Responsibility accounting is an essential part of any effective system of budgetary control. The reporting of costs and revenues under responsibility accounting differs from budgeting in two ways:

1. A distinction is made between controllable and noncontrollable items.
2. Performance reports either emphasize or include only the items that can be controlled by the individual manager.

Responsibility accounting is used in both profit and not-for-profit entities. The former try to maximize net income. The latter want to minimize the cost of providing services.

BUSINESS INSIGHT ▶ Service Company Perspective

In 2001, SR Telecom Inc., a Montreal-based manufacturer of broadband fixed wireless networks seemed doomed to the fate of many high-tech companies at that time. It was spending too much and carrying a huge debt load. However, the company soon turned its fortunes around by streamlining its operations and using the market turmoil to cheaply acquire assets that broadened its product portfolio. The company was basically a one-product operation providing wireless connections to carry data to rural and remote regions, mainly in developing nations, where the installation of copper or fibre cable was too costly. But, with the growth of the Internet, demand for broadband access increased and wireless technologies had advanced, providing SR Telecom with new opportunities.

In order to grow, though, the company needed to improve its operations. Its production cycle was too slow, and it was making too much equipment before orders even came in. The company was stockpiling large inventories, while its accounts receivable were too high. As the inventories were gradually worked off, contracts with suppliers of components and raw materials were renegotiated to get just-in-time delivery. Production began only on orders that could be shipped out once they were finished. This reduced working inventory on the production floor at any one time to $1.5 million, from approximately $10 million, and cut the company's 10-week production cycle down to three weeks. These significant improvements were the result of employee teams that renewed their efforts to control costs at every level.

Source: Andrew Wahl, "Out of the Wilderness," *Canadian Business*, May 26, 2003.

Controllable versus Noncontrollable Revenues and Costs

In all costs and revenues can be controlled at some level of responsibility in a company. This truth emphasizes the adage used by the CEO of any organization that "the buck stops here." Under responsibility accounting, the critical issue is whether or not the cost or revenue can be controlled at the level of responsibility that it is associated with.

A cost is considered to be **controllable** at a particular level of managerial responsibility if the manager has the power to incur it in a specific period of time. From this criterion, the following can be concluded:

1. All costs are controllable by top management because of its broad range of authority.
2. Fewer costs are controllable as one moves down to each lower level of managerial responsibility because the manager's authority decreases at each level.

In general, costs that are incurred directly by a level of responsibility can be controlled at that level. In contrast, costs that are incurred indirectly and allocated to a responsibility level are considered to be **noncontrollable** at that level.

Responsibility Reporting System

In a **responsibility reporting system**, a report is prepared for each level of responsibility in the company's organization chart. To illustrate such a system, we will use the partial organization chart and production departments of Francis Chair Company in Illustration 10-18.

The responsibility reporting system begins with the lowest level of responsibility for controlling costs and moves upward to each higher level. The connections between levels are shown in Illustration 10-19.

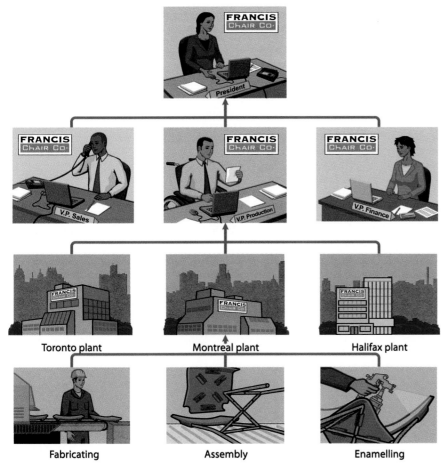

Illustration 10-18 ◄

Partial organization chart

Report A

President sees summary data of vice-presidents.

Report B

Vice-president sees summary of controllable costs in his/her functional area.

Report C

Plant manager sees summary of controllable costs for each department in the plant.

Report D

Department manager sees controllable costs of his/her department.

A brief description of the four reports for Francis Chair Company is as follows:

1. **Report D** is typical of reports that go to managers at the lowest level of responsibility shown in the organization chart—department managers. Similar reports are prepared for the managers of the fabricating, assembling, and enamelling departments.
2. **Report C** is an example of reports that are sent to plant managers. It shows the costs of the Montreal plant that are controllable at the second level of responsibility. In addition, Report C shows summary data for each department that is controlled by the plant manager. Similar reports are prepared for the Toronto and Halifax plant managers.
3. **Report B** is a report at the third level of responsibility. It shows the controllable costs of the vice-president of production and summary data on the three assembly plants that this officer is responsible for.
4. **Report A** is typical of the reports that go to the top level of responsibility—the president. This report shows the controllable costs and expenses of this position and summary data on the vice-presidents who are accountable to the president.

A responsibility reporting system makes it possible to use management by exception at each level of responsibility. In addition, each higher level of responsibility can obtain the detailed report for each lower level of responsibility. For example, the vice-president of production in the Francis Chair Company may ask to see the Montreal plant manager's report because this plant is $5,300 over budget.

This type of reporting system also makes it possible to do comparative evaluations. In Illustration 10-19, the Montreal plant manager can easily rank each department manager's effectiveness in controlling manufacturing costs. Comparative rankings provide further incentive for a manager to control costs. For example, the Toronto plant manager will want to continue to be number one in the report to the vice-president of production. The Montreal plant manager will not want to remain number three in future reporting periods.

Illustration 10-19 ▶

Responsibility reporting system

Report A

President sees summary data of vice-presidents.

REPORT A

To: President   Month: January

Controllable Costs:	Budget	Actual	Fav./Unfav.
President	$ 150,000	$ 151,500	$ 1,500 U
Vice-president:			
Sales	185,000	187,000	2,000 U
Production	1,179,000	1,186,300	7,300 U
Finance	100,000	101,000	1,000 U
Total	$1,614,000	$1,625,800	$11,800 U

Report B

Vice-president sees summary of controllable costs in his/her functional area.

REPORT B

To: Vice-President Production   Month: January

Controllable Costs:	Budget	Actual	Fav./Unfav.
VP Production	$ 125,000	$ 126,000	$ 1,000 U
Assembly Plants:			
Toronto	420,000	418,000	2,000 F
Montreal	304,000	309,300	5,300 U
Halifax	330,000	333,000	3,000 U
Total	$1,179,000	$1,186,300	$ 7,300 U

Report C

Plant manager sees summary of controllable costs for each department in the plant.

REPORT C

To: Plant Manager–Montreal   Month: January

Controllable Costs	Budget	Actual	Fav./Unfav.
Montreal Plant	$ 110,000	$ 113,000	$ 3,000 U
Departments:			
Fabricating	84,000	85,300	1,300 U
Enamelling	62,000	64,000	2,000 U
Assembly	48,000	47,000	1,000 F
Total	$ 304,000	$ 309,300	$ 5,300 U

Report D

Department manager sees controllable costs of his/her department.

REPORT D

To: Fabricating Department Manager   Month: January

Controllable Costs	Budget	Actual	Fav./Unfav.
Direct materials	$ 20,000	$ 20,500	$ 500 U
Direct labour	40,000	41,000	1,000 U
Overhead	24,000	23,800	200 F
Total	$ 84,000	$ 85,300	$ 1,300 U

Types of Responsibility Centres

There are three basic types of responsibility centres: cost centres, profit centres, and investment centres. These centres indicate the degree of responsibility the manager has for the performance of the centre.

A **cost centre** incurs costs (and expenses) but does not directly generate revenues. Managers of cost centres have the authority to incur costs. They are evaluated on their ability to control costs. **Cost centres are usually either production departments or service departments.** The former participate directly in making the product. The latter provide only support services. In a Ford Motor Company of Canada automobile plant, the welding, painting, and assembling departments are production departments; the maintenance, cafeteria, and human resources departments are service departments. All of them are cost centres.

A **profit centre** incurs costs (and expenses) and also generates revenues. Managers of profit centres are judged on the profitability of their centres. Examples of profit centres include the individual departments of a retail store, such as clothing, furniture, and automotive products, and branch offices of banks.

Like a profit centre, an **investment centre** incurs costs (and expenses) and generates revenues. In addition, an investment centre has control over the investment funds that are available for use. Managers of investment centres are evaluated on both the profitability of the centre and the rate of return earned on the funds invested. Investment centres are often associated with product lines and subsidiary companies. For example, General Mills' product lines include cereals, helper dinner mixes, fruit snacks, popcorn, and yogurt. And, in our feature story, Petro-Canada has five operating divisions: North American Gas, East Coast Oil, Oil Sands, International, and Refining and Marketing. The manager of an investment centre (product line) is able to control or significantly influence investment decisions for such matters as plant expansion and entry into new market areas. These three types of responsibility centres are shown in Illustration 10-20.

The evaluation of a manager's performance in each type of responsibility centre is explained in the remainder of this chapter.

Helpful Hint (1) Is the jewellery department of The Bay a profit centre or a cost centre? (2) Is the props department of a movie studio a profit centre or a cost centre? Answers: (1) Profit centre. (2) Cost centre.

Types of Responsibility Centres

Expenses   Re̶ve̶nu̶es

Cost Centre

Expenses + Revenues

Profit Centre

Expenses + Revenues + Return on Investments

Investment Centre

Illustration 10-20 ◄

Types of responsibility centres

Responsibility Accounting for Cost Centres

study objective 5

Indicate the features of responsibility reports for cost centres.

A manager's performance in a cost centre is evaluated based on his or her ability to meet budgeted goals for controllable costs. **Responsibility reports for cost centres compare actual controllable costs with flexible budget data.**

A responsibility report is shown in Illustration 10-21. The report is adapted from the flexible budget report for Fox Manufacturing Company in Illustration 10-16. It assumes that the finishing department manager is able to control all manufacturing overhead costs except amortization, property taxes, and his own monthly salary of $6,000. The remaining $4,000 of supervision costs are assumed to be for other supervisory personnel in the finishing department, whose salaries the manager can control.

Illustration 10-21 ▶

Responsibility report for a cost centre

FOX MANUFACTURING COMPANY
Responsibility Report
Finishing Department
Month Ended January 31, 2005

Controllable Cost	Budget	Actual	Difference: Favourable (F)/ Unfavourable (U)
Indirect materials	$13,500	$14,000	$ 500 U
Indirect labour	18,000	17,000	1,000 F
Utilities	4,500	4,600	100 U
Supervision	4,000	4,000	0
	$40,000	$39,600	$ 400 F

Only controllable costs are included in the report, and no distinction is made between variable and fixed costs. The responsibility report continues the concept of management by exception. In this case, top management may want an explanation for the $1,000 favourable difference in indirect labour and/or the $500 unfavourable difference in indirect materials.

Responsibility Accounting for Profit Centres

study objective 6

Identify the content of responsibility reports for profit centres.

To evaluate the performance of a manager of a profit centre, detailed information is needed about both the controllable revenues and the controllable costs. The operating revenues that are earned by a profit centre, such as sales, are controllable by the manager. All variable costs (and expenses) that are incurred by the centre can also be controlled by the manager because they vary with sales. However, to determine the controllability of fixed costs, it is necessary to distinguish between direct and indirect fixed costs.

Direct and Indirect Fixed Costs

A profit centre may have both direct and indirect fixed costs. **Direct fixed costs** are costs that are specifically for one centre and are incurred for the benefit of that centre alone. Examples of such costs include the salaries established by the profit centre manager for supervisory personnel and the cost of a timekeeping department for the centre's employees. Since these fixed costs can be traced directly to a centre, they are also called **traceable costs**. **Most direct fixed costs are controllable by the profit centre manager.**

In contrast, **indirect fixed costs** are for a company's overall operating activities and are incurred for the benefit of more than one profit centre. Indirect fixed costs are allocated to profit centres according to some type of equitable basis. For example, property taxes on a building that is occupied by more than one centre may be allocated based on the square feet of floor space used by each centre. Or, the costs of a company's human resources department may be allocated to profit centres based on the number of employees in each centre. Because these fixed costs apply to more than one centre, they are also called **common costs**. **Most indirect fixed costs cannot be controlled by the profit centre manager.**

Responsibility Report

The responsibility report for a profit centre shows the budgeted and actual **controllable revenues and costs**. The report is prepared using the cost-volume-profit income statement explained in Chapter 5 and has these features:

1. Controllable fixed costs are deducted from the contribution margin.
2. The amount by which the contribution margin is greater than the controllable fixed costs is identified as the **controllable margin**.
3. Noncontrollable fixed costs are not reported.

The responsibility report for the manager of the marine division, a profit centre of Mantle Manufacturing Company, is shown in Illustration 10-22. For the year, the marine division also had $60,000 of indirect fixed costs that were not controllable by the profit centre manager.

Illustration 10-22 ◄

Responsibility report for profit centre

MANTLE MANUFACTURING COMPANY
Responsibility Report
Marine Division
Year Ended January 31, 2005

	Budget	Actual	Difference: Favourable (F)/ Unfavourable (U)
Sales	$1,200,000	$1,150,000	$50,000 U
Variable costs			
Cost of goods sold	500,000	490,000	10,000 F
Selling and administrative expenses	160,000	156,000	4,000 F
Total	660,000	646,000	14,000 F
Contribution margin	540,000	504,000	36,000 U
Controllable fixed costs			
Cost of goods sold	100,000	100,000	0
Selling and administrative expenses	80,000	80,000	0
Total	180,000	180,000	0
Controllable margin	$ 360,000	$ 324,000	$36,000 U

Helpful Hint Note that we are emphasizing financial measures of performance. These days, companies are also trying to stress non-financial performance measures, such as product quality, labour productivity, market growth, materials' yield, manufacturing flexibility, and technological capability.

The controllable margin is considered to be the best measure of the manager's performance **in controlling revenues and costs**. This report shows that the manager's performance was below budgeted expectations by 10 percent ($36,000 ÷ $360,000). Top management would likely investigate the causes of this unfavourable result. Note that the report does not show the marine division's noncontrollable fixed costs of $60,000. These costs would be included in a report on the profitability of the profit centre.

Responsibility reports for profit centres may also be prepared monthly. In addition, they may include cumulative year-to-date results.

Helpful Hint Responsibility reports are helpful tools for evaluating managerial performance. Too much emphasis on profits or investments, however, can be harmful because it ignores other important performance issues, such as quality and social responsibility.

Decision Toolkit

Decision Checkpoints	Info Needed for Decision	Tools to Use for Decision	How to Evaluate Results
Have the individual managers been held accountable for the costs and revenues under their control?	Relevant costs and revenues, where the individual manager has authority to make day-to-day decisions about the items	Responsibility reports focused on cost centres, profit centres, and investment centres, as appropriate	Compare the budget to actual costs and revenues for controllable items.

the navigator

BEFORE YOU GO ON . . .

▶ Review It

1. What conditions are essential for responsibility accounting?
2. What is involved in a responsibility reporting system?
3. What is the primary objective of a responsibility report for a cost centre?
4. How does the contribution margin differ from the controllable margin in a responsibility report for a profit centre?

▶ Do It

Midwest Division operates as a profit centre. It reports the following actual results for the year: sales $1,700,000; variable costs $800,000; controllable fixed costs $400,000; noncontrollable fixed costs $200,000. The annual budgeted amounts were $1,500,000; $700,000; $400,000; and $200,000; respectively. Prepare a responsibility report for Midwest Division at December 31, 2005.

Action Plan

- Deduct variable costs from sales to show the contribution margin.
- Deduct controllable fixed costs from the contribution margin to show the controllable margin.
- Do not report noncontrollable fixed costs.

Solution

MIDWEST DIVISION
Responsibility Report
Year Ended December 31, 2005

	Budget	Actual	Difference: Favourable (F)/ Unfavourable (U)
Sales	$1,500,000	$1,700,000	$200,000 F
Variable costs	700,000	800,000	100,000 U
Contribution margin	800,000	900,000	100,000 F
Controllable fixed costs	400,000	400,000	0
Controllable margin	$ 400,000	$ 500,000	$100,000 F

Related exercise material: BE10-7 and E10–10.

Responsibility Accounting for Investment Centres

As explained earlier, an investment centre manager can control or significantly influence the investment funds that are available for use. Thus, the main basis for evaluating the performance of a manager of an investment centre is the **return on investment (ROI)**. The return on investment is considered to be a useful performance measurement because it shows the **how effectively the manager uses the assets at his or her disposal**.

Return on Investment (ROI)

The formula for calculating the ROI for an investment centre, using assumed data, is shown in Illustration 10-23. Both factors in the formula can be controlled by the investment centre manager. Operating assets consist of the current assets and plant assets that are used in operations by the centre and are controlled by the manager. Non-operating assets, such as idle plant assets and land held for future use, are excluded. Average operating assets are usually based on the cost or book value of the assets at the beginning and end of the year.

Illustration 10-23 ▶

ROI formula

Responsibility Report

The range of the investment centre manager's responsibility significantly affects the content of the performance report. Since an investment centre is an independent entity for operating purposes, **all fixed costs are controllable by its manager**. This means, for example, that the manager is even responsible for amortization on the investment centre's assets. This also means that—compared to performance reports for profit centre managers—there are more fixed costs that are classified as being controllable in performance reports for investment centre managers. The report also shows the budgeted and actual ROI on a line beneath the controllable margin.

To illustrate this responsibility report, we will now assume that the marine division of Mantle Manufacturing Company is an investment centre. It has budgeted and actual average operating assets of $2 million. We also assume that the manager can control the $60,000 of fixed costs that were not controllable when the division was a profit centre. The responsibility report is shown in Illustration 10-24.

MANTLE MANUFACTURING COMPANY
Responsibility Report
Marine Division
Year Ended December 31, 2005

	Budget	Actual	Difference: Favourable (F)/ Unfavourable (U)
Sales	$1,200,000	$1,150,000	$50,000 U
Variable costs			
Cost of goods sold	500,000	490,000	10,000 F
Selling and administrative expenses	160,000	156,000	4,000 F
Total	660,000	646,000	14,000 F
Contribution margin	540,000	504,000	36,000 U
Controllable fixed costs			
Cost of goods sold	100,000	100,000	0
Selling and administrative expenses	80,000	80,000	0
Other fixed costs	60,000	60,000	0
Total	240,000	240,000	0
Controllable margin	$ 300,000	$ 264,000	$36,000 U
Return on investment	15% [a]	13.2% [b]	1.8% U [c]

[a] $\frac{\$300,000}{\$2,000,000}$ [b] $\frac{\$264,000}{\$2,000,000}$ [c] $\frac{\$36,000}{\$2,000,000}$

Illustration 10-24 ◀

Responsibility report for investment centre

The report shows that the manager's performance based on the ROI was 12 percent (1.8% ÷ 15%) below budget expectations. Top management would likely want to know the reasons for this unfavourable result.

Judgmental Factors in ROI

The return on investment approach includes two judgmental factors:

1. **Valuation of operating assets.** Operating assets may be valued at their acquisition cost, book value, appraised value, or market value. The first two values are easily found in the accounting records.
2. **Margin (income) measure.** This measure may be the controllable margin, income from operations, or net income.

Each of the alternative values for operating assets can be a reliable basis for evaluating a manager's performance, as long as it is consistently used between reporting periods. However, the use of income measures other than the controllable margin will not result in a valid basis for evaluating the performance of an investment centre manager.[1]

Improving ROI

The manager of an investment centre can improve the ROI in two ways: (1) increase the controllable margin, and/or (2) reduce the average operating assets. To illustrate, we will use the data in Illustration 10-25 for the marine division of Mantle Manufacturing.

Illustration 10-25 ▶

Assumed data for Marine Division

Sales	$2,000,000
Variable cost	1,100,000
Contribution margin (45%)	900,000
Controllable fixed costs	300,000
Controllable margin (a)	$ 600,000
Average operating assets (b)	$5,000,000
Return on investment (a) ÷ (b)	12%

Increasing the Controllable Margin.   The controllable margin can be increased by increasing sales or by reducing the variable and controllable fixed costs as follows:

1. **Increase sales by 10 percent.** Sales increase by $200,000 ($2,000,000 × 0.10). Assuming that there is no change in the contribution margin percentage of 45 percent, the contribution margin will increase by $90,000 ($200,000 × 0.45). The controllable margin will increase by the same amount because the controllable fixed costs will not change. Thus, the controllable margin becomes $690,000 ($600,000 + $90,000). The new ROI is 13.8 percent, calculated as in Illustration 10-26.

Illustration 10-26 ▶

ROI calculation—increase in sales

$$\text{ROI} = \frac{\text{Controllable margin}}{\text{Average operating assets}} = \frac{\$690,000}{\$5,000,000} = 13.8\%$$

An increase in sales benefits both the investment centre and the company if it results in new business. It would not benefit the company if the increase was achieved by taking something away from other investment centres.

2. **Decrease variable and fixed costs by 10 percent.** Total costs decrease by $140,000 [($1,100,000 + $300,000) × 0.10]. This reduction will result in a corresponding increase in the controllable margin. Thus, the controllable margin becomes $740,000 ($600,000 + $140,000). The new ROI is 14.8 percent, calculated as in Illustration 10-27.

Illustration 10-27 ▶

ROI calculation—decrease in costs

$$\text{ROI} = \frac{\text{Controllable margin}}{\text{Average operating assets}} = \frac{\$740,000}{\$5,000,000} = 14.8\%$$

This type of action is clearly beneficial if it eliminates waste and inefficiencies. But a reduction in such vital costs as required maintenance and inspections is not likely to be acceptable to top management.

Reducing the Average Operating Assets.   Assume that the average operating assets are reduced 10 percent or $500,000 ($5,000,000 × 0.10). The average operating assets become $4.5 million ($5,000,000 − $500,000). Since the controllable margin remains unchanged at $600,000, the new ROI is 13.3 percent, as calculated in Illustration 10-28.

Illustration 10-28 ▶

ROI calculation—decrease in operating assets

$$\text{ROI} = \frac{\text{Controllable margin}}{\text{Average operating assets}} = \frac{\$600,000}{\$4,500,000} = 13.3\%$$

---

[1] Although the ROI approach is often used in evaluating investment performance, it has some disadvantages. The appendix to this chapter illustrates a second method for evaluation, referred to as the residual income approach.

Reductions in operating assets may or may not be wise. It is good to eliminate excessive inventories and to dispose of unneeded plant assets. However, it is unwise to reduce inventories below expected needs or to dispose of essential plant assets.

Decision Toolkit

Decision Checkpoints	Info Needed for Decision	Tools to Use for Decision	How to Evaluate Results
Has the investment centre performed up to expectations?	The controllable margin (contribution margin minus controllable fixed costs), and average investment centre operating assets	Return on investment	Compare the actual ROI to the expected ROI.

Principles of Performance Evaluation

Performance evaluation is at the centre of responsibility accounting. **Performance evaluation** is a management function that compares actual results to budget goals. Performance evaluation uses both behavioural and reporting principles.

Behavioural Principles

The human factor is critical in evaluating performance. Behavioural principles include the following:

1. **Managers of responsibility centres should be directly involved in setting budget goals for their areas of responsibility.** Without such involvement, managers may view the goals as unrealistic or arbitrarily set by top management. Such views can decrease the managers' motivation to meet the targeted objectives.
2. **The evaluation of performance should be based entirely on matters that can be controlled by the manager being evaluated.** Criticism of a manager for matters that he or she cannot control reduces the effectiveness of the evaluation process. It leads to negative reactions by the manager and to doubts about the fairness of the company's evaluation policies.
3. **Top management should support the evaluation process.** As explained earlier, the evaluation process begins at the lowest level of responsibility and extends upward to the highest level of management. Managers quickly lose trust in the process when top management ignores, overrules, or bypasses established procedures for evaluating a manager's performance.
4. **The evaluation process must allow managers to respond to their evaluations.** Evaluation is not a one-way street. Managers should have the opportunity to defend their performance. Evaluation without feedback is impersonal and ineffective.
5. **The evaluation should identify both good and poor performance.** Praise for good performance is a powerful motivating factor for a manager. This is especially true when a manager's compensation includes rewards for meeting budget goals.

Reporting Principles

Performance evaluation under responsibility accounting should be based on certain reporting principles. These principles relate mostly to the internal reports that provide the basis for evaluating performance. Performance reports should:

1. Contain only data that are controllable by the manager of the responsibility centre
2. Provide accurate and reliable budget data to measure performance
3. Highlight significant differences between actual results and budget goals
4. Be tailor-made for the intended evaluation
5. Be prepared at reasonable intervals

BEFORE YOU GO ON . . .

▶ Review It

the
navigator

1. What is the formula for calculating the return on investment (ROI)?
2. Identify three actions that a manager may take to improve the ROI.

APPENDIX 10A ▶ RESIDUAL INCOME—ANOTHER PERFORMANCE MEASUREMENT

study objective 8

Explain the difference between ROI and residual income.

Illustration 10A-1 ▶

ROI formula

Although most companies use the ROI in evaluating their investment performance, the ROI has a significant disadvantage. To illustrate, let's look at the marine division of Mantle Manufacturing Company. It has an ROI of 20 percent as calculated in Illustration 10A-1.

Controllable Margin	÷	Average Operating Assets	=	Return on Investment (ROI)
$1,000,000	÷	$5,000,000	=	20%

The marine division is considering producing a new product for its boats, a GPS satellite tracker. To produce the tracker, operating assets will have to increase by $2 million. The tracker is expected to generate an additional $260,000 of controllable margin. A comparison to show how the tracker will affect the ROI is presented in Illustration 10A-2.

Illustration 10A-2 ▶

ROI comparison

	Without Tracker	For Tracker	With Tracker
Controllable margin (a)	$1,000,000	$260,000	$1,260,000
Average operating assets (b)	$5,000,000	$2,000,000	$7,000,000
Return on investment [(a) ÷ (b)]	20%	13%	18%

The investment in the tracker reduces the ROI from 20 percent to 18 percent.

Let's suppose that you are the manager of the marine division and must decide if you should produce the tracker. If you were evaluated using the ROI, you probably would not produce the tracker because your ROI would drop from 20 percent to 18 percent. The problem with this ROI analysis is that it ignores an important variable, the minimum rate of return on a company's operating assets. The **minimum rate of return** is the rate at which the marine division can cover its costs and earn a profit. Assuming that the marine division has a minimum rate of return of 10 percent, it should invest in the tracker because its ROI of 13 percent is greater than 10 percent.

Residual Income Compared to ROI

To evaluate performance using the minimum rate of return, companies use the residual income approach. **Residual income** is the income that remains after subtracting from the controllable margin the minimum rate of return on a company's average operating assets. The residual income for the tracker would be calculated as in Illustration 10A-3.

Illustration 10A-3 ▶

Residual income formula

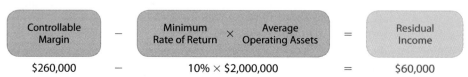

Controllable Margin	−	Minimum Rate of Return × Average Operating Assets	=	Residual Income
$260,000	−	10% × $2,000,000	=	$60,000

As shown, the residual income from the tracker investment is $60,000. Illustration 10A-4 indicates how the residual income changes as the additional investment is made.

	Without Tracker	For Tracker	With Tracker
Controllable margin (a)	$1,000,000	$260,000	$1,260,000
Average operating assets × 10% (b)	500,000	200,000	700,000
Return on investment [(a) − (b)]	$ 500,000	$ 60,000	$ 560,000

Illustration 10A-4 ◄

Residual income formula

This example shows how performance evaluation that is based on the ROI can be misleading and can even cause managers to reject projects that would actually increase income for the company. As a result, many companies use residual income to evaluate investment alternatives and measure company performance.

The residual income amount can be calculated in several ways, depending on how we define the terms used. The following variant on residual income is often referred as the Economic Value[1] Added (EVA) approach. EVA is similar to residual income as a measure of the income created by the investment centre above the cost of invested assets. However, the EVA approach differs from the residual income approach in two ways. First, the weighted-average cost of capital is used for EVA instead of the minimum rate of return on the invested assets. Second, the EVA calculates an investment centre's profit after tax. Basically, the EVA is calculated by deducting the total cost of capital (equity and borrowing) from the net income after tax. Illustration 10A-5 shows how the EVA is calculated.

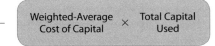

Illustration 10A-5 ◄

Economic Value Added (EVA) formula

If this EVA result is positive, the company has added economic value. If it is negative, the company has lost capital. Many Canadian corporations have used the EVA approach in evaluating their investment centres, including Equifax Canada, Domtar, Husky Injection Molding Systems Ltd., and Alcan Aluminium.

BUSINESS INSIGHT ▶ Management Perspective

The Canadian Imperial Bank of Commerce and Royal Bank of Canada are the most undervalued of the Big Five banks in terms of their market values, according to analyst Robert Wessel. They are below their deserved market price by 10 percent and 6 percent respectively. The Royal Bank remains the most profitable bank based on the Economic Value Added (EVA) method. Wessel found that it has a "disciplined approach to capital management" and has been the most consistent performer, with only one negative EVA quarter in the past three years.

Source: *Financial Post*, December 15, 2001, p. FP6.

Residual Income Weakness

The goal of the residual income approach is to focus efforts on maximizing the total amount of residual income. This goal, however, ignores the fact that one division might use substantially fewer assets to attain the same level of residual income as another division. For example, we know that to produce the tracker, the marine division of Mantle Manufacturing used $2 million of average operating assets to generate $260,000 of controllable margin. Now let's say a different division produced a product called SeaDog, and it used $4 million to generate $460,000 of controllable margin, as shown in Illustration 10A-6.

---

[1] EVA was established by Stern, Steven & Co. in the U.S.A.

	Tracker	SeaDog
Controllable margin (a)	$260,000	$460,000
Average operating assets × 10% (b)	200,000	400,000
Residual income [(a) − (b)]	$ 60,000	$ 60,000

If the performance of these two investments were evaluated using the residual income approach, they would be considered equal: both products have the same total residual income amount. This ignores, however, the fact that SeaDog required twice as much in operating assets to achieve the same level of residual income.

▦ Using the Decision Toolkit

The manufacturing overhead budget for Reebles Company has the following items:

Variable costs	
Indirect materials	$25,000
Indirect labour	12,000
Maintenance	10,000
Manufacturing supplies	6,000
Total variable costs	$53,000

Fixed costs	
Supervision	$17,000
Inspections	1,000
Insurance	2,000
Amortization	15,000
Total fixed costs	$35,000

The budget was based on an estimated production of 2,000 units. During November, 1,500 units were produced, and the following costs were incurred:

Variable costs	
Indirect materials	$25,200
Indirect labour	13,500
Maintenance	8,200
Manufacturing supplies	5,100
Total variable costs	$52,000

Fixed costs	
Supervision	$19,300
Inspections	1,200
Insurance	2,200
Amortization	14,700
Total fixed costs	$37,400

Instructions

(a) Determine which items would be controllable by Ed Lopat, the production manager. (Assume that "supervision" does not include Lopat's own salary.)
(b) How much should have been spent during the month for the manufacture of the 1,500 units?
(c) Prepare a flexible manufacturing overhead budget report for Mr. Lopat.
(d) Prepare a responsibility report. Include only the costs that would have been controllable by Mr. Lopat. In an attached memo, describe clearly for Mr. Lopat the areas in which his performance needs to be improved.

Solution

(a) Ed Lopat should be able to control all the variable expenses and the fixed expenses of supervision and inspection. Insurance and amortization ordinarily are not the responsibility of the department manager.

(b) The total variable cost per unit is $26.50 ($53,000 ÷ 2,000). The total budgeted cost during the month to manufacture 1,500 units is variable costs of $39,750 (1,500 × $26.50) plus fixed costs of $35,000, for a total of $74,750 ($39,750 + $35,000).

(c)

REEBLES COMPANY
Production Department
Manufacturing Overhead Budget Report (flexible)
Month Ended November 30, 2005

	Budget at 1,500 units	Actual at 1,500 units	Difference: Favourable (F)/ Unfavourable (U)
Variable costs			
Indirect materials	$18,750	$25,200	$ 6,450 U
Indirect labour	9,000	13,500	4,500 U
Maintenance	7,500	8,200	700 U
Manufacturing supplies	4,500	5,100	600 U
Total variable costs	39,750	52,000	12,250 U
Fixed costs			
Supervision	17,000	19,300	2,300 U
Inspections	1,000	1,200	200 U
Insurance	2,000	2,200	200 U
Amortization	15,000	14,700	300 F
Total fixed costs	35,000	37,400	2,400 U
Total costs	$74,750	$89,400	$14,650 U

(d) Because a production department is a cost centre, the responsibility report should include only the costs that the production manager can control. In this type of report, no distinction is made between variable and fixed costs. Budget data in the report should be based on the units that are actually produced.

REEBLES COMPANY
Production Department
Responsibility Report
Month Ended November 30, 2005

Controllable Costs	Budget	Actual	Difference: Favourable (F)/ Unfavourable (U)
Indirect materials	$18,750	$25,200	$ 6,450 U
Indirect labour	9,000	13,500	4,500 U
Maintenance	7,500	8,200	700 U
Manufacturing supplies	4,500	5,100	600 U
Supervision	17,000	19,300	2,300 U
Inspections	1,000	1,200	200 U
Total costs	$57,750	$72,500	$14,750 U

To: Mr. Ed Lopat, Production Manager

From: _____ , Vice-President of Production

Subject: Performance Evaluation for November

Your performance in controlling costs that are your responsibility was very disappointing in the month of November. As indicated in the accompanying responsibility report, total costs were $14,750 over budget. On a percentage basis, costs were 26% over budget. As you can see, actual costs were over budget for every cost item. In three instances, costs were significantly over budget (indirect materials 34%, indirect labour 50%, and supervision 14%).

Ed, it is imperative that you get costs under control in your department as soon as possible.

I think we need to talk about ways to implement more effective cost-control measures. I would like to meet with you in my office at 9 a.m. on Wednesday to discuss possible alternatives.

Summary of Study Objectives

1. **Describe the concept of budgetary control.** Budgetary control consists of (1) preparing periodic budget reports that compare actual results with planned objectives, (2) analyzing the differences to determine their causes, (3) taking appropriate corrective action, and (4) modifying future plans, if necessary.

2. **Evaluate the usefulness of static budget reports.** Static budget reports are useful for evaluating the progress toward planned sales and profit goals. They are also good for assessing a manager's effectiveness in controlling fixed costs and expenses when (1) actual activity closely approximates the master budget activity level, and/or (2) the costs respond to changes in activity in a fixed way.

3. **Explain the development of flexible budgets and the usefulness of flexible budget reports.** To develop the flexible budget, it is necessary to do the following:
   1. Identify the activity index and the relevant range of activity.
   2. Identify the variable costs, and determine the budgeted variable cost per unit of activity for each cost.
   3. Identify the fixed costs, and determine the budgeted amount for each cost.
   4. Prepare the budget for selected increments of activity within the relevant range.

Flexible budget reports make it possible to evaluate a manager's performance in controlling production and costs.

4. **Describe the concept of responsibility accounting.** Responsibility accounting involves accumulating and reporting revenues and costs that relate to the individual manager who has the authority to make the day-to-day decisions about the cost items. The evaluation of a manager's performance is based on the matters that are directly under the manager's control. In responsibility accounting, it is necessary to distinguish between controllable and noncontrollable fixed costs and to identify three types of responsibility centres: cost, profit, and investment.

5. **Indicate the features of responsibility reports for cost centres.** Responsibility reports for cost centres compare actual costs with flexible budget data. The reports show only controllable costs, and no distinction is made between variable and fixed costs.

6. **Identify the content of responsibility reports for profit centres.** Responsibility reports show the contribution margin, controllable fixed costs, and controllable margin for each profit centre.

7. **Explain the basis and formula that are used for evaluating performance in investment centres.** The primary basis for evaluating performance in investment centres is the return on investment (ROI). The formula for calculating the ROI for investment centres is as follows: controllable margin ÷ average operating assets.

8. **Explain the difference between ROI and residual income (Appendix 10A).** ROI is the controllable margin divided by average operating assets. Residual income is the income that remains after subtracting the minimum rate of return on a company's average operating assets. ROI sometimes provides misleading results because profitable investments are often rejected if they would reduce the ROI but increase overall profitability.

Decision Toolkit—A Summary

Decision Checkpoints	Info Needed for Decision	Tools to Use for Decision	How to Evaluate Results
Are the increased costs that result from increased production reasonable?	Variable costs projected at different levels of production	Flexible budget	After considering different production levels, results are favourable if expenses are less than the budgeted amounts.
Have the individual managers been held accountable for the costs and revenues under their control?	Relevant costs and revenues, where the individual manager has authority to make day-to-day decisions about the items	Responsibility reports focused on cost centres, profit centres, and investment centres, as appropriate	Compare the budget to actual costs and revenues for controllable items.
Has the investment centre performed up to expectations?	The controllable margin (contribution margin minus controllable fixed costs), and average investment centre operating assets	Return on investment	Compare the actual ROI to the expected ROI.

Glossary

Key Term Matching Activity

Budgetary control The use of budgets to control operations. (p. 416)

Controllable costs Costs that a manager has the authority to incur within a specific period of time. (p. 426)

Controllable margin The contribution margin less controllable fixed costs. (p. 431)

Cost centre A responsibility centre that incurs costs but does not directly generate revenues. (p. 429)

Decentralization The situation that exists when control of operations is given to many managers throughout the organization. (p. 426)

Direct fixed costs Costs that relate specifically to a responsibility centre and are incurred for the benefit of that centre alone. (p. 430)

Economic Value Added (EVA) The after-tax controllable margin minus the weighted average cost of the total capital used. (p. 437)

Flexible budget A projection of budget data for various levels of activity. (p. 418)

Indirect fixed costs Costs that are incurred for the benefit of more than one profit centre. (p. 430)

Investment centre A responsibility centre that incurs costs, generates revenues, and has control over the investment funds that are available for use. (p. 429)

Management by exception A review of budget reports by top management that focuses entirely or mostly on differences between actual results and planned objectives. (p. 424)

Noncontrollable costs Costs that are incurred indirectly and are allocated to a responsibility centre that cannot control them. (p. 426)

Profit centre A responsibility centre that incurs costs and also generates revenues. (p. 429)

Residual income The income that remains after subtracting from the controllable margin the minimum rate of return on a company's operating assets. (p. 436)

Responsibility accounting A part of management accounting that involves accumulating and reporting revenues and costs that relate to the manager who has the authority to make the day-to-day decisions about the cost items. (p. 425)

Responsibility reporting system The preparation of reports for each level of responsibility in the company's organization chart. (p. 427)

Return on investment (ROI) A measure of management's effectiveness in using assets at its disposal in an investment centre. (p. 432)

Segment An area of responsibility in decentralized operations. (p. 426)

Static budget A projection of budget data at one level of activity. (p. 417)

Demonstration Problem

Animated Demonstration Problem

Glenda Company uses a flexible budget for manufacturing overhead that is based on direct labour hours. For 2005, the master overhead budget for the packaging department at its normal capacity of 300,000 direct labour hours was as follows:

Variable Costs		Fixed Costs	
Indirect labour	$360,000	Supervision	$ 60,000
Supplies and lubricants	150,000	Amortization	24,000
Maintenance	210,000	Property taxes	18,000
Utilities	120,000	Insurance	12,000
	$840,000		$114,000

During July, 24,000 direct labour hours were worked. The company incurred the following variable costs in July: indirect labour $30,200; supplies and lubricants $11,600; maintenance $17,500; and utilities $9,200. Actual fixed overhead costs were the same as monthly budgeted fixed costs.

Instructions

Prepare a flexible budget report for the packaging department for July.

Action Plan

- Use budget data for actual direct labour hours worked.
- Classify each cost as variable or fixed.
- Determine the difference between budgeted and actual costs.
- Identify the difference as favourable or unfavourable.
- Determine the difference in total variable costs, total fixed costs, and total costs.

Solution to Demonstration Problem

GLENDA COMPANY
Manufacturing Overhead Budget Report (flexible)
Packaging Department
Month Ended July 31, 2005

	Budget	Actual	Difference: Favourable (F)/ Unfavourable (U)
Direct labour hours	24,000	24,000	
Variable costs			
Indirect labour	$28,800	$30,200	$1,400 U
Supplies and lubricants	12,000	11,600	400 F
Maintenance	16,800	17,500	700 U
Utilities	9,600	9,200	400 F
Total variable costs	67,200	68,500	1,300 U
Fixed costs			
Supervision	5,000	5,000	0
Amortization	2,000	2,000	0
Property taxes	1,500	1,500	0
Insurance	1,000	1,000	0
Total fixed costs	9,500	9,500	0
Total costs	$76,700	$78,000	$1,300 U

the navigator

Note: All questions, exercises, and problems below with an asterisk (*) relate to material in Appendix 10A

Self-Study Questions

Additional Self-Study Questions

Answers are at the end of the chapter.

(SO 1) 1. Budgetary control involves all of the following except:
   (a) modifying future plans.
   (b) analyzing differences.
   (c) using static budgets.
   (d) determining differences between actual and planned results.

(SO 2) 2. A static budget is useful in controlling costs when the cost behaviour is:
   (a) mixed.   (c) variable.
   (b) fixed.   (d) linear.

(SO 3) 3. At zero direct labour hours in a flexible budget graph, the total budgeted cost line intersects the vertical axis at $30,000. At 10,000 direct labour hours, a horizontal line drawn from the total budgeted cost line intersects the vertical axis at $90,000. The fixed and variable costs may be expressed as:
   (a) $30,000 fixed plus $6 per direct labour hour variable.
   (b) $30,000 fixed plus $9 per direct labour hour variable.
   (c) $60,000 fixed plus $3 per direct labour hour variable.
   (d) $60,000 fixed plus $6 per direct labour hour variable.

(SO 3) 4. At 9,000 direct labour hours, the flexible budget for indirect materials is $27,000. If $28,000 of indirect materials costs are incurred at 9,200 direct labour hours, the flexible budget report should show the following difference for indirect materials:
   (a) $1,000 unfavourable.
   (b) $1,000 favourable.
   (c) $400 favourable.
   (d) $400 unfavourable.

(SO 4) 5. Under responsibility accounting, the evaluation of a manager's performance is based on matters that the manager:
   (a) directly controls.
   (b) directly and indirectly controls.
   (c) indirectly controls.
   (d) has shared responsibility for with another manager.

(SO 4) 6. Responsibility centres include:
   (a) cost centres.
   (b) profit centres.
   (c) investment centres.
   (d) all of the above.

(SO 5) 7. Responsibility reports for cost centres:
   (a) distinguish between fixed and variable costs.
   (b) use static budget data.
   (c) include both controllable and noncontrollable costs.
   (d) include only controllable costs.

(SO 6) 8. In a responsibility report for a profit centre, controllable fixed costs are deducted from the contribution margin to show the:
   (a) profit centre margin.
   (b) controllable margin.
   (c) net income.
   (d) income from operations.

(SO 7) 9. In the formula for return on investment (ROI), the factors for the controllable margin and operating assets are, respectively:
   (a) the controllable margin percentage and total operating assets.
   (b) the controllable margin dollars and average operating assets.
   (c) the controllable margin dollars and total assets.
   (d) the controllable margin percentage and average operating assets.

(SO 7) 10. A manager of an investment centre can improve the ROI by:
   (a) increasing average operating assets.
   (b) reducing sales.
   (c) increasing variable costs.
   (d) reducing variable and/or controllable fixed costs.

(SO 8) *11. In the formula for residual income, the factors for calculating the residual income are:
   (a) the contribution margin, controllable margin, and average operating assets.
   (b) the controllable margin, average operating assets, and ROI.
   (c) the controllable margin, average operating assets, and minimum rate of return.
   (d) the controllable margin, ROI, and minimum rate of return.

the navigator

Questions

1. (a) What is budgetary control?
   (b) Tony Crespino is describing budgetary control. What steps should he include in his description?

2. The following purposes are part of a budgetary reporting system: (a) Determine the efficient use of materials. (b) Control overhead costs. (c) Determine whether income objectives are being met. For each purpose, indicate the name of the report, the frequency of the report, and the primary recipient(s) of the report.

3. How may a budget report for the second quarter differ from a budget report for the first quarter?

4. Don Cox has doubts about the usefulness of a master sales budget in evaluating sales performance. Is Don's concern justified? Explain.

5. Under what circumstances may a static budget be an appropriate basis for evaluating a manager's effectiveness in controlling costs?

6. "A flexible budget is really a series of static budgets." Is this true? Explain.

7. The static manufacturing overhead budget based on 40,000 direct labour hours shows budgeted indirect labour costs of $56,000. During March, the department incurs $66,000 of indirect labour costs while working 45,000 direct labour hours. Is this a favourable or unfavourable performance? Why?

8. A static overhead budget based on 40,000 direct labour hours shows factory insurance of $6,500 as a fixed cost. At the 50,000 direct labour hours worked in March, factory insurance costs were $6,200. Is this a favourable or unfavourable performance? Why?

9. Kate Coulter is confused about how a flexible budget is prepared. Identify the steps for Kate.

10. Alou Company has prepared a graph of flexible budget data. At zero direct labour hours, the total budgeted cost line intersects the vertical axis at $25,000. At 10,000 direct labour hours, the line drawn from the total budgeted cost line intersects the vertical axis at $85,000. How may the fixed and variable costs be expressed?

11. The flexible budget formula shows fixed costs of $40,000 plus variable costs of $2 per direct labour hour. What is the total budgeted cost at (a) 9,000 hours and (b) 12,345 hours?

12. What is management by exception? What criteria may be used in identifying exceptions?

13. What is responsibility accounting? Explain the purpose of responsibility accounting.

14. Anne Lemieux is studying for an accounting examination. Describe for Anne the conditions that are necessary for responsibility accounting to be used effectively.

15. Distinguish between controllable and noncontrollable costs.

16. How do responsibility reports differ from budget reports?

17. What is the relationship, if any, between a responsibility reporting system and a company's organization chart?

18. Distinguish among the three types of responsibility centres.

19. (a) What costs are included in a performance report for a cost centre? (b) In the report, are variable and fixed costs identified?

20. How do direct fixed costs differ from indirect fixed costs? Are both types of fixed costs controllable?

21. Lori Quan is confused about the controllable margin reported in an income statement for a profit centre. How is this margin calculated, and what is its main purpose?

22. What is the main basis for evaluating the performance of an investment centre's manager? Indicate the formula for this basis.

23. Explain the ways that ROI can be improved.

24. Indicate two behavioural principles that relate to (a) the manager being evaluated and (b) top management.

*25. What is a major disadvantage of using the ROI to evaluate investment and company performance?

*26. What is the residual income approach, and what is one of its major weaknesses?

Brief Exercises

BE10–1 For the quarter ended March 31, 2005, Westphal Company accumulates the following sales data for its product, Garden-Tools: $315,000 budgeted; $304,000 actual. Prepare a static budget report for the quarter.

Prepare static budget report.
(SO 2)

BE10–2 Data for Westphal Company are given in BE10–1. In the second quarter, budgeted sales were $380,000, and actual sales were $386,000. Prepare a static budget report for the second quarter and for the year to date.

Prepare static budget reports.
(SO 2)

BE10–3 In Hinsdale Company, direct labour is $20 per hour. The company expects to operate at 10,000 direct labour hours each month. In January 2005, direct labour totalling $205,000 is incurred in working 10,400 hours. Prepare (a) a static budget report and (b) a flexible budget report. Evaluate the usefulness of each report.

Show usefulness of flexible budgets in evaluating performance.
(SO 2, 3)

BE10–4 Dukane Company expects to produce 1.2 million units of Product XX in 2005. Monthly production is expected to range from 80,000 to 120,000 units. Budgeted variable manufacturing costs per unit are as follows: direct materials $4, direct labour $6, and overhead $9. Budgeted fixed manufacturing costs per unit for amortization are $2 and for supervision $1. Prepare a flexible manufacturing budget for the relevant range value using increments of 20,000 units.

Prepare flexible budget for manufacturing costs.
(SO 3)

BE10–5 Data for Dukane Company are given in BE10–4. In March 2005, the company incurs the following costs in producing 100,000 units: direct materials $425,000, direct labour $590,000, and variable overhead $915,000. Prepare a flexible budget report for March. Were costs controlled?

Prepare flexible budget report.
(SO 3)

BE10–6 In the assembly department of Osaka Company, budgeted and actual manufacturing overhead costs for the month of April 2005 were as follows:

	Budget	Actual
Indirect materials	$15,000	$14,300
Indirect labour	20,000	20,800
Utilities	10,000	10,750
Supervision	5,000	5,000

All costs can be controlled by the department manager. Prepare a responsibility report for April for the cost centre.

Prepare responsibility report for cost centre.
(SO 5)

BE10–7 Advent Manufacturing Company accumulates the following summary data for the year ending December 31, 2005, for its water division. The division operates as a profit centre: sales—$2,000,000 budgeted, $2,080,000 actual; variable costs—$1,000,000 budgeted, $1,030,000 actual; and controllable fixed costs—$300,000 budgeted, $310,000 actual. Prepare a responsibility report for the water division.

Prepare responsibility report for profit centre.
(SO 6)

BE10–8 For the year ending December 31, 2005, Sanjay Company accumulates the following data for the plastics division, which it operates as an investment centre: contribution margin—$700,000 budgeted, $715,000 actual; controllable fixed costs—$300,000 budgeted, $305,000 actual. Average operating assets for the year were $2 million. Prepare a responsibility report for the plastics division, beginning with the contribution margin.

Prepare responsibility report for investment centre.
(SO 7)

BE10–9 For its three investment centres, Stahl Company accumulates the following data:

	Centre I	Centre II	Centre III
Sales	$2,000,000	$3,000,000	$ 4,000,000
Controllable margin	1,200,000	2,000,000	3,000,000
Average operating assets	6,000,000	8,000,000	10,000,000

Calculate the return on investment (ROI) for each centre.

Calculate return on investment using ROI formula.
(SO 7)

BE10–10 Data for the investment centres for Stahl Company are given in BE10–9. The centres expect the following changes in the next year: (Centre I) 15% increase in sales; (Centre II) $200,000 decrease in costs; (Centre III) $400,000 decrease in average operating assets. Calculate the expected return on investment (ROI) for each centre. Assume Centre I has a contribution margin percentage of 80%.

Calculate return on investment under changed conditions.
(SO 7)

Calculate ROI and residual income.
(SO 8)

*BE10−11   Wasson, Inc. reports the following financial information:

Average operating assets	$3,000,000
Controllable margin	$600,000
Minimum rate of return	9%

Calculate the return on investment and the residual income.

Calculate ROI and residual income.
(SO 8)

*BE10−12   Presented below is information for the Prince George division of Cut Wood, Inc.:

Contribution margin	$1,200,000
Controllable margin	$800,000
Average operating assets	$3,200,000
Minimum rate of return	16%

Calculate the division's return on investment and residual income.

Exercises

Prepare flexible manufacturing overhead budget.
(SO 3)

E10−1   Mrsic Company uses a flexible budget for manufacturing overhead that is based on direct labour hours. The variable manufacturing overhead costs per direct labour hour are as follows:

Indirect labour	$1.00
Indirect materials	0.60
Utilities	0.40

Fixed overhead costs per month are as follows: supervision $4,000; amortization $1,500; and property taxes $800. The company believes it will normally operate in a range of 7,000 to 10,000 direct labour hours per month.

Instructions

Prepare a monthly flexible manufacturing overhead budget for 2005 for the expected range of activity, using increments of 1,000 direct labour hours.

Prepare flexible budget reports for manufacturing overhead costs, and comment on findings.
(SO 3)

E10−2   Using the information in E10−1, assume that in July 2005, Mrsic Company incurs the following manufacturing overhead costs:

Variable Costs		Fixed Costs	
Indirect labour	$8,700	Supervision	$4,000
Indirect materials	5,300	Amortization	1,500
Utilities	3,200	Property taxes	800

Instructions

(a) Prepare a flexible budget performance report, assuming that the company worked 9,000 direct labour hours during the month.
(b) Prepare a flexible budget performance report, assuming that the company worked 8,500 direct labour hours during the month.
(c) ◖▤▤▤▷ Comment on your findings.

Prepare flexible selling expenses budget.
(SO 3)

E10−3   Vincent Company uses flexible budgets to control its selling expenses. Monthly sales are expected to range from $170,000 to $200,000. Variable costs and their percentage relationship to sales are as follows: sales commissions 6%; advertising 4%; travelling 3%; and delivery 2%. Fixed selling expenses consist of sales salaries $32,000; amortization on delivery equipment $7,000; and insurance on delivery equipment $1,000.

Instructions

Prepare a monthly flexible budget for each $10,000 increment of sales within the relevant range for the year ending December 31, 2005.

E10–4 The actual selling expenses incurred in March 2005 by Vincent Company are as follows:

Prepare flexible budget reports for selling expenses.
(SO 3)

Variable Expenses		Fixed Expenses	
Sales commissions	$11,000	Sales salaries	$32,000
Advertising	7,000	Amortization	7,000
Travel	5,100	Insurance	1,000
Delivery	3,500		

Instructions

(a) Prepare a flexible budget performance report for March using the budget data in E10–3, assuming that March sales were $170,000. Expected and actual sales are the same.
(b) Prepare a flexible budget performance report, assuming that March sales were $180,000. Expected sales and actual sales are the same.
(c) ▭▭▭▶ Comment on the importance of using flexible budgets in evaluating the sales manager's performance.

E10–5 Sublette Company's manufacturing overhead budget for the first quarter of 2005 contained the following data:

Prepare flexible budget report and responsibility report for manufacturing overhead.
(SO 3, 5)

Variable Costs		Fixed Costs	
Indirect materials	$12,000	Supervisory salaries	$36,000
Indirect labour	10,000	Amortization	7,000
Utilities	8,000	Property taxes and insurance	8,000
Maintenance	5,000	Maintenance	5,000

Actual variable costs were as follows: indirect materials $13,800; indirect labour $9,600; utilities $8,700; and maintenance $4,200. Actual fixed costs equalled the budgeted costs except for property taxes and insurance, which were $8,400. All costs are considered controllable by the production department manager except for amortization, property taxes, and insurance.

Instructions

(a) Prepare a flexible overhead budget report for the first quarter.
(b) Prepare a responsibility report for the first quarter.

E10–6 As sales manager, Kajsa Keyser was given the following static budget report for selling expenses in the clothing department of Dunham Company for the month of October:

Prepare and discuss flexible budget report.
(SO 2, 3)

DUNHAM COMPANY
Clothing Department
Budget Report
Month Ended October 31, 2005

	Budget	Actual	Difference: Favourable (F)/ Unfavourable (U)
Sales in units	8,000	10,000	2,000 F
Variable costs			
Sales commissions	$ 2,000	$ 2,600	$600 U
Advertising expense	800	850	50 U
Travel expense	4,400	4,900	500 U
Free samples given out	1,600	1,300	300 F
Total variable costs	8,800	9,650	850 U
Fixed costs			
Rent	1,500	1,500	0
Sales salaries	1,200	1,200	0
Office salaries	800	800	0
Amortization—vehicles (sales staff)	500	500	0
Total fixed costs	4,000	4,000	0
Total costs	$12,800	$13,650	$850 U

As a result of this budget report, Kajsa was called into the president's office and congratulated on her fine sales performance. She was reprimanded, however, for allowing her costs to get out of control. Kajsa knew something was wrong with the performance report that she had been given. However, she was not sure what to do, and has come to you for advice.

Instructions

(a) Prepare a budget report based on flexible budget data to help Kajsa.
(b) Should Kajsa have been reprimanded? Explain.

Prepare and discuss responsibility report.
(SO 3, 5)

E10–7   Pronto Plumbing Company is a newly formed company that specializes in plumbing services for home and business. The owner, Paul Pronto, had divided the company into two segments: Home Plumbing Services and Business Plumbing Services. Each segment is run by its own supervisor, while basic selling and administrative services are shared by both segments.

Paul has asked you to help him create a performance reporting system that will allow him to measure each segment's performance in terms of its profitability. The following information has been collected on the Home Plumbing Services segment for the first quarter of 2005:

	Budget	Actual
Service revenue	$25,000	$26,000
Allocated portion of costs		
Building amortization	11,000	11,000
Advertising	5,000	4,200
Billing	3,500	3,000
Property taxes	1,200	1,000
Materials and supplies	1,500	1,200
Supervisory salaries	9,000	9,400
Insurance	4,000	3,500
Wages	3,000	3,300
Gas and oil	2,700	3,400
Equipment amortization	1,600	1,300

Instructions

(a) Prepare a responsibility report for the first quarter of 2005 for the Home Plumbing Services segment.
(b) ▭▬▬▶ Write a memo to Paul Pronto in which you discuss the principles that should be used when performance reports are prepared.

Calculate costs using total budgeted cost formulas, and prepare flexible budget graph.
(SO 3)

E10–8   Sherrer Company has two production departments: fabricating and assembling. At a department managers' meeting, the controller uses flexible budget graphs to explain the total budgeted costs. Separate graphs based on direct labour hours are used for each department. The graphs show the following:

1. At zero direct labour hours, the total budgeted cost line and the fixed cost line intersect the vertical axis at $40,000 in the fabricating department and at $35,000 in the assembling department.
2. At normal capacity of 50,000 direct labour hours, the line drawn from the total budgeted cost line intersects the vertical axis at $160,000 in the fabricating department, and $110,000 in the assembling department.

Instructions

(a) State the total budgeted cost formula for each department.
(b) Calculate the total budgeted cost for each department, assuming actual direct labour hours worked were 53,000 and 47,000 in the fabricating and assembling departments, respectively.
(c) Prepare the flexible budget graph for the fabricating department, assuming the maximum direct labour hours in the relevant range is 100,000. Use increments of 10,000 direct labour hours on the horizontal axis and increments of $50,000 on the vertical axis.

Prepare responsibility reports for cost centres.
(SO 4)

E10–9   Marcum Company's organization chart includes the president; the vice-president of production; three assembly plants—Vancouver, Hamilton, and Saint John; and two departments within each plant—machining and finishing. Budgeted and actual manufacturing cost data for July 2005 are as follows:

1. Finishing Department—Vancouver: direct materials, $41,000 actual, $45,000 budgeted; direct labour, $83,000 actual, $82,000 budgeted; manufacturing overhead, $51,000 actual, $49,200 budgeted.
2. Machining Department—Vancouver: total manufacturing costs, $220,000 actual, $214,000 budgeted.
3. Hamilton Plant: total manufacturing costs, $424,000 actual, $421,000 budgeted.
4. Saint John Plant: total manufacturing costs, $494,000 actual, $499,000 budgeted.

The Vancouver plant manager's office costs were $95,000 actual and $92,000 budgeted. The vice-president of production's office costs were $132,000 actual and $130,000 budgeted. Office costs are not allocated to departments and plants.

Instructions

Using the format on page 428, prepare the reports in a responsibility system for (a) the finishing department—Vancouver, (b) the plant manager—Vancouver, and (c) the vice-president of production.

E10–10 Longhead Manufacturing Inc. has three divisions which are operated as profit centres. Actual operating data for the divisions are as follows:

Calculate missing amounts in responsibility reports for three profit centres, and prepare report.
(SO 6)

Operating Data	Women's Shoes	Men's Shoes	Children's Shoes
Contribution margin	$250,000	(c)	$170,000
Controllable fixed costs	100,000	(d)	(e)
Controllable margin	(a)	$ 90,000	96,000
Sales	600,000	450,000	(f)
Variable costs	(b)	320,000	250,000

Instructions

(a) Calculate the missing amounts. Show your calculations.
(b) Prepare a responsibility report for the Women's Shoe Division assuming (1) the data are for the month ended June 30, 2005, and (2) all data match the budgeted amounts, except variable costs, which are $10,000 over budget.

E10–11 The Green Division of Campana Company reported the following data for the current year:

Calculate ROI for current year and for possible future changes.
(SO 7)

Sales	$3,000,000
Variable costs	1,800,000
Controllable fixed costs	600,000
Average operating assets	5,000,000

Top management is unhappy with the investment centre's return on investment (ROI). It asks the manager of the Green Division to submit plans to improve the ROI in the next year. The manager believes it is reasonable to consider each of the following independent courses of action.

1. Increase sales by $320,000 with no change in the contribution margin percentage.
2. Reduce variable costs by $100,000.
3. Reduce average operating assets by 4%.

Instructions

(a) Calculate the return on investment (ROI) for the current year.
(b) Using the ROI formula, calculate the ROI under each of the proposed courses of action. (Round to one decimal.)

E10–12 The Medina and Haley Dental Clinic provides both preventive and orthodontic dental services. The two owners, Martin Medina and Cybil Haley, operate the clinic as two separate investment centres: Preventive Services and Orthodontic Services. Each owner is in charge of one centre: Martin for Preventive Services and Cybil for Orthodontic Services. Each month they prepare an income statement on the two centres to evaluate performance and make decisions about how to improve the operational efficiency and profitability of the clinic.

Prepare responsibility report for investment centre.
(SO 7)

Recently, they have been concerned about the profitability of the Preventive Services operations. For several months, the centre has been reporting a loss. Shown below is the responsibility report for the month of May 2005:

	Actual	Difference from Budget
Service revenue	$40,000	$1,000 F
Variable costs		
Filling materials	5,000	100 U
Novocain	4,000	200 U
Supplies	2,000	250 F
Dental assistant wages	2,500	0
Utilities	500	50 U
Total variable costs	14,000	100 U
Fixed costs		
Allocated portion of receptionist's salary	3,000	200 U
Dentist salary	10,000	500 U
Equipment amortization	6,000	0
Allocated portion of building amortization	15,000	1,000 U
Total fixed costs	34,000	1,700 U
Operating income (loss)	$ (8,000)	$ 800 U

In addition, the owners know that the investment in operating assets at the beginning of the month was $82,400, and it was $77,600 at the end of the month. They have asked for your help in evaluating their current performance reporting system.

Instructions

(a) Prepare a responsibility report for an investment centre as illustrated in the chapter.
(b) ▭▭▭▶ Write a memo to the owners in which you discuss the weaknesses of their current reporting system.

Determine missing amounts in responsibility reports for three investment centres.
(SO 7)

E10–13 The Transamerica Transportation Company uses a responsibility reporting system to measure the performance of its three investment centres: planes, taxis, and limos. Segment performance is measured using a system of responsibility reports and return on investment calculations. The allocation of resources within the company and the segment managers' bonuses are based in part on the results shown in these reports.

Recently, the company was the victim of a computer virus that deleted portions of its accounting records. This was discovered when the current period's responsibility reports were being prepared. The printout of the actual operating results appeared as follows:

	Planes	Taxis	Limos
Service revenue	$ (a)	$500,000	$ (b)
Variable costs	5,500,000	(c)	320,000
Contribution margin	(d)	200,000	480,000
Controllable fixed costs	1,500,000	(e)	(f)
Controllable margin	(g)	80,000	240,000
Average operating assets	25,000,000	(h)	1,600,000
Return on investment	12%	10%	(i)

Instructions

Determine the missing amounts.

Calculate and compare ROI and residual income.
(SO 8)

*E10–14 Presented below is selected information for three regional divisions of Yono Company:

	Divisions		
	North	West	South
Contribution margin	$300,000	$500,000	$400,000
Controllable margin	$150,000	$400,000	$225,000
Average operating assets	$1,000,000	$2,000,000	$1,500,000
Minimum rate of return	13%	16%	10%

Instructions

(a) Calculate the return on investment for each division.

(b) Calculate the residual income for each division.

(c) Assume that each division has an investment opportunity that would provide a rate of return of 19%. If the ROI is used to measure performance, which division or divisions will probably make the additional investment?

(d) Assume the same opportunity as in (c), except that residual income is used to measure performance. Which division or divisions will probably make the additional investment?

*E10–15   Presented below is selected financial information for two divisions of Capital Brewery. Determine the missing amounts.

Determine missing amounts for residual income.
(SO 8)

	Lager	Lite Lager
Contribution margin	$500,000	$300,000
Controllable margin	$200,000	(c)
Average operating assets	(a)	$1,000,000
Minimum rate of return	(b)	13%
Return on investment	25%	(d)
Residual income	$90,000	$200,000

Problems: Set A

P10–16A   Alcore Company estimates that 240,000 direct labour hours will be worked during 2005 in the assembly department. Based on that, the following budgeted manufacturing overhead data are calculated:

Prepare flexible budget and budget report for manufacturing overhead.
(SO 3, 5)

Variable Overhead Costs		Fixed Overhead Costs	
Indirect labour	$ 72,000	Supervision	$ 72,000
Indirect materials	48,000	Amortization	36,000
Repairs	24,000	Insurance	9,600
Utilities	38,400	Rent	9,000
Lubricants	9,600	Property taxes	6,000
	$192,000		$132,600

It is estimated that the direct labour hours worked each month will range from 18,000 to 24,000 hours.

During January, 20,000 direct labour hours were worked and the following overhead costs were incurred:

Variable Overhead Costs		Fixed Overhead Costs	
Indirect labour	$ 6,200	Supervision	$ 6,000
Indirect materials	3,600	Amortization	3,000
Repairs	1,600	Insurance	800
Utilities	2,500	Rent	800
Lubricants	830	Property taxes	500
	$14,730		$11,100

Instructions

(a) Prepare a monthly flexible manufacturing overhead budget for each increment of 2,000 direct labour hours over the relevant range for the year ending December 31, 2005.

(b) Prepare a manufacturing overhead budget report for January.

(c) ✏▶ Comment on management's efficiency in controlling the manufacturing overhead costs in January.

P10–17A   Kitchen Care Inc. (KCI) is a manufacturer of toaster ovens. To improve control over operations, the president of KCI wants to begin using a flexible budgeting system, rather than use only the current master budget. The following data are available for KCI's expected costs at production levels of 90,000, 100,000, and 110,000 units:

Prepare flexible budget report for cost centre.
(SO 3)

Variable costs	
Manufacturing	$6 per unit
Administrative	$3 per unit
Selling	$1 per unit
Fixed costs	
Manufacturing	$150,000
Administrative	$80,000

Instructions

(a) Prepare a flexible budget for each of the possible production levels: 90,000, 100,000, and 110,000 units.
(b) If KCI sells the toaster ovens for $15 each, how many units will it have to sell to make a profit of $250,000 before taxes?

(CGA-adapted)

Prepare flexible budget, budget report, and graph for manufacturing overhead.
(SO 3, 5)

P10−18A High Arctic Manufacturing Company produces one product, Kebo. Because of wide fluctuations in the demand for Kebo, the assembly department has significant variations in its monthly production levels.

The annual master manufacturing overhead budget is based on 300,000 direct labour hours. In July, 27,500 labour hours were worked. The master manufacturing overhead budget for the year and the actual overhead costs incurred in July are as follows:

Overhead Costs	Master Budget (annual)	Actual in July
Variable		
Indirect labour	$ 300,000	$26,000
Indirect materials	210,000	17,000
Utilities	90,000	8,100
Maintenance	60,000	5,400
Fixed		
Supervision	180,000	15,000
Amortization	120,000	10,000
Insurance and taxes	60,000	5,000
Total	$1,020,000	$86,500

Instructions

(a) Prepare a monthly flexible overhead budget for the year ending December 31, 2005, assuming monthly production levels range from 22,500 to 30,000 direct labour hours. Use increments of 2,500 direct labour hours.
(b) Prepare a budget performance report for the month of July 2005, comparing actual results with budgeted data based on the flexible budget.
(c) ▭▬▭▷ Were costs controlled effectively? Explain.
(d) State the formula for calculating the total monthly budgeted costs in High Arctic Company.
(e) Prepare a flexible budget graph showing total budgeted costs at 25,000 and 27,500 direct labour hours. Use increments of 5,000 on the horizontal axis and increments of $10,000 on the vertical axis.

Prepare flexible budget report; compare flexible and fixed budgets.
(SO 2, 3)

P10−19A Doggone Groomers is in the dog-grooming business. Its operating costs are described by the following formulas:

Grooming supplies (variable)	$y = \$0 + \$4.00x$
Direct labour (variable)	$y = \$0 + \$12.00x$
Overhead (mixed)	$y = \$8,000 + \$1.00x$

Puli, the owner, has determined that direct labour is the cost driver for all three categories of costs.

Instructions

(a) Prepare a flexible budget for activity levels of 550, 600, and 700 direct labour hours.
(b) ▭▭▭▷ Explain why the flexible budget is more informative than the fixed budget.
(c) Calculate the total cost per direct labour hour at each of the activity levels specified in part (a).
(d) The groomers at Doggone normally work a total of 650 direct labour hours during each month. Each grooming job normally takes a groomer 1¼ hours. Puli wants to earn a profit equal to 40% of the costs incurred. Determine what she should charge each pet owner for grooming.

(CGA-adapted)

P10–20A Laesecke Company uses budgets to control costs. The May 2005 budget report for the company's packaging department is as follows:

State total budgeted cost formula, and prepare flexible budget reports for two time periods. (SO 2, 3, 5)

LAESECKE COMPANY
Budget Report
Packaging Department
Month Ended May 31, 2005

Manufacturing Costs	Budget	Actual	Difference: Favourable (F)/ Unfavourable (U)
Variable costs			
Direct materials	$ 35,000	$ 37,500	$2,500 U
Direct labour	50,000	53,000	3,000 U
Indirect materials	15,000	15,200	200 U
Indirect labour	12,500	13,000	500 U
Utilities	7,500	7,100	400 F
Maintenance	5,000	5,200	200 U
Total variable costs	125,000	131,000	6,000 U
Fixed costs			
Rent	8,000	8,000	0
Supervision	9,000	9,000	0
Amortization	5,000	5,000	0
Total fixed cost	22,000	22,000	0
Total costs	$147,000	$153,000	$6,000 U

The monthly budget amounts in the report were based on an expected production of 50,000 units per month or 600,000 units per year.

The company president was unhappy with the department manager's performance. The department manager, who thought he had done a good job, could not understand the unfavourable results. In May, 55,000 units were produced.

Instructions

(a) State the total budgeted cost formula.
(b) Prepare a budget report for May, using flexible budget data. Why does this report provide a better basis for evaluating performance than the report based on static budget data?
(c) In June, 40,000 units were produced. Prepare the budget report using flexible budget data, assuming (1) each variable cost was 20% less in June than its actual cost in May, and (2) fixed costs were the same in the month of June as in May.

P10–21A Korene Manufacturing Inc. operates the home appliance division as a profit centre. Operating data for this division for the year ended December 31, 2005, are shown in the following table:

Prepare responsibility report for profit centre. (SO 6)

	Budget	Difference from Budget
Sales	$2,400,000	$80,000 U
Cost of goods sold		
Variable costs	1,200,000	47,000 U
Controllable fixed costs	200,000	10,000 F
Selling and administrative expenses		
Variable costs	240,000	8,000 F
Controllable fixed costs	60,000	6,000 U
Noncontrollable fixed costs	50,000	2,000 U

In addition, Korene Manufacturing incurred $150,000 of indirect fixed costs that were budgeted at $155,000. Twenty percent of these costs are allocated to the home appliance division. None of these costs can be controlled by the division manager.

Instructions

(a) Prepare a responsibility report for the home appliance division for the year.
(b) ◖▬▬▬▷ Comment on the manager's performance in controlling revenues and costs.
(c) Identify any costs that were excluded from the responsibility report and explain why they were excluded.

Prepare responsibility report for investment centre, and calculate ROI.
(SO 7)

P10–22A Chudzik Manufacturing Company makes garden and lawn equipment. The company operates through three divisions. Each division is an investment centre. Operating data for the lawn mower division for the year ended December 31, 2005, and relevant budget data are as follows:

	Actual	Comparison with Budget
Sales	$3,000,000	$150,000 unfavourable
Variable cost of goods sold	1,400,000	100,000 unfavourable
Variable selling and administrative expenses	300,000	50,000 favourable
Controllable fixed cost of goods sold	270,000	On target
Controllable fixed selling and administrative expenses	130,000	On target

Average operating assets for the year for the lawn mower division were $5 million, which was also the budgeted amount.

Instructions

(a) Prepare a responsibility report (in thousands of dollars) for the lawn mower division.
(b) ◖▬▬▬▷ Evaluate the manager's performance. Which items will likely be investigated by top management?
(c) Calculate the expected ROI in 2006 for the lawn mower division, assuming the following independent changes:
   1. The variable cost of goods sold decreases by 15%.
   2. The average operating assets decrease by 20%.
   3. Sales increased by $500,000 and this increase is expected to increase the contribution margin by $200,000.

Discuss impact of ROI and residual income on manager performance.
(SO 7)

P10–23A Iqaluit Corporation recently announced a bonus plan to be awarded to the manager of the most profitable division. The three managers are to choose whether the ROI or residual income will be used to measure profitability. In addition, they must decide whether investments will be measured using the gross book value or net book value of assets. Iqaluit defines income as operating income and investments as total assets. The following information is available for the year just ended:

Division	Gross Book Value of Assets	Accumulated Amortization	Operating Income
A	$800,000	$400,000	$100,000
B	750,000	450,000	85,000
C	250,000	50,000	50,000

Iqaluit uses a required rate of return of 10% on investments to calculate residual income.

Instructions

Which method for calculating performance did each vice-president use if each one wanted to show that his or her division had the best performance?

(CMA Canada-adapted)

P10–24A Kojak Company uses a responsibility reporting system. It has divisions in Calgary, Winnipeg, and Sudbury. Each division has three production departments: cutting, shaping, and finishing. Responsibility for each department belongs to a manager who reports to the division production manager. Each division manager reports to the vice-president of production. There are also vice-presidents for marketing and finance. All vice-presidents report to the president.

Prepare reports for cost centres under responsibility accounting, and comment on performance of managers. (SO 4, 5)

In January 2005, controllable budgeted and actual manufacturing overhead costs for the departments and divisions were as follows:

Manufacturing Overhead	Budget	Actual
Individual costs—cutting department—Winnipeg		
Indirect labour	$ 70,000	$ 73,000
Indirect materials	46,000	46,700
Maintenance	18,000	20,500
Utilities	17,000	20,100
Supervision	20,000	22,000
	$171,000	$182,300
Total costs		
Shaping department—Winnipeg	$148,000	$158,000
Finishing department—Winnipeg	208,000	210,000
Calgary division	673,000	676,000
Sudbury division	715,000	722,000

Additional overhead costs were incurred as follows: Winnipeg division production manager—actual costs $52,500, budgeted $51,000; vice-president of production—actual costs $65,000, budgeted $64,000; president—actual costs $76,400, budgeted $74,200. These expenses are not allocated.

The vice-presidents who report to the president, other than the vice-president of production, had the following expenses:

	Budget	Actual
Marketing	$130,000	$133,600
Finance	105,000	108,000

Instructions

(a) Using the format on page 428, prepare the following responsibility reports:
  1. Manufacturing overhead—cutting department manager—Winnipeg division
  2. Manufacturing overhead—Winnipeg division manager
  3. Manufacturing overhead—vice-president of production
  4. Manufacturing overhead and expenses—president

(b) ▭▭▭▷ Comment on the comparative performances of: (1) the department managers in the Winnipeg division, (2) the division managers, and (3) the vice-presidents.

*P10–25A Haniwall Industries has manufactured prefabricated houses for over 20 years. The houses are constructed in sections that are assembled on customers' lots. Haniwall expanded into the precut housing market when it acquired Miramichi Company, one of its suppliers. In this market, various types of lumber are precut into the appropriate lengths, banded into packages, and shipped to customers' lots for assembly. Haniwall designated the Miramichi division as an investment centre.

Calculate ROI and residual income and discuss impact on manager performance. (SO 8)

Haniwall uses the return on investment (ROI) as a performance measure and defines investment as the average operating assets. Management bonuses are based in part on the ROI. All investments are expected to earn a minimum rate of return of 16%. Miramichi's ROI has ranged from 20.1% to 23.5% since it was acquired. Miramichi had an investment opportunity in 2005 that had an estimated ROI of 19%. Miramichi's management decided against the investment because it believed the investment would decrease the division's overall ROI.

Selected financial information for Miramichi are presented below. The division's average operating assets were $12.3 million for the year 2005.

MIRAMICHI DIVISION
Selected Financial Information
Year Ended December 31, 2005

Sales	$26,000,000
Contribution margin	9,100,000
Controllable margin	2,460,000

Instructions

(a) Calculate the following performance measures for 2005 for the Miramichi division: (1) return on investment (ROI), and (2) residual income.
(b) ◁▦▦▶ Would the management of the division have been more likely to accept the investment opportunity it had in 2005 if residual income had been used as a performance measure instead of the ROI? Explain your answer.

(CMA-adapted)

Calculate ROI and residual income and discuss impact on manager performance.
(SO 7, 8)

*P10–26A Lawton Industries, founded by a former vice-president of Haniwall Industries in P10–25A, has been manufacturing prefabricated houses for the past five years. To compete with Haniwall, Lawton also expanded into the precut housing market by acquiring one of its suppliers, Presser Company. After designating Presser as an investment centre, Lawton next decided to use the ROI as a performance measure and to give managers bonuses that are partly based on the ROI. Lawton defines investments as average productive assets and expects a minimum return of 15% before income taxes. Presser's ROI has averaged 19.5% since it was acquired.

In 2005, Presser found an investment opportunity that would have an estimated ROI of 18%. After analyzing the opportunity, Presser's management finally decided not to make the investment because management did not want the division's overall ROI to decrease.

The 2005 income statement for Presser follows. The division had operating assets of $25.2 million at the end of 2005, which was a 5% increase over the 2004 year-end balance.

PRESSER DIVISION
Income Statement
Year Ended June 30, 2005
(in thousands)

Sales revenue		$48,000
Cost of goods sold		31,600
Gross margin		16,400
Operating expenses		
Administrative	$4,280	
Selling	7,200	11,480
Income from operations before income taxes		$ 4,920

Instructions

(a) Calculate the following performance measures for 2005 for the Presser division: (1) the return on investment (ROI), and (2) the residual income.
(b) Would the management of Presser division have been more likely to accept the investment opportunity it had in 2005 if residual income had been used as a performance measure instead of the ROI? Explain your answer.
(c) The Presser division is a separate investment centre within Lawton Industries. Identify several items that Presser should control so that it can be evaluated fairly by either the ROI or residual income performance measures.

(CMA Canada-adapted)

Calculate ROI and residual income, identify responsibility centres and discuss impact on manager performance.
(SO 5, 6, 7, 8)

*P10–27A National Motors is a major car manufacturer with a wide variety of models, including its most recent one, the *Mountaineer*. The new model uses parts and components from external suppliers, as well as some from the following divisions of National Motors:

Division S:
This division manufactures stainless steel components for the *Mountaineer* and other models sold by National Motors. Sales of components for the *Mountaineer* represent 25% of the division's revenue.

Division F:

This division produces different wipers that fit a wide variety of car models manufactured by National Motors and other major car manufacturers. Sales of wipers for the *Mountaineer* are negligible. Division F has total assets of $250 million. Last year's revenues were $150 million with operating expenses of $117.5 million.

Division D:

This division uses all its capacity to manufacture engines for the *Mountaineer.* The division manager is strictly responsible for choosing the inputs used to produce the engines.

National Motors uses the return on investment (ROI) to evaluate the performance of the division managers. The required rate of return of 14% is the same for all divisions.

At the last meeting of the division managers, Mr. Goodman, manager of Division D, was not happy because he thought that he was not evaluated fairly. The chief executive officer of National Motors did not understand why Mr. Goodman's evaluation would be unfair as she thought that the ROI was the best measure available to evaluate performance.

Instructions

(a) Calculate the residual income for Division F based on last year's results and investment. Show your calculations.
(b) Identify which type of responsibility centre each of the three divisions should be. Briefly explain your reasoning.
(c) Is the ROI appropriate to evaluate the performance of Mr. Goodman and Division D? Briefly explain your answer.

(CGA-adapted)

Problems: Set B

P10–28B   Oakley Company estimates that 360,000 direct labour hours will be worked during 2005 in the packaging department. Based on that, the following budgeted manufacturing overhead cost data are calculated for the year.

Prepare flexible budget and budget report for manufacturing overhead. (SO 3, 5)

Fixed Overhead Costs		Variable Overhead Costs	
Supervision	$90,000	Indirect labour	$144,000
Amortization	60,000	Indirect materials	90,000
Insurance	30,000	Repairs	54,000
Rent	36,000	Utilities	72,000
Property taxes	18,000	Lubricants	18,000
	$234,000		$378,000

It is estimated that the direct labour hours worked each month will range from 27,000 to 36,000 hours.

During October, 27,000 direct labour hours were worked and the following overhead costs were incurred:

1. Fixed overhead costs: supervision $7,500; amortization $5,000; insurance $2,470; rent $3,000; and property taxes $1,500
2. Variable overhead costs: indirect labour $11,760; indirect materials $6,400; repairs $4,000; utilities $5,700; and lubricants $1,640

Instructions

(a) Prepare a monthly flexible manufacturing overhead budget for each increment of 3,000 direct labour hours over the relevant range for the year ending December 31, 2005.
(b) Prepare a flexible budget report for October.
(c) ✏️ Comment on management's efficiency in controlling manufacturing overhead costs in October.

P10–29B   Finesse Company manufactures tablecloths. Sales have grown rapidly over the past two years. As a result, the president has installed a budgetary control system for 2005. The following data were used in developing the master manufacturing overhead budget for the ironing department. The budget is based on an activity index of direct labour hours.

Prepare flexible budget, budget report, and graph for manufacturing overhead. (SO 3, 5)

Variable Costs	Rate per Direct Labour Hour	Annual Fixed Costs	
Indirect labour	$0.40	Supervision	$30,000
Indirect materials	0.60	Amortization	18,000
Factory utilities	0.30	Insurance	12,000
Factory repairs	0.20	Rent	24,000

The master overhead budget was prepared on the expectation that 480,000 direct labour hours would be worked during the year. In June, 42,000 direct labour hours were worked. At that level of activity, actual costs were as follows:

1. Variable—per direct labour hour: indirect labour $0.43; indirect materials $0.58; factory utilities $0.32; and factory repairs $0.24
2. Fixed: same as budgeted

Instructions

(a) Prepare a monthly flexible manufacturing overhead budget for the year ending December 31, 2005, assuming production levels range from 35,000 to 50,000 direct labour hours. Use increments of 5,000 direct labour hours.
(b) Prepare a budget performance report for June, comparing actual results with budgeted data based on the flexible budget.
(c) Were costs effectively controlled? Explain.
(d) State the formula for calculating the total budgeted costs for Finesse Company.
(e) Prepare a flexible budget graph, showing total budgeted costs at 35,000 and 45,000 direct labour hours. Use increments of 5,000 direct labour hours on the horizontal axis and increments of $10,000 on the vertical axis.

Prepare flexible budget reports for varying situations using total budgeted cost formula.
(SO 2, 3, 5)

P10–30B Yaeger Company uses budgets in controlling costs. The August 2005 budget report for the company's assembling department is as follows:

YAEGER COMPANY
Budget Report
Assembling Department
Month Ended August 31, 2005

Manufacturing Costs	Budget	Actual	Difference: Favourable (F)/ Unfavourable (U)
Variable costs			
Direct materials	$ 48,000	$ 47,000	$1,000 F
Direct labour	66,000	62,700	3,300 F
Indirect materials	24,000	24,200	200 U
Indirect labour	18,000	17,500	500 F
Utilities	15,000	14,900	100 F
Maintenance	9,000	9,200	200 U
Total variable costs	180,000	175,500	4,500 F
Fixed costs			
Rent	12,000	12,000	0
Supervision	17,000	17,000	0
Amortization	7,000	7,000	0
Total fixed costs	36,000	36,000	0
Total costs	$216,000	$211,500	$4,500 F

The monthly budget amounts in the report were based on an expected production of 60,000 units per month or 720,000 units per year. The assembling department manager is pleased with the report and expects a raise, or at least praise for a job well done. The company president, however, is unhappy with the results for August, because only 58,000 units were produced.

Instructions

(a) State the total monthly budgeted cost formula.
(b) Prepare a budget report for August using flexible budget data. Why does this report provide a better basis for evaluating performance than the report based on static budget data?

(c) In September, 64,000 units were produced. Prepare the budget report using flexible budget data, assuming (1) each variable cost was 10% higher than its actual cost in August, and (2) fixed costs were the same in September as in August.

P10–31B Henning Manufacturing Inc. operates its patio furniture division as a profit centre. Operating data for this division for the year ended December 31, 2005, are as follows:

Prepare responsibility report for a profit centre. (SO 6)

	Budget	Difference from Budget
Sales	$2,500,000	$70,000 F
Cost of goods sold		
Variable costs	1,300,000	33,000 F
Controllable fixed costs	200,000	5,000 U
Selling and administrative expenses		
Variable costs	220,000	7,000 U
Controllable fixed costs	50,000	2,000 U
Noncontrollable fixed costs	70,000	4,000 U

In addition, Henning Manufacturing incurs $180,000 of indirect fixed costs that were budgeted at $175,000. Twenty percent of these costs are allocated to the patio furniture division.

Instructions

(a) Prepare a responsibility report for the patio furniture division for the year.
(b) ▭▭▭▷ Comment on the manager's performance in controlling revenues and costs.
(c) Identify any costs that have been excluded from the responsibility report and explain why they were excluded.

P10–32B Alosio Manufacturing Company manufactures a variety of tools and industrial equipment. The company operates three divisions. Each division is an investment centre. Operating data for the home division for the year ended December 31, 2005, and relevant budget data are as follows:

Prepare responsibility report for investment centre, and calculate ROI. (SO 7)

	Actual	Comparison with Budget
Sales	$1,550,000	$100,000 favourable
Variable cost of goods sold	700,000	70,000 unfavourable
Variable selling and administrative expenses	125,000	25,000 unfavourable
Controllable fixed cost of goods sold	170,000	On target
Controllable fixed selling and administrative expenses	100,000	On target

Average operating assets for the year for the home division were $2.5 million, which was also the budgeted amount.

Instructions

(a) Prepare a responsibility report (in thousands of dollars) for the home division.
(b) ▭▭▭▷ Evaluate the manager's performance. Which items will likely be investigated by top management?
(c) Calculate the expected ROI in 2006 for the home division, assuming the following independent changes to actual data:
  1. The variable cost of goods sold is decreased by 6%.
  2. The average operating assets are decreased by 10%.
  3. Sales are increased by $200,000, and this increase is expected to increase the contribution margin by $90,000.

*P10–33B The Fun Time Entertainment Division (FTED) of Mason Industries manufactures go-karts and other recreational vehicles. FTED is considering building a new plant in 2005. The investment will cost $5 million. The expected revenues and costs for the new plant in 2005 are as follows:

Compare ROI and residual income with supporting calculations. (SO 7, 8)

Revenues	$4,800,000
Variable costs	1,600,000
Fixed costs	2,350,000
Operating income	$ 850,000

FTED's ROI in 2005 is 24%. The ROI is defined as operating income divided by total assets. The bonuses of Jack John, the division manager of FTED, and other division managers are based on division ROI.

Instruction

(a) If Mason Industries uses the ROI to evaluate division managers, explain why FTED would be reluctant to build the new plant. Show all calculations.
(b) Suppose Mason Industries uses residual income as the basis for awarding bonuses to FTED's managers. Suppose also that the required rate of return on investment is 15%. Would FTED be more willing to build the new plant? Explain.

(CMA Canada-adapted)

Calculate ROI and residual income and rank department performances. (SO 7, 8)

*P10–34B   Northern Pride Inc., a diversified company, operates four departments. The company has collected the following departmental information for 2005:

Department	Sales	Cost of Goods Sold	Operating Expenses	Current Investment
1	$ 200,000	$ 150,000	$ 15,000	$ 175,000
2	90,000	35,000	23,500	210,000
3	1,500,000	1,173,000	195,000	1,100,000
4	1,250,000	750,000	276,000	1,400,000

Instructions

(a) Rank the four departments based on their return on investment.
(b) Rank the four departments based on their residual income. Assume that the company requires a minimum return on the current investment of 10%.
(c) ▭▤▤▤▷ Explain why the rankings in part (a) and part (b) are similar or different.

(CGA-adapted)

Discuss impact of ROI and residual income on manager performance. (SO 8)

*P10–35B   Kappa Company has three divisions: A, B, and C. Each year the vice-president in charge of the best performing division is entitled to a sizeable bonus. The results for the year are now in and each vice-president has claimed that the bonus should be his or hers, using some version of return on investment (ROI) or residual income (RI), and basing their calculations on either the net book value (defined as original/historical cost less accumulated amortization) or the gross book value (GBV), defined as original/historical cost *without* any amortization of the asset base.

The vice-presidents based their claims on the following information:

Division	GBV at Start of Year	Controllable Income
A	$400,000	$47,500
B	380,000	46,000
C	250,000	30,800

All divisions have fixed assets with a 20-year useful life and no disposal value. The fixed assets were purchased 10 years ago. Kappa's cost of capital is 10%. The company's three divisions all use beginning-of-the-year values for invested capital in the ROI or RI calculation. Assume straight-line amortization.

Instructions

Which method for evaluating performance did each vice-president use in order to show that his or her division had the best performance?

(CGA-adapted)

Compare and contrast performances under ROI and residual income. (SO 7, 8)

*P10–36B   Return on investment (ROI) is often expressed as follows:

$$\text{ROI} = \frac{\text{Controllable margin}}{\text{Average operating assets}} = \frac{\text{Controllable margin}}{\text{Sales}} \times \frac{\text{Sales}}{\text{Average operating assets}}$$

Instructions

(a) Explain the advantages of breaking down the ROI calculation into two separate components.
(b) 1. Comparative data on three companies operating in the same industry follow. The minimum required ROI is 10% for all three companies. Determine the missing amounts.

	Company A	Company B	Company C
Sales	$1,000,000	$500,000	(a)
Net operating income	$100,000	$50,000	(b)
Average operating assets	$500,000	(c)	$5,000,000
Profit margin	(d)	(e)	0.5%
Assets turnover	(f)	(g)	2
Return on investment (ROI)	(h)	1%	(i)
Residual income	(j)	(k)	(l)

2. Compare and contrast the performance of the three companies, with reference to their relative performance as measured by the ROI and residual income.

(CGA-adapted)

Additional Cases

Cases

C10–37   Z-Bar Pastures is a 160-hectare farm on the outskirts of Swift Current, Saskatchewan, specializing in the boarding of brood mares and their foals. A recent economic downturn in the thoroughbred industry has led to a decline in breeding activities, and it has made the boarding business extremely competitive. To meet the competition, Z-Bar Pastures planned in 2005 to entertain clients, advertise more extensively, and absorb expenses formerly paid by clients, such as veterinary and blacksmith fees.

The budget report for 2005 is presented below. As shown, the static income statement budget for the year is based on an expected 21,900 boarding days at $25 per mare. The variable expenses per mare per day were budgeted as follows: feed $5; veterinary fees $3; blacksmith fees $0.30; and supplies $0.70. All other budgeted expenses were either semi-fixed or fixed.

During the year, management decided not to replace a worker who quit in March, but it did issue a new advertising brochure and entertained clients more.[2]

Z-BAR PASTURES
Static Budget Income Statement
Year Ended December 31, 2005

	Master Budget	Actual	Difference
Number of mares	60	52	8 U
Number of boarding days	21,900	18,980	2,920 U
Sales	$547,500	$379,600	$167,900 U
Less variable expenses			
Feed	109,500	104,390	5,110 F
Veterinary fees	65,700	58,838	6,862 F
Blacksmith fees	6,570	6,074	496 F
Supplies	15,330	12,954	2,376 F
Total variable expenses	197,100	182,256	14,844 F
Contribution margin	350,400	197,344	153,056 U
Less fixed expenses:			
Amortization	40,000	40,000	0
Insurance	11,000	11,000	0
Utilities	14,000	12,000	2,000 F
Repairs and maintenance	11,000	10,000	1,000 F
Labour	96,000	88,000	8,000 F
Advertisement	8,000	12,000	4,000 U
Entertainment	5,000	7,000	2,000 U
Total fixed expenses	185,000	180,000	5,000 F
Net income	$165,400	$ 17,344	$148,056 U

---

[2] Data for this case are based on Hans Sprohge and John Talbott, "New Applications for Variance Analysis," *Journal of Accountancy* (April 1989), pp. 137–141.

Instructions

With the class divided into groups, answer the following.

(a) Based on the static budget report:
1. What was (were) the primary cause(s) of the loss in net income?
2. Did management do a good, average, or poor job of controlling expenses?
3. Were management's decisions to stay competitive sound?
(b) Prepare a flexible budget report for the year.
(c) Based on the flexible budget report, answer the three questions in part (a) above.
(d) What course of action do you recommend for the management of Z-Bar Pastures?

C10–38   Castle Company manufactures expensive watch cases that are sold as souvenirs. Three of its sales departments are retail sales, wholesale sales, and outlet sales. The retail sales department is a profit centre. The wholesale sales department is a cost centre. Its managers merely take orders from customers who purchase through the company's whole-sale catalogue. The outlet sales department is an investment centre, because each manager is given full responsibility for an outlet store location. The manager can hire and dismiss employees; purchase, maintain, and sell equipment; and in general is fairly independent of company control.

Sara Sutton is a manager in the retail sales department. Gilbert Lewis manages the whole-sale sales department. José Lopez manages the Club Cartier outlet store in Montreal. The following are the budget responsibility reports for each of the three departments:

Budget			
	Retail Sales	Wholesale Sales	Outlet Sales
Sales	$ 750,000	$ 400,000	$200,000
Variable costs			
Cost of goods sold	150,000	100,000	25,000
Advertising	100,000	30,000	5,000
Sales salaries	75,000	15,000	3,000
Printing	10,000	20,000	5,000
Travel	20,000	30,000	2,000
Fixed costs			
Rent	50,000	30,000	10,000
Insurance	5,000	2,000	1,000
Amortization	75,000	100,000	40,000
Investment in assets	1,000,000	1,200,000	800,000

Actual Results			
	Retail Sales	Wholesale Sales	Outlet Sales
Sales	$ 750,000	$ 400,000	$200,000
Variable costs			
Cost of goods sold	195,000	120,000	26,250
Advertising	100,000	30,000	5,000
Sales salaries	75,000	15,000	3,000
Printing	10,000	20,000	5,000
Travel	15,000	20,000	1,500
Fixed costs			
Rent	40,000	50,000	12,000
Insurance	5,000	2,000	1,000
Amortization	80,000	90,000	60,000
Investment in assets	1,000,000	1,200,000	800,000

Instructions

(a) Determine which of the items should be included in the responsibility report for each of the three managers.
(b) Compare the budgeted measures with the actual results. Decide which results should be brought to the attention of each manager.

C10–39   The manufacturing overhead budget for Dillons Company contains the following items:

Variable expenses

Indirect materials	$28,000
Indirect labour	12,000
Maintenance expenses	10,000
Manufacturing supplies	6,000
Total variable expenses	$56,000

Fixed expenses

Supervision	$18,000
Inspection costs	1,000
Insurance expenses	2,000
Amortization	15,000
Total fixed expenses	$36,000

The budget was based on an estimated 2,000 units being produced. During the past month, 1,500 units were produced, and the following costs were incurred.

Variable expenses

Indirect materials	$28,200
Indirect labour	13,500
Maintenance expenses	8,200
Manufacturing supplies	5,100
Total variable expenses	$55,000

Fixed expenses

Supervision	$19,300
Inspection costs	1,200
Insurance expenses	2,200
Amortization	14,700
Total fixed expenses	$37,400

Instructions

(a) Determine which items would be controllable by Hideko Shitaki, the production manager.

(b) How much should have been spent during the month for the manufacture of the 1,500 units?

(c) Prepare a flexible manufacturing overhead budget report for Ms. Shitaki.

(d) Prepare a responsibility report. Include only the costs that Ms. Shitaki could have controlled. In an attached memo, describe clearly for Ms. Shitaki the areas in which her performance needs to be improved.

C10–40   The Madison Company purchased the Tek Company three years ago. Before the acquisition, Tek manufactured and sold plastic products to a wide variety of customers. Tek has since become a division of Madison and now manufactures only plastic Tek for products made by Madison's Macon division. Macon sells its products to hardware wholesalers.

Madison's corporate management gives the Tek division management a considerable amount of authority in running the division's operations. However, corporate management retains authority for decisions about capital investments, price setting on all products, and the quantity of each product to be produced by the Tek division.

Madison has a formal performance evaluation program for the management of all of its divisions. The performance evaluation program relies heavily on each division's return on investment. The income statement below for the Tek division is the basis for evaluating Tek's management.

The financial statements for the divisions are prepared by the corporate accounting staff. Costs for corporate general services are allocated to each division based on their sales dollars. The computer department's actual costs are allocated to the divisions based on usage. The net division investment includes the division's fixed assets at net book value (cost less amortization), division inventory, and corporate working capital that is allocated to each based on the division's sales dollars.

TEK DIVISION OF MADISON COMPANY
Income Statement
Year Ended March 31, 2005
(in thousands)

Sales		$4,000
Costs and expenses		
Product costs		
Direct materials	$ 500	
Direct labour	1,100	
Factory overhead	1,300	
Total	2,900	
Less: Increase in inventory	350	2,550
Engineering and research		120
Shipping and receiving		240
Division administration		
Manager's office	$ 210	
Cost accounting	40	
Personnel	82	332
Corporate costs		
Computer	$ 48	
General services	230	278
Total costs and expenses		3,520
Divisional operating income		$ 480
Net plant investment		$1,600
Return on investment		30%

Instructions

(a) Discuss Madison Company's financial reporting and performance evaluation program as it relates to the responsibilities of the Tek division.

(b) Based on your anwer to (a), recommend appropriate revisions of the financial information and reports that are used to evaluate the performance of Tek's management. If revisions are not necessary, explain why they are not needed.

(CMA Canada-adapted)

*C10–41　Raddington Industries produces tool and die machinery for manufacturers. In 2001, the company acquired one of its suppliers of alloy steel plates, Reigis Steel Company. In order to manage the two separate businesses, the operations of Reigis are reported separately as an investment centre.

Raddington monitors its divisions based on their divisional contribution margin and return on average investment (ROI), with investment defined as the average operating assets employed. Management bonuses are based on the ROI. The average cost of capital is 11% of the operating investment.

Reigis's cost of goods sold is considered to be entirely variable, while the division's administrative expenses are not dependent on volume. Selling expenses are a mixed cost, with 40% attributed to the sales volume. Reigis recently contemplated a capital acquisition with an estimated ROI of 11.5%; however, division management decided against the investment because it believed that the investment would decrease Reigis's overall ROI. The 2005 operating statement for Reigis follows. The division used operating assets of $15.75 million at June 30, 2005, a 5% increase over the 2004 year-end balance.

REIGIS STEEL DIVISION
Operating Statement
Year Ended June 30, 2005
(in thousands)

Sales revenue		$25,000
Less expenses:		
Cost of goods sold	$16,500	
Administrative expenses	3,955	
Selling expenses	2,700	23,155
Income from operations before income taxes		$ 1,845

Information

(a) Calculate the following performance measures for 2005 for the Reigis Steel Division: (1) the ROI before tax, and (2) the residual income

(b) Explain why management of the Reigis Steel Division would have been more likely to accept the capital acquisition if residual income rather than the ROI had been used as a performance measure.

(c) The Reigis Steel Division is a separate investment centre within Raddington Industries. Identify several items that Reigis should control if it is to be evaluated fairly by either the ROI or residual income performance measures.

(CMA Canada-adapted)

*C10–42 The performance of the division manager of Rarewood Furniture is measured by the ROI, defined as divisional segment income divided by the gross book value of total divisional assets. For existing operations, the division's projections for the coming year are as follows:

Sales	$ 20,000,000
Expenses	(17,500,000)
Segment income	$ 2,500,000

The gross book value of the total assets now used in operations is $12.5 million. Currently, the manager is evaluating an investment in a new product line that would, according to her projections, increase 2005 segment income by $200,000. The cost of the investment has not yet been determined. The company's cost of capital is 10%.

Instructions

(a) Calculate the ROI for 2005 without the new investment.

(b) Assuming the new product line would require an investment of $1.1 million, calculate the revised projected ROI for the division in 2005 with the new investment. Would the manager likely accept or reject the investment? Explain.

(c) How much would the investment have to cost for the manager the be indifferent about making it?

(d) Create a brief example with numbers to explain and illustrate how the use of residual income as a performance measure may encourage a manager to accept a project that is good for of the company, but that he or she might otherwise reject. (*Hint*: You may use above situation as an example for your explanation.)

(CGA-adapted)

C10–43 A company operates five different plants, located in Vancouver, Edmonton, Toronto, Montreal, and Halifax. The total company operating income is $1,900,275. The following information was collected for each location:

	Vancouver	Edmonton	Toronto	Montreal	Halifax
Sales	$3,750,000	$4,700,000	$1,800,875	$800,000	$500,250
Materials	1,600,950	1,500,450	500,450	150,450	100,450
Direct labour	800,900	1,590,900	590,900	150,900	280,500
Variable overhead	470,000	170,000	140,000	30,000	40,900
Other operating expenses	600,500	280,000	230,000	352,600	70,000
Current investment	4,550,000	5,500,000	2,000,000	700,000	300,000

Instructions

(a) Based on your calculations of the return on investments (ROI), which plant has the highest ROI? Show your calculations.
(b) Assume that the company requires a minimum return of 10% on the current investment. Which plant has the highest residual income? Show your calculations.
(c) Compare your answers in parts (a) and (b) and emphasize whether they are the same or different. Explain why.

(CGA-adapted)

C10–44   Canadian Products Corporation participates in a highly competitive industry. To compete successfully and reach its profit goals, the company has chosen the decentralized form of organization. Each manager of a decentralized investment centre is evaluated based on the centre's profit contribution, market penetration, and return on investment. When managers fail to meet the objectives set by corporate management, they are either demoted or dismissed.

An anonymous survey of managers in the company revealed that the managers feel pressured to compromise their personal ethical standards in order to reach corporate objectives. For example, at certain plant locations there was pressure to reduce quality control to a level which could not ensure that all unsafe products would be rejected. Also, sales personnel were encouraged to use questionable sales tactics to obtain orders, including gifts and other incentives to purchasing agents.

The chief executive officer is disturbed by the survey findings. In his opinion, such behaviour cannot be condoned by the company. He concludes that the company should do something about this problem.

Instructions

(a) Who are the stakeholders in this situation?
(b) Identify the ethical implications, conflicts, or dilemmas in the situation.
(c) What might the company do to reduce the pressure on managers and eliminate the ethical conflicts?

(CMA-adapted)

Answers to Self-Study Questions

1. c   2. b   3. a   4. d   5. a   6. d   7. d   8. b   9. b   10. d   11. c

Remember to go back to the Navigator Box at the beginning of the chapter to check off your completed work.

CHAPTER 11

Standard Costs and Balanced Scorecard

High Performance Is More Than Child's Play

Anyone who has played with or shopped for a child in recent years is familiar with Mega Bloks®. The simple interlocking building-block system has put the Montreal-based toy manufacturer in the upper ranks of the industry. Mega Bloks has become one of the top 10 toy brands in North America, winning several awards for its mixture of fun, creativity, and learning.

The Mega Bloks plant in Montreal produces more than 20 billion blocks a year, which represented about 55 to 60 percent of the company's total production in 2003. Mega Bloks outsources the remaining production to several companies in Asia. With volumes of this size, the company must keep tight control over manufacturing costs. An important part of the manufacturing process is determining how much direct materials, labour, and overhead should cost. This establishes standard costs that can then be compared to actual costs to assess performance efficiency.

Since Mega Bloks' toys are essentially plastic, the main raw materials that go into manufacturing them are the basic components of plastic resin: polyethylene, polystyrene, ABS (a copolymer of acrylonitrile, butadiene, and styrene), and polypropylene. Manufacturing overhead, meanwhile, includes facilities, machine maintenance, supervision, and quality control.

Although demand for the toys varies throughout the year according to the season, volume levels and thus labour rates are predictable, says Éric Phaneuf, director of finance and investor relations. "We are linked with our retailers regarding retail sales," he says. "So in the planning process, we look at both the sell-in (shipments to retailers) as well as retail sell-through." Mega Bloks determines the standard costs used to assess performance through a mix of the previous year's costs and current market price.

the navigator

THE NAVIGATOR

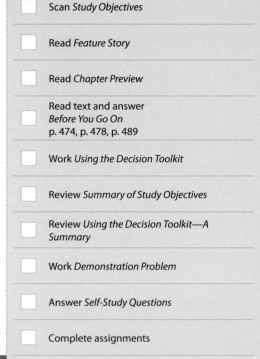

- ☐ Scan *Study Objectives*

- ☐ Read *Feature Story*

- ☐ Read *Chapter Preview*

- ☐ Read text and answer *Before You Go On* p. 474, p. 478, p. 489

- ☐ Work *Using the Decision Toolkit*

- ☐ Review *Summary of Study Objectives*

- ☐ Review *Using the Decision Toolkit—A Summary*

- ☐ Work *Demonstration Problem*

- ☐ Answer *Self-Study Questions*

- ☐ Complete assignments

STUDY OBJECTIVES

After studying this chapter, you should be able to:

1. Distinguish between a standard and a budget.
2. Identify the advantages of standard costs.
3. Describe how standards are set.
4. State the formulas for determining direct materials and direct labour variances.
5. State the formulas for determining manufacturing overhead variances.
6. Discuss the reporting of variances.
7. Prepare an income statement for management under a standard cost system.
8. Describe the balanced scorecard approach to performance evaluation.
9. Identify the features of a standard cost accounting system (Appendix 11A).

the navigator

Standards are a fact of life. You met the admission standards for the school you are attending. The vehicle that you drive had to meet certain governmental emissions standards. The hamburgers and salads you eat in a restaurant have to meet certain health and nutritional standards before they can be sold. And, as described in our feature story, Mega Bloks develops standards for the costs of its materials, labour, and overhead, which it compares with its actual costs. The reason for standards in these cases is very simple: they help to ensure that overall product quality is high. Without standards, quality control is lost.

In this chapter, we continue to study controlling costs. You will learn how to develop standard costs that can be used to evaluate performance.

The chapter is organized as follows:

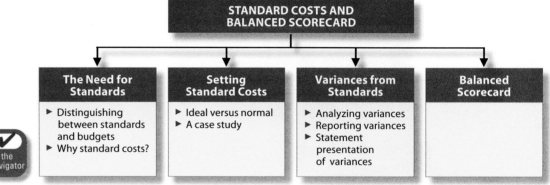

The Need for Standards

Standards are common in business. The standards that are imposed by government agencies are often called **regulations**. In Canada, most regulations fall under provincial jurisdiction, for example, in Ontario, the *Employment Standards Act* and *Ontario Human Rights Code*. Standards that are established internally by a company may include standards for personnel matters—such as employee absenteeism and ethical codes of conduct—quality control standards for products, and standard costs for goods and services. In managerial accounting, **standard costs** are predetermined unit costs that are used as measures of performance.

We will focus on manufacturing operations in the remainder of this chapter. But you should know that standard costs also apply to many types of service businesses as well. For example, a fast-food restaurant such as McDonald's, knows the price it should pay for pickles, beef, buns, and other ingredients. It also knows how much time it should take an employee to flip hamburgers. If too much is paid for pickles or too much time is taken to prepare Big Macs, the deviations are noticed and corrective action is taken. Standard costs can also be used in not-for-profit enterprises, such as universities, charitable organizations, and government agencies.

Distinguishing between Standards and Budgets

study objective 1

Distinguish between a standard and a budget.

In theory, standards and budgets are essentially the same. Both are predetermined costs, and both contribute to management planning and control. There is a difference, however, in the way the terms are expressed. A standard is a unit amount. A budget is a total amount. Thus, it is customary to state, for example, that the standard cost of direct labour for a unit of product is $10. If 5,000 units of the product are produced, the $50,000 of direct labour is the budgeted labour cost. A standard is the budgeted cost per unit of product. A standard is therefore concerned with each individual cost component that makes up the entire budget.

There are important accounting differences between budgets and standards. Except for when manufacturing overhead is applied to jobs and processes, budget data are not journalized in cost accounting systems. In contrast, as will be illustrated in the appendix to this chapter, standard costs are sometimes used in cost accounting systems. Also, a company may report its inventories at standard cost in its financial statements, but it would not report inventories at budgeted costs.

Why Standard Costs?

study objective 2

Identify the advantages of standard costs.

Standard costs offer several advantages to an organization, as shown in Illustration 11-1. These advantages are only available when standard costs are carefully established and prudently used. Using standards only as a way of placing blame can have a negative effect on managers and employees. In an effort to minimize this effect, many companies offer money incentives to employees who meet their standards.

Advantages of standard costs

Illustration 11-1 ◄

Advantages of standard costs

Facilitate management planning

Promote greater economy by making employees more "cost-conscious"

Help set selling prices

Contribute to management control by providing basis for evaluation of cost control

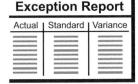

Help highlight variances in management by exception

Simplify costing of inventories and reduce clerical costs

Setting Standard Costs—A Difficult Task

study objective 3

Describe how standards are set.

Setting standards for the costs to produce a unit of product is a difficult task. It requires input from all persons who have responsibility for costs and quantities. To determine the standard cost of direct materials, management may have to consult purchasing agents, product managers, quality control engineers, and production supervisors. In setting the cost standard for direct labour, pay rate data are obtained from the payroll department, and the labour time requirements may be determined by industrial engineers. The managerial accountant provides important input for management in the standard-setting process by accumulating historical cost data and by knowing how costs respond to changes in activity levels.

To be effective in controlling costs, standard costs need to be up to date at all times. Thus, standards should be reviewed continuously. They should be changed whenever it is determined that the existing standard is not a good measure of performance. Circumstances that could cause the revision of a standard include changed wage rates resulting from a new union contract, a change in product specifications, or the use of a new manufacturing method.

Ideal versus Normal Standards

Standards may be set at one of two levels: ideal or normal. **Ideal standards** represent optimum levels of performance under perfect operating conditions. **Normal standards** represent efficient levels of performance that are attainable under expected operating conditions.

Some managers believe ideal standards will stimulate workers to constant improvement. However, most managers believe that ideal standards lower the morale of the entire workforce because they are so difficult, if not impossible, to meet. Very few companies use ideal standards.

Helpful Hint When standards are set too high, employees sometimes feel pressure to act unethically to meet these standards.

Most companies that use standards set them at a normal level. When they are properly set, normal standards are **rigorous but attainable**. Normal standards allow for rest periods, machine breakdowns, and other "normal" contingencies in the production process. It will be assumed in the remainder of this chapter that standard costs are set at a normal level.

A Case Study

To establish the standard cost of producing a product, it is necessary to establish standards for each manufacturing cost element—direct materials, direct labour, and manufacturing overhead. The standard for each element is determined from the standard price to be paid and the standard quantity to be used. To illustrate, we will look at a case study of how standard costs are set. In this extended example, we will assume that Xonic, Inc. wants to use standard costs to measure performance in filling an order for 1,000 kilograms of Grow!, a fertilizer concentrate.

Direct Materials

The **direct materials price standard** is the cost per unit of direct materials that should be incurred. This standard should be based on the purchasing department's best estimate of the **cost of raw materials**. This is often based on current purchase prices. The price standard should also include an amount for related costs, such as receiving, storing, and handling the material. Illustration 11-2 shows the calculation of the materials price standard per litre of material for Xonic's concentrate.

Illustration 11-2 ▶

Setting direct materials price standard

Item	Price
Purchase price, net of discounts	$2.70
Freight	0.20
Receiving and handling	0.10
Standard direct materials price per litre	$3.00

The **direct materials quantity standard** is the quantity of direct materials that should be used per unit of finished goods. This standard is expressed as a physical measure, such as kilograms, barrels, or litres. In setting the standard, management should consider both the quality and quantity of materials that are required to manufacture the product. The standard should include allowances (extra amounts) for unavoidable waste and normal spoilage. The standard quantity per unit for Xonic, Inc. is calculated in Illustration 11-3.

Illustration 11-3 ▶

Setting direct materials quantity standard

Item	Quantity (litres)
Required materials	3.5
Allowance for waste	0.4
Allowance for spoilage	0.1
Standard direct materials quantity per unit	4.0

The standard direct materials cost per unit is the standard direct materials price times the standard direct materials quantity. For Xonic, Inc., the standard direct materials cost per kilogram of concentrate is $12.00 ($3.00 × 4.0 litres).

Direct Labour

Alternative Terminology The direct labour price standard is also called the *direct labour rate standard*.

The **direct labour price standard** is the rate per hour that should be incurred for direct labour. This standard is based on current wage rates and is adjusted for expected changes, such as cost of living adjustments (COLAs). The price standard also generally includes employer payroll taxes and benefits, such as paid holidays and vacations. For Xonic, Inc., the direct labour price standard is given in Illustration 11-4.

Illustration 11-4 ◄

Setting direct labour price standard

Item	Price
Hourly wage rate	$ 7.50
COLA	0.25
Payroll taxes	0.75
Fringe benefits	1.50
Standard direct labour rate per hour	$10.00

The **direct labour quantity standard** is the time that should be required to make one unit of the product. This standard is especially critical in labour-intensive companies. Allowances should be made in this standard for rest periods, cleanup, machine setup, and machine downtime. Illustration 11-5 shows Xonic's direct labour quantity standard.

Illustration 11-5 ◄

Setting direct labour quantity standard

Item	Quantity (Hours)
Actual production time	1.5
Rest periods and cleanup	0.2
Setup and downtime	0.3
Standard direct labour hours per unit	2.0

The **standard direct labour cost per unit is the standard direct labour rate times the standard direct labour hours.** For Xonic, Inc., the standard direct labour cost per litre of concentrate is $20 ($10.00 × 2.0 hours).

Manufacturing Overhead

For manufacturing overhead, a **standard predetermined overhead rate** is used in setting the standard. This overhead rate is determined by dividing budgeted overhead costs by an expected standard activity index. Standard direct labour hours and standard machine hours are two examples of standard activity indexes.

As discussed in Chapter 4, many companies use activity-based costing (ABC) to allocate overhead costs. Because ABC uses multiple activity indexes to allocate overhead costs, it results in a better correlation between the activities and costs that are incurred. As a result, the use of ABC can significantly improve the usefulness of a standard cost system for management decision-making.

Xonic, Inc. uses standard direct labour hours as its activity index. The company expects to produce 13,200 kilograms of Grow! concentrate during the year at normal capacity. Since it takes two direct labour hours for each kilogram, the total standard direct labour hours is 26,400 (13,200 × 2). At this level of activity, overhead costs are expected to be $132,000. Of that amount, $79,200 is variable and $52,800 is fixed. The standard predetermined overhead rates are calculated as shown in Illustration 11-6.

Illustration 11-6 ◄

Calculating predetermined overhead rates

Budgeted Overhead Costs	Amount	Standard Direct Labour Hours	Overhead Rate per Direct Labour Hour
Variable	$ 79,200	26,400	$3.00
Fixed	52,800	26,400	2.00
Total	$132,000	26,400	$5.00

The **standard manufacturing overhead rate per unit is the predetermined overhead rate times the activity index quantity standard.** For Xonic, Inc., which uses direct labour hours as its activity index, the standard manufacturing overhead rate per kilogram of concentrate is $10 ($5 × 2 hours).

Total Standard Cost per Unit

Now that the standard quantity and price have been established per unit of product, the total standard cost can be determined. The total standard cost per unit is the sum of the standard costs of direct materials, direct labour, and manufacturing overhead. For Xonic, Inc., the total standard cost per kilogram of Grow! concentrate is $42, as shown on the standard cost card in Illustration 11-7.

Illustration 11-7 ▶

Standard cost per kilogram
of Grow! concentrate

Product: Grow!		Unit Measure: Kilogram	
Manufacturing Cost Elements	Standard Quantity	Standard Price	Standard Cost
Direct materials	4 litres	$ 3.00	$12.00
Direct labour	2 hours	10.00	20.00
Manufacturing overhead	2 hours	5.00	10.00
			$42.00

A standard cost card is prepared for each product. This card becomes the basis for determining variances from standards.

BUSINESS INSIGHT ▶ Management Perspective

Setting standards can be difficult. And sometimes the standard costs that an organization uses need to be changed. Canadian Pacific Railway (CPR) recognized that a good way to increase its bottom line was to look at its purchases. With the exception of labour, most corporate expenditures, including long-term capital investments, flow through the purchasing department, so it is not surprising that there are opportunities for costs savings there. A reduction in third-party spending would have a direct impact on net profits and income, since a dollar saved on expenses goes straight to the bottom line, whereas a dollar in revenue will contribute only a portion, depending on the operating ratio (expenses over revenue).

CPR used strategic sourcing to re-examine corporate purchasing behaviour and analyze current purchasing practices. It focused on third-party spending — how much was spent, with whom, at what time of year, etc. Costs were then separated into spending streams, from which easy targets for cost reduction were focused on. The emphasis was on alternatives, such as substitute parts or alternative processes. Cost savings quickly accumulated. And CPR found itself at that point which often leads to conflict. Once standard costs are adjusted, budgets also need to be adjusted, and few departments like to see their funding cut.

Source: Robert Lepine, CMA, and Ken Rawson, "Strategic Savings on the Right Track," *CMA Management Magazine,* February 2003.

BEFORE YOU GO ON . . .

▶ Review It

1. How do standards differ from budgets?
2. What are the advantages of standard costs for an organization?
3. Distinguish between normal standards and ideal standards. Which kind is used more often? Why?

▶ Do It

The management of Arapahoe Company has decided to use standard costs. Management asks you to explain the components that are used in setting the standard cost per unit for direct materials, direct labour, and manufacturing overhead.

Action Plan

• Differentiate between the two components of each standard: price and quantity.

Solution

The standard direct materials cost per unit is the standard direct materials price times the standard direct materials quantity. The standard direct labour cost per unit is the standard direct labour rate times the standard direct labour hours. The standard manufacturing overhead rate per unit is the standard predetermined overhead rate times the activity index quantity standard.

Related exercise material: BE11–2, BE11–3, and E11–1.

Variances from Standards

One of the major management uses of standard costs is to identify variances from standards. **Variances** are the differences between total actual costs and total standard costs. To illustrate, we will assume that in producing 1,000 kilograms of Grow! concentrate in the month of June, Xonic, Inc. incurred the costs shown in Illustration 11-8.

Alternative Terminology In business, the term variance is also used to indicate differences between total budgeted costs and total actual costs.

Illustration 11-8 ◀

Actual production costs

Direct materials	$13,020
Direct labour	20,580
Variable overhead	6,500
Fixed overhead	4,400
Total actual costs	$44,500

Total standard costs are determined by multiplying the units produced by the standard cost per unit. The total standard cost of Grow! is $42,000 (1,000 kilograms × $42). Thus, the total variance is $2,500, as shown in Illustration 11-9.

Illustration 11-9 ◀

Calculation of total variance

Actual costs	$44,500
Less: Standard costs	42,000
Total variance	$ 2,500

Note that the variance is expressed in total dollars and not on a per unit basis.

When actual costs are higher than standard costs, the variance is **unfavourable**. The $2,500 variance in June for Grow! is unfavourable. An unfavourable variance has a negative connotation. It suggests that too much was paid for one or more of the manufacturing cost elements or that the elements were used inefficiently.

If actual costs are less than standard costs, the variance is **favourable**. A favourable variance has a positive connotation. It suggests there is efficient management of manufacturing costs and efficient use of direct materials, direct labour, and manufacturing overhead. However, be careful: a favourable variance could be obtained by using inferior materials. In printing wedding invitations, for example, a favourable variance could result from using an inferior grade of paper. Or, a favourable variance might be achieved in installing tires on an automobile assembly line by tightening only half of the lug bolts. A variance is not favourable if quality control standards have been sacrificed.

Analyzing Variances

To properly interpret the significance of a variance, you must analyze it to determine the underlying factors. Analyzing variances begins by determining the cost elements that comprise the variance. **For each manufacturing cost element, a total dollar variance is calculated. Then this variance is analyzed into a price variance and a quantity variance.** The relationships are shown in Illustration 11-10.

Illustration 11-10 ◀

Variance relationships

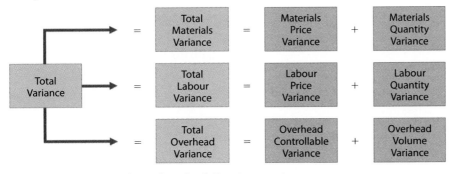

Each of the variances is explained in the following sections.

study objective 4

State the formulas for determining direct materials and direct labour variances.

Direct Materials Variances

In completing the order for 1,000 kilograms of concentrate, Xonic used 4,200 litres of direct materials. These were purchased at a cost of $3.10 per unit. The **total materials variance** is calculated using the formula in Illustration 11-11.

Illustration 11-11 ▶

Formula for total materials variance

Actual Quantity (AQ) × Actual Price (AP)	−	Standard Quantity (SQ) × Standard Price (SP)	=	Total Materials Variance (TMV)

For Xonic, the total materials variance is $1,020 unfavourable ($13,020 − $12,000), as shown below:

$$(4,200 \times \$3.10) - (4,000 \times \$3.00) = \$1,020 \text{ U}$$

Next, the total variance is analyzed to determine the amount that is attributable to price (costs) and to quantity (use). The **materials price variance** is calculated using the formula in Illustration 11-12.[1]

Illustration 11-12 ▶

Formula for materials price variance

Actual Quantity (AQ) × Actual Price (AP)	−	Actual Quantity (AQ) × Standard Price (SP)	=	Materials Price Variance (MPV)

For Xonic, Inc., the materials price variance is $420 ($13,020 − $12,600) unfavourable as shown below:

$$(4,200 \times \$3.10) - (4,200 \times \$3.00) = \$420 \text{ U}$$

Helpful Hint The alternative formula is: $AQ \times (AP - SP) = MPV$

The calculation in Illustration 11-12 is based on the fact that all of the material purchased during the month of June was used during the month. However, if the material purchased during the month is different from the material used during the month, the price variance should be calculated by multiplying the actual quantity purchased by the difference between the actual and standard price per unit. Using this formula, the calculation for Xonic would be $4,200 \times (\$3.10 - \$3.00) = \$420$ U. In general, most firms calculate the material price variance at the point of purchase, rather than at the point of use in production. This practice gives timely variance reports and the materials can be carried in the inventory accounts at their standard costs.

The **materials quantity variance** is determined using the formula in Illustration 11-13.

Illustration 11-13 ▶

Formula for materials quantity variance

Actual Quantity (AQ) × Standard Price (SP)	−	Standard Quantity (SQ) × Standard Price (SP)	=	Materials Quantity Variance (MQV)

For Xonic, the materials quantity variance is $600 unfavourable ($12,600 − $12,000), as shown below:

$$(4,200 \times \$3.00) - (4,000 \times \$3.00) = \$600 \text{ U}$$

Helpful Hint The alternative formula is: $SP \times (AQ - SQ) = MQV$

The quantity variance can also be calculated by applying the standard price to the difference between the actual and standard quantities used. The calculation in this example is $3.00 × (4,200 − 4,000) = $600 U.

The total materials variance of $1,020 (unfavourable), therefore, consists of the amounts shown in Illustration 11-14.

---

[1] We will assume that all materials purchased during the period are used in production and that no units remain in inventory the end of the period.

Materials price variance	$ 420 U	
Materials quantity variance	600 U	
Total materials variance	$1,020 U	

Illustration 11-14 ◄

Summary of materials variances

A matrix is sometimes used to analyze a variance. **When a matrix is used, the formulas for each cost element are calculated before the variances are calculated.**

The completed matrix for the direct materials variance for Xonic is shown in Illustration 11-15. The matrix provides a convenient structure for determining each variance.

Illustration 11-15 ▼

Matrix for direct materials variances

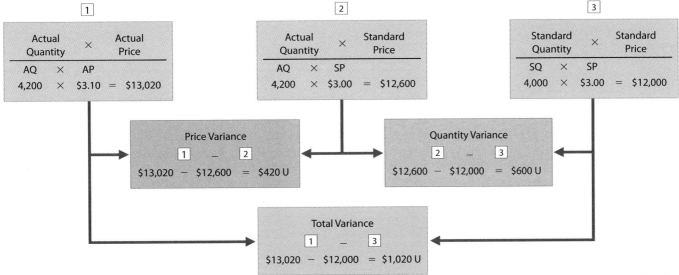

Causes of Materials Variances. What are the causes of a variance? The causes may be both internal and external factors. **The investigation of a materials price variance usually begins in the purchasing department.** Many factors affect the price paid for raw materials. These include the delivery method used, the availability of quantity and cash discounts, and the quality of the materials requested. If these factors have been considered in setting the price standard, the purchasing department should be responsible for any variances.

However, a variance may be beyond the control of the purchasing department. Sometimes, for example, prices may rise faster than expected. Moreover, actions by groups that the company cannot control, such as the OPEC nations' oil price increases, may cause an unfavourable variance. There are also times when a production department may be responsible for the price variance. This can occur when a rush order forces the company to pay a higher price for the materials.

The starting point for determining the cause(s) of an unfavourable **materials quantity variance** is in the **production department**. If the variances are due to inexperienced workers, faulty machinery, or carelessness, the production department would be responsible. However, if the materials obtained by the purchasing department were of inferior quality, then the purchasing department should be responsible.

"What caused the material price variances?"

Purchasing Dept.

"What caused the material quality variances?"

Production Dept.

Decision Toolkit

Decision Checkpoints	Info Needed for Decision	Tools to Use for Decision	How to Evaluate Results
Has management accomplished its price and quantity objectives for materials?	The actual cost and standard cost of materials	Materials price and materials quantity variances	Positive (favourable) variances suggest that the price and quantity objectives have been met.

BEFORE YOU GO ON . . .

▶ Review It

1. What are the three main components of the total variance from standard cost?
2. What are the formulas for calculating the total, price, and quantity variances for direct materials?

▶ Do It

The standard cost of Product XX includes two units of direct materials at $8.00 per unit. During July, 22,000 units of direct materials are purchased at $7.50 and are used to produce 10,000 units. Calculate the total, price, and quantity variances for the materials.

Action Plan

Use the formulas for calculating each of the materials variances:

- Total materials variance = (AQ × AP) − (SQ × SP)
- Materials price variance = (AQ × AP) − (AQ × SP)
- Materials quantity variance = (AQ × SP) − (SQ × SP)

Solution

Substituting amounts into the formulas, the variances are as follows:

Total materials variance = (22,000 × $7.50) − (20,000 × $8.00) = $5,000 unfavourable.
Materials price variance = (22,000 × $7.50) − (22,000 × $8.00) = $11,000 favourable.
Materials quantity variance = (22,000 × $8.00) − (20,000 × $8.00) = $16,000 unfavour-able.

Related exercise material: BE11–4, E11–2, E11–5, and E11–6.

Direct Labour Variances

The process of determining direct labour variances is the same as for determining the direct materials variances. In completing the Grow! order, Xonic incurred 2,100 direct labour hours at an average hourly rate of $9.80. The standard hours allowed for the units produced were 2,000 hours (1,000 units × 2 hours). The standard labour rate was $10 per hour. The **total labour variance** is obtained using the formula in Illustration 11-16

Illustration 11-16 ▶

Formula for total labour variance

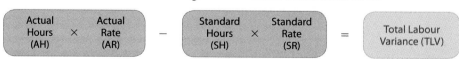

The total labour variance is $580 unfavourable ($20,580 − $20,000), as shown below.

(2,100 × $9.80) − (2,000 × $10.00) = $580 U

Illustration 11-17 the formula for the **labour price variance.**

Illustration 11-17 ◀

Formula for labour price variance

| Actual Hours (AH) | × | Actual Rate (AR) | − | Actual Hours (AH) | × | Standard Rate (SR) | = | Labour Price Variance (LPV) |

For Xonic, the labour price variance is $420 favourable ($20,580 − $21,000), as shown below:

$$(2{,}100 \times \$9.80) - (2{,}100 \times \$10.00) = \$420 \text{ F}$$

The labour price variance can also be calculated by multiplying the actual hours worked by the difference between the actual pay rate and the standard pay rate. The calculation in this example is $2{,}100 \times (\$10.00 - \$9.80) = \$420$ F.

The **labour quantity variance** is derived using the formula in Illustration 11-18.

Helpful Hint The alternative formula is: AH × (AR − SR) = LPV

Illustration 11-18 ◀

Formula for labour quantity variance

| Actual Hours (AH) | × | Standard Rate (SR) | − | Standard Hours (SH) | × | Standard Rate (SR) | = | Labour Quantity Variance (LQV) |

For Xonic, the labour quantity variance is $1,000 unfavourable ($21,000 − $20,000) as shown below:

$$(2{,}100 \times \$10.00) - (2{,}000 \times \$10.00) = \$1{,}000 \text{ U}$$

The same result can be obtained by multiplying the standard rate by the difference between the actual hours worked and standard hours allowed. In this case, the calculation is $\$10.00 \times (2{,}100 - 2{,}000) = \$1{,}000$ U.

The total direct labour variance of $580 (unfavourable), therefore, consists of the amounts shown in Ilustration 11-19.

Helpful Hint The alternative formula is: SR × (AH − SH) = LQV

Illustration 11-19 ◀

Summary of labour variances

Labour price variance	$ 420 F
Labour quantity variance	1,000 U
Total direct labour variance	$ 580 U

Illustration 11-20 ▼

Matrix for direct labour variances

These results can also be obtained from the matrix in Illustration 11-20.

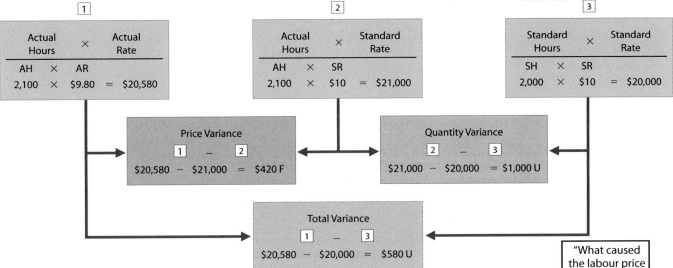

Causes of Labour Variances. Labour price variances usually result from two factors: (1) paying workers **higher wages than expected**, and (2) a **misallocation of workers**. In companies where pay rates are determined by union contracts, there should not be many labour price variances. When workers are not unionized, there is a much higher likelihood of such variances. The manager who authorized the wage increase is responsible for these variances.

"What caused the labour price variances?"

Personnel decisions

"What caused the labour quantity variances?"

Production Dept.

Misallocation of the workforce means using skilled workers instead of unskilled workers, and vice versa. The use of an inexperienced worker instead of an experienced one will result in a favourable price variance because of the lower pay rate of the unskilled worker. An unfavourable price variance would result if a skilled worker were substituted for an inexperienced one. The production department is generally responsible for labour price variances that results from misallocation of the workforce.

Labour quantity variances relate to the **efficiency of workers**. The cause of a quantity variance generally can be traced to the production department. The causes of an unfavourable variance may be poor training, worker fatigue, faulty machinery, or carelessness. These causes are the responsibility of the **production department**. However, if the excess time is due to inferior materials, the production department is not responsible.

Decision Toolkit

Decision Checkpoints	Info Needed for Decision	Tools to Use for Decision	How to Evaluate Results
Has management accomplished its price and quantity objectives for labour?	The actual cost and standard cost of labour	Labour price and labour quantity variance	Positive (favourable) variances suggest that the price and quantity objectives have been met.

BUSINESS INSIGHT ▶ Service Company Perspective

At United Parcel Service (UPS), performance standards for many tasks that are done by UPS employees are set by industrial engineers. For example, a UPS driver is expected to walk at a pace of three feet per second when going to a customer's door and knock rather than take the time to look for a doorbell. UPS executives attribute the company's success to its ability to manage and hold labour accountable.

Manufacturing Overhead Variances

study objective 5

State the formulas for determining manufacturing overhead variance.

The calculation of the manufacturing overhead variances is mostly the same as the calculation of the materials and labour variances. However, the task is more challenging for manufacturing overhead because both variable and fixed overhead costs must be considered.

Total Overhead Variance.   The **total overhead variance** is the difference between actual overhead costs and the overhead costs applied to work done. As indicated earlier, the manufacturing overhead costs incurred by Xonic were $10,900, as calculated in Illustration 11-21.

Illustration 11-21 ▶

Total overhead incurred

Variable overhead	$ 6,500
Fixed overhead	4,400
Total actual overhead	$10,900

Under a standard cost system, manufacturing overhead costs are applied to work in process based on the **standard hours allowed** for the work done. **Standard hours allowed** means the hours that should have been worked to produce the units that were produced. For the Grow! order, the standard hours allowed are 2,000. The predetermined overhead rate is $5 per direct labour hour. Thus, the overhead applied is $10,000 (2,000 × $5). Note that the actual hours of direct labour (2,100) are not used in applying manufacturing overhead.

Illustration 11-22 gives the formula for the total overhead variance:

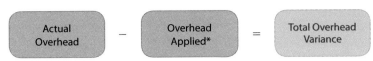

* Based on direct labour hours

Illustration 11-22 ◀

Formula for total overhead variance

Thus, for Xonic, the total overhead variance is $900 unfavourable, as shown below:

$$\$10,900 - \$10,000 = \$900\ U$$

The overhead variance is generally analyzed by examining the variable overhead variance and the fixed overhead variance. In general, the name usually given to the variable overhead variance is the **overhead controllable variance**. The fixed overhead variance is often referred to as the **overhead volume variance** because fixed overhead costs are usually known at the time the budget is prepared. Therefore, the fixed overhead controllable variance, which is the difference between the actual fixed overhead costs and the budget fixed overhead costs, is zero.

Overhead Controllable Variance. The **overhead controllable variance** shows whether overhead costs were effectively controlled. To calculate this variance, the actual overhead costs incurred are compared with budgeted costs for the **standard hours allowed**. The budgeted costs are determined from the flexible manufacturing overhead budget, which was presented in Chapter 10. For Xonic, the budget formula for manufacturing overhead was its variable manufacturing overhead cost of $3 per hour of labour plus its fixed manufacturing overhead costs of $4,400. Xonic's budget is given in Illustration 11-23.

Alternative Terminology
The overhead controllable variance is also called the *budget* or *spending variance.*

Illustration 11-23 ◀

Flexible budget using standard direct labour hours

XONIC INC.
Flexible Manufacturing Overhead Budget

Activity Index				
Standard direct labour hours	1,800	2,000	2,200	2,400
Costs				
Variable Costs				
Indirect materials	$1,800	$ 2,000	$ 2,200	$ 2,400
Indirect labour	2,700	3,000	3,300	3,600
Utilities	900	1,000	1,100	1,200
Total variable costs	5,400	6,000	6,600	7,200
Fixed costs				
Supervision	3,000	3,000	3,000	3,000
Amortization	1,400	1,400	1,400	1,400
Total fixed costs	4,400	4,400	4,400	4,400
Total costs	$9,800	$10,400	$11,000	$11,600

As shown, the budgeted costs for 2,000 standard hours are $10,400 ($6,000 variable and $4,400 fixed).

Illustration 11-24 provides the formula for the overhead controllable variance.

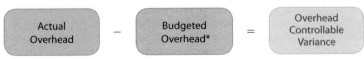

* Based on standard hours allowed

Illustration 11-24 ◀

Formula for overhead controllable variance

The overhead controllable variance for Xonic is $500 unfavourable, as shown below:

$$\$10,900 - \$10,400 = \$500\ U$$

Most controllable variances involve variable overhead costs, which are controllable costs. At Xonic, reason for the variance is found by comparing the actual variable overhead costs ($6,500) with the budgeted variable costs ($6,000).

This variable overhead controllable (VOH) variance of $500 (unfavourable) can also be analyzed into a spending (price) variance and an efficiency (quantity) variance. The formula for the spending variance is given in Illustration 11-25.

Illustration 11-25 ▶

Formula for variable overhead spending (price) variance

| Actual Variable Overhead (AH) × (AR) | − | Actual Hours* at Standard Variable Overhead Rate (AH) × (SR) | = | Variable Overhead Spending (Price) Variance (VOHS) |

* Based on direct labour hours

For Xonic, the variable overhead spending variance is $200 unfavourable ($6,500 − $6,300), as shown below:

$$\$6,500 - (2,100 \times \$3) = \$200 \text{ U}$$

The variable overhead efficiency variance is derived using the formula in Illustration 11-26.

Illustration 11-26 ▶

Formula for variable overhead efficiency (quantity) variance

| Actual Hours* at Standard Variable Overhead Rate (AH) × (SR) | − | Standard Hours* at Standard Variable Overhead Rate (SH) × (SR) | = | Variable Overhead Efficiency Variance (VOHE) |

* Based on direct labour hours

For Xonic, the variable overhead efficiency variance is $300 unfavourable ($6,300 − $6,000), as shown below:

$$(2,100 \times \$3) - (2,000 \times \$3) = \$300 \text{ U}$$

Helpful Hint The alternative formula is:
$SR \times [AH - SH] = VOHE$

The same result can be obtained by multiplying the standard rate by the difference between the actual hours worked and standard hours allowed. In this case, the calculation is $3.00 × (2,100 − 2,000) = $300 U.

The total variable overhead variance of $500 (unfavourable), therefore, consists of the amounts shown in Illustration 11-27.

Illustration 11-27 ▶

Summary of controllable overhead variances

Variable overhead spending variance	$200 U
Variable overhead efficiency variance	300 U
Total variable overhead variance	$500 U

Illustration 11-28 ▼

Matrix for variable overhead variances

These results can also be obtained from the matrix in Illustration 11-28.

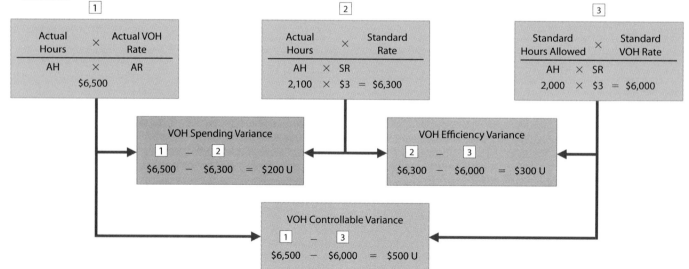

Management can compare the actual and budgeted overhead for each manufacturing overhead cost that contributes to the controllable variance. In addition, cost and quantity variances can be developed for each overhead cost, such as indirect materials and indirect labour.

Fixed Overhead Variance. The **fixed overhead variance** is the difference between the actual fixed overhead and the standard hours allowed times the fixed overhead rate. This fixed overhead (FOH) variance can also be analyzed into a controllable (spending) variance and a volume variance. The fixed overhead controllable variance shows whether spending on fixed costs was under or over the budgeted fixed costs for the year. Illustration 11-29 gives the formula for the spending variance.

* Based on direct labour hours

Illustration 11-29 ◄

Formula for fixed overhead spending variance

For Xonic, the fixed overhead spending variance is $0 ($4,400 − $4,400), as shown below:

$$\$4,400 - (2,200 \times \$2) = \$0$$

The fixed overhead volume variance shows whether fixed costs were under- or overapplied during the year. For example, the overhead volume variance answers the question of whether Xonic effectively used its fixed costs. If Xonic produces less concentrate than normal capacity would allow, an unfavourable variance results. Conversely, if Xonic produces more Grow! concentrate than what is considered normal capacity, a favourable variance results.

The formula for calculating the overhead volume variance is in Illustration 11-30.

Illustration 11-30 ◄

Formula for overhead volume variance

To illustrate the fixed overhead rate calculation, recall that Xonic budgeted a fixed overhead cost for the year of $52,800 (Illustration 11-6). At normal capacity, 26,400 standard direct labour hours are required. The fixed overhead rate is therefore $2 ($52,800 ÷ 26,400).

Next, Xonic produced 1,000 units of Grow! concentrate in June. As indicated earlier, the standard hours allowed for the 1,000 units produced in June is 2,000 (1,000 units × 2 hours). For Xonic, the standard direct labour hours for June at normal capacity is 2,200 (26,400 annual hours ÷ 12 months). The calculation of the overhead volume variance for June is therefore as shown in Illustration 11-31.

Illustration 11-31 ◄

Calculation of overhead volume variance

In Xonic's case, a $400 unfavourable volume variance results. The volume variance is unfavourable because Xonic did not produce up to the normal capacity level in the month of June. As a result, it underapplied its fixed overhead for that period.

The total fixed overhead variance of $400 (unfavourable), therefore, consists of the amounts shown in Illustration 11-32.

Fixed overhead controllable (spending) variance	$ 0 U
Fixed overhead volume variance	400 U
Total fixed overhead variance	$400 U

Illustration 11-32 ◄

Summary of fixed overhead variances

These results can also be obtained from the matrix in Illustration 11-33.

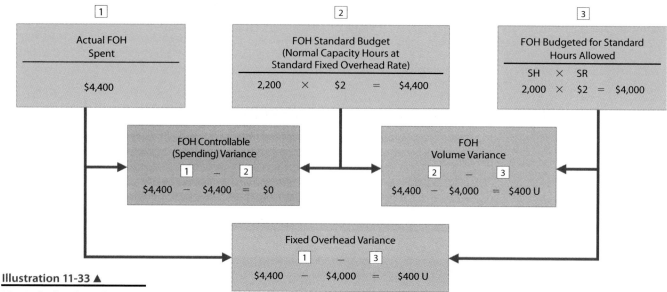

Illustration 11-33 ▲

Matrix for fixed overhead variances

Having investigated these specific variances, we can now see that, in summary, the total overhead variance of $900 (unfavourable) consists of the amounts shown in Illustration 11-34.

Illustration 11-34 ►

Summary of total overhead variances

Variable overhead spending variance	$200 U	
Variable overhead efficiency variance	300 U	
Total variable overhead variance		$500 U
Fixed overhead spending variance	$ 0	
Fixed overhead volume variance	400 U	
Total fixed overhead variance		400 U
Total overhead variances		$900 U

Illustration 11-35 ▼

Matrix for overhead costs

These results can also be obtained from the matrix in Illustration 11-35.

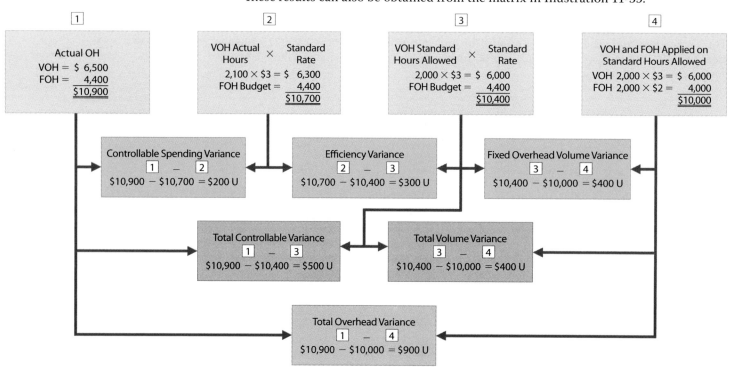

In calculating the overhead variances, it is important to remember the following:

1. The standard hours allowed are used in each of the variances.
2. Budgeted costs for the controllable variance are derived from the flexible budget.
3. The controllable variance generally relates to variable costs.
4. The volume variance relates only to fixed costs.

Causes of Manufacturing Overhead Variances.   Since the **controllable variance** relates to variable manufacturing costs, the **production department** is responsible for the variance. The cause of an unfavourable variance may be (1) a **higher-than-expected use** of indirect materials, indirect labour, and factory supplies, or (2) **increases in indirect manufacturing costs**, such as fuel and maintenance costs.

The **production department** is also responsible for the overhead volume variance if the cause is either inefficient use of direct labour or machine breakdowns. When the cause is a **lack of sales orders**, the production department is not responsible.

"What caused the manufacturing overhead variances?"

	Overhead
Controllable	**Volume**
Variance	**Variance**
Production Department	Production or Sales Department

Decision Toolkit

Decision Checkpoints	Info Needed for Decision	Tools to Use for Decision	How to Evaluate Results
Has management accomplished its price and quantity objectives for overhead?	The actual cost and standard cost of overhead	The overhead controllable variance and overhead volume variance	Positive (favourable) variances suggest that the price and quantity objectives have been met.

Reporting Variances

All variances should be reported to appropriate levels of management as soon as possible. The sooner management is informed, the sooner problems can be evaluated and corrective actions can be taken, if necessary.

The form, content, and frequency of variance reports vary considerably among companies. One approach is to prepare a weekly report for each department that has primary responsibility for cost control. Under this approach, materials price variances are reported to the purchasing department, and all other variances are reported to the production department that did the work. The report in Illustration 11-36 for Xonic, Inc., with the type of materials for the concentrate order listed first, shows this approach.

study objective 6

Discuss the reporting of variances.

Illustration 11-36 ◀

Materials price variance report

XONIC, INC.
Variance Report—Purchasing Department
Week Ended June 8, 2005

Type of Materials	Quantity Purchased	Actual Price	Price Standard	Price Variance	Explanation
X 100	4,200 litres	$3.10	$3.00	$420 U	Rush order
X 142	1,200 units	2.75	2.80	60 F	Quantity discount
A 85	600 doz.	5.20	5.10	60 U	Regular supplier on strike
Total price variance				$420 U	

The explanation column is completed after the purchasing department manager has been consulted.

Variance reports make it easier to use the "management by exception" approach explained in Chapter 10. For example, the vice-president of purchasing can use the report shown above to evaluate the effectiveness of the purchasing department manager. Or the vice-president of production can use production department variance reports to determine how well each production manager is controlling costs. In using variance reports, top management normally looks for **significant variances**. These may be judged based on some quantitative measure, such as more than 10 percent of the standard or more than $1,000.

BUSINESS INSIGHT ▶ *e*-Business Perspective

Computerized standard cost systems are among the most complex accounting systems to develop and maintain. The standard cost system must be fully integrated into the general ledger. It must allow for the creation and timely maintenance of the database of standard usage and costs for every product. It must perform variance calculations. And it must also produce variance reports by product, department, or employee. With the increased use of automation and robotics, the computerized standard cost system may even be connected directly to these automated systems to gather variance information.

Statement Presentation of Variances

study objective 7

Prepare an income statement for management under a standard cost system.

In income statements **prepared for management** under a standard cost accounting system, the **cost of goods sold is stated at standard cost and the variances are disclosed separately**, as shown in Illustration 11-37. The statement shown is based entirely on the production and sale of concentrate. It assumes selling and administrative costs of $3,000. Notice that each variance is shown, as well as the total net variance. In this example, variations from standard costs reduced net income by $2,500.

Illustration 11-37 ▶

Variances in income statement for management

XONIC, INC. Income Statement Month Ended June 30, 2005		
Sales		$60,000
Cost of goods sold (at standard)		42,000
Gross profit (at standard)		18,000
Variances unfavourable		
Materials price	$ 420	
Materials quantity	600	
Labour price	(420)	
Labour quantity	1,000	
Overhead controllable (spending and efficiency)	500	
Overhead volume	400	
Total variance unfavourable		2,500
Gross profit (actual)		15,500
Selling and administrative expenses		3,000
Net income		$12,500

In financial statements prepared for shareholders and other external users, standard costs may be used. The costing of inventories at standard costs is in accordance with generally accepted accounting principles when there are no significant differences between actual costs and standard costs. Hewlett-Packard and Jostens, Inc., for example, report their inventories at standard costs. However, if there are significant differences between actual and standard costs, inventories and the cost of goods sold must be reported at actual costs.

Variances can also be shown in an income statement prepared in the contribution margin format. To do so, it is necessary to analyze the overhead variances into variable and fixed components. This type of analysis is explained in cost accounting textbooks.

Balanced Scorecard

Financial measures (measurements of dollars), such as variance analysis and the return on investment (ROI), are useful tools for evaluating performance. However, many companies now use non-financial measures as well as financial measures in order to better assess performance and be ready for future results. For example, airlines like Air Canada and WestJet use capacity utilization as an important measure to understand and predict future performance. And publishers of such newspapers as the *National Post* or *La Presse* use circulation figures as another measure for evaluating performance. Some key non-financial measures that are used in various industries are listed in Illustration 11-38.

study objective 8

Describe the balanced scorecard approach to performance evaluation.

Industry		Measure
Automobiles		Capacity utilization of plants Average age of key assets Impact of strikes Brand-loyalty statistics
Chemicals		Market profile of customer end-products Number of new products Employee stock ownership percentages Number of scientists and technicians used in R&D
Computer Systems		Customer satisfaction data Factors affecting customer product selection Number of patents and trademarks held Customer brand awareness
Banks		Number of ATMs by province Number of products used by average customer Percentage of customer service calls handled by interactive voice response units Personnel cost per employee Credit card retention rates

Illustration 11-38 ◀

Non-financial measures used in various industries

Most companies recognize that both financial and non-financial measures can provide useful insights into what is happening in the company. As a result, many companies now use a broad-based approach to performance measurement, called the balanced scorecard, to evaluate performance. The **balanced scorecard** uses financial and non-financial measures in an integrated system that links performance measurement and a company's strategic goals. The balanced scorecard concept is very popular: nearly 50 percent of the largest companies in Canada and the United States, including Alcan, Bombardier, Unilever, Chase, and Wal-Mart, are using this approach.

The balanced scorecard evaluates company performance from a series of "perspectives." The four most commonly used perspectives are as follows:

1. The **financial perspective** is the most traditional view of the company. It uses the financial measures of performance that are used by most firms.
2. The **customer perspective** evaluates how well the company is performing from the viewpoint of those people who buy and use its products or services. This view measures how well the company compares to competitors in terms of price, quality, product innovation, customer service, and other dimensions.
3. The **internal process perspective** evaluates the internal operating processes that are critical to success. All critical aspects of the value chain—including product development, production, delivery, and after-sale service—are evaluated to ensure that the company is operating effectively and efficiently.
4. The **learning and growth perspective** evaluates how well the company develops and retains its employees. This would include an evaluation of such things as employee skills, employee satisfaction, training programs, and the communication of information.

The four perspectives of the balanced scorecard are linked to each other by a flow of influence. The linkage starts with the learning and growth perspective. Corporate success begins with well-trained and happy employees. If employees are well-trained, then the company will have good internal processes. If the company's internal processes are functioning well, then customers will be satisfied. If customers are satisfied, then the company should experience financial success. Illustration 11-39 shows this flow.

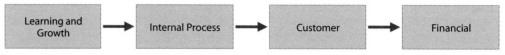

Within each perspective, the balanced scorecard identifies objectives that will contribute to attaining the strategic goals. Illustration 11-40 shows examples of objectives within each perspective.

Financial perspective
Return on assets
Net income
Credit rating
Share price
Profit per employee

Customer perspective
Percentage of customers who would recommend the product to a friend
Customer retention
Response time per customer request
Brand recognition
Customer service expenses per customer

Internal process perspective
Percentage of defect-free products
Stockouts
Labour use rates
Waste reduction
Planning accuracy

Learning and growth perspective
Percentage of employees leaving in less than one year
Number of cross-trained employees
Ethics violations
Training hours
Reportable accidents

The objectives are linked across the perspectives so that performance measurement is tied to company goals. The financial objectives are normally set first, and then objectives are set in the other perspectives that will help accomplish the financial objectives. For example, within the financial perspective, a common goal is to increase the profit per dollar invested as measured by the ROI. In order to increase the ROI, a customer perspective objective might be to increase customer satisfaction as measured by the percentage of customers who would recommend the product to a friend. In order to increase customer satisfaction, an objective for the internal process perspective might be to increase product quality as measured by the percentage of defect-free units. Finally, in order to increase the percentage of defect-free units, the objective for the learning and growth perspective might be to reduce factory employee turnover as measured by the percentage of employees leaving in under one year. Through this linked process, the company can better understand how to achieve its goals and what measures to use to evaluate performance.

In summary, the balanced scorecard does the following:

1. Employs both financial and non-financial measures (e.g., ROI is a financial measure; employee turnover is a non-financial measure)
2. Creates links so that high-level corporate goals can be communicated all the way down to the shop floor
3. Provides measurable objectives for such non-financial measures as product quality, rather than such vague statements as "We would like to improve quality"
4. Integrates all of the company's goals into a single performance measurement system, so that too much weight will not be placed on any single goal

BEFORE YOU GO ON . . .

► Review It

1. What are the formulas for calculating the total, price, and quantity variances for direct labour?
2. What are the formulas for calculating the total, controllable, and volume variances for manufacturing overhead?
3. How are standard costs and variances reported in income statements prepared for management?
4. What are the basic characteristics of the balanced scorecard?

APPENDIX 11A ► STANDARD COST ACCOUNTING SYSTEM

A **standard cost accounting system** is a double-entry system of accounting. In this system, standard costs are used in making entries, and variances are formally recognized in the accounts. A standard cost system may be used with either job-order or process costing. At this point, we will explain and illustrate a **standard cost job-order cost accounting system**. The system is based on two important assumptions: (1) Variances from standards are recognized at the earliest opportunity. (2) The Work in Process account is maintained using only standard costs. In practice, there are many variations among standard cost systems. The system described here should prepare you for systems you will see in the workplace.

study objective 9

Identify the features of a standard cost accounting system.

Journal Entries

We will use the transactions of Xonic, Inc. to illustrate the journal entries. As you study the entries, note that the major difference between the entries here and those for the job-order cost accounting system in Chapter 2 is the **variance accounts**. The transactions and entries are as follows:

1. Purchased raw materials on account for $13,020 when the standard cost is $12,600.

Raw Materials Inventory	12,600	
Materials Price Variance	420	
Accounts Payable		13,020
To record purchase of materials.		

The inventory account is debited for the actual quantities at standard cost. This enables the perpetual materials records to show actual quantities. The price variance, which is unfavourable, is debited to Materials Price Variance.

2. Incurred direct labour costs of $20,580 when the standard labour cost is $21,000.

Factory Labour	21,000	
Labour Price Variance		420
Wages Payable		20,580
To record direct labour costs.		

Like the raw materials inventory account, Factory Labour is debited for the actual hours worked at the standard hourly rate of pay. In this case, the labour variance is favourable. Thus, Labour Price Variance is credited.

3. Incurred actual manufacturing overhead costs of $10,900.

Manufacturing Overhead	10,900	
Accounts Payable/Cash/Acc. Amortization		10,900
To record overhead incurred.		

The controllable overhead variance is not recorded at this time. It depends on the standard hours applied to work in process. This amount is not known at the time the overhead is incurred.

4. Issued raw materials for production at a cost of $12,600 when the standard cost is $12,000.

Work in Process Inventory	12,000	
Materials Quantity Variance	600	
Raw Materials Inventory		12,600
To record issue of raw materials.		

Work in Process Inventory is debited for standard materials quantities used at standard prices. The variance account is debited because the variance is unfavourable. Raw Materials Inventory is credited for the actual quantities at standard prices.

5. Assigned factory labour to production at a cost of $21,000 when the standard cost is $20,000.

Work in Process Inventory	20,000	
Labour Quantity Variance	1,000	
Factory Labour		21,000
To assign factory labour to jobs.		

Work in Process Inventory is debited for standard labour hours at standard rates. The unfavourable variance is debited to Labour Quantity Variance. The credit to Factory Labour produces a zero balance in this account.

6. Applied $10,000 of manufacturing overhead to production.

Work in Process Inventory	10,000	
Manufacturing Overhead		10,000
To assign overhead to jobs.		

Work in Process Inventory is debited for the standard hours allowed multiplied by the standard overhead rate.

7. Transferred $42,000 of completed work to finished goods.

Finished Goods Inventory	42,000	
Work in Process Inventory		42,000
To record transfer of completed work to		
finished goods.		

In this example, both inventory accounts are at standard cost.

8. The 1,000 kilograms of Grow! concentrate are sold for $60,000.

Accounts Receivable	60,000	
Cost of Goods Sold	42,000	
Sales		60,000
Finished Goods Inventory		42,000
To record sale of finished goods and the cost		
of goods sold.		

Cost of Goods Sold is debited at standard cost. Gross profit, in turn, is the difference between sales and the standard cost of goods sold.

9. Recognized unfavourable overhead variances: controllable, $500; volume, $400.

Overhead Controllable Variance	500	
Overhead Volume Variance	400	
Manufacturing Overhead		900
To recognize overhead variances.		

Before this entry, there was a debit balance of $900 in Manufacturing Overhead. This entry therefore produces a zero balance in the account. The information needed for this entry is often not available until the end of the accounting period.

Ledger Accounts

The cost accounts for Xonic, after posting the entries, are shown in Illustration 11A-1. Note that six variance accounts are included in the ledger. The remaining accounts are the same as those illustrated for a job-order cost system in Chapter 2, in which only actual costs were used.

Raw Materials Inventory

(1)	12,600	(4)	12,600

Materials Price Variance

(1)	420		

Work in Process Inventory

(4)	12,000	(7)	42,000
(5)	20,000		
(6)	10,000		

Factory Labour

(2)	21,000	(5)	21,000

Materials Quantity Variance

(4)	600		

Finished Goods Inventory

(7)	42,000	(8)	42,000

Manufacturing Overhead

(3)	10,900	(6)	10,000
		(9)	900

Labour Price Variance

		(2)	420

Cost of Goods Sold

(8)	42,000		

Labour Quantity Variance

(5)	1,000		

Overhead Controllable Variance

(9)	500		

Overhead Volume Variance

(9)	400		

Illustration 11A-1 ◀

Cost accounts with variances

Helpful Hint All debit balances in variance accounts indicate unfavourable variances; all credit balances indicate favourable variances.

Using the Decision Toolkit

Assume that during the past month, Fineway produced 10,000 cartons of Sharpline highlighters. Sharpline offers a translucent barrel and cap with a visible ink supply for see-through colour. The special fluorescent ink is fade- and water-resistant. Each carton contains 100 boxes of markers, and each box contains five markers. The markers come in boxes of one of five fluorescent colours—orange, blue, yellow, green, and pink—and in a five-colour set.

The standard cost for one carton of 500 markers is as follows:

Manufacturing Cost Elements	Quantity	Standard Price		Cost
Direct materials				
Tips (boxes of 500)	500	× $0.03	=	$ 15.00
Translucent barrels and caps (boxes of 500)	500	× $0.09	=	45.00
Fluorescent ink (5-litre containers)	5 litre	× $6.40	=	32.00
Total direct materials				92.00
Direct labour	0.25 hours	× $ 9.00	=	2.25
Overhead	0.25 hours	× $48.00	=	12.00
				$106.25

During the month, the following transactions occurred in manufacturing the 10,000 cartons of highlighters:

1. Purchased 10,000 boxes of tips for $148,000 ($14.80 per 500 tips); purchased 10,200 boxes of translucent barrels and caps for $453,900 ($44.50 per 500 barrels and caps); and purchased 9,900 containers of fluorescent ink for $328,185 ($33.15 per 5 litres).
2. All materials purchased during the period were used to make markers during the period.
3. A total of 2,300 direct labour hours were worked at a total labour cost of $20,240 (an average hourly rate of $8.80).
4. The variable manufacturing overhead incurred was $34,600, and the fixed overhead incurred was $84,000.

The manufacturing overhead rate of $48.00 is based on a normal capacity of 2,600 direct labour hours. The total budget at this capacity is $83,980 fixed and $40,820 variable.

Instructions

Determine whether Fineway met its price and quantity objectives for materials, labour, and overhead.

Solution

To determine whether Fineway met its price and quantity objectives, calculate the total variance and the variances for each of the manufacturing cost elements.

Total Variance		
Actual cost incurred:		
Direct materials		
Tips	$148,000	
Translucent barrels and caps	453,900	
Fluorescent ink	328,185	
Total direct materials		$ 930,085
Direct labour		20,240
Overhead		118,600
Total actual costs		1,068,925
Standard cost (10,000 × $106.25)		1,062,500
Total variance		$ 6,425 U

Direct Materials Variances

Total	= $930,085	− $920,000 (10,000 × $92)	= $10,085 U
Price (tips)	= $148,000 (10,000 × $14.80)	− $150,000 (10,000 × $15.00)	= $2,000 F
Price (barrels and caps)	= $453,900 (10,200 × $44.50)	− $459,000 (10,200 × $45.00)	= $5,100 F
Price (ink)	= $328,185 (9,900 × $33.15)	− $316,800 (9,900 × $32.00)	= $11,385 U
Quantity (tips)	= $150,000 (10,000 × $15.00)	− $150,000 (10,000 × $15.00)	= $0
Quantity (barrels and caps)	= $459,000 (10,200 × $45.00)	− $450,000 (10,000 × $45.00)	= $9,000 U
Quantity (ink)	= $316,800 (9,900 × $32.00)	− $320,000 (10,000 × $32.00)	= $3,200 F

Direct Labour Variances

Total	= $20,240 (2,300 × $8.80)	− $22,500 (2,500 × $9.00)	= $2,260 F
Price	= $20,240 (2,300 × $8.80)	− $20,700 (2,300 × $9.00)	= $460 F
Quantity	= $20,700 (2,300 × $9.00)	− $22,500 (2,500 × $9.00)	= $1,800 F

Overhead Variances

Total	= $118,600 ($84,000 + $34,600)	− $120,000 (2,500 × $48)	= $1,400 F
Controllable	= $118,600 ($84,000 + $34,600)	− $123,230 [(2,500 × $15.70) + $83,980]	= $4,630 F
Volume	= $123,230 [(2,500 × $15.70) + $83,980]	− $120,000 (2,500 × $48)	= $3,230 U

The same result of overhead variances can also be obtained by the following analysis:

Overhead Variances

Total	= $118,600 ($84,000 + $34,600)	− $120,000 (2,500 × $48)	= $1,400 F
Variable overhead spending	= $34,600 $34,600	− $36,110 (2,300 × $15.70)	= $1,510 F*
Variable overhead efficiency	= $36,110 (2,300 × $15.70)	− $39,250 (2,500 × $15.70)	= $3,140 F*
Fixed overhead spending	= $84,000 $84,000	− $83,980 (2,600 × $32.30)	= $20 U*
Fixed overhead volume	= $83,980 (2,600 × $32.30)	− $80,750 (2,500 × $32.30)	= $3,230 U

* Overhead controllable variance = ($1,510 F + $3,140 F) − $20 U = $4,630 F

Fineway's total variance was an $6,425 unfavourable. The unfavourable materials variance outweighed the favourable labour and overhead variances. The main causes were an unfavourable price variance for ink and an unfavourable quantity variance for barrels and caps.

Summary of Study Objectives

1. **Distinguish between a standard and a budget.** Both standards and budgets are predetermined costs. The main difference is that a standard is a unit amount, whereas a budget is a total amount. A standard may be regarded as the budgeted cost per unit of product.

2. **Identify the advantages of standard costs.** Standard costs offer several advantages. They facilitate management planning, promote greater economy and efficiency, are useful in setting selling prices, contribute to management control, permit "management by exception," simplify the costing of inventories, and reduce clerical costs.

3. **Describe how standards are set.** The direct materials price standard should be based on the delivered cost of raw materials plus an allowance for receiving and handling. The direct materials quantity standard should establish the required quantity plus an allowance for waste and spoilage. The direct labour price standard should be based on current wage rates and expected adjustments, such as COLAs. It also generally includes payroll taxes and fringe benefits. Direct labour quantity standards should be based on required production time plus an allowance for rest periods, cleanup, machine setup, and machine downtime. For manufacturing overhead, a standard predetermined overhead rate is used. It is based on an expected standard activity index, such as standard direct labour hours or standard direct labour cost.

4. **State the formulas for determining direct materials and direct labour variances.** The formulas for the direct materials variances are:

$$\left(\begin{array}{c}\text{Actual}\\\text{quantity}\end{array} \times \begin{array}{c}\text{Actual}\\\text{price}\end{array}\right) - \left(\begin{array}{c}\text{Standard}\\\text{quantity}\end{array} \times \begin{array}{c}\text{Standard}\\\text{price}\end{array}\right) = \begin{array}{c}\text{Total materials}\\\text{variance}\end{array}$$

$$\left(\begin{array}{c}\text{Actual}\\\text{quantity}\end{array} \times \begin{array}{c}\text{Actual}\\\text{price}\end{array}\right) - \left(\begin{array}{c}\text{Actual}\\\text{quantity}\end{array} \times \begin{array}{c}\text{Standard}\\\text{price}\end{array}\right) = \begin{array}{c}\text{Materials price}\\\text{variance}\end{array}$$

$$\left(\begin{array}{c}\text{Actual}\\\text{quantity}\end{array} \times \begin{array}{c}\text{Standard}\\\text{price}\end{array}\right) - \left(\begin{array}{c}\text{Standard}\\\text{quantity}\end{array} \times \begin{array}{c}\text{Standard}\\\text{price}\end{array}\right) = \begin{array}{c}\text{Materials}\\\text{quantity variance}\end{array}$$

The formulas for direct labour are:

$$\left(\begin{array}{c}\text{Actual}\\\text{hours}\end{array} \times \begin{array}{c}\text{Actual}\\\text{rate}\end{array}\right) - \left(\begin{array}{c}\text{Standard}\\\text{hours}\end{array} \times \begin{array}{c}\text{Standard}\\\text{rate}\end{array}\right) = \begin{array}{c}\text{Total labour}\\\text{variance}\end{array}$$

$$\left(\begin{array}{c}\text{Actual}\\\text{hours}\end{array} \times \begin{array}{c}\text{Actual}\\\text{rate}\end{array}\right) - \left(\begin{array}{c}\text{Actual}\\\text{hours}\end{array} \times \begin{array}{c}\text{Standard}\\\text{rate}\end{array}\right) = \begin{array}{c}\text{Labour price}\\\text{variance}\end{array}$$

$$\left(\begin{array}{c}\text{Actual}\\\text{hours}\end{array} \times \begin{array}{c}\text{Standard}\\\text{rate}\end{array}\right) - \left(\begin{array}{c}\text{Standard}\\\text{hours}\end{array} \times \begin{array}{c}\text{Standard}\\\text{rate}\end{array}\right) = \begin{array}{c}\text{Labour quantity}\\\text{variance}\end{array}$$

5. **State the formulas for determining manufacturing overhead variances.** The formulas for the manufacturing overhead variances are:

$$\begin{array}{c}\text{Actual}\\\text{overhead}\end{array} - \begin{array}{c}\text{Overhead}\\\text{applied}\end{array} = \begin{array}{c}\text{Total overhead}\\\text{variance}\end{array}$$

$$\begin{array}{c}\text{Actual}\\\text{overhead}\end{array} - \begin{array}{c}\text{Overhead}\\\text{budgeted}\end{array} = \begin{array}{c}\text{Overhead}\\\text{controllable}\\\text{variance}\end{array}$$

$$\begin{array}{c}\text{Fixed}\\\text{overhead}\\\text{rate}\end{array} \times \left(\begin{array}{c}\text{Normal}\\\text{capacity}\\\text{hours}\end{array} - \begin{array}{c}\text{Standard}\\\text{hours}\\\text{allowed}\end{array}\right) = \begin{array}{c}\text{Overhead}\\\text{volume variance}\end{array}$$

6. **Discuss the reporting of variances.** Variances are reported to management in variance reports. The reports aid management by exception by highlighting significant differences.

7. **Prepare an income statement for management under a standard cost system.** Under a standard cost system, an income statement prepared for management will report the cost of goods sold at standard cost and then disclose each variance separately.

8. **Describe the balanced scorecard approach to performance evaluation.** The balanced scorecard uses financial and non-financial measures in an integrated system that links performance measurement and a company's strategic goals. It uses four perspectives: financial, customer, internal processes, and learning and growth. Objectives are set within each of these perspectives and they link to objectives in the other perspectives.

9. **Identify the features of a standard cost accounting system (Appendix 11A).** In a standard cost accounting system, standard costs are journalized and posted, and separate variance accounts are maintained in the ledger. When actual costs and standard costs do not differ significantly, inventories may be reported at standard costs.

Decision Toolkit—A Summary

Decision Checkpoints	Info Needed for Decision	Tools to Use for Decision	How to Evaluate Results
Has management accomplished its price and quantity objectives for materials?	The actual cost and standard cost of materials	Materials price and materials quantity variances	Positive (favourable) variances suggest that the price and quantity objectives have been met.
Has management accomplished its price and quantity objectives for labour?	The actual cost and standard cost of labour	Labour price and labour quantity variances	Positive (favourable) variances suggest that the price and quantity objectives have been met.
Has management accomplished its price and quantity objectives for overhead?	The actual cost and standard cost of overhead	The overhead controllable variance and overhead volume variance	Positive (favourable) variances suggest that the price and quantity objectives have been met.

Glossary

www.wiley.com/canada/managerial

Key Term Matching Activity

the navigator

Balanced scorecard An approach that uses financial and non-financial measures in an integrated system that links performance measurement and a company's strategic goals. (p. 487)

Customer perspective A viewpoint used in the balanced scorecard to evaluate the company from the perspective of those people who buy and use its products or services. (p. 487)

Direct labour price standard The rate per hour that should be incurred for direct labour. (p. 472)

Direct labour quantity standard The time that should be required to make one unit of product. (p. 473)

Direct materials price standard The cost per unit of direct materials that should be incurred. (p. 472)

Direct materials quantity standard The quantity of direct materials that should be used per unit of finished goods. (p. 472)

Financial perspective A viewpoint used in the balanced scorecard to evaluate a company's performance, and using financial measures. (p. 487)

Fixed overhead variance The difference between the actual fixed overhead and the standard hours allowed times the fixed overhead rate. (p. 483)

Ideal standards Standards based on the optimum level of performance under perfect operating conditions. (p. 471)

Internal process perspective A viewpoint used in the balanced scorecard to evaluate the effectiveness and efficiency of a company's value chain, including product development, production, delivery, and after-sale service. (p. 487)

Labour price variance The difference between the actual hours of labour times the actual labour rate, and the actual hours times the standard rate. (p. 478)

Labour quantity variance The difference between the actual hours of labour of times the standard labour rate, and standard hours times the standard rate. (p. 479)

Learning and growth perspective A viewpoint used in the balanced scorecard to evaluate how well a company develops and retains its employees. (p. 487)

Materials price variance The difference between the actual quantity of materials times the actual price of materials, and the actual quantity times the standard price. (p. 476)

Materials quantity variance The difference between the actual quantity of materials times the standard price of materials, and the standard quantity times the standard price. (p. 476)

Normal standards Standards based on an efficient level of performance that are attainable under expected operating conditions. (p. 471)

Overhead controllable variance The difference between the actual overhead incurred and the overhead budgeted for the standard hours allowed. (p. 481)

Overhead volume variance The difference between the overhead budgeted for the standard hours allowed and the overhead applied. (p. 481)

Standard cost accounting system A double-entry system of accounting in which standard costs are used in making entries and variances are recognized in the accounts. (p. 489)

Standard costs   Predetermined unit costs which are used as measures of performance. (p. 470)

Standard hours allowed   The hours that should have been worked for the units produced. (p. 480)

Standard predetermined overhead rate   An overhead rate that is determined by dividing the budgeted overhead costs by an expected standard activity index. (p. 473)

Total labour variance   The difference between the actual hours of labour times the actual labour rate and the standard hours times the standard rate. (p. 476)

Total materials variance   The difference between the actual quantity of materials times the actual price of materials and the standard quantity times the standard price. (p. 476)

Total overhead variance   The difference between actual overhead costs and the overhead costs applied to work done. (p. 480)

Variances   The difference between total actual costs and total standard costs. (p. 475)

Demonstration Problem

www.wiley.com/canada/managerial

**Animated
Demonstration
Problem**

Manlow Company makes a pasta sauces for the restaurant industry. The standard cost for one tub of sauce is as follows:

Manufacturing Cost Elements	Standard Quantity	Standard Price	Standard Cost
Direct materials	6 litre	$0.90	$5.40
Direct labour	0.5 hrs.	$12.00	6.00
Manufacturing overhead	0.5 hrs.	$4.80	2.40
			$13.80

During the month, the following transactions occurred in manufacturing 10,000 tubs of sauce:

1. A total of 58,000 ounces of materials were purchased at $1.00 per litre.
2. All the materials purchased were used to produce the 10,000 tubs of sauce.
3. A total of 4,900 direct labour hours were worked at a total labour cost of $56,350.
4. The variable manufacturing overhead incurred was $15,000 and the fixed overhead incurred was $10,400.

The manufacturing overhead rate of $4.80 is based on a normal capacity of 5,200 direct labour hours. The total budget at this capacity is $10,400 fixed and $14,560 variable.

Instructions

Calculate the total variance and the variances for each of the manufacturing cost elements.

Action Plan

- Check to make sure the total variance and the sum of the individual variances are equal.
- Find the price variance first, then the quantity variance.
- Base the budgeted overhead costs on the flexible budget data.
- Base the overhead applied on the standard hours allowed.
- Ignore the actual hours worked in calculating the overhead variances.
- Relate the overhead volume variance only to the fixed costs.

Solution to Demonstration Problem

Total Variance

Actual costs incurred	
Direct materials	$ 58,000
Direct labour	56,350
Manufacturing overhead	25,400
	139,750
Standard cost (10,000 × $13.80)	138,000
Total variance	$ 1,750 U

Direct Materials Variances

Total	= $58,000	− $54,000	= $4,000 U	
	(58,000 × $1.00)	(60,000 × $0.90)		
Price	= $58,000	− $52,200	= $5,800 U	
	(58,000 × $1.00)	(58,000 × $0.90)		
Quantity	= $52,200	− $54,000	= $1,800 F	
	(58,000 × $0.90)	(60,000 × $0.90)		

Direct Labour Variances

Total	=	$56,350 (4,900 × $11.50)	−	$60,000 (5,000 × $12.00)	= $3,650 F
Price	=	$56,350 (4,900 × $11.50)	−	$58,800 (4,900 × $12.00)	= $2,450 F
Quantity	=	$58,800 (4,900 × $12.00)	−	$60,000 (5,000 × $12.00)	= $1,200 F

Overhead Variances

Total	=	$25,400 ($15,000 + $10,400)	−	$24,000 (5,000 × $4.80)	= $1,400 U
Controllable	=	$25,400 ($15,000 + $10,400)	−	$24,400 ($14,000 + $10,400)	= $1,000 U
Volume	=	$24,400 ($14,000 + $10,400)	−	$24,000 (5,000 × $4.80)	= $400 U

The same result of overhead variances can also be obtained by the following analysis:

Overhead Variances

Total	=	$25,400 ($15,000 + $10,400)	−	$24,000 (5,000 × $4.80)	= $1,400 U
Variable overhead spending	=	$15,000 $15,000	−	$13,720 (4,900 × $2.80)	= $1,280 U*
Variable overhead efficiency	=	$13,720 (4,900 × $2.80)	−	$14,000 (5,000 × $2.80)	= $280 F*
Fixed overhead spending	=	$10,400 $10,400	−	$10,400 (5,200 × $2.00)	= $0 U*
Fixed overhead volume	=	$10,400 (5,200 × $2.00)	−	$10,000 (5,000 × $2.00)	= $400 U

* Overhead controllable variance = $1,280 U − $280 F + $0 = $1,000 U

Note: All questions, exercises, and problems below with an asterisk (*) relate to material in Appendix 11A.

Self-Study Questions

www.wiley.com/canada/managerial

Additional Self-Study Questions

Answers are at the end of the chapter.

(SO 1) 1. Standards differ from budgets as:
(a) budgets but not standards may be used in valuing inventories.
(b) budgets but not standards may be journalized and posted.
(c) budgets are a total amount and standards are a unit amount.
(d) only budgets contribute to management planning and control.

(SO 2) 2. The advantages of standard costs include all of the following except:
(a) management by exception may be used.
(b) management planning is made easier.
(c) the costing of inventories is made simpler.
(d) management must use a static budget.

(SO 3) 3. The setting of standards is:
(a) a managerial accounting decision.
(b) a management decision.

(c) a worker decision.
(d) preferably set at the ideal level of performance.

4. Each of the following formulas is correct except: (SO 4)
(a) Labour price variance = (actual hours × actual rate) − (actual hours × standard rate).
(b) Overhead controllable variance = actual overhead − overhead budgeted.
(c) Materials price variance = (actual quantity × actual cost) − (standard quantity × standard cost).
(d) Overhead volume variance = overhead budgeted − overhead applied.

5. In producing product AA, 6,300 kilograms of (SO 4) direct materials were used at a cost of $1.10 per kilogram. The standard was 6,000 kilograms at $1 per kilogram. The direct materials quantity variance is:
(a) $330 unfavourable. (c) $600 unfavourable.
(b) $300 unfavourable. (d) $630 unfavourable.

(SO 4) 6. In producing product ZZ, 14,800 direct labour hours were used at a rate of $8.20 per hour. The standard was 15,000 hours at $8.00 per hour. Based on these data, the direct labour:
(a) quantity variance is $1,600 favourable.
(b) quantity variance is $1,600 unfavourable.
(c) price variance is $2,960 favourable.
(d) price variance is $3,000 unfavourable.

(SO 5) 7. Which of the following is correct about overhead variances?
(a) The controllable variance generally relates to fixed overhead costs.
(b) The volume variance relates only to variable overhead costs.
(c) The standard hours actually worked are used in each variance.
(d) Budgeted overhead costs are based on the flexible overhead budget.

(SO 5) 8. The formula for calculating the total overhead variance is:
(a) actual overhead less overhead applied.
(b) overhead budgeted less overhead applied.
(c) actual overhead less overhead budgeted.
(d) No correct answer is given.

9. Which of the following is incorrect about variance reports?   (SO 6)
(a) They aid "management by exception."
(b) They should only be sent to the top level of management.
(c) They should be prepared as soon as possible.
(d) They may vary in form, content, and frequency in different companies.

10. Which of the following would *not* be an objective   (SO 8) used in the customer perspective of the balanced scorecard approach?
(a) The percentage of customers who would recommend the product to a friend
(b) Customer retention
(c) Brand recognition
(d) Earnings per share

*11. Which of the following is incorrect about a standard cost accounting system?   (SO 9)
(a) It can be used with job-order costing.
(b) It can be used with process costing.
(c) It is a single-entry system.
(d) It keeps separate accounts for each variance.

Questions

1. (a) "Standard costs are the expected total cost of completing a job." Is this correct? Explain.
(b) "A standard imposed by a government agency is known as a regulation." Do you agree? Explain.

2. (a) Explain the similarities and differences between standards and budgets.
(b) Contrast the accounting for standards and budgets.

3. Standard costs help management planning. What are the other advantages of standard costs?

4. Contrast the roles of the management accountant and management in setting standard costs.

5. Distinguish between an ideal standard and a normal standard.

6. What factors should be considered in setting (a) the direct materials price standard and (b) the direct materials quantity standard?

7. "The objective in setting the direct labour quantity standard is to determine the combined time required to make one unit of product." Do you agree? What allowances should be made in setting this standard?

8. How is the predetermined overhead rate determined when standard costs are used?

9. What is the difference between a favourable cost variance and an unfavourable cost variance?

10. In each of the following formulas, give the words that should replace each number.

(a) (Actual quantity × 1) − (Standard quantity × 2) = Total materials variance
(b) (3 × Actual price) − (Actual quantity × 4) = Materials price variance
(c) (Actual quantity × 5) − (6 × Standard price) = Materials quantity variance

11. In the direct labour variance matrix, there are three factors: (1) actual hours × actual rate, (2) actual hours × standard rate, and (3) standard hours × standard rate. Using the numbers, indicate the formulas for each of the direct labour variances.

12. Keene Company's standard predetermined overhead rate is $8.00 per direct labour hour. For the month of June, 26,000 actual hours were worked, and 27,500 standard hours were allowed. Normal capacity hours were 28,000. How much overhead was applied?

13. If the $8.00 per hour overhead rate in question 12 includes $5.00 of variable overhead, and the actual overhead costs were $218,000, what is the overhead controllable variance for June? Is the variance favourable or unfavourable?

14. Using the data in questions 12 and 13, what is the overhead volume variance for June? Is the variance favourable or unfavourable?

15. What is the purpose of calculating the overhead volume variance? What is the basic formula for this variance?

16. Nancy Morgan does not understand why the overhead volume variance indicates that fixed overhead costs are underapplied or overapplied. Clarify this for Nancy.

17. Mia Antonucci is trying to outline the important points about overhead variances on a class examination. List four points that Mia should include in her outline.

18. How often should variances be reported to management? What principle may be used with variance reports?

19. What circumstances may cause the purchasing department to be responsible for both an unfavourable materials price variance and an unfavourable materials quantity variance?

20. What four perspectives are used in the balanced scorecard? Describe each one, and how they are linked.

21. Sanjiv Mehta says that the balanced scorecard was created to replace financial measures as the primary mechanism for performance evaluation. He says that it uses only non-financial measures. Is this true?

22. What are some examples of non-financial measures that companies use to evaluate performance?

*23. (a) Explain the basic features of a standard cost accounting system. (b) What type of balance will exist in the variance account when (1) the materials price variance is unfavourable and (2) the labour quantity variance is favourable?

*24. (a) How are variances reported in income statements prepared for management? (b) Is it okay to use standard costs in preparing financial statements for shareholders? Explain.

Brief Exercises

BE11–1 Valdez Company uses standards and budgets. For the year, estimated production of Product X is 500,000 units. The total estimated costs for materials and labour are $1 million and $1.6 million, respectively. Calculate the estimates for (a) a standard cost and (b) a budgeted cost.

Distinguish between standard and budget costs. (SO 1)

BE11–2 Hideo Company accumulates the following data concerning raw materials in making one unit of finished product: (1) Price—net purchase price $3.20, freight in $0.20, and receiving and handling $0.10. (2) Quantity—required materials 2.6 kilograms, allowance for waste and spoilage 0.4 kilograms. Calculate the following:

(a) standard direct materials price per unit
(b) standard direct materials quantity per unit
(c) total standard material cost per unit

Determine direct materials standard. (SO 3)

BE11–3 Labour data for making one unit of finished product in Hideo Company are as follows: (1) Price—hourly wage rate $10.00, payroll taxes $0.80, and fringe benefits $1.20. (2) Quantity—actual production time 1.2 hours, rest periods and cleanup 0.25 hours, and setup and downtime 0.15 hours. Calculate the following:

(a) standard direct labour rate per hour
(b) standard direct labour hours per unit
(c) standard labour cost per unit

Determine direct labour standard. (SO 3)

BE11–4 Sprague Company's standard materials cost per unit of output is $10 (2 kilograms × $5.00). During July, the company purchases and uses 3,300 kilograms of materials costing $16,731 in making 1,500 units of finished product. Calculate the total, price, and quantity materials variances.

Calculate direct materials variances. (SO 4)

BE11–5 Talbot Company's standard labour cost per unit of output is $20 (2 hours × $10.00 per hour). During August, the company incurs 1,900 hours of direct labour at an hourly cost of $9.60 per hour in making 1,000 units of finished product. Calculate the total, price, and quantity labour variances.

Calculate direct labour variances. (SO 4)

BE11–6 In October, Russo Company reports 21,000 actual direct labour hours, and it incurs $96,000 of manufacturing overhead costs. Standard hours allowed for the work done is 20,000 hours. The predetermined overhead rate is $5.00 per direct labour hour. Calculate the total manufacturing overhead variance.

Calculate total manufacturing overhead variance. (SO 5)

Calculate manufacturing overhead controllable variance.
(SO 5)

BE11–7 Overhead data for Russo Company are given in BE11–6. In addition to that data, the flexible manufacturing overhead budget shows that budgeted costs are $4.00 variable per direct labour hour and $25,000 fixed. Calculate the manufacturing overhead controllable variance.

Calculate overhead volume variance.
(SO 5)

BE11–8 Using the data in BE11–6 and BE11–7, calculate the manufacturing overhead volume variance. Normal capacity was 25,000 direct labour hours.

Match objectives to perspectives in Balanced Scorecard.
(SO 8)

BE11–9 The four perspectives in the balanced scorecard are (1) financial, (2) customer, (3) internal process, and (4) learning and growth. Match each of the following objectives with the perspective it is most likely associated with: (a) plant capacity utilization, (b) employee work days missed due to injury, (c) return on assets, and (d) brand recognition.

Prepare journal entries for material variances.
(SO 9)

***BE11–10** Journalize the following transactions for McBee Manufacturing:
(a) Purchased 6,000 units of raw materials on account for $11,500. The standard cost was $12,000.
(b) Issued 5,600 units of raw materials for production. The standard units were 5,800.

Prepare journal entries for labour variances.
(SO 9)

***BE11–11** Journalize the following transactions for Worrel Manufacturing:
(a) Incurred direct labour costs of $24,000 for 3,000 hours. The standard labour cost was $24,600.
(b) Assigned 3,000 direct labour hours costing $24,000 to production. Standard hours were 3,100.

Exercises

Calculate standard materials costs.
(SO 3)

E11–1 Raul Mondesi manufactures and sells homemade wine, and he wants to develop a standard cost per litre. The following are required for production of a 200-litre batch:

90 litres of grape concentrate at $1.35 per litre
27 kilograms of granulated sugar at $0.60 per kilogram
60 lemons at $0.60 each
50 yeast tablets at $0.25 each
50 nutrient tablets at $0.20 each
75 litres of water at $0.10 per litre

Raul estimates that 4% of the grape concentrate is wasted, 10% of the sugar is lost, and 20% of the lemons cannot be used.

Instructions

Calculate the standard cost of the ingredients for one litre of wine. (Do calculations to three decimal places.)

Calculate materials price and quantity variances.
(SO 4)

E11–2 The standard cost of Product B manufactured by Gomez Company includes three units of direct materials at $5.00 per unit. During June, 27,600 units of direct materials are purchased at a cost of $4.70 per unit, and 27,600 units of direct materials are used to produce 9,000 units of Product B.

Instructions

(a) Calculate the materials variance, and the price and quantity variances.
(b) Repeat (a), assuming the purchase price is $5.20 and the quantity purchased and used is 26,400 units.

Calculate labour price and quantity variances.
(SO 4)

E11–3 Pagley Company's standard labour cost of producing one unit of Product DD is four hours at the rate of $12.00 per hour. During August, 40,500 hours of labour are incurred at a cost of $12.10 per hour to produce 10,000 units of Product DD.

Instructions

(a) Calculate the total labour variance.
(b) Calculate the labour price and quantity variances.
(c) Repeat (b), assuming the standard is 4.2 hours of direct labour at $12.20 per hour.

E11-4 Rapid Repair Services, Inc. is trying to establish the standard labour cost of a typical oil change. The following data have been collected from time and motion studies conducted over the past month:

Calculate materials and labour variances. (SO 3, 4)

Actual time spent on the oil change	1.0 hour
Hourly wage rate	$10.00
Payroll taxes	10% of wage rate
Setup and downtime	10% of actual labour time
Cleanup and rest periods	30% of actual labour time
Fringe benefits	25% of wage rate

Instructions

(a) Determine the standard direct labour hours per oil change.
(b) Determine the direct labour hourly rate.
(c) Determine the direct labour cost per oil change.
(d) If an oil change took 1.5 hours at the standard hourly rate, what was the direct labour quantity variance?

E11-5 Kopecky Inc., which produces a single product, has prepared the following standard cost sheet for one unit of the product:

Calculate materials and labour variances. (SO 4)

Direct materials (8 kilograms at $2.50 per kilograms)	$20.00
Direct labour (3 hours at $12 per hour)	$36.00

During the month of April, the company manufactures 240 units and incurs the following actual costs:

Direct materials (1,900 kilograms)	$4,940
Direct labour (700 hours)	$8,120

Instructions

Calculate the total, price, and quantity variances for materials and labour.

E11-6 The following direct materials and direct labour data are for the operations of Batista Manufacturing Company for the month of August:

Calculate materials and labour variances and list reasons for unfavourable variances. (SO 4, 6)

Costs		Quantities	
Actual labour rate	$13.00 per hour	Actual hours incurred and used	4,250 hours
Actual materials price	$128.00 per tonne	Actual quantity of materials purchased and used	1,250 tonnes
Standard labour rate	$12.00 per hour	Standard hours used	4,300 hours
Standard materials price	$130.00 per tonne	Standard quantity of materials used	1,200 tonnes

Instructions

(a) Calculate the total, price, and quantity variances for materials and labour.
(b) ▭▭▭▷ Provide two possible explanations for each of the unfavourable variances calculated in (a), and suggest which department might be responsible for the unfavourable result.

E11-7 The following information was taken from the annual manufacturing overhead cost budget of Fernetti Company:

Calculate overhead variances and list reasons for unfavourable variances. (SO 5, 6)

Variable manufacturing overhead costs	$33,000
Fixed manufacturing overhead costs	$21,450
Normal production level in labour hours	16,500
Normal production level in units	4,125
Standard labour hours per unit	4

During the year, 4,000 units were produced, 16,100 hours were worked, and the actual manufacturing overhead was $54,000. Actual fixed manufacturing overhead costs equalled the budgeted fixed manufacturing overhead costs. Overhead is applied based on direct labour hours.

Instructions

(a) Calculate the total, fixed, and variable predetermined manufacturing overhead rates.
(b) Calculate the total, controllable, and volume overhead variances.
(c) ▭▭▭▷ Briefly interpret the overhead controllable and volume variances calculated in (b).

Determine missing amounts for overhead variances.
(SO 5)

E11–8   The loan department of Your Local Bank uses standard costs to determine the overhead cost of processing loan applications. During the current month, a fire occurred, and the accounting records for the department were mostly destroyed. The following data were salvaged from the ashes:

Standard variable overhead rate per hour	$ 9.00
Standard hours per application	2
Standard hours allowed	2,000
Standard fixed overhead rate per hour	$6
Actual fixed overhead cost	$13,200
Variable overhead budget based on standard hours allowed	$18,000
Fixed overhead budget	$13,200
Overhead controllable variance	$1,500 U

Instructions

(a) Determine the following:

  1. Total actual overhead cost
  2. Actual variable overhead cost
  3. Variable overhead cost applied
  4. Fixed overhead cost applied
  5. Overhead volume variance

(b) Determine how many loans were processed.

Calculate overhead variances.
(SO 5)

E11–9   Manufacturing overhead data for the production of Product H by Rondell Company are as follows:

Overhead incurred for 52,000 actual direct labour hours worked	$213,000
Overhead rate (variable $3.00; fixed $1.00) at normal capacity of 54,000 direct labour hours	$ 4.00
Standard hours allowed for work done	52,000

Instructions

Calculate the total, controllable, and volume overhead variances.

Prepare variance report for direct labour.
(SO 4, 6)

E11–10   During March 2005, Garner Tool & Die Company worked on four jobs. A review of the direct labour costs reveals the following summary data:

	Actual		Standard		Total
Job Number	Hours	Costs	Hours	Costs	Variance
A257	220	$ 4,400	225	$4,500	$ 100 F
A258	450	10,350	430	8,600	1,750 U
A259	300	6,150	300	6,000	150 U
A260	115	2,070	110	2,200	130 F
Total variance					$1,670 U

Analysis reveals that Job A257 was a repeat job. Job A258 was a rush order that required overtime work at premium rates of pay. Job A259 required a more experienced replacement worker on one shift. Work on Job A260 was done for one day by a new trainee when a regular worker was absent.

Instructions

Prepare a report for the plant supervisor on direct labour cost variances for March. The report should have columns for the following headings: (1) Job No., (2) Actual Hours, (3) Standard Hours, (4) Labour Quantity Variance, (5) Actual Rate, (6) Standard Rate, (7) Labour Price Variance, and (8) Explanations.

Prepare variance reports.
(SO 6)

E11–11   Imperial Landscaping plants grass seed as basic landscaping for business terrains. During a recent month, the company worked on three projects (Ames, Korman, and Stilles). The company is interested in controlling its material costs—grass seed costs—for these planting projects.

In order to provide management with useful cost control information, the company uses standard costs and prepares monthly variance reports. Analysis reveals that the purchasing agent mistakenly purchased poor-quality seeds for the Ames project. The Korman project, however, received seed that was on sale but was higher than standard quality. The

Stilles project received standard seeds; however, the price had increased and a new employee was used to spread the seed.

Shown below are quantity and cost data for each project:

	Actual		Standard		Total
Project	Quantity	Costs	Quantity	Costs	Variance
Ames	500 kg	$1,175	460 kg	$1,150	$ 25 U
Korman	400	960	410	1,025	65 F
Stilles	500	1,300	480	1,200	100 U
Total variance					$ 60 U

Instructions

(a) Prepare a variance report for the purchasing department with the following column headings: (1) Project, (2) Actual Kilograms Purchased, (3) Actual Price, (4) Standard Price, (5) Price Variance, and (6) Explanation.

(b) Prepare a variance report for the production department with the following column headings: (1) Project, (2) Actual Kilograms, (3) Standard Kilograms, (4) Standard Price, (5) Quantity Variance, and (6) Explanation.

E11–12 Carlos Company uses a standard cost accounting system. During January, the company reported the following manufacturing variances:

Prepare income statement for management.
(SO 7)

Materials price variance	$1,250 debit	Labour quantity variance	$ 725 debit
Materials quantity variance	700 credit	Overhead controllable variance	200 credit
Labour price variance	525 debit	Overhead volume variance	1,000 debit

In addition, 6,000 units of product were sold at $8 per unit. Each unit sold had a standard cost of $6. Selling and administrative expenses were $6,000 for the month.

Instructions

Prepare an income statement for management for the month ending January 31, 2005.

E11–13 The following is a list of terms related to performance evaluation:

Identify performance evaluation terminology.
(SO 1, 8)

1. Balanced scorecard
2. Variance
3. Learning and growth perspective
4. Non-financial measures
5. Customer perspective
6. Internal process perspective
7. Ideal standards
8. Normal standards

Instructions

Match each of the following descriptions with one of the terms above.

(a) The difference between total actual costs and total standard costs.

(b) An efficient level of performance that is attainable under expected operating conditions.

(c) An approach that uses financial and non-financial measures in an integrated system that links performance measurement and a company's strategic goals.

(d) A viewpoint used in the balanced scorecard to evaluate how well a company develops and retains its employees.

(e) An evaluation tool that is not based on dollars.

(f) A viewpoint used in the balanced scorecard to evaluate the company from the perspective of those people who buy and use its products or services.

(g) An optimum level of performance under perfect operating conditions.

(h) A viewpoint used in the balanced scorecard to evaluate the efficiency and effectiveness of the company's value chain.

Determine missing entries and balances for variances.
(SO 4, 5, 9)

*E11−14   Tovar Company uses a standard cost accounting system. Some of the ledger accounts have been destroyed in a fire. The controller asks for your help in reconstructing some missing entries and balances.

Instructions

(a) Materials Price Variance shows a $3,000 favourable balance. Accounts Payable shows $128,000 of raw materials purchases. What was the amount debited to Raw Materials Inventory for raw materials purchased?

(b) Materials Quantity Variance shows a $3,000 unfavourable balance. Raw Materials Inventory shows a zero balance. What was the amount debited to Work in Process Inventory for direct materials used?

(c) Labour Price Variance shows a $1,500 unfavourable balance. Factory Labour shows a debit of $150,000 for wages incurred. What was the amount credited to Wages Payable?

(d) Factory Labour shows a credit of $150,000 for direct labour used. Labour Quantity Variance shows a $900 unfavourable balance. What was the amount debited to Work in Process for direct labour used?

(e) Overhead applied to Work in Process totalled $165,000. If the total overhead variance was $1,000 unfavourable, what was the amount of overhead costs debited to Manufacturing Overhead?

(f) Overhead Controllable Variance shows a debit balance of $1,500. What was the amount and type of balance (debit or credit) in Overhead Volume Variance?

Journalize entries for materials and labour variances.
(SO 9)

*E11−15   Data for Kopecky Inc. are given in E11−5.

Instructions

Journalize the entries to record the materials and labour variances.

Journalize overhead variances.
(SO 9)

*E11−16   Data for Rondell Company are given in E11−9.

Instructions

(a) Journalize the incurrence of the overhead costs and the application of overhead to the job, assuming a standard cost accounting system is used.

(b) Prepare the adjusting entry for the overhead variances.

Journalize entries in standard cost accounting system.
(SO 9)

*E11−17   Marley Company installed a standard cost system on January 1. Selected transactions for the month of January are as follows:

1. Purchased 18,000 units of raw materials on account at a cost of $4.50 per unit. Standard cost was $4.25 per unit.

2. Issued 18,000 units of raw materials for jobs that required 17,600 standard units of raw materials.

3. Incurred 15,200 actual hours of direct labour at an actual rate of $4.80 per hour. The standard rate is $5.25 per hour. (*Note*: Credit Wages Payable.)

4. Performed 15,200 hours of direct labour on jobs when standard hours were 15,400.

5. Applied overhead to jobs at 100% of the direct labour cost for the standard hours allowed.

Instructions

Journalize the January transactions.

Problems: Set A

Determine amounts from variance report.
(SO 4, 5)

P11−18A   You have been given the following information about the production of Gamma Co., and are asked to provide the plant manager with information for a meeting with the vice-president of operations:

Standard Cost Card

Direct materials (6 kg at $3 per kg)	$18.00
Direct labour (0.8 hrs. at $5)	4.00
Variable overhead (0.8 hrs. at $3 per hr.)	2.40
Fixed overhead (0.8 hrs at $7 per hr.)	5.60
	$30.00

The following is a production report for the most recent period of operations:

Costs	Total Standard Cost	Price/ Rate	Spending/ Budget	Quantity/ Efficiency	Volume
Direct materials	$405,000	$6,900 F		$9,000 U	
Direct labour	90,000	4,850 U		7,000 U	
Variable overhead	54,000		$1,300 F	?	
Fixed overhead	126,000		500 F		$14,000 U

(header: Variances)

Instructions

(a) How many units were produced during the period?
(b) How many kilograms of raw material were purchased and used during the period?
(c) What was the actual cost per kilogram of raw materials?
(d) How many actual direct labour hours were worked during the period?
(e) What was the actual rate paid per direct labour hour?
(f) What was the actual variable overhead cost incurred during the period?
(g) What is the total fixed cost in the company's flexible budget?
(h) What were the budget hours for the last period?

(CGA-adapted)

P11–19A Inman Corporation manufactures a single product. The standard cost per unit of product is as follows:

Calculate variances. (SO 4, 5)

Direct materials—2 kilograms of plastic at $5 per kilogram	$10.00
Direct labour—2 hours at $12 per hour	24.00
Variable manufacturing overhead	12.00
Fixed manufacturing overhead	6.00
Total standard cost per unit	$52.00

The master manufacturing overhead budget for the month based on the normal productive capacity of 15,000 direct labour hours (7,500 units) shows total variable costs of $90,000 ($6 per labour hour) and total fixed costs of $45,000 ($3 per labour hour). Normal productive capacity is 15,000 direct labour hours. Overhead is applied based on direct labour hours. Actual costs for producing 7,600 units in November were as follows:

Direct materials (15,000 kilograms)	$ 73,500
Direct labour (14,900 hours)	181,780
Variable overhead	88,990
Fixed overhead	44,000
Total manufacturing costs	$388,270

The purchasing department normally buys the quantities of raw materials that are expected to be used in production each month. Raw materials inventories, therefore, can be ignored.

Instructions

Calculate all of the materials, labour, and overhead variances.

P11–20A Soriano Manufacturing Company uses a standard cost accounting system to account for the manufacturing of exhaust fans. In July 2005, it accumulates the following data for 1,500 units started and finished:

Calculate variances, and prepare income statement. (SO 4, 5, 7)

Cost and Production Data	Actual	Standard
Raw materials		
Units purchased	17,400	
Units used	17,400	18,000
Unit cost	$3.40	$3.00
Direct labour		
Hours worked	2,900	3,000
Hourly rate	$11.80	$12.20
Manufacturing overhead		
Incurred	$87,500	
Applied		$93,750

Manufacturing overhead was applied based on direct labour hours. Normal capacity for the month was 2,800 direct labour hours. At normal capacity, budgeted overhead costs were $20 per labour hour variable and $11.25 per labour hour fixed. Total budgeted fixed overhead costs were $31,500.

Jobs finished during the month were sold for $240,000. Selling and administrative expenses were $25,000.

Instructions

(a) Calculate all of the variances for direct materials, direct labour, and manufacturing overhead.

(b) Prepare an income statement for management showing the variances. Ignore income taxes.

Prepare flexible budget, determine standard costs, calculate variances.
(SO 3, 4, 5)

P11–21A   Under a contract with the provincial government, ChemLabs Inc. analyzes the chemical and bacterial composition of well water in various municipalities in the interior of British Columbia. The contract price is $25.20 per test performed. The normal volume is 10,000 tests per month. Each test requires two testing kits, which have a standard price of $3.80 each. Direct labour to perform the test is 10 minutes at $22.80 per hour. At normal volume, the overhead costs are as follows:

Variable overhead costs		
Indirect labour	$18,000	
Utilities	4,000	
Labour-related costs	15,000	
Laboratory maintenance	11,000	$ 48,000
Fixed overhead costs		
Supervisor	30,000	
Amortization	28,000	
Base utilities	9,000	
Insurance	2,000	69,000
Total overhead		$117,000

Overhead is allocated based on direct labour hours.

During May 2005, 9,000 tests were performed. The records show the following actual costs and production data:

	Activity	Actual Cost
Number of test kits purchased	19,000	$70,300
Number of test kits used	18,500	
Direct labour	1,623 hours	37,646
Total overhead costs		
Variable		45,200
Fixed		68,500

Test kits are kept in inventory at standard cost. At the end of May, no tests were in process.

Instructions

(a) Prepare a flexible overhead budget based on 80% of the normal volume.
(b) Prepare a standard cost card for a water test.
(c) Calculate the direct materials price and quantity variances and the direct labour rate and efficiency variances for May 2000, indicating whether they are favourable or unfavourable.
(d) Calculate the laboratory variable overhead variances for the month, indicating whether they are favourable or unfavourable.

(CGA-adapted)

P11–22A Kohler Clothiers manufactures women's business suits. The company uses a standard cost accounting system. In March 2005, 11,800 suits were made. The following standard and actual cost data applied to the month of March when normal capacity was 15,000 direct labour hours. All materials purchased were used in production:

Calculate variances, identify significant variances, and discuss causes.
(SO 4, 5, 6)

Cost Element	Standard (per unit)	Actual
Direct materials	5 metres at $7 per metre	$410,400 for 57,000 metres ($7.20 per metre)
Direct labour	1 hour at $12 per hour	$125,440 for 11,200 hours ($11.20 per hour)
Overhead	1 hour at $9.30 per hour (fixed $6.30; variable $3.00)	$90,000 fixed overhead $42,000 variable overhead

Overhead is applied based on direct labour hours. At normal capacity, budgeted fixed overhead costs were $94,500, and budgeted variable overhead costs were $45,000.

Instructions

(a) Calculate the total, price, and quantity variances for materials and labour, and calculate the total, controllable, and volume variances for manufacturing overhead.
(b) ✏️ Which of the materials and labour variances should be investigated if management considers a variance of more than 6% from standard to be significant? Discuss the potential causes of this variance.

P11–23A You have been given the following information about Kirkland Co. Ltd., which uses a standard cost system in accounting for its one product:

Calculate various amounts from standard costs and variances.
(SO 4, 5)

1. In the month of November 2005, 5,000 units were produced.
2. The annual overhead budget includes $750,000 for variable and $1,050,000 for fixed overhead items. Budgeted production for the year is 50,000 units. Overhead is applied based on direct labour hours.
3. The materials standard per unit is 20 litres at $1.
4. The direct labour standard per unit is 3 hours at $10.
5. The actual price paid for material was $0.99.
6. The actual direct labour rate was $10.50.
7. Actual fixed overhead costs totalled $88,000.
8. The following variances have already been calculated:

Materials price	600 F
Materials quantity	1,600 U
Labour rate	7,400 U
Variable overhead spending	1,800 U

Instructions

Calculate the following:

(a) The quantity of material purchased
(b) The quantity of material used
(c) The actual direct labour hours worked
(d) The labour efficiency variance
(e) The variable overhead efficiency variance
(f) The actual variable overhead
(g) The fixed overhead budget variance
(h) The fixed overhead production volume variance

Answer questions about variances.
(SO 4, 5)

P11–24A Crede Manufacturing Company uses a standard cost accounting system. In 2005, 33,000 units were produced. Each unit took several kilograms of direct materials and 1⅓ standard hours of direct labour at a standard hourly rate of $12. Normal capacity was 42,000 direct labour hours. During the year, 132,000 kilograms of raw materials were purchased at $0.90 per kilogram. All materials purchased were used during the year.

Instructions

(a) If the materials price variance was $3,960 unfavourable, what was the standard materials price per kilogram?
(b) If the materials quantity variance was $2,871 favourable, what was the standard materials quantity per unit?
(c) What were the standard hours allowed for the units produced?
(d) If the labour quantity variance was $8,400 unfavourable, what were the actual direct labour hours worked?
(e) If the labour price variance was $4,470 favourable, what was the actual rate per hour?
(f) If total budgeted manufacturing overhead was $327,600 at normal capacity, what was the predetermined overhead rate?
(g) What was the standard cost per unit of product?
(h) How much overhead was applied to production during the year?
(i) If the fixed overhead rate was $2.50, what was the overhead volume variance?
(j) If the overhead controllable variance was $3,000 favourable, what were the total variable overhead costs incurred?
(k) Using selected answers above, what were the total costs assigned to work in process?

Calculate variances and prepare income statement.
(SO 4, 5, 7)

P11–25A Hi-Tek Labs performs steroid testing services for high schools, colleges, and universities. Because the company works only with educational institutions, the price of each test is strictly regulated. Therefore, the costs incurred must be carefully monitored and controlled. Shown below are the standard costs for a typical test:

Direct materials (1 Petri dish at $2 per dish)	$ 2.00
Direct labour (0.5 hours at $20 per hour)	10.00
Variable overhead (0.5 hours at $8 per hour)	4.00
Fixed overhead (0.5 hours at $3 per hour)	1.50
Total standard cost per test	$17.50

The lab does not maintain an inventory of Petri dishes. Therefore, the dishes purchased each month are used that month. Actual activity for the month of May 2005, when 2,000 tests were conducted, resulted in the following:

Direct materials (2,020 dishes)	$ 4,242
Direct labour (995 hours)	20,895
Variable overhead	8,100
Fixed overhead	3,400

Monthly budgeted fixed overhead is $3,600. Revenues for the month were $45,000, and selling and administrative expenses were $2,000.

Instructions

(a) Calculate the price and quantity variances for direct materials and direct labour, and the controllable and volume variances for overhead.
(b) Prepare an income statement for management.
(c) ✏️▷ Provide possible explanations for each unfavourable variance.

Calculate variances.
(SO 5)

P11–26A Pointe Claire Company applies overhead based on direct labour hours. Two direct labour hours are required for each unit of product. Planned production for the period was set at 9,000 units. Manufacturing overhead is budgeted at $135,000 for the period (20% of this cost is fixed). The 17,200 hours worked during the period resulted in the production of 8,500 units. The variable manufacturing overhead cost incurred was $108,500 and the fixed manufacturing overhead cost was $28,000.

Instructions

(a) Calculate the variable overhead spending variance for the period.
(b) Calculate the variable overhead efficiency (quantity) variance for the period.

(c) Calculate the fixed overhead budget (spending) variance for the period.
(d) Calculate the fixed overhead volume variance for the period.

(CMA Canada-adapted)

*P11-27A   Fayman Manufacturing Company uses standard costs with its job-order cost accounting system. In January, an order (Job 84) was received for 3,900 units of Product D. The standard cost of one unit of Product D is as follows:

Journalize and post standard cost entries, and prepare income statement.
(SO 4, 5, 7, 9)

Direct materials—1.4 kilograms at $4 per kilogram	$ 5.60
Direct labour—1 hour at $9 per hour	9.00
Overhead—1 hour (variable $7.40; fixed $10.00)	17.40
Standard cost per unit	$32.00

Overhead is applied based on direct labour hours. Normal capacity for the month of January was 4,500 direct labour hours. During January, the following transactions applicable to Job No. 84 occurred:

1. Purchased 6,200 kilograms of raw materials on account at $3.60 per kilogram.
2. Requisitioned 6,200 kilograms of raw materials for production.
3. Incurred 3,700 hours of direct labour at $9.25 per hour.
4. Worked 3,700 hours of direct labour on Job No. 84.
5. Incurred $73,650 of manufacturing overhead on account.
6. Applied overhead to Job No. 84 based on the direct labour hours.
7. Transferred Job No. 84 to finished goods.
8. Billed customer for Job No. 84 at a selling price of $250,000.
9. Incurred selling and administrative expenses of $61,000 on account.

Instructions

(a) Journalize the transactions.
(b) Post to the job-order cost accounts.
(c) Prepare the entry to recognize the overhead variances.
(d) Prepare the income statement for management for January 2005.

Problems: Set B

P11-28B   Ranier Corporation manufactures a single product. The standard cost per unit of product is shown below:

Calculate variances.
(SO 4, 5)

Direct materials—1 kilogram of plastic at $7 per kilogram	$ 7.00
Direct labour—1.5 hours at $12 per hour	18.00
Variable manufacturing overhead	11.25
Fixed manufacturing overhead	3.75
Total standard cost per unit	$40.00

The predetermined manufacturing overhead rate is $10 per direct labour hour ($15.00 ÷ 1.5). This rate was calculated from a master manufacturing overhead budget based on normal production of 7,500 direct labour hours (5,000 units) for the month. The master budget showed total variable costs of $56,250 ($7.50 per hour) and total fixed costs of $18,750 ($2.50 per hour). Actual costs for October in producing 4,800 units were as follows:

Direct materials (5,100 kilograms)	$ 37,230
Direct labour (7,000 hours)	87,500
Variable overhead	56,170
Fixed overhead	19,680
Total manufacturing costs	$200,580

The purchasing department normally buys the quantities of raw materials that are expected to be used in production each month. Raw materials inventories can therefore be ignored.

Instructions

Calculate all of the materials, labour, and overhead variances.

Calculate variances, and prepare income statement.
(SO 4, 5, 7)

P11–29B   Finley Manufacturing Corporation accumulates the following data for jobs started and finished during the month of June 2005:

Costs and Production Data	Actual	Standard
Raw materials unit cost	$2.25	$2.00
Raw materials units used	10,400	10,000
Direct labour payroll	$124,100	$120,000
Direct labour hours worked	14,600	15,000
Manufacturing overhead incurred	$182,500	
Manufacturing overhead applied		$189,000
Machine hours expected to be used at normal capacity		42,500
Budgeted fixed overhead for June		$51,000
Variable overhead rate per hour		$3.00
Fixed overhead rate per hour		$1.20

Overhead is applied based on standard machine hours. Three hours of machine time are required for each direct labour hour. The jobs were sold for $400,000. Selling and administrative expenses were $40,000. Assume that the amount of raw materials purchased equalled the amount used.

Instructions

(a) Calculate all of the variances for direct materials, direct labour, and manufacturing overhead.

(b) Prepare an income statement for management. Ignore income taxes.

Calculate variances, and identify significant variances.
(SO 4, 5)

P11–30B   Sasha Clothiers is a small company that manufactures oversize suits. The company uses a standard cost accounting system. In May 2005, 11,200 suits were produced.

The following standard and actual cost data applied to the month of May when normal capacity was 14,000 direct labour hours. All materials purchased were used.

Cost Element	Standard (per unit)	Actual
Direct materials	8 metres at $4.50 per metre	$371,050 for 90,500 metres ($4.10 per metre)
Direct labour	1.2 hours at $13 per hour	$201,630 for 14,300 hours ($14.10 per hour)
Overhead	1.2 hours at $6 per hour (fixed $3.50; variable $2.50)	$49,000 fixed overhead $36,000 variable overhead

Overhead is applied based on direct labour hours. At normal capacity, the budgeted fixed overhead costs are $49,000, and the budgeted variable overhead is $35,000.

Instructions

(a) Calculate the total, price, and quantity variances for materials and labour, and the total, controllable, and volume variances for manufacturing overhead.

(b) ✏▶ Which of the materials and labour variances should be investigated if management considers a variance of more than 7% from standard to be significant?

Calculate variances.
(SO 4, 5)

P11–31B   Milberg Co. uses absorption costing and standard costing to improve cost control.

In 2005, the total budgeted overhead rate was $1.55 per direct labour hour. When the budget was being prepared, Milberg expected a monthly activity level of 10,000 direct labour hours. The monthly variable overhead cost budgeted for this level of activity was $9,500.

The following data on actual results are provided for the month of November 2005.

Materials purchased	20,000 units
Direct labour costs incurred	$36,000
Total of direct labour rate and efficiency variances	$500 F
Actual wage rate ($0.20 less than standard)	$4.80
Under applied variable overhead costs	$1,065 U
Total underapplied fixed and variable overhead costs	$2,256 U
Materials price variance	$200 F
Materials efficiency variance	$610 F
Price of purchased materials	$0.60 per unit
Materials used	15,000 units

Instructions

Identify and calculate as many different variances as you can for 2005.

(CGA-adapted)

P11–32B Harbaugh Manufacturing Company uses a standard cost accounting system. In 2005, 30,000 units were produced. Each unit took several kilograms of direct materials and 1½ standard hours of direct labour at a standard hourly rate of $12. Normal capacity was 50,000 direct labour hours. During the year, 133,000 kilograms of raw materials were purchased at $0.92 per kilogram. All materials purchased were used during the year.

Answer questions about variances.
(SO 4, 5)

Instructions

(a) If the materials price variance was $5,320 favourable, what was the standard materials price per kilogram?
(b) If the materials quantity variance was $3,840 unfavourable, what was the standard materials quantity per unit?
(c) What were the standard hours allowed for the units produced?
(d) If the labour quantity variance was $7,200 unfavourable, what were the actual direct labour hours worked?
(e) If the labour price variance was $9,120 favourable, what was the actual rate per hour?
(f) If total budgeted manufacturing overhead was $340,000 at normal capacity, what was the predetermined overhead rate?
(g) What was the standard cost per unit of product?
(h) How much overhead was applied to production during the year?
(i) If the fixed overhead rate was $2, what was the overhead volume variance?
(j) If the overhead controllable variance is $3,000 unfavourable, what were the total variable overhead costs incurred?
(k) Using one or more answers above, what were the total costs assigned to work in process?

P11–33B The Multi-Tool Manufacturing Company uses a standard cost system and applies overhead to products using an average activity overhead rate. Proposals have been made to change to a practical capacity rate or to an expected activity rate for product 200519X1.

Calculate overhead variances and discuss meaning.
(SO 5)

Average activity is 75% of practical capacity. The expected activity for 2005 is only 60% of practical capacity. An overhead rate of $10.50 per direct labour hour has been calculated for 2005 using an overhead budget at average activity. The overhead budget at an average activity of 13,500 direct labour hours (per year) is as follows:

Variable overhead	$ 60,750
Fixed overhead	81,000
Total budgeted overhead	$141,750

$$\text{Overhead rate} = \frac{\$141,750}{13,500} = \$10.50 \text{ per direct labour hour}$$

The actual activity in the month of January was 1,050 direct labour hours. Standard direct labour hours for output produced were 1,075 hours. The actual overhead for January was $11,635. Assume that January is one-twelfth of the year.

Instructions

(a) Calculate the overhead rate if practical capacity is used as the base activity.
(b) Calculate the overhead rate if expected activity for 2005 is used as the base activity.
(c) Calculate the combined overhead spending variance for January.
(d) Calculate the volume variance, assuming the use of (1) an expected activity overhead rate and (2) a practical capacity overhead rate.
(e) Briefly discuss the meaning of the variances determined in (d).

(CMA Canada-adapted)

P11–34B Farm Labs, Inc. provides mad cow disease testing for both provincial and federal government agriculture agencies. Because the company's customers are government agencies, prices are strictly regulated. Farm Labs must therefore constantly monitor and control its testing costs. Shown below are the standard costs for a typical test:

Calculate variances and prepare income statement.
(SO 4, 5, 7)

Direct materials (2 test tubes @ $1.50 per tube)	$ 3.00
Direct labour (1 hour @ $25 per hour)	25.00
Variable overhead (1 hour @ $5 per hour)	5.00
Fixed overhead (1 hour @ $10 per hour)	10.00
Total standard cost per test	$43.00

The lab does not maintain an inventory of test tubes. The tubes purchased each month are used that month. Actual activity for the month of November 2005, when 1,500 tests were conducted, resulted in the following:

Direct materials (3,050 test tubes)	$ 3,050
Direct labour (1,600 hours)	36,800
Variable overhead	7,400
Fixed overhead	14,000

Monthly budgeted fixed overhead is $14,000. Revenues for the month were $75,000, and selling and administrative expenses were $4,000.

Instructions

(a) Calculate the price and quantity variances for direct materials and direct labour, and the controllable and volume variances for overhead.
(b) Prepare an income statement for management.
(c) ◖▭▭▭▷ Provide possible explanations for each unfavourable variance.

Calculate variances.
(SO 4, 5)

P11–35B   Ronaldo Manufacturing Company uses a standard cost system in accounting for the cost of one of its products. The budgeted monthly production is 1,650 units per month. The standard direct labour cost is 15 hours per unit at $5 per hour. The budgeted cost for manufacturing overhead is set as follows:

Fixed overhead per month	$173,250
Variable overhead per month	74,250
Total budgeted overhead	$247,500

The manufacturing overhead rate is 200% of the direct labour cost.

During the month of April, the plant produced 1,604 units and the cost of production was as follows:

Direct materials (87,000 litres)	$ 870,000
Direct labour (24,610 hrs.)	125,511
Fixed manufacturing overhead	186,000
Variable manufacturing overhead	61,300
	$1,242,811

Instructions

Calculate the following:

(a) Labour price and quantity variances
(b) Variable overhead spending and quantity variances
(c) Fixed overhead spending and volume variances

(CMA Canada-adapted)

Journalize and post standard cost entries, and prepare income statement.
(SO 4, 5, 9)

*P11–36B   Berman Corporation uses standard costs with its job-order cost accounting system. In January, an order (Job No. 12) for 1,950 units of Product B was received. The standard cost of one unit of Product B is as follows:

Direct materials	3 kilograms at $1 per kilogram	$ 3.00
Direct labour	1 hour at $8 per hour	8.00
Overhead	2 hours (variable $4 per machine hour; fixed $2.25 per machine hour)	12.50
Standard cost per unit		$23.50

Normal capacity for the month was 4,200 machine hours. During January, the following transactions applicable to Job No. 12 occurred:

1. Purchased 6,250 kilograms of raw materials on account at $1.04 per kilogram.
2. Requisitioned 6,250 kilograms of raw materials for Job No. 12.
3. Incurred 2,200 hours of direct labour at a rate of $7.75 per hour.

4. Worked 2,200 hours of direct labour on Job No. 12.
5. Incurred manufacturing overhead of $25,800 on account.
6. Applied overhead to Job No. 12 based on standard machine hours used.
7. Completed Job No. 12.
8. Billed customer for Job No. 12 at a selling price of $70,000.
9. Incurred selling and administrative expenses of $2,000 on account.

Instructions

(a) Journalize the transactions.
(b) Post to the job-order cost accounts.
(c) Prepare the entry to recognize the overhead variances.
(d) Prepare the January 2005 income statement for management.

*P11–37B   Azim Shirts Inc. manufactures sweatshirts for large stores. The standard costs for a dozen sweatshirts are as follows:

Calculate variances and prepare journal entries.
(SO 4, 5, 9)

Direct materials	24 metres	×	$1.10 per metre	=	$26.40
Direct labour	3 hours	×	$7.35 per hour	=	$22.05

During February, Azim worked on three separate orders of sweatshirts. Job cost records for the month disclose the following:

Lot	Units in Lot	Materials Used	Hours Worked
4503	1,000 dozen	24,100 metres	2,980
4504	1,700 dozen	40,440 metres	5,130
4505	1,200 dozen	28,825 metres	2,890

You have been able to gather the following information:

1. Azim purchased 95,000 metres of material during February at a cost of $106,400. The material price variance is recorded when goods are purchased, and all inventories are carried at standard cost.
2. The payroll department reported that production employees were paid $7.50 per hour.
3. There was no beginning work in process. During February, lots 4503 and 4504 were completed, and all materials were issued for lot 4505, which was 80% complete as to labour.

Instructions

(a) Calculate the material price variance and make the appropriate journal entry.
(b) Calculate the remaining relevant variances for total production.
(c) Prepare journal entries to charge materials and labour to production.

(CGA-adapted)

www.wiley.com/canada/managerial

Additional Cases

Cases

C11–38   Agmar Professionals, a management consulting firm, specializes in strategic planning for financial institutions. Tim Agler and Jill Marlin, partners in the firm, are assembling a new strategic planning model for clients to use. The model is designed to be used on most personal computers and replaces a rather lengthy manual model currently marketed by the firm. To market the new model, Tim and Jill will need to provide clients with an estimate of the number of labour hours and the computer time needed to operate the model. The model is currently being test-marketed at five small financial institutions. These financial institutions are listed below, along with the number of combined computer/labour hours used by each institution to run the model once:

Financial Institutions	Computer/Labour Hours Required
Canadian National	25
First Funds	45
Financial Federal	40
Pacific Coast	30
Lakeview Savings	30
Total	170
Average	34

Any company that purchases the new model will need to purchase user manuals to access and operate the system. Also required are specialized computer forms that are sold only by Agmar Professionals. User manuals will be sold to clients in cases of 20, at a cost of $300 per case. One manual must be used each time the model is run because each manual includes a non-reusable computer password for operating the system. The specialized computer forms are sold in packages of 250, at a cost of $50 per package. One application of the model requires the use of 50 forms. This amount includes two forms that are generally wasted in each application due to printer alignment errors. The overall cost of the strategic planning model to user clients is $12,000. Most clients will use the model four times each year.

Agmar Professionals must provide its clients with estimates of ongoing costs that are incurred in operating the new strategic planning model. They would like to provide this information in the form of standard costs.

Instructions

With the class divided into groups, answer the following:

(a) What factors should be considered in setting a standard for computer/labour hours?
(b) What alternatives for setting a standard for computer/labour hours might be used?
(c) What standard for computer/labour hours would you select? Justify your answer.
(d) Determine the standard materials cost associated with the user manuals and computer forms for each application of the strategic planning model.

C11–39 Mo Coughlin and Associates is a medium-sized company located near a large metropolitan area in the Prairies. The company manufactures cabinets of mahogany, oak, and other fine woods for use in expensive homes, restaurants, and hotels. Although some of the work is custom, many of the cabinets are a standard size.

One non-custom model is called the Luxury Base Frame. Normal production is 1,000 units per month. Each unit has a direct labour hour standard of five hours. Overhead is applied to production based on standard direct labour hours. During the most recent month, only 900 units were produced; 4,500 direct labour hours were allowed for standard production, but only 4,000 hours were used. Standard and actual overhead costs were as follows:

	Standard (1,000 units)	Actual (900 units)
Indirect materials	$ 12,000	$ 12,300
Indirect labour	48,000	51,000
Manufacturing supervisors, salaries (fixed)	22,000	22,000
Manufacturing office employees, salaries (fixed)	13,000	11,500
Engineering costs (fixed)	26,000	25,000
Computer costs	10,000	10,000
Electricity	2,500	2,500
Manufacturing building amortization (fixed)	8,000	8,000
Machinery amortization (fixed)	3,000	3,000
Trucks and forklift amortization (fixed)	1,500	1,500
Small tools	700	1,400
Insurance (fixed)	500	500
Property taxes (fixed)	300	300
Total	$147,500	$149,000

Instructions

(a) Determine the overhead application rate.
(b) Determine how much overhead was applied to production.

(c) Calculate the controllable overhead variance and the overhead volume variance.
(d) Decide which overhead variances should be investigated.
(e) Discuss the causes of the overhead variances. What can management do to improve its performance next month?

C11–40   Company A applies fixed and variable overhead based on machine hours. Below are the results of Company A for the month just past:

The activity in machine hours	40,000
Flexible budget variable overhead per machine hour	$2.80
Actual variable overhead cost incurred	$117,000
Actual fixed overhead cost incurred	302,100
Variable overhead cost applied to production	117,600
Variable overhead efficiency variance (unfavourable)	8,400
Fixed overhead budget variance (unfavourable)	2,100

Instructions

(a) Calculate the following:
   1. Budgeted fixed overhead
   2. Fixed portion of the predetermined overhead rate
   3. Standard hours allowed for units produced
   4. Fixed overhead volume variance
   5. Fixed overhead cost applied to production
   6. Variable overhead spending variance
   7. Actual machine hours worked
   8. Underapplied (overapplied) overhead
   (*Note:* Show all your supporting calculations.)
(b) Why is it important to separate the spending variance from the efficiency variance in variable overhead variance analysis?
(c) What does the volume variance mean in fixed overhead variance analysis?

(CGA-adapted)

C11–41   You have started working as a cost accountant for a firm which has only been in business for one month. The firm is able to buy a new type of biodegradable plastic at a fixed price of $100 per roll. The plastic is then cut and sealed to make garbage bags. Fixed factory overhead is estimated to be $125,000 per month. During this past month, 8,000 cartons of garbage bags were produced, which represents 80% of the activity volume. You are given the following information:

Rolls of plastic used	40
Variable overhead incurred	$61,000
Overhead efficiency variance	$5,000 U

Standard costs per carton of garbage bags:

Labour hours	2
Wage rate	$8 per hour
Total overhead	$20
Rolls of plastic	0.004 rolls

Instructions

Calculate the following:

(a) Applied overhead per direct labour hour
(b) Standard direct labour hours allowed for units produced
(c) The activity volume
(d) Predetermined fixed overhead rate
(e) Fixed overhead applied
(f) Variable overhead spending variance
(g) Actual number of direct labour hours incurred
(h) Labour efficiency variance
(i) Materials quantity variance
(j) Fixed overhead budget variance
(k) Fixed overhead volume variance

(CGA-adapted)

C11–42   The Kohler Chemical Manufacturing Company produces two primary chemical products to be used as base ingredients for a variety of products. The 2005 budget for the two products (in thousands) was as follows:

	LX-4	ABC-8	Total
Level of production in litres	1,800	1,800	3,600
Direct materials	$4,500	$5,625	$10,125
Direct labour	2,700	2,700	5,400
Total direct manufacturing cost	$7,200	$8,325	$15,525

The following planning assumptions were used for the budget: (1) a direct materials yield of 96%, and (2) a direct labour rate of $6 per hour.

The actual results for 2005 were as follows (in thousands):

Total litres produced	1,710	1,974	3,684
Direct materials	$4,104.00	$6,415.50	$10,519.50
Direct labour	2,808.00	3,276.00	6,084.00
Total direct manufacturing cost	$6,912.00	$9,691.50	$16,603.50

The actual production yield was 95% for LX-4 and 94% for ABC-8. The direct labour cost per hour for both products was $6.50.

Instructions

(a) Calculate for product LX-4: (1) the direct materials price variance, and (2) the direct materials efficiency (yield) variance.
(b) Calculate for product ABC-8: (1) the direct labour rate variance, and (2) the direct labour efficiency variance.

(CMA Canada-adapted)

C11–43   Delta Manufacturing Company uses a standard cost system in accounting for the cost of its main product. The following standards have been established for the direct manufacturing costs per unit:

Direct materials (1 kg at $5/kg)	$5.00 per unit
Direct labour (2 hrs. at $4/hr.)	$8.00 per unit

Budgeted overhead for the month of April (based on expected activity of 4,000 direct labour hours) is as follows:

Variable overhead	$19,000
Fixed overhead	8,000
Total overhead	$27,000

Overhead is applied based on labour hours. The average activity per month is 5,000 direct labour hours. The company calculates overhead rates based on average activity. Results for the month of April are as follows:

Units produced	2,100
Direct materials used (2,500 kg)	$11,000
Direct labour (4,320 hrs.)	18,144
Variable overhead	21,410
Fixed overhead	8,125
Total costs	$58,679

There was no beginning or ending work in process inventory.

Instructions

Calculate the following:
(a) Direct materials price, usage, and budget variances
(b) Labour price, usage, and budget variances
(c) Variable overhead spending, quantity, and budget variances
(d) Fixed overhead spending and volume variances

C11−44 At Camden Manufacturing Company, production workers in the painting department are paid based on productivity. The labour time standard for a unit of production is established through periodic time studies conducted by Foster Management. In a time study, the actual time a worker requires to complete a specific task is observed. Allowances are then made for preparation time, rest periods, and cleanup time. Dan Renfro is one of several veterans in the painting department. Dan is informed by Foster Management that he will be used in the time study for the painting of a new product. The findings will be the basis for establishing the labour time standard for the next six months. During the test, Dan deliberately slows his normal work pace in an effort to obtain a labour time standard that will be easy to meet. Because it is a new product, the Foster Management representative who conducted the test is unaware that Dan did not give the test his best effort.

Instructions

(a) Who was benefited and who was harmed by Dan's actions?
(b) Was Dan ethical in the way he performed the time-study test?
(c) What measure(s) might the company take to obtain valid data for setting the labour time standard?

Answers to Self-Study Questions

1. c   2. d   3. b   4. c   5. b   6. a   7. d   8. a   9. b   10. d   *11. c

Remember to go back to the Navigator Box at the beginning of the chapter to check off your completed work.

CHAPTER 12

Planning for Capital Investments

A Billion-Dollar Expansion

When a substantial nickel deposit was found in the wilderness 350 kilometres north of Goose Bay, Labrador, a mining operation was needed to take on the challenge of developing the area. Enter Toronto-based Inco Ltd., one of the world's leading nickel producers.

"Voisey's Bay is a key component in Inco's growth strategy," said chairman and chief executive officer Scott Hand in an interview with *The Globe and Mail*. "Our objective is to be the world's leading nickel company, not just a leading nickel company."

After acquiring the rights to the Voisey's Bay property in 1996, Inco began a long process of negotiation with the Government of Newfoundland and Labrador and with two Labrador-based aboriginal groups—the Labrador Inuit Association and the Innu Nation. In June 2002, the company announced that it had reached agreement in principle with the province to develop Voisey's Bay and had also successfully completed Impact and Benefits Agreements with both aboriginal groups.

Inco's subsidiary Voisey's Bay Nickel Company is developing a $909-million mine and processing plant at Voisey's Bay, and is putting more than $176 million toward research and development, including the construction of a hydrometallurgical demonstration plant at Argentia, Newfoundland. Scheduled to be operating by 2006, the demonstration plant is the first step toward the development of a commercial hydrometallurgical processing facility by the end of 2011. In the meantime, the company will ship nickel-in-concentrate from Voisey's Bay to Inco's operations in Manitoba and Ontario. This will generate the cash flow that is needed to finance the project. Total estimated capital costs for the project are $2.3 billion. Cash payback is expected in 6.3 years from January 1, 2006.

The nickel production at Voisey's Bay will cost less than other Inco operations. "We currently estimate that the cash costs for our Voisey's Bay operation over the life of the mine will be approximately $1.10 to $1.15 per pound," Mr. Hand explained. Compare this to Inco's current overall costs of $2 per pound for the first quarter of 2004.

With more than 30 million tons of proven and probable reserves, Voisey's Bay could generate substantial profits, although precise estimates are not available. Once in operation in 2006, the mine is expected to produce 110 million pounds of nickel concentrate annually. With demand for nickel continuing to rise, Inco's substantial investment will likely pay off.

Voisey's Bay Nickel Company Limited: www.vbnc.com
Inco. Limited: www.inco.com

THE NAVIGATOR

- [ ] Scan *Study Objectives*

- [ ] Read *Feature Story*

- [ ] Read *Chapter Preview*

- [ ] Read text and answer *Before You Go On* p. 527, p. 535

- [ ] Work *Using the Decision Toolkit*

- [ ] Review *Summary of Study Objectives*

- [ ] Review *Using the Decision Toolkit—A Summary*

- [ ] Work *Demonstration Problem*

- [ ] Answer *Self-Study Questions*

- [ ] Complete assignments

STUDY OBJECTIVES

After studying this chapter, you should be able to:

1. Discuss the capital budgeting evaluation process, and explain what inputs are used in capital budgeting.
2. Describe the cash payback technique.
3. Explain the net present value method.
4. Identify the challenges presented by intangible benefits in capital budgeting.
5. Describe the profitability index.
6. Indicate the benefits of performing a post-audit.
7. Explain the internal rate of return method.
8. Describe the annual rate of return method.

the navigator

Companies like Inco Ltd. must constantly determine how to invest their resources. Other examples: Hollywood studios recently built 25 new sound stage projects to allow for additional filming in future years. Starwood Hotels and Resorts Worldwide, Inc. committed a total of $1 billion to renovate its existing hotel properties, while, at roughly the same time, the hotel industry cancelled about $2 billion worth of new construction. And Union Pacific Resources Group Inc. announced that it would cut its planned capital expenditures by 19 percent in order to use the funds to reduce its outstanding debt.

The process of making such capital expenditure decisions is called capital budgeting. **Capital budgeting** involves choosing among various capital projects to find the one(s) that will maximize a company's return on its financial investment. This chapter discusses the various techniques that are used to make effective capital budgeting decisions.

The chapter is organized as follows:

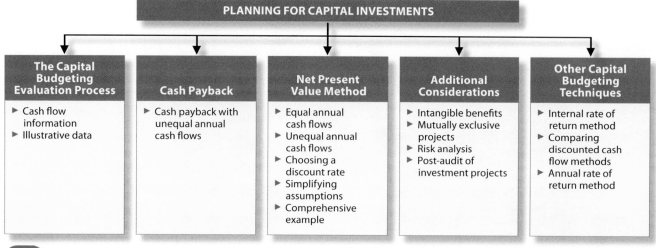

PLANNING FOR CAPITAL INVESTMENTS

The Capital Budgeting Evaluation Process	Cash Payback	Net Present Value Method	Additional Considerations	Other Capital Budgeting Techniques
► Cash flow information ► Illustrative data	► Cash payback with unequal annual cash flows	► Equal annual cash flows ► Unequal annual cash flows ► Choosing a discount rate ► Simplifying assumptions ► Comprehensive example	► Intangible benefits ► Mutually exclusive projects ► Risk analysis ► Post-audit of investment projects	► Internal rate of return method ► Comparing discounted cash flow methods ► Annual rate of return method

the navigator

The Capital Budgeting Evaluation Process

study objective 1

Discuss the capital budgeting evaluation process, and explain what inputs are used in capital budgeting.

Many companies follow a carefully set process in capital budgeting. At least once a year, proposals for projects are requested from each department. The proposals are examined by a capital budgeting committee, which submits its findings to the officers of the company. The officers, in turn, choose the projects that they believe are the most worthy of funding. They submit this list of projects to the board of directors. Ultimately, the directors approve the capital expenditure budget for the year. This process is shown in Illustration 12-1.

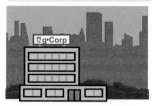

1. Project proposals are requested from departments, plants, and authorized personnel.

2. Proposals are examined by a capital budget committee.

3. Officers determine which projects are worthy of funding.

4. The board of directors approves the capital budget.

Illustration 12-1 ▲

Corporate capital budget authorization process

The involvement of top management and the board of directors in the process shows how important capital budgeting decisions are. These decisions often have a significant impact on a company's future profitability. In fact, poor capital budgeting decisions can cost a lot of money. Inco's Voisey's Bay project is costing about $909 million for the mine and processing plant and more than $176 million is going toward research and development. Such decisions, when they turn out bad, have led to the bankruptcy of some companies.

BUSINESS INSIGHT ▶ Management Perspective

Monitoring capital expenditure amounts is one way to learn about a company's growth potential. Few companies can grow without making large capital investments. Here are four well-known Canadian companies and the amounts and types of capital expenditures they made in the year 2003:

Company Name	Amount	Types of Expenditures
Voisey's Bay Nickel Company	$909 million	Acquisitions and plant expansions
The Hudson's Bay Company	$133.1 million	The Bay, Zeller's, software, and information systems
Canadian Tire	$279 million	Retail stores, real estate, and other expenses
Alcan	$838 million	Expansion of the Alouette smelter and construction of the Alma smelter in Quebec

Cash Flow Information

In this chapter, we will look at several methods that help companies make effective capital budgeting decisions. Most of these methods use **cash flow numbers**, rather than accrual accounting revenues and expenses. Remember from your financial accounting course that accrual accounting records *revenues* and *expenses*, rather than cash inflows and cash outflows. In fact, revenues and expenses that are measured during a period often differ significantly from their cash flow counterparts. Accrual accounting has advantages over cash accounting in many contexts. **But for purposes of capital budgeting, estimated cash inflows and outflows are the preferred inputs.** Why? Because ultimately, the value of all financial investments is determined by the value of the cash flows received and paid.

Sometimes cash flow information is not available. In this case, adjustments can be made to accrual accounting numbers to estimate cash flow. Often, net annual cash flow is estimated by adding amortization expense back to net income. Amortization expense is added back because it is an expense that does not require an outflow of cash. Accordingly, the amortization expense that is deducted in determining net income is added back to net income to determine net annual cash flow. Suppose, for example, that Reno Company's net income of $13,000 includes a charge for amortization expense of $26,000. Its estimated net annual cash flow would be $39,000 ($13,000 + $26,000).

Some typical cash outflows and inflows related to equipment purchases and replacement are listed in Illustration 12-2.

Cash Outflows
Initial investment
Repairs and maintenance
Increased operating costs
Overhaul of equipment

Cash Inflows
Sale of old equipment
Increased cash received from customers
Reduced cash outflows for operating costs
Salvage value of equipment when project is complete

Illustration 12-2 ◀

Typical cash flows relating to capital budgeting decisions

These cash flows are the inputs that are considered relevant in capital budgeting decisions.

The capital budgeting decision, under any technique, depends in part on a variety of considerations:

- **The availability of funds:** Does the company have unlimited funds, or will it have to ration capital investments?
- **Relationships among proposed projects:** Are proposed projects independent of each other, or does the acceptance or rejection of one depend on the acceptance or rejection of another?
- **The company's basic decision-making approach:** Does the company want to produce an accept-reject decision, or a ranking of desirability among possible projects?

- **The risk associated with a particular project:** How certain are the projected returns? The certainty of estimates varies, depending on market considerations or the length of time before returns are expected.

Illustrative Data

For our discussion of quantitative techniques, we will use an ongoing example, as this will make it easier to compare the results of the various techniques. Assume that Stewart Soup Company is considering an investment of $130,000 in new equipment. The new equipment is expected to last 10 years. It will have zero salvage value at the end of its useful life. The annual cash inflows are $200,000, and the annual cash outflows are $176,000. These data are summarized in Illustration 12-3.

Illustration 12-3 ▶

Investment information for Stewart Soup company

Initial investment	$130,000
Estimated useful life	10 years
Estimated salvage value	0
Estimated annual cash flows	
Cash inflows from customers	$200,000
Cash outflows for operating costs	176,000
Net annual cash flow	$ 24,000

In the following two sections, we will examine two popular techniques for evaluating capital investments: the cash payback and net present value methods.

Cash Payback

study objective 2

Describe the cash payback technique.

The **cash payback technique** identifies the time period required to recover the cost of the capital investment from the net annual cash flow produced by the investment. Illustration 12-4 shows the formula for calculating the cash payback period.

Illustration 12-4 ▶

Cash payback formula

Cost of Capital Investment	÷	Net Annual Cash Flow	=	Cash Payback Period

The cash payback period in the Stewart Soup example is 5.42 years, calculated as follows:

$$\$130,000 \div \$24,000 = 5.42 \text{ years}$$

The evaluation of the payback period is often related to the expected useful life of the asset. For example, assume that at Stewart Soup a project is unacceptable if the payback period is longer than 60 percent of the asset's expected useful life. The 5.42-year payback period in this case is a bit over 50 percent of the project's expected useful life. Thus, the project is acceptable.

It follows, therefore, that when the payback technique is used to decide among acceptable alternative projects, **the shorter the payback period, the more attractive the investment.** This is true for two reasons: (1) The earlier the investment is recovered, the sooner the cash funds can be used for other purposes. (2) The risk of loss from obsolescence and changed economic conditions is less in a shorter payback period.

The calculation of the cash payback period above assumes there will be the same net annual cash flows in each year of the investment's life. In many cases, this assumption is not valid. In the case of **uneven** net annual cash flows, the cash payback period is determined when the cumulative net cash flows from the investment equal the cost of the investment. To illustrate, assume that Chan Company proposes an investment in a new website that is estimated to cost $300,000. The proposed investment cost, net annual cash flows, cumulative net cash flows, and cash payback period are shown in Illustration 12-5.

Helpful Hint Net annual cash flow can also be approximated by "Net cash provided by operating activities" from the statement of cash flows.

Illustration 12-5 ◀

Cash inflow schedule

Year	Investment	Net Annual Cash Flow	Cumulative Net Cash Flow
0	$300,000		
1		$ 60,000	$ 60,000
2		90,000	150,000
3		90,000	240,000
4		120,000	360,000
5		100,000	460,000

Cash payback period = 3.5 years

As indicated from Illustration 12-5, at the end of year 3, the cumulative cash inflow of $240,000 is less than the investment cost of $300,000, but at the end of year 4 the cumulative cash inflow of $360,000 is higher than the investment cost. The cash inflow needed in year 4 to equal the investment cost is $60,000 ($300,000 − $240,000). Assuming the cash inflow occurred evenly during year 4, this amount is then divided by the net annual cash flow in year 4 ($120,000) to determine the point during the year when the cash payback occurs. Thus, the result is 0.5 ($60,000 ÷ $120,000), or half of the year, and the cash payback period is 3.5 years.

Cash Payback with Unequal Annual Cash Flows

When annual cash flows are unequal, we cannot use the simple payback formula given above. Instead, the annual cash flows must be accumulated on a year-to-year basis until the accumulation equals the initial investment. To illustrate, assume that Stewart Soup management expects the same aggregate annual cash flows ($240,000), but also a declining market demand for the new product over the life of the equipment. The annual cash flows are shown in illustration 12-6, which also presents the payback calculation for the project. The initial investment will be covered in year 5.

Illustration 12-6 ◀

Payback period with unequal annual cash flows.

Year	Assumed Annual Cash Flows	Accumulated Cash Flows
0	$130,000 initial investment	
1	$ 34,000	$ 34,000
2	30,000	64,000
3	27,000	91,000
4	25,000	116,000
5	24,000	140,000
6	22,000	
7	21,000	
8	20,000	
9	19,000	
10	18,000	
	$240,000	Cash payback period 5 years

Cash Payback: Pros and Cons

The cash payback technique may be useful as an initial screening (evaluation) tool for projects. It also may be the most critical factor in the capital budgeting decision for a company that wants a fast turnaround on its investment because of a weak cash position. Finally, it is fairly easy to calculate and understand.

However, the cash payback technique should not ordinarily be the only basis for the capital budgeting decision, because it ignores the expected profitability of the project after the payback period. To illustrate, assume that Projects A and B have the same payback period, but Project A's useful life is double the useful life of Project B. Project A's earning power, therefore, is twice as long as Project B's. Another disadvantage of the cash payback technique is that it ignores the time value of money.

Net Present Value Method

Recognition of the time value of money can make a significant difference in the long-term impact of the capital budgeting decision. For example, cash flows that occur early in the life of an investment will be worth more than those that occur later—because of the time value of money. It is therefore useful to recognize the timing of cash flows when evaluating projects.

Capital budgeting techniques that consider both the time value of money and the estimated net cash flow from an investment are called **discounted cash flow techniques**. They are generally recognized as the most informative and best-conceived approaches to making capital budgeting decisions. The expected net cash flow that is used in discounting cash flows consists of the annual net cash flows plus the estimated liquidation proceeds (salvage value) when the asset is sold at the end of its useful life.

The most common discounted cash flow technique is called **net present value**. A second method, discussed later in the chapter, is the **internal rate of return**. Before you read on, **we recommend that you read the Time Value of Money Appendix on the text companion site** to review time value of money concepts, which these methods are based on.

Under the **net present value (NPV) method**, net cash flows are discounted to their present value and then compared with the capital required by the investment. The difference between these two amounts is referred to as the **net present value (NPV)**. The interest rate used in discounting the future net cash flows is a rate determined by management. This rate, often called the **discount rate** or required rate of return, is discussed in a later section.

The rule for making a decision is as follows: **a proposal is acceptable when the net present value is zero or positive.** At either of those values, the rate of return on the investment equals or exceeds the discount rate (required rate of return). When the net present value is negative, the project is unacceptable. Illustration 12-7 shows the net-present-value decision criteria.

Illustration 12-7 ▶

Net-present-value decision criteria

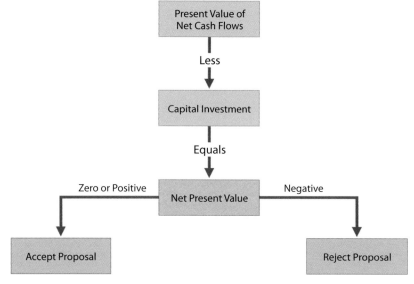

The rule to follow when choosing among acceptable proposals is this: **the higher the positive net present value, the more attractive the investment.** This method is used with the two cases in the next sections. In each case, we will assume that the investment has no salvage value at the end of its useful life.

Equal Annual Cash Flows

Stewart Soup's net annual cash flows are $24,000. If we assume this amount **is uniform over the asset's useful life**, the present value of the net annual cash flows can be calculated by using the present value of an annuity of 1 for 10 periods (from Table 4, Appendix 12A). Assuming a discount rate of 12 percent, the present value of net cash flows is calculated as in Illustration 12-8 (rounded to the nearest dollar).

	Present Value at 12%
Discount factor for 10 periods	5.65022
Present value of net cash flows: $24,000 × 5.65022	$135,605

Illustration 12-9 shows the analysis of the proposal using the net present value method.

	12%
Present value of net cash flows	$135,605
Capital investment	130,000
Net present value	$ 5,605

The proposed capital expenditure is acceptable at a required rate of return of 12 percent because the net present value is positive.

Unequal Annual Cash Flows

When net annual cash flows are unequal, we cannot use annuity tables to calculate their present value. Instead, tables showing the **present value of a single future amount must be applied to each annual cash flow**. To illustrate, assume that Stewart Soup management expects the same total net cash flows of $240,000 over the life of the investment. But because of a declining market demand for the new product over the life of the equipment, the net annual cash flows are higher in the early years and lower in the later years. The present value of the net annual cash flows is calculated as in Illustration 12-10, using Table 3 in Appendix 12A.

Year	Assumed Annual Net Cash Flows (1)	Discount Factor 12% (2)	Present Value 12% (1) × (2)
1	$ 34,000	0.89286	$ 30,357
2	30,000	0.79719	23,916
3	27,000	0.71178	19,218
4	25,000	0.63552	15,888
5	24,000	0.56743	13,618
6	22,000	0.50663	11,146
7	21,000	0.45235	9,499
8	20,000	0.40388	8,078
9	19,000	0.36061	6,852
10	18,000	0.32197	5,795
	$240,000		$144,367

Therefore, the analysis of the proposal by the net present value method is as shown in Illustration 12-11.

	12%
Present value of net cash flows	$144,367
Capital investment	130,000
Net present value	$ 14,367

In this example, the present value of the net cash flows is greater than the $130,000 capital investment. Thus, the project is acceptable at a 12-percent required rate of return (discount rate). The difference between the present values using the 12-percent rate under equal cash flows ($135,605) and unequal cash flows ($144,367) is due to the pattern of the flows. Since more money is received sooner under this particular uneven cash flow scenario, its present value is greater.

Choosing a Discount Rate

Helpful Hint Cost of capital is the rate that management expects to pay on all borrowed and equity funds. It does not relate to the cost of funding a *specific* project.

Now that you understand how the net present value method is applied, it is logical to ask a related question: How is a discount rate (required rate of return) chosen in real capital budgeting decisions? In most instances, a company uses a discount rate that is equal to its **cost of capital**—that is, the rate that it must pay to obtain funds from creditors and shareholders.

The cost of capital is a weighted average of the rates paid on borrowed funds as well as on funds that are provided by investors in the company's common and preferred shares. If a project is believed to be of higher risk than the company's usual line of business, the discount rate should be increased. That is, the discount rate has two elements, a cost of capital element and a risk element. Often, companies assume the risk element is equal to zero.

Using an incorrect discount rate can lead to incorrect capital budgeting decisions. Consider again the Stewart Soup example in Illustration 12-9, where we used a discount rate of 12 percent. Suppose that this discount rate does not take into account the fact that this project is riskier than most of the company's investments. A more appropriate discount rate, given the risk, might be 15 percent. Illustration 12-12 compares the net present values at the two rates. At the higher, more appropriate discount rate of 15 percent, the net present value is negative, and the company should reject the project.

Illustration 12-12 ▶

Comparison of net present values at different discount rates

	Present Values at Different Discount Rates	
	12%	15%
Discount factor for 10 periods	5.65022	5.01877
Present value of net cash flows:		
$24,000 × 5.65022	$135,605	
$24,000 × 5.01877		$120,450
Capital investment	130,000	130,000
Positive (negative) net present value	$ 5,605	$ (9,550)

The discount rate is often given other names, including the **hurdle rate**, the **required rate of return**, and the **cut-off rate**. Determination of the cost of capital varies somewhat, depending on whether the entity is a for-profit or not-for-profit enterprise. Calculation of the cost of capital is discussed more fully in advanced accounting and finance courses.

Simplifying Assumptions

In our examples of the net present value method, we have made a number of simplifying assumptions:

- **All cash flows come at the end of each year.** In reality, cash flows will come at uneven intervals throughout the year. However, it is far simpler to assume that all cash flows come at the end (or in some cases the beginning) of the year. In fact, this assumption is frequently made in practice.
- **All cash flows are immediately reinvested in another project that has a similar return.** In most capital budgeting situations, cash flows are received during each year of a project's life. To determine the return on the investment, some assumption must be made about how the cash flows are reinvested in the year that they are received. It is customary to assume that cash flows received are reinvested in some other project that has a similar return until the end of the project's life.
- **All cash flows can be predicted with certainty.** The outcomes of business investments are full of uncertainty. There is no way of knowing how popular a new product will be, how long a new machine will last, or what competitors' reactions might be to changes in a product. But, in order to make investment decisions, analysts must estimate future outcomes. In this chapter, we have assumed that future amounts are known with certainty.[1] In reality, little is known with certainty. More advanced capital budgeting techniques deal with uncertainty by considering the probability that various outcomes will occur.

BEFORE YOU GO ON . . .

▶ Review It

1. What is the cash payback technique? What are its strengths and weaknesses?
2. What is the net present value decision rule to determine whether a project is acceptable?
3. What common assumptions are made in capital budgeting decisions?

▶ Do It

Watertown Paper Corporation is considering adding another machine for the manufacture of corrugated cardboard. The machine would cost $800,000. It would have an estimated life of seven years and a salvage value of $40,000. It is estimated that annual cash inflows would increase by $400,000 and that annual cash outflows would increase by $190,000. Management believes a discount rate of 9 percent is appropriate. Using the net present value method, should the project be accepted?

Action Plan

- Use the NPV method to calculate the difference between the present value of net cash flows and the initial investment.
- Accept the project if the net present value is positive.

Solution

Estimated annual cash inflows	$400,000	
Estimated annual cash outflows	190,000	
Net annual cash flow	$210,000	

	Cash Flows	×	9% Discount Factor	=	Present Value
Present value of net annual cash flows	$210,000	×	5.03295 [a]	=	$1,056,920
Present value of salvage value	$40,000	×	0.54703 [b]	=	21,881
Present value of net cash flows					1,078,801
Capital investment					800,000
Net present value					$ 278,801

[a] Table 4, Appendix 12A.
[b] Table 3, Appendix 12A.

Since the net present value is positive, the project is acceptable.

Related exercise material: BE12–2, BE12–3, BE12–4, BE12-5, E12–1, E12–2, and E12–3.

the navigator

Comprehensive Example

Best Taste Foods is considering investing in new equipment to produce fat-free snack foods. Management believes that although demand for these foods has levelled off, fat-free foods are here to stay. Illustration 12-13 shows the estimated cost flows, cost of capital, and cash flows that were determined in consultation with the marketing, production, and finance departments.

Illustration 12-13 ◄

Investment information for Best Taste Foods

Initial investment	$1,000,000
Cost of equipment overhaul in 5 years	$200,000
Salvage value of equipment in 10 years	$20,000
Cost of capital	15%
Estimated annual cash flows	
Cash inflows received from sales	$500,000
Cash outflows for cost of goods sold	$200,000
Maintenance costs	$30,000
Other direct operating costs	$40,000

[1] One exception is a brief discussion of sensitivity analysis later in the chapter.

Remember that we are using cash flows in our analysis, not accrual revenues and expenses. The direct operating costs, therefore, would not include amortization expense, since amortization expense does not use cash. Illustration 12-14 presents the calculation of the net annual cash flows of this project.

Illustration 12-14 ▶

Calculation of net annual cash flows

Cash inflows received from sales	$ 500,000
Cash outflows for cost of goods sold	(200,000)
Maintenance costs	(30,000)
Other direct operating costs	(40,000)
Net annual cash flow	$ 230,000

The calculation of the net present value for this proposed investment is shown in Illustration 12-15.

Illustration 12-15 ▶

Calculation of net present value for Best Taste Foods investment

Event	Time Period	Cash Flow ×	15% Discount Factor =	Present Value
Equipment purchase	0	$1,000,000	1.00000	$(1,000,000)
Equipment overhaul	5	200,000	0.49718	(99,436)
Net annual cash flow	1–10	230,000	5.01877	1,154,317
Salvage value	10	20,000	0.24719	4,944
Net present value				$ 59,825

Because the net present value of the project is positive, the project should be accepted.

Decision Toolkit

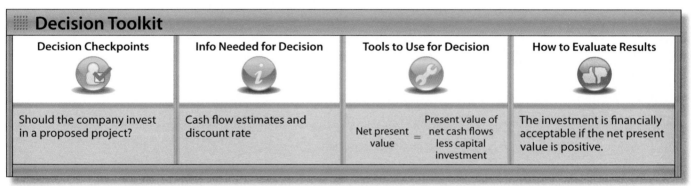

Decision Checkpoints	Info Needed for Decision	Tools to Use for Decision	How to Evaluate Results
Should the company invest in a proposed project?	Cash flow estimates and discount rate	Net present value = Present value of net cash flows less capital investment	The investment is financially acceptable if the net present value is positive.

Additional Considerations

study objective 4

Identify the challenges presented by intangible benefits in capital budgeting.

Now that you understand how the net present value method works, we can add some "wrinkles." Specifically, these are the impact of intangible benefits, a way to compare mutually exclusive projects, refinements that take risk into account, and the need to conduct post-audits of investment projects.

Intangible Benefits

The NPV evaluation techniques we have used so far rely on tangible costs and benefits that are fairly easy to measure. Some investment projects, especially high-tech projects, fail to make it through initial capital budget screens because only the project's "tangible" benefits are considered. But by ignoring intangible benefits, such as increased quality, improved safety, or greater employee loyalty, capital budgeting techniques might incorrectly eliminate projects that could be financially beneficial to the company.

To avoid rejecting projects that actually should be accepted, two possible approaches are suggested:

1. Calculate net present value ignoring intangible benefits. Then, if the NPV is negative, ask whether the intangible benefits are worth at least the amount of the negative NPV.

2. Make rough, conservative estimates of the value of the intangible benefits, and incorporate these values into the NPV calculation.

Example

Assume that Berg Company is considering the purchase of a new robot for soldering electrical connections. The estimates for this proposed purchase are shown in Illustration 12-16.

Initial investment	$200,000			
Annual cash inflows	$50,000			
Annual cash outflows	20,000			
Net annual cash flow	$30,000			
Estimated life of equipment	10 years			
Discount rate	12%			
	Cash Flows	×	12% Discount Factor	=	Present Value
Present value of net cash flows	$30,000 ×	5.65022	=	$169,507
Initial investment				200,000
Net present value				$(30,493)

Illustration 12-16 ◄

Investment information for Berg Company

Based on the negative net present value of $30,493, the proposed project is not acceptable. This calculation, however, ignores important information. First, the company's engineers believe that purchasing this machine will dramatically improve the electrical connections in the company's products. As a result, future warranty costs will be reduced. Also, the company believes that higher quality will translate into higher future sales. Finally, the new machine will be much safer than the previous one.

This new information can be brought into the capital budgeting decision in the two ways mentioned above. First, one might simply ask whether the reduced warranty costs, increased sales, and improved safety benefits have an estimated total present value to the company of at least $30,493. If yes, then the project is acceptable.

Alternatively, an estimate of the annual cash flows of these benefits can be made. In our initial calculation, each of these benefits was assumed to have a value of zero. It seems likely that their actual values are much higher than zero. Given the difficulty of estimating these benefits, however, conservative values should be assigned to them. If, after using conservative estimates, the net present value is positive, the project should be accepted.

To illustrate, assume that Berg estimates a sales increase of $10,000 annually as a result of an increase in quality from the customer's perspective. Berg also estimates that cost outflows would be reduced by $5,000 as a result of lower warranty claims, reduced injury claims, and fewer worker absences. Consideration of the intangible benefits results in the revised NPV calculation in Illustration 12-17.

Initial investment	$200,000			
Annual cash inflows (revised)	$60,000			
Annual cash outflows (revised)	15,000			
Net annual cash flow	$45,000			
Estimated life of equipment	10 years			
Discount rate	12%			
	Cash Flows	×	12% Discount Factor	=	Present Value
Present value of net cash flows	$45,000 ×	5.65022	=	$254,260
Initial investment				200,000
Net present value				$ 54,260

Illustration 12-17 ◄

Revised investment information for Berg Company, including intangible benefits

Using these conservative estimates of the value of the additional benefits, it appears that Berg should accept the project.

Mutually Exclusive Projects

In theory, all projects with positive NPVs should be accepted. However, companies rarely are able to adopt all positive-NPV proposals. First, proposals are often **mutually exclusive**. This means that if the company adopts one proposal, it would be impossible also to adopt the other proposal. For example, a company may be considering the purchase of a new packaging machine and is looking at various brands and models. Only one packaging machine is needed. Once the company has determined which brand and model to purchase, the others will not be purchased—even though they may also have positive net present values.

Even in instances where projects are not mutually exclusive, managers often must choose between various positive-NPV projects because the company's resources are limited. For example, the company might have ideas for two new lines of business, each of which has a projected positive NPV. However, both of these proposals require skilled personnel, and the company determines that it will not be able to find enough skilled personnel to staff both projects. Management will have to choose the project that it thinks is a better option.

When choosing between alternative proposals, it is tempting simply to choose the project with the higher NPV. Consider the two mutually exclusive projects in Illustration 12-18. Each is assumed to have a 10-year life and a 12-percent discount rate.

Illustration 12-18 ▶

Investment information for mutually exclusive projects

	Project A	Project B
Initial investment	$40,000	$90,000
Net annual cash inflow	10,000	19,000
Salvage value	5,000	10,000
Net present value	18,112	20,574

Project B has the higher NPV, and so it would seem that the company should adopt it. Note, however, that Project B also requires more than twice the original investment of Project A. In choosing between the two projects, the company should also include in its calculations the amount of the original investment.

One relatively simple method of comparing alternative projects is the **profitability index**. This method considers both the size of the original investment and the discounted cash flows. The profitability index is calculated by dividing the present value of cash flows that occur after the initial investment by the initial investment. Illustration 12-19 shows the formula.

Illustration 12-19 ▶

Formula for profitability index

$$ \boxed{\text{Present Value of Net Cash Flows}} \div \boxed{\text{Initial Investment}} = \boxed{\text{Profitability Index}} $$

The profitability index makes it possible to compare the relative desirability of projects that require different initial investments. Note that any project with a positive NPV will have a profitability index above 1. Applying the profitability index to the preceding example, we get the present values in Illustration 12-20.

Illustration 12-20 ▶

Revised investment information for mutually exclusive projects

	Project A	Project B
Initial investment	$40,000	$90,000
Net annual cash inflow	10,000	19,000
Present value of net cash flows:		
($10,000 × 5.65022) + ($5,000 × 0.32197)	58,112	
($19,000 × 5.65022) + ($10,000 × 0.32197)		110,574

The profitability index for the two projects is calculated in Illustration 12-21.

Illustration 12-21 ▶

Calculation of profitability index

$$ \text{Profitability Index} = \frac{\text{Present Value of Net Cash Flows}}{\text{Initial Investment}} $$

Project A	Project B
$\dfrac{\$58,112}{\$40,000} = 1.45$	$\dfrac{\$110,574}{\$90,000} = 1.23$

In this case, the profitability index of Project A exceeds that of Project B. Thus, Project A is more desirable. Again, if these were not mutually exclusive projects, and if resources were not limited, then the company should invest in both projects, since both have positive NPVs. Additional matters to consider in preference decisions are discussed in more advanced courses.

Decision Toolkit

Decision Checkpoints	Info Needed for Decision	Tools to Use for Decision	How to Evaluate Results
Which investment proposal should a company accept?	The estimated cash flows and discount rate for each proposal	$$\text{Profitability index} = \frac{\text{Present value of net cash flows}}{\text{Initial investment}}$$	The investment proposal with the highest profitability index should be accepted.

Risk Analysis

A simplifying assumption made by many financial analysts is that projected results are known with certainty. In reality, projected results are only estimates that are based on the forecaster's belief about what is most likely to happen. One approach for dealing with such uncertainty is **sensitivity analysis**. Sensitivity analysis uses several outcome estimates to get a sense of the variability among potential returns. An example sensitivity analysis was presented in Illustration 12-12, where we illustrated the impact on NPV of different discount rate assumptions. A higher-risk project would be evaluated using a higher discount rate.

Similarly, to take into account the fact that cash flows that are further away are often more uncertain, a higher discount rate can be used to discount more distant cash flows. Other techniques to handle uncertainty are discussed in more advanced courses.

Post-Audit of Investment Projects

Any well-run organization should perform an evaluation, called a **post-audit**, of its investment projects after they are completed. A post-audit is a thorough evaluation of how well a project's actual performance matches the original projections. In a recent story about Campbell Soup, a decision to invest in the Intelligent Quisine line was made based on management's best estimates of future cash flows. During the development phase of the project, an outside consulting firm was hired to evaluate the project's potential for success. Because actual results during the initial years were far below the estimated results, and because the future did not look promising either, the project was terminated.

Performing a post-audit is important for many reasons. First, if managers know that their estimates will be compared to actual results, they will be more likely to submit reasonable and accurate data when they make investment proposals. This clearly is better for the company than having managers submit overly optimistic estimates in an effort to get their favourite projects approved. Second, a post-audit provides a formal mechanism for deciding whether existing projects should be supported or terminated. Third, post-audits improve future investment proposals because, by evaluating past successes and failures, managers improve their estimation techniques.

A post-audit uses the same evaluation techniques that were used in making the original capital budgeting decision—for example, the NPV method. The difference is that, in the post-audit, actual figures are inserted because they are known, and estimations of future amounts are revised based on new information. The managers responsible for the estimates used in the original proposal must explain the reasons for any significant differences between their estimates and actual results.

study objective 6

Indicate the benefits of performing a post-audit.

Post-audits are not foolproof. When Campbell Soup abandoned a new line of convenient meals called Intelligent Quisine, some observers suggested that the company was too quick to drop the project. Industry analysts suggested that with more time and more advertising expenditures, the company might have enjoyed a success.

BUSINESS INSIGHT ▶ Management Perspective

In November 2003, about half of Canadian households still did not have a DVD player. But that year's holiday season saw a dramatic growth in DVD sales, matched only by the dramatic drop in prices. Brand leaders like Sony and Panasonic were probably not the ones who filled that potential market, though, since models produced by less well-known companies were often selling for half their prices. The DVD players available for $80 or less are in fact a preview of a trend in consumer electronics. Previously, these manufacturers' products made their way to Canadian stores only under another company's brand. But, like South Korea's Samsung, several Chinese contract manufacturers are now trying to become brands in their own right, taking a bigger portion of the profits in the process.

Source: Ian Austen, "Spin Masters," *Canadian Business*, November 24, 2003.

Other Capital Budgeting Techniques

Some companies use capital budgeting techniques other than, or in addition to, the cash payback and net present value methods. In this section, we will briefly discuss these other approaches.

Internal Rate of Return Method

The **internal rate of return method** differs from the net present value method as it finds the **interest yield of the potential investment**. The **internal rate of return** is the interest rate that will cause the present value of the proposed capital expenditure to equal the present value of the expected net annual cash flows. This means that it finds the rate that results in an NPV equal to zero. Note that because it recognizes the time value of money, the internal rate of return method is (like the NPV method) a discounted cash flow technique.

How does one determine the internal rate of return? One way is to use a financial (business) calculator or computerized spreadsheet to solve for this rate. If a calculator or computer spreadsheet is not used, a trial-and-error procedure is used.

To illustrate, assume that Brock Company is considering the purchase of a new front-end loader at a cost of $244,371. Net annual cash flows from this loader are estimated to be $100,000 a year for three years. To determine the internal rate of return on this front-end loader, we find the discount rate that results in a net present value of zero. As shown in Illustration 12-22, at a rate of return of 10 percent, Brock has a positive net present value of $4,315. At a rate of return of 12 percent, it has a negative net present value of $4,188. At an 11-percent rate, the net present value is zero, and this rate therefore is the internal rate of return for this investment.

Illustration 12-22 ▼

Determination of internal rate of return

Year	Annual Cash Flows	Discount Factor 10%	Present Value 10%	Discount Factor 11%	Present Value 11%	Discount Factor 12%	Present Value 12%
1	$100,000	0.90909	$ 90,909	0.90090	$ 90,090	0.89286	$ 89,286
2	100,000	0.82645	82,645	0.81162	81,162	0.79719	79,719
3	100,000	0.75132	75,132	0.73119	73,119	0.71178	71,178
			248,686		244,371		240,183
Less: Initial investment			244,371		244,371		244,371
Net Present value			$ 4,315		$ 0		$ (4,188)

An easier approach to solving for the internal rate of return can be used if the net annual cash flows are **equal**, as in the Brock Company example. In this special case, we can find the internal rate of return using the following equation:

$$\$244,371 \ = \ \$100,000 \ \times \ \text{Present value of } \$100,000 \text{ for 3 years at x percent}$$

Solving for the interest rate, we find:

$$\frac{\$244,371}{\$100,000} \ = \ 2.44371 \ = \ \text{Present value of } \$100,000 \text{ for 3 years at x percent}$$

We then look up the factor 2.44371 in Table 4 of Appendix 12A in the three-period row and find it under 11%. Row 3 is reproduced below for your convenience.

Table 4 Present Value of an Annuity of 1												
(n) Periods	2%	2.5%	3%	4%	5%	6%	8%	9%	10%	11%	12%	15%
3	2.88388	2.85602	2.82861	2.77509	2.72325	2.67301	2.57710	2.53130	2.48685	2.44371	2.40183	2.28323

(Note that if the cash flows are **uneven**, then a trial-and-error approach or a financial calculator or computerized spreadsheet must be used.) Once we know the internal rate of return, we compare it to management's required rate of return (the discount rate). The decision rule is as follows: **Accept the project when the internal rate of return is equal to or greater than the required rate of return. Reject the project when the internal rate of return is less than the required rate of return.** These relationships are shown in Illustration 12-23.

Alternative Terminology
The minimum required rate of return is sometimes referred to as the *hurdle rate or the cut-off rate.*

Illustration 12-23 ◄

Internal rate of return decision criteria

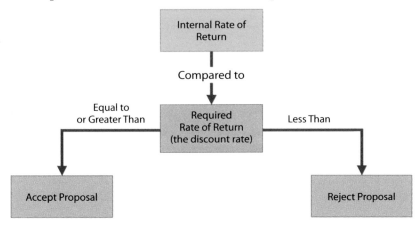

The internal rate of return method is widely used. Most managers find the internal rate of return easy to interpret.

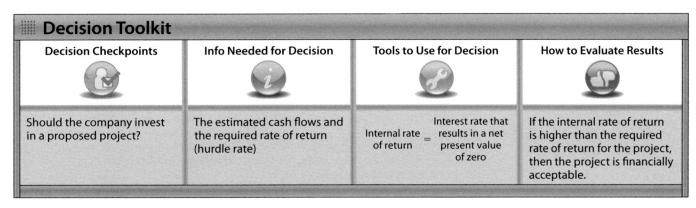

▦ Decision Toolkit

Decision Checkpoints	Info Needed for Decision	Tools to Use for Decision	How to Evaluate Results
Should the company invest in a proposed project?	The estimated cash flows and the required rate of return (hurdle rate)	Internal rate of return = Interest rate that results in a net present value of zero	If the internal rate of return is higher than the required rate of return for the project, then the project is financially acceptable.

Comparing Discounted Cash Flow Methods

A comparison of the two discounted cash flow methods—net present value and internal rate of return—is presented in Illustration 12-24. When properly used, either method will provide management with relevant quantitative data for making capital budgeting decisions.

However, the net present value method does have two advantages. First, we can use the NPV method in situations where the discount rate varies over the life of the project because of risk considerations. In the internal rate of return method, we cannot use more than one discount rate to make risk adjustments. The internal rate of return solves for only a single discount rate over the life of the project. Second, in evaluating different combinations of individual projects, we can add the NPVs of the individual projects in each combination to estimate the effect of accepting or rejecting a combination of projects. We can do this because the result of the NPV method is a dollar amount, not a percentage.

Illustration 12-24 ▶

Comparison of discounted cash flow methods

	Net Present Value	Internal Rate of Return
Objective:	Calculate net present value (a dollar amount).	Calculate the internal rate of return (a percentage).
Decision rule:	If the net present value is zero or positive, accept the proposal. If the net present value is negative, reject the proposal.	If the internal rate of return is equal to or greater than the required rate of return, accept the proposal. If the internal rate of return is less than the required rate of return, reject the proposal.

BUSINESS INSIGHT ▶ *@*-business Perspective

Dan Gelbart, co-founder and chief technology officer of Vancouver-based Creo Inc., has been described as a modern-day Johannes Gutenberg, the inventor of the printing press. Gelbart's development of digital prepress and computer-to-plate technology has revolutionized printing.

Creo products and systems are not cheap, however. They don't save printers money. Rather, they allow them to use their presses more efficiently and increase revenues by taking on more work. Creo's revenues are driven by capital spending in the printing industry, which in turn is driven by the health of the industry and the economy. That meant Creo's performance was not stellar in the early 2000s.

Still, the market potential was encouraging, since many printers had not yet converted to digital technology—something that was becoming essential for staying competitive. In any list of capital expenditures that printers would make, investment in prepress technologies was going to be at the top.

In the meantime, Creo was investigating how to make its technology more accessible to smaller printers, who would find it more difficult to justify the huge capital investment. The company is now offering a line of simpler, less expensive systems, along with financing deals to make them easier to buy.

As one printer put it, "Last year, Creo's products were about increasing profits. Today, they mean survival."

Source: Zena Olijnyk, "Stop the Presses!" *Canadian Business*, Sept. 2, 2002.

Annual Rate of Return Method

study objective 8

Describe the annual rate of return method.

The final capital budgeting technique we will look at is the **annual rate of return method**. It is based directly on accrual accounting data rather than on cash flows. It indicates the **profitability of a capital expenditure** by dividing the expected annual net income by the average investment. This method has many different names, including simple rate of return, accounting rate of return, unadjusted rate of return, and rate of return on assets. The formula for calculating the annual rate of return is shown in Illustration 12-25.

Illustration 12-25 ▶

Annual rate of return formula

Expected Annual Net Income ÷ Average Investment = Annual Rate of Return

Assume that Reno Company is considering an investment of $130,000 in new equipment. The new equipment is expected to last five years and have zero salvage value at the end of its useful life. The straight-line method of amortization is used for accounting purposes. The expected annual revenues and costs of the new product that will be produced from the investment are shown in Illustration 12-26.

Sales		$200,000
Less: Costs and expenses		
Manufacturing costs (not including amortization)	$132,000	
Amortization expense ($130,000 ÷ 5)	26,000	
Selling and administrative expenses	22,000	180,000
Income before income taxes		20,000
Income tax expense		7,000
Net income		$ 13,000

Illustration 12-26 ◀

Estimated annual net income from Reno Company's capital expenditure

Reno's expected annual net income is $13,000. Illustration 12-27 gives the formula for determining the average investment.

$$\text{Average investment} = \frac{\text{Original investment} + \text{Value at end of useful life}}{2}$$

Illustration 12-27 ◀

Formula for calculating average investment

The value at the end of the useful life is equal to the asset's salvage value, if any.

For Reno, the average investment is $65,000 [($130,000 + $0) ÷ 2]. The expected annual rate of return on Reno's investment in new equipment is therefore 20 percent, calculated as follows:

$$\$13,000 \div \$65,000 = 20\%$$

Management then compares the annual rate of return with its required rate of return for investments of similar risk. The required rate of return is generally based on the company's cost of capital. The decision rule is this: **A project is acceptable if its rate of return is greater than management's required rate of return.** It is unacceptable when the reverse is true. When the annual rate of return technique is used in deciding among several acceptable projects, **the higher the rate of return for a particular risk, the more attractive the investment.**

Annual Rate of Return Method: Pros and Cons

The main advantages of this method are the simplicity of its calculation and management's familiarity with the accounting terms used in the calculation. A major limitation of the annual rate of return method is that it does not consider the time value of money. For example, no consideration is given as to whether cash inflows will occur early or late in the life of the investment. As explained in the **Time Value of Money Appendix**, the time value of money can make a significant difference between the future value and the discounted present value of an investment. A second disadvantage is that this method relies on accrual accounting numbers rather than expected cash flows.

Helpful Hint A capital budgeting decision based on only one technique may be misleading. It is often wise to analyze an investment from different perspectives.

BEFORE YOU GO ON . . .

▶ Review It

1. When is a proposal acceptable under (a) the net present value method and (b) the internal rate of return method?
2. How does the internal rate of return method differ from the net present value method?
3. What is the formula for and the decision rule in using the annual rate of return method? What are the drawbacks of this method?

APPENDIX 12A ▶ TIME VALUE OF MONEY

TABLE 1
Future Value of 1
(Future Value of a Single Sum)

$$FVF_{n,i} = (1 + i)^n$$

(n) Periods	2%	2.5%	3%	4%	5%	6%	8%	9%	10%	11%	12%	15%
1	1.02000	1.02500	1.03000	1.04000	1.05000	1.06000	1.08000	1.09000	1.10000	1.11000	1.12000	1.15000
2	1.04040	1.05063	1.06090	1.08160	1.10250	1.12360	1.16640	1.18810	1.21000	1.23210	1.25440	1.32250
3	1.06121	1.07689	1.09273	1.12486	1.15763	1.19102	1.25971	1.29503	1.33100	1.36763	1.40493	1.52088
4	1.08243	1.10381	1.12551	1.16986	1.21551	1.26248	1.36049	1.41158	1.46410	1.51807	1.57352	1.74901
5	1.10408	1.13141	1.15927	1.21665	1.27628	1.33823	1.46933	1.53862	1.61051	1.68506	1.76234	2.01136
6	1.12616	1.15969	1.19405	1.26532	1.34010	1.41852	1.58687	1.67710	1.77156	1.87041	1.97382	2.31306
7	1.14869	1.18869	1.22987	1.31593	1.40710	1.50363	1.71382	1.82804	1.94872	2.07616	2.21068	2.66002
8	1.17166	1.21840	1.26677	1.36857	1.47746	1.59385	1.85093	1.99256	2.14359	2.30454	2.47596	3.05902
9	1.19509	1.24886	1.30477	1.42331	1.55133	1.68948	1.99900	2.17189	2.35795	2.55803	2.77308	3.51788
10	1.21899	1.28008	1.34392	1.48024	1.62889	1.79085	2.15892	2.36736	2.59374	2.83942	3.10585	4.04556
11	1.24337	1.31209	1.38423	1.53945	1.71034	1.89830	2.33164	2.58043	2.85312	3.15176	3.47855	4.65239
12	1.26824	1.34489	1.42576	1.60103	1.79586	2.01220	2.51817	2.81267	3.13843	3.49845	3.89598	5.35025
13	1.29361	1.37851	1.46853	1.66507	1.88565	2.13293	2.71962	3.06581	3.45227	3.88328	4.36349	6.15279
14	1.31948	1.41297	1.51259	1.73168	1.97993	2.26090	2.93719	3.34173	3.79750	4.31044	4.88711	7.07571
15	1.34587	1.44830	1.55797	1.80094	2.07893	2.39656	3.17217	3.64248	4.17725	4.78459	5.47357	8.13706
16	1.37279	1.48451	1.60471	1.87298	2.18287	2.54035	3.42594	3.97031	4.59497	5.31089	6.13039	9.35762
17	1.40024	1.52162	1.65285	1.94790	2.29202	2.69277	3.70002	4.32763	5.05447	5.89509	6.86604	10.76126
18	1.42825	1.55966	1.70243	2.02582	2.40662	2.85434	3.99602	4.71712	5.55992	6.54355	7.68997	12.37545
19	1.45681	1.59865	1.75351	2.10685	2.52695	3.02560	4.31570	5.14166	6.11591	7.26334	8.61276	14.23177
20	1.48595	1.63862	1.80611	2.19112	2.65330	3.20714	4.66096	5.60441	6.72750	8.06231	9.64629	16.36654
21	1.51567	1.67958	1.86029	2.27877	2.78596	3.39956	5.03383	6.10881	7.40025	8.94917	10.80385	18.82152
22	1.54598	1.72157	1.91610	2.36992	2.92526	3.60354	5.43654	6.65860	8.14028	9.93357	12.10031	21.64475
23	1.57690	1.76461	1.97359	2.46472	3.07152	3.81975	5.87146	7.25787	8.95430	11.02627	13.55235	24.89146
24	1.60844	1.80873	2.03279	2.56330	3.22510	4.04893	6.34118	7.91108	9.84973	12.23916	15.17863	28.62518
25	1.64061	1.85394	2.09378	2.66584	3.38635	4.29187	6.84847	8.62308	10.83471	13.58546	17.00006	32.91895
26	1.67342	1.90029	2.15659	2.77247	3.55567	4.54938	7.39635	9.39916	11.91818	15.07986	19.04007	37.85680
27	1.70689	1.94780	2.22129	2.88337	3.73346	4.82235	7.98806	10.24508	13.10999	16.73865	21.32488	43.53532
28	1.74102	1.99650	2.28793	2.99870	3.92013	5.11169	8.62711	11.16714	14.42099	18.57990	23.88387	50.06561
29	1.77584	2.04641	2.35657	3.11865	4.11614	5.41839	9.31727	12.17218	15.86309	20.62369	26.74993	57.57545
30	1.81136	2.09757	2.42726	3.24340	4.32194	5.74349	10.06266	13.26768	17.44940	22.89230	29.95992	66.21177
31	1.84759	2.15001	2.50008	3.37313	4.53804	6.08810	10.86767	14.46177	19.19434	25.41045	33.55511	76.14354
32	1.88454	2.20376	2.57508	3.50806	4.76494	6.45339	11.73708	15.76333	21.11378	28.20560	37.58173	87.56507
33	1.92223	2.25885	2.65234	3.64838	5.00319	6.84059	12.67605	17.18203	23.22515	31.30821	42.09153	100.69983
34	1.96068	2.31532	2.73191	3.79432	5.25335	7.25103	13.69013	18.72841	25.54767	34.75212	47.14252	115.80480
35	1.99989	2.37321	2.81386	3.94609	5.51602	7.68609	14.78534	20.41397	28.10244	38.57485	52.79962	133.17552
36	2.03989	2.43254	2.89828	4.10393	5.79182	8.14725	15.96817	22.25123	30.91268	42.81808	59.13557	153.15185
37	2.08069	2.49335	2.98523	4.26809	6.08141	8.63609	17.24563	24.25384	34.00395	47.52807	66.23184	176.12463
38	2.12230	2.55568	3.07478	4.43881	6.38548	9.15425	18.62528	26.43668	37.40434	52.75616	74.17966	202.54332
39	2.16474	2.61957	3.16703	4.61637	6.70475	9.70351	20.11530	28.81598	41.14479	58.55934	83.08122	232.92482
40	2.20804	2.68506	3.26204	4.80102	7.03999	10.28572	21.72452	31.40942	45.25926	65.00087	93.05097	267.86355

TABLE 2
Present Value of 1
(Present Value of a Single Sum)

$$PVF_{n,i} = \frac{1}{(1+i)^n} = (1+i)^{-n}$$

(n) Periods	2%	2.5%	3%	4%	5%	6%	8%	9%	10%	11%	12%	15%
1	0.98039	0.97561	0.97087	0.96154	0.95238	0.94340	0.92593	0.91743	0.90909	0.90090	0.89286	0.86957
2	0.96117	0.95181	0.94260	0.92456	0.90703	0.89000	0.85734	0.84168	0.82645	0.81162	0.79719	0.75614
3	0.94232	0.92860	0.91514	0.88900	0.86384	0.83962	0.79383	0.77218	0.75132	0.73119	0.71178	0.65752
4	0.92385	0.90595	0.88849	0.85480	0.82270	0.79209	0.73503	0.70843	0.68301	0.65873	0.63552	0.57175
5	0.90573	0.88385	0.86261	0.82193	0.78353	0.74726	0.68058	0.64993	0.62092	0.59345	0.56743	0.49719
6	0.88797	0.86230	0.83748	0.79031	0.74622	0.70496	0.63017	0.59627	0.56447	0.53464	0.50663	0.43233
7	0.87056	0.84127	0.81309	0.75992	0.71068	0.66506	0.58349	0.54703	0.51316	0.48166	0.45235	0.37594
8	0.85349	0.82075	0.78941	0.73069	0.67684	0.62741	0.54027	0.50187	0.46651	0.43393	0.40388	0.32690
9	0.83676	0.80073	0.76642	0.70259	0.64461	0.59190	0.50025	0.46043	0.42410	0.39092	0.36061	0.28426
10	0.82035	0.78120	0.74409	0.67556	0.61391	0.55839	0.46319	0.42241	0.38554	0.35218	0.32197	0.24718
11	0.80426	0.76214	0.72242	0.64958	0.58468	0.52679	0.42888	0.38753	0.35049	0.31728	0.28748	0.21494
12	0.78849	0.74356	0.70138	0.62460	0.55684	0.49697	0.39711	0.35554	0.31863	0.28584	0.25668	0.18691
13	0.77303	0.72542	0.68095	0.60057	0.53032	0.46884	0.36770	0.32618	0.28966	0.25751	0.22917	0.16253
14	0.75788	0.70773	0.66112	0.57748	0.50507	0.44230	0.34046	0.29925	0.26333	0.23199	0.20462	0.14133
15	0.74301	0.69047	0.64186	0.55526	0.48102	0.41727	0.31524	0.27454	0.23939	0.20900	0.18270	0.12289
16	0.72845	0.67362	0.62317	0.53391	0.45811	0.39365	0.29189	0.25187	0.21763	0.18829	0.16312	0.10687
17	0.71416	0.65720	0.60502	0.51337	0.43630	0.37136	0.27027	0.23107	0.19785	0.16963	0.14564	0.09293
18	0.70016	0.64117	0.58739	0.49363	0.41552	0.35034	0.25025	0.21199	0.17986	0.15282	0.13004	0.08081
19	0.68643	0.62553	0.57029	0.47464	0.39573	0.33051	0.23171	0.19449	0.16351	0.13768	0.11611	0.07027
20	0.67297	0.61027	0.55368	0.45639	0.37689	0.31180	0.21455	0.17843	0.14864	0.12403	0.10367	0.06110
21	0.65978	0.59539	0.53755	0.43883	0.35894	0.29416	0.19866	0.16370	0.13513	0.11174	0.09256	0.05313
22	0.64684	0.58086	0.52189	0.42196	0.34185	0.27751	0.18394	0.15018	0.12285	0.10067	0.08264	0.04620
23	0.63416	0.56670	0.50669	0.40573	0.32557	0.26180	0.17032	0.13778	0.11168	0.09069	0.07379	0.04017
24	0.62172	0.55288	0.49193	0.39012	0.31007	0.24698	0.15770	0.12641	0.10153	0.08170	0.06588	0.03493
25	0.60953	0.53939	0.47761	0.37512	0.29530	0.23300	0.14602	0.11597	0.09230	0.07361	0.05882	0.03038
26	0.59758	0.52623	0.46369	0.36069	0.28124	0.21981	0.13520	0.10639	0.08391	0.06631	0.05252	0.02642
27	0.58586	0.51340	0.45019	0.34682	0.26785	0.20737	0.12519	0.09761	0.07628	0.05974	0.04689	0.02297
28	0.57437	0.50088	0.43708	0.33348	0.25509	0.19563	0.11591	0.08955	0.06934	0.05382	0.04187	0.01997
29	0.56311	0.48866	0.42435	0.32065	0.24295	0.18456	0.10733	0.08216	0.06304	0.04849	0.03738	0.01737
30	0.55207	0.47674	0.41199	0.30832	0.23138	0.17411	0.09938	0.07537	0.05731	0.04368	0.03338	0.01510
31	0.54125	0.46511	0.39999	0.29646	0.22036	0.16425	0.09202	0.06915	0.05210	0.03935	0.02980	0.01313
32	0.53063	0.45377	0.38834	0.28506	0.20987	0.15496	0.08520	0.06344	0.04736	0.03545	0.02661	0.01142
33	0.52023	0.44270	0.37703	0.27409	0.19987	0.14619	0.07889	0.05820	0.04306	0.03194	0.02376	0.00993
34	0.51003	0.43191	0.36604	0.26355	0.19035	0.13791	0.07305	0.05340	0.03914	0.02878	0.02121	0.00864
35	0.50003	0.42137	0.35538	0.25342	0.18129	0.13011	0.06763	0.04899	0.03558	0.02592	0.01894	0.00751
36	0.49022	0.41109	0.34503	0.24367	0.17266	0.12274	0.06262	0.04494	0.03235	0.02335	0.01691	0.00653
37	0.48061	0.40107	0.33498	0.23430	0.16444	0.11579	0.05799	0.04123	0.02941	0.02104	0.01510	0.00568
38	0.47119	0.39128	0.32523	0.22529	0.15661	0.10924	0.05369	0.03783	0.02674	0.01896	0.01348	0.00494
39	0.46195	0.38174	0.31575	0.21662	0.14915	0.10306	0.04971	0.03470	0.02430	0.01708	0.01204	0.00429
40	0.45289	0.37243	0.30656	0.20829	0.14205	0.09722	0.04603	0.03184	0.02210	0.01538	0.01075	0.00373

TABLE 3
Future Value of an Ordinary Annuity of 1

$$fVF - OA_{n,i} = \frac{(1 + i)^n - 1}{i}$$

(n) Periods	2%	2.5%	3%	4%	5%	6%	8%	9%	10%	11%	12%	15%
1	1.00000	1.00000	1.00000	1.00000	1.00000	1.00000	1.00000	1.00000	1.00000	1.00000	1.00000	1.00000
2	2.02000	2.02500	2.03000	2.04000	2.05000	2.06000	2.08000	2.09000	2.10000	2.11000	2.12000	2.15000
3	3.06040	3.07563	3.09090	3.12160	3.15250	3.18360	3.24640	3.27810	3.31000	3.34210	3.37440	3.47250
4	4.12161	4.15252	4.18363	4.24646	4.31013	4.37462	4.50611	4.57313	4.64100	4.70973	4.77933	4.99338
5	5.20404	5.25633	5.30914	5.41632	5.52563	5.63709	5.86660	5.98471	6.10510	6.22780	6.35285	6.74238
6	6.30812	6.38774	6.46841	6.63298	6.80191	6.97532	7.33592	7.52334	7.71561	7.91286	8.11519	8.75374
7	7.43428	7.54743	7.66246	7.89829	8.14201	8.39384	8.92280	9.20044	9.48717	9.78327	10.08901	11.06680
8	8.58297	8.73612	8.89234	9.21423	9.54911	9.89747	10.63663	11.02847	11.43589	11.85943	12.29969	13.72682
9	9.75463	9.95452	10.15911	10.58280	11.02656	11.49132	12.48756	13.02104	13.57948	14.16397	14.77566	16.78584
10	10.94972	11.20338	11.46388	12.00611	12.57789	13.18079	14.48656	15.19293	15.93743	16.72201	17.54874	20.30372
11	12.16872	12.48347	12.80780	13.48635	14.20679	14.97164	16.64549	17.56029	18.53117	19.56143	20.65458	24.34928
12	13.41209	13.79555	14.19203	15.02581	15.91713	16.86994	18.97713	20.14072	21.38428	22.71319	24.13313	29.00167
13	14.68033	15.14044	15.61779	16.62684	17.71298	18.88214	21.49530	22.95339	24.52271	26.21164	28.02911	34.35192
14	15.97394	16.51895	17.08632	18.29191	19.59863	21.01507	24.21492	26.01919	27.97498	30.09492	32.39260	40.50471
15	17.29342	17.93193	18.59891	20.02359	21.57856	23.27597	27.15211	29.36092	31.77248	34.40536	37.27971	47.58041
16	18.63929	19.38022	20.15688	21.82453	23.65749	25.67253	30.32428	33.00340	35.94973	39.18995	42.75328	55.71747
17	20.01207	20.86473	21.76159	23.69751	25.84037	28.21288	33.75023	36.97371	40.54470	44.50084	48.88367	65.07509
18	21.41231	22.38635	23.41444	25.64541	28.13238	30.90565	37.45024	41.30134	45.59917	50.39593	55.74971	75.83636
19	22.84056	23.94601	25.11687	27.67123	30.53900	33.75999	41.44626	46.01846	51.15909	56.93949	63.43968	88.21181
20	24.29737	25.54466	26.87037	29.77808	33.06595	36.78559	45.76196	51.16012	57.27500	64.20283	72.05244	102.44358
21	25.78332	27.18327	28.67649	31.96920	35.71925	39.99273	50.42292	56.76453	64.00250	72.26514	81.69874	118.81012
22	27.29898	28.86286	30.53678	34.24797	38.50521	43.39229	55.45676	62.87334	71.40275	81.21431	92.50258	137.63164
23	28.84496	30.58443	32.45288	36.61789	41.43048	46.99583	60.89330	69.53194	79.54302	91.14788	104.60289	159.27638
24	30.42186	32.34904	34.42647	39.08260	44.50200	50.81558	66.76476	76.78981	88.49733	102.17415	118.15524	184.16784
25	32.03030	34.15776	36.45926	41.64591	47.72710	54.86451	73.10594	84.70090	98.34706	114.41331	133.33387	212.79302
26	33.67091	36.01171	38.55304	44.31174	51.11345	59.15638	79.95442	93.32398	109.18177	127.99877	150.33393	245.71197
27	35.34432	37.91200	40.70963	47.08421	54.66913	63.70577	87.35077	102.72314	121.09994	143.07864	169.37401	283.56877
28	37.05121	39.85980	42.93092	49.96758	58.40258	68.52811	95.33883	112.96822	134.20994	159.81729	190.69889	327.10408
29	38.79223	41.85630	45.21885	52.96629	62.32271	73.63980	103.96594	124.13536	148.63093	178.39719	214.58275	377.16969
30	40.56808	43.90270	47.57542	56.08494	66.43885	79.05819	113.28321	136.30754	164.49402	199.02088	241.33268	434.74515
31	42.37944	46.00027	50.00268	59.32834	70.76079	84.80168	123.34587	149.57522	181.94343	221.91317	271.29261	500.95692
32	44.22703	48.15028	52.50276	62.70147	75.29883	90.88978	134.21354	164.03699	201.13777	247.32362	304.84772	577.10046
33	46.11157	50.35403	55.07784	66.20953	80.06377	97.34316	145.95062	179.80032	222.25154	275.52922	342.42945	664.66553
34	48.03380	52.61289	57.73018	69.85791	85.06696	104.18376	158.62667	196.98234	245.47670	306.83744	384.52098	765.36535
35	49.99448	54.92821	60.46208	73.65222	90.32031	111.43478	172.31680	215.71076	271.02437	341.58955	431.66350	881.17016
36	51.99437	57.30141	63.27594	77.59831	95.83632	119.12087	187.10215	236.12472	299.12681	380.16441	484.46312	1,014.34568
37	54.03425	59.73395	66.17422	81.70225	101.62814	127.26812	203.07032	258.37595	330.03949	422.98249	543.59869	1,167.49753
38	56.11494	62.22730	69.15945	85.97034	107.70955	135.90421	220.31595	282.62978	364.04343	470.51056	609.83053	1,343.62216
39	58.23724	64.78298	72.23423	90.40915	114.09502	145.05846	238.94122	309.06646	401.44778	523.26673	684.01020	1,546.16549
40	60.40198	67.40255	75.40126	95.02552	120.79977	154.76197	259.05652	337.88245	442.59256	581.82607	767.09142	1,779.09031

TABLE 4
Present Value of an Ordinary Annuity of 1

$$PVF - OA_{n,i} = \frac{1 = \dfrac{1}{(1+i)^n}}{i}$$

(n) Periods	2%	2.5%	3%	4%	5%	6%	8%	9%	10%	11%	12%	15%
1	0.98039	0.97561	0.97087	0.96154	0.95238	0.94340	0.92593	0.91743	0.90909	0.90090	0.89286	0.86957
2	1.94156	1.92742	1.91347	1.88609	1.85941	1.83339	1.78326	1.75911	1.73554	1.71252	1.69005	1.62571
3	2.88388	2.85602	2.82861	2.77509	2.72325	2.67301	2.57710	2.53129	2.48685	2.44371	2.40183	2.28323
4	3.80773	3.76197	3.71710	3.62990	3.54595	3.46511	3.31213	3.23972	3.16986	3.10245	3.03735	2.85498
5	4.71346	4.64583	4.57971	4.45182	4.32948	4.21236	3.99271	3.88965	3.79079	3.69590	3.60478	3.35216
6	5.60143	5.50813	5.41719	5.24214	5.07569	4.91732	4.62288	4.48592	4.35526	4.23054	4.11141	3.78448
7	6.47199	6.34939	6.23028	6.00205	5.78637	5.58238	5.20637	5.03295	4.86842	4.71220	4.56376	4.16042
8	7.32548	7.17014	7.01969	6.73274	6.46321	6.20979	5.74664	5.53482	5.33493	5.14612	4.96764	4.48732
9	8.16224	7.97087	7.78611	7.43533	7.10782	6.80169	6.24689	5.99525	5.75902	5.53705	5.32825	4.77158
10	8.98259	8.75206	8.53020	8.11090	7.72173	7.36009	6.71008	6.41766	6.14457	5.88923	5.65022	5.01877
11	9.78685	9.51421	9.25262	8.76048	8.30641	7.88687	7.13896	6.80519	6.49506	6.20652	5.93770	5.23371
12	10.57534	10.25776	9.95400	9.38507	8.86325	8.38384	7.53608	7.16073	6.81369	6.49236	6.19437	5.42062
13	11.34837	10.98319	10.63496	9.98565	9.39357	8.85268	7.90378	7.48690	7.10336	6.74987	6.42355	5.58315
14	12.10625	11.69091	11.29607	10.56312	9.89864	9.29498	8.24424	7.78615	7.36669	6.98187	6.62817	5.72448
15	12.84926	12.38138	11.93794	11.11839	10.37966	9.71225	8.55948	8.06069	7.60608	7.19087	6.81086	5.84737
16	13.57771	13.05500	12.56110	11.65230	10.83777	10.10590	8.85137	8.31256	7.82371	7.37916	6.97399	5.95423
17	14.29187	13.71220	13.16612	12.16567	11.27407	10.47726	9.12164	8.54363	8.02155	7.54879	7.11963	6.04716
18	14.99203	14.35336	13.75351	12.65930	11.68959	10.82760	9.37189	8.75563	8.20141	7.70162	7.24967	6.12797
19	15.67846	14.97889	14.32380	13.13394	12.08532	11.15812	9.60360	8.95012	8.36492	7.83929	7.36578	6.19823
20	16.35143	15.58916	14.87747	13.59033	12.46221	11.46992	9.81815	9.12855	8.51356	7.96333	7.46944	6.25933
21	17.01121	16.18455	15.41502	14.02916	12.82115	11.76408	10.01680	9.29224	8.64869	8.07507	7.56200	6.31246
22	17.65805	16.76541	15.93692	14.45112	13.16300	12.04158	10.20074	9.44243	8.77154	8.17574	7.64465	6.35866
23	18.29220	17.33211	16.44361	14.85684	13.48857	12.30338	10.37106	9.58021	8.88322	8.26643	7.71843	6.39884
24	18.91393	17.88499	16.93554	15.24696	13.79864	12.55036	10.52876	9.70661	8.98474	8.34814	7.78432	6.43377
25	19.52346	18.42438	17.41315	15.62208	14.09394	12.78336	10.67478	9.82258	9.07704	8.42174	7.84314	6.46415
26	20.12104	18.95061	17.87684	15.98277	14.37519	13.00317	10.80998	9.92897	9.16095	8.48806	7.89566	6.49056
27	20.70690	19.46401	18.32703	16.32959	14.64303	13.21053	10.93516	10.02658	9.23722	8.54780	7.94255	6.51353
28	21.28127	19.96489	18.76411	16.66306	14.89813	13.40616	11.05108	10.11613	9.30657	8.60162	7.98442	6.53351
29	21.84438	20.45355	19.18845	16.98371	15.14107	13.59072	11.15841	10.19828	9.36961	8.65011	8.02181	6.55088
30	22.39646	20.93029	19.60044	17.29203	15.37245	13.76483	11.25778	10.27365	9.42691	8.69379	8.05518	6.56598
31	22.93770	21.39541	20.00043	17.58849	15.59281	13.92909	11.34980	10.34280	9.47901	8.73315	8.08499	6.57911
32	23.46833	21.84918	20.38877	17.87355	15.80268	14.08404	11.43500	10.40624	9.52638	8.76860	8.11159	6.59053
33	23.98856	22.29188	20.76579	18.14765	16.00255	14.23023	11.51389	10.46444	9.56943	8.80054	8.13535	6.60046
34	24.49859	22.72379	21.13184	18.41120	16.19290	14.36814	11.58693	10.51784	9.60858	8.82932	8.15656	6.60910
35	24.99862	23.14516	21.48722	18.66461	16.37419	14.49825	11.65457	10.56682	9.64416	8.85524	8.17550	6.61661
36	25.48884	23.55625	21.83225	18.90828	16.54685	14.62099	11.71719	10.61176	9.67651	8.87859	8.19241	6.62314
37	25.96945	23.95732	22.16724	19.14258	16.71129	14.73678	11.77518	10.65299	9.70592	8.89963	8.20751	6.62882
38	26.44064	24.34860	22.49246	19.36786	16.86789	14.84602	11.82887	10.69082	9.73265	8.91859	8.22099	6.63375
39	26.90259	24.73034	22.80822	19.58448	17.01704	14.94907	11.87858	10.72552	9.75696	8.93567	8.23303	6.63805
40	27.35548	25.10278	23.11477	19.79277	17.15909	15.04630	11.92461	10.75736	9.77905	8.95105	8.24378	6.64178

▦ Using the Decision Toolkit

Stewart's Soup is considering expanding its international presence. It sells 38 percent of the soup consumed in Canada, but only 2 percent of soup worldwide. Thus the company believes that it has great potential for international sales. Recently, 20 percent of Stewart's sales were in foreign markets (and nearly all of that was in Europe). Its goal is to have 30 percent of its sales in foreign markets. In order to accomplish this goal, the company will have to invest heavily.

In recent years Stewart has spent between $300 and $400 million on capital expenditures. Suppose that Stewart is interested in expanding its South American presence by building a new production facility there. After considering tax, marketing, labour, transportation, and political issues, Stewart has determined that the most desirable location is either Buenos Aires or Rio de Janeiro. The following estimates have been provided:

	Buenos Aires	Rio de Janeiro
Initial investment	$2,500,000	$1,400,000
Estimated useful life	20 years	20 years
Annual revenues (accrual)	$500,000	$380,000
Annual expenses (accrual)	$200,000	$180,000
Annual cash inflows	$550,000	$430,000
Annual cash outflows	$222,250	$206,350
Estimated salvage value	$500,000	$0
Discount rate	9%	9%

Instructions

Evaluate each of these mutually exclusive proposals using (1) the cash payback, (2) the net present value, (3) the profitability index, (4) the internal rate of return, and (5) the annual rate of return. Discuss the implications of your findings.

Solution

(1) Cash payback

Buenos Aires	Rio de Janeiro
$\dfrac{\$2,500,000}{\$327,750} = 7.63$ years	$\dfrac{\$1,400,000}{\$223,650} = 6.26$ years

(2) Net present value

	Buenos Aires	Rio de Janerio
Present value of net cash flows		
$327,750 × 9.12855	= $2,991,882	$223,650 × 9.12855 = $2,041,600
$500,000 × 0.17843	= 89,215	
	3,081,097	
Less: Initial investment	2,500,000	1,400,000
Net present value	$ 581,097	$ 641,600

(3) Profitability index

Buenos Aires	Rio de Janeiro
$\dfrac{\$3,081,097}{\$2,500,000} = 1.23$	$\dfrac{\$2,041,600}{\$1,400,000} = 1.46$

(4) Internal rate of return: The internal rate of return can be approximated by experimenting with different discount rates to see which one comes the closest to resulting in a net present value of zero. Doing this, we find that Buenos Aires has an internal rate of return of approximately 12%, while the internal rate of return of the Rio de Janeiro location is approximately 15%, as shown below. Rio, therefore, is preferable.

Internal rate of return

Buenos Aires					Rio de Janeiro			
Cash Flows	×	12% Discount Factor	=	Present Value	Cash Flows	×	15% Discount Factor	=	Present Value

$327,750 ×	7.46944	= $2,448,109	$223,650 ×	6.25933	= $1,399,899
$500,000 ×	0.10367	= 51,835			
		2,499,944			
Less: Capital investment		2,500,000			1,400,000
Net present value		$ (56)			$ (101)

(5) Annual rate of return

Buenos Aires	Rio de Janeiro

Average investment
$$\frac{(\$2,500,000 + \$500,000)}{2} = \$1,500,000 \qquad \frac{(\$1,400,000 + \$0)}{2} = \$700,000$$

Annual rate of return
$$\frac{\$300,000}{\$1,500,000} = 0.20 = 20\% \qquad \frac{\$200,000}{\$700,000} = 0.286 = 28.6\%$$

Implications: Although the annual rate of return is higher for Rio de Janeiro, this method has the disadvantage of ignoring the time value of money, as well as using accrual numbers rather than cash flows. The cash payback of Rio de Janeiro is also shorter, but this method also ignores the time value of money. Thus, while these two methods can be used for a quick assessment, neither should be relied upon as the only evaluation tool.

From the net present value calculation, it would appear that the two projects are nearly identical in their acceptability. However, the profitability index indicates that the Rio de Janeiro investment is far more desirable because it generates its cash flows with a much smaller initial investment. A similar result is found by using the internal rate of return. Overall, assuming that the company will invest in only one project, it would appear that the Rio de Janeiro project should be chosen.

the navigator

Summary of Study Objectives

1. **Discuss the capital budgeting evaluation process, and explain what inputs are used in capital budgeting.** Project proposals are gathered from each department and submitted to a capital budget committee, which screens the proposals and recommends worthy projects. Company officers decide which projects to fund, and the board of directors approves the capital budget. In capital budgeting, estimated cash inflows and outflows, rather than accrual-accounting numbers, are the preferred inputs.

2. **Describe the cash payback technique.** The cash payback technique identifies the time period it will take to recover the cost of the investment. The formula when net annual cash flows are the same is as follows: cost of capital expenditure divided by estimated net annual cash inflow equals cash payback period. The shorter the payback period, the more attractive the investment.

3. **Explain the net present value method.** Under the net present value method, the present value of future cash inflows is compared with the capital investment to determine the net present value. The decision rule is as follows: Accept the project if the net present value is zero or positive. Reject the project if the net present value is negative.

4. **Identify the challenges presented by intangible benefits in capital budgeting.** Intangible benefits are difficult to measure, and thus are often ignored in capital budgeting decisions. This can result in incorrectly rejecting some projects. One method for considering intangible benefits is to calculate the NPV, ignoring intangible benefits; if the resulting NPV is below zero, evaluate whether the benefits are worth at least the amount of the negative net present value. Alternatively, intangible benefits can be included in the NPV calculation, using conservative estimates of their value.

5. **Describe the profitability index.** The profitability index is a tool for comparing the relative merits of two alternative capital investment opportunities. It is calculated by dividing the present value of net cash

flows by the initial investment. The higher the index, the more desirable the project.

6. **Indicate the benefits of performing a post-audit.** A post-audit is an evaluation of a capital investment's actual performance. Post-audits create an incentive for managers to make accurate estimates. Post-audits are also useful for determining whether a project should be continued, expanded, or terminated. Finally, post-audits provide feedback that is useful for improving estimation techniques.

7. **Explain the internal rate of return method.** The objective of the internal rate of return method is to find the interest yield of the potential investment, which is expressed as a percentage rate. The decision rule is this: Accept the project when the internal rate of return is equal to or greater than the required rate of return. Reject the project when the internal rate of return is less than the required rate of return.

8. **Describe the annual rate of return method.** The annual rate of return uses accounting data to indicate the profitability of a capital investment. It is calculated by dividing the expected annual net income by the amount of the average investment. The higher the rate of return, the more attractive the investment.

Decision Toolkit—A Summary

Decision Checkpoints	Info Needed for Decision	Tools to Use for Decision	How to Evaluate Results
Should the company invest in a proposed project?	Cash flow estimates and discount rate	$\text{Net present value} = \dfrac{\text{Present value of net cash flows}}{\text{less capital investment}}$	The investment is financially acceptable if the net present value is positive.
Which investment proposal should a company accept?	The estimated cash flows and discount rate for each proposal	$\text{Profitability index} = \dfrac{\text{Present value of net cash flows}}{\text{Initial investment}}$	The investment proposal with the highest profitability index should be accepted.
Should the company invest in a proposed project?	The estimated cash flows and the required rate of return (hurdle rate)	$\text{Internal rate of return} = \begin{array}{c}\text{Interest rate that}\\ \text{results in a net}\\ \text{present value}\\ \text{of zero}\end{array}$	If the internal rate of return is higher than the required rate of return for the project, then the project is financially acceptable.

Key Term Matching Activity

Glossary

Annual rate of return method   A method for determining how profitable a capital expenditure is, calculated by dividing expected annual net income by the average investment. (p. 534)

Capital budgeting   The process of making capital expenditure decisions in business. (p. 520)

Cash payback technique   A capital budgeting technique that identifies the time period needed to recover the cost of a capital investment from the annual cash inflow produced by the investment. (p. 522)

Cost of capital   The average rate of return that the firm must pay to obtain borrowed and equity funds. (p. 526)

Discounted cash flow technique   A capital budgeting technique that considers both the estimated total cash inflows from the investment and the time value of money. (p. 524)

Discount rate   The interest rate used in discounting the future net cash flows to determine the present value. (p. 524)

Internal rate of return   The rate that will cause the present value of the proposed capital expenditure to equal the present value of the expected annual cash inflows. (p. 532)

Internal rate of return method   A method used in capital budgeting that results in finding the interest yield of the potential investment. (p. 532)

Net present value   The difference that results when the original capital outlay is subtracted from the discounted cash inflows. (p. 524)

Net present value method A method used in capital budgeting in which cash inflows are discounted to their present value and then compared to the capital investment. (p. 524)

Post-audit A thorough evaluation of how well a project's actual performance matches the projections made when the project was proposed. (p. 531)

Profitability index A method of comparing alternative projects that considers both the size of the investment and its discounted future cash flows. It is calculated by dividing the present value of net future cash flows by the initial investment. (p. 530)

Demonstration Problem

Sierra Company is considering a long-term capital investment project called ZIP. ZIP will require an investment of $120,000, and it will have a useful life of four years. Annual net income is expected to be $9,000 a year. Amortization is calculated by the straight-line method with no salvage value. The company's cost of capital is 12 percent. (*Hint:* Assume cash flows can be calculated by adding back the amortization expense.)

Instructions

(Round all calculations to two decimal places.)

(a) Calculate the cash payback period for the project. (Round to two decimals.)
(b) Calculate the net present value for the project. (Round to nearest dollar.)
(c) Calculate the annual rate of return for the project.
(d) Should the project be accepted? Why?

Animated Demonstration Problem

Solution to Demonstration Problem

(a) $120,000 ÷ $39,000[a] = 3.08 years

(b)

	Present Value at 12%
Discount factor for 4 periods	3.03735
Present value of net cash flows:	
$39,000 × 3.03735	$118,457
Capital investment	120,000
Negative net present value	$ (1,543)

[a] $9,000 + $30,000

(c) $9,000 ÷ $60,000[b] = 15%

(d) The annual rate of return of 15% is good. However, the cash payback period is 77% of the project's useful life, and the net present value is negative. The recommendation is to reject the project.

[b] $120,000 ÷ 2

the navigator

Action Plan

- Calculate the time it will take to pay back the investment: the cost of the investment divided by net annual cash flows.

- When calculating the NPV, remember that net annual cash flow equals annual net income plus annual amortization expense.

- Be careful to use the correct discount factor in using the net present value method.

- Calculate the annual rate of return: expected annual net income divided by the average investment.

Self-Study Questions

Answers are at the end of the chapter.

(SO 1) 1. Which of the following is not an example of a capital budgeting decision?
(a) Decision to build a new plant
(b) Decision to renovate an existing facility
(c) Decision to buy a piece of machinery
(d) All of these are capital budgeting decisions.

(SO 1) 2. Which of the following shows the correct order for when the parties get involved in the capital budgeting authorization process?
(a) Plant managers, officers, capital budget committee, board of directors
(b) Board of directors, plant managers, officers, capital budget committee
(c) Plant managers, capital budget committee, officers, board of directors
(d) Officers, plant managers, capital budget committee, board of directors

(SO 2) 3. One weakness of the cash payback approach is that:
(a) it uses accrual-based accounting numbers.
(b) it ignores the time value of money.
(c) it ignores the useful life of alternative projects.
(d) Both (b) and (c) are true.

(SO 3) 4. Which is a true statement about using a higher discount rate to calculate the net present value of a project?
(a) It will make it less likely that the project will be accepted.
(b) It will make it more likely that the project will be accepted.
(c) It is appropriate to use a higher rate if the project is seen as being less risky than other projects being considered.
(d) It is appropriate to use a higher rate if the project will have a short useful life compared to other projects being considered.

(SO 3) 5. A positive net present value means that the:
(a) project's rate of return is less than the cut-off rate.
(b) project's rate of return exceeds the required rate of return.

(c) project's rate of return equals the required rate of return.
(d) project is unacceptable.

6. Which of the following is not an alternative name   (SO 3)
for the discount rate?
(a) Hurdle rate
(b) Required rate of return
(c) Cut-off rate
(d) All of these are alternative names for the discount rate.

7. If a project has intangible benefits whose value is   (SO 4)
hard to estimate, the best thing to do is:
(a) ignore these benefits, since any estimate of their value will most likely be wrong.
(b) include a conservative estimate of their value.
(c) ignore their value in your initial net present value calculation, but then estimate whether their potential value is worth at least the amount of the net present value deficiency.
(d) Both (b) and (c) are correct.

8. A post-audit of an investment project should be   (SO 6)
performed:
(a) on all significant capital expenditure projects.
(b) on all projects that management feels might be financial failures.
(c) on randomly selected projects.
(d) only on projects that are a tremendous success.

9. A project should be accepted if its internal rate of   (SO 7)
return exceeds:
(a) zero.
(b) the rate of return on a government bond.
(c) the company's required rate of return.
(d) the rate the company pays on borrowed funds.

10. Which of the following is incorrect about the   (SO 8)
annual rate of return technique?
(a) The calculation is simple.
(b) The accounting terms used are familiar to management.
(c) The timing of the cash inflows is not considered.
(d) The time value of money is considered.

Questions

1. Describe the process a company may use in screening and approving the capital expenditure budget.

2. What are the advantages and disadvantages of the cash payback technique?

3. Walter Shea claims the formula for the cash payback technique is the same as the formula for the annual rate of return technique. Is Walter correct? What is the formula for the cash payback technique?

4. Two types of present value tables may be used with the discounted cash flow technique. Identify the tables and the circumstance(s) when each table should be used.

5. What is the decision rule for the net present value method?

6. Discuss the factors that determine the appropriate discount rate to use when calculating the net present value.

7. What simplifying assumptions were made in the chapter in the calculation of net present value?

8. What are some examples of potential intangible benefits of investment proposals? Why do these intangible benefits complicate the capital budget evaluation process? What might happen if intangible benefits are ignored in a capital budget decision?

9. What steps can be taken to include intangible benefits in the capital budget evaluation process?

10. What advantages does the profitability index provide compared to the net present value method when two projects are being compared?

11. What is a post-audit? What are the potential benefits of a post-audit?

12. Identify the steps in using the internal rate of return method.

13. Waterville Company uses the internal rate of return method. What is the decision rule for this method?

14. What are the strengths of the annual rate of return approach? What are its weaknesses?

15. Your classmate, Karen Snyder, is confused about the factors that are included in the annual rate of return technique. What is the formula for this technique?

16. Stella Waite is trying to understand the term "cost of capital." Define the term and indicate its relevance to the decision rule under the annual rate of return technique.

Brief Exercises

BE12–1 Marcus Company is considering purchasing new equipment for $450,000. It is expected that the equipment will produce net annual cash flows of $55,000 over its 10-year useful life. Annual amortization will be $45,000. Calculate the cash payback period.

Calculate cash payback period for capital investment.
(SO 2)

BE12–2 Nien Company accumulates the following data for a proposed capital investment: cash cost $220,000; net annual cash flows $40,000; present value factor of cash inflows for 10 years, 5.65 (rounded). Determine the net present value, and indicate whether the investment should be made.

Calculate net present value of investment.
(SO 3)

BE12–3 Timo Corporation, an amusement park, is considering a capital investment in a new ride. The ride would cost $136,000 and have an estimated useful life of five years. It will be sold for $70,000 at that time. (Amusement parks need to rotate rides to keep people interested.) It will be expected to increase net annual cash flows by $25,000. The company's borrowing rate is 8%. Its cost of capital is 10%. Calculate the net present value of this project to the company.

Calculate net present value of investment.
(SO 3)

BE12–4 Michener Bottling Corporation is considering the purchase of a new bottling machine. The machine would cost $200,000 and has an estimated useful life of eight years with zero salvage value. Management estimates that the new bottling machine will provide net annual cash flows of $35,000. Management also believes that the new machine will save the company money because it is expected to be more reliable than other machines, and thus will reduce downtime. How much would the reduction in downtime have to be worth in order for the project to be acceptable? Assume a discount rate of 9%. (*Hint*: Calculate the net present value.)

Calculate net present value with intangible benefits.
(SO 3, 4)

Calculate net present value and profitability index.
(SO 3, 5)

BE12–5   Harry Company is considering two different, mutually exclusive capital expenditure proposals. Project A will cost $395,000, has an expected useful life of 10 years, a salvage value of zero, and is expected to increase net annual cash flows by $70,000. Project B will cost $270,000, has an expected useful life of 10 years, a salvage value of zero, and is expected to increase net annual cash flows by $50,000. A discount rate of 9% is appropriate for both projects. Calculate the net present value and profitability index of each project. Which project should be accepted?

Perform post-audit.
(SO 3, 6)

BE12–6   Martelle Company is performing a post-audit of a project completed one year ago. The initial estimates were that the project would cost $250,000, would have a useful life of nine years, and zero salvage value, and would result in net annual cash flows of $45,000 per year. Now that the investment has been in operation for one year, revised figures indicate that it actually cost $260,000, will have a useful life of 11 years, and will produce net annual cash flows of $37,000 per year. Evaluate the success of the project. Assume a discount rate of 10%.

Calculate internal rate of return.
(SO 7)

BE12–7   Frost Company is evaluating the purchase of a rebuilt spot-welding machine to be used in the manufacture of a new product. The machine will cost $170,000, has an estimated useful life of seven years, and a salvage value of zero, and will increase net annual cash flows by $33,740. What is its approximate internal rate of return?

Calculate internal rate of return.
(SO 7)

BE12–8   Vintech Corporation is considering investing in a new facility. The estimated cost of the facility is $2,045,000. It will be used for 12 years, then sold for $600,000. The facility will generate annual cash inflows of $400,000 and will need new annual cash outflows of $160,000. The company has a required rate of return of 7%. Calculate the internal rate of return on this project, and discuss whether the project should be accepted.

Calculate annual rate of return.
(SO 8)

BE12–9   Engles Oil Company is considering investing in a new oil well. It is expected that the oil well will increase annual revenues by $130,000 and will increase annual expenses by $80,000, including amortization. The oil well will cost $490,000 and will have a $10,000 salvage value at the end of its 10-year useful life. Calculate the annual rate of return.

Exercises

Calculate cash payback and net present value.
(SO 2, 3)

E12–1   Dobbs Corporation is considering purchasing a new delivery truck. The truck has many advantages over the company's current truck (not the least of which is that it runs). The new truck would cost $56,000. Because of the increased capacity, reduced maintenance costs, and increased fuel economy, the new truck is expected to generate cost savings of $8,000. At the end of eight years, the company will sell the truck for an estimated $28,000. Traditionally, the company has used a general rule that a proposal should not be accepted unless it has a payback period that is less than 50% of the asset's estimated useful life. Hal Michaels, a new manager, has suggested that the company should not rely only on the payback approach, but should also use the net present value method when evaluating new projects. The company's cost of capital is 8%.

Instructions

(a) Calculate the cash payback period and net present value of the proposed investment.
(b) Does the project meet the company's cash payback criteria? Does it meet the net present value criteria for acceptance? Discuss your results.

Calculate cash payback period and net present value.
(SO 2, 3)

E12–2   Jack's Custom Manufacturing Company is considering three new projects. Each one requires an equipment investment of $21,000, will last for three years, and will produce the following net annual cash flows:

Year	AA	BB	CC
1	$ 7,000	$ 9,500	$13,000
2	9,000	9,500	10,000
3	15,000	9,500	9,000
Total	$31,000	$28,500	$32,000

The equipment's salvage value is zero, and Jack uses straight-line amortization. Jack will not accept any project with a payback period over two years. Jack's required rate of return is 15%.

Instructions

(a) Calculate each project's payback period, indicating the most desirable project and the least desirable project using this method. (Round to two decimals and use average annual cash flows in your calculations.)
(b) Calculate the net present value of each project. Does your evaluation change? (Round to the nearest dollar.)

E12–3 TLC Corp. is considering purchasing one of two new diagnostic machines. Either machine would make it possible for the company to bid on jobs that it currently is not equipped to do. Estimates for each machine follow:

Calculate net present value and profitability index.
(SO 3, 5)

	Machine A	Machine B
Original cost	$78,000	$190,000
Estimated life	8 years	8 years
Salvage value	0	0
Estimated annual cash inflows	$20,000	$40,000
Estimated annual cash outflows	$5,000	$9,000

Instructions

Calculate the net present value and profitability index of each machine. Assume a 9% discount rate. Which machine should be purchased?

E12–4 Kendra Corporation is involved in the business of injection moulding of plastics. It is considering the purchase of a new computer-aided design and manufacturing machine for $425,000. The company believes that with this new machine it will improve productivity and increase quality, resulting in an increase in net annual cash flows of $95,000 for the next six years. Management requires a 10% rate of return on all new investments.

Determine internal rate of return.
(SO 7)

Instructions

Calculate the internal rate of return on this new machine. Should the investment be accepted?

E12–5 Summer Company is considering three capital expenditure projects. Relevant data for the projects are as follows:

Determine internal rate of return.
(SO 7)

Project	Investment	Annual Income	Life of Project
22A	$240,000	$15,000	6 years
23A	270,000	24,400	9 years
24A	280,000	21,000	7 years

Annual income is constant over the life of the project. Each project is expected to have zero salvage value at the end of the project. Summer Company uses the straight-line method of amortization.

Instructions

(a) Determine the internal rate of return for each project. (Round to three decimals.)
(b) If Summer Company's required rate of return is 11%, which projects are acceptable?

E12–6 Mane Event is considering opening a new hair salon in Lethbridge, Alberta. The cost of building a new salon is $300,000. A new salon will normally generate annual revenues of $70,000, with annual expenses (including amortization) of $40,000. At the end of 15 years, the salon will have a salvage value of $75,000.

Calculate annual rate of return.
(SO 8)

Instructions

Calculate the annual rate of return on the project.

E12–7 Dryden Service Centre just purchased an automobile hoist for $41,000. The hoist has an eight-year life and an estimated salvage value of $3,000. Installation costs and freight charges were $3,300 and $700, respectively. Dryden uses straight-line amortization.

The new hoist will be used to replace mufflers and tires on automobiles. Dryden estimates that the new hoist will enable its mechanics to replace five extra mufflers per week.

Calculate cash payback period and annual rate of return.
(SO 2, 8)

Each muffler sells for $72, installed. The cost of a muffler is $34, and the labour cost to install a muffler is $12.

Instructions

(a) Calculate the payback period for the new hoist.
(b) Calculate the annual rate of return for the new hoist. (Round to one decimal.)

Calculate annual rate of return, cash payback period, and net present value.
(SO 2, 3, 8)

E12–8   Morgan Company is considering a capital investment of $180,000 in additional productive facilities. The new machinery is expected to have a useful life of six years with no salvage value. Amortization is by the straight-line method. During the life of the investment, annual net income and net annual cash flows are expected to be $20,000 and $50,000, respectively. Morgan has a 15% cost of capital rate, which is also the minimum acceptable rate of return on the investment.

Instructions

(Round to two decimals.)

(a) Calculate (1) the cash payback period and (2) the annual rate of return on the proposed capital expenditure.
(b) Using the discounted cash flow technique, calculate the net present value.

Problems: Set A

Calculate annual rate of return, net present value, and apply decision rules.
(SO 2, 3, 8)

P12–9A   The Three Stages partnership is considering three long-term capital investment proposals. Each investment has a useful life of five years. Relevant data on each project are as follows:

	Project Main	Project Lane	Project Crane
Capital investment:	$150,000	$160,000	$120,000
Annual net income:			
Year 1	$13,000	$18,000	$27,000
2	13,000	17,000	22,000
3	13,000	16,000	21,000
4	13,000	12,000	13,000
5	13,000	9,000	12,000
Total	$65,000	$72,000	$95,000

Amortization is calculated by the straight-line method and there is no salvage value. The company's cost of capital is 15%. (Use average net annual cash flows in your calculations.)

Instructions

(a) Calculate the cash payback period for each project. (Round to two decimals.)
(b) Calculate the net present value for each project. (Round to the nearest dollar.)
(c) Calculate the annual rate of return for each project. (Round to two decimals.)
(d) Rank the projects based on each of your answers for (a), (b), and (c). Which project do you recommend?

Calculate payback period, annual rate of return, net present value, and apply decision rules.
(SO 2, 3, 8)

P12–10A   ALGS Inc. wants to purchase a new machine for $20,000, including $1,500 of installation costs. The old machine was bought five years ago and had an expected economic life of 10 years without salvage value. This old machine now has a book value of $2,000 and ALGS Inc. expects to sell it for that amount. The new machine would decrease operating costs by $8,000 each year of its economic life. The straight-line amortization method would be used for the new machine, for a five-year period with no salvage value. The company's tax rate is 30%.

Instructions

(a) Determine the cash payback period (ignore income taxes).
(b) Calculate the annual rate of return.
(c) Calculate the net present value assuming a 10% rate of return (ignore income taxes).
(d) State your conclusion on whether the new machine should be purchased.

(CGA-adapted)

P12–11A Tony Siebers is an accounting major at a Maritimes university located approximately 60 kilometres from a major city. Many of the students attending the university are from the metropolitan area and visit their homes regularly on the weekends. Tony, an entrepreneur at heart, realizes that few good commuting alternatives are available for students doing weekend travel. He believes that a weekend commuting service could be organized and run profitably from several suburban and downtown shopping mall locations. Tony has gathered the following investment information:

Calculate payback period, annual rate of return, net present value, and discuss findings.
(SO 2, 3, 8)

1. Five used vans would cost a total of $75,000 to purchase and would have a three-year useful life with almost no salvage value. Tony plans to use straight-line amortization.
2. Ten drivers would have to be employed at a total payroll expense of $48,000.
3. Other annual out-of-pocket expenses associated with running the commuter service would include gasoline $16,000; maintenance $4,300; repairs $5,000; insurance $5,200; and advertising $2,500.
4. Tony has visited several financial institutions to discuss funding for his new venture. The best interest rate he has been able to negotiate is 8%. Use this rate for the cost of capital.
5. Tony expects each van to make ten round trips weekly and carry an average of six students each trip. The service is expected to operate 30 weeks each year, and each student will be charged $12 for a round-trip ticket.

Instructions

(a) Determine (1) the annual net income and (2) the net annual cash flows for the commuter service.
(b) Calculate (1) the cash payback period and (2) the annual rate of return. (Round to two decimals.)
(c) Calculate the net present value of the commuter service. (Round to the nearest dollar.)
(d) ◁▭▭▭▷ What should Tony conclude from these calculations?

P12–12A Madden Limited is the largest Canadian producer of dairy-products. The company needs to replace its equipment. The current equipment was purchased 18 years ago at a cost of $2 million, and it was amortized over a 20-year period using the straight-line method, assuming no expected salvage value. Management believes that, currently, the equipment could be sold for $150,000.

Calculate initial investment, cash payback, and net present value.
(SO 2, 3)

The new equipment would cost $2.85 million and have an expected residual value of $525,000 at the end of its estimated life of 10 years. With the new equipment, the current operating costs of $1.5 million would decrease by 30% in year 1, remain at that level for year 2 and year 3, decrease by another 10% in year 4, and remain at that level for the remaining life of the asset. With the new equipment, the company would have to hire another operator at an annual cost of $30,000. The company's cost of capital is 12%.

Instructions

(a) Assuming that the company decides to buy the new equipment now, calculate the initial investment.
(b) Calculate the total net savings in operating costs over the expected life of the new equipment. Show your calculations.
(c) Calculate the net present value of investing in the new equipment. Show your calculations.
(d) If the maximum acceptable payback period for the company is eight years, should the company replace the equipment now? Explain your rationale and show your calculations.

(CGA-adapted)

P12–13A Berens River Clinic is considering investing in new heart monitoring equipment. It has two options: Option A would have an initial lower cost but would require a significant expenditure for rebuilding after four years. Option B would require no rebuilding expenditure, but its maintenance costs would be higher. Since the option B machine is of a higher initial quality, it is expected to have a salvage value at the end of its useful life. The following estimates were made of the cash flows:

Calculate net present value, profitability index, and internal rate of return.
(SO 3, 5, 7)

	Option A	Option B
Initial cost	$160,000	$227,000
Annual cash inflows	75,000	80,000
Annual cash outflows	35,000	30,000
Cost to rebuild (end of year 4)	60,000	0
Salvage value	0	12,000
Estimated useful life	8 years	8 years

The company's cost of capital is 11%.

Instructions

(a) Calculate the (1) net present value, (2) profitability index, and (3) internal rate of return for each option. (*Hint*: To solve for the internal rate of return, experiment with alternative discount rates to arrive at a net present value of zero.)

(b) Which option should be accepted?

Calculate payback, annual rate of return, and net present value.
(SO 2, 3, 8)

P12–14A   MCA Corporation is reviewing an investment proposal. The initial cost and estimates of the book value of the investment at the end of each year, the net cash flows for each year, and the net income for each year are presented in the schedule below. All cash flows are assumed to take place at the end of the year. The salvage value of the investment at the end of each year is equal to its book value. There would be no salvage value at the end of the investment's life.

Investment Proposal

Year	Initial Cost and Book Value	Annual Cash Flows	Annual Net Income
0	$105,000		
1	70,000	$50,000	$15,000
2	42,000	45,000	17,000
3	21,000	40,000	19,000
4	7,000	35,000	21,000
5	0	30,000	23,000

MCA Corporation uses a 15% target rate of return for new investment proposals.

Instructions

(a) What is the cash payback period for this proposal?

(b) What is the annual rate of return for the investment?

(c) What is the net present value of the investment?

(CMA Canada-adapted)

Calculate net present value considering intangible benefits.
(SO 3, 4)

P12–15A   Prestige Auto Care is considering the purchase of a new tow truck. The garage currently has no tow truck, and the $60,000 price tag for a new truck would be a major expenditure for the garage. Jenna Lind, owner of the garage, has compiled the following estimates in trying to determine whether the tow truck should be purchased:

Initial cost	$60,000
Estimated useful life	8 years
Annual cash inflows from towing	$8,000
Overhaul costs (end of year 4)	$5,000
Salvage value	$15,000

Jenna's good friend, Reid Shaw, stopped by. He is trying to convince Jenna that the tow truck will have other benefits that Jenna has not even considered. First, he says, cars that need towing need to be fixed. Thus, when Jenna tows them to her facility, her repair revenues will increase. Second, he notes that the tow truck could have a plow mounted on it, thus saving Jenna the cost of plowing her parking lot. (Reid will give her a used plow blade for free if Jenna will plow Reid's driveway.) Third, he notes that the truck will generate goodwill; that is, people who are rescued by Jenna and her tow truck will feel grateful and might be more inclined to use her service station in the future, or buy gas there. Fourth, the tow truck will have "Prestige Auto Care" on its doors, hood, and back tailgate—a form of free advertising wherever the tow truck goes.

Reid estimates that, at a minimum, these benefits would be worth the following:

Additional annual net cash flows from repair work	$3,000
Annual savings from plowing	500
Additional annual net cash flows from customer goodwill	1,000
Additional annual net cash flows resulting from free advertising	500

The company's cost of capital is 9%.

Instructions

(a) Calculate the net present value, ignoring the additional benefits described by Reid. Should the tow truck be purchased?

(b) Calculate the net present value, including the additional benefits suggested by Reid. Should the tow truck be purchased?

(c) Suppose Reid has been overly optimistic in his assessment of the value of the additional benefits (perhaps because he wants his driveway plowed). At a minimum, how much would the additional benefits have to be worth in order for the project to be accepted?

P12–16A The Taylor Company Limited reported a cost of goods sold of $576,000 last year, when 18,000 units were produced and sold. The cost of goods sold was 35% materials, 42% direct labour, and 23% overhead.

Calculate net present value and payback period.
(SO 2, 3)

The company is considering the purchase of a machine costing $100,000, with an expected useful life of five years and a salvage value at that time of $10,000. The machine would have a maximum capacity of 25,000 units per year and is expected to reduce direct labour costs by 25%; however, it would require an additional supervisor at a cost of $40,000 per year. The machine would be amortized over the five years using the straight-line method.

Production and sales for the next five years are expected to be as follows:

Year	Production and Sales
2005	18,000 units
2006	18,000 units
2007	20,000 units
2008	20,000 units
2009	20,000 units

Instructions

(a) Should the company purchase the machine if the company has a minimum desired rate of return of 12%?

(b) What is the payback on this investment?

(c) At 12%, how high must the salvage value be before recommending that the investment be made?

(CMA Canada-adapted)

P12–17A Bonita Corp. is thinking about opening a soccer camp in southern Ontario. In order to start the camp, the company would need to purchase land, and build four soccer fields and a dormitory-type sleeping and dining facility to house 150 soccer players. Each year, the camp would be run for eight sessions of one week each. The company would hire college soccer players as coaches. The camp attendees would be male and female soccer players aged 12 to 18. Property values in southern Ontario have enjoyed a steady increase in value. It is expected that after using the facility for 20 years, Bonita can sell the property for more than it was originally purchased for. The following amounts have been estimated:

Calculate net present value and internal rate of return with sensitivity analysis.
(SO 3, 7)

Cost of land	$300,000
Cost to build dorm and dining facility	$600,000
Annual cash inflows assuming 150 players and 8 weeks	$950,000
Annual cash outflows	$840,000
Estimated useful life	20 years
Salvage value	$1,500,000
Discount rate	8%

Instructions

(a) Calculate the net present value of the project.

(b) To gauge the sensitivity of the project to these estimates, assume that if only 130 players attend each week, revenues will be $800,000 and expenses will be $770,000. What is the net present value using these alternative estimates? Discuss your findings.

(c) Assuming the original facts, what is the net present value if the project is actually riskier than first assumed, and an 11% discount rate is more appropriate?

(d) ⬛▭▭▶ Assume that during the first five years the annual net cash flows each year were only $45,000. At the end of the fifth year, the company is running low on cash, so management decides to sell the property for $1.3 million. What was the actual internal rate of return on the project? Explain how this return was possible if the camp did not appear to be successful.

Calculate incremental cash flow and net present value.
(SO 2, 3)

P12–18A   Saskatoon First Company must expand its manufacturing capabilities to meet the growing demand for its products. The first alternative is to expand its current manufacturing facility, which is located next to a vacant lot in the heart of the city. The second alternative is to convert a warehouse, already owned by the company, located 20 kilometres outside the city. Saskatoon First's controller obtains the following information to evaluate both proposals.

The plant and equipment investment to expand the current manufacturing facility is $19 million, while a $22-million investment is required to convert the warehouse. At either site, Saskatoon First needs to invest $3 million in working capital. Cash revenues from products made in the new facility are expected to equal $13 million each year. If the warehouse is converted, cash operating costs are expected to be $10 million per year. Expanding the current facility will increase efficiency: annual cash operating costs, if the current facility is expanded, will be $1 million lower than the cash operating costs if the warehouse is converted. The controller uses a 10-year period and a 14% required rate of return to evaluate manufacturing investments. The estimated disposal price of the new facility (including a recovery of working capital of $3 million) at the end of 10 years is $8 million at both locations. Saskatoon First amortizes the investment in plant and equipment using straight-line amortization over 10 years on the difference between the initial investment and the disposal price.

Instructions

Calculate the net present value of the proposals to expand the current manufacturing facility and to convert the warehouse. Which project should Saskatoon First choose based on the NPV calculations?

(CMA Canada-adapted)

Problems: Set B

Calculate annual rate of return, payback period, net present value and apply decision rules.
(SO 2, 3, 8)

P12–19B   The partnership of Lou and Bud is considering three long-term capital investment proposals. Relevant data on each project are as follows:

	Project Brown	Project Red	Project Yellow
Capital investment:	$200,000	$225,000	$250,000
Annual net income:			
Year 1	$25,000	$ 20,000	$ 26,000
2	16,000	20,000	24,000
3	13,000	20,000	23,000
4	10,000	20,000	22,000
5	8,000	20,000	20,000
Total	$72,000	$100,000	$115,000

The salvage value is expected to be zero at the end of each project. Amortization is calculated by the straight-line method. The company's required rate of return is the company's cost of capital, which is 12%. (Use average net annual cash flows in your calculations.)

Instructions

(a) Calculate the cash payback period for each project. (Round to two decimals.)
(b) Calculate the net present value for each project. (Round to the nearest dollar.)
(c) Calculate the average annual rate of return for each project. (Round to two decimals.)
(d) Rank the projects on each of your answers in (a), (b), and (c). Which project do you recommend?

P12–20B Biotec Inc. wants to replace its R&D equipment with new high-tech equipment. The existing equipment was purchased five years ago at a cost of $125,000. At that time, the equipment had an expected life of 10 years, with no expected salvage value. The equipment is being amortized on a straight-line basis. Currently, the market value of the old equipment is $57,500.

Calculate initial investment, cash payback, and net present value.
(SO 2, 3)

The new equipment can be bought for $160,000 including installation. Over its 10-year life, it will reduce raw material usage and overhead, and as a result R&D costs will decrease from $159,000 to $138,000 for the first six years, and from $124,000 to $95,200 for the last four years. Net working capital requirements will also increase by $23,000 at the time of replacement.

It is estimated that the new equipment can be sold for $40,000 at the end of its life. Since the new equipment's cash flows are relatively certain, the project's cost of capital is set at 10%, compared to 15% for an average-risk project. The firm's maximum acceptable payback period is five years.

Instructions

(a) Calculate the initial investment amount.
(b) Calculate the project's cash payback period.
(c) Calculate the project's net present value.
(d) State whether or not the company should replace the old R&D equipment with the new high-tech equipment. Justify your answer.

(CGA-adapted)

P12–21B Jo Quick is managing director of the Lots a Tots Daycare Centre. Lots a Tots is currently set up as a full-time child care facility for children between the ages of 12 months and six years. Jo Quick is trying to determine whether the centre should expand its facilities to incorporate a newborn care room for infants between the ages of six weeks and 12 months. The necessary space already exists. An investment of $20,000 would be needed, however, to purchase cribs, high chairs, etc. The equipment purchased for the room would have a five-year useful life with zero salvage value.

Calculate annual rate of return, cash payback, and net present value.
(SO 2, 3, 8)

The newborn nursery would be staffed to handle 11 infants on a full-time basis. The parents of each infant would be charged $125 weekly, and the facility would operate 52 weeks each year. Staffing the nursery would require two full-time specialists and five part-time assistants at an annual cost of $60,000. Food, diapers, and other miscellaneous supplies are expected to total $6,000 annually.

Instructions

(a) Determine (1) the annual net income and (2) the net annual cash flows for the new nursery.
(b) Calculate (1) the cash payback period for the new nursery and (2) the annual rate of return. (Round to two decimals.)
(c) Calculate the net present value of incorporating a newborn care room. (Round to the nearest dollar.) Lots a Tots' cost of capital is 10%.
(d) What should Jo Quick conclude from these calculations?

P12–22B A company presently sells 850,000 units per year of a product to one customer at a price of $0.80 per unit. The customer requires that the product be exclusive and expects no increase in sales during the next year. The product is manufactured with a machine that was purchased seven years ago at a cost of $500,000. Currently, the machine has a book value of $150,000 but the market value is only $30,000. The machine is expected to last another three years, after which it will have no salvage value. Last year, the production costs per unit were as follows:[1]

Calculate net present value and apply decision rule.
(SO 3)

Direct materials	$0.20
Direct labour	0.12
Variable overhead	0.08
Fixed overhead	0.15
Total cost per unit	$0.55

[1] Based on an annual activity of 200,000 machine hours. Each product requires 0.5 machine hours. Fixed overhead includes amortization.

The president of the company is considering the replacement of the old machine with a new one that would cost $400,000. The new machine is expected to last five years. At the end of that period, the salvage value will be $50,000. The president expects to save 10% of the company's total variable costs with the new machine.

Instructions

Assume that the company's desired rate of return is 12%. Using the net present value method, determine if the company should replace the old machine with the new one, and briefly explain why or why not. Show your calculations.

(CGA-adapted)

Calculate net present value, profitability index, and internal rate of return.
(SO 3, 5, 7)

P12−23B   Aqua Tech Testing is considering investing in a new testing device. It has two options: Option A would have an initial lower cost but would require a significant expenditure for rebuilding after five years. Option B would require no rebuilding expenditure, but its maintenance costs would be higher. Since the option B machine is of a higher initial quality, it is expected to have a salvage value at the end of its useful life. The following estimates were provided:

	Option A	Option B
Initial cost	$80,000	$170,000
Annual cash inflows	$180,000	$140,000
Annual cash outflows	$160,000	$108,000
Cost to rebuild (end of year 5)	$26,500	$0
Salvage value	$0	$27,500
Estimated useful life	8 years	8 years

The company's cost of capital is 9%.

Instructions

(a) Calculate the (1) net present value, (2) profitability index, and (3) internal rate of return for each option. (*Hint*: To solve for the internal rate of return, experiment with alternative discount rates to arrive at a net present value of zero.)
(b) Which option should be accepted?

Calculate net present value and apply decision rule.
(SO 3)

P12−24B   Vorteck Inc. manufactures snowsuits. Vorteck is considering purchasing a new sewing machine at a cost of $2.5 million. Its existing machine was purchased five years ago at a price of $1.8 million, and six months ago Vorteck spent $55,000 to keep it operational. The existing sewing machine can be sold today for $260,000. The new sewing machine would require a one-time, $85,000 training cost. Operating costs would decrease by the following amounts for years 1 to 7:

Year 1	$390,000
2	400,000
3	411,000
4	426,000
5	434,000
6	435,000
7	436,000

The new sewing machine would be amortized according to the declining-balance method at a rate of 20%. The salvage value is expected to be $380,000. This new equipment would require maintenance costs of $95,000 at the end of the fifth year. The cost of capital is 9%.

Instructions

Use the net present value method to determine whether Vorteck should purchase the new machine to replace the existing machine, and state the reason for your conclusion.

(CGA-adapted)

Calculate net present value considering intangible benefits and sensitivity analysis.
(SO 3, 4)

P12−25B   The Fort McMurchy Sanitation Company is considering the purchase of a garbage truck. The $77,000 price tag for a new truck would represent a major expenditure for the company. Kalia Vang, owner of the company, has compiled the following estimates in trying to determine whether the garbage truck should be purchased:

Initial cost	$77,000
Estimated useful life	10 years
Net annual cash flows	$12,000
Overhaul costs (end of year 5)	$7,000
Salvage value	$15,000

One of the company's employees is trying to convince Kalia that the truck has other merits that have not been considered in the initial estimates. First, the new truck will be more efficient, with lower maintenance and operating costs. Second, the new truck will be safer. Third, the new truck has the ability to handle recycled materials at the same time as trash, thus offering a new revenue source. Estimates of the minimum value of these benefits follow:

Annual savings from reduced operating costs	$400
Annual savings from reduced maintenance costs	800
Additional annual net cash savings from reduced employee absence	500
Additional annual net cash inflows from recycling	300

The company's cost of capital is 10%.

Instructions

(a) Calculate the net present value, ignoring the additional benefits. Should the truck be purchased?
(b) Calculate the net present value, including the additional benefits. Should the truck be purchased?
(c) Suppose management has been overly optimistic in assessing the value of the additional benefits. At a minimum, how much would the additional benefits have to be worth in order for the project to be accepted?

P12–26B Benjamin Corp. is thinking about opening a hockey camp in Barrie. In order to start the camp, the company would need to purchase land, and build two ice rinks and a dormitory-type sleeping and dining facility to house 200 players. Each year, the camp would be run for eight sessions of one week each. The company would hire college hockey players as coaches. The camp attendees would be male and female hockey players aged 12 to 18. Property values in this area have enjoyed a steady increase in recent years. Benjamin Corp. expects that after using the facility for 15 years, the rinks will have to be dismantled, but the land and buildings will be worth more than they were originally purchased for. The following amounts have been estimated:

Calculate net present value with sensitivity analysis and discuss findings.
(SO 3)

Cost of land	$300,000
Cost to build dorm and dining hall	$600,000
Annual cash inflows assuming 200 players and 8 weeks	$920,000
Annual cash outflows	$760,000
Estimated useful life	15 years
Salvage value	$1,200,000
Discount rate	11%

Instructions

(a) Calculate the net present value of the project.
(b) To evaluate how sensitive the project is to these estimates, assume that if only 170 players attend each week, revenues will be $700,000 and expenses will be $650,000. What is the net present value using these alternative estimates? Discuss your findings.

Cases

www.wiley.com/canada/managerial

Additional Cases

C12–27 Migami Company is considering the purchase of a new machine. The invoice price of the machine is $117,000, freight charges are estimated to be $3,000, and installation costs are expected to be $5,000. The salvage value of the new equipment is expected to be zero after a useful life of four years. Existing equipment could be retained and used for an additional four years if the new machine is not purchased. At that time, the salvage value of the equipment would be zero. If the new machine is purchased now, the existing machine would have to be scrapped. Migami's accountant, Caitlyn Lahr, has accumulated the following data regarding annual sales and expenses with and without the new machine:

1. Without the new machine, Migami can sell 10,000 units of product annually at a per unit selling price of $100. If the new unit is purchased, the number of units produced and sold would increase by 20%, and the selling price would remain the same.
2. The new machine is faster than the old machine, and it is more efficient in its usage of materials. With the old machine, the gross profit rate is 28.5% of sales, whereas the rate will be 30% of sales with the new machine.
3. Annual selling expenses are $160,000 with the current equipment. Because the new equipment would produce a greater number of units to be sold, annual selling expenses are expected to increase by 10% if it is purchased.
4. Annual administrative expenses are expected to be $100,000 with the old machine, and $112,000 with the new machine.
5. The current book value of the existing machine is $30,000. Migami uses straight-line amortization.
6. Migami management has a required rate of return of 15% on its investments and a payback period of no more than three years.

Instructions

With the class divided into groups, answer the following. (Ignore income tax effects.)

(a) Calculate the annual rate of return for the new machine. (Round to two decimals.)
(b) Calculate the payback period for the new machine. (Round to two decimals.)
(c) Calculate the net present value of the new machine. (Round to the nearest dollar.)
(d) Based on your answer above, would you recommend that Migami buy the machine? Why or why not?

C12–28 The City of Craston has recently turned its attention to the apparent problem of a shortage of public transportation. In the last few years, more and more complaints have surfaced with regard to inadequate bus services or difficulties in obtaining taxi services in the suburbs.

To operate a taxi in the city, a special licence is required; the city council's Taxi Commission issues these licences. No new licences have been issued since a freeze was instituted in 1995. There are currently only 1,750 licences still in use out of 4,500. The freedom exists, however, to transfer ownership of a licence. Such transactions have been recently quoted at $1,750 on the open market.

The addition of an airport on the outskirts of the city and three hotels in the city has created an apparent shift by taxi drivers to the core of the city and to the airport routes, resulting in poor services in the suburban areas. In contemplating this situation, the City of Craston recognizes two viable alternatives to correct the problem. Either the city can increase the number of buses serving the suburban areas, or it can issue additional taxi licences.

The Commission regulates taxi fares. Tax revenues are currently being collected from taxi drivers at a rate of 3 percent of gross revenues. The average trip is estimated to be 10 kilometres. This year, the fare consists of a $1.10 flat rate plus $0.50 for every kilometre. It has been determined that each taxi driver collects revenues from 19,200 trips per year. The City estimates that in order to get the desired results, 85 licences would have to be issued at the given open market price. In addition, an incentive of $0.10 per kilometre would have to be placed on the flat rate trips originating in the suburban areas to attract taxi drivers. Accordingly, the ratio of suburban to core city and airport trips would be 1 to 4.

The other alternative cited above is to increase the number of buses serving the suburban areas. Public transit fares are $1 per ride. The City estimates that if it increased the number of buses, at a cost of $1.4 million, the number of single trips would increase by 1.5 million per year. The buses would have an expected life of five years, at which time their combined salvage value would equal $100,000. The buses would be amortized on a straight-line basis. For the duration of five years, five additional workers would have to be employed, each at an annual salary of $30,000, and maintenance costs would increase by $36,000 per year.

So far, investigation of these alternatives has revealed that if additional taxi licences are issued, the public transit revenues will drop by $350,000 per year.

Instructions

The city of Craston has asked you to evaluate the two proposals and provide a recommendation. In your analysis, assume that the rates charged for public transit and taxi fares will remain constant for the five-year period and that all cash flows occur at year end. The city of Craston currently has a 12-percent required rate of return.

(CMA Canada-adapted)

C12–29 The owners of Les Tigres de Trois-Rivières hockey club are considering a deal with an older, established club whereby they can acquire the services of Pierre Luc, a very high scorer and great gate attraction, in exchange for Robert McCain (currently paid $15,000 annually). The established club would also receive $500,000 cash from Les Tigres.

The owners' accountants have assembled the following data:

Estimated useful life of Luc	5 years
Estimated residual value of Luc	$20,000
Estimated useful life of McCain	5 years
Estimated residual value of McCain	None
Current cash offer for McCain received from another club	$50,000
Applicable desired rate of return	10%

Other information:

Year	Luc's Salary	Additional Gate Receipts Because of Luc	Additional Expenses of Handling Higher Volume
1	$60,000	$330,000	$33,000
2	70,000	300,000	30,000
3	80,000	200,000	20,000
4	80,000	100,000	10,000
5	72,000	40,000	4,000

Instructions

Based on your analysis of the data, recommend whether or not the club should acquire the services of Pierre Luc.

(CMA Canada-adapted)

C12–30 Lapides Ltd. is a small company that is currently analyzing capital expenditure proposals for the purchase of equipment. The capital budget is limited to $250,000, which Lapides believes is the maximum capital it can raise.

The financial adviser is preparing an analysis of four projects that the company is considering, as follows:

	Project A	Project B	Project C	Project D
Net initial investment:	$200,000	$190,000	$250,000	$210,000
Projected cash inflows:				
Year 1	$50,000	$40,000	$75,000	$75,000
2	50,000	50,000	75,000	75,000
3	50,000	70,000	60,000	60,000
4	50,000	75,000	80,000	40,000
5	50,000	75,000	100,000	20,000

Instructions

(a) Calculate the cash payback period for each of the four projects.
(b) Calculate the net present value for each project at a cost of capital of 12%.
(c) Which projects, if any, would you recommend funding, and why?

(CMA Canada-adapted)

C12–31 Ms. Cookie Corporation is a company specializing in selling cookies for fund-raising activities. One year ago, the company purchased a special cookie-cutting machine. However, to have more efficient operations, Ms. Cookie is considering the purchase of a more advanced machine. The new machine would be acquired on December 31, 2005, and management expects that it would sell 500,000 dozen cookies in each of the next six years. The selling price of the cookies is expected to average $4.15 per dozen.

Ms. Cookie has two options: continue to operate the old machine, or sell the old machine and purchase the new machine. The following information has been collected to help management decide which option is more profitable:

	Old Machine	New Machine
Original cost of machine at acquisition	$180,000	$340,000
Remaining useful life as of December 31, 2005	6 years	6 years
Expected annual cash operating expenses		
Variable cost per dozen	$0.50	$0.25
Total fixed costs	$40,000	$30,000
Estimated cash value of machine		
December 31, 2005	$40,000	$340,000
December 31, 2011	$10,000	$10,000

Assume that all operating revenues and expenses occur at the end of the year.

Instructions

Use the net present value method to determine whether Ms. Cookie should keep the old machine or acquire the new one. The company has a 10% required rate of return on its investments.

(CMA Canada-adapted)

C12–32   Tony Skateboards is considering building a new plant. James Bott, the company's marketing manager, is an enthusiastic supporter of the new plant. Alyssa Minh, the company's chief financial officer, is not so sure that the plant is a good idea. Currently, the company purchases its skateboards from foreign manufacturers. The following figures were estimated for the construction of a new plant:

Cost of plant	$4,000,000
Annual cash inflows	4,000,000
Annual cash outflows	3,550,000
Estimated useful life	15 years
Salvage value	$2,000,000
Discount rate	11%

James believes that these figures understate the true potential value of the plant. He suggests that by manufacturing its own skateboards the company will benefit from a "buy Canadian" patriotism that he believes is common among skateboarders. He also notes that the firm has had numerous quality problems with the skateboards manufactured by its suppliers. He suggests that the inconsistent quality has resulted in lost sales, increased warranty claims, and some costly lawsuits. Overall, he believes sales will be $200,000 higher each year than projected above, and that the savings from lower warranty costs and legal costs will be $80,000 per year. He also believes that the project is not as risky as assumed above, and that a 9% discount rate is more reasonable.

Instructions

(a) Calculate the net present value of the project based on the original projections.
(b) Calculate the net present value including James's estimates of the value of the intangible benefits, but still using the 11% discount rate.
(c) Calculate the net present value using the original estimates, but using the 9% discount rate that James suggests is more appropriate.
(d) Comment on your findings.

C12–33   Impro Company operates in a province where corporate taxes and workers' compensation insurance rates have recently doubled. Impro's president has just assigned you the task of preparing an economic analysis and making a recommendation about whether or not to move the company's entire operation to New Brunswick. The president is slightly in favour of such a move because New Brunswick is his boyhood home and he also owns a fishing lodge there.

You have just completed building your dream house, moved in, and sodded the lawn. Your children are all doing well in school and sports and they and your spouse want no part of a move to New Brunswick. If the company does move, so will you because the town where you now live is a one-industry community and you and your spouse will have to move to have employment. Moving when everyone else does will cause you to take a big loss on the sale of your house. The same hardships will be suffered by your co-workers, and the town will be devastated.

In gathering the costs of moving versus not moving, you have a lot of freedom in the assumptions you make, the estimates you calculate, and the discount rates and time periods you project. You are in a position to influence the decision in a major way.

Instructions

(a) Who are the stakeholders in this situation?
(b) What are the ethical issues in this situation?
(c) What would you do in this situation?

Answers to Self-Study Questions

1. d   2. c   3. d   4. a   5. b   6. d   7. d   8. a   9. c   10. d

Remember to go back to the Navigator Box at the beginning of the chapter to check off your completed work.

Photo Credits

Company Index

Subject Index